The Complete
Professional Corporation
Desk Book

The Complete Professional Corporation Desk Book

HARRY V. LAMON, Jr., J.D., C.L.U.

and

J. ALSTON THOMPSON, Jr., J.D., LL. M.

Prentice-Hall, Inc. • Englewood Cliffs, New Jersey

Prentice-Hall International, Inc., *London*
Prentice-Hall of Australia, Pty. Ltd., *Sydney*
Prentice-Hall of Canada, Ltd., *Toronto*
Prentice-Hall of India Private Ltd., *New Delhi*
Prentice-Hall of Japan, Inc., *Tokyo*
Prentice-Hall of Southeast Asia Pte. Ltd., *Singapore*
Whitehall Books, Ltd., *Wellington, New Zealand*

© 1982 *by*

Prentice-Hall, Inc.
Englewood Cliffs, N.J.

Library of Congress Cataloging in Publication Data

Lamon, Harry V., Jr.
  Complete professional corporation desk book.
  Bibliography: p.
  Includes index.
  1. Professional corporations—United States.
I. Thompson, J. Alston, Jr.   II. Title.
KF2901.L35   346.73'064   81-15395
                        347.30664   AACR2

ISBN 0-13-162305-2

Printed in the United States of America

**To
Ada and Penny
whose sacrifices
made this book
possible**

THE AUTHORS

Harry V. Lamon, Jr.

Harry V. Lamon, Jr. is a member of the firm of Lamon, Elrod and Harkleroad, P.C., Atlanta, and he has been engaged in the practice of tax law for more than twenty years.

Mr. Lamon is past president and founder of both the Southern Federal Tax Institute and Southern Pension Conference. His professional memberships include Atlanta Bar Association, Atlanta Estate Planning Council, District of Columbia Bar, State Bar of Georgia, Lawyers Club of Atlanta, Old Warhorse Lawyers Club, Inc., Atlanta Chapter, American Society of Pension Actuaries and the American Pension Conference.

The author is a frequent lecturer before legal groups and is a contributor to Prentice-Hall's loose leaf services. An adjunct Professor of Law, Emory University School of Law, Mr. Lamon is co-author with Ray of *Fiduciary Responsibility Under the New Pension Reform Law*, Michigan CLE. He was graduated from Davidson College and Emory University Law School, J.D.

J. Alston Thompson, Jr.

J. Alston Thompson, Jr. is an attorney specializing in the practice of taxation and corporation law, both domestic and international and he is a member of the firm of Lamon, Elrod and Harkleroad, P.C., Atlanta.

Mr. Thompson is a member of the Georgia and New York bars, the American Bar Association, the New York Bar Association, the State Bar of Georgia, the Atlanta Bar Association, the Lawyers Club of Atlanta, and The Group, an association of attorneys interested in the professional corporation area.

The author is a member of the advisory board of *The Virginia Tax Review*, published by the University of Virginia School of Law, Charlottesville, Virginia, and is a contributor to legal periodicals, as well as a popular seminar lecturer.

Mr. Thompson received his B.A. Degree from Vanderbilt University, a J.D. Degree from the University of Virginia School of Law and an LL. M. (in taxation) from New York University School of Law.

A Word from the Authors

PURPOSE OF THE DESK BOOK

Since professional corporations were given the "green light" by the Internal Revenue Service in 1970 with the issuance of Rev. Rul. 70-101,[1] a number of works have been published regarding the formation and operation of professional corporations. However, most of these works were prepared during the early years of the professional corporation struggle and, although they define the problems and pitfalls, they do little to guide the practitioner into the safe harbors which have been established. The purpose of the Desk Book is to consolidate the authors' more than twenty years of experience in the professional corporation area and to provide a working Desk Book with practical answers and forms.

The Desk Book will cover all of the major areas of corporate and tax law involved in the establishment and operation of professional corporations and will be a practical reference aid rather than a treatise. In other words, this Desk Book is a "how to" book for the professional corporation advisor which heretofore did not exist. In consolidating the lessons of the first decade of unrestricted professional corporations, the Desk Book provides definite recommendations for those professional advisors who are counseling professional corporations, be they lawyers, accountants, or business managers, and it also provides options for the implementation of the recommendations set forth.

Obviously, those individuals who are considering incorporation, or are already incorporated, must be successful professionals. Consequently, it would be reasonable to assume that such individuals have diverse needs and desires and sufficiently large egos to accompany those needs and desires. For this reason, this Desk Book discusses the personal interrelationships which are involved incorporating and operating a professional corporation and gives guidelines regarding the manner in which these needs and desires may be met. However, in some cases it is impossible to meet all of the needs and desires, and to fulfill all of the egos, and, consequently, professional corporations break up. This aspect of professional corporations is also extensively covered in this Desk Book.

SHORT HISTORY OF
PROFESSIONAL CORPORATIONS

The story of professional corporations has its genesis in the group practice of medicine as it developed after World War II. During the years prior to 1970, the Internal Revenue Service and professional groups played a game of "cat and mouse" which was eventually won by the professionals. The general objective of professional group practice was to obtain qualified retirement plans comparable to those of business corporations, and the Internal Revenue Service sought to frustrate this attempt. The various stages in this game of "cat and mouse" are as follows:

1. Prior to the 1960's, both ethical and legal restraints imposed by state laws prohibited professionals from practicing through corporations. Consequently, most professional groups practiced as unincorporated associations. The initial reaction of the Internal Revenue Service to such associations was to postulate that such associations were taxable as corporations and not as partnerships and, consequently, federal income taxes should be paid at both the corporate and individual levels. In *Pelton v. Commissioner*,[1a] the Commissioner argued, and the Seventh Circuit agreed, that a group of three physicians organized as a trust was taxable as a corporation.

2. Under corporate qualified retirement plans, benefits may only be accrued for common-law "employees" and not for self-employed individuals or partners.[2] Even though most state laws prohibited the incorporation of professionals, professional group practices in many ways resembled corporations. Because of the need for professionals to be characterized as "employees" many professional groups sought to be considered corporations as the Commissioner had described in *Pelton*. This quest was supported by the "resemblance test," which had been espoused by the Internal Revenue Service and judicially sanctioned in *Morrissey v. Commissioner*.[3] Under the resemblance test, it appeared that professionals had found a way for their professional associations to be considered corporations for tax purposes (even though they were not entitled to incorporate under state law) and, consequently, to provide corporate retirement plans for their "employees."

3. As the Internal Revenue Service began to realize that taxing professional associations as corporations would create a loss of tax revenues, the Commissioner's attitude toward professional groups did an abrupt about-face. Consequently, the Internal Revenue Service began to challenge the right of professional associations to be taxed as corporations, and in *United States v. Kintner*,[4] the Internal Revenue Service argued that a medical group formed as a common-law association was not entitled to adopt a corporate-type retirement plan because a

corporation could not maintain the personal relationships required in the practice of medicine. The Ninth Circuit, following *Morrissey* and *Pelton*, held that the medical group was taxable as a corporation. A similar result was obtained in *Galt v. United States*.[5]

4. Following its losses in *Kintner* and *Galt*, the Treasury, on November 15, 1960, adopted Regulations under Section 7701 which were designed to negate the effect of *Kintner* and *Galt*. Because these Regulations were specifically aimed at the *Kintner* case, they are sometimes known as the "Kintner Regulations." Under these Regulations, it was very difficult for associations to be considered taxable as corporations because the Regulations stressed the effect of local law. The Kintner Regulations took the position that an association or partnership which was subject to the Uniform Partnership Act (as adopted by the appropriate state) could never achieve the corporate characteristics which had previously been contained in the Regulations under the 1939 Code which had been obtained from *Morrissey*, that is, (1) continuity of life, (2) centralization of management, (3) limited liability, and (4) free transferability of interest. The Internal Revenue Service, obviously, declined to follow the *Kintner* decision.[6] At this point it appeared that the Internal Revenue Service had frustrated the attempts of professionals to obtain the benefits of corporate retirement plans.

5. Beginning in 1961, several states began to consider adopting statutes which would permit professionals to form professional associations which were not subject to the state-adopted Uniform Partnership Act. This would enable professional associations to avoid the 1960 Kintner Regulations. At the same time, efforts of professionals to obtain the benefits of corporate retirement plans were ongoing in Congress. In 1962, the self-employed Individuals' Tax Retirement Act, H.R. 10, generally known as the Keogh Act, was passed.[7] Unfortunately for professionals, the benefits under an H.R. 10 plan were severely limited and the amount of deductible contributions on behalf of a self-employed individual was the lesser of $2,500 or 10% of his earned income.

6. Professionals continued the struggle, and in the early 1960's many states began adopting professional corporation statutes which specifically permitted professionals to incorporate and be subject to the state's general corporation laws. It should be noted that at the present time all states and the District of Columbia allow all or some specified professions to practice as professional corporations or professional associations.[8]

7. The Treasury Department was, however, relentless and, in 1965, the Regulations under Section 301.7701 were amended to "clarify the tax treatment for professional service organizations" by the issuance of T.D. 6797.[9] Section 301.7701-1 was amended by revising Paragraph (c) to provide that "the labels applied by local law to organizations . . . are in and of themselves of no importance to the classification of such organizations for the purposes of taxation under the

Internal Revenue Code.'' The Regulations further stated that a professional service organization formed under the law of a state authorizing professional corporations would not be classified as a corporation merely because the organization was so labeled under local law. The result of the new Regulations was that most professional corporations were not considered professional corporations for tax purposes. However, the sparring was not over and professionals took the Treasury Department to task, litigating the 1965 Regulations. The courts considered the novel concept espoused by the 1965 Regulations, that a corporation validly chartered under state law would not be taxed as a corporation for federal income tax purposes, and held for the professional groups.[10]

8. On August 8, 1969, Technical Information Release 1019 announced that the Internal Revenue Service was conceding that professional service organizations established under state professional corporation acts will, generally, be treated as corporations for tax purposes. Revenue Ruling 70-101[11] supplemented T.I.R. 1019 and provides in part as follows:

> (1) In light of recent decisions of the Federal Courts, the Service generally will treat organizations of doctors, lawyers and other professional people organized under state professional association acts as corporations for tax purposes.

> (2) In addition, a professional service organization that meets the requirements for corporate classification under Section 301.7701-2 of the Regulations, exclusive of the 1965 Amendments (§301.7701-2[h] of the Regulations) made thereto, in its organization and operation will be classified as a corporation.

> (3) A professional service organization must be both organized and operated as a corporation to be classified as such. See *Jerome J. Roubik and Joan M. Roubik, et al. v. Commissioner*.[12]

Revenue Ruling 70-455[13] supplemented Rev. Rul. 70-101 and provided in part that, ''It is held that a professional service organization that is organized and operated under . . . the [state professional corporation statutes] will be treated as a corporation.''

9. In T.D. 7515 (42 Fed. Reg. 55611, October 18, 1977), the Service revoked the 1965 amendments to the Kintner Regulations (§§301.7701-1 and 2) which denied corporate tax treatment to professional corporations. These Regulations were revoked to reflect the current position of the Service that the 1965 amendments do not control the tax classification of professional corporations. Also, in Rev. Rul. 77-31,[14] the Service ruled that a professional service organization formed and operated under the professional service corporation act of a state listed in Rev. Rul. 70-101 will be considered a corporation for federal income tax purposes and the detailed criteria of Regulations §7701 need not be examined. However, the American Bar Association Committee on Professional Service Cor-

porations has reported that some agents have recently sought to apply the Kintner regulations despite Rev. Rul. 70-101 and Rev. Rul. 77-31.[15]

WHAT LIES AHEAD FOR PROFESSIONAL CORPORATIONS?

The professional corporation advisor should realize that, while professional corporations have been sanctioned by the Internal Revenue Service, professional corporations are no panacea. If structured properly, they may provide the tax benefits sought by the professionals, the primary benefit being the establishment of qualified retirement plans.

As professionals differ in their financial needs and desires, so, too, the advisors to professional corporations differ in their advice concerning professional corporations. The authors believe that an aggressive approach should be taken in planning and operating professional corporations, but that this aggressiveness should not push the planning to the point where the federal income tax return becomes a first offer (i.e., many taxpayers expect their return to be their "first offer" to the Internal Revenue Service!). Consequently, the authors feel that it is incumbent upon the advisor to the professional client to obtain for the client all benefits which are available from the professional corporation without ignoring current and possible future positions of the Internal Revenue Service.

In the late 1960's and early 1970's, the question presented to the advisor for professional corporations was, "Can we incorporate?" Now the question becomes "Should we incorporate?" However, since the initial battle with the Internal Revenue Service regarding incorporation is over, do professional corporations simply face smooth sailing or are there squalls, and even hurricanes, ahead? Recognizing that tax lawyers are often imbued with a slight case of paranoia regarding the Internal Revenue Service, the authors still feel that the second decade of professional corporations will show a concerted effort on the part of the Internal Revenue Service to examine, and often attack, existing professional corporations if they have not been organized and operated in accordance with the strict formalities of corporate and tax law.

The importance of corporate planning and adherence to state corporate laws and the federal tax laws and regulations cannot be over-emphasized. With proper corporate and tax planning, the chances of the Internal Revenue Service successfully attacking a professional corporation can be substantially minimized. Throughout this Desk Book, the authors will specifically point out those areas which are vulnerable to attack.

Harry V. Lamon, Jr.
J. Alston Thompson, Jr.

NOTES TO "A WORD FROM THE AUTHORS"

1. 1970-1 C.B. 278.

1ª 82 F.2d 473 (7th Cir. 1936).

2. Treas. Reg. §31.3401(c)-1(a) through (c); Section 401(a) of the Code; Rev. Rul. 61-157, 1961-2 C.B. 67 (declared obsolete by Rev. Rul. 72-488, 972-2 C.B. 649.

3. 296 U.S. 344 (1935).

4. 216 F.2d 418 (9th Cir. 1954).

5. 175 F. Supp. 360 (N.D. Tex. 1959).

6. Rev. Rul. 56-23, 1956-1 C.B. 598 (declared obsolete by Rev. Rul. 72-92, 1972-1 C.B. 407).

7. Public Law No. 87-792, 76 STAT. 809 (1962).

8. 4 Cavitch, *Business Organizations*, Section 82.01; and Prentice-Hall *Professional Corporation Guide*, Volume 2, Section 30,001, *et seq.*

9. 1965-1 C.B. 553.

10. *Kurzner v. United States*, 413 F.2d 97 (5th Cir. 1969) (one-man orthopedic corporation); *O'Neill v. United States*, 410 F.2d 888 (6th Cir. 1969) (medical professional corporation); *United States v. Empey*, 406 F.2d 157 (10th Cir. 1969) (four-man legal corporation); *Smith v. United States*, 301 F. Supp. 1016 (S.D. Fla. 1969) (four-man medical corporation); *Van Epps v. United States*, 301 F. Supp. 256 (D. Ariz. 1969) (three-man medical corporation); *Ahola v. United States*, 300 F. Supp. 1055 (D. Minn. 1969) (medical business trust); *Williams v. United States*, 300 F. Supp. 928 (D. Minn. 1969) (217-employee medical clinic); *Cochran v. United States*, 299 F. Supp. 1113 (D. Ariz. 1969) (large medical corporation); *Ryan v. United States,* 69-2 U.S.T.C. ¶9684 (W.D. Mich. 1969); *Kelsey v. United States*, 69-2 U.S.T.C. ¶9642 (W.D. Ark. 1969) (three-man medical associaiton); *Mendelsohn v. United States*, 69-2 U.S.T.C. ¶9577 (W.D. Ark. 1969) (medical corporation); *Fowler v. United States*, 69-2 U.S.T.C. ¶9561 (N.D. Ohio 1969); *First National Bank & Trust Co. v. United States*, 69-1 U.S.T.C. ¶9296 (N.D. Okla. 1969) (trustee for profit sharing trust of medical corporation); *Wallace v. United States*, 294 F. Supp. 1225 (E.D. Ark. 1968) (three-man medical corporation); *Holder v. United States*, 289 F. Supp. 160 (N.D. Ga. 1968), *aff'd per curiam,* 412 F.2d 1189 (5th Cir. 1969) (large medical professional association); *Foreman v. United States,* 232 F. Supp. 134 (S.D. Fla. 1964) (two-man medical association).

11. See note 1, *supra.*

12. 53 T.C. 365 (1969); see generally section [9.01], *infra.*

13. 1970-2 C.B. 297.

14. 1977-1 C.B. 409.

15. For a general discussion of this topic, see:

    Kalish and Lewis, "Professional Corporations Revisited" (After the employee Retirement Income Security Act of 1974), Vol. 28, No. 3, *Tax Lawyer,* 471.

Lamon, "Current Survey of Professional Corporations," *Law Notes*, October, 1971, Vol. 8, Page 1.

Haddleton, "Kintner Regs. Now Block Professional Corporations; Final H.R. 10 Regulations Analyzed," 20 *J. Taxation* 74 (1964).

Fischer, "Classification Under Section 7701—the Past, Present and Prospects for the Future," 30 *Tax Lawyer* 627 (1977).

Nota bene: Throughout the Desk Book, the Internal Revenue Service will be referred to as the "Service," the Internal Revenue Code of 1954, as amended, will be referred to as the "Code," references to the Code are sometimes cited by "Section" only, Treasury Regulations will be cited as "Regulations,"the Prentice-Hall *Professional Corporation Guide* is referred to herein as the *Professional Corporation Guide,* the Employee Retirement Income Security Act of 1974 is referred to as "ERISA," and the Economic Recovery Tax Act of 1981 is referred to as "ERTA."

All notes in the Desk Book appear at the conclusion of each chapter.

CONTENTS

CONTENTS

PART II—OPERATING TECHNIQUES

CONTENTS

CONTENTS

CONTENTS

LIST OF ILLUSTRATIONS AND FORMS

LIST OF ILLUSTRATIONS AND FORMS

The authors wish to express their gratitude to Daniel G. Calugar, Esq., Doris Walker, and Carol Cameron of Lamon, Elrod & Harkleroad, P.C., for their assistance in the preparation of the Desk Book.

The authors advise that this Desk Book is not an attempt to provide specific legal advice for a particular fact situation but, rather, is a compilation of those forms and techniques which have proven successful for them in situations which they have encountered. Each fact situation encountered by the professional corporation advisor will require advice based on the particular facts, state law, and individuals involved.

Harry V. Lamon, Jr.
J. Alston Thompson, Jr.

The Complete

Professional Corporation

Desk Book

PART I

INCORPORATION

CHAPTER **1**

Advantages of Incorporation

In 1935, in the famous case of *Gregory v. Helvering,* [1] Mr. Justice Sutherland stated:

> The legal right of a taxpayer to decrease the amount of what otherwise would be his taxes, or altogether avoid them, by means which the law permits, cannot be doubted.

This passage is one of the most often quoted statements regarding taxpayers' responsibilities for the payment of federal income taxes, and it is specifically applicable in the professional corporation area. If professionals can utilize the advantages which may be obtained from incorporating, they should definitely consider doing so. On the other hand, it is not necessary that incorporation be prompted solely for tax motives, since there are a number of non-tax benefits available. Care should be taken, however, by the professional corporation advisor to assure that corporate documents, particularly the minutes of the first meeting of the Board of Directors of the corporation (see section 6.02, *infra*) specifically delineate the substantial business reasons for incorporating the professional practice.

A general description of the advantages of incorporating follows. The benefits which may be provided by a professional corporation are discussed more completely in the remaining chapters of the Desk Book.

[1.01] QUALIFIED RETIREMENT PLANS

The establishment of qualified retirement plans is one of the primary benefits obtainable through incorporating a professional practice. Obviously, the

3

larger the investment (amount of contributions) placed in a tax-exempt trust of a qualified retirement plan, the larger the investment pool upon retirement. Consequently, maximizing retirement plan contributions is a major goal in most professional corporations and qualified corporate retirement plans permit this, whereas plans available to partnerships and sole proprietorships, H.R. 10 plans (Keogh plans), place severe limits on contributions. Further, corporate plans permit a wide degree of flexibility in structuring benefits and the operational provisions of plans, whereas H.R. 10 plans do not. On the other hand, most of the favorable rules relating to the tax treatment of distributions from qualified corporate plans, such as lump sum treatment under Section 402(e) and estate tax exclusion under Section 2039(c), also apply to H.R. 10 plans. Also, where H.R. 10 plans cover one or more "owner-employees" there are further limitations placed on H.R. 10 plans. Under Section 401(c)(3), an "owner-employee" is an employee who either owns the entire unincorporated trade or business or a partner owning more than 10% of either the capital or profits interest in a professional partnership.

QUALIFIED RETIREMENT PLANS

Aspect of the Plan	H.R. 10 Plans	Non-Subchapter S Corporate Plans
Contributions	A. Defined Contribution Plans	A. Defined Contribution Plans
	Contributions for Self-employed participants limited to 15% of earned income from the business not to exceed $7,500. Where a profit sharing plan is adopted, a definite formula for contributions must be provided. Section 401(d)(2)(B). Also, a higher percentage of compensation cannot be contributed for owner-employees. Compensation in excess of $100,000 cannot be taken into account in allocating contributions. Section 401(a)(17).	An employer may contribute 15% of compensation under a profit sharing plan or 25% of compensation under a money purchase pension plan. The combined maximum which may be contributed under a profit sharing plan and money purchase pension plan is 25%. Profit sharing plans may have totally discretionary contribution formulas and different percentages may be contributed for officers and shareholders due to integration with Social Security benefits. Also, Section 415 of the Code limits the annual allocation on account of participants to
	For taxable years beginning after December 31, 1981, ERTA increases the contribution limit to $15,000	

Aspect of the Plan	H.R. 10 Plans	Non-Subchapter S Corporate Plans
Contributions	and the compensation limit is increased from $100,000 to $200,000 (however, if compensation in excess of $100,000 is taken into account, the rate of contributions for common-law participants cannot be less than 7½% of compensation).	$41,500 for 1981 (which will be increased annually by the cost of living).
	B. Defined Benefit Pension Since the adoption of ERISA, it is possible for defined benefit H.R. 10 pensions to be adopted which would permit benefits funded by contributions in excess of the $7,500 limit. Section 401(j). However, the maximum benefit will be considerably smaller than the maximum benefit permitted under defined benefit corporate plans. For taxable years beginning after December 31, 1981, ERTA increases the amount of compensation which may be taken into account from $50,000 to $100,000 (this change provides an increase similar to the $7,500 to $15,000 increase for defined contribution plans).	B. Defined Benefit Pension Plans Deductible contributions to defined benefit pension plans are limited to the amount necessary to satisfy funding requirements, or if greater an amount that permits accelerated funding of past service liabilities. The annual benefit, expressed as a straight life annuity (disregarding the value of a qualified joint and survivor annuity) which may be paid from such plan, may not (for 1981) exceed the lesser of $124,500 or 100% of the participant's average compensation for his three highest consecutive years. Where an employer maintains both a defined benefit and a defined contribution plan, the allowable contribution is computed as follows: The sum of (a) the ratio of the projected annual benefit

5

Aspect of the Plan	H.R. 10 Plans	Non-Subchapter S Corporate Plans
		under the defined benefit plan to the maximum possible benefit and (b) the ratio of the aggregate annual additions actually made under the defined contribution plan to the maximum annual additions that could have been made for all years of employment may not exceed 1.4.
Investments	Investments must be held by insurance company accounts, mutual funds, U.S. Retirement Plan Bonds, special "custodial accounts" with banks, or with qualified trustees (usually a bank). Also, investments in collectibles (stamps, coins, diamonds, art, etc.) are not permitted after December 31, 1981.	Any individual or qualified corporation may act as the trustee of the plan and investments are limited only by the prudence and diversification rules of ERISA. Also, investments in collectibles (stamps, coins, diamonds, art, etc.) are not permitted after December 31, 1981.
Participation	Where owner-employees participate in the plan, all full-time employees with three years of service (other than owner-employees) must participate in the plan. Section 401(d)(3).	All employees with one year of service who have attained age 25 must participate in the plan. Through the use of dual entry dates, participation may be postponed until approximately 18 months after the date of employment. The plan may, however, exclude employees under any nondiscriminatory classification not based on age or years of service requirements more strict than age 25 and one year of service.

Aspect of the Plan	H.R. 10 Plans	Non-Subchapter S Corporate Plans
Vesting	Where owner-employees participate in the plan, there must be full and immediate vesting upon participation.	Any acceptable method under Section 411, but usually ''4-40'' vesting.
Distributions	Benefits may not be distributed to owner-employees before age 59½ without penalties and distributions to participants must begin not later than age 70½, or in the case of non-owner-employees, upon a later separation from service.	There are no minimum or maximum age vesting restrictions upon distributions to shareholder-employees of professional corporations and distributions may be made in accordance with the provisions of the plan without penalties. However, pension plan benefits may not be payable prior to death, disability, separation from service or attainment of normal retirement age.
Voluntary Contributions	Voluntary contributions by owner-employees are limited to the lesser of: 10% of earned income from the business, such lesser percentage that is applicable to non-owner-employees, or $2,500; provided that if all participants are owner-employees, voluntary contributions are not permitted. Section 4972(c).	Voluntary employee contributions may be made at any time, the limitations being 10% of covered compensation (cumulative) and the annual Section 415 allocation limits. In any event, 6% of compensation may always be contributed without affecting the Section 415 limitation.
Loans to Participants	No loans may be made to owner-employees, and under ERTA (effective for taxable years beginning after December 31, 1981, loans may not be made to any partners.	Permitted as specified under Section 408(b)(1) of ERISA.

7

Aspect of the Plan	H.R. 10 Plans	Non-Subchapter S Corporate Plans
Integration with Social Security Benefits	If no contributions or benefits for owner-employees are provided, integration with Social Security benefits is permitted [Regulations §1.401-11(c)(2)]. A defined contribution plan which provides contributions for owner-employees may be integrated only if the deductible contributions allocated to owner-employees do not exceed one-third of the total deductible contributions and self-employment Social Security taxes attributable to owner-employees are treated as contributions allocable to such employees. Section 401(d)(6). A defined benefit pension plan may not be integrated with Social Security if it provides benefits for owner-employees. Section 401(j)(4).	Integration with Social Security benefits is permitted.
Excess Contributions	Produce penalties. Section 4972.	Subject to Section 415 limitations, usually produce no penalties and are carried over to, and deducted in, following years.

A professional corporation may also take advantage of other types of plans, such as thrift plans and cash or deferred profit sharing plans. The establishment of qualified retirement plans, which provide substantial benefits, may also help satisfy the obligation which a professional group may feel to provide its career employees with reasonable pensions to permit comfortable retirement.

8

[1.02]   HEALTH AND MEDICAL PLANS

(1)   Uninsured Medical Reimbursement Plans

After December 31, 1979, the amendments made by the Revenue Act of 1978 severely restricted the use of uninsured health and medical reimbursement plans. However, if such a plan covers all employees of the professional corporation on a nondiscriminatory basis (such that each employee is entitled to the same dollar amount of benefits), the benefits paid under the plan will be deductible by the corporation and not includable in the employee's income. Such plans may provide for the payment by the corporation of any medical costs which would be deductible by the employee and which have been incurred on behalf of the employee or any of his dependents. Nondiscriminatory uninsured health and medical reimbursement plans may still be advantageous for very small professional corporations. Health and medical reimbursement plans may also be established on a discriminatory basis for officers, shareholders, and highly compensated individuals, but only for annual physicals and other ''diagnostic'' procedures. For a general discussion, see section [14.03], *infra*.

(2)   Health and Medical Insurance

A professional corporation may provide hospitalization and major medical insurance for its employees. The premium for such insurance is deductible by the corporation and not includable in the income of the employees as long as the premiums are paid under a ''plan'' of insurance, Section 105. Since hospitalization and major medical insurance are actually ''insurance,'' the rules relating to uninsured health and medical plans are not applicable. Consequently, benefits under health and medical insurance may discriminate in favor of one class of employees, making it possible to provide separate levels of benefits for officers and for staff employees. For a general discussion, see section [14.03], *infra*.

(3)   Disability Insurance

A professional corporation may also provide disability insurance for some or all of its employees under a ''plan'' of providing health benefits. The premiums paid by the corporation for disability insurance are deductible by the corporation and are not includable in the employee's income. However, if the premiums for disability insurance are paid by the corporation, any benefits paid under the policy must be includable in the gross income of the disabled employee when received. For a general discussion, see section [14.02], *infra*.

(4) Wage Continuation Plans

A corporation may also provide wage continuation plans for employees who are unable to work. This tax-favored benefit is unavailable to self-employed individuals. However, the Tax Reform Act of 1976 places substantial limitations on the ability of an employee to exclude "sick pay" under wage continuation plans from his gross income. An employee who is under age 65 and is absent from work due to disability can generally exclude up to $100 per week from his gross income if the payments are wages or payments in lieu of wages. However, this exclusion is reduced dollar for dollar by the amount in which the employee's adjusted gross income exceeds $15,000; consequently, where an employee's adjusted gross income exceeds $20,500, no exclusion is allowed. For a general discussion, see section [14.06], *infra*.

[1.03] LIFE INSURANCE

(1) Group Term Life Insurance

Under Section 79 of the Code, an employer may provide group term life insurance for its employees in an amount up to $50,000. The premiums for such insurance are deductible by the employer and are not includable in the gross income of the employee. The employer may also provide group term insurance in addition to $50,000 and the employee will be taxed on the favorable Table I costs contained under Regulations §1.79-3. In certain circumstances, the employer may also provide group permanent insurance for its employees, and the employee will only be taxed on the portion of the insurance relating to the permanent aspect. In general, group term insurance provides insurance protection for employees at a very low cost to the employer. For a general discussion, see section [14.02](1), *infra*.

(2) Retired Lives Reserve

The employer may also, under Section 79 of the Code, provide insurance for an employee which will yield a paid-up policy upon his retirement. Such insurance is generated through the retired lives reserve concept and provides a deductible premium payment for the employer which need not be included in the employee's income. For a general discussion, see section [14.02](3), *infra*.

(3) Key Man Insurance

Generally, members of a professional group will obtain insurance on the lives of the other professionals in order to permit the orderly purchase of a deceased professional's stock. This is generally done through the purchase by the professional corporation of insurance, which is owned by and payable to the professional corporation, i.e., "key man" insurance. The premiums on this insurance are paid by the professional corporation with after-tax dollars (and are not taxable to the professionals) and, usually, a tax savings is generated because the tax rate of the professional corporation is usually less than that of the respective professionals. Proceeds received by the professional corporation are not includable in the income of the professional corporation or the professionals and may be used to purchase the stock of a deceased professional. For a general discussion, see section [14.02](5), *infra*.

(4) Split Dollar Insurance

Split dollar insurance provides a vehicle for a shareholder, or his family, to own whole life insurance while producing a tax savings. Under the typical split dollar arrangement, an employee, his wife, or possibly a trust, will be the owner of a whole life insurance policy on the life of the employee. The professional corporation which employs the professional will agree to advance all (or a portion) of the premium to the employee, wife, or trust in order to permit the annual premiums to be paid. Although the funds advanced by the professional corporation must be obtained from after-tax dollars, the split dollar approach normally results in a tax savings because the corporation is in a lower tax bracket than the professional (the professional would also have had to pay the premiums with after-tax dollars). The funds advanced to pay the premium are not considered income to the employee and, upon the death of the professional or the termination of the split dollar arrangement, the corporation must be reimbursed for the funds which it has advanced toward the payment of the premiums. For a general discussion, see section [14.02](4), *infra*.

[1.04]   USE OF THE CORPORATE SURTAX EXEMPTION

Under Section 11 of the Code, as amended by the Economic Recovery Tax Act of 1981, reduced tax rates apply to the first $100,000 of taxable income of a corporation, as follows: 16% on the first $25,000, 19% on the next $25,000, 30% on the next $25,000, and 40% on the next $25,000. All taxable income in excess of $100,000 is taxed at 46%. In years after 1982, the rate will be 15% on the first $25,000 and 18% on the next 25,000. The surtax exemption will result in an average corporate tax rate of 26¾% for the first $100,000 in taxable income of a corporation and permits a corporation to retain funds for capital expenditures at a tax rate which is usually lower than that of the professionals. Under ERTA the corporate tax rates for the first two $25,000 income brackets will be reduced 1% in 1982 and 1983, producing rates of 16% (1982) and 15% (1983) on the first $25,000 and 19% (1982) and 18% (1983) on the next $25,000. The illustration of the advantages of the corporate surtax exemption set forth in Chapter 3, *infra*, provides an example of the retention of corporate earnings for the purchase of capital equipment. Also see section [8](11) *infra*.

Under Section 243, a "dividends received deduction" is established for corporations which receive dividends from other corporations. When this deduction is used in conjunction with the corporate surtax exemption, significant tax benefits may be obtained through the use of a professional corporation as an investment vehicle. For example, if funds retained in a professional corporation are invested in stocks of other corporations and dividends are paid to the professional corporation, 85% of the dividend is excludable from the professional corporation's income, leaving 15% to be taxable. If, then, the professional corporation is in a 15% tax bracket, the effective tax rate on the inter-corporate dividends received by the professional corporation will be 2.25%.

Also, a professional corporation may have a different fiscal year from that of the shareholder professional, which may permit the income of the professionals to be deferred from one calendar year to another without requiring the deferral from one corporate fiscal year to another.

[1.05] $5,000 DEATH BENEFIT

Section 101(b) provides that a corporation may provide a $5,000 death benefit to the spouse or family of a deceased employee. This benefit may be provided for the professionals employed by a professional corporation, and the payment of the benefit is deductible by the professional corporation and is not includable in the income of the recipient.

[1.06] ADMISSION OF NEW SHAREHOLDERS

When a new shareholder is admitted to a professional corporation, he is usually sold a number of shares of stock in the professional corporation. These shares of stock represent his capital interest in the corporation but not, necessarily, his income interest. His income interest may vary from his capital interest and a change in his income interest need not require an adjustment in his capital interest. Thus, the professional corporation provides an easier mechanism than the partnership for adjusting capital and income interests.

Also, the capital and income interests of a shareholder in a professional corporation may vary from his voting interest if different types of voting stock are used.

[1.07] RETIREMENT OF SHAREHOLDERS

The professional corporation provides a mechanism whereby the interest of a retiring shareholder may be redeemed (or purchased by other shareholders) without the possible dissolution of the firm, which may occur in partnerships under Section 708.

[1.08] BUSINESS EXPENSES

A professional corporation should not provide any specific benefit over and above that of a partnership with regard to the deductibility of business expenses, because any such expenses deductible by a professional corporation would also be deductible by the partnership (or by the partners). However, many accountants feel that the use of a professional corporation eliminates certain questions which the Service might otherwise raise on audit.

[1.09] NONTAX ADVANTAGES

Many partnerships of professionals operate in a very loose fashion, often meetings are held sporadically and usually no minutes of meetings are taken. The use of a professional corporation requires that certain corporate formalities be met. Consequently, if a professional corporation is formed, board meetings should be held on a regular basis and minutes should be kept of those meetings. This often obviates misunderstandings. Also, a professional corporation must have a president who usually functions as the "managing partner." The corporate form establishes a mechanism for the professionals to raise and review the question of officers at least annually. Also, upon the establishment of a professional corporation, all employees of the corporation will be placed on salaries and federal income tax withholding will be withheld from the compensation paid to them. For a professional who has difficulty in managing his assets, federal income tax withholding is often a benefit because, once an accurate withholding level is established, the professional can be assured that his income tax liabilities will be met.

The liabilities of the shareholders of a professional corporation for tort and contract obligations of the corporation and the other shareholders are also substantially limited. In general, each partner in a general partnership is jointly and severally liable for the negligent acts of his partners and for the contractual obligations of the partnership. However, in most states, there are limits on collateral malpractice liability in professional corporations. In other words, a professional is generally responsible for his own malpractice and that of professionals under his direct supervision but not for the malpractice of the other shareholders. The professional corporation will, of course, be responsible for the malpractice liability of all professionals. Further, unless under state law, the "veil" of the corporation can be pierced, the corporation (and not the shareholders) is solely liable for general and contractual liabilities.

NOTES TO CHAPTER 1

1. 293 U.S. 465 (1935).
2. 89 F.2d 473 (7th Cir. 1936).
3. Treas. Regs. §31.3401(c)-1(a) through (c); Code Section 401(a); Rev. Rul. 61-157, 1961-2 C.B. 67 (declared obsolete by Rev. Rul. 72-488 1972-2 C.B. 649).

CHAPTER **2**

Potential Problems and Disadvantages Created By Incorporation

[2.01] UNREASONABLE COMPENSATION

When a professional corporation is established, there is an opportunity for the Service to apply a double tax, first on the corporation and then on the shareholders. If the Service can establish that the compensation paid to a shareholder is "unreasonable," the unreasonable portion of the compensation will be taxed to the corporation as earnings (the compensation deduction will be disallowed) and then will be taxed to the respective shareholder as dividends. Unreasonable compensation should, however, generally not be a problem in professional corporations. For a general discussion of reasonable compensation, see Chapter 13, *infra*.

[2.02] PERSONAL HOLDING COMPANY TAX

It is possible that, in certain circumstances, professional corporations may be treated as personal holding companies and any accumulated earnings which are not paid out to shareholders may be subject to the 70% (50% in 1982 and thereafter) personal holding company tax. The personal holding company tax should, generally, not be a problem for professional corporations if contracts with hospitals and other institutions are drafted properly, naming the professional corporation as the provider of the services, and if all income is paid to the professional corporation and not to the professionals. The Service has relaxed its view of the applicability of the personal holding company provisions to one-man professional corporations. For a general discussion of the personal holding company tax, see section [9.02], *infra*.

[2.03] ACCUMULATED EARNINGS TAX

Any corporation may run afoul of the accumulated earnings tax provisions of Section 534 of the Code where earnings in excess of $150,000 ($250,000 during 1982 and thereafter under ERTA for regular corporations) are accumulated. The accumulated earnings tax is also a problem for professional corporations but may be avoided by limiting the amount of earnings which are accumulated. For a general discussion, see section [9.04], *infra*.

[2.04] SECTION 482, SECTION 269, AND EARNER OF INCOME PROBLEMS

Where a corporation is not operated with proper corporate formalities, where there is a misallocation of funds between the shareholders and the corporation, or where the corporation is used strictly for tax avoidance, it is possible for the Service to attack the existence of the corporation and attempt to tax the income of the corporation directly to the shareholders. If this occurs, obviously, the qualified retirement plans of the professional corporation will be jeopardized. These problems can usually be eliminated if the corporation is operated properly. For a general discussion, see sections [9.01] and [9.03], *infra*.

[2.05] TRANSFER OF RECEIVABLES AND PAYABLES UPON INCORPORATION

The incorporation of any business (including a professional practice) is subject to the very technical rules of Section 351 of the Code. Enormous tax liabilities may be created upon incorporation by the transfer of accounts receivable and accounts payable to the corporation. However, where the professional seeks competent tax advice prior to the incorporation, these problems can be eliminated. For a general discussion, see section [5.10](1), *infra*.

[2.06] BUNCHING OF INCOME UPON INCORPORATION

Where a professional partnership incorporates, it is possible for more than one year's income to be "bunched" into one taxable year of a professional. This occurs because, in a partnership, the entire income of the partnership is taxed to the partner in the calendar year in which the partnership ends. For example, in the case of a partnership with a January 31 fiscal year end, the entire income for the fiscal year ended January 31, 1981, will be taxed in each partner's 1981 calendar year, even though the income was probably distributed pro rata during the partnership year. Consequently, if incorporation occurs on February 1, 1981, and the professionals are paid a salary during each month of calendar year 1981, the professionals will be taxed on 23 months of income during calendar year 1981. This problem usually occurs only when a fiscal year partnership is incorporated and it may be minimized by proper tax planning. For a general discussion, see section [5.14], *infra*.

[2.07]   POSSIBLE INCREASES IN FICA AND FUTA TAXES

Probably the largest out-of-pocket expense which will be encountered upon the incorporation of a professional practice is the increase in FICA and FUTA taxes. Upon the incorporation of a professional practice, the professionals will be considered employees of the professional corporation. Consequently, the corporation and the professionals must pay FICA and FUTA taxes on the salaries paid to the professionals. The table below indicates that the joint FICA taxes which must be paid by the professional and by the professional corporation will substantially exceed the self-employment tax which would be levied only against the professional. The total tax difference for 1981 is $1,188, and the decision of whether to incorporate should be based on tax savings of at least that amount, plus $180, the amount of FUTA taxes payable (3.4% of the first $6,000 in wages).

Year	FICA Tax Rate	Wage Base	Amount Payable By Each	Total	Self-Employed Tax Rate	Tax	Difference
1980	6.13%	$25,900	$1,587.67	$3,175.34	8.10%	$2,097.90	$1,077.44
1981	6.65%	29,700	1,975.05	3,950.10	9.30%	2,762.10	1,188.00
1982	6.70%	31,800	2,130.60	4,261.20	9.35%	2,973.30	1,287.90
1983	6.70%	33,900	2,271.30	4,542.60	9.35%	3,169.65	1,372.95
1984	6.70%	36,000	2,412.00	4,824.00	9.35%	3,366.60	1,458.00
1985	7.05%	38,100	2,686.05	5,372.10	9.90%	3,771.90	1,600.20

It should be realized, however, that the FICA and FUTA taxes payable by the corporation are deductible and, consequently, should reduce the net out-of-pocket expense. However, as FICA taxes increase during the coming years, the FICA tax may become a factor.

[2.08]   DEPRECIATION AND INVESTMENT TAX CREDIT

Upon the transfer of assets from a professional to his professional corporation, no recapture of depreciation will occur, but the corporation will not be entitled to use the double declining balance method of depreciation on taxable personal property or real property because it will not be considered the "first user" of the property. However, the professional corporation can use other accelerated methods of depreciation on tangible personal property.[1] Also, for property placed in service during or after 1981, the Accelerated Cost Recovery System of ERTA will reduce the impact of the loss of accelerated depreciation rates. The investment tax credit previously taken by the professional should not be recaptured on incorporation. For further discussion, see section [5.07], *infra*.

[2.09] MISCELLANEOUS TAXES

Incorporation of a professional practice will also create an increase in workmen's compensation taxes because all employees (including the new professional employees) must be covered by workmen's compensation. Also, the professional corporation will be subject to state and local income taxes and franchise taxes, where applicable, and the stock in the professional corporation which is owned by the professionals may be subject to state and local transfer taxes and intangible taxes.

[2.10] NONTAX DISADVANTAGES

(1) Malpractice Insurance Increases

Upon incorporation, it is possible for the malpractice insurance premiums of professional practices to increase, sometimes as much as 25 percent. For some reason, insurance companies that underwrite malpractice insurance feel that the professional corporation is another insured which must be covered by the policy at an additional cost.

(2) More Governmental Regulation

Incorporation may subject the professional practice to further governmental regulation. For example, if wage and price controls are implemented, they will, probably, cover professional corporations; whereas, wage controls generally have, in the past, not covered professional partnerships. Also, under some state laws, corporations are required to file an annual report with the Secretary of State or Department of Commerce and such a provision may make the professional corporation's balance sheet available for public inspection.

(3) Lost Individuality

Upon incorporation, some "partners" feel that they have lost their individuality. Further, some individuals simply refuse to follow the federal income tax withholding requirements even though withholding does eliminate the "feast or famine" syndrome created by the requirement that partners pay their estimated federal income tax on a quarterly basis.

(4) Adherence to Corporate Formalities

Upon incorporation, the shareholders and the corporation must commence strict adherence to corporate formalities and record keeping. This often results in increased legal and accounting fees and also additional fees for the administration of the qualified retirement plans.

(5) Decreased Spendable Income

The incorporation of a professional practice will, if the benefits available from incorporation are obtained, produce a decreased amount of spendable income for each professional employee due to the forced savings produced through the qualified retirement plans. This is illustrated in the example contained in the following section, but it must be noted that the professional will actually have a net savings over what would occur if he were to attempt to save personally the same amount of funds which are set aside in the qualified retirement plans.

(6) Time Required

Probably the most important practical disadvantage of incorporating, next to the out-of-pocket cost for FICA and FUTA taxes, is the amount of time which must be expended by the professionals in reviewing documents and establishing criteria for the professional corporation. It is for this reason that the authors highly recommend that the professional, be he doctor, lawyer, accountant, or other professional, seek competent professional advice in the specialized area of professional corporations. The authors, on many occasions, have represented law firms which have incorporated, and it has been related to the authors by those firms that the fees expended in seeking adequate professional advice have been more than offset by the peace of mind generated by such advice.

NOTE TO CHAPTER 2

1. Rev. Rul. 57-352, 1957-2 C.B. 150, and Rev. Rul. 56-256, 1956-1, C.B. 129.

CHAPTER **3**

Who Should Incorporate?

One of the most important steps an advisor can take in counseling his professional client regarding incorporation is to determine, with the help of his client, whether incorporation is economically feasible. The authors feel that, if the following three questions can be answered in the affirmative, the professional should seriously consider incorporating. If the first question is answered in the negative, incorporation is definitely not appropriate. If the answer to the first question is affirmative, but if either the second or the third question is answered in the negative, the professional should not consider incorporating.

[3.01] CAN YOUR CLIENT AFFORD TO INCORPORATE?

Simply put, if the professional practice does not generate sufficient income to provide for the professional's personal needs and to utilize the employee benefits available through a professional corporation, the practice should not be incorporated. The authors feel that a professional should, generally, have a minimum income (net of professional expenses) of $75,000 before seriously considering incorporating. This minimum level of income will, of course, fluctuate (usually up and not down) based upon the life style of the professional and the amount the professional will require for living expenses, such as private schools and college educations. The authors feel that it is always best to begin the answer to this question at the bottom line, i.e., how much does the professional need to support himself and his family? This answer should be computed with the help of the professional's accountant and then the accountant, the attorney, and the professional should work backward to determine what income will be necessary to provide the professional's support needs and the employee benefits generated by a professional corporation. In most cases, the spouse of the professional should at least be considered, if not consulted, in making these computations.

In some cases where the computations indicate that a professional should not incorporate because of insufficient funds (over and above support needs) to utilize the employee benefits available through a professional corporation, the authors have found it advisable to proceed with the incorporation based on an anticipated increase in professional income. This course of action, however, should be undertaken, only if there is a substantial likelihood that the professional's income will justify incorporation within the next three years, and then with the full advice and consent of the professional and his accountant. Early incorporation permits the professional to become acquainted with the general operation of a professional corporation prior to the establishment of the retirement plans.

[3.02] IF THE PROFESSIONAL CAN AFFORD TO INCORPORATE, IS HE WILLING TO FUND QUALIFIED RETIREMENT PLANS?

The qualified retirement plans available to a corporation, and consequently to a professional corporation, continue to be the primary benefit obtainable through the incorporation of a professional practice. The comparison of corporate plans with H.R. 10 plans in section [1.01], *supra*, clearly indicates that not only can contributions to corporate plans be increased substantially, but that the plans can be significantly more flexible. However, unless the professional is willing to make significant contributions to the qualified retirement plans (in the opinion of the authors, at least $15,000 per year), the benefit of incorporating is diminished. It should be realized, however, that even if a professional contributes an amount equal to the H.R. 10 limit to his accounts under the professional corporation's qualified retirement plans, the flexibility of corporate retirement plans may still favor incorporating. Further, in considering the use of qualified retirement plans, the professional should determine whether he is willing to make the contributions which will be required on behalf of the staff employees. In order to make this determination, the authors recommend that a *pro forma* be prepared showing different levels of contributions for the professional and the corresponding required contributions for the staff employees.

[3.03] IF THE PROFESSIONAL CAN INCORPORATE AND IS WILLING TO FUND QUALIFIED RETIREMENT PLANS, IS HE WILLING TO COMPLY WITH CORPORATE FORMALITIES?

Professional corporations are just like all business corporations, and normal corporate formalities required under state law must be met. Consequently, the professional corporation must keep adequate books and records, hold annual shareholders' and directors' meetings, and adopt and comply with bylaws for the operation of the corporation. The professional must be willing to exert the effort and expend the time necessary to assure that corporate business is properly conducted. Also, shortly after incorporation, a substantial number of changes must be made, such as bank account numbers and names, letterheads, signs on the office space, etc., and the professional will necessarily be charged with these duties.

As the years pass, the professional will also be effectively charged with the duty of monitoring changes in the law affecting professional corporations, which will certainly occur from time to time. In order to do this, it will be necessary for the professional to employ adequate accounting and legal services on a continuing basis, and the professional must make a firm commitment to pay the legal and accounting fees necessary to perpetuate the professional corporation. A professional corporation which operates without adequate legal and accounting advice is simply a smoldering time bomb.

The incorporated professional must also adjust his psyche so that he will be in a position to consider himself no longer a "partner" but an "employee" of the professional corporation. Along with his new status as an employee will come federal income tax withholding on a regular basis. This will mean that, generally, the professional will no longer be required to make quarterly estimated payments for federal income tax purposes. It will also mean that, at each pay period, the professional will take home less money than he would have received when, as a partner, no federal income taxes had been withheld. Some professionals appear to be incapable of adjusting to federal income tax withholding while others thrive on it. The authors feel that the consequences of federal income tax withholding should specifically be discussed with the professional because, in many cases where professionals have found themselves incapable of effectively managing their money, federal income tax withholding is an advantage.

The above questions are focused on the individual professional who is considering incorporating. However, where a group of professionals is considering incorporating, the questions are the same but the answers are more difficult to resolve. Each professional has divergent needs and desires, both financial and professional, which must be met. It has been the authors' experience that, in professional groups containing more than 10 partners, it is very often impossible to incorporate because it is impossible to satisfy the partners' different desires. This occurs even where all of the professionals agree that incorporation is the right course of action to take. For this reason, many groups of professionals are now considering forming partnerships which consist of several professional corporations. In this manner, each professional can establish the retirement plans and employee benefits which he desires for himself in his own professional corporation. This concept is discussed more fully in Chapter 19, *infra*.

The following example clearly indicates that, if the answer to the three questions above is in the affirmative, incorporation should definitely be considered.

[3.04] ILLUSTRATION OF THE TAX ADVANTAGES OF INCORPORATING A PROFESSIONAL PRACTICE

The following comparison illustrates the tax benefits that may be realized through a professional corporation which are not available through a proprietorship or partnership. The subject of the comparison is a 40-year old physician who maintains a medical practice which grosses $250,000 per year. He employs four staff persons whose combined annual payroll equals $30,000. The comparison is also based on the following assumptions:

(1) In the proprietorship form, the professional maintains a defined contribution H.R. 10 plan and makes the maximum allowable yearly contribution to the plan. Similarly, the professional corporation maintains a qualified money purchase pension plan (which is integrated with Social Security benefits at a $20,000 level) and a profit sharing plan, and contributes amounts sufficient to provide the maximum allowable allocation under Section 415 of the Code (exclusive of forfeitures).

(2) The professional is paid an annual salary equal to the net income of the corporation after deducting the retirement plan contributions.

(3) Wherever applicable, the tax rates and limitations are those effective during the calendar year 1982. It is assumed that the professional files a joint return with his spouse and claims $5,000 in itemized deductions and two exemptions. It should be realized that the increase from $7,500 to $15,000 for H.R. 10 plan contributions under ERTA will make incorporation less attractive for some professionals. However, even if the professional anticipates contributing only $15,000 to his plans, the flexibility of corporate plans (vesting schedules, etc.) should favor incorporation. Also, the ERTA reduction (1% in 1982 and 1% in 1983) in the first two corporate tax brackets ($1- $25,000 and $25,001-$50,000) should favor incorporation.

	PROPRIETORSHIP	CORPORATION
Income		
Gross Receipts	$250,000	$250,000
Deductions Not Affected by Incorporation		
Operating expenses	$ 40,000	$ 40,000
Salaries—staff	30,000	30,000
Payroll taxes—staff		
Unemployment	816	816
FICA	1,839	1,839
	(72,655)	(72,655)

Deductions Affected by Incorporation	PROPRIETORSHIP	CORPORATION
Retirement plan deduction:		
H.R. 10 plan		
Staff (approximate)	(3,000)	
Professional	(15,000)	
Money purchase pension and profit sharing plans		
Staff (approximate)		(5,800)
Professional (approximate)		(34,000)
Accident and health insurance		(1,000)
Disability insurance		(500)
Group-term life insurance ($100,000 of coverage)		(350)
Medical reimbursement plan		(150)
Payroll taxes—professional		
Unemployment		(200)
FICA		(2,130)
Net income before salary	$159,345	$133,215
Salary	N/A	(133,215)
Taxable income	$159,345	$ -0-

Tax Liability Comparison

Corporate income tax		$ -0-
Self-employment tax	$ 2,973	
FICA—employee's share		$ 2,130
Additional income tax due on Table I—Cost of $50,000 of group term life insurance		70
Personal income tax on proprietorship share or corporate salary	63,622	$ 50,557
Total Federal tax liability	$ 66,595	$ 52,757

Cash Flow Comparison

Proprietorship share or corporate salary	$159,345	$133,215
Federal tax liability	(66,595)	(52,767)
Nondeductible payments for medical and health benefits equivalent to		

	PROPRIETORSHIP	CORPORATION
those provided by the Corporation	(2,000)	
Net Disposable Income	$90,750	$ 80,458
Cash set aside for investments	(19,000)	N/A
Net spendable income	$71,750	$ 80,458

As the foregoing example indicates, the use of the corporate form permits the professional to obtain tax deductible insurance benefits and, at the same time, fund a personal retirement benefit equal to $34,000, or $19,000 more than the corresponding amount contributed to the H.R. 10 plan. In obtaining these substantial economic benefits, the professional must understand the following:

(1) the larger contributions to the corporate retirement plans result in a net disposable income to the professional which is $10,292 less than that produced from the proprietorship;

(2) the professional should determine if the net disposable income available after incorporation is sufficient to meet his personal living needs;

(3) the required contributions to the corporate retirement plans on behalf of the staff personnel exceed the corresponding contributions to the H.R. 10 plan by $2,800;

(4) assuming that the professional will make contributions of $34,000 to the retirement plans on his behalf for 20 years and that those contributions earn an average annual return of 8%, the corporation will produce a retirement fund of approximately $1,555,000, as compared to approximately $745,000 in the H.R. 10 plan if contributions equal $15,000 for 20 years; and

(5) if the professional attempts to save $19,000 for investment (the difference between the contributions to corporate plans and the H.R. 10 plan), the *proprietor has approximately $9,000 less in net spendable income than does the employee of the professional corporation.*

In this example, the professional has withdrawn all of the corporate net income as salary in order to avoid corporate income taxes. Suppose, however, that the corporation must purchase a new X-ray machine costing $20,000. In that event, the professional's salary must be reduced by approximately $24,000 in order to leave sufficient funds in the corporation to finance the purchase of the equipment. This means, of course, that the professional's personal taxable income will decrease by $24,000. Since salary is earned income and is taxed at a maximum rate of 50%, the $24,000 salary reduction will decrease the professional's personal tax liability by $12,000. The additional corporate income will be taxed to the corporation at the following rates:

Taxable Income	Rate	
$0 - $25,000	17%	(16% in 1982 and 15% in 1983)
$25,001 - $50,000	20%	(19% in 1982 and 18% in 1983)
$50,001 - $75,000	30%	
$75,001 - $100,000	40%	
In excess of $100,000	46%	

Accordingly, the $24,000 of corporate income will generate a corporate tax liability of $4,080. Thus, by having the corporation, rather than the professional purchase the equipment, the net cost of the equipment has been reduced from $40,000 (50% tax paid to produce $20,000 purchase price) in the proprietorship to $24,000 in the corporation.

Other matters which deserve comment:

(1) Although a proprietorship has been used in this comparison, the analysis is equally applicable where a partnership is considering incorporation.

(2) Congress has severely curtailed the extent to which medical reimbursement plans may be used to benefit only the highly paid employees or the owners of a corporation. However, a plan may be established which benefits only those persons if reimbursement is limited to expenses for diagnostic services, such as physicals or routine dental care, and the plan envisioned in the example above is so limited.

(3) The cost of the first $50,000 of group-term insurance is not taxed to the professional, although it is deductible by the corporation. With regard to the second $50,000 of coverage, the professional must report $138 as taxable income.

(4) Incorporation results in increased unemployment and Social Security taxes on the professional's salary. However, when one considers the fact that such taxes are a deductible expense of the corporation, as well as the fact that the income of a sole proprietor is subject to self-employment taxes at a rate which is approximately 2% higher than the Social Security rates applicable to employees, the payroll tax expense after incorporation is only slightly greater than as a proprietorship.

(5) It has been assumed that the proprietor purchases medical, disability, and life insurance policies which provide benefits similar to those provided by the corporation. These expenses, which are deductible if incurred by the corporation, are nondeductible personal expenses of the proprietor.

(6) The impact of state and local income and franchise taxes has been ignored.

CHAPTER 4

How to Advise the Client

Probably the most important meeting between a professional corporation advisor and a professional considering incorporating is the initial conference, and probably the most important aspect of the initial conference is the tone of the conference as set by the professional corporation advisor. By the time the professional has reached the point of discussing this matter with his advisors, he has probably been approached by several get-rich-quick men, several insurance agents, and several stock brokers, each with a presentation on the benefits from incorporation and the establishment of qualified retirement plans. Because of these contacts, the professional is usually very uncertain about which way to proceed and is seeking a definite, independent review of the matter by his professional advisor. For that reason, the professional advisor should review the advantages and disadvantages of incorporating, as set forth in Chapters 1 and 2, *supra*, and should be as decisive as possible in outlining the advantages and disadvantages. The authors have found that, by and large, professionals who are considering incorporation do not want to make the final decision themselves and simply ask "Please tell me what to do." In this situation, the professional corporation advisor must simply make his recommendation and be prepared to defend that recommendation if it happens to conflict with those of others with whom the professional may have discussed this matter. However, if the three questions provided under sections [3.01-3.03], *supra*, were answered in the affirmative, the question of whether or not to incorporate would appear to be rhetorical.

The initial meeting with a professional considering incorporation should be held at least one month prior to the date on which the anticipated professional corporation will be formed. This will permit the professional advisor sufficient time to have additional meetings (which will be necessary) prior to the formation of the corporation. At the initial meeting, at least the accountant and attorney for the professional should be present. Also, prior to that meeting, the accountant should have made the computations necessary to answer the question set forth in section [3.02], *supra* (i.e., can the professional afford to incorporate). This question should be discussed in detail by the professional, the accountant, and the attorney. If the answer is yes, the attorney should then submit a list of advantages and disadvantages of incorporating which can be discussed. The authors have found that submitting a list of advantages and disadvantages in the form of a memorandum, such as that attached below, facilitates discussion.

MEMORANDUM

TO:

FROM:

DATE:

  RE: Advantages and Disadvantages of Incorporation

To facilitate your consideration of the incorporation of your medical practice, we have, below, outlined the various advantages and disadvantages which are inherent in the operation of a professional practice in corporate form. This outline is intentionally abbreviated and the general topics listed below will be discussed in detail at our meeting with you.

ADVANTAGES

1. Qualified Retirement Plans:

a.	Defined Contribution Plans	v	H.R. 10 Plan
	Maximum contribution of Lesser of 25% or $41,500	v	Maximum Contribution of 15% or $7,500, ($15,000) in 1982
	Possible Use of:		
	(1) Profit Sharing Plan		
	(2) Money-Purchase Pension Plan		
	(3) Thrift Plan		
	(4) Cash or Deferred Plan		
b.	Corporate Defined Benefit Plan, Maximum Benefit of $124,500 or 100% of Compensation	v	H.R. 10 Defined Benefit Plan

2. Health and Medical Plans:

Contributions are deductible by the Corporation and not taxable as income to employees.

   a. Medical Expense Reimbursement Plan (Restricted use after 12/31/79)

   b. Hospitalization and Major Medical Insurance

3. Group Term Life Insurance:

Premiums are deductible by Corporation and not taxable as income to employees on first $50,000 of coverage, excess coverage available at a low "tax" cost.

4. Disability Insurance:

Premiums are deductible by Corporation and not taxable as income to employees.

5. Split-Dollar Insurance:

Reduced cost for insurance protection, with major portion of premiums being paid by Corporation with after-tax dollars.

6. Tax shelter via Corporate Form:

   a. Surtax exemption: 17% (16% in 1982 and 15% in 1983) on first $25,000, 20% (19% in 1982 and 18% in 1983) on next $25,000, 30% on next $25,000, 40% on next $25,000, and 46% on all taxable income in excess of $100,000.

   b. 85% dividends received deduction.

   c. Deferral possibilities where Corporation has fiscal year.

7. $5,000 Death Benefit:

Deductible by Corporation and not taxable to employee's estate as income.

8. Retirement of Shareholder:

Corporation provides flexible medium for the retirement of a shareholder.

   a. Key-man insurance

   b. Nonqualified deferred compensation

9. Business Expenses:

Some benefit in deducting business expenses at corporate level.

10. Nontax Advantages:

   a. Discipline of corporate form, management, income tax withholding, etc.

   b. Withdrawal, retirement or addition of associates and partners without dissolution.

   c. Limitations on liability: (i) creditors of corporation and (ii) negligent acts of employees.

DISADVANTAGES

1. Potential double tax—Unreasonable compensation and loans to shareholders.

2. Personal Holding Company Tax—Proper execution of contracts.

3. Accumulated earnings tax, Section 269, and Section 482.

4. Transfer of receivables and payables.

5. Income bunching and incorporation—Especially where fiscal year partnership.

6. Corporateness—Possible disqualification of plans. *Roubik*.

7. Multiple corporation problem—Discrimination under corporate retirement plans. Section 414.

8. Possible increase in malpractice insurance.

9. Increased FICA and FUTA taxes. However, corporation's share is deductible, thus reducing the cost.

10. Nontax Disadvantages:

    a. Psychological (loss of individuality).

    b. Strict adherence to corporate formalities.

    c. Increased accounting fees and fees for administration of retirement plans.

At the initial meeting, the professional, the accountant, and the attorney should also discuss the various types of qualified retirement plans and should obtain an answer to the question listed in section [3.03], *supra*, (i.e., will the professional make adequate use of the corporate retirement plans available?). The authors have found that professionals are interested in the amount of contributions which can be allocated to their accounts and also the amount of contributions which they "have to" make on account of the staff employees. The authors feel that any fears which the professional may have regarding the funding of "enormous" retirement benefits for staff employees can be ameliorated by a discussion of the effect of the integration of the plans with Social Security and the effect of the vesting schedule, coupled with the turnover rate of staff employees. The authors often submit, at the initial meeting, the following illustration of the allocations which will be required under various defined contribution plans:

ILLUSTRATION OF THE ALLOCATION OF
CONTRIBUTIONS AMONG PARTICIPANTS
UNDER CERTAIN
DEFINED CONTRIBUTION PLANS

PREPARED FOR:

Assume that a P.C. which maintains a Profit Sharing Plan employs two physicians who each earn $110,000 per year, two nurses who each earn $10,000 per year, and three staff members who earn $9,000, $8,000 and $7,000 per year. Also assume sufficient profits to permit a Profit Sharing Plan contribution equal to 15% of the total payroll of $264,000, or $39,600, which would be made for a given plan year. The Profit Sharing Plan contribution would be allocated on a pro rata basis as follows:

Participant	Contribution Allocation
Physician	$16,500
Physician	16,500
Nurse	1,500
Nurse	1,500
Staff @ $9,000	1,350
Staff @ $8,000	1,200
Staff @ $7,000	1,050
TOTAL	$39,600

A Profit Sharing Plan may be integrated with the Social Security Wage base, in which case the allocation of the same $39,600 would be as follows:

Participant	Contribution Allocation
Physician	$17,550.00
Physician	17,550.00
Nurse	1,022.72
Nurse	1,022.72
Staff @ $9,000	920.45
Staff @ $8,000	818.19
Staff @ $7,000	715.92
TOTAL	$39,600.00

For purposes of this example, the integration level has been fixed at $20,000, rather than using the actual Social Security Wage Base currently in effect.

Under a fully integrated Money-Purchase Pension Plan, the contribution formula would be an amount equal to (a) 3% of each participant's compensation up to the Social Security Wage Base (or $20,000 whichever is lesser) plus (b) 10% of compensation in excess of the Social Security Wage Base (or $20,000 whichever is lesser).

Using the same compensation as in the prior examples, and once again fixing the integration rate at $20,000, a contribution in the amount of $20,520 would be required and the allocation would be as follows:

Participant	Contribution Allocation
Physician	$9,600
Physician	9,600
Nurse	300
Nurse	300
Staff @ $9,000	270
Staff @ $8,000	240
Staff @ $7,000	210
TOTAL	$20,520

The following example represents total contributions allocated where the Corporation maintains a non-integrated Profit Sharing Plan and an integrated Money-Purchase Pension Plan:

Participant	Profit Sharing Plan	Money-Purchase Pension Plan	Total Allocation
Physician	$16,500	$ 9,600	$26,100
Physician	16,500	9,600	26,100
Nurse	1,500	300	1,800
Nurse	1,500	300	1,800
Staff @ $9,000	1,350	270	1,620
Staff @ $8,00	1,200	240	1,440
Staff @ $7,000	1,050	210	1,260
TOTAL	$39,600	$20,520	$60,120

Obviously, maintaining both a Profit Sharing Plan and an integrated Money-Purchase Pension Plan permits a greater contribution to be made on behalf of the physicians than may be made under the Profit Sharing Plan alone, while the contribution for the physicians, (the lesser of 25% of salary or $41,500) the Profit addition of the Money-Purchase Pension Plan gives the nurses and staff members additional security that they would not have if the P.C. maintained only a Profit Sharing Plan, as the P.C. will be required to make this fixed obligation contribution each year.

If the P.C. should desire to contribute up to the maximum deductible contribution for the physicians, (the lesser of 25% of salary or $36,875) the Profit Sharing Plan contribution can be increased accordingly.

It is also incumbent upon the attorney, at the initial meeting with the professional, to discuss the anticipated legal fees which will be charged for incorporating the professional practice. A complete discussion of the additional legal and accounting fees which arise upon incorporation is more fully discussed in section [8.08](6), *infra*. However, the authors have found that the fees charged will vary in accordance with the type of professional group involved and the number of professionals, with fees usually falling in a $1,500 to $7,500 range, depending upon the number and complexity of retirement plans prepared. The professional corporation advisor should also consider the different questions and problems which various professions may generate. As a general rule, and without attempting to categorize professionals, the authors have generally found the following:

Physicians

Physicians are usually willing to move ahead with incorporation after sufficient explanation has been given by the attorney and accountant. However, they usually do not understand the corporate and tax aspects of incorporation and/or do not have the time or inclination to do so. Physicians simply retain competent advisors and rely upon them.

Attorneys

Attorneys usually understand the general nature of the benefits to be gained from incorporating but not the technical aspects. However, for one reason or another, attorneys seem to be less willing to move forward with incorporation than do physicians. Some attorneys view the practice of law through professional corporations as somehow quasi unethical, while others simply feel that "we've been doing okay, why change?"

Accountants

Accountants usually understand both the general and technical nature of incorporation and, once a decision has been made to incorporate, they are willing to proceed. However, for some reason, some accountants do not view as important the corporate formalities, including the execution of employment agreements, stock retirement agreements, etc., and these items are often neglected unless the attorney constantly monitors the situation.

Following the initial meeting, the attorney should write a confirming letter to the professional briefly outlining some of the more important advantages and disadvantages of incorporating. This letter should specifically state the services which the attorney will perform for the professional and the fees which will be charged. The letter should be structured so that the professional will agree to the fee arrangement in the letter and return one executed copy of the letter to the attorney for his files. A copy of a letter which may be used for this purpose follows. The authors cannot overemphasize the importance of obtaining from the professional a signed copy of the fee agreement letter. This will preclude misunderstandings over fees. It is also often appropriate for the attorney's fee letter to specifically state those duties which will be performed by the accountant, since at times the attorney's and accountant's functions overlap. The attorney and accountant should always have a clear understanding of who will perform the various functions, and this understanding should be reached prior to incorporation.

EXAMPLE OF FEE AGREEMENT LETTER

RE: PROFESSIONAL CORPORATION

Dear _____:

We were happy to have the opportunity to discuss with you the formation of a professional corporation. We would like to confirm some of the major aspects of professional corporations which we discussed in our last meeting on _____.

Incorporation of your legal practice has a great number of advantages from a tax standpoint. The single, most important advantage that a professional corporation holds over its unincorporated counterpart is the availability of a qualified retirement plan. Under a retirement plan that qualifies under Section 401(a) of the Internal Revenue Code, amounts contributed to the plan may be deducted in the year contributed, and the employees are not taxed on benefits provided by the plan until those benefits are paid or otherwise made available to them—usually after retirement age. Furthermore, the trust fund, which enjoys exempt status under Section 501(a) of the Code, is not taxable upon the earnings realized on the contributions that have been made to the fund. Since these earnings are not taxed at the time realized, the compounded growth of the fund is greatly enhanced. This growth in principal helps to fund additional retirement benefits for you upon retirement. In addition, any interest that an employee may have in a qualified plan will be excluded from his gross estate at the time of his death if not paid in a lump sum, and, if he should exercise any of his options whereby payments of benefits become payable to a beneficiary other than his estate at or after his death, such an election is excluded from the gift tax provisions of the Internal Revenue Code.

A comparison between a qualified retirement plan for a corporation and a qualified H.R. 10 Plan for a partnership reveals clearly the advantages that the corporate plan has over the H.R. 10 Plan. In an H.R. 10 Plan, the employer's contributions are limited to the lower of 15% of compensation or $7,500 ($15,000 in 1982 and thereafter) per owner-employee. On the other hand, the maximum deductible contribution to a corporate profit sharing plan is 15% of the compensation of the employees covered by the plan; and the maximum deductible contribution to a combination of a profit sharing plan and a pension plan is 25% of the employees' compensation.

In addition, ERISA limits the total amount that may be contributed for each employee who is a participant in both a profit sharing plan and a money purchase pension plan to 25% of compensation or $41,500 per year, whichever is less.* Such a limitation is considerably more liberal than the limitation on H.R. 10 Plan contributions.

There are other important distinctions between a corporate plan and an H.R. 10 Plan that should be recognized. In a corporate plan, a reasonable vesting schedule may be imposed, whereas in an H.R. 10 Plan the vesting of a participant's benefits must occur immediately after the participant meets the eligibility require-

---

*This maximum dollar figure must be adjusted for forfeitures and, within limits, for certain voluntary contributions. Also, the amount is subject to cost of living increases each year.

ments. No benefits may be paid under an H.R. 10 Plan before an owner-employee reaches age 59½, but under a corporate plan earlier benefits, such as early retirement, may be provided for employees. If an owner-employee should need to borrow funds from the plan, such a borrowing would be treated as a distribution to him, and therefore taxable, under an H.R. 10 Plan. Within certain limits, loans to participants would not be treated as a distribution under a corporate plan. Also, distribution of benefits must begin under a H.R. 10 Plan at age 70½, but there is no such rule covering corporate plans.**

Aside from the retirement plan itself, there are a number of other tax advantages that corporations enjoy over partnerships. For example, under sections 105 and 106 of the Internal Revenue Code, a corporation may provide health and accident insurance plans. Payments under such plans will be allowed as a deduction to the corporation but will not be included in the income of the recipients. This is particularly advantageous to the employee, since payments for such expenses by the employee are deductible only to the extent of one-half of the payments made for medical insurance premiums (not to exceed $150.00), and to the extent that all other medical expenses exceed 3% of the employee's adjusted gross income with a further limitation that expenses for drugs must be in excess of 1% of the employee's adjusted gross income before they may be counted toward the 3% floor on medical deductions.

Somewhat analogous to the medical expense area is the ability of the corporation to provide disability insurance for its employees. The premiums paid for such insurance are deductible by the corporation, and are not included in the income of the employee-beneficiary. The only requirements that need be met for such treatment are that the corporation may not be a beneficiary of the policy or hold any right of ownership in the policy; premiums must be paid in consideration of personal services so that the arrangement is designed for the benefit of the employees rather than stockholders; and the premiums paid, when combined with other forms of compensation, must not be unreasonable in amount.

Another benefit available to a corporation is coverage for its employees under a group-term life insurance policy, the premium payments for which are fully deductible by the corporation. The corporation may carry as much as $50,000 in group-term life insurance on each of its employees, and the premiums paid by the corporation will not be includable in the employee's income. Furthermore, the proceeds of the policy may be excluded from the employee's gross estate at his death if the insurance is payable to someone other than his estate, and the employee has transferred the policy so that he no longer possesses any incidents of ownership. Such life insurance coverage may exceed $50,000 per employee, but the cost of insurance in excess of $50,000 will be included in the employee's gross income; however, it should be pointed out that the amount included under the income tax regulations may be considerably less than what it would actually cost to purchase such additional term life insurance on the open market.

Another income tax benefit afforded to employees of a corporation is that the corporation may, at the death of the employee, pay his or her spouse up to $5,000

**Since the maximum contribution permitted for an Individual Retirement Account ("IRA") is $1,500.00 ($2,000 in 1982 and thereafter) each year, we have omitted discussion of IRA's as being inadequate.

as a death benefit. The corporation will be permitted to deduct the payment, while the spouse may exclude the full amount of the payment from his or her gross income under Section 101(b) of the Internal Revenue Code.

But there are some tax pitfalls attendant to incorporation. The small professional corporation will face the same difficulties as a larger corporation, but may also be more susceptible in the following areas:

1. Section 482 of the Code relating to the attribution of professional income of the corporation to the lawyer as an individual.

2. Sections 351 and 357 relating to certain tax problems in the transferring of receivables from the partnership or sole practice to the new corporation and the assumption of liabilities by the new corporation.

3. Sections 162 and 212 of the Code relating to the ordinary and necessary business expenses of a corporation, particularly with respect to the deduction of reasonable compensation by the corporation.

4. An attack on the corporate status of the organization itself.

We list the above problems to indicate some of the major areas of dispute which exist at this time between the Internal Revenue Service and professional corporations. The establishment of a professional corporation can provide many important tax benefits to a professional organization. However, as indicated above, unless everything is done correctly, it can be a tax trap for the unwary. Furthermore, you must realize that the entire area of professional corporations and the tax benefits which now flow therefrom could be modified or eliminated by subsequent changes in the Federal Tax Laws.

In order that you will have a clear understanding concerning the services we will perform incident to the incorporation of your legal practice and the fees we will charge, set forth below are the services which we have agreed to perform:

The incorporation of your legal practice will include the following:

1. Incorporation

Design and drafting of all incorporation documents, including:

   a. Articles of Incorporation
   b. Minutes of Organizational Meeting
   c. Waiver of Notice for Organizational Meeting
   d. Stock Subscription Agreements
   e. Transfer Agreements
   f. Consent of Registered Agent
   g. Issuance of Stock Certificates
   h. Bylaws
   i. Health and Medical Reimbursement Plan, if desired

This, of course, includes filing all documents with the Secretary of State, arranging for newspaper notice, obtaining the corporate seal, compiling minute books, and all other steps incident to incorporation.

This also includes the conferences and research necessary to deal with those problems incident to the termination of your existing partnership (disposition of accounts receivable, etc.) and to discuss the tax impact and operation of the Health and Medical Reimbursement Plan. We anticipate that our fees for this aspect of the incorporation of your legal practice will be approximately $_____.

2. Employment Agreements and Stock Retirement Agreement

We anticipate that it will be necessary that employment and stock agreements be drafted for the shareholders of the new corporation, and possibly for the associates. Our fee for drafting these agreements is not included in our $_____ incorporation fee because it will, undoubtedly, be necessary to tailor the agreements for each of the shareholder employees, especially the senior partners. The tailoring of such agreements can often involve numerous conferences and many hours of work; therefore, we anticipate that our fee for drafting these agreements will be $_____, but our fee could exceed this amount because our time expended in connection with these agreements will be billed on an hourly basis as required.

3. Retirement Plans

Our incorporation fee also does not include the drafting of qualified retirement plans for the new corporation. The legal work involved with the preparation of qualified retirement plans and trusts is quite extensive, and we anticipate that several conferences with you and the Internal Revenue Service may be necessary. We will design and draft one qualified retirement plan and trust agreement of the defined contribution type (money purchase pension plan or profit sharing plan) and draft the Summary Plan Description for the Plan for a fee of $_____. Our work will, of course, include all necessary discussions and conferences with the IRS in order to achieve qualification of the Plan. If it is desired, we will design and draft an additional defined contribution plan for the new corporation for a fee of $_____.

As you can see, the cost for incorporating your law practice will probably range between $_____ and $_____ depending on the complexity of your employment agreements and stock retirement agreements and the number of retirement plans adopted. Also, all out-of-pocket expenses will be paid by the corporation. We believe that our fees are in line with those charged by lawyers who are equally as experienced and knowledgeable in the area of professional corporations and business planning.

We are enclosing a copy of this letter to be signed by you and returned to us if the fee arrangement set forth herein is agreeable to you. We will look forward to meeting with you again to discuss these matters in more detail.

Sincerely,

_____

The fees set forth above are hereby accepted and approved this _____ day of _____, 19____.

_____

CHAPTER 5

Tax Aspects of Incorporation

After the decision to incorporate is made it must be determined what assets will be transferred to the new professional corporation and what steps must be taken to assure that the transfer will be considered a tax-free exchange.

[5.01] TECHNICAL RULES OF SECTION 351 OF THE CODE

In general, the exchange by an individual of property for stock in a corporation will constitute a taxable exchange under Section 1012 of the Code. The gain realized by the individual will be the difference between the value of the stock received and the adjusted basis of the property transferred. An exception to this general rule is provided in Section 351 of the Code which provides for nonrecognition treatment where property is transferred to a corporation solely in exchange for stock or securities of that corporation and, immediately after the exchange, the transferor (or transferors) is in control of the corporation. The rules of Section 351 of the Code are very technical and require precise compliance. Upon the incorporation of a professional practice, the professional advisor should definitely seek to bring the incorporation within the nonrecognition rules of Section 351 of the Code. Only on rare occasions will a taxable incorporation be advantageous, since a taxable incorporation will result in the immediate recognition of income on all accounts receivable transferred to the new professional corporation. There are also substantial reporting requirements under Regulations §1.351-3 which should be reviewed by the accountant for the professional corporation.

(1) Stock or Securities

In a transfer under Section 351 of the Code, the transferor must receive solely "stock" or "securities" in exchange for the property transferred. The receipt of other property constitutes "boot" which, in a Section 351 transfer, will be taxable (recognized) to the transferor to the extent that gain is realized on the exchange. The professional corporation advisor should understand the difference between "realized" gain and "recognized" gain. In all Section 351 exchanges, a gain is "realized" by the transfer of property in exchange for stock and securities. However, Section 351 of the Code provides that the realized gain will not be "recognized," except to the extent of boot received by the transferor. Where boot is received in a Section 351 transaction, the character of the gain to be recognized is determined with reference to the assets which have been transferred.[1]

The requirement that the transferor receive "stock" will generally not be a problem upon the incorporation of a professional practice. Since there will usually be no sophisticated capitalization of a professional corporation, including stock rights or warrants, many of the more esoteric questions encountered under Section 351 of the Code may be avoided.

However, the definition of the term "security" will be important upon the incorporation of a professional practice. Generally, upon the incorporation of a business, it is important to assure that the business has not been "thinly" capitalized and that it has sufficient capital to operate.

In situations of thin capitalization, loans and other obligations from the transferor to the corporation will usually be considered as capital contributions. See Regulations §1.385. Also, for state law purposes, it is important to assure that a corporation has sufficient capital to conduct business. If it can be shown that a corporation is not adequately capitalized for the purpose for which it is formed, it may be possible for creditors of the corporation to "pierce" the corporate veil, thus destroying the limited liability established by the corporate form and reaching the assets of the shareholders. See section [5.10], *infra*, with regard to structuring the capital of a professional corporation. Once the hurdle of thin capitalization for general tax and state law purposes has been satisfied, a professional corporation should generally not be overly endowed with assets because, although the assets of the practice are necessary for the conduct of the practice, it is not essential that the professional corporation have a large net worth. Because there is no need for a large capital base in a professional corporation, the incorporation of a professional practice is an opportune time for the professional to set up a mechanism for the tax-free withdrawal of funds from the practice. This can occur through the issuance by the professional corporation of debt obligations.

For purposes of Section 351 of the Code, the term "security" includes debt obligations of the corporation. Generally, courts have looked at the term of the obligation to determine whether it is a security. Normally, debt obligations with a term of 10 years or more have been considered securities and debt obligations with a term of five years or less have not. Characterization of obligations in excess of five years in duration but less than 10 depends upon the facts and circumstances of each particular case.[2]

The example contained in section [5.10](4), *infra*, illustrates how debt obligations of the professional corporation may be issued in a Section 351 exchange. An example of a promissory note which may be issued as "debt" in a Section 351 exchange is attached to this section as Exhibit 2.

(2) Control

In order for the nonrecognition provisions of Section 351 to apply, the transferor or transferors must be in "control" of the transferee corporation immediately after the exchange. The term "control" is defined in Section 368 (c) as:

> Ownership of stock possessing at least 80% of the total combined voting power of all classes of stock entitled to vote and at least 80% of the total number of shares of all other classes of stock of the corporation.

The control requirement should not present a problem upon the incorporation of a professional practice. However, in the event that the professional corporation is formed by an existing partnership, with the transfer of partnership assets to the corporation in exchange for stock, followed by the liquidation of the partnership and the distribution of the stock to the partners, a question may arise with regard to whether the partnership was in control of the corporation "immediately after the exchange." As described more fully in section [5.11], *infra*, the Service has indicated that this will not be a problem.

(3) Assumption of Liabilities by a Corporation

Where, in a Section 351 exchange, the transferee corporation assumes liabilities of the transferors, gain will usually not be recognized. However, gain will be recognized in the following two events: (i) the principal purpose of the incorporation is the avoidance of federal income taxes under Section 357(b); or (ii) the liabilities assumed by the corporation in the exchange exceed the adjusted basis of the transferor in the property transferred under Section 357(c).

In general, the recognition of income due to the tax avoidance requirements of Section 357(b) of the Code should not be a problem upon the incorporation of the professional practice. However, where the incorporation has not been properly planned and executed, where there has not been sufficient emphasis given to the business motives for incorporating, and where the minutes of the initial meeting of the Board of Directors were not properly drafted, it may be possible for the Service to contend that the professional corporation was incorporated simply to avoid federal income taxes. There are, however, no cases dealing with this particular issue in the professional corporation context.

On the other hand, it is entirely possible for professional corporations to run afoul of the rules of Section 357(c) of the Code. Because it is the general practice to transfer all assets and liabilities of the professional practice to the new professional corporation, it is entirely possible, that, without adequate advance structuring, the liabilities assumed by the new professional corporation will exceed the adjusted basis of the property transferred. This is particularly true with accounts receivables and trade payables, which are more fully discussed in sections [5.02] and [5.03], *infra*. Potential problems may also arise if there are obligations due to banks which have been incurred to finance the purchase of equipment or if there are liabilities to retired professionals.

[5.02] DEDUCTIBILITY OF LIABILITIES
ASSUMED BY A CORPORATION

The provisions of Section 351 and Section 362 (which deal with the corporation's basis in property acquired) do not provide for an increase in the corporation's basis in the property acquired due to liabilities assumed by the corporation. Also, the court decisions which have specifically considered the question of whether such liabilities assumed are deductible by the corporation have held that the corporation's payment of such liabilities does not give rise to a deduction because the liabilities represented capital expenditures incurred by the corporation in acquiring property.[3] This analysis will, if accurate, require that the benefit of any deduction attributable to the corporation's payment of such liabilities be irretrievably lost, unless gain is recognized on the Section 351 transaction.

However, it has been indicated, or at least inferred, by several courts that a cash basis corporation may deduct cash basis accounts payable which have been transferred to it if, along with the transfer, accounts receivable are also transferred.[4]

The Service has, for a number of years, issued private letter rulings on this issue and the Service will, generally, rule that a corporation may deduct the payment of liabilities assumed by it in a Section 351 transaction if: (1) the accounts payable would have been deductible by the transferor had they been paid by it; (2) there is a valid business purpose for the transfer of the payables upon incorporation; and (3) the result does not distort the income of the transferor or transferee.[5] In conjunction with such private letter rulings, the Service generally requires that the corporation enter into a closing agreement which sets forth the agreed-upon results. A copy of a private letter ruling and a closing agreement relating to the incorporation of a professional practice are attached as Exhibit 1 to this section. In the past, most commentators have recommended caution in this area and that the transferee obtain a private letter ruling prior to the incorporation.[6]

There are, however, a number of reasons why it is usually not practical to obtain a private letter ruling and closing agreement in the professional corporation setting. Generally, a professional corporation will have only a small amount of accounts payable, and these payables may be eliminated prior to incorporation, thus disposing of the problem. On the other hand, if enough of accounts payable and loans do exist, these obligations (such as bank loans and obligations to retiring professionals) may be left outside the professional corporation. Further, even if such obligations are placed in the professional corporation, there is authority to support the proposition that the payment of such obligations is deductible by the corporation. For example, private letter rulings issued to taxpayers, while not binding on the Service, are an indication of the current position taken by the Service. Also, in an article published while he was Chief Counsel of the Service, K. Martin Worthy indicated that it would be inconsistent for the Service to contend that deductions were not allowable.[7] Further, in the Revenue Act of 1978, Section 357(c) of the Code was specifically amended to provide that the assumption of liabilities for trade payables and amounts due to retired professionals would not be considered ''liabilities'' assumed by the corporation if such payments would have been deductible by the transferor if paid by him. The assumption of the amendment is, obviously, that in practice these liabilities are generally assumed by corporations. It would also be reasonable to infer from the amendment to Section 357(c) that Congress assumed that corporations would also receive a deduction for such payments. Although this question is still undecided, the weight of authority favors granting a deduction to the corporation for such liabilities assumed.

[5.03] DEALING WITH ACCOUNTS RECEIVABLE

Accounts receivable and work in process usually represent the largest asset of a professional practice and, therefore, may present one of the biggest problems upon incorporation. If the accounts receivable are not transferred to the new professional corporation, there will almost certainly be a cash flow shortage in the new professional corporation due to the three-to-five-month lag time in billing and collecting for current work done. Also, if the accounts receivable are maintained outside of the new professional corporation, it is presumably the employees of the new professional corporation who will bill and collect these accounts receivable. Consequently, the new professional corporation should be compensated for these services and, unless very accurate records are maintained, it is possible that the old accounts receivable will simply become mingled with the new. For this reason, upon the incorporation of almost all professional corporations, the accounts receivable are transferred to the new corporation. The transfer of accounts receivable has, in the past, created two potential problems which, thankfully, appear to have been resolved.

For some years, the Service took the position that the transfer of accounts receivable to a new corporation created an assignment of income problem. Because accounts receivable have not been reported as income, they have a zero basis to a cash basis taxpayer, and the Service sought to tax the receivables to the professional personally when income was received by the professional corporation.[8] This position of the Service has, however, not been sustained by the courts and has been rejected by at least one Commissioner of Internal Revenue.[9] Most practitioners now feel that the assignment of income question is a moot point in a properly structured professional corporation.

Because accounts receivable have a zero basis, a potential problem is created upon the incorporation of a professional practice where both accounts receivable and accounts payable are transferred. For years, the Service took the position that, under Section 357(c) of the Code, the transfer of accounts receivable to a corporation did not offset transferred accounts payable and, consequently, gain could be recognized where the amount of the accounts payable exceeded the adjusted basis of the tangible assets transferred. This "Catch 22" was espoused by the Service and that position led to a number of cases, some of which were lost by taxpayers.[10]

The Revenue Act of 1978 has, finally, resolved this problem by providing that trade payables and amounts due to retired professionals will not be considered as "liabilities" under Section 357(c) where the payment would have been deductible (when paid) by the transferor.[11] The revisions to Section 357(c) of the Code and the issuance of Rev. Rul. 80-198[12] should eliminate the need for a closing agreement when applying for a private letter ruling regarding the assignment of income theory for accounts receivable. A closing agreement may still be necessary, however, to assure the deductibility of liabilities assumed by the professional corporation.

[5.04] TAX BENEFIT RULE

The tax benefit rule provided under Section 111 of the Code provides that a taxpayer must recapture the amount of previous deductions which have created a tax benefit. Upon incorporation, the tax benefit rule will apply to create taxable income for amounts which have previously been deducted, such as supplies. However, the Treasury Regulations specifically provide [13] that the tax benefit rule is not applicable to depreciation recapture and, generally, the recapture provided by the tax benefit rule provides no (or a very small) problem for the incorporating professional.

[5.05] SECTION 1239 OF THE CODE

Under Section 1239 of the Code, any gain recognized as a result of a sale or exchange of depreciable property between an individual and his controlled corporation will be characterized as ordinary income. The Service also takes the position that this rule applies between a partnership and a corporation incorporated by it.[14] Consequently, any gain realized in a Section 351 transfer will generally be considered ordinary income in its entirety.[15] In order to avoid this result, the incorporation should be structured so that it will be entirely tax-free under Section 351.

[5.06] TAX ATTRIBUTES OF THE NEW PROFESSIONAL CORPORATION

The basis of the property received by the new professional corporation in the Section 351 transfer will be a "carryover basis" under Section 362 of the Code. In other words, the basis for depreciation and other purposes of the professional corporation will carry over from the hands of the transferor and will be equal to the basis of the property in the hands of the transferor increased by any gain recognized on the transfer.

Sections 167(b)(2), (3) and (4) of the Code provide for certain accelerated methods of depreciation. These methods are, however, only available for property of which the owner is the "first user" under Section 167(c)(2) of the Code. Since the new professional corporation will not be the first user of the property, these accelerated methods of depreciation will not be available. However, the new professional corporation will be entitled to use accelerated depreciation not in excess of 150% of the straight line method on tangible personal property.[16]

Upon the issuance of its stock in exchange for the property under Section 351 of the Code, the new professional corporation will not recognize gain under Section 1032 of the Code.

[5.07] RECAPTURE OF INVESTMENT TAX CREDIT

Section 47 of the Code generally provides that investment tax credit will be recaptured upon the disposition of property on which the credit was taken. However, Section 47(b) provides that the investment tax credit will not be recaptured where there is a "change in form of conducting [the] trade or business as long as the property is retained in such trade or business as Section 38 property and the taxpayer retains a substantial interest in such trade or business." Under Regulations §1.47-3(f)(1)(ii), such a change in form occurs where (1) the basis of the property in the hands of the corporation is determined in whole or in part by reference to its basis in the hands of the professional, (2) the property is retained for use in the professional practice, (3) the professional retains a substantial interest in the corporation, and (4) substantially all the assets necessary to operate the professional practice are transferred to the professional corporation.

Obviously, no recapture will occur where all of the assets of the professional practice are transferred to the new professional corporation and all of the existing professionals retain a substantial interest in the new corporation.[17] However, where a substantial portion of the assets (for example, the office building in which the professional practice has been conducted) are not transferred, it is possible that the Service could contend that recapture should occur. However, the Service has not taken this position in one letter ruling,[18] where the Service found that holding and renting the building was a separate trade or business distinct from the law practice. Therefore, the building need not be transferred to the professional corporation in order to avoid recapture on the professional equipment.

Even if recapture does not occur because there has been simply a change in the form of conducting the profession, it is possible for investment tax credit recapture to occur on equipment which is retained in the hands of the professionals. Section 46(e)(3) of the Code was introduced in 1971 to eliminate tax shelter investments where noncorporate lessors entered into net leases. Any property maintained by the professionals and leased to the professional corporation will be subject to the rules of Section 46(e)(3) and investment tax credit recapture will occur if the term of the least is 50% or more of the useful life of the property and if the expenses incurred during the first 12 months of the lease (solely by reason of Section 162, i.e., excluding taxes, etc.) do not exceed 15% of the rentals under the lease. Section 46(e)(3) appears to disallow the investment tax credit regardless of when the lease was entered into. However Regulations §1.46-4(d)(1) provides that recapture is inapplicable to property used by the taxpayer in the trade or business for at least 24 months prior to the time at which the lease was entered into. Consequently, professional corporation advisors should be aware that property retained outside the new professional corporation and leased to the professional corporation may constitute property on which the investment tax credit is recaptured, unless the property has been used in the professional practice for two years or more or unless the net lease requirements are met.

[5.08] SECTION 482 OF THE CODE

Section 482 of the Code was enacted to permit the Service to reallocate income to related taxpayers where the allocation chosen by the related taxpayers materially distorts income. For example, when an individual transferred farming operations to a new corporation immediately prior to harvest, it was held that the deductions taken by the individual in producing the crop should be reallocated to the corporation.[19] Also, where income from a long-term construction contract was reported on the completed contract method (which postpones reporting income until the contract is completed) and the construction business was incorporated toward the end of the life of a long-term contract, Section 482 can be used to allocate to the unincorporated business an appropriate amount of income from the contract.[20]

Section 482 is generally of little applicability to professional corporations.

However, where an attorney has been working a number of years on a contingent fee case, it is possible that the Service could take a position similar to that taken on construction contracts, under the completed contract method. Consequently, the facts and circumstances of each particular professional corporation should be examined in light of Section 482 prior to incorporation.

[5.09] BASIS TO TRANSFEROR

The professional (or the partnership) which transfers property under Section 351 to the new professional corporation will take a "substituted" basis under Section 358 of the Code. That is, the existing basis of the transferor in the property transferred will become its basis in the stock received, decreased by the fair market value of any "boot" received and increased by any gain recognized.

[5.10] STEPS INCIDENT TO INCORPORATION

(1) Accounts Receivable and Accounts Payable

Due to the problems with transferring accounts receivable and payable to a new corporation under Section 351, the preferred method of handling accounts payable is to reduce them as much as possible by using cash on hand. Any accounts payable which cannot be paid currently may be transferred to the professional corporation. If accounts payable are transferred to the corporation, the professionals should be advised of the risk involved (relating to the deductibility of the payments of these liabilities). In the alternative, the professional partnership could be kept intact and the accounts payable could be retained by it, with sufficient accounts receivable retained in the partnership to cover accounts payable. Also, if the professional would prefer not to place the professional office and office equipment in the professional corporation, it can be retained outside the professional corporation and leased to the professional corporation.

(2) Transfer of Other Assets

Assuming that accounts payable have been reduced to a minimum and that there are insufficient tangible assets to warrant retaining them in the hands of the professionals, essentially all property of the professional practice will be transferred to the new professional corporation, including accounts receivable and work in process. If accounts receivable are not transferred, presumably the new professional corporation will collect them and will charge a fee for the collection.

(3) Issuance of Stock

Stock in the new professional corporation will usually be issued on the depreciated basis of the property transferred to the corporation in the Section 351 exchange. Consequently, no stock will be issued for accounts receivable and only stock of a par value equal to the depreciated book value of all transferred property is issued. A discussion of the issuance of stock in accordance with the professionals' shares of earnings and other matters relating to capitalization is contained in Chapter 7 *infra*. In conjunction with the capitalization of the corporation, it may be desirable, as discussed in section [5.01](1), *supra*, to issue securities (i.e., a ten-year note) to the professionals upon incorporating. This will permit them to obtain a tax-free return of some of the existing capital. A copy of a note which may be used to effectuate the issuance of such security is included in this chapter as Exhibit 2. This note should be made to run for at least ten years and should prohibit prepayment during at least the first five years. The note should also carry a commercially standard rate of interest and otherwise be an ''arm's-length'' note.

(4) Illustration of Proper Disposition of Assets Upon Incorporation

Dr. X has been practicing as a proprietor for approximately 1½ years. He has determined, in conjunction with his accountant and attorney, that a professional corporation would be preferable. Dr. X intends to incorporate on November 1, 1980, and the balance sheet of his proprietorship appears as follows:

(A PROPRIETORSHIP)
BALANCE SHEET
October 31, 1980
ASSETS

CURRENT ASSETS:

Cash		$ 50.00	
Accounts Receivable		47,205.85	
Investments		9,023.46	
Total Current Assets			$56,279.31

FIXED ASSETS:	Cost	Accumulated Depreciation	Net Book Value	
Furniture and Fixtures	$10,080.00	$1,848.68	$ 8,231.32	
Auto	5,777.00	2,647.86	3,129.14	
Total Fixed Assets	15,857.00	4,496.54		$11,360.46

OTHER ASSETS:

Deposits	$1,912.40
TOTAL ASSETS	$69,552.17

LIABILITIES AND OWNER'S EQUITY

CURRENT LIABILITIES:

Accounts Payable	$ 1.88	
Note Payable to Bank	25,000.00	
Current Portion of Long-Term Debt	1,889.23	
Current Portion of Capitalized Lease	1,217.37	
Accrued Payroll Taxes	303.12	
Deferred Revenue (To Offset Accounts Receivable)	47,205.85	
Total Current Liabilities		$75,617.45

LONG-TERM DEBT:

Long-Term Debt, Net of Current Portion	$ 3,257.90	
Capitalized Lease, Net of Current	923.89	
Total Long-Term Debt		$ 4,181.79

OWNER'S EQUITY:

Owner's Equity—Opening Balance	($16,796.59)	
Less Withdrawals:		
Personal	68,712.29	
Contributions	110.00	
Net Income (Loss)	75,371.81	
Total Owner's Equity		($10,247.07)
Total Liabilities and Owner's Equity		$69,552.17

The following disposition will be made of the assets and liabilities of Dr. X's proprietorship:

Cash:	Kept by Dr. X.
Accounts Receivable:	Transferred to the new professional corporation at a zero basis.
Investments:	Kept by Dr. X.

Fixed Assets:

Transferred to the corporation at net book value of $11,360.

Deposits:

Transferred to the corporation.

Accounts Payable:

Paid by Dr. X.

Note Payable to Bank:

This represents an initial loan from the bank for working capital. Because a transfer of this liability to the corporation would create a liability in excess of basis, Dr. X has agreed to maintain this loan in his personal name.

Current Portion of
   Long Term Debt:

Transferred to corporation.

Current Portion of
   Capitalized Lease:

Transferred to corporation.

Accrued Payroll Taxes:

Transferred to corporation.

Deferred Revenue:

This figure has no impact on the incorporation because it is ''contra-account'' placed in the balance sheet to offset the accounts receivable as an asset. Accounts receivable do not normally appear on a cash basis balance sheet.

Long-Term Debt:

Transferred to new corporation.

Long-Term Portion
   of Capitalized Lease:

Transferred to new corporation.

This disposition of assets produces a net equity in the new professional corporation of $5,681.35 (fixed assets of $11,360.46, plus deposits of $1,912.40, less current portion of long-term debt of $1,889.23, less current portion of capitalized lease of $1,217.37, less long-term debt of $3,257.90, and less capitalized lease of $923.89). The payroll taxes (since they will be deductible when paid) are offset against the accounts receivable.

The authors feel that a new professional corporation should have capital paid in for stock of at least $1,500 to $2,000. Any additional amounts contributed may, depending on the circumstances, be used to create debt obligations (in the above example, $2,500 of paid-in capital for which stock is issued and $3,181.35 of long-term debt should suffice).

[5.11] ALTERNATIVE METHODS OF INCORPORATING A PARTNERSHIP

There are basically three methods which can be employed to incorporate a professional practice which exists as a partnership, and they are as follows:

Alternative 1: The partnership will transfer its assets to the newly formed professional corporation in a Section 351 transfer and, immediately thereafter, distribute the stock and securities received in the transfer to the partners.

Alternative 2: The partnership will liquidate, distributing assets to the partners, and the partners will, immediately, contribute these assets to the newly formed professional corporation in a Section 351 transfer in exchange for stock and securities.

Alternative 3: The partners will contribute under Section 351 their partnership interests to the newly-formed professional corporation and the professional corporation will, then, continue to operate as a partner of the partnership or liquidate the partnership into itself.

The Service has taken the position in Rev. Rul. 70-239[21] that the tax consequences of all three alternatives are the same. Thus, the Service regards the incorporation of a partnership as essentially the transfer under Section 351 of the Code by the partnership of all of its assets, subject to its liabilities, to the corporation in exchange for all of the outstanding stock of the corporation. While it is easy to see the rationale of the Service, since the end result is substantially the same in all three alternatives, one is tempted not to look farther into this issue. However, the provisions of Subchapter K of the Code are very technical and, when viewed against the three alternatives, it becomes apparent that the same result is not reached in each of the three alternatives. Commentators generally feel that the position of the Service in Rev. Rul. 70-239 is questionable.[22]

Because of the different results which may be obtained in the incorporation of a partnership, it is incumbent upon the professional advisors to review each of the alternatives and the potential results. It can be said, generally, that in the event the bases of the partners in their partnership interests equal the basis of the partnership in its property, there will be no untoward results under Subchapter K; however, there still may be potential problems with regard to the status of the corporation as a

Subchapter S corporation, a professional corporation, or a corporation issuing Section 1244 stock.

(1) Effect of Alternative upon Gain Realized Under Section 351(b)

The method of incorporation chosen may affect the amount of gain recognized under Section 351(b) of the Code (where boot is received) if the bases of the partners in their interests differ from the partnership's basis in its assets. For example, where one partner has a higher basis in his interest than the other partners (such as from the purchase or inheritance of his partnership interest), that partner will recognize less gain from boot received upon incorporation under Alternatives 2 and 3. On the other hand, if Alternative 1 is chosen, all of the partners will recognize their pro rata portion of the gain (because partnership property is transferred and the bases of the partners are irrelevant). Whether the partnership transfers assets to the newly formed corporation or whether the partners transfer their partnership interests to the newly formed corporation may also affect the character of the gain recognized.

(2) Effect of Alternative upon Shareholders' Bases and Corporation's Basis

The method selected for incorporation will also have an effect upon the corporation's basis in the contributed property where one or more of the partners has acquired an increased basis in his interest by purchase or inheritance and no election was made under Section 754 of the Code which would permit the partnership to increase correlatively its basis in its assets. Because the aggregate bases of the partners will, in this situation, exceed the basis of the partnership in its assets, under Alternative 1 the corporation will take a smaller "carryover" basis, when the initial Section 351 transfer is made by the partnership, than when the transfer is made by partners under the other Alternatives. Also, in the event that the partners form the new corporation under Alternatives 2 or 3, the allocation of the corporation's basis to the various assets may be different from that under Alternative 1.

(3) Subchapter S Election by New Corporation

A corporation cannot be a validly electing Subchapter S corporation as long as a partnership is one of its stockholders. Consequently, the use of Alternative 1 may prohibit the newly formed professional corporation from immediately electing Subchapter S status. However, if the partnership is liquidated quickly under Alternative 1, it may be possible for the newly formed corporation to make a subsequent Subchapter S election (within the first 30 days of its first taxable year) and be considered a validly electing Subchapter S corporation. Regulation §1.1372-1(a) provides that the existence of a nonqualified shareholder prior to the election date does not disqualify an otherwise electing corporation.

(4) Status of the New Corporation as a Professional Corporation

Under many state laws, only licensed professionals can be shareholders of a corporation incorporated under the professional corporation statutes, and in those states the corporation formed under Alternative 1 cannot, initially, be a professional corporation. This may be rectified following formation, however, if the partnership liquidates and transfers the stock in the corporation to the partners. At that time, the stock will be held by qualified professionals and the Articles of Incorporation could be amended under state law to create a professional corporation (this amendment to the Articles of Incorporation should be performed prior to the corporation's commencement of business).

(5) Issuance of 1244 Stock by the New Corporation

Under Section 1244 of the Code, stock which is originally issued as Section 1244 stock will continue to retain its status only as long as it remains in the hands of the initial recipient. Consequently, if Alternative 1 is followed, any stock which is distributed from the partnership to the partners will, under the plain meaning of Section 1244 and the regulations thereunder, not be considered Section 1244 stock. It could be argued, however, that the transitory nature of the incorporation and the substance-over-form rationale expressed in Rev. Rul. 70-239[23] would support the conclusion that the partnership should be ignored for purposes of Section 1244 and the stock should be considered as issued directly from the new professional corporation to the professionals. The authors believe that it may be difficult to sustain such a rationale because, at the time of incorporation, the new corporation begun under Alternative 1 cannot be a professional corporation and, consequently, the status of the corporation will change for state law purposes after the stock has been distributed to the professionals.

(6) Conclusion

If any of the points raised in this section appear to be important upon the incorporation of a partnership, they should be reviewed in detail with competent tax counsel. There are several excellent treatises covering this area which should be reviewed at that time.[24] Also, in the event that a partnership is incorporated, care should be taken to assure that the partnership is dissolved for federal tax purposes and for state law purposes. Many states require that notice be published in the local newspaper regarding the dissolution of a partnership and this should not be overlooked.

[5.12] MERGING PROFESSIONAL PRACTICES

With the proliferation of professional corporations, it is not likely that, from time to time, professional practices will merge. This creates a problem where the surviving practice is incorporated and the merged practice is not. Where a smaller practice will be merging with a larger, incorporated practice, potential problems are created under the technical requirements of Section 351 of the Code. Specifically, if the smaller practice transfers its accounts receivable and assets to the larger practice in exchange for stock, the requirements for Section 351 will not be met unless, immediately after the transfer, the professionals of the smaller practice control (the 80% test) the larger practice. Consequently, the transfer of a smaller practice to a larger practice in exchange for stock may result in a taxable transaction. It is also possible that the Service would seek, in such a situation, to increase the value of the stock received by some amount attributable to the "good will" of the ongoing larger practice.

In order to avoid the taxable transaction which may occur upon merging practices, the smaller practice may, prior to the merger, incorporate. Thus, the merger could be effected on a tax-free basis as a general corporate merger under Section 368(a)(1)(A). However, such a transaction is subject to attack if the smaller practice has not maintained its independent corporate status for a period of time or if the incorporation of the larger practice was made with a view to the merger. The Service could take the position that, upon a merger immediately following the incorporation of the larger practice, there was not "control" of the larger practice immediately after the incorporation because of the subsequent merger.

Another alternative which should be considered is the creation of an entirely new professional corporation to which the existing professional corporation and the unincorporated professional would transfer assets. Since both of the transferors would be, technically, in control immediately after the transaction, the requirements of Section 351 of the Code would appear to be met. This alternative may also present problems and should be reviewed in advance by competent tax counsel.

Probably the easiest manner of merging professional practices would be to avoid the Section 351 requirements altogether. In this manner, the merger would be accomplished by simply permitting the independent professional to retain his independent practice which would be wound down through the collection of receivables previously generated. The professional would then purchase stock in the existing larger professional corporation and become an employee of that corporation (presumably at a lower or insignificant salary during the first three to four months while collections commence). The independent professional could, then, either sell his operating assets to the larger professsional corporation or transfer those assets to the corporation at an agreed price in exchange for stock.

[5.13] INCORPORATION OF SEVERAL PARTNERS OF A PARTNERSHIP

As professionals seek to satisfy their own tax planning needs and desires, from time to time the situation will occur in which several partners of the partnership desire to become professional corporations. This matter is more fully discussed in Chapter 10, *infra*. The professional advisors should understand that there is no basic problem with a partner transferring his partnership interest to a professional corporation which then becomes a partner in the partnership. Most state professional corporation laws provide that professional corporations are subject to the general corporate laws of that state and, under most general corporate laws, corporations can be members of a general partnership.

The incorporating partner should be aware of the possibilities which are available to obtain additional funds. He should not overlook the possibility of obtaining debt securities upon the incorporation of the new professional corporation. Also, the incorporating partner should seriously consider receiving a distribution from the partnership, prior to incorporation, which will reduce his basis in his partnership interest. Generally, this distribution will be tax-free under Section 731 of the Code, even if the partnership is required to borrow funds in order to make the distribution. This will permit the incorporating partner to receive a substantial tax-free distribution of cash which can be "repaid" by the corporation to the partnership in later years at lower rates under the corporate surtax exemption.

Upon the incorporation of one or more partners in a partnership, care should be taken to assure that the partnership is not terminated under Section 708(b) (sale or exchange of 50% or more of the partnership interests) and that the fiscal year rules of Section 706 are met.

[5.14] BUNCHING OF INCOME

The date of incorporation, the parties' accounting methods, the professional corporation's taxable year, the predecessor partnership's taxable year, and the professionals' taxable years (usually calendar years) will all affect the "bunching" of income problem, i.e., placing more than one year's income into a partner/shareholder's taxable year, thus, increasing his taxable income and his income tax rate. Bunching typically occurs when the taxable years of the predecessor partnership and the partner/shareholder are different. For example, where a February 28 fiscal year partnership is incorporated, there is a potential bunching of 22 months' income in a partner/shareholder's year in which the incorporation occurs. That is, if the incorporation were to occur, effective March 1, 1981, all income earned by the partnership from March 1, 1980, through February 28, 1981, will be taxable to the partners in their taxable calendar years ending December 31, 1981. Section 706(a) of the Code provides that partners will be taxed on the taxable income of the partnership (irrespective of when distributions occur) during the taxable year in which the partnership's year ends. In addition, if the new professional corporation were to pay monthly salaries to the shareholders from March through December of 1981, these salaries would also be taxable to the shareholders in their taxable years ending December 31, 1981. Accordingly, 22 months of earnings would be taxable in one taxable year. Such bunching usually creates a cash flow problem for the professionals, because normally the partnership would have distributed funds on a monthly basis (in 1980) and, consequently, much of that income has been spent and is not available for the payment of taxes.

It is advantageous for partnerships to have fiscal years because the establishment of a fiscal year results in an initial deferral of taxable income from the partners' calendar year of the partners. Consequently, partners in a February 28 partnership are usually paying taxes ten months in arrears, and, when the partnership is finally terminated, the deferral comes to an end. Even though changes in Section 706(b)(1) of the Code make it much more difficult for partnerships to have a fiscal year other than that of the majority of the partners, there are a surprising number of fiscal year partnerships still in existence. The bunching problem, although it is a natural consequence of the use of a fiscal year partnership, may create such cash flow problems that incorporation is postponed or rejected altogether.

Bunching results in: (1) the creation of a cash flow drain upon the professional because more than one year's taxes will be due in one taxable year; and (2) an increase in the tax rate of the professionals (up to 50% on earned income and as high as 70% on unearned income). Bunching is, thus, a timing problem and there is no way it can be totally avoided. There are, however, a number of ways to soften the blow and delay the impact of bunching. When a fiscal year partnership is encountered, each of the following methods of delaying the effect of bunching should be examined.

(1) Use of Loans and Delayed Salaries

The most obvious method of delaying the impact of bunching is to delay the initial salaries from the new professional corporation and permit the professionals to live off savings or loans obtained from banks (or from the professional corporation). For example, assume that a fiscal year partnership with a year ended February

28, 1981, is terminated on that date and a new professional corporation is formed on March 1, 1981. A partner's share of distributable income for the February 28, 1981, fiscal year of the partnership was $100,000, and it is anticipated that his income for the next three years will be approximately $100,000 each year. If the partner/shareholder's salary for the first ten months of incorporation (from March 1, 1981, through December 31, 1981) is reduced to $30,000 (from what would normally be $83,333 for that period) his total taxable income for 1981 would be $130,000. The corporation would then adopt a February 28 fiscal year-end and $70,000 would be paid to the partner/shareholder in January and February of 1980 prior to the corporation's fiscal year-end. The salary for the remainder of the calendar year 1982 could be set at $60,000, producing a total taxable income for his calendar year 1982 of $130,000. The shareholder would then be paid $40,000 during January and February of 1983, making his total compensation for the corporate fiscal year ending February 28, 1983, equal to $100,000. During the remainder of the calendar year 1983, the shareholder would be paid $90,000 (which would approximate his normal monthly salary), thus creating a taxable income for him in the calendar year 1983 of $130,000. This example illustrates how the effects of bunching may be lessened by spreading the additional income over several years.

Professional corporation advisors should, however, be aware that avoiding the bunching problem in this manner may create potential difficulties with the Service if there is no substantial business purpose to justify the deferral of salaries which occur, primarily, in the first year of incorporation. Such deferrals may, however, be rationalized on the grounds that it is anticipated that the corporation will encounter a cash flow shortage during its initial months of operation and, therefore, will defer salaries of all officers until the point in time in which the cash flow shortage is overcome and the fiscal year of the corporation is chosen. If loans are required in order to enable the partners/shareholders to meet living expenses during the intitial months of incorporation, the authors recommend that such loans be made from independent third parties such as banks or insurance companies (loans against insurance policies). If loans are made to the partners/shareholders from the corporation during the initial months of incorporation, the argument that a cash flow shortage may exist is obviously weakened by the existence of sufficient funds to make loans. The Service may, consequently, construe such loans as constructive dividends to the shareholders.

Also, some advisors also recommend that qualified retirement plans be established upon incorporation and that advanced funding take place during the early months of incorporation. These advisors also recommend that a rapid vesting schedule be employed (or possibly that past service with the partnership be included for vesting service) and that the plans permit loans to participants. The authors do not recommend this approach because they feel that advance funding of plans during the first year where salaries have not been established is unwise, and, together with extensive loans to the shareholders, may permit the Service to argue that the plans should be disqualified because they have not been operated for the "exclusive benefit" of the participants. A more detailed discussion of participants' loans is contained in section [14.04](2), *infra*.

(2) Leaving Partnership in Existence

Another readily apparent solution to the bunching problem involves leaving the existing professional partnership in existence, with most of the accounts receivable remaining with the professional partnership, instead of being transferred to the professional corporation. However, a small amount of accounts receivable could be transferred to the professional corporation to permit some cash flow during the early months or the professional corporation could obtain bank loans to provide working capital. Following the example discussed in section [5.14](1), *supra*, the accounts receivable which are collected through the partnership would be paid out as follows:

Assuming that incorporation took place on March 1, 1981, the partners/shareholders would be taxable in 1981 on their proportionate share of earnings of the partnership as of February 28, 1981, or $100,000. Because there would be few receivables in the professional corporation during the first several months of operation, the salaries paid to the partners/shareholders could, justifiably, be very low, thereby avoiding excessive bunching in calendar year 1981. In 1982, the partners/shareholders would be taxable on their shares of the earnings from the partnership for the partnership year ended February 28, 1982, and the partnership could be terminated at that time because most of the receivables should be either collectable or considered worthless. During 1982, the partners/shareholders' salaries could be increased. This method of approaching the bunching problem provides a result similar to the salary delay and loan method described in section [5.14](1), *supra*.

It should be recognized, however, that this method of approaching the bunching problem is also subject to the business purpose and constructive dividend questions described in section [5.14](1), *supra*, and also to the question of whether the prior partnership has actually terminated. Under Section 708 of the Code, the partnership is considered terminated if *no part* of the business or financial operation of the partnership continues to be carried on by the partners. For this reason, it would be advisable to assure that the previous partnership is, during its continued existence after incorporation, more than simply a shell. In at least one case, the Tax Court has ruled favorably in a comparable situation holding that a pre-incorporation partnership which continues to hold notes received has not been terminated but continues in existence.[25]

However, it is not clear that the de facto termination of a partnership can be postponed by the retention of nominal assets, and the professionals should seek to maintain more than just passive activity (collection of accounts receivable) in the partnership, if possible.

(3) Tax Shelters

The use of tax shelters may also help ameliorate the impact of bunching. Most tax shelters (such as real estate investments, equipment leasing, and oil and gas drilling ventures) simply result in deferral of taxes. Consequently, in the example in section [5.14](1), *supra*, it is possible to permit the partner/shareholder to report the entire 22 months of income in 1981 and, through the purchase of the tax shelters, defer the tax on that income until later years. As with any tax shelter, the professional should choose ''bunching'' shelters not only for the shelter provided, but for the investment potential. Many professionals (primarily physicians) historically have had a bad track record in choosing good tax shelters; any shelter chosen to spread the bunching problem should be very carefully reviewed by both the attorney and the accountant.

(4) Changing the Fiscal Year of the Individual

It is also possible to soften the blow of bunching by changing the partners' fiscal years to coincide with that of the partnership. This does involve, however, obtaining the approval of the Service.[26] While the bunching of income into the taxpayer's first taxable year of incorporated practice will certainly be lessened by this approach, a cash squeeze produced by the accelerated payment of taxes is usually the byproduct.

Assuming, in the example described in section [5.14](1), *supra*, that the fiscal year partnership will incorporate on March 1, 1981, and that each partner will change his taxable year to a March 1 - February 28 taxable year effective March 1, 1981, the following would obtain:

1. During 1980, the partners would continue on a calendar year basis and each partner's return for 1980 would be due on April 15, 1981, and would include the entire income of the partnership year ended February 28, 1980.
2. During 1981, the partners would have a short first taxable year beginning January 1, 1981, and ending February 28, 1981. This short year would include the partnership income for the entire partnership beginning March 1, 1980, and ending February 28, 1981, and the return and taxes would be due on June 15, 1981, for this year.
3. The first full year of the partner/shareholder on his new fiscal year would begin March 1, 1981, and would continue until February 28, 1982, during which he would be paid a salary.

Obviously, this method may also necessitate bank borrowings in order to pay accelerated income taxes, and the authors feel that the problems encountered with this method, such as the requirement of filing with the Service for approval and the psychological impact on the partner/shareholder when he must consider a February 28 year-end as opposed to a calendar year-end, generally make this alternative a less favorable one.

(5) Subchapter S Election

The election of Subchapter S status for the new professional corporation also offers a means whereby the problems associated with bunching may be deferred. If Subchapter S treatment is elected for the new professional corporation and the new professional corporation adopts a fiscal year ending in the following year (February 28, 1982, in the example which has been discussed in this section) and no salaries are paid during the first fiscal year, the "undistributed taxable income" of the new corporation will be taxable to the partners/shareholders in 1982 at the end of the corporation's first fiscal year. The use of a Subchapter S election defers income in much the same manner as the other alternatives but, due to the particular problems associated with Subchapter S treatment, this approach should be chosen only after a full examination of all the ramifications of Subchapter S. A further discussion of Subchapter S is contained in the following section.

[5.15] SUBCHAPTER S ELECTION

The general rules which apply to Subchapter S corporations also apply to professional corporations which elect treatment under Subchapter S of the Code. Generally, Subchapter S corporations are not taxed as entities and the income generated by a Subchapter S corporation is taxed to its shareholders, whether paid out to them or retained by the corporation. Losses generated in the Subchapter S corporation are deductible by the shareholders on their individual tax returns to the extent of their bases in the stock of the corporation.[27]

Although the use of a Subchapter S corporation does eliminate certain problems, such as the potential personal holding company and accumulated earnings taxes, the authors feel that the election of Subchapter S treatment is generally not advisable for professional corporations. The authors see the following problems and drawbacks which may impair or eliminate the benefits which are normally sought under Subchapter S by a professional corporation.

(1) Technical Nature of the Rules

The rules of Subchapter S are very technical in nature and must be followed precisely, particularly those rules relating to previously taxed income. Even if the rules relating to Subchapter S can be mastered, Subchapter S corporations are limited to 15 shareholders (under ERTA this limit is raised to 25 for 1982 and thereafter) and to the issuance of one class of stock. Obviously, larger professional corporations will be precluded from using Subchapter S. Also, those corporations which intend to use different classes of stock, for voting purposes and other reasons, will be precluded from using Subchapter S.

(2) Retirement Plans

The rules relating to corporate retirement plans gernerally apply to the retirement plans adopted by Subchapter S corporations. There are, however, severe restrictions upon the benefits which may be obtained by "shareholder employees" of Subchapter S corporations. Shareholder employees are those individuals who are officers of the corporation or who own over 5% of the stock of the corporation. The benefits available to shareholder-employees are restricted as follows:[28]

(1) Under Section 1379(b)(1), contributions on behalf of shareholder-employees are limited to the lesser of 15% of compensation or $7,500 (under ERTA this limit is raised to $15,000 for 1982 and thereafter). Contributions in excess of those amounts are taxable to the shareholder-employee and are deductible by the corporation. Such additional contributions are considered to be voluntary contributions on behalf of the shareholder-employee.

(2) Under Section 1379(a) forfeitures in the accounts of participants in the plan may not be allocated to the shareholder-employees.

(3) Under Section 401(a)(17), only the first $100,000 (under ERTA this is increased to $200,000 for 1982 and thereafter) of a shareholder-employee's compensation may be taken into account.

(3) Reasonable Compensation

Some commentators feel that the reasonable compensation question, which is more fully discussed in Chapter 13, *infra*, is eliminated by the election of Subchapter S because all income will be taxable to the shareholders during the year. The authors feel, however, that the election of Subchapter S does not insulate the shareholders of the corporation from attacks by the Service regarding the reasonableness of their compensation.[29] The Service may always increase the taxes due by recasting compensation as dividends. Further, dividends received from a Subchapter S corporation are not subject to the dividends exclusion ($200 per individual and $400 on a joint return for 1981, but under ERTA, $100 per individual and $200 per joint return for 1982 and thereafter) under Section 116 of the Code.

(4) Surtax Exemption and Dividends-Received Deduction

Since all income of the Subchapter S corporation will be taxable on an annual basis to its shareholders, Subchapter S corporation do not benefit from the corporate surtax exemption. Consequently, it is impossible for Subchapter S corporation to retain earnings for expansion and other purposes at the lower corporate rates which are generally available. Although professional corporations do not require an enormous amount of working capital, earnings must generally be retained for expansion and equipment purchases. Unless all fixed assets of the professional corporation are placed in a separate partnership or corporation (which would not elect Subchapter S treatment) a professional corporation which elects Subchapter S treatment would not have the very favorable advantage of retaining funds at lower corporate surtax rates. Also, the dividends-received deduction available under Section 243 of the Code is not available to corporations electing treatment under Subchapter S. Further, because Subchapter S corporations may not retain earnings under the corporate surtax exemption, some of the benefit of purchasing key man insurance in the corporation or entering into split dollar insurance agreements with employees or their spouses is also eliminated.

The surtax exemption, the dividends-received deduction, and the use of key man and split dollar insurance are certainly not benefits which, in and of themselves, would provide the sole reason for incorporating. They are, however, benefits which should not be lost once a professional has incorporated his practice.

(5) State Laws

It is possible that some state laws do not recognize the taxation of corporations under Subchapter S and, in this case, a professional corporation electing Subchapter S status may be forced to file two separate types of income tax returns.

(6) Investment Tax Credit Recapture

At certain times, the sale or other disposition of stock of a Subchapter S corporation may generate investment tax credit recapture.[30]

Although these drawbacks to the election of Subchapter S status will generally militate against its election on a long-term basis, the election of Subchapter S treatment may help ease the problem generated by income bunching which occurs upon the incorporation of a fiscal year partnership (see section [5.14], *supra*), and may be beneficial during the first year of incorporation where the professionals seek to deduct losses and start up expenses. With the exception of the use of Subchapter S status in such start-up situations, the authors see no benefits which warrant considering the indefinite use of Subchapter S status for professional corporations.[31]

EXHIBIT 1

PRIVATE LETTER RULING AND CLOSING STATEMENT

Letter Ruling 7801008

Gentlemen:

This is in reply to a letter dated June 23, 1977, requesting a ruling as to the federal income tax consequences of a consummated transaction. Additional information was submitted in letters dated June 24, July 21, July 25, August 3, and September 6, 1977. The information submitted for consideration is substantially as set forth below.

Transferor is a partnership which was formed in 1967, and was engaged in the practice of public accounting from then until July of 1977. Transferor employs the cash method of accounting on a calendar year basis. D, E, and F shared equally in the partnership profits. In addition, G, a former partner in Transferor who retired in April of 1975, shared on an equal basis with D, E, and F in any accounts receivable and subsequently billed work-in-process that existed at the date of his retirement. Pursuant to an agreement with G, Transferor is also obligated to pay G the sum of $10,175.28 per year for a period of five years which began four months after G's retirement. As of April 30, 1977, there was an unpaid balance of $33,069.66 due G pursuant to this agreement.

X was incorporated in July of 1975 as a professional corporation, and has been engaged in the practice of public accounting from then until the present. X employs the cash method of accounting on the basis of a fiscal year ending June 30. As of June 23, 1977, X had 100 shares of no par value common stock, its only class of stock, issued and outstanding. A, B, and C each owned 33 1/3 shares of this stock.

D, E, F, and X wish to combine the operations of Transferor and X. The increased size of the resulting firm will enhance its ability to attract larger clients, as well as its ability to retain higher grade employees. In order to accomplish these goals, the following action was taken:

(A) On July 1, 1977, Transferor transferred to X all of its assets, except for accounts receivable, in an amount sufficient to liquidate Transferor's trade accounts payable and the balance of the unpaid amount due G, solely in exchange for 120 shares of X stock and the assumption by X of certain liabilities of Transferor. The assets transferred from Transferor to X in the transaction included cash, accounts receivable, work in process, employee advances, prepaid expenses, furniture and fixtures. D, E, and F each received 40 of the shares issued to Transferor.

(B) Simultaneously with the above-described transaction, A, B, and C each transferred $700 to X in exchange for a total of 20 additional shares of X stock, or 6⅔ shares each. When added to their previous holdings, this gave A, B, and C each 40 shares of X stock. It has been represented that the cash transferred by A, B, and C to X, as described above, is equal to or in excess of 10% of the fair market value of the X stock owned by each of them immediately before the transfer.

62

(C) Upon the consummation of the transactions described above in subparagraphs (A) and (B), X changed its name to Transferee.

Transferor will remain in existence until its trade accounts payable and liability to G are satisfied.

With regard to the consummated transaction, the following representations have been made.

(a) The adjusted basis and the fair market value of the assets transferred by Transferor, A, B, and C ("the transferors") to Transferee in the transaction, in each instance, exceeded the sum of the amount of the liabilities of the transferors assumed by Transferee plus the amount of the liabilities to which such assets were subject.

(b) The liabilities of the transferors assumed by Transferee in the transaction were incurred in the ordinary course of business and were associated with the assets transferred.

(c) The fair market value of the stock of Transferee issued to the transferors in the transaction is approximately equal to the fair market value of the assets transferred.

(d) The transferors have no plan or intention to sell or otherwise dispose of the stock of Transferee received by them in the transaction, or to liquidate Transferee.

(e) Transferee has no plan or intention to sell or otherwise dispose of the assets received by it in the transaction, other than in the ordinary course of business.

(f) Transferee will retain and use the assets transferred by the transferors to it in the transaction in the practice of public accounting.

(g) The transferors did not retain any rights or interests in the assets transferred to Transferee.

(h) Transferee has no present plans to issue shares other than those issued in connection with the transaction.

(i) Each of the parties to the transaction paid its own expenses, if any, arising out of or incurred in the transaction.

(j) Transferor neither accumulated its receivables nor made any extraordinary payment of its payables in anticipation of the transaction.

(k) Transferee has no intention of making the election under Section 1372(a) of the Internal Revenue Code of 1954 to be taxed as a "small business corporation" as defined in Section 1371 of the Code.

(l) The Reserve for Bad Debts as shown on the balance sheet of Transferor was for its financial accounting purposes only, and not for federal income tax accounting purposes.

(m) Transferee did not issue any evidences of its indebtedness in connection with the transaction. All property received by Transferee in the transaction was received solely in exchange for Transferee stock.

Based solely on the information and representations submitted, and provided that the cash transferred by A, B, and C to Transferee is equal to or in excess of 10% of the fair market value of the Transferee stock owned by each of them immediately before the transaction described above, it is held as follows:

(1) No gain or loss will be recognized to Transferor A, B, and C upon the transfer of the assets described in subparagraphs (A) and (B) above, to Transferee solely in exchange for Transferee stock and the assumption by Transferee of the liabilities described in subparagraph (A) above (Rev. Rul. 70-239, 1970-1 C.B. 74, and Sections 351(a) and 357(a).

(2) No gain or loss will be recognized to Transferee upon receipt of the assets transferred to it by Transferor, A, B, and C in the transaction in exchange for Transferee stock (Section 1032(a)).

(3) The basis of the assets of Transferor received by Transferee in the transaction will be the same as the basis of such assets in the hands of Transferor immediately prior to the exchange (Section 362(a)).

(4) The basis of the Transferee stock received by Transferor in the transaction will be the same as the basis of the assets exchanged therefor decreased by the sum of the amount of the liabilities of Transferor assumed by Transferee and the amount of the liabilties to which such assets are subject; and the basis of the Transferee stock received by A, B, and C, respectively, in the transaction will be the same as the amount of cash transferred by each of them in exchange therefor (Section 358(a)).

(5) With respect to the public accounting practice carried on by Transferor that has been transferred to Transferee, items of income and deduction will neither be duplicated nor omitted as between Transferor and Transferee.

(6) Items, which, but for the transfer, would have resulted in income or deduction to Transferor in a period subsequent to the transfer will constitute items of income or deduction to Transferee when received or paid by it. Transferee will have a zero basis for the income items so transferred. The proceeds received in collection of the income items will be included as ordinary income in computing the taxable income of Transferee. If Transferee disposes of all or any portion of the income items (other than by collection in the ordinary course of business) in any manner including but not limited to (a) a sale; (b) an assignment; (c) a pledge; (d) a taxable exchange; (e) a nontaxable exchange (except in a transaction to which Section 381 of the Code applies); (f) a gift or donation; (g) a dividend distribution; or (h) a distribution in partial or in complete liquidation, Transferee will include the face amount of the income items so disposed of in its gross income in the taxable year of the disposition. The amount so included in gross income will thereupon become the basis for income tax purposes of the income item in the hands of Transferee at the time of disposition. Where the income item does not have a face value, the sales proceeds in the case of an arm's-length sale or fair market value in all other cases will be included in income in the taxable year of disposition. The term "items" is not limited to accounts receivable but includes any item the sale, exchange or disposition of which would have resulted in ordinary income in the hands of Transferor.

All of the above rulings are premised on the condition that Transferee enters into a closing agreement, which closing agreement has been prepared in triplicate and is enclosed. In pursuance of our practice with respect to all such closing agreements, the agreements contain a stipulation to the effect that any change or modification of applicable statutes will render the agreements ineffective to the extent that they are dependent upon such statutes.

The original, duplicate and triplicate of the closing agreement should be dated and signed with the corporate name followed by the signature and title of the officer, or officers, authorized by the Board of Directors of Transferee to act in such matters.

The executed agreements should be returned to this office for the attention of T:C:R:1:3. After the agreements have been approved, a copy will be forwarded to you.

No determination or verification has been made as to whether the cash transferred by A, B, and C to Transferee, as described above in subparagraph (B), was equal to or in excess of 10% of the fair market value of the stock of Transferee already owned by each of them as required by Section 1.351-1(a)(1)(ii) of the Income Tax Regulations and Rev. Proc. 76-22, 1976-1 C.B. 562. A determination or verification of this matter is specifically reserved until the federal income tax returns for the taxpayers involved have been filed for the year in which the transaction was consummated.

No opinion is expressed about the tax treatment of the transaction under other provisions of the Code and Regulations or about the tax treatment of any conditions existing at the time of, or effects resulting from, the transaction that are not specifically covered by the above rulings.

A copy of this letter and closing agreement should be attached to the federal income tax returns of the taxpayers involved for the taxable year in which the transaction covered by this ruling was consummated.

Sincerely yours,

_____

Assistant Commissioner (Technical)

CLOSING AGREEMENT AS TO FINAL DETERMINATION COVERING SPECIFIC MATTERS

THIS CLOSING AGREEMENT, made in triplicate under and in pursuance of Section 7121 of the Internal Revenue Code of 1954 by and between _____ and the Commissioner of Internal Revenue:

WHEREAS, based on information submitted on behalf of _____ _____ (hereinafter referred to as "Transferor") in the request for ruling dated June 23, 1977, and in additional letters dated June 24, July 21, and July 25, August 3, and September 6, 1977, and in the absence of other material circumstances as part of the consummated transaction, it has been determined for federal income tax purposes that under the circumstances stated in the Assistant Commissioner's Letter to Transferee dated September 30, 1977, a copy of which is attached hereto and made a part hereof, that:

(1) With respect to the public accounting practice carried on by transferor which was Transferred to Transferee, items of income and deduction will neither be duplicated or omitted as between Transferor and Transferee.

(2) Items which, but for the transfer, would have resulted in income or deduction to Transferor in a period subsequent to the transfer will constitute items of income or deduction to Transferee when received or paid by it. Transferee will have a zero basis for the income items so transferred. The proceeds received in collection of the income items will be included as ordinary income in computing the taxable income of Transferee. If Transferee disposes of all or any portion of the income items other than by collection in the ordinary course of business) in any manner including but not limited to (a) a sale; (b) an assignment; (c) a pledge; (d) a taxable exchange; (e) a nontaxable exchange (except in a transaction to which Section 381 of the code applies); (f) a gift or donation; (g) a dividend distribution; or (h) a distribution in partial or in complete liquidation, Transferee will include the face amount of the income items so disposed of in its gross income in the taxable year of the disposition. The amount so included in gross income will thereupon become the basis for income tax purposes of the income item in the hands of Transferee at the time of the disposition. Where the income item does not have a face value, the sales proceeds in the case of an arm's-length sale or fair market value in all other cases will be included in income in the taxable year of disposition. The term "items" is not limited to accounts receivable but includes any item the sale, exchange or disposition of which would have resulted in ordinary income in the hands of the Transferor.

(3) Transferee will notify the District Director of the occurrence of any event which is specified in paragraph (2) of this closing agreement in the form of a separate statement attached to its federal income tax return for the year in which the event specified in paragraph (2) occurs. In the event Transferee fails to notify the District Directors as specified above, then notwithstanding the provisions of Section 6501 of the Code (relating to the period of limitation on assessment) the Commissioner under this closing agreement may assess any deficiency (including interest and additions to the tax) due to the occurrence of any event specified in paragraph (2) as if, on the date notification by Transferee is received by the District Director, one year remained before the expiration of the period of limitation upon assessment for the taxable year in which the event specified in paragraph (2) occurred.

WHEREAS, the determinations set forth above are agreed to by said taxpayer:

NOW, THIS CLOSING AGREEMENT WITNESSETH, that the said taxpayer and said Commissioner of Internal Revenue hereby mutually agree that the determinations set forth above shall be final and conclusive, subject, however, to reopening in the event of fraud, malfeasance, or misrepresentation of material fact, and provided that any change or modification of applicable statutes will render this agreement ineffective to the extent that it is dependent upon such statutes.

IN WITNESS WHEREOF, the above parties have subscribed their names to these presents, in triplicate.

Signed this _____ day of _____, 19____.

_____
Taxpayer

_____

By: _____

_____
(Title)

Commissioner of Internal Revenue

By: _____

_____
(Title)

EXHIBIT 2

PROMISSORY NOTE

Principal   Atlanta, Georgia
$_____   _____ (Date)

FOR VALUE RECEIVED, the undersigned, _____, (hereinafter referred to as ''Maker'' promises to pay to the order of _____ _____ (hereinafter, together with any other holder hereof, referred to as ''Holder'') the principal sum of _____ Dollars and _____ ($ _____), with interest from the date hereof at the rate _____ per centum (____%) per annum on said principal sum, or on so much thereof as may from time to time remain unpaid; said principal and interest being payable one (1) year from the date of this Note in lawful money of the United States, in the following installments:

DATE	PAYMENT	PRINCIPAL	INTEREST	REMAINING PRINCIPAL BALANCE

Each installment, when paid, will be applied first to the payment of interest accrued on unpaid principal, and the residue thereof to be credited on the principal.

Principal and interest are payable at the Holder's offices located at _____ or at such other place as the Holder hereof may designate in writing.

After the sixth anniversary of this Note, the entire unpaid balance of this Note, or partial payments in even hundreds of dollars, may be paid at any time prior to maturity, with interest to the date of payment on said prepayment, without penalty.

If, for any reason, any of the installments are not paid promptly on or before the due date, the Maker shall be in default hereunder. Upon default and at any time thereafter, the Holder may declare the entire unpaid balance of this Note, with interest, immediately due and payable without presentment, demand, protest, or notice of any kind, all of which are hereby expressly waived. Upon default, and in case the Holder should elect, on account of such default, to declare the unpaid balance of the principal sum due and payable, said principal sum, or so much thereof as may remain unpaid at the time of such default, shall bear interest at the rate of _____ per centum (____%) per annum from the date of such default. If this Note be placed in the hands of an attorney for collection, the Maker will pay all costs of collection incurred by the Holder, including a reasonable attorney's fee.

And each of us, whether maker, endorser, guarantor, or surety, hereby severally waives and renounces, for himself and family, any and all exemption rights either of us, or the family of either of us, may have under or by virtue of the Constitution or laws of Georgia, or any other state, or the United States, as against the debt or any renewal thereof; and each of us further waives demand, protest, and notice of demand, protest, and nonpayment.

Time is of the essence of this Note, and this Note is to be construed in all respects and enforced according to the laws of the State of Georgia.

Executed this _____ day of _____, 19___.

_____

(CORPORATE SEAL)

ATTEST:

By: _____
                President

_____
Secretary
Signed, sealed and delivered
in the presence of:

_____
Witness

_____
Witness

NOTES TO CHAPTER 5

1. Rev. Rul. 68-55, 1968-1 C.B. 140 and Rev. Rul. 67-19, 1962-1 C.B. 29.3.

2. *Camp Wolters Enterprises, Inc.,* 22 T.C. 737 (1954), *aff'd,* 230 F.2d 555 (5th Cir. 1956), cert. den. 352 U.S. 826 (1957) (Notes maturing five to nine years after issuance were held to be securities); *L&F Sterne, Inc. v. Commissioner,* 107 F.2d 390 (2d Cir. 1939) (Bonds maturing on an average of 2½ years were not held to be securities); *U.S. v. Hertwig,* 398 F.2d 452 (5th Cir. 1968) (10 year bonds deemed to be securities); *Turner Construction Co. v. U.S.,* 364 F.2d 525 (2d Cir. 1966) (Securities of five years or less deemed to be boot). See Bittker & Eustice, *Federal Income Taxation of Corporations and Shareholders,* §3.04 (4th Ed.).

3. *Holdcroft Transportation Company v. Commissioner,* 153 F.2d 323 (8th Cir. 1946); *Haden Company v. Commissioner,* 165 F.2d 588 (5th Cir. 1948); *Rodney, Inc., v. Commissioner,* 145 F.2d 692 (6th Cir. 1944).

4. See *U.S. v. Smith,* 418 F.2d 589 (5th Cir. 1979); *U.S. v. Hempt Brothers,* 490 F.2d 1175 (3rd Cir. 1974), cert. denied, 419 U.S. 826; R. Pearlman, "Corporations - Assumption of Liabilities," A-40 *Tax Management Portfolio,* No. 233-2d, 1975.

5. See, for example, Letter ruling 7838133 where 42 professionals incorporated.

6. See McKee, Nelson and Whitmire, *Federal Taxation of Partnerships and Partners* at ¶17.02[3].

7. Worthy, "IRS Chief Counsel Outlines What Lies Ahead for Professional Corporations," 32 *Journal of Taxation* 88, 90-91 (1971).

8. The Service has also sought, on certain occasions, to cause cash basis taxpayers to recognize income on accounts receivable at the time of transfer to the corporation. This contention has, however, been rejected, *Thomas W. Briggs,* 15 T.C.M. 440, ¶56,086 P-H Memo T.C. (1956). Also see generally, Rothman, "Transfers to Controlled Corporations: Related Problems," *Tax Management Portfolio,* No. 348, 1979. Also see L.R. 8022071 where the Service ruled that no assignment of income occurred where a broker incorporated his proprietorship and transferred commission contracts (payable in installments over 25 years) to the corporation. There should also be no problem with acceleration of income on accounts receivable under Section 751, since any distribution of receivables to partners (prior to the transfer of the professional corporation under Section 351) should be on a pro rata basis.

9. *U.S. v. Hempt Brothers,* note 1-8, supra; *Roberts Co., Inc.,* 5 T.C. 1 (1945) acq. 1945 C.B. 6; Worthy, note 7, *supra.*

10. *Peter Raich,* 46 T.C. 604 (1966) (taxpayer required to report gain); *Bongiovanni v. Commissioner,* 470 T.C. 921 (2d Cir. 1972) (cash method accounts payable are not liabilities under Section 357(c)); *David Rosen,* 62 T.C. 11 (1974), affirmed without opinion (3rd Cir. 1975) (*Raich,* affirmed); *Wilfred E. Thatcher,* 61 T.C. 28 (1973) (*Raich* affirmed) reversed on this issue, 533 F.2d 1114 (9th Cir. 1976); *Donald O. Focht,* 68 T.C. 223 (1977).

11. Rev. Rul. 80-199, 1980-30 I.R.B. 11, and Rev. Rul. 80-198, 1980-30 I.R.B. 10.

12. *Id.*

13. Treas. Regs. §1.111-1(a).

14. Rev. Rul. 72-172, 1972-1 C.B. 265.

15. Rev. Rul. 60-302, 1960-2 C.B. 223.

16. Rev. Rul. 57-352, 1957-2 C.B. 150, amplified by Rev. Rul. 59-389, 1959-2 C.B. 89, clarified by Rev. Rul. 67-248, 1967-2 C.B. 98. Also see Rev. Rul. 56-256, 1956-1, C.B. 29.

17. *Letter Ruling 8034171·*

The sole proprietor of a plumbing business wants to incorporate. He lives in a community property state and his assets were acquired during his marriage. The sole proprietor and his wife will receive all the shares in the new corporation. He used Section 38 property in his business and has taken investment credits.

The service has ruled that the transfer of Section 38 property to the new corporation, assuming the transfer qualified under section 351, is not an early disposition. Thus, the investment credit will not be recaptured. The Service reasoned that there has been a mere change in the form of the business. It said that the proprietor's 50% ownership after incorporation satisfied the requirement in Treas. Reg. §1.47-3(f)(ii)(b) that the transferor retain a substantial interest in the business.

18. Letter Ruling 8016047.

19. *Runy v. U.S.,* 305 F.2d 681 (9th Cir. 1962).

20. *Jud Plumbing & Heating Co.,* 5 T.C. 127 (1945), *aff'd,* 153 F.2d 681 (5th Cir. 1946).

21. 1970-1 C.B. 74.

22. McKee, *supra,* note 6 ¶17.03[1], and Willis, *Partnership Taxation* at ¶72.05 (2d Ed.)

23. See note 21, *supra.*

24. McKee, *supra,* note 6 at Chapter 17 and Willis, *supra,* note 24 at Sections 72.05 and 72.06.

25. *David A. Foxman,* 41 T.C. 535 (1964), *aff'd,* 352 F.2d 466 (3rd Cir. 1965); also see *Baker Commodities, Inc. v. Commissioner,* 415 F.2d 519 (9th Cir. 1969), aff'g, 48 T.C. 374 (1967), *cert. denied,* 397 U.S. 988 (No termination of partnership until all activity ends and all assets distributed); *Ginsbury v. U.S.,* 396 F.2d 983 (Ct. Cl. 1968) (no termination of partnership even when primary activity ends).

26. Treas. Regs. §1.442-1(b)(2)(ii).

27. For a complete discussion of the general rules under which Subchapter S corporations operate, see Section 6501 of *The Professional Corporation Guide* and Prentice-Hall *Federal Taxes* at ¶33,361 *et seq.*

28. See Prentice-Hall *Pension and Profit Sharing Service,* at ¶8666.

29. In *Gary N. Cromer*, 40 T.C.M. 701, ¶80,263 P-H Memo T.C. (1980), the Tax Court recognized that unreasonable compensation may exist in a Subchapter S corporation. Also see Worthy, *supra*, note 7 at 91; *Byrne v. Commissioner*, 45 T.C. 151 (1965), *aff'd* 361 F.2d 939 (7th Cir. 1966); *Bianchi v. Commissioner*, 66 T.C. 324 (1976), *aff'd* 553 F.2d 93 (2d Cir. 1977); and *LaMastro v. Commissioner*, 72 T.C. 377 (1979).

30. Treas. Regs. §1.47-4(a)(2)].

31. Also see Worthy, *supra*, note 7 at 91.

CHAPTER 6

The Fine Points of

Corporate Documents

[6.01] INCORPORATION WORK SHEET

One of the most important practical aspects of incorporating a professional practice is gathering the information needed for incorporation as quickly as possible without repeated telephone calls and conferences. This can be done most easily by the use of a detailed work sheet which can be completed when meeting with the professional and his other advisors. Since the incorporation of a professional practice involves various aspects, other than the tax aspects of incorporation, it is important that a clear understanding exists between all of the advisors involved— attorney, accountant, stockbroker, insurance agent, and business consultant—regarding the tasks each advisor will perform. The use of a work sheet helps to coordinate this aspect of incorporation and will also act as the attorney's record of what agreements were made with regard to the delegation of responsibilities. Of course, it is also advisable for the attorney to write a letter to the professional outlining his understanding of the delegation of duties.

The form of work sheet included in this chapter is coordinated with the documents contained in other sections of the Desk Book (articles of incorporation, employment agreements, and stock retirement agreements, etc.); the various aspects of those agreements are discussed in later sections of the Desk Book.

All of the documents relating to the incorporation (bylaws, employment agreements, stock retirement agreements, etc.) should be prepared in advance of the incorporation and submitted to the professional (and to those of his advisors whom he designates) so that they may be reviewed and any questions answered and any amendments made. Shortly after incorporation (within two weeks), the original meeting of the Board of Directors should be held and all of the incorporation documents should be executed in multiple copies, with one executed copy going to each shareholder of the professional corporation and one copy being placed in the corporation's minute book.

Obviously, at the meeting in which the questions enumerated in the work-sheet are answered, a number of very basic decisions must be made so that the nature of the professional corporation can be established. It is important to bring all of the important issues (particularly those which normally generate disputes among professionals) before the professionals *prior to incorporation* so that they may be resolved. In the case of a one-man professional corporation, this simply means describing the tax risks incident to incorporation and delineating the employee benefits that the professional desires. On the other hand, in the case of a professional corporation which will have two or more shareholders, uncertainties in the following areas should definitely be resolved prior to incorporation:

a. The type of stock to be issued and the control of the corporation. Will there be any shareholder agreements regarding the voting of stock? See Chapter 7, *infra*.

b. Compensation and general provisions of employment agreements. Professionals will definitely be interested in, and disputes may occur over, provisions relating to compensation and bonuses, vacations and time off for professional meetings, amounts paid upon termination of employment, and the use of covenants against competition. See section [10.01], *infra*.

c. The manner in which entertainment and other professional expenses are handled and whether the professional corporation will purchase automobiles for the professionals. For some reason, the handling of automobiles appears to be a particularly common stumbling block for professionals. See, generally, section [10.01], *infra*.

d. All provisions relating to the retirement of a shareholder's stock upon his death, disability, retirement, or termination of employment. See, generally, Chapter 11, *infra*.

e. The type of qualified retirement plans which will be established and the nature of the benefits provided under those plans. Problems in this area arise primarily because of the different needs and desires of the professionals which are usually generated by age and financial position. See, generally, Chapter 15, *infra*.

To say that it is impossible to incorporate a professional practice without a work sheet such as the one contained in this chapter is, of course, an overstatement. However, a work sheet vastly simplifies the task at hand, jogs memories, and alerts individuals to the responsibilities which they must undertake.

CORPORATION WORK SHEET

Date: _____

Date Documents
Needed _____

Meeting Held on: _____
Location: _____
Persons Present: _____
_____
_____

1. Name: _____
_____

2. County of Incorporation: _____

3. Date of Incorporation: _____

4. Business Address of Corporation: _____
_____
_____

5. Telephone Number: _____

6. Principal Office Address (if different from No. 4):
_____
_____
_____

7. Registered Office Address (if different from No. 4):
_____
_____
_____

8. Registered Agent at Above Address: _____
_____

9. Purpose (or area of specialization): _____
_____

10. Stock: _____
    Par Value: _____
    Shares to be Authorized: _____
    Shares to be Outstanding: _____
    Classes: _____
    Property to be Transferred for Shares:
        Cash: _____
        Tangible Property—attach list with description and adjusted basis.
        Accounts Receivable: _____
        Other Assets: _____
        Accounts Payable and Liabilities: _____

11. Incorporator's Name: Address:

_____

_____

_____

_____

12. Shareholders (Subscribers):

Name	Address	Shares	Consideration

13. Board of Directors: _____

_____

_____

14. Officers:

President: _____

Secretary: _____

Treasurer: _____

Vice Presidents: _____

_____

_____

15. Name of Newspaper for publication:

_____

16. Persons Authorized to Sign Checks: _____

_____

17. Date of Organizational Meeting: _____

Persons Present: _____

Location: _____

Chairman: _____

Secretary: _____

18. Date of Documents to be Executed: _____

19. Date Documents to be Effective: _____

20. Fiscal Year: _____

Will first year be a short year? _____

21. Name and Address of Accountant:

Name	Address

22. Who will get tax ID numbers? Federal: _____

State: _____

23. Name and Address of Corporation's Bank and Account Representative:
    Name   Address

    _____
    _____
    _____

24. Who will secure Bank Resolution and signature cards; who will open check-
    ing accounts? _____
    _____

25. Name and Address of Insurance Agents:
    Name   Address   Type of Insurance
    _____   Life Insurance
    _____   Malpractice
    _____   General Insurance
    _____   Medical
    _____   Disability

    Who will notify insurance carriers of incorporation?
    _____

    If insurance is obtained, who will prepare the insurance plan and prepare
    corporate resolutions? _____
    Group term life: _____
    Disability: _____
    Group medical: _____

26. Name and Business Address of Stock Broker, Investment Manager, Business
    Consultant, etc.:

    Name   Function   Address

    _____
    _____
    _____
    _____

27. Clinic Manager, if any, or person to be contacted regarding questions: ___
    _____

28. Calculation of net spendable income for professionals during first year of
    incorporation: _____
    Gross income from practice: _____
    Practice expenses: _____
    Net income from practice before compensation: _____
    Additional expenses associated with incorporation: _____

    Anticipated retirement plan contributions for professionals and staff: _____
    Retained earnings for capital improvement: _____
    Net available for salaries of professionals: _____

Will this amount meet the living needs of the professionals?

Salary Requirements of each professional:

Name	Monthly	Annually

29. Name of holding corporation, if any, which will own all major equipment and building and lease to the corporation:

30. Are there any special contracts (with hospitals, etc.) which must be amended or re-executed with corporation? If so, obtain copies.: _____

31. Does anyone now have an H.R. 10 plan? _____

    Will plans be frozen or transferred to corporate retirement plans? _____

32. Is there a partnership or practice agreement, if so obtain a copy. _____

    How will the new corporation be formed: (a) by transfer of assets from partnership followed by distribution of stock to partners? (b) by liquidation of partnership and partners' transfer of assets to corporation? (c) by transfer of partnership interests to corporation? Discuss attributes of each method. ___

    Who will assure state law requirements regarding notice, etc., have been met regarding liquidation of partnership?

    Will partnership remain in existence, if so, how long?

    Will capital accounts in partnership correspond to stock holdings, if not, how will adjustments be made?

33. Controlled Group Problem: Do any of the professionals have interests in other corporations, partnerships, joint returns, or proprietorships, which are engaged in the active conduct of a trade or business and which have employees?

34. Has there been a change in accounting method within the last ten years? __

35. Do any ethical problems exist and should any state professional association be
contacted? _____
_____

EMPLOYMENT CONTRACTS

SHAREHOLDER EMPLOYMENT CONTRACTS

	Name	Social Security Number

For: 1) _____
2) _____
3) _____
4) _____
5) _____
6) _____
7) _____
8) _____
9) _____
10) _____

Term: From: _____ To: _____

Monthly Salary: Stated Amount: _____
Production Formula: _____
Excess Carried Over or Canceled: _____
Oswald Clause: _____

Bonuses:

Will contract provide for stated discretionary or production bonus? _____

Expenses: Normally paid by Employee but Employer may pay for: _____
Professional Societies: _____

Meetings & Post Graduate Courses: _____
Normally employer pays cost of tuition only, employee pays living
expenses:

or

Stated amount: _____

Auto Insurance: $100,000 - $300,000: _____

Vacation: _____

Time off for attendance at professional meetings: _____

Outside Personal Professional Activities:
Employee can keep income: _____

or

Cannot keep income: _____

Sick pay period (usually 60 days): _____

Salary continuation on disability (tie in with disability insurance waiting
period—normally not to extend beyond 12 months): _____

78

Number of Months Salary Continues: _____ Percent of Salary: _____

Extended period for provision of hospitalization, major medical and group term life insurance: _____

Military leave provisions: _____

Terminations: (__ day's notice): _____

    Salary continuation: _____

        If employer terminates: _____

           For cause, what cause? _____

        If employee terminates: _____

        At or after normal retirement age: _____

        On death: _____

(Salary continuation usually corresponds to receivables on books in the case of a medical practice, i.e., three to five months, in other professions this point is negotiated.)

$5,000 death benefit: _____

Noncompetition clause: _____

Special provision for vacation, night, weekend, or holiday duty: _____

NONSHAREHOLDER EMPLOYMENT CONTRACTS

		Name	Monthly Salary
For:	1)	_____	_____
	2)	_____	_____
	3)	_____	_____
	4)	_____	_____
	6)	_____	_____
	7)	_____	_____
	8)	_____	_____
	9)	_____	_____

Term: From: _____ To: _____

    Compensation: If employee will not be paid a monthly salary, will compensation depend upon production? _____

Bonus: Discretionary or based on production?

Payment of professional society dues: _____

_____

Meetings and postgraduate courses:

      Usually only tuition: _____

                or

      Flat amount: _____

Vacation: _____

_____

Sick leave: _____

_____

One afternoon off per week: _____

Special time off (teaching, etc.): _____

_____

Outside Professional activities:

      May   or   May Not   Keep Compensation

Termination: _____ days' notice.

    Payment for Receivables: _____

_____

    Death Payment: _____

_____

    Incentive compensation to be paid: _____

Disability insurance: Amount: _____

Major Medical Insurance: _____

Group Term Life Insurance: _____

Stock Purchase: _____

      When: _____

      Formula for price: _____

      Percentage to be Sold: _____

      Change in name of corporation: _____

      Equality in salary: When: _____

Noncompetition clause: _____

_____

STOCK RETIREMENT AGREEMENT

Cross-Purchase or Redemption Agreement: _____

Amount of purchase price: _____

    Voluntary retirement: _____

    Quits: (Is there to be a reduction?): _____

    Total disability (tie in with employment contract) _____

_____

    Death: _____

Will agreement require mandatory redemption in all events?

_____

Will agreement require mandatory redemption upon death, disability, or retirement but optional redemption (with first refusal) upon termination of employment prior to retirement? _____

_____

How will value be determined? Formula (book value) or annually agreed-upon value? _____

What special adjustments will be made to value? Will key man insurance proceeds be added to value? Will equipment be valued at the greater of depreciated value or cost? _____

How will purchase price be paid? Lump sum or in installments (no. of years: _____ ; interest_____)?

Will the payment of purchase price be over a longer period of time at reduced rate of interest if caused by termination of employment prior to retirement? ___

Will stockholder be entitled to retain a security interest in stock? _____

Will life insurance be puchased on lives of stockholders? Will agreement require that proceeds of insurance be used to make lump sum payment toward purchase price? _____

Will shareholders guarantee the Corporation's obligation to purchase the stock?

HEALTH AND MEDICAL REIMBURSEMENT PLAN

Effective Date: _____

Employees Covered: _____

Title/Office: _____

Will the plan be discriminatory or nondiscriminatory?

_____

Participation (3 years of service and age 25)? _____

Benefits: Discriminatory—diagnostic
 Nondiscriminatory— _____

Percentage or Stated Amount: _____

ESTIMATE OF LEGAL FEES FOR INCORPORATION

Incorporation and other related documents: _____

Stock retirement agreements, employment agreements: _____
_____

Retirement plans: _____
TOTAL FEE: _____

How much of fee is for "tax advice?" _____ —
Estimated out-of-pocket expenses: _____ —
Fee for private letter ruling, if any: _____ —
How will time for extraordinary work be charged?
(hourly basis) _____ —

[6.02] ARTICLES OF INCORPORATION

Each professional corporation must have articles of incorporation, for it is the articles of incorporation which generate the existence of the professional corporation under state law. Under the laws of most states, the articles of incorporation of a professional corporation will be identical to those of a business corporation with a few minor variations, such as the required statement that the corporation is formed to engage in a certain profession. The discussion contained in this section is not meant as a complete guide to the preparation of articles of incorporation under the laws of the various states, but rather as a guide to those provisions which normally appear in articles of incorporation. The *Professional Corporation Guide* (at §25,001) contains examples of articles of incorporation for various states. In some states, professions are incorporated as professional "associations," which represents a carryover from the early 1960's when unincorporated associations sought corporate tax status.

The principal rule to be followed when drafting articles of incorporation for professional corporations is to keep them short and straightforward without omitting provisions that protect the shareholders. The articles of incorporation which follow have been prepared under Georgia law and comprise approximately three pages when finalized. The comments following each section of the articles describe the reasons for the section and possible additional provisions which may be required under the laws of other states.

ARTICLES OF INCORPORATION OF
XYZ, P.C.

I.

The name of the corporation is: XYZ, P.C.

Comment:

The choice of the name to be adopted by the professional corporation is, generally, up to the professionals. It may be a generic name, such as Georgia

Neurosurgical Associates, P.C., or it may be a name comprised of the names of the professionals, followed by the appropriate corporate designation. Most states require a designation following a professional corporation of either "P.C." or "P.A." or a variation, such as, "A Professional Corporation, "or "A Professional Law Corporation." It is also permissible in most states to include "Inc.," "Incorporated," or "Co." in the title of a professional corporation in lieu of the "P.C." or "P.A." designation.

In most states, the name chosen must be approved by the state official or authority charged with the duty of administering the state's corporation laws (the Secretary of State or the Corporation Commissioner). Also, in some states, the name must be approved by the local professional association and a certificate of good standing for the incorporating professionals must be obtained from the state licensing authority, such as the state bar. In addition, some states require a definite designation following the name of the professional corporation which indicates the profession for which the corporation is licensed (such as "A Professional Law Corporation"). On the other hand, a number of states, such as Georgia, do not require such a designation, except that in the case of physicians, the use of the term "Dr." is not sufficient and the name must specifically state the degree to which the person is entitled, such as "M.D." or "D.D.S" Some professionals feel that it is an excellent idea to include in the name of the professional corporation some indication of the profession practiced, even though it is not required by state law. The authors, however, feel that this is a question of personal choice to be made by the professionals.

II.

The corporation shall have perpetual duration.

Comment:

For many years, a number of states continued to follow the practice of limiting the duration of corporations. Now, almost all states provide that corporations, including professional corporations, may have perpetual existence. Unless there is a compelling reason to structure a professional corporation with a limited life, the authors recommend that the articles of incorporation of a professional corporation state that the corporation will have perpetual duration.

III.

The corporation is organized under the Georgia Business Corporation Code and hereby elects to become subject to the Georgia Professional Corporation Act, Ga. Laws, 1970, No. 943, p. 243, for the following purposes:

To engage in every phase and aspect of the business of rendering the same professional services to the public that a Doctor of Medicine, duly licensed under the laws of the State of Georgia, is authorized to render, but such professional service shall be rendered only through officers, employees, and agents who are duly licensed under the laws of the State of Georgia to practice medicine within this State;

To own real and personal property necessary or appropriate for the rendering of the professional services authorized by this Article and to invest the funds of this corporation in real estate, mortgages, stocks, bonds, or any other type of investment whatsoever;

To do all and everything necessary and proper for the accomplishment of any of the purposes or the attaining of any of the objects or the furtherance of the purposes and objects enumerated in these Articles of Incorporation or any amendment thereof, necessary or incidental to the protection and benefit of this corporation, and, in general, either alone or in association with other associations, corporations, firms, or individuals, to carry on any lawful pursuit necessary or incidental to the accomplishment of the purposes or the attainment of the objects or the furtherance of such purposes or objects of this corporation; and

To enter into any other lawful businesses from time to time, without limitation.

Comment:

The activities in which a professional corporation may engage are prescribed by the various state professional corporation statutes. Almost all state statutes require language comparable to that in the above paragraph which states that the corporation will practice a certain profession but that such professional services must be rendered only through officers, employees, or agents who are duly licensed under the laws of that state to practice the profession for which the corporation is incorporated. Under most state professional corporation acts, professional corporations are governed by general business corporation rules, but are specifically restricted from engaging in general business activities. On the other hand, it is, under most state statutes, permissible for professional corporations to own and operate the real and personal property necessary and appropriate for rendering the professional services for which the corporation is formed. The authors feel that the articles of incorporation of a professional corporation should specifically state that the professional corporation is entitled to enter any other lawful business.

In a number of states, certain professionals have the option of choosing either a regular business corporation or a professional corporation. For example, under the Georgia Professional Corporation Act,[1] architects are considered "professionals" and are entitled to incorporate. Architects are also covered by the general provisions of the Georgia Code dealing with professionals and may incorporate their business under the Georgia Business Corporation Code.[2] Consequently, the professional contemplating incorporation should consider what type of corporation to employ, a "business" or a "professional" corporation. Generally, the business corporation rules are less restrictive than the professional corporation rules; and, consequently, a professional having such a choice would normally choose a business corporation.

IV.

The corporation shall have authority to issue not more than 100,000 shares of common stock of one dollar ($1.00) par value each.

Comment:

The articles of incorporation must state the amount and par value of authorized stock. For a further discussion of the type of stock normally issued by professional corporations, see Chapter 7, *infra*. State statutes differ with regard to the other characteristics of stock which must be contained in the articles of incorporation. Generally, where the articles of incorporation authorize several classes of stock, the specific rights and privileges of the various classes must be stated in the articles of incorporation. Similarly, certain state statutes provide that restrictions relating to stock may be contained either in the articles of incorporation or the bylaws. The authors recommend that, where this option is granted, such restrictions generally be contained in the bylaws, as it is normally easier to amend the bylaws than the articles of incorporation. In addition, many state statutes, require that the articles of incorporation specifically state whether the shareholders have preemptive rights in additional shares. Generally, it is advisable to grant shareholders preemptive rights unless specific classes of shares are being issued to certain stockholders in order to maintain a certain capital and voting structure.

V.

The corporation shall not commence business until it shall have received consideration valued at not less than $500.00 in payment for the issuance of shares of stock.

Comment:

The general business statutes of almost every state require a minimum paid-in capital before a corporation can commence business, and this requirement is also applicable to professional corporations. It is very important that this requirement be met and is not overlooked in the haste to incorporate. The authors have encountered situations where several years have passed before shares have actually been issued. Ignoring such corporate formalities potentially subjects a professional corporation to attack by the Service. See Chapter 9, *infra*, with regard to the various lines of attack open to the Service.

VI.

The initial registered office of the corporation shall be at _____.
The initial registered agent of the corporation at such address shall be .

_____ .

Comment:

Almost every state statute requires that a corporation designate a registered agent for service of process. Normally, this registered agent will either be an officer of the corporation, the attorney for the corporation, or a corporation specifically designated to act as the registered agent, such as the Prentice-Hall *Corporation Service*. The choice of this registered agent is generally up to the professional corporation, but it is important to assure that the registered agent chosen will react in a timely fashion to any complaints or other papers served on him in connection with law suits pending against the corporation. The designated registered agent must, generally, file with the appropriate state authority a form under which he consents to serve.

VII.

The intitial Board of Directors shall consist of ____ (____) members whose names and addresses are:

_____

_____

_____

_____.

Comment:

The initial board of directors will generally consist of the intitial professional shareholders of the corporation. In some states, membership on the board of a professional corporation is limited solely to professionals licensed to practice the profession for which the professional corporation is formed. Also, most states require a certain minimum number of directors, such as three, but usually that number may be less than the specified minimum if the number of shareholders is less than the specified minimum. Where a professional corporation has a sufficient number of shareholder-professionals to constitute the board of directors, it is generally best to name all of the shareholder-professionals as directors (possibly designating certain members of the board to constitute special committees of the board). Naming spouses of shareholder-professionals to the board (if not prohibited under state law) generally provides no definite advantage and often imposes impediments to the holding of corporate meetings and other actions by the board. Also, in recent years, rather strict fiduciary responsibilities have been imposed upon directors by courts and various governmental agencies. For this reason, accountants and attorneys are less willing to serve, if not precluded from serving, on the boards of their clients.

VIII.

The names and addresses of the incorporators are:

_____

_____

_____

_____

Comment:

Due to the fiduciary standards that are being imposed upon attorneys and accountants by the courts, various agencies of the federal government, and their respective associations, it is generally unadvisable for either the attorney or the accountant to act as the incorporator of a professional corporation. It is normally acceptable under state law for one or more of the professionals to act as the incorporator and this should generally be done.

Some state statutes require compliance with various other rules prior to incorporation, such as the submission, along with the articles of incorporation, of certificates of good standing which must be obtained from appropriate state licensing authorities.

[6.03] MINUTES OF THE FIRST MEETING OF THE BOARD OF DIRECTORS.

Having a meeting of, and preparing minutes for, the initial meeting of the board of directors is another essential step in the proper incorporation of a professional practice. However, due to the number of meetings which have usually been held prior to incorporation and the time which has previously been spent, the tendency is not to hold a formal initial meeting but simply to prepare a set of minutes and have them signed and placed in the minute book. The authors are convinced that holding a first meeting of the board is necessary because it gives the attorney and accountant the opportunity to reiterate important points, it permits the professionals to review in a single sitting all the activites which have taken place, and it permits a setting in which final documents, such as employment agreements and stock retirement agreements, may be executed by all of the participating professionals. Also, at the initial meeting of the board of directors, the stock in the corporation should be issued to the subscribing stockholders. It is preferable to hold the initial meeting of the board of directors on the actual date of incorporation, but, if this is not possible, the initial meeting of the board should be held within two weeks after date of incorporation.

At the initial meeting of the Board of Directors of the new professional corporation, the following matters should be discussed and reflected in the minutes.

(1) Business Reasons for Incorporation

While the incorporation of a professional practice does generate substantial tax benefits, there are also business reasons for incorporation and it is important to document these reasons. This documentation should take place in the minutes of the first meeting of the board of directors where the directors should discuss the tax and nontax advantages of incorporation. The absence of such documentation may weaken the corporation's case at a later date if the Service attacks the existence of the corporation. See section [9.01], *infra*.

The courts have generally recognized valid business purposes for the formation of professional corporations. For example, in *Holder v. U.S.*,[3] the court stated, "The principal purpose for forming the associaiton was the business purpose of controlling the sizable and unwieldy organization and to obtain other benefits, such as limited liability, provided by the Georgia Professional Association Act." As one might expect, the Treasury Department contended that the business reasons for incorporation stated by the taxpayers were merely inconsequential byproducts of an incorporation which took place solely for tax purposes. Thus, while such documentation contained in the minutes of the first meeting of the board of directors may be refuted by the Service, it is damaging if such documentation is omitted. Consequently, the authors recommend that the minutes of the first meeting of the board of directors contain a discussion of nontax reasons for incorporating, such as the discipline and management afforded by a professional corporation, the ease of admitting and retiring professionals, and the limitations on liability.

(2) Adoption of Bylaws.

The bylaws of the professional corporation (which are discussed more completely in section [6.04], *infra*) should be presented to the board at the first meeting of directors and adopted. It is important that the bylaws, which are the working rules of the corporation, should actually be adopted because they further support the existence and operation of a bona fide professional corporation.

(3) Adoption of Corporate Seal.

While in recent years the use of the corporate seal has not been as actively required as it was in the past, it is normally advisable to obtain a corporate seal for the corporation (one can be obtained for a minimum charge of $10 to $15). Under most state statutes, the corporate seal, when affixed to a document which has been signed by a duly authorized officer and attested by another officer, merely permits the introduction of that document into evidence without extrinsic proof as to the validity of the signatures and the authority for signing. Consequently, the seal is not a required element in a professional corporation, but, generally, a useful one. It is also necessary to obtain a corporate seal because banks and financial institutions normally require it to be affixed to resolutions authorizing the opening of accounts.

(4) Election of Officers.

The officers of the corporation should be elected at the first meeting of the board of directors because, without officers, the corporation cannot function properly. Many professional corporation statutes generally place restrictions upon the election of officers and the qualifications of the persons who may be elected. Consequently, the appropriate state statute should be reviewed. In general, professional corporation statutes may place no restrictions on the election of officers, require that all officers be duly licensed professionals, or may require that all officers except administrative officers be duly licensed professionals. Also, in most states the general corporation law prohibits the president and secretary from being the same individual, for the obvious reason that it is important to have the president's signature attested by another individual. In some states, however, professional corporation statutes permit the president and secretary to be the same individual in one-man professional corporations. In states where the president and secretary must be different individuals, the tendency in most one-man professional corporations is to appoint the spouse of the professional as the secretary or to appoint the office manager as the secretary. From a practical point of view, it is probably easier to appoint someone in the office as the secretary so that the professional will not be continuously required to take documents home for signature.

(5) Issuance of Stock

At the first meeting of the directors, the professionals should submit their stock subscription and transfer agreements, both of which should be accepted by the corporation. Upon the payment of the consideration stated in the transfer agreement, the corporation should issue the subscribed shares. The minutes of the first meeting should also reflect that the value of the consideration stated in the stock transfer agreement is accurate and should also indicate the disposition of the accounts receivable, i.e., will they be transferred to the professional corporation or will the professional retain them?

If the stock to be issued by the professional corporation will be Section 1244 stock (more fully described in section [7.08], *infra*), the initial minutes of the board should contain an appropriate Section 1244 resolution, although Section 1244 no longer requires one.

(6) Employment Agreements

At the initial meeting of the board, the employment agreements for the professional employees of the corporation should be reviewed and executed. Also, if it is intended that salaries be initially postponed, in order to avoid the bunching problem (discussed at section [5.14], *supra*) or in order to take advantage of tax deferral through the choice of a fiscal year (discussed at section [8.03], *infra*), the minutes should reflect a discussion of the reasons for the deferral.

(7) Stock Retirement Agreement

Upon the issuance of stock at the initial meeting of the board, the stock retirement agreement (more completely discussed at section [11.02], *infra*) should be reviewed by the stockholders and executed. It is very important to have this agreement executed upon the issuance of stock in order to fix the rights of the shareholders. Also, in the event that there are any other shareholder agreements, these agreement should also be adopted at the initial meeting of the board of directors.

(8)   Office Space

If the office space of the predecessor professional practice was leased from a third party, the lease on that space is usually assigned to the new professional corporation and the board should ratify and affirm such assignment. On the other hand, if the office occupied by the predecessor professional practice is owned by the professionals and is not transferred to the professional corporation, arrangements must be made to enter into a new lease and that new lease should be reviewed and ratified at the first meeting.

(9)   Retirement Plans

If qualified retirement plans are adopted at the time of incorporation, the minutes of the initial meeting of the board should contain appropriate resolutions authorizing the adoption of those plans and their submission to the Service for qualification.

(10)   Bank Resolutions

In order to open bank accounts, most banks require a certified copy of a corporate board resolution stating that certain individuals will have signature and other powers over the accounts opened. Generally, the bank will use a standard form resolution, which should be adopted in the minutes of the initial meeting of the board of directors.

(11)   Group Insurance and Medical Benefits

If a medical reimbursement plan, group term insurance plan, disability insurance plan, or group health insurance plan is to be adopted by the corporation, the appropriate time to do so is at the initial meeting of the board. Often, however, such plans are not finalized by the time of the initial meeting and, consequently, must be adopted later.

(12)   Power Delegated to Officers

The initial minutes should also delegate to the appropriate officers of the corporation the power to act on behalf of the corporation.

(13) Choice of Fiscal Year

If the fiscal year can be determined at the time of the incorporation, it should be adopted in the minutes of the first meeting of the board. It is customary, however, to postpone the adoption of a fiscal year. If this is the case, the minutes of the first meeting of the board should reflect such postponement.

(14) Special Contracts

Any special contracts which are required to continue the existing professional practice, such as contracts with hospitals and government agencies, should be assigned to the new professional corporation.

(15) Approval of Acts of Incorporator

The minutes of the first meeting of the board should also approve the acts of the incorporator, who has technically acted on behalf of the board prior to incorporation.

Contained below is an example of the minutes of the first meeting of the board of directors. These minutes contain all of the items described above, including appropriate alternative language.

EXHIBIT 1

MINUTES OF FIRST ORGANIZATION MEETING
OF BOARD OF DIRECTORS OF

_____

The first meeting of the Board of Directors of _____ was held at the offices of _____, on _____, 19___, pursuant to a waiver of notice, signed by all of said Directors, which is attached hereto, marked Exhibit "A" and made a part hereof.

The following Directors were present in person, to-wit: _____ _____ constituting all of the members of the Board of Directors of the Corporation named in the Articles of Incorporation. Also present at the meeting at the invitation of the Board of Directors were: _____

Upon motion duly made, seconded and unanimously adopted, _____ was elected Chairman of the meeting and _____was elected Secretary of the meeting.

The Chairman thereupon reported that the Corporation was duly incorporated under the laws of the State of Georgia on _____, 19___, by the filing of Articles of Incorporation in the office of the Secretary of State.

A copy of said Articles of Incorporation, with the Certificate of the Secretary of State of the State of Georgia attached thereto, was presented to the meeting; and, upon motion duly made and seconded, said Articles of Incorporation were unanimously accepted and ordered filed with the records of the Corporation. A copy of said Articles of Incorporation, together with a copy of the Certificate of the Secretary of State of the State of Georgia, is attached hereto, marked Exhibit "B" and made a part hereof.

The Chairman then noted that the Corporation was incorporated to carry on the professional practice of Doctor X [XYZ Partnership]. The Chairman also noted that during the past several months, the members of the Board have discussed in great detail with their attorney and accountant the advantages and disadvantages of incorporating the professional practice. It was noted that in reaching the final decision to incorporate, the Directors recognized the potential disadvantages, but felt that the advantages available from incorporation outweighed the disadvantages. The Board then discussed the advantages which are available to a professional practice which operates in corporate form, which are as follows:

1. The corporate form permits a more disciplined and organized operation of a professional practice and is conducive to the implementation of normal management techniques. It provides economic and managerial efficiency and continuity of management.

2. The use of the corporate form in a professional practice provides a medium whereby new owners of the corporation may be admitted and the interest of retired owners may be purchased without causing a dissolution of the practice and without creating an undue hardship upon the remaining owners.

3. The operation through a professional corporation permits the professional employees to limit their professional liability solely to their acts and the acts performed by those employees of the corporation who are under their supervision. The professional employees of the corporation will not be responsible for the improper or negligent acts of their fellow professionals, nor will they be liable for the general debts of the corporation.

4. The use of a professional corporation permits a wide range of employee benefits and the ability to provide these benefits will enhance the ability of the corporation to attract qualified professionals and will assist in perpetuating the duration of the corporation.

While the Directors recognized the importance of providing additional employee benefits to employees of the Corporation, they noted that the Corporation was formed primarily to take advantage of the general benefits available from operating in corporate form, such as the limitation on liability and the ability to manage the activities of the Corporation in an efficient manner.

The Chairman then presented a form of Bylaws for the regulation of the affairs of the Corporation, which were read section by section. After discussion, and upon motion duly made and seconded, the following resolution was unanimouly adopted:

RESOLVED, the the Bylaws presented to this meeting, a copy of which is attached to these minutes as Exhibit "C" and made a part hereof, be, and the same hereby are, adopted as the Bylaws of the Corporation, and the Secretary of the Corporation is hereby instructed to cause a copy of said Bylaws, certified by him, to be placed in the records of the Corporation, together with the Corporation's Articles of Incorporation.

The Chairman presented to the meeting a seal for the Corporation bearing the following words, to-wit:

CORPORATE SEAL
GEORGIA

the impression of which seal appears on the margin of these minutes, and, upon motion duly made and seconded, the same was unanimously adopted as the seal of the Corporation.

The Chairman then presented a form of stock certificate for the one dollar ($1.00) par value common stock of the Corporation and, upon motion duly made and seconded, the same was unanimously adopted as the form of stock certificate to be used by the corporation for its common stock. A copy of said form of stock certificate, identified as Exhibit ''D'', was ordered attached to these minutes and made a part hereof.

The Chairman reported that the common stock of the Corporation could be issued so as to qualify under Section 1244 of the Internal Revenue Code of 1954. He noted that this Section permits ordinary loss treatment when the holder of Section 1244 stock either sells or exchanges such stock at a loss, or when such stock becomes worthless. After discussion, upon motion duly made and seconded, the following resolution, constituting a plan to issue stock pursuant to Section 1244 of the Internal Revenue Code of 1954, was unanimously adopted:

WHEREAS, there is no prior offer outstanding by this Corporation to sell or issue any of its common stock; and

WHEREAS, this Corporation is a ''small business corporation'' as defined in Section 1244 (c)(3) of the Internal Revenue Code of 1954; and

WHEREAS, it is deemed desirable that the offer, sale, and issuance of the common stock of this Corporation be effectuated in such manner that qualified shareholders may receive the benefits of Section 1244 of the Internal Revenue Code of 1954;

NOW, THEREFORE, BE IT RESOLVED, that this Corporation offer, sell, and issue up to 100,000 shares of its common stock pursuant to the provisions of Section 1244 of the Internal Revenue Code of 1954; the maximum amount to be received by the Corporation in consideration for such stock shall not be in excess of $1,000,000 in money or other property; and said stock shall be known as ''Section 1244 stock.''

The Chairman then presented to the meeting Stock Subscription Agreements signed by the subscribers for _____ shares of the common stock of the Corporation. Said Stock Subscription Agreements are attached to these minutes as Exhibit ''E'' and made a part hereof. Upon motion duly made and seconded, said Stock Subscription Agreements were unanimously accepted, and it was ordered that, upon said common stock being fully paid for in conformity with the terms of said

Stock Subscription Agreements, the Corporation, through its proper corporate officers, issue and deliver to said subscribers a certificate representing such shares, which shares shall be fully-paid and nonassessable.

The Chairman then presented to the meeting Transfer Agreements for _____ shares of the common stock of the Corporation. Said Transfer Agreements are attached to these minutes as Exhibit "E-1" and made a part hereof. After examining said Transfer Agreements and upon motion duly made and seconded, the following resolutions were unanimously adopted:

> RESOLVED, that the Transfer Agreements presented to this meeting be, and the same hereby are, accepted in full payment from the following subscribers for the number of shares indicated:
>
> _____   _____
>
> _____   _____
>
> FURTHER RESOLVED, that the Board of Directors has determined that the fair market value of the property listed on such Transfer Agreements is not less than the amount shown.

Thereupon, _____ shares of the common stock of the Corporation were duly issued to the above-named subscribing shareholders.

Because the subscribers for the common stock of the Corporation had transferred their existing accounts receivable to the Corporation as part of the consideration for the issuance of stock, the Board discussed the necessity of notifying all outstanding accounts of such transfer. However, it was determined by the Board that such notification was not necessary because the patients (clients) of the subscribers had been notified of the incorporation of the professional practice and it was felt that such notice might lead to confusion. Consequently, it was agreed that amounts paid on account of those accounts receivable would be indorsed and deposited to the Corporation's account as received.

[The Chairman noted that the accounts receivable of the existing professional practice of Doctor X [XYZ Partnership] would not be transferred to the Corporation and that the Corporation had been requested by Doctor X [XYZ Partnership] to act as the collecting agent for those accounts receivable. It was further noted that Doctor X [XYZ Partnership] would continue in business until all such accounts receivable are collected, written off, or otherwise disposed of. The Board then discussed this request by Doctor X [XYZ Partnership] to act as a collecting agent and, upon motion duly made and seconded it was unanimously:

> RESOLVED, that the President of the Corporation is authorized to enter into an agreement with Doctor X [XYZ Partnership] under which the corporation will act as a collecting agent for an amount equal to ____% of the amounts collected by the corporation.]

Upon motion duly made and seconded, the following were unanimously elected as the officers of the Corporation to serve until the next annual meeting of the Board of Directors or until their successors shall be elected and qualified, each to serve at the pleasure of the Board of Directors:

President   _____
Vice President   _____
Secretary   _____
Treasurer   _____

Upon motion duly made, seconded, and unanimously carried, it was:

RESOLVED, that either one of the following officers, to-wit: the President or Vice President of the Corporation be, and such officer hereby is, authorized and empowered to execute, for and on behalf and in the name of the Corporation, any and all contracts and agreements of every nature whatsoever, relating to any of the affairs or business of the Corporation, and such contracts and agreements shall contain such terms, provisions and limitations as may be agreed upon by such officer.

(OPTION FOR ONE PROFESSIONAL EMPLOYEE)

The Chairman then presented to the meeting a proposed Employment Agreement between the Corporation and its professional employee. The Employment Agreement was read section by section after which a general discussion was had. Thereupon, upon motion duly made and seconded, the following resolution was unanimously adopted:

BE IT RESOLVED, that the President or Vice President of the Corporation be, and such officers hereby are, authorized and empowered for and on behalf and in the name of the Corporation to execute an Employment Agreement between the Corporation and its professional employee, effective _____, 19____, containing such terms and provisions and in such form as is attached hereto as Exhibit "F" and made a part hereof.

Thereupon, the Employment Agreement for the professional employee was executed by the corporation and the professional employee.

(OPTION FOR MORE THAN ONE PROFESSIONAL EMPLOYEE)

The Chairman then presented to the meeting proposed Employment Agreements between the Corporation and each of its professional employees. The Employment Agreements were read section by section after which a general discussion was had. Thereupon, upon motion duly made and seconded, the following resolution was unanimously adopted to-wit:

BE IT RESOLVED that the President or Vice President of the Corporation be, and such officers hereby are, authorized and empowered for and on behalf and in the name of the Corporation to execute Employment Agreements between the Corporation and each of its professional employees, effective _____, 19____, containing such terms and provisions and in such forms as are attached hereto as Exhibit "F" and made a part hereof.

Thereupon, the Employment Agreements for the professional employees of the corporation were executed by the corporation and the professional employees.

The Board of Directors then discussed the fact that the salaries contained in the employment agreements for the professional employees have been initially established at a very low level. The Chairman noted that the low salaries for the professional employees had been established on the advice of the Corporation's accountant in order to assure that the Corporation would have sufficient working capital to operate during the initial months following incorporation. The Board discussed this matter and agreed that it was very important to assure that the Corporation begin activities on a strong foundation with sufficient working capital to meet the demands, both anticipated and unanticipated, which may arise during the months following incorporation. In noting that the initial salaries were set at a very low level, the Board unanimously agreed that the professional employees of the corporation were deserving of, and would eventually be granted, higher salaries. Then, upon motion duly made and seconded, it was unanimously:

> RESOLVED, that the salaries of the professional employees of the Corporation of _____ dollars per month shall continue for a period of _____ months or until the Board of Directors determines that the corporation has established a sufficient amount of working capital; and
> FURTHER RESOLVED, that when the Board of Directors has established that the Corporation has accumulated sufficient working capital, the salaries of the professional employees of the Corporation shall be raised to the following levels: _____

After noting that the stock of the Corporation had been duly issued to the subscribers therefor, the Chairman then presented to the meeting a proposed stock retirement agreement between the Corporation and its shareholders. The stock retirement agreement was then read section by section, after which a general discussion was had. Thereupon and upon motion duly made and seconded, the following resolution was unanimously adopted:

> RESOLVED, that the President or Vice President of the Corporation be, and such officers hereby are, authorized and empowered for and on behalf and in the name of the Corporation to execute a Stock Retirement Agreement between the Corporation and its shareholders, effective _____, containing such terms and provisions and in such form as is attached hereto as Exhibit ___ and made a part hereof.

The Corporation and the shareholders then executed the Stock Retirement Agreement and also executed the Schedule A to the Stock Retirement Agreement setting the value of the common stock of the Corporation at _____ dollars per share.

Upon motion duly made, seconded, and unanimously carried, it was:

> RESOLVED, that the _____ be designated as the banking depository of the Corporation.
> FURTHER RESOLVED, that said bank's usual resolution in the form presented to the meeting, a copy of which is attached to these minutes as Exhibit "G" and made a part hereof, designating the persons who may borrow money and whose signatures shall be required on checks and drafts withdrawing funds from said depository and covering related matters, is unanimously adopted.

(OPTION FOR TWO RETIREMENT PLANS)

Upon motion duly made, seconded, and unanimously adopted, it was:

RESOLVED, that the Board of Directors of _____ does hereby authorize the President and Secretary of the Corporation to execute on behalf of the Corporation a Profit Sharing Plan and Trust Agreement and a Money Purchase Pension Plan and Trust Agreement for the employees of ____ which are to be prepared by Lamon, Elrod & Harkleroad, P.C., attorneys for the Corporation; and under which _____ shall act as Trustee;

FURTHER RESOLVED, that the Board of Directors herby contributes to the Trustee the like sum of One Hundred and 00/100 Dollars ($100.00) to constitute the initial contribution under each Plan;

FURTHER RESOLVED, that for purposes of Section 415 of the Internal Revenue Code, the limitation year of such Plans shall be the ''Plan Year'' as defined in the Plans,

FURTHER RESOLVED, that Lamon, Elrod & Harkleroad, P.C., Attorneys at Law, 2500 Peachtree Center, 229 Peachtree St. N.E., Atlanta, Georgia 30043, is hereby authorized to proceed with the qualification of said Plans in accordance with the provisions of Section 401(a) and 501(a) of the Internal Revenue Code, and that the President and Vice President of the Corporation are hereby authorized and directed to execute an appropriate Power of Attorney for this purpose;

FURTHER RESOLVED, that the Plan Administrator of each Plan shall be _____;

FURTHER RESOLVED, that the Plans be announced to all employees upon their execution and that the Corporation shall comply with all provisions of the Employee Retirement Income Security Act of 1974; and

FINALLY RESOLVED, that all employees be furnished a description of the benefits provided by the Plans in accordance with the Employee Retirement Income Security Act of 1974.

(OPTION FOR ONE RETIREMENT PLAN)

Upon motion duly made, seconded, and unanimously adopted, it was:

RESOLVED, that the Board of Directors of _____ does hereby authorize the President and Secretary to execute on behalf of the Corporation a _____ for the employees of _____ which is to be prepared by Lamon Elrod & Harkleroad, P.C., attorneys for the Corporation; and under which the_____ shall act as Trustee;

FURTHER RESOLVED, that the Board of Directors hereby contributes to the Trustee the like sum of One Hundred and 00/100 Dollars ($100.00) to constitute the initial contribution under such Plan;

FURTHER RESOLVED, that for purposes of Section 415 of the Internal Revenue Code, the limitation year of such Plan shall be the ''Plan Year'' as defined in the Plan;

FURTHER RESOLVED, that Lamon, Elrod & Harkleroad, P.C., Attorneys at Law, 2500 Peachtree Center, 229 Peachtree St. N.E., Atlanta,

Georgia 30043, is hereby authorized to proceed with the qualification of said Plan in accordance with the provisions of Section 401(a) and 501(a) of the Internal Revenue Code, and that the President and Vice President of the Corporation are hereby authorized and directed to execute an appropriate Power of Attorney for this purpose;

FURTHER RESOLVED, that the Plan Administrator of said Plan shall be _____ ;

FURTHER RESOLVED, that the Plan be announced to all employees upon its execution and that the Corporation shall comply with all provisions of the Employee Retirement Income Security Act of 1974; and

FINALLY RESOLVED, that all employees be furnished a description of the benefits provided by the Plan in accordance with the Employee Retirement Income Security Act of 1974.

The Chairman then presented and read a Medical Reimbursement Plan for the _____ of the Corporation. After considerable discussion and upon motion duly made, seconded and unanimously carried, it was:

RESOLVED, that the Medical Reimbursement Plan presented to this meeting, a copy of which is attached to these minutes as Exhibit "H" and made a part hereof, be and the same hereby is approved, accepted, and adopted by the Corporation.

Upon motion duly made, seconded, and unanimously adopted, it was:

RESOLVED, that in accordance with the Articles of Incorporation the registered office of the Corporation in Georgia be established and maintained at _____ and that, _____, a resident of the State of Georgia, be and hereby is appointed as the registered agent of the Corporation in charge of such office and of the books required by law to be kept in that office.

The Chairman noted that, although the Corporation will be carrying on the professional practice of Doctor X [XYZ Partnership], the Corporation was not the owner of the office space in which the professional practice of Doctor X [XYZ Partnership] had been conducted. He then recommended to the Board that they consider the possibility of continuing the professional practice in the same office space as previously occupied by Doctor X [XYZ Partnership] and the Board discussed this matter. After a general discussion, the Board agreed to authorize the President of the Corporation to enter into negotiations with the owners of the office space previously rented by Doctor X [XYZ Partnership] and, upon motion duly made and seconded, it was unanimously:

RESOLVED, that the President of the Corporation is hereby instructed and authorized to enter into negotiations to lease the office space previously leased by Doctor X [XYZ Partnership] so that the Corporation may continue its professional practice in that office space; and

FURTHER RESOLVED, that the President of the Corporation is authorized to negotiate a lease, upon terms and conditions which are favorable to the Corporation, for a monthly rental not to exceed _____ dollars per month, under which the Corporation will pay all utilities and expenses of operating the office space; and

FURTHER RESOLVED, that the Board does hereby agree that a rental rate of _____ dollars per month for the office space previously occupied by Doctor X [XYZ Partnership] is the arm's-length, fair rental value of that property and is comparable to the rent being charged for similar property.

After a general discussion, it was the consensus of all of the Directors that the fiscal year of the Corporation should be determined at a later date. Therefore, upon motion duly made, seconded and unanimously adopted, the determination of the Corporation's fiscal year was deferred.

It was then moved, seconded and unanimously approved, that the Corporation commence business as of _____.

The Board of Directors than reviewed the contractual agreements which Doctor X [XYZ Partnership] had had with ABC Hospital for the operation of that hospital's anesthesiology department, and the Board agreed that such agreement should be assigned to the Corporation so that the Corporation could continue the medical practice of Doctor X [XYZ Partnership] at ABC Hospital. Thereupon, the Chairman submitted to the Board an agreement assigning that the contract to the Corporation and, upon motion duly made and seconded, it was unanimously:

RESOLVED, that the President is hereby authorized and empowered to enter into an assignment of that certain contract between Dr. X [XYZ Partnership] and ABC Hospital in the form attached hereto as Exhibit

_____.

The Board then discussed the possibility of providing certain group insurance coverage for the employees of the Corporation and agreed to provide group accident and health insurance, disability insurance, and group term life insurance for the employees of the Corporation. With regard to the adoption of a plan for the provision of accident and health insurance for the employees of the Corporation, Mr. _____ stated that such insurance is normally provided by corporations as an employee benefit for employees in order to eliminate the disastrous financial effect which may occur upon the illness of an employee. It was then agreed by the Board that the Corporation would pay the premiums for the accident and health insurance for the officers of the Corporation and their families and that the Corporation would also pay the premiums for the individual coverage of all non-officer employees of the Corporation. It was noted that many of the non-officer employees of the Corporation had working spouses and that these spouses were covered under separate insurance plans at their places of employment and that coverage under the Corporation's plan would be an unnecessary duplication. Then, upon motion duly made and seconded, it was unanimously:

RESOLVED, that the Corporation shall adopt a plan of providing group accident and health insurance as more specifically set forth in Exhibit

_____.

The Board then discussed the desirability of providing disability insurance coverage for the employees of the Corporation. With regard to this, Mr. _____

99

stated that it was his recommendation that disability insurance coverage be provided for the officers of the Corporation, with the monthly disability benefits being not more than_____ dollars per month after a sixty (60) day waiting period. Then, upon motion duly made and seconded, it was unanimously:

RESOLVED, that the Corporation does hereby adopt the plan of providing disability insurance for the officers of the Corporation and that such insurance shall provide monthly disability benefits in an amount not to exceed _____ dollars per month after a sixty (60) day elimination period, as more specifically set forth in the plan attached as Exhibit _____ hereto.

The Board of Directors then discussed the possibility of providing group term life insurance for all of the employees of the Corporation. It was recommended by Mr. _____ that all of the employees of the Corporation be covered under this plan, a copy of which is attached hereto as Exhibit _____. The plan was then discussed in its entirety by the Board and, upon motion duly made and seconded, it was unanimously:

RESOLVED, that the plan for providing group-term life insurance protection for the employees of the Corporation, as attached hereto as Exhibit _____, is hereby adopted.

Upon motion duly made, seconded, and unanimously carried, it was:

RESOLVED, that the Treasurer's action in paying all fees and expenses incident and necessary to the organization of the Corporation be, and hereby is, approved;

FURTHER RESOLVED, that the officers of the Corporation be, and they hereby are, further authorized and empowered to do any and all other and further things and matters, of every nature whatsoever, which such officers, in their sole and unlimited discretion, shall deem necessary or proper for the purpose of effectuating and carrying out the intent and purposes of the resolutions adopted at this meeting looking towards the completion of all acts and matters in connection with the full organization and operation of the corporation; and

FURTHER RESOLVED, that all acts and things heretofore done for and on behalf and in the name of the Corporation by the Incorporator, _____ , and the law firm of Lamon, Elrod & Harkleroad, P.C. be, and the same hereby are, ratified and affirmed in each, all, and every respect.

There being no further business to come before the meeting, the same was, upon motion duly made and carried, adjourned.

_____
                                                                Secretary

APPROVED:

_____
Chairman

EXHIBIT "A"

WAIVER OF NOTICE OF
MEETING OF BOARD OF DIRECTORS OF

_____

We, the undersigned, being all of the members of the Board of Directors of
_____, a Georgia Professional Corporation, do hereby severally
waive notice of the time, place and purposes of the first meeting of the Board of
Directors of said Corporation and do hereby consent that the same be held at the
offices of _____, on the _____ day of _____, 19___, for the transaction of any
business which may properly come before the meeting.

_____

_____

[6.04] BYLAWS

All professional corporations should adopt bylaws at the first meeting of the
Board of Directors. Bylaws provide general operating rules for the corporation,
such as the provisions for the issuance of stock, the calling and holding of
shareholders' and directors' meetings, and the election and duties of the officers of
the corporation. Bylaws may be kept rather simple, along the lines of the form
bylaws contained at the end of this section, or they may be tailored to fit the
individual situation. In most cases, it is not necessary to revise extensively the form
bylaws. The following items are those which should be considered by the shareholders and directors and may require revisions to the form bylaws.

(1) State Law Professional Corporation Rules

Many state professional corporation statutes go beyond simply permitting
the incorporation of professionals and require certain special operating procedures.
For example, most state statutes require some type of notice to be placed on the
stock certificate indicating that the transfer of the stock is restricted to professionals, and it is generally advisable to place a form of this notice in the bylaws. Also,
state statutes often limit to professionals those persons who may be officers or
directors. Further, some state statutes permit non-professionals (for estates of
professionals) to hold stock in a professional corporation but non-professional
stockholders are not entitled to vote. Any such provisions of the state's professional
corporation laws should be contained in the bylaws.

(2)   Indemnification

Most state corporation laws permit corporations to indemnify officers, directors and employees of the corporation who have suffered losses (due to lawsuits or otherwise) brought about by actions they have taken on behalf of the corporation in good faith. Such indemnification provisions are, generally, available to professional corporations and should be adopted in the bylaws.

(3)   Buy-Sell Agreements

Some professional corporations do not adopt separate buy-sell agreements for the stock in the professional corporation (as described in section[11.02], *infra*). Rather, the restrictions on the transfer of the stock of the corporation and requirements that stock be repurchased upon the death, disability, or termination of employment are contained in the bylaws of the corporation. Rather than complicating the bylaws, which should set out the general operating rules of the corporation, the authors feel that any agreement relating to the repurchase of stock should be set forth in a separate agreement which is executed by all of the stockholders. This assures that all of the stockholders have agreed to the stock restriction provisions; the bylaws of the corporation can generally be changed by a majority vote of the shareholders and directors and it would be unfair to permit the majority of the shareholders and directors to unilaterally change the provisions of any buy-sell agreement. For this reason, if the buy-sell agreement is contained in the bylaws, the bylaws should also contain a special provision requiring that any change to that portion of the bylaws will not be effective until approved by a unanimous vote of the shareholders. Where the general buy-sell agreement is contained outside the bylaws, it is, however, advisable to place a short stock restriction and transfer provision in the bylaws to take effect in the event that no independent agreement exists.

(4)   Oswald Provisions

One of the methods employed to counteract the "reasonable compensation" problem, which is more fully discussed in Chapter 13, *infra*, is the use of an "Oswald" clause. In the *Oswald* case,[4] the Tax Court permitted a taxpayer to return the unreasonable portion of his compensation to the corporation and obtain a deduction therefor. While some practitioners feel that an Oswald clause is an indispensable element in refuting a claim of unreasonable compensation, other practitioners do not. Because there is a question regarding the efficacy of Oswald clauses, some practitioners feel that it is best if they are not placed in employment agreements and are, instead, placed in the bylaws, where they will be binding upon the corporation but will not be readily apparent to an examining IRS agent. The form bylaws contained in this section contain an Oswald clause in Article 9.5.

(5) Executive Committees

With larger professional corporation groups, management often becomes unwieldy and it is important to establish executive committees of the Board in such areas as management, finance, compensation, and hiring. The authors' experience has shown that executive committees are probably not necessary until a professional corporation employs approximately ten professionals but, in certain circumstances, they may be helpful even in smaller professional corporations. A provision establishing an executive committee could be adopted as follows:

> The Executive Committee of the Board of Directors of the Corporation shall consist of the President, the Secretary, and the Treasurer (in the alternatives, specific names of individuals may be listed). Any vacancy on the committee shall be filled by the vote of Directors holding 80% of the voting shares of the Corporation. Any member of the Executive Committee may be removed only by the unanimous vote of the Executive Committee, excluding the vote of the affected member of the Committee. The following actions of the Executive Committee shall be final and binding upon the Board of Directors and the entire Board may not act thereon except to ratify the actions of the Executive Committee:
>
> (1) To terminate the employment, with or without cause, of any professional employee of the Corporation, or
> (2) To fix or change the compensation of any professional employee of the Corporation, or
> (3) To take any action affecting the relationship between any member of the Executive Committee and the Corporation, its directors, shareholders, and officers.
>
> In each of the matters described in Paragraphs (1), (2), and (3) above, the vote of the affected member of the Executive Committee shall not be counted, but the action of the members of the Executive Committee must be unanimous.

(6) Arrangements Regarding Voting

In certain instances, as with the use of a stock retirement provision contained in the bylaws as noted above, it is important to provide in the bylaws special rules regarding how the stock of the corporation will be voted in certain matters. Under most state statutes, a majority vote of a quorum of the shareholders or directors of the corporation may control the business at a meeting. This means, generally, that a majority of the shareholders or directors will constitute a "quorum" for purposes of holding a meeting and that a majority of the quorum present at a particular meeting will control the actions of the corporation. This permits, in some cases, the control of the corporation by a relatively small number of votes. In professional corporations, it is sometimes advisable to provide that a majority vote of all of the shareholders and directors is required to accomplish certain acts, such as the dissolution of the corporation, terminating or hiring professionals, adopting or terminating qualified retirement plans, granting employee benefits to professionals, determining compensation formulae, and acquiring real estate and expensive office equipment. To the extent that there are a substantial number of such special requirements, it may be advisable to adopt a Shareholders' Agreement as described in the following section.

BYLAWS OF

(A Georgia Professional Corporation)

ARTICLE 1
CAPITAL STOCK

1.1 Stock Certificates. Certificates of stock shall be numbered consecutively in the order in which they are issued. They shall be signed by the President and Secretary and the Seal of the corporation shall be affixed thereto. In an appropriate place in the corporate records shall be entered the name of the person owning the shares, the number of shares, and the date of issue. Certificates of stock exchanged or returned shall be canceled by the Secretary and placed in the corporate records.

1.2 Transfer of Stock. Transfers of stock shall be made on the stock books of the corporation by the holder in person or by power of attorney, or by surrender of the old certificate for such shares, duly assigned. Certificates of stock shall be issued, held, transferred, redeemed and canceled in strict conformity with the requirements of the Georgia Professional Corporation Act. Certificates of stock shall bear the following Notice:

"NOTICE

SHARES IN THIS PROFESSIONAL CORPORATION MAY BE ISSUED TO, HELD BY, OR TRANSFERRED ONLY TO A PERSON WHO IS LICENSED TO PRACTICE THE PROFESSION FOR WHICH THE CORPORATION IS ORGANIZED AND WHO, UNLESS DISABLED, IS ACTIVELY ENGAGED IN SUCH PRACTICE, EXCEPT AS OTHERWISE PROVIDED IN SECTION 5 OF THE GEORGIA PROFESSIONAL CORPORATION ACT. SHARES STANDING IN THE NAME OF A DISQUALIFIED PERSON, OR IN THE NAME OF THE PERSONAL REPRESENTATIVE OF A DECEASED PERSON, EXCEPT DURING THE HOLDING PERIOD PROVIDED IN SECTION 5 OF THIS ACT, ARE VOID."

1.3 Voting. The holders of the common stock shall be entitled to one vote for each share of stock standing in their name.

1.4 <u>Shareholders of Record</u>. For the purpose of determining shareholders entitled to notice of, or entitled to vote at, any meeting of shareholders or any adjournment thereof, or shareholders entitled to receive payment of any dividend, or in order to make a determination of shareholders for any other proper purpose, the date on which notice of the meeting is mailed or the date on which the resolution of the Board of Directors declaring such dividend is adopted, as the case may be, shall be the record date for such determination, unless a record date is fixed in advance, or the stock transfer books are closed for such purpose, within the statutory time periods. The corporation shall keep at its registered office or principal place of business, or at the office of its transfer agent or registrar, a record of its shareholders, giving the names and addresses of all shareholders, and the number and class of the shares held by each. A list of shareholders as of the record date shall be open for inspection at any meeting of shareholders.

ARTICLE 2
SHAREHOLDER MEETINGS

2.1 <u>Annual Meetings</u>. An annual meeting of the shareholders shall be held within or without the State of Georgia at such place, date and time as shall be designated from time to time by the Board of Directors and stated in the notice of the meeting. If an annual meeting has not been called or held for any continuous eighteen month period any shareholder may call such meeting upon proper notice.

2.2 <u>Special Meetings</u>. Special meetings of the shareholders may be called at any time by the Chairman of the Board of Directors, the President or the Secretary or by the Board of Directors. A special meeting of the shareholders may also be called, as provided by law, at the request of the holders of not less than one-fourth of all the shares entitled to vote.

2.3 <u>Place of Meeting</u>. Shareholder meetings shall be held at the registered office of the corporation in Georgia or at such other place as is designated by the Board of Directors or person or persons calling the meeting in the notice of the meeting.

2.4 <u>Notice Requirements</u>. Written notice stating the place, day and hour of a meeting and, in the case of a special meeting, in general terms, the purpose or purposes for which the meeting is called, shall be delivered by or at the direction of the President, the Secretary or the person or persons calling the meeting, to each shareholder of record entitled to vote at such meeting. Such notice shall be given not less than ten (10) or more than fifty (50) days before the date of the meeting, either by hand-delivering a copy or sending a copy through the United States mail. If mailed, such notice shall be deemed to be delivered when deposited in the United States mail addressed to the shareholder at his address as it appears on the stock transfer books of the corporation, with first class postage thereon prepaid.

2.5 <u>Waiver of Notice</u>. Notice of a meeting need not be given to any shareholder who signs a written waiver of notice, in person or by proxy, either before or after the meeting; and a shareholder's waiver shall be deemed the equivalent of giving proper notice. Attendance of a shareholder at a meeting, either in person or by proxy, shall of itself constitute waiver of notice of the meeting and waiver of any and all objections to the place of the meeting, the time of the meeting, or the manner in which it has been called or convened, except when a shareholder attends a meeting solely for the express purpose of stating, at the beginning of the meeting, any such objection or objections to the transaction of business. Except as required in the notice of a special meeting, neither the business transacted nor the purpose of the meeting need be specified in the waiver.

2.6 Quorum. The majority of the shares of the corporation entitled to vote, represented in person or by duly executed proxy, shall constitute a quorum at any and all meetings of the shareholders. If a quorum is present, the affirmative vote of the majority of shares represented at the meeting and entitled to vote on any subject matter shall be the act of the shareholders. When a quorum is once present to organize a meeting, it is not broken by the subsequent withdrawal of any of those present. A meeting may be adjourned despite the absence of a quorum.

2.7 Voting. Every shareholder of record shall be entitled at each meeting of shareholders, and upon each proposal presented at such meeting, to one vote for each paid-up share of stock having the right to vote which is standing in his name on the books of the corporation. Unless otherwise provided by law, the Articles of Incorporation, or the Bylaws, whenever any corporate action is to be taken by a vote of the shareholders it shall be by a majority of the shares represented at a meeting at which a quorum is present or represented and entitled to vote thereon.

2.8 Proxies. A shareholder entitled to vote may vote in person or by proxy executed in writing by the shareholder or by his attorney-in-fact. A proxy shall not be valid after eleven (11) months from the date of its execution unless a longer period is expressly stated in such proxy.

2.9 Action by Consent. Any action required or permitted to be taken by vote at a meeting of the shareholders may be taken without a meeting if written consent setting forth the action so taken is signed by all the shareholders entitled to vote thereon, and filed with the Secretary of the corporation. Such consent shall have the same force and effect as a unanimous vote of the shareholders.

ARTICLE 3
DIRECTORS

3.1 Powers. Subject to these bylaws, or any lawful agreement between the shareholders, the full and entire management of the affairs and business of the corporation shall be vested in the Board of Directors, which shall have and may exercise all of the powers that may be exercised or performed by the corporation.

3.2 Number. The corporation shall have such number of Directors as is set in the Articles of Incorporation or as set from time to time by resolution of the shareholders, but not less than the lesser of three (3) or the number of shareholders of record and not more than seven (7).

3.3 Election and Term. Directors shall be elected at the first annual meeting of shareholders and at each annual meeting thereafter, each Director to hold office until the next annual meeting or thereafter until such later date when his successor has been elected and qualified.

3.4 <u>Vacancies</u>. The Directors may fill the place of any Director which may become vacant prior to the expiration of his term, such appointment by the Directors to continue until the expiration of the term of the Director whose place has become vacant. A vacancy occurring in the Board for any reason need not be filled unless the remaining Directors are fewer in number than that required by law; any vacancy shall be filled by vote of a majority of the Directors then in office or, if the Directors do not act, by the shareholders.

3.5 <u>Removal.</u> Any or all of the Directors may be removed without assignment of cause by vote of a majority of all the shares entitled to vote.

3.6 <u>Compensation.</u> Directors shall not receive a salary for their services as Directors; but, by resolution of the Board, a fixed sum and expenses of attendance may be allowed for attendance at each meeting of the Board. A Director may serve the corporation in a capacity other than that of Director and receive compensation for the services rendered in that other capacity.

3.7 <u>Chairman.</u> The Board of Directors may elect one of the Directors as Chairman of the Board by majority vote. The term of the Chairman shall be the same as the term of a Director. The Chairman shall preside at all meetings of the Board of Directors and shall have such other duties as the Board may from time to time prescribe.

ARTICLE 4
DIRECTOR MEETINGS

4.1 <u>Place of Meetings</u>. The meetings of the Board of Directors may be held at the registered office of the corporation, or at any place within or without the State of Georgia that a majority of the Board of Directors may from time to time by resolution designate, or that may be designated in any notice of a meeting by the person calling the meeting.

4.2 <u>Annual Meeting</u>. The Board of Directors shall hold an annual meeting each year, immediately following the annual meeting of the shareholders for the purpose of electing officers and for the consideration of other business.

4.3 <u>Special Meetings</u>. Special meetings of the Board of Directors may be called at any time by the Chairman of the Board, the President or by any one of the Directors.

4.4 <u>Notice of Meetings</u>. Written notice of any meeting, setting forth the time, place and date of the meeting, shall be given to each Director not less than three (3) days before the meeting. Such notice shall be given either by hand-delivering a copy or sending a copy through the United States mail. If mailed, such notice shall be deemed delivered when deposited in the United States mail, addressed to the Director at his address as shown in the records of the corporation, with first class postage thereon prepaid.

4.5 <u>Waiver of Notice</u>. Notice of a meeting need not be given to any Director who signs a written waiver of notice either before or after the meeting; and a

Director's waiver shall be deemed the equivalent of giving proper notice. Attendance of a Director at a meeting shall of itself constitute a waiver of notice of such meeting, and a waiver of any and all objections to the place of the meeting, the time of the meeting or the manner in which it has been called or convened, except where a Director states at the beginning of the meeting any such objection or objections to the transaction of business. The signature of any Director approving the minutes of any meeting of the Board of Directors, entered thereon, shall be effective to the same extent as if such Director had been present at such meeting.

4.6 Quorum. At all meetings of the Board of Directors, a majority of the number of Directors fixed by the shareholders shall constitute a quorum for the transaction of business. If a quorum is present, the affirmative vote of a majority of the Directors in attendance shall be the act of the Board and all resolutions adopted and all business transacted by the Board of Directors shall require the affirmative vote of a majority of the Directors present at the meeting. When a quorum is once present to organize a meeting it is not broken by the subsequent withdrawal of any of those present. A meeting may be adjourned despite the absence of a quorum.

4.7 Presumption of Asset. A Director who is present at a meeting of the Board of Directors shall be presumed to have concurred in any action taken at the meeting, unless his dissent to such action shall be entered in the minutes of the meeting or unless he shall submit his written dissent to the person acting as the Secretary of the meeting before the adjournment of the meeting or shall forward such dissent by registered or certified mail to the Secretary of the corporation within twenty-four (24) hours after the adjournment of the meeting. Such right to dissent shall not apply to a Director who, being present at the meeting, failed to vote against such action.

4.8 Action by Consent. Any action to be taken at a meeting of the Directors, or any action that may be taken at a meeting of the Directors, may be taken without a meeting if a consent which may be in the form of minutes of a meeting, in writing, setting forth the action so taken, shall be signed by all of the Directors.

ARTICLE 5
OFFICERS

5.1 Titles of Officers. The corporation shall have a President, a Secretary, a Treasurer and such other officers as the Board of Directors may designate and elect. One person may be elected to more than one office, except that the offices of President and Secretary may not be held by the same person.

5.2 Election. The officers shall be elected by the Board of Directors and shall serve at the pleasure of the Board.

5.3 Removal and Vacancies. Any officer may be removed by a vote of a majority of the entire Board whenever in its judgment the best interests of the corporation will be served thereby, but such removal shall be without prejudice to the contract rights, if any, of the person so removed. Election or appointment of an officer shall not of itself create contract rights. Any vacancy, however occurring, shall be filled by the Board.

5.4 <u>President.</u> The President shall be the chief executive officer of the corporation and shall have general and active management of the corporation. He shall be responsible for the administration of the corporation, including general supervision of its policies, general and active management of its financial affairs and shall execute bonds, mortgages or other contracts under the Seal of the Corporation. He shall only borrow money on behalf of the corporation pursuant to authority which may be general authority from the Board of Directors. The President shall have the authority to institute or defend legal proceedings when the Directors are deadlocked. He shall preside at all meetings of shareholders and discharge the duties of a presiding officer, shall present at each annual meeting of the shareholders a report of the business of the corporation for the preceding fiscal year, and shall perform whatever other duties the Board of Directors may from time to time prescribe.

5.5 <u>Vice President.</u> The Vice President or, if more than one Vice President is elected, the Vice Presidents in the order designated by the Board of Directors, shall exercise the functions of the President during the absence or disability of the President. Each Vice President shall have such other duties as are assigned to him from time to time by the Board of Directors.

5.6 <u>Secretary</u>. The Secretary shall keep minutes of all meetings of the shareholders and Directors and have charge of the minute books, stock books and Seal of the Corporation and shall perform such other duties and have such other powers as may from time to time be delegated to him by the President or the Board of Directors.

5.7 <u>Treasurer</u>. The Treasurer shall be charged with the management of the financial affairs of the corporation and shall have the power to recommend action concerning the corporation's financial affairs to the President and shall perform such other duties and have such other powers as may from time to time be delegated to him by the President or Board of Directors.

5.8 <u>Other Officers</u>. Any other officers designated and elected by the Board of Directors shall have such duties as shall be delegated to them by the President or the Board of Directors.

5.9 <u>Compensation</u>. The Board of Directors shall fix the compensation of the officers of the corporation. The compensation of other agents and employees of the corporation may be fixed by the Board of Directors or by an officer to whom that function has been delegated by the Board.

ARTICLE 6

INDEMNIFICATION

6.1 <u>Persons Indemnified</u>. Any person who was or is a party or is threatened to be made a party to any threatened, pending or completed action, suit or proceeding, whether civil, criminal, administrative or investigative (other than an action by the corporation) by reason of the fact that he is or was a director, officer, employee or agent of this corporation, or in a similar position for another corporation, partnership, joint venture, trust or other enterprise at the request of this corporation, shall be indemnified by this corporation, against all expenses (including attorneys' fees), judgments, fines and amounts paid in settlement, actually and reasonably incurred by him in the defense, settlement or otherwise in connection with such action, suit or proceeding, if he acted in a manner he reasonably believed to be in or not opposed to the best interests of this corporation, and with respect to any criminal action or proceeding, if he had not reasonable cause to believe his conduct was unlawful. The termination of any action, suit or proceeding by judgment, order, settlement, conviction, or upon a plea of *nolo contendere* or its equivalent, shall not, of itself, create a presumption that the person did not act in a manner which he reasonably believed to be in or not opposed to the best interests of the corporation, and, with respect to any criminal action or proceeding, that he had reasonable cause to believe that his conduct was unlawful.

6.2 <u>Indemnification Right</u>. Determination of the right to such indemnification and the amount thereof may be made, at the option of the person to be indemnified, pursuant to procedure set forth from time to time in the bylaws or by any of the following procedures: (a) order of the court or administrative body or agency having jurisdiction of the action, suit or proceeding; (b) resolution adopted by a majority of a quorum of the Board of Directors of the corporation without counting in such majority or quorum any Directors who have incurred expenses in connection with such action, suit or proceeding; (c) resolution adopted by a majority of a quorum of the stockholders entitled to vote at any meeting; or (d) order of any court having jurisdiction over the corporation. Any such determination that a payment by way of indemnity should be made shall be binding upon the corporation. Such right of indemnification shall not be exclusive of any other right which such directors, officers and employees of the corporation and the other persons above mentioned may have or hereafter acquire and, without limiting the generality of such statement, they shall be entitled to their respective rights or indemnification or reimbursement under any bylaw, agreement, vote of stockholders, provision of law, insurance policy, or otherwise, as well as their rights under this Article 6. The provisions of this Article 6 shall apply to any member of any committee appointed by the Board of Directors as fully as though such person had been a director, officer or employee of the corporation.

6.3 <u>Payment</u>. A disinterested majority of the Board of Directors of this corporation or a majority of a quorum of the shareholders entitled to vote at a meeting shall be authorized to pay to any person entitled to indemnification under this Article 6, all actual expenses incurred in connection with such action, suit, or proceeding during the pendency thereof.

6.4 <u>Intent</u>. It is the intention of this corporation that this Article 6 of the bylaws of this corporation and the indemnification hereunder shall extend the maximum indemnification possible under the laws of the State of Georgia, and if any one or more words, phrases, clauses, sentences, or sections of this Article 6 should be held unenforceable for any reason, all remaining portions of this Article 6 shall remain of full force and effect.

ARTICLE 7

AMENDMENT

These bylaws may be amended at any meeting of the shareholders by the affirmative vote of a majority of all shares entitled to vote, or may be amended by a unanimous vote of the Board of Directors provided that such amendment shall be ineffective after the date of the next meeting of the shareholders unless approved at that meeting by an affirmative vote of a majority of all shares entitled to vote.

ARTICLE 8

TRANSFER OF STOCK IN PROFESSIONAL CORPORATION

8.1 Stock. Except as otherwise provided herein, stock in this corporation may only be issued to, held by, or transferred to a person who is licensed to practice medicine in the state and who, unless disabled, is actively engaged in such practice.

8.2 Disqualification. If a shareholder of this professional corporation becomes legally disqualified to practice medicine in this state, he shall, within ninety (90) days after being disqualified, transfer his shares of stock to an individual who is legally qualified to practice medicine in this state or offer to sell his stock to this professional corporation. After such disqualification, such shareholder shall not be entitled to vote his stock or participate in any decision concerning the practice of medicine. If a shareholder dies or retires, his stock shall, within six (6) months after the date of death or retirement, be transferred to an individual who is legally qualified to practice medicine in this state, or offered for sale to this corporation.

8.3 Price. The purchase price to be paid by this professional corporation to a shareholder for his shares of common stock of this professional corporation, in case of his disqualification, death, or retirement shall be determined in the following manner:

The Board of Directors shall, at its annual meeting immediately following the annual meeting of the share-holders, and at such other times as it sees fit, determine by majority vote the purchase price of each share of stock of this corporation. Until such time as the Board of Directors shall make such a determination, the price of each such share of stock is hereby initially set at $1.00 per share. The purchase price as so determined from time to time in accordance with this Article 8 shall be conclusively binding upon all of the shareholders and upon this corporation.

If a determination of the purchase price of said stock of this corporation has not been made as herein provided, within the twelve-(12) month period immediately preceding a shareholder's disqualification, death or retirement, then the Board of Directors shall make such a determination

111

in the manner herein provided within thirty (30) days after the happening of such event, and the purchase price as so determined shall be conclusively binding upon a shareholder or the personal representative of the estate of a deceased shareholder and upon this corporation.

The purchase price fixed by the procedure described in these bylaws shall be in lieu of the purchase price fixed by the procedure described in Section 5 of the Georgia Professional Corporation Act.

8.4 Purchase. If the stock of any such shareholder is offered to this corporation pursuant to this Article 8, it shall be purchased by this corporation at the price determined in accordance with Section 8.3 of this Article 8; and such purchase price as so determined shall be paid by this corporation in cash within thirty (30) days following the date of the offer. There shall be credited against the purchase price the amount of any indebtedness due and payable to this corporation by the shareholder. Upon payment of the purchase price, such shareholder or his personal representative, as the case may be, shall deliver such stock certificate, duly endorsed, to this corporation free and clear of all liens and encumbrances.

8.5 Stock Retirement Agreement. The provisions in this Article 8 relating to the transfer of stock in this corporation may, to the extent permitted by law, be superseded by a stock retirement agreement between this corporation and its shareholders.

ARTICLE 9

MISCELLANEOUS

9.1 Seal. The Seal of the corporation shall be in such form as the Board of Directors may from time to time determine, and shall initially be in the following form:

CORPORATE SEAL
GEORGIA

In the event it is inconvenient to use such a seal at any time, the signature of the company followed by the word ''SEAL'' enclosed in parentheses or scroll, shall be deemed the Seal of the corporation. The Seal shall be in the custody of the Secretary and affixed by him or any Assistant Secretary on the certificates of stock and such other papers as may be directed by law, by these bylaws or by the President or by the Board of Directors. The presence or absence of the Corporate Seal on any instrument, or its addition thereto, shall not affect the character, validity, or legal effort of the instrument in any respect.

9.2 Stock in Other Companies. In the absence of other arrangement by the Board, the President of the corporation may vote, endorse for transfer or take any other action necessary with respect to shares of stock and securities issued by any other corporation and owned by this corporation; and he may make, execute and deliver any proxy, waiver or consent with respect thereto.

9.3 <u>Registered Office</u>. The initial address of the registered office and name of the registered agent of the corporation are stated in the Articles of Incorporation. The registered office and registered agent of the corporation may be changed from time to time by the Board of Directors. The corporation may establish offices at such other place or places both within and without the State of Georgia as the Board of Directors may from time to time determine.

9.4 <u>Interested Directors</u>. No contract or other transaction between this corporation and any other firm, association or corporation shall be affected or invalidated by the fact that any of the members of the Board of Directors of this corporation are interested in or are members, shareholders, governors, directors or officers of such firm, association or corporation; and no contract, act or transaction of this corporation with any individual, firm, association or corporation shall be affected or invalidated by the fact that any members of the Board of Directors of this corporation are parties to or interested in such contract, act or transaction or are in any way connected with such individual, firm, association or corporation. Each and every individual who may become a member of the Board of Directors of this corporation is hereby relieved from any liability that might otherwise exist from contracting with this corporation for the benefit of himself or any firm, association or corporation in which he may in any way be interested.

9.5 <u>Payments Disallowed</u>. Any payments made to an officer of the corporation such as compensation, bonuses, commissions, interest or rent, or any entertainment expense incurred by him which shall be disallowed in whole or in part by the Internal Revenue Service as a deductible expense of the corporation, shall be repaid by such officer to the corporation to the full extent of such allowance. It shall be the duty of the Directors, as a Board, to enforce repayment of each such amount disallowed. Such disallowed amount shall be repaid to the corporation within one (1) year after the date on which the corporation paid the deficiency with respect to such compensation. It is further understood that the corporation shall not be required to legally defend any proposed disallowance by the Internal Revenue Service and the amount required to be reimbursed by the officer shall be the amount, as finally determined by agreement or otherwise, actually disallowed as a deduction. The officer shall be obligated to make such repayments only if the amounts so repaid to the corporation will be deductible or excludable from the gross income of the officer under the Internal Revenue Code of 1954, as amended, and if such repayment is determined not to be deductible or excludable by the officer, such repayment shall be refunded by the corporation to the officer within ninety (90) days from the date of such determination.

9.6 <u>Headings</u>. The Article and Section headings contained herein are for convenience and reference only, and shall in no manner be construed as a part of these bylaws.

9.7 <u>Professional Practice</u>. The Board of Directors shall be charged with the responsibility of allocating the professional practice and the patients of the Corporation among the professional employees of the Corporation in order to assure that proper professional care is rendered.

I, _____, Secretary of _____ formed and existing under the laws of Georgia, do hereby certify that the foregoing is a true and complete copy of the bylaws of this professional corporation as submitted to, read to and adopted at the Organizational Meeting of the Board of Directors held on the _____ day of _____, 19____.

IN WITNESS WHEREOF, I have hereunder subscribed my name and affixed the Seal of this Corporation, this ____ day of _____, 19____.

(CORPORATE SEAL)   _____
                                                            Secretary

[6.05] SHAREHOLDER OPERATING AGREEMENTS

Due to the personalities involved or the size of the professional group, it is often advantageous to establish a Shareholders' Operating Agreement which will determine the respective rights and obligations of the parties with regard to certain important matters. This Agreement should be established at the time of incorporation in order that the shareholders reach a consensus on such matters as who will be the officers and directors of the corporation, the compensation to be paid to the shareholders, the employee benefits to be established for the shareholders, the hiring and termination of employment of shareholders, the use of corporate funds and the acquisition of capital equipment or real property, the granting of non-qualified deferred compensation to any shareholder, the deferring of salaries, the hiring and firing of staff employees, the handling of business expenses by professionals, and the ultimate disposition of the name of the corporation and its offices upon the dissolution of the professional corporation. If there are relatively few of these special items which the shareholders feel must be addressed, it is advisable to place special provisions in the bylaws and avoid a separate agreement.

Professionals and their advisors should understand that a shareholder operating agreement is no panacea and will not assure a properly functioning professional corporation, nor will it hold a floundering professional corporation together. Shareholder operating agreements, consequently, perform the following two functions:

1. Such agreements set forth the professionals' understanding of the way in which the professional corporation is intended to be run, and
2. Such agreements determine who, if anyone, will be entitled to certain assets of the corporation, such as its name, upon the breakup of the professional corporation.

Professionals are, to say the least, unique individuals, and, if professionals decide that they will not work together, they will not, no matter what written agreements provide. The primary task of the professional corporation advisor is, then, to create a professional corporation which will be flexible enough to meet the needs of each professional and will also provide a framework in which the egos of the professionals can exist without creating a conflict that will break up the professional corporation. If it appears to the professional corporation advisor that a shareholders' operating agreement will help serve this goal, one should be implemented. A sample Shareholders Operating Agreement follows.

SHAREHOLDERS' OPERATING AGREEMENT

THIS AGREEMENT, made and entered into this _____ day of _____, 19_____, by and between_____ ,_____ , and _____ (hereinafter referred to as the "Shareholders") with the acknowledgement and consent of _____, P.C., a Georgia Professional Corporation (hereinafter referred to as the "Corporation").

WHEREAS, _____, _____, and _____, own all of the outstanding capital stock of the corporation; and

WHEREAS, the Shareholders have entered into this Agreement for the purpose of setting the basis for the initial organization and the continued management and operation of the corporation; and

WHEREAS, this Agreement is made as a Shareholders' Agreement pursuant to the provisions of Section 22-611 of the Georgia Business Corporation Code;

NOW, THEREFORE, for and in consideration of the sum of $_____ in hand paid by each party to the others and for other good and valuable consideration, the receipt and sufficiency of which are hereby acknowledged, the parties hereto agree as follows:

1. Duration.

The term of this Agreement shall be from _____ to _____, unless sooner terminated in accordance with the provisions hereof. At the end of such initial term, this Agreement shall be automatically extended and renewed on a year-to-year basis, until terminated as provided herein.

2. Voting of Shares.

The initial organization and continued management and operation of the Corporation shall at all times be in compliance with this Agreement. During the term of this Agreement, each Shareholder agrees to vote his shares in accordance with the provisions of this Agreement. In addition, any Shareholder who is also an officer, director, or member of any committee of the Board of Directors of the corporation (the Board of Directors of the Corporation is hereinafter referred to as the "Board" and the members of the Board are hereinafter referred to as the "Directors") agrees, during the term of this Agreement, to vote in such capacity in accordance with the provisions of this Agreement. Without limiting the generality of the foregoing, whenever this Agreement requires a certain vote to accomplish any matter, the provisions of this Agreement with reference to the required vote shall control as between the Shareholders, and any contrary provisions of the Articles of Incorporation or Bylaws of the Corporation shall be of no effect.

3. Election of Directors.

The Board shall at all times consist of the Shareholders. Persons hereafter becoming shareholders of the Corporation shall be elected to the Board. In the event that any person who is a Shareholder ceases to hold shares in the Corporation, then the Shareholders agree to take such action to remove such person from the Board.

4. Officers.

The Officers of the Corporation shall be as follows:

President: _____;
Vice President: _____;
Secretary: _____;
Treasurer: _____.

Such officers may be changed from time to time by the Board, provided that each Director shall hold an office in the Corporation. No person other than a Director shall be an officer of the Corporation without the unanimous consent of the Directors.

5. Corporate Funds.

All funds of the Corporation shall be deposited in its name in such bank accounts as shall be designated by the Board. All withdrawals from such accounts shall be made with a check or other instrument, signed by two (2) officers of the Corporation or by such other person or persons as may be designated by the unanimous agreement of the Board.

6. Fiscal Year and Corporate Records.

The fiscal year of the Corporation shall be determined by the Board. The Corporation's books shall be kept on a cash basis and such books shall be maintained at the principal office of the Corporation (or at the office of the Corporation's accountants, if the Board so determines) and each Shareholder shall at all time shave access thereto.

7. Powers.

Each officer of the Corporation shall have the same rights and powers as any other officer of the Corporation and the Board shall not, except by unanimous vote, provide to any officer of the Corporation any right or power not given to any other officer. No Director shall, unless authorized by unanimous consent of the Board, make, draw, accept, or endorse any promissory note or other engagement for the payment of money, or guarantee any debt or account on behalf of the Corporation, or pledge the credit of the Corporation in any way.

8. Specific Matters.

All decisions regarding the operation of the Corporation shall be made by the board except those matters which are specifically required by law to be made by the Shareholders. In making such decisions, the board shall be governed by the following:

    A. Unanimous approval of the Directors shall be required:

        i. To employ and establish the compensation for professional employees of the Corporation who are not shareholders;

ii. To amend the Bylaws of the Corporation or any agreement between the Corporation and the Shareholders which relates to the Corporation's redemption of a Shareholder's shares or to the transfer by a Shareholder of his shares in the Corporation;

iii. For the issuance by the Corporation of any shares of stock of the Corporation or for the transfer by a Shareholder of any shares of stock in the Corporation;

iv. To amend the Articles of Incorporation of the Corporation;

v. To expand the existing professional practice of the Corporation, or to lease office space or move the Corporation's offices, or to acquire real estate, or to acquire fixed assets in any fiscal year of the Corporation with an aggregate value in excess of $5,000;

vi. To adopt, amend, or terminate any qualified retirement plan;

vii. To provide, increase, decrease, or terminate any key man life insurance owned by the Corporation on the life of any Shareholder or any employee benefits of any Shareholder, including, but not limited to, group health and accident insurance, group life insurance, or disability insurance;

viii. To grant any non-qualified deferred compensation or salary continuation to any Shareholder; and

ix. To amend, terminate, or refuse to renew or extend any employment agreement between the Corporation and any Director, all of which agreements shall be deemed automatically extended and renewed until such unanimous consent is made; provided, however, that the termination of the employment of a Director "for cause" (as that term is defined in his respective Employment Agreement), may occur only after the approval of all Directors, except the Director whose termination for cause is being considered.

B. It is acknowledged that the Corporation has entered into employment agreements with the Directors. Such employment agreements shall, at all times, impose substantially similar duties and requirements upon all Directors. Further, the compensation to be paid to all Directors under such employment agreements shall, at all times, be equal, except the Board may establish a compensation or bonus formula based on production, which formula shall be agreed to by all Directors. If, in any fiscal year of the Corporation, a majority of the Shareholders determines that there are not sufficient funds to pay the entire compensation due to the Directors as set forth in such employment agreements, then and in that event, the compensation to be paid to the Directors shall be determined by a majority of the Shareholders and waivers of unpaid compensation for such fiscal year shall be signed by all Directors.

C. Except as otherwise provided in this Agreement, all other decisions to be made by the Board shall require a two-thirds majority vote of the Directors, unless the Articles of Incorporation, Bylaws, or the Georgia Business Corporation Code shall require a larger vote for a particular matter.

When a majority vote of the Board is referred to in this Agreement, such reference shall mean a two-thirds majority vote of all Directors and not merely a majority of a quorum present at any meeting.

9. Staff Employees.

Each Director shall have the right to employ and discharge the non-physician employees of the Corporation whose work is directly supervised by him, subject to the advance approval of a majority of the Board, with the salary to be paid to non-physician employees being subject to the salary scales established from time to time by the Board. Those non-professsional employees of the corporation who are not directly supervised by any Director shall be employed and discharged by the Board by majority vote or by the office manager of the Corporation with the consent of a majority of the Board.

10. Malpractice Insurance Coverage.

The Corporation shall carry and pay the premiums for professional liability insurance coverage in such amounts as shall be determined by the Board and the coverage for all Directors shall be equal.

11. Expenses.

Unless otherwise approved by the unanimous vote of the Board, no Director shall charge to the Corporation, or submit to the Corporation for reimbursement, any expenses for automobiles, entertainment, conventions, post graduate courses, charitable contributions, club dues, or any item connected with the operation or maintenance of his home; provided, however, that the Directors are encouraged to conduct, at their own expense, such professional entertainment as they deem appropriate for the Corporation's professional development; and, further provided, however, that each Director is required to own and maintain an automobile for use in the performance of his services as an employee of the Corporation. The Corporation shall pay all dues for the professional societies and organizations of which all of the Directors are members. The dues for any professional societies or organizations of which all of the Directors are not members shall be paid by the Directors individually.

12. Corporate Name, Offices, and Telephone Number.

Should the Corporation be dissolved or otherwise cease the active practice of medicine, no Shareholder shall have the right to continue to use the name _____, or any substantially similar name, nor shall any Shareholder have the right to use the existing offices or telephone number of the Corporation.

13. Qualified Retirement Plans.

Prior to the end of the Corporation's first fiscal year, the Corporation shall adopt the following qualified retirement plans: _____. The Board of Directors shall determine the specific provisions of such Plans, with the assistance of its attorney and accountant, and the contribution to such Plans shall be determined annually by the Board in accordance with the terms of such Plans. The administrative committee for such Plans shall consist of all of the Directors, unless any Director waives his right to serve as a member of that committee. Investment decisions for such Plans shall be determined by a majority vote of the members of the administrative committee.

14. Other Shareholders.

As a condition precedent to purchasing stock in the Corporation, an individual shall have executed this Agreement or shall have executed a document, in form satisfactory to the Board, agreeing to be bound by all of the provisions of this Agreement.

15. Stock Legends.

Stock certificates issued by the Corporation representing shares owned by the Shareholders shall bear an appropriate legend that such shares are subject to and must be voted in accordance with the terms and conditions of this Agreement.

16. Amendment and Termination.

This Agreement may not be amended without the written, unanimous consent of the Shareholders. This Agreement shall be terminated only upon the following events:

    a. written, unanimous consent of all Shareholders; or

    b. bankruptcy, insolvency, or cessation of the business of the Corporation.

17. Applicability of Agreement.

This Agreement shall be applicable to all shares owned or hereafter acquired by any Shareholder. This Agreement shall be made in and shall be construed in accordance with the laws of the State of Georgia, and this Agreement shall be binding upon and inure to the benefit of the parties hereto, their respective heirs, representatives, executors, administrators, successors, and assigns.

18. Corporation's Consent.

The Corporation has consented to and acknowledged this Agreement and agrees that all of its operations and activities shall be subject to and governed by the terms and provisions of this Agreement.

IN WITNESS WHEREOF, the parties hereunto have caused this Agreement to be executed as of the day and year first above set forth.

CORPORATION

By: _____
    President

(CORPORATE SEAL)

    SHAREHOLDERS

ATTEST:

By: _____
    Secretary

_____

_____

_____

NOTES TO CHAPTER 6

1. Ga. Code Ann. Chapter 84-54.

2. Ga. Code Ann. §84-302.

3. 289 F.Supp. 160 (N.D. Ga.), aff'd, 412 F.2d 1189 (5th Cir. 1969). Also see *O'Neill v. U.S.*, 281 F. Supp. 359 (N.D. Ohio 1960), *aff'd,* 410 F.2d 888 (6th Cir. 1969), and *Cochran v. U.S.,* 299 F. Supp. 1113 (D. Ariz. 1969).

4. *Vincent T. Oswald*, 49 T.C. 645 (1968). See section [13.04] (7).

CHAPTER 7

Shares, Shareholder Rights and Capitalization

[7.01] SHARES AND CAPITALIZATION

The capitalization of a corporation and the issuance of shares serve a somewhat different function from that of ownership of an income interest in a partnership. Generally, in a partnership a partner's income interest will correspond to his voting interest and his income interest may have little or no relation to his capital account. Further, the income interest of a partner will guarantee that the partner will receive a percentage of all income earned by the partnership. On the other hand, a shareholder's interest in a corporation entitles him to own shares in the corporation, to receive his share of the retained earnings of the corporation upon liquidation, and to vote such shares if such shares have voting rights. The ownership of stock in a corporation generally has no relationship to the compensation paid to the shareholder. These general rules for business corporations also hold true for professional corporations.

A problem can arise in a professional corporation if an attempt is made to equate stockholdings with income interests. In initially capitalizing a professional corporation, the attorney should seek, where possible, to keep the capitalization relatively simple. A sufficient number of shares of stock should be authorized to cover the anticipated shares to be issued on incorporation and also shares which may be issued in the future. The only reason that a substantial number of shares should not be authorized upon incorporation is the imposition, in some states, of a franchise tax based upon the authorized capital stock. It should be remembered that the "authorized capital stock" places a maximum limit on the amount of capital stock which may be "outstanding," and it is usually the practice that the authorized capital stock will substantially exceed the outstanding capital stock at any particular point in time (this permits the issuance of additional shares without the necessity of amending the Articles of Incorporation to authorize additional shares). Usually, in a professional corporation, only one class of stock is authorized, and that stock would be voting common stock and would have a par value which would permit easy computation, such as one dollar or ten dollars per share.

In determining the number of shares which should be subscribed in the initial offering to effectuate the incorporation, under most state laws there is no required number of shares which must be issued, except that the corporation must have a minimum paid-in capital to begin operation. In all situations, it is preferable to have stock issued for the initial paid-in capital. Also, the amount of capital stock which will be issued is determined by issuing stock as follows:

Cash   Stock issued so that the par value of common stock issued equals the amount of cash contributed.

Property   Stock issued so that the par value of stock issued equals depreciated book value of property contributed.

Generally, in issuing stock in a professional corporation, no value is attributed to accounts receivable which may be contributed to the new corporation (although some commentators feel that this is unwise),[1] and accounts payable assumed by the corporation are offset against the accounts receivable. Further, in determining the value of the property contributed, liabilities assumed by the corporation upon incorporation (other than accounts payable) should be deducted from the amount of the cash and the adjusted basis of the property contributed. For an example of the calculation of the stock to be issued upon incorporation, see section [5.10], *supra*.

There is also no specific amount of capital which must be contributed to a professional corporation, as long as the minimum capital requirement is met under state law. The corporation must have sufficient capital to avoid the thin corporation rules of federal income tax law and the rules under state law regarding the ability of creditors of the corporation to pierce the corporate veil when a corporation is thinly capitalized. Amounts contributed to the capital of a professional corporation will be allocated as follows: to "paid in capital" an amount equal to the par value of the stock and the "capital surplus" the remainder. For example, where $5,000 is contributed for 5,000 shares of capital stock with a par value of $.01 per share, $50 will be allocated to paid in capital and $4,950 will be allocated to capital surplus.

The Service has finally issued proposed regulations under Section 385 of the Code relating to what constitutes debt and what constitutes equity in a corporation. These proposed regulations will have very little impact upon a properly formed professional corporation which issues appropriate debt and equity securities under Section 351 during incorporation. Generally, however, a professional corporation has no great need for a substantial amount of equity since the corporation simply provides personal services and is not required to build up a substantial inventory. Also, accumulating a large equity will make the purchase of stock by new shareholders more difficult. See section [11.01], *infra*.

[7.02]   CLASSES OF STOCK AND SHAREHOLDER RIGHTS

In most professional corporations a single class of stock is issued and all shares are entitled to vote. It is also common for professional corporations to issue the same number of shares to each shareholder or to base shareholdings in the professional corporation upon existing capital accounts in the predecessor partnership. On the other hand, where the senior members of the practice desire to retain control of the professional corporation, they may purchase the majority of the stock and, thereby, retain effective control of the corporation.

The control of a professional corporation may also be adjusted by the issuance of non-voting stock. Typically, those persons holding non-voting stock would be the junior members of the professional corporation and would be elected as directors of the corporation. As directors, the junior members of the corporation would be entitled to vote only upon matters affecting routine administration and not matters affecting the issuance or transfer of shares, the admission of additional directors, the expulsion or discharge of directors, the establishment of, or contributions to, employee benefit plans, the election of officers, the sale of stock to new shareholders, or any change in the structure of the corporation.

Similar control may be retained by the senior professionals through the use of executive committees of the Board of Directors (see section [6.04](5), *supra*), shareholder agreements (see section [6.05], *supra*), and voting trusts and proxies (see section [7.05], *infra*).

[7.03]   SHARES TO BE ISSUED

As discussed above in this section, shares of stock in a professional corporation may be issued without regard to compensation paid to the professionals. In fact, it is general practice not to issue shares in accordance with compensation because the amount of compensation paid annually may change and the issuance and/or redemption of shares required by changes in compensation would create an undue burden on the corporation. Consequently, upon the incorporation of a partnership, shares are usually issued either in accordance with previously existing capital accounts or on an equal basis to all shareholders.

Where the professional corporation retains substantial funds (retained earnings) for the purchase of equipment and office buildings, it may be advisable to adjust periodically shareholdings to correspond to changes in the compensation paid to the shareholders. Such adjustments are often only employed in larger professional corporations. For example, if attorney A receives a $100,000 salary in 1981 which constitutes 10% of all compensation paid to all shareholder-attorneys in 1981, attorney A should be entitled to 10% of the $200,000 retained earnings in 1981. That is, the earnings retained by the professional corporation in 1981 could have been distributed to the attorneys but were, instead, retained. If the 1981 earnings had been distributed as compensation in 1981, attorney A would have received $20,000. On the other hand, if attorney A owns only 5% of the stock of the professional corporation, the $200,000 retained earnings will only increase attorney A's stock value by $10,000. In order to be fair to attorney A, should attorney A's share interest be increased to 10%? Without such adjustments (which are not dissimilar from adjustments to capital and profits interests in a partnership), it could be argued that attorney A is treated unfairly. On the other hand, the stock holdings could remain the same and attorney A could be given a bonus of $10,000 to make him "whole." If such a bonus is made, what should be done where some attorneys share profits in a smaller percentage than they share stock? For example, if attorney A is given a bonus, is attorney B required to contribute to the capital of the corporation where he receives a $100,000 salary (10%) but owns 20% of the stock? That is, attorney B will share in 20% of the $200,000 retained earnings (or $40,000) when, based upon his 1981 earnings, he should have only shared in 10% ($20,000). Must attorney B contribute $20,000 to the corporation? There appear to be no conclusive answers to these questions.

[7.04] EQUALIZING THE PARTNERS' CAPITAL ACCOUNTS

Where the capital accounts of the partners in the predecessor partnership are not maintained in the same ratio as are their voting and income interests, a potential problem exists if the capital accounts cannot be brought into proportion prior to incorporation. For example, assume that A and B incorporate their professional practice and, at the time of incorporation, their capital accounts, voting, and income interests are as follows:

	Capital Accounts	Voting Interests	Income Interests
A	0	50%	50%
B	$10,000	50%	50%

Assuming that A and B transfer all of the assets of the partnership to the new professional corporation, B will have, in effect, transferred to the new corporation $10,000 of assets, whereas A will have transferred no assets. In this example, how should the stock in the professional corporation be issued? If the stock is issued according to capital accounts, B will receive all of the stock in the new corporation.

Thus, B will have all of the voting rights in the new corporation and will be entitled to all of the retained earnings of the new corporation. On the other hand, if the stock in the new professional corporation is issued in accordance with the voting and profits interests of the predecessor partnership, A and B will share evenly in the voting rights and retained earnings of the new professional corporation, but A has received a windfall that may produce unforeseen tax consequences. There is authority under Section 351 of the Code to support the position that, since A is not an actual transferor of the new corporation and B (the transferor) does not control 80% of the corporation, A's receipt of the stock in the new professional corporation is taxable to him.[2] Also, A's receipt of stock in the new corporation could be considered as additional compensation paid to him,[3] could be considered as a gift by B to A, or could create potential income tax problems under Section 751 of the Code, depending upon the manner of the incorporation of the partnership.

Consequently, where a partnership is to be incorporated and the stock of the professional corporation will be issued in accordance with prior income interests, the capital accounts of the partners must exist in the same percentage as the income interests. If this cannot be accomplished prior to incorporation, one of the following alternatives (on the facts of the above example) should be considered:

(1)   Retention of Assets by B

Partner B could withhold assets with a value of $10,000 and those assets could be leased to the new corporation. This will permit B's capital account to be reduced prior to incorporation and, then, partners B and A could both contribute an equal amount of cash to the professional corporation.

(2)   Distribution of Notes to B

In the incorporation, partner A and partner B would contribute an equal amount of cash to the new corporation. Also, partner B would contribute the $10,000 in assets of the partnership and, in receipt therefor, would receive a note from the new professional corporation which would constitute a security under Section 351 of the Code. This will permit the incorporation to be tax-free and permit partner B to be paid (tax-free) an amount reflecting his capital account in the predecessor partnership.

(3)   Distribution of Cash to B

The partnership could distribute cash to partner B, reducing his capital account to zero. Partners A and B could then contribute their partnership interests to the new professional corporation. It is likely, however, that the partnership will not have an amount of cash equal to B's capital account and, consequently, it may be necessary for the partnership to borrow funds to generate the cash to distribute to B. Care should be taken to assure that the adjusted basis of the properties transferred to the new corporation is in excess of the liabilities assumed by the new corporation.

(4)   Uses of Different Classes of Stock

It may also be possible to segregate B's existing capital account into a second class of stock which will be repaid to him at a later date. For example, upon the incorporation of the partnership, both A and B would be issued the same number of shares of class A stock, providing for a one dollar par, voting rights, and the right to receive dividends. The class A stock would be subordinated upon liquidation to the rights of a class B preferred stock of the corporation. The class B stock would have no voting rights, not be entitled to dividends, and the shareholders of that stock would be entitled to a preferential distribution equal to the par value of that stock upon liquidation ($10,000). The issuance of class B preferred stock to B will isolate B's equity interest in a frozen account in which A will not participate, and this will permit the admission of shareholders at a later date without their obligation to purchase a portion of B's prior equity. This alternative reaches the same result as distributing a promissory note to B upon incorporation; and, if the corporation will be in a position to pay B the amount of his existing capital account upon incorporation, the issuance of a promissory note qualifying as a security upon incorporation is probably the preferable route.

[7.05]   VOTING TRUSTS AND PROXIES

The control of a corporation may also be obtained through the use of voting trusts and the granting of proxies. However, it should be recognized that some states specifically prohibit the use of voting trusts and proxies in professional corporations. Also, almost all states severely restrict the use of irrevocable voting trusts and proxies and prescribe specific time limits and other rules which must be met in the use of voting trusts and proxies. Therefore, the authors recommend that, while voting trusts and proxies may provide a means to control a professional corporation, there are more effective and less cumbersome methods of controlling corporate activities, such as the use of several classes of stock, the implementation of shareholder agreements, and the provision of certain voting requirements in the bylaws of the corporation. In addition, it should be remembered that rigid limitations on voting rights may produce resentment by junior members of the firm as their income production increases. Since most professionals need to vent their feelings and participate in the direction of the professional corporation, the authors feel it is usually advisable to grant all shareholders in the corporation some form of voting rights on all matters, even though the effectiveness of the voting rights granted may be restricted by the diminished number of shares issued.

[7.06]   STOCK SUBSCRIPTIONS AND
TRANSFER AGREEMENTS

The issuance of stock in a professional corporation is no different from that in a regular business corporation, and the general corporate formalities normally followed by business corporations should be observed. For this reason, it is advisable that a shareholder wishing to purchase shares of a professional corporation submit a formal subscription in which he requests to purchase shares of the professional corporation. Shares offered in a professional corporation are not given a blanket exemption from federal or most state securities laws. The sale of shares of a professional corporation must be registered with federal and local securities authorities, unless an exemption from registration can be found. Such an exemption is available under Section 4(2) of the Securities Act of 1933 and is also available under most state securities laws, for example, Section 9(m) of the Georgia Securities Act of 1973. Consequently, the stock subscription submitted by the prospective stockholder should contain language sufficient to permit the professional corporation to issue the stock, relying on the representations of the prospective stockholder, under the relevant exemptions. While it is unlikely that a professional employee would seek rescission of the purchase of his stock and sue for securities fraud, this is a possibility where a corporate separation occurs soon after incorporation. For this reason, the authors feel that it is prudent and not a matter of "overkill" to provide appropriate stock subscription agreements. Copies of an appropriate stock subscription and stock sales agreements are included in this chapter as Exhibits 1 and 2, respectively.

Also, upon the purchase of stock, the purchasing stockholder should submit to the corporation an appropriate transfer agreement which delineates the assets to be transferred in exchange for the stock which will be issued. The transfer agreement serves the purpose of acting as a bill of sale for the assets received by the corporation and also lists the assets and liabilities transferred in exchange for the stock. Further, outlining the assets in the transfer agreement forces the attorney and accountant to review the application of Section 351 to the transaction as a whole. A form of transfer agreement is included in this chapter as Exhibit 3.

[7.07] STOCK LEGENDS

The stock certificates issued by a professional corporation should contain legends which relate to the restrictive nature of the stock. These legends should appear on the face of the stock certificate or, if this is impossible (which in many cases it is), the following inscriptions should appear on the face of the certificate and the legend should appear on the reverse side:

> "The transfer of the shares represented by this certificate is restricted—See restrictive legends on reverse side."

Stock certificates of professional corporations should contain at least the following restrictive legends:

(1) Legends Required Under State Law Regarding Ownership of the Stock by Professional. See Article 1.2 of the form Bylaws contained in section [6.04], *supra*, for an example of such a restriction.

(2) Voting Restrictions and Restrictions Under Stock Retirement Agreements. See Article 8 of the Stock Retirement Agreement contained in section [11.04], *infra*, which provides an example of such a restriction.

(3) Federal Securities Law Restriction. The following notice should be placed upon all stock certificates:

NOTICE: The shares of common stock represented by this certificate were issued and sold in reliance on the exemption from registration under Section 4(2) of the Securities Act of 1933 as amended (the "1933 Act") and have not been the subject of a registration statement under the 1933 Act. These shares may not be sold or otherwise transferred except in a transaction that is exempt under the 1933 Act or pursuant to an effective registration statement under the 1933 Act or in a transaction which is otherwise in compliance with the 1933 Act.

(4) State Securities Law Notices. All stock certificates should also contain an appropriate state securities law notice such as the following:

NOTICE: The shares of common stock represented by this certificate were issued and sold in a transaction that is exempt from registration under the Georgia Securities Act of 1973 in reliance upon Section 9(m) of that Act. Such securities may not be resold or transferred except in a transaction that is exempt under that Act or pursuant to an effective registration statement under that Act or in a transaction which is otherwise in compliance with that Act.

[7.08] SECTION 1244 STOCK

Section 1244 of the Code provides that, where a loss is incurred upon the sale or other disposition of stock in a small business corporation, the loss on that stock, up to $50,000 on an individual return and up to $100,000 on a joint return, will be treated as an ordinary and not a capital loss. The provisions of Section 1244 are available to professional corporations.

Upon the incorporation of a professional corporation, the steps necessary to effectuate the issuance of Section 1244 stock are often overlooked, simply because it is never envisioned that the professional corporation will suffer substantial losses and be liquidated. Since, generally, only successful professionals incorporate, it could be argued that the issuance of Section 1244 stock is of no practical use in the professional corporation setting. However, the authors feel that since there is so little effort involved in the issuance of qualifiying Section 1244 stock, all professional corporation should issue stock under Section 1244 in the event, however unlikely it may be, a loss may be incurred.

Prior to the Revenue Act of 1978, Section 1244 contained a series of rather intricate requirements which required exact compliance in order to effectuate the issuance of Section 1244 stock. Section 1244 was one of the true "traps for the unwary" and, consequently, in the Revenue Act of 1978 Section 1244 was substantially amended to facilitate the issuance of Section 1244 stock. In order to create the existence of Section 1244 stock, the following requirements must be met:

(1) The corporation must qualify as a "small business corporation" under Section 1244(c)(3) of the Code which requires that the corporation have paid in capital of $1,000,000 or less.
(2) The stock must be issued in exchange for money or other property, not services.
(3) The corporation, during its five most recent taxable years ending before the date the loss on the stock was sustained, derived more than 50% of its aggregate gross receipts from sources other than rents, royalties, dividends, interest, annuities, and sales or exchanges of stocks or securities.

It should be noted that the benefits provided under Section 1244 are available only to the person to whom the stock was originally issued and are not available to any transferee of the stock. Thus, if stock in a professional corporation which was originally issued as Section 1244 stock is sold by one of the professionals to an incoming professional shareholder, the incoming shareholder will not receive the benefits of Section 1244.

Also, prior to the revisions made to Section 1244 of the Code, there was a requirement which specifically provided that stock issued under Section 1244 must be issued under a "plan" to provide Section 1244 stock. Although this requirement no longer exists, the authors feel that the issuance of Section 1244 stock be memorialized in an appropriate corporate resolution, such as that contained in the form minutes of the first organizational meeting of the board of directors contained in section [6.03], *supra*.

EXHIBIT 1

STOCK SUBSCRIPTION AGREEMENT

DATE _____

TO THE BOARD OF DIRECTORS OF _____

The undersigned hereby subscribes for the one dollar ($1.00) par value capital stock of your corporation in the amount and for the consideration set out below:

Name	Consideration	Shares
_____	_____	_____
_____	_____	_____

Tendered herewith is the consideration for the shares subscribed. This subscription shall expire three (3) months from the date hereof unless accepted by the corporation prior to that time. [It is understood and agreed that _____ shall not be entitled to certificates for nor entitled to vote the shares hereby subscribed until such shares are fully paid].

Very truly yours,

_____

ACCEPTED:

_____

By: _____
  Secretary

Date: _____

EXHIBIT 2

STOCK SALES AGREEMENT

THIS AGREEMENT, made and entered this ____ day of _____, _____, by and between _____, ("Seller") and _____ ("Purchaser").

WHEREAS, Seller owns all of the issued and outstanding stock of _____, a Georgia professional corporation (the Corporation"), consisting of _____, shares of $____ par value voting common stock (the "Stock");

WHEREAS, Purchaser is currently an employee of the Corporation;

WHEREAS, Seller desires to sell Purchaser certain shares of Stock and Purchaser desire to purchase such Stock from Seller, all on the terms and conditions hereinafter set forth; and

WHEREAS, Seller has provided or made available to Purchaser all financial or other information regarding the Corporation which Purchaser has requested;

NOW THEREFORE, for and in consideration of the promises, covenants, and agreements hereinafter set forth, the parties hereto agree as follows:

1. Sale. Seller hereby agrees to sell to Purchaser ____ shares of Stock and Purchaser hereby agrees to purchase such ____ shares of Stock from Seller.

2. Purchase Price. The purchase price for the ____ shares of Stock is _____ Dollars ($____).

3. Closing. The closing of the sale of Stock to the Purchaser shall take place at the office of the Corporation in _____, Georgia on _____, _____, with the sale to be effective as of _____, _____. At the closing;

 (a) Seller shall deliver to Purchaser a certificate representing ___ shares of Stock duly endorsed, free and clear of all liens, claims and encumbrances.

(b) Purchaser shall deliver to Seller a certified or cashier's check for the full amount of the purchase price set forth in Paragraph 2.

4. <u>Title.</u> Seller covenants and represents that he is the sole owner of and has the right to sell the Stock covered by this Agreement and that all such Stock is free and clear of all liens, claims and encumbrances. Seller further represents and warrants that:

(a) Other than the Stock, no preferred stock, stock options, or other equity interests in the Corporation are outstanding;

(b) The stock transfer records of the Corporation are accurate and reflect all requests to date for registration for shares of Stock; and

(c) The Corporation has no outstanding bonds, debentures, or other debt instruments of any type that are convertible into Stock.

5. <u>Representations, Warranties, and Acknowledgments.</u> The following representations, warranties and acknowledgments relating to the Stock covered by this Agreement are hereby made:

(a) Purchaser warrants that he is receiving the Stock for his own account without the participation of any other person and with the intent to hold the Stock for investment and without the intent of participating directly or indirectly in the distribution of the Stock, or any portion thereof, and not with a view to, or for sale in connection with, the distribution of the Stock, or any portion thereof.

(b) Purchaser acknowledges that the Stock has not been registered under (i) the Georgia Securities Act of 1973, as amended, in reliance upon an exemption from registration thereunder; (ii) the Securities Act of 1933, as amended, in reliance upon an exemption from registration thereunder, or (iii) the securities laws of any other jurisdiction and, in connection therewith, Purchaser covenants and agrees that he will not offer, sell or otherwise transfer the Stock, or any portion thereof, other than in compliance with that certain Stock Retirement Agreement entered into between Seller, Purchaser and the Corporation, dated _____ , 19___ , (the "Stock Retirement Agreement").

(c) Purchaser acknowledges and agrees that the Stock is subject to restrictions on transfer and to the terms and conditions of the Stock Retirement Agreement and represents and warrants that he has read and comprehends the Stock Retirement Agreement and has or will voluntarily become a party thereto and bound thereby.

(d) Purchaser acknowledges that the Stock may only be issued to, held by, or transferred to a person who is licensed to practice the profession for which the Corporation is organized and who, unless disabled, is actively engaged in such practice, except as otherwise provided in Section 5 of the Georgia Professional Corporation Act, Ga. Code Ann. §§84-5401 to 5407. Purchaser further acknowledges that any transfer of Stock by him in violation of the Georgia Professional Corporation Act shall be void.

(e) The agreements, representations and acknowledgments made by the Purchaser herein extend to and apply to all of the Stock acquired by Purchaser. Acceptance of the certificates evidencing any of the Stock shall constitute a confirmation by Purchaser that all agreements, representations and acknowledgments made herein shall be true and correct at such time.

(f) Purchaser acknowledges that Seller has made available to Purchaser such financial and other information regarding the Corporation as Purchaser has requested.

(g) Purchaser further acknowledges that Seller and the Corporation are relying upon the truth and accuracy of each of the foregoing representations, warranties and acknowledgments. Purchaser hereby covenants and agrees to indemnify, defend and hold harmless Seller and the Corporation, and each of them, from and against all liabilities, costs, claims, expenses (including, without limitation, reasonable attorneys' fees), damages, demands, actions, causes of action, suits or proceedings, resulting from the untruth, inaccuracy or breach of any such representation, warranty or acknowledgment.

6. Benefit. This Agreement shall be binding upon and shall inure to the benefit of the parties, their legal representatives, and assigns.

7. Waiver of Breach or Violation not Deemed Continuing. The waiver by either party of a breach or violation of any provisions of this Agreement shall not operate as or be construed to be a waiver of any subsequent breach hereof.

8. Governing Law. This Agreement shall be interpreted, construed and governed according to the laws of the State of Georgia.

9. Paragraph Headings. The paragraph headings contained in this Agreement are for convenience only and shall in no manner be construed as a part of this Agreement.

10. Entire Agreement. This Agreement constitutes the sole and entire agreement of the parties with respect to the matters contained herein, and any representation, inducement, promise, or agreement, whether oral or written, which pertains to such matters and is not embodied herein shall be of no force or effect.

11. Counterparts. This Agreement is executed in multiple counterparts, each of which shall be deemed an original and together shall constitute one and the same agreement, with one counterpart being delivered to each party thereto.

IN WITNESS WHEREOF, the parties have executed this Agreement, all being done in duplicate originals with one original being delivered to each party on the day and year first above written.

Signed, sealed, and
delivered this _____
day of_____ , 19___ ,

_____
Witness

Seller

_____

Purchaser:

_____

EXHIBIT 3

TRANSFER AGREEMENT

WHEREAS, Dr. X has practiced as a _____ through _____, 19____, and

WHEREAS, Dr. X desires to transfer and assign all of the assets specifically enumerated in Schedule A attached hereto for ____ shares of $1.00 par value common stock of _____, and the assumption of the liabilities of _____ by _____;

NOW, THEREFORE, in consideration of the mutual agreements contained herein and for other good and valuable consideration, the parties hereto enter into this Transfer Agreement.

Dr. X transfers and assigns all of his right, title and interest in and to any and all the assets specifically enumerated in Schedule A attached hereto for and in consideration of _____ shares of the $1.00 par value common stock of _____, and the assumption of all liabilities relating to the medical practice of said _____ pursuant to Section 351 of the Internal Revenue Code of 1954, as amended.

2.

This Agreement shall be effective as of _____, 19____, and shall constitute a transfer in accordance with Section 351 of the Internal Revenue Code since said transfer is solely in exchange for stock of the transferee and does not include the receipt of "money or other property" as that phrase is defined in Section 357(a) of the Internal Revenue Code, and immediately after the exchange _____ is in control of the corporation as defined in Section 368(c) of the Internal Revenue Code.

IN WITNESS WHEREOF, the parties hereto have affixed their hands and seal this ____ day of _____, 19____.

_____

DR. X

(CORPORATE SEAL)   ACCEPTED BY:

ATTEST:
                                    _____
_____
Secretary   By: _____
                                    President

NOTES TO CHAPTER 7

1. Eaton, *Business Organizations—Professional Corporations and Associations*, Vol. 17 at §12.05[10].
2. *William A. James*, 53 T.C. 63 (1969).
3. Treas. Regs. §1.351-1(b).

CHAPTER 8

Practical Aspects of Incorporation

[8.01] MISCELLANEOUS ITEMS WHICH MUST BE CHANGED UPON INCORPORATION

There are a number of bookkeeping and other operational matters which must be accomplished at the time of incorporation. Professional corporation advisors sometimes forget to mention all of the various items which must be changed and, even if they are mentioned to the professional, professionals often forget them. A number of these items, such as the filing of tax returns and beginning new books, are indispensable elements to the proper operation of the new corporation. On the other hand, some of the items, such as changing the name of the practice in the building directory, are not absolutely necessary for the valid existence of the professional corporation but do indicate that a separate and distinct corporation exists apart from the professionals. For these reasons, it is generally best for the attorney to prepare a short list of the general items which must be accomplished at the time of incorporation and deliver this list to the professional and his other advisors. An example of such a list is attached to this section as Exhibit 1.

[8.02] MODIFIED LIMITED LIABILITY

Under the partnership laws of most states, which correspond to the Uniform Partnership Act, general partners are jointly and severally liable for the torts committed by their partners and jointly liable for the contractual obligations of their partners, both of which must, of course, occur within the scope of the partnership's operation. Consequently, professionals who operate in partnerships have basically no insulation from the potential malpractice liability of their partners, other than the professional malpractice insurance which is carried. Since many states permit a form of modified limited liability for professional corporations, a very important nontax factor for incorporation exists. This factor has been recognized by the courts as being a very important aspect of the incorporation of a professional practice[1] and, as a practical matter, will become more important as areas of specialization increase within the same professional group. The modified limited liability provisions of state professional corporation acts eliminate "collateral" liability where one professional will be liable for the acts of another. (However, many states are silent on the issue of collateral liability and the elimination of collateral liability must be inferred from the general corporation law). Generally, under state professional corporation acts, a professional will be liable only for his own negligent acts and for those of others who work directly under his instruction. The corporation will, obviously, be liable for all negligent acts of its employees and agents. See Section 11 of the Model Professional Corporation Act attached as Exhibit 2 of this chapter.

It can be argued that the modified limited liability available through professional corporations is of no practical importance because sufficient malpractice insurance is obtainable. However, with the litigious society in which we live, malpractice premiums are becoming increasingly expensive and larger judgments against professionals are becoming more numerous. In July of 1980, for example, a $35.5 million judgement was awarded against a prestigious New York law firm. The possibility of malpractice claims is also becoming more likely as the complexity of professions increases. For these reasons, the authors feel that the modified limited liability which may be obtained through a professional corporation is a benefit which should not be overlooked.

On the other hand, some professionals feel that it is inappropriate for a professional to seek, in any way, to limit his own personal liability for the acts of his "partners" in a professional corporation. The Ohio Supreme Court rule which permits lawyers to incorporate provides, "The participation by an individual as a shareholder of a legal professional association shall be on the condition that such individual shall, and by such participation does, guarantee the financial responsibility of the association for its breach of any duty, whether or not rising out of the attorney-client relationship."[2] Also, at least four states do permit modified limited liability for professionals.[3] As with tort liabilities, the contractual liability of a corporation is limited. The corporation alone is subject to the obligations under contracts which it executes (unless the professionals have guaranteed those obligations).

In order to obtain the benefits which are available through the use of a professional corporation, the professional should take several steps to assure that the existence of the corporation is recognized. First, the corporation should be properly formed and corporate stock should be issued. If the professionals receive competent legal and accounting advice upon the formation of a professional corporation, this should not present a problem. Second, the corporation should be capitalized so as not to violate the thin capitalization rules under state law and permit creditors of the corporation to "pierce the corporate veil" and reach the assets of the shareholders. If a professional group receives competent tax and accounting advice upon incorporation, this should also generally not present a problem, especially where accounts receivable and fixed assets are transferred to the professional corporation. Third, the professional corporation should, following incorporation, be operated as an independent legal entity and not as the "hip pocket" of the professionals. To the extent that the professionals do not adequately recognize the independent existence of the corporation, the creditors of the corporation will be in a position to contend that the existence of the corporation should be ignored and that the shareholders are, in fact, partners in a joint enterprise and should be jointly responsible for the liabilities of the corporation. A professional corporation operated with proper legal and accounting advice, where adequate documentation is kept, should be in a position to refute any such contention.

[8.03]   CHOICE OF FISCAL YEAR

During its first year of operation, any new corporation, including a professional corporation, may choose its taxable year. Within the parameters provided by Sections 441 and 443 of the Code, the taxable year may be any twelve-month period ending on the last day of any month. The choice of the taxable year is made during the first year of operation by simply cutting short the first year of operation. For example, if a professional corporation is incorporated on September 1 and anticipates operating on a March 1 - February 28 fiscal year, the first year of operation of the professional corporation will be from September 1 until the following February 28 at which time the first fiscal year will be terminated. The fiscal year of a corporation is generally chosen by the filing of a federal income tax return for that year. In the past, however, there have been some attempts by the Service to contend that a corporation's fiscal year is chosen upon the filing of various procedural forms such as the Form SS-4 (for obtaining an employer identification number), which requires a statement of the fiscal year end. Consequently, when such procedural forms are filed early in the existence of the corporation, the attorneys and accountants for the corporation should specifically state in the designated spaces on those forms that the fiscal year has not yet been determined and thus avoid the possibility of the Service contending that another fiscal year has been chosen.

The authors have found that approximately 75% of all professional corporation choose to employ a non-calendar fiscal year. The choice of a fiscal year depends upon many factors. As a practical matter, the end of the fiscal year should normally be at the seasonal low point of the profession, if any occurs, and at a point at which the accountant has sufficient time to give adequate attention to the affairs of the corporation. Typically, accounting firms are extraordinarily busy at the end of the year and during April when tax returns must be filed. Consequently, it is advisable to discuss with the accountant when he would recommend the fiscal year to end. Generally, for a cash basis professional corporation, a fiscal year ending in the early part of the calendar year (January, February, or March) provides a mechanism whereby the professionals may undertake basic tax planning. This occurs because most professionals are, personally, calendar year taxpayers. The Service has even privately ruled that a professional corporation may choose an initial fiscal year even though a material distortion of income may occur.[4]

The choice of a corporate fiscal year ending in the early part of the year will permit a possible deferral of income from one taxable year to another. For example, where a calendar year professional incorporates and establishes a February 28 fiscal year end for the professional corporation, the corporation may elect to defer the payment of salaries which would normally occur late in the calendar year (November and December) into January or February of the next calendar year. This postponement of salaries will result in a deferral of federal and state income taxes because the salaries have been deferred into another taxable year of the professionals but remain in the same taxable year of the corporation. Such a postponement will result in a one-time benefit because the deferral in taxes will eventually be made up. For example, if during the second year (when the extra salary is paid) the corporation continues to pay normal monthly salaries, the professional will report fourteen months of salary (the normal twelve months of salary plus the two months of salary from the previous November and December). However, if the corporation continues to defer November and December salaries for an indefinite period of time, the professional can obtain what results in an interest-free loan of the taxes which would be due to the government. Any such deferral should, however, be based upon valid business purposes, such as the reduced cash flow of the professional corporation at the end of the year, because deferral may give rise to the contention by the Service that the existence of the corporation should be ignored because it is being operated as a mere tax device for the professional. The choice of a fiscal year may also help eliminate the problem of bunching of income which occurs upon the incorporation of a fiscal year partnership, as described in section [5.14], *supra*.

Where the professional corporation chooses an accrual method of accounting, as more completely described in the following section, it is often advantageous to choose a fiscal year ending in the later part of the calendar year, such as October or November. Under Section 267 of the Code, any payment of compensation or bonuses to an individual who controls a corporation, where the corporation and the individual are on different accounting methods, must be made to the individual within two and one-half months following the close of the fiscal year in order to be accruable and deductible by the corporation. Thus, a professional corporation with a November fiscal year end could accrue and deduct a bonus or salary payment which is not actually made to the professional until January of the following year.

Where a newly formed professional corporation has an inordinate amount of income during the early months of incorporation through the unexpected early collection of accounts receivable or through the collection of large contingent fees, the professionals should consider closing the first taxable year of the corporation following the receipt of that income and establishing qualified retirement plans for that year. Other income received after the close of the first fiscal year could then be deferred until later calendar years of the professionals.

[8.04] METHOD OF ACCOUNTING

A new professsional corporation is not bound by the accounting method of its predecessor where the corporation is created under Section 351 of the Code. Consequently, a new professional corporation is entitled to select whatever accounting method its Board of Directors deems advisable.

There are two basic methods of accounting which are available to professional corporations. The cash method, which is predominant, requires that income be reported by the corporation only after it is actually or constructively received by the corporation and that deductions for expenses of the corporation may not be claimed until actually paid.[5] On the other hand, the accrual method of accounting requires a corporation to include in income, and to expense as deductions, items of income at the time bills are rendered therefor and expenses at the time they become noncontingent obligations of the corporation.

The cash method of accounting is generally chosen by professional corporations due to its simplicity and due to some of the adverse consequences which may result under the accrual method of accounting. The accrual method of accounting may be particularly disadvantageous for a professional corporation with a large amount of accounts receivable which must be reported as income at the time bills are submitted for the services rendered, thus, substantially accelerating the income of the professional corporation. It will be possible, however, for the professional corporation to utilize a bad debt reserve which should assist in alleviating some of the problems of accelerated income.[6]

In the past, one advantage of choosing the accrual method of accounting was the ability to fund qualified retirement plans following the end of the fiscal year. Prior to ERISA, contributions made to a qualified retirement plan of a cash basis professional corporation were required to be made on or before the last day of the end of the fiscal year. On the other hand, accrual basis corporations were permitted, under the then existing version of Section 404(a)(6) of the Code, to make retirement plan contributions on or before the due date for filing the corporate income tax return, plus extensions of time to file. With the enactment of ERISA in

1974, the general rule available for accrual basis corporations was also made available to cash basis corporations. Consequently, the retirement plan contributions of a cash basis corporation will be deductible in a year if made on or before the time for filing the federal income tax return for that year (plus extensions of time), if the contributions are allocated to participants on account of that year, and if the contributions are deducted in the federal income tax return filed for that year.[7] This change has eliminated one of the substantial benefits which had been obtainable from electing the accrual method of accounting.

It should also be remembered that Section 267 of the Code applies to accrual method professional corporations. This provision requires that, where the corporation and a controlling shareholder are on different accounting methods, any deductible salaries or bonuses paid to that controlling shareholder after the end of the corporation's fiscal year must be paid within two and one-half months of the end of that fiscal year in order to be deductible in that fiscal year.

The cash method of accounting does, however, also have drawbacks; the primary drawback being the inability of the professionals to perform precise corporate planning prior to the end of the fiscal year. Generally, professionals desire to reduce the income of the professional corporation to a very low level at the end of each fiscal year. However, since salaries and bonuses paid to the professionals must, in order to be deductible, be paid prior to the end of the fiscal year, it is very difficult to determine without some very hectic, last-minute calculations, the exact position of the corporation on the final day of its fiscal year. Also, the Internal Revenue Service has taken the position[8] that employment taxes which are due and owing to the federal government at the end of the fiscal year of a cash method corporation and are not paid by the end of that fiscal year (but are paid within the time prescribed for payment) are not deductible in the year in which the liability was generated. Cash basis accounting and law firms should also seek to assure that advance retainers received by the professional corporation are set up in proper trust accounts and will, consequently, not be considered income prior to being earned.

Because of the simplicity of the cash method of accounting, the authors feel that there is usually very little reason not to choose it. However, it is often advantageous to prepare and review an accrual statement for a professional corporation, even though the cash method is chosen; an accrual statement may be used in computing the value of the corporation and in obtaining bank loans because it does reflect accounts receivable (and possibly work in process) and anticipated expenses.

The method of accounting is chosen for tax purposes when the first income tax return is filed for the professional corporation, but, as a practical matter, the method of accounting should be chosen when the corporation is formed.

[8.05] SOLO PRACTITIONERS

During the early struggle with the Service regarding the status of professional corporations, some advisors recommended against the formation of professional corporations involving only one professional. Now that the Service has recognized professional corporations, most advisors feel that the general rules relating to professional corporation also apply to one-man professional corporation and, consequently, do not oppose the formation of one-man professional corporations.

It should be recognized, however, that a one-man professional corporation may present a situation which is particularly susceptible to Service scrutiny. For example, the Service may, with a one-man corporation, have a stronger case with regard to assignment of income, the application of Section 482, or the argument that the corporation is a mere sham. These concepts are more completely discussed in Chapter 9. This occurs because some of the major nontax benefits associated with the formation of a professional corporation are not available in a one-man professional corporation, such as the modified limitation on professional malpractice liability (although contractual liability limits still exist), the nonexistence of continuity of existence (because for all practical purposes the corporation will cease to exist when the professional terminates his employment or dies), and the structural benefit of centralization of management and admitting and removing shareholders without the dissolution of the corporation. In certain instances of abusive practices, the Service has taken specific note of the one-man professional corporation. For example, in Rev. Rul. 75-35[9] a professional incorporated his sole practice and isolated his staff employees in a separate corporation in order to exclude those employees from participation in the qualified retirement plans of the professional corporation. The Service stated that the professional controlled the second corporation and, consequently, the employees should participate in the professional corporation's plans. The Service could, also, have attacked the substance of the professional corporation and contended that it was only formed for tax purposes and, therefore, should be ignored.

Even with these potential problems, the Service has appeared to give the green light to solo practitioners who wish to incorporate. In his much cited article,[10] the then Commissioner of Internal Revenue, K. Martin Worthy, stated that the Service would not attack the existence of a professional corporation merely because there is only one professional employee employed by the corporation. Since that article, the Service has apparently adopted that position.[11] In Rev. Rul. 72-4,[12] the Service stated that the qualified status of a corporate retirement plan will not be withheld simply because it can be established that the corporation is operated for the purposes of selling services, abilities, or talents of only one employee who is also the principal or sole shareholder. Such a qualified retirement plan, obviously, provides benefits for all employees of the professional corporation. In addition, in 1975, the Service issued Rev. Rul. 75-67 which some practitioners feel is the death knell for the long-anticipated attack on one-man professional corporations.[13] In Rev. Rul. 75-67, the Service held that a one-man professional corporation will not be considered a personal holding company unless the professional will provide specific services for the client and does not have the right to substitute another professional. The ruling also contends that, if the services of the professional are sufficiently specialized so that it would be impossible for another professional to perform those services, the corporation may be considered a personal holding company. The application of the personal holding company rules to professional corporations is more fully discussed in section [9.02], *infra*.

The benefits of operating as a professional corporation should, consequently, be available to the cautious sole practitioner. However, because the one-man professional corporation presents a unique opportunity for the Service to attack the existence of the corporation, the sole practitioner who incorporates should take steps to assure that the integrity of the professional corporation is observed. The corporate minute book should be scrupulously maintained; annual minutes should be drafted and an appropriate employment agreement should be executed. Further, all contracts with third parties should be in the name of the professional corporation, and the professionals should never specifically agree in writing (or otherwise) to personally perform (to the exclusion of other professionals) services so as to run afoul of Rev. Rul. 75-67. The potential problems with one-man professional corporations are heightened where the professional is employed by an institution, such as a hospital, which provides office space and complete staff services. In this situation, the only employee of the professional corporation may be the professional employee. Consequently, this situation presents an opportunity for the professional to lapse into unattentiveness and, himself, disregard the existence of the professional corporation.

[8.06]   PROFESSIONAL ADVISORS AND THEIR FEES

Because professionals are normally engrossed by their work, the choice of their advisors is crucial. It is their advice which will create the professional corporation vehicle that will provide the tax benefits and retirement planning for the professional. For this reason, the professional should generally seek to hire *unrelated* advisors. Although there are ethical and legal restraints upon the ability to practice law or to become a certified public accountant, there are often no restraints or basic standards which must be met by some of the so-called "consultants" who make their services available to professionals. Some consultants offer "package deals" in which the consulting firm provides the consultant, the lawyer, and the accountant. It is generally advisable to avoid such arrangements because it is not always clear in whose direction the loyalties lie. For example, if an attorney is hired by a consulting firm, how can he also represent the professional? Is there not an implicit conflict of interest? The authors have found that, generally, the best results are obtained where all of the advisors are independent and are free to provide advice which is not tainted by other allegiances. The authors, in fact, advise their clients that often the best results are reached where the advisors initially disagree on the matter and then, by working together, reach a common ground which is satisfactory to the professional.

(1) Types of Advisors

In operating a professional corporation, the professional will definitely need the advice of an attorney and an accountant, plus possibly a pension consultant and a financial advisor if a corporate retirement plan is adopted. In hiring these advisors, the professional should review the following points:

(a) *The Pension Consultant*

Where a professional corporation adopts a defined benefit pension plan, it will be necessary to employ the services of an actuary to give advice regarding the structure of the benefits to be derived from the plan. On the other hand, where the professional corporation adopts qualified defined contribution plans, such as a money purchase pension and profit sharing plans, it is likely that the attorney will have sufficient knowledge to advise the professional regarding the benefits which may be obtained from such plans. Once the qualified reitirement plans are established, the professional must acquire assistance in administering the plans. For defined benefit pension plans, the actuary retained to design the plan should be employed to perform the annual actuarial study. For defined contributions plans the accountant, the institutional trustee of the plans (if any), or an independent retirement plan consulting firm can compute the annual allocations. A more complete discussion of the administrative and investment work, including the choice of the trustee for retirement plans, is contained in section [15.02], *infra*.

(b) *The Accountant*

It is imperative that the newly-formed professional corporation retain the services of a qualified accountant who is familiar with the operation of professional corporations and retirement plans of the type which will be adopted. The accountant, or someone else in his firm, should also have a detailed knowledge of the tax aspects of incorporating a professional practice. Although the attorney is primarily responsible for the incorporation of the professional corporation, it is the accountant who continues to advise on a monthly or quarterly basis. It is the bookkeeping or accounting system established by the accountant and his review of the accounting systems that will help solve problems and eliminate the possibility of employee theft. Without adequate accounting assistance, a professional corporation will certainly flounder. The incorporation of a professional practice is, consequently, a time when the services of the existing accountant should be analyzed and when a new accountant should be retained, if necessary.

Once the accountant for the professional corporation has been selected, it is often advisable for the accountant for the corporation to serve as the accountant for the individual professionals. This usually does not create a conflict of interest and permits the professionals to coordinate their individual and corporate planning.

(c) *Financial Advisors*

Many professionals retain financial advisors to assist them concerning insurance, investments, and income and estate planning. The need for such advisors will only be increased by incorporating, and their participation in the incorporation process should not be neglected. Areas of importance to financial advisors will be life and disability insurance coverage following incorporation, investment of funds maintained in qualified retirement plans, and the estate planning impact of incorporation.

(d) *The Attorney*

In selecting an attorney to assist in the incorporation of a professional practice, professionals should choose an attorney (or a law firm) who either specializes in or has substantial experience in incorporating professionals. The incorporation of a professional practice and the establishment of qualified retirement plans should generally not be left to the lawyer engaged in general practice, even if he is "my next door neighbor." The choice of an attorney experienced in the professional corporation area does not necessarily mean that a large law firm must be employed. There are a substantial number of small firms and even sole practitioners who engage in a significant amount of professional corporation work.

(2) Fees Charged by Professionals

In considering fees to be paid to professional advisors, the professional should be aware of the old adage, "You get what you pay for." This is not to say that the professional should hire the advisors with the highest fees but that, on the contrary, he should not necessarily hire the ones with the lowest fees. The incorporation of a professional practice is an area which, as indicated in the previous section, involves the overlapping of professional and non-professional advisors. Professional advisors, such as attorneys and accountants, must charge for their fees, whereas the non-professional advisors often provide "free advice" and their fees are actually made up through commissions earned on the products sold to the professional. Consequently, in interviewing advisors, the professional should obtain a clear understanding of what services will be rendered by the advisor and what fee will be charged.

It was estimated in 1970 that the total fee for incorporating a one-man professional corporation would range from $2,200 to $4,600 and that the fees for incorporating a three-or four-man professional practice would range from $3,150 to $6,300.[14] A more recent article has indicated that, as late at 1976, the legal fees for incorporating a professional practice will vary from $1,200 to $4,500.[15] It has been the author's experience that the legal fees for incorporating a professional medical practice will range from a low of $2,500 for the one-man professional practice with one qualified retirement plan to a high of approximately $7,500 for a professional corporation with several professional employees, two qualified retirement plans, and a detailed stock retirement agreement. Incorporating a "partnership of professional corporations" and establishing qualified retirement plans may generate legal fees of from $5,000 to $15,000, depending upon the number of professional corporations. Also, the additional accounting fees charged upon incorporation (for meetings to discuss incorporation and for closing the old books of the practice and opening new corporate books) will average $1,000 to $2,500.

The attorney should attempt to provide a "turnkey" incorporation package for a stated price. A sufficient amount of experience in the professional corporation area should permit the attorney to give a relatively close estimate of the cost of incorporation and the establishment of qualified retirement plans, excluding such matters as obtaining private letter rulings from the Service, negotiating contracts with hospitals, etc., and any unexpected matters. The attorney should also express to the professional that fees may be kept in line by having the professional perform fact gathering on his own, although the authors have found that the attorney and the accountant are generally faced with the prospect of discovering most of the facts.

In determining the fees which will be charged, the attorney should also consider that a significant portion of the fees that relate to the incorporation of a professional practice should be considered for tax advice, and, as such, will be deductible. Consequently, the fee charged by the attorney should be divided into the following three elements:

(1) Fee for incorporation which must be capitalized and amortized over 60 months under Section 248 of the Code.[16]
(2) Tax advice, which may be immediately deductible, and
(3) Preparation of retirement plans, employment and other agreements, the fees for which are also immediately deductible.[17]

Once the professsional corporation has been established, the professionals should be made aware that they should continue to engage their accountant and attorney on a continuing basis, at least annually, to review year-end planning. The authors recommend that, following the incorporation of a professional practice, the attorney be place on retainer for at least the next two years in order to encourage the professional to seek proper legal advice. It has been the authors' experience that, unless such a retainer is established, the professionals are hesitant to call the attorney, even when problems arise. The retainer established should be an estimate of fees necessary to enable the attorney to meet with the professionals once after the first six months of incorporation, immediately prior to the end of the first fiscal year, and at the end of the second fiscal year (plus answering various questions and handling telephone calls during the year). These meetings, which should include the accountant, are crucial. A monthly retainer of $200 should suffice for the first two years. After the first two years of incorporation, many professionals have sufficient knowledge and awareness of the professional corporation to operate it themselves. It is, however, generally an excellent idea for the accountant and attorney to continue to meet with the professionals during the last month of each fiscal year in order to discuss tax planning and the funding of the retirement plans.[18]

(3) Do-It-Yourself Kits

The authors strongly advise professionals to avoid those offering ''free advice'' regarding incorporation and form books promising the incorporation of a professional practice for ''$29.95 without the use of a lawyer.'' The establishment of a professional corporation can and will provide substantial economic and retirement benefits to professionals if it is properly incorporated and run. The incorporation of a professional practice is not something that should be taken lightly; if the Service chooses to ignore the existance of the professional corporation or to disqualify the corporation's qualified retirement plans, the tax consequences will be disastrous. For this reason, if a professional has determined to incorporate, he should also face the fact that it will be necessary to hire a competent attorney, accountant, and other advisors and to pay their fees. The fees of such advisors are simply part of the cost of incorporating, as is the additional federal unemployment tax that must be paid on the compensation of the professionals after incorporation.

[8.07] CHOICE OF NAME AND USE OF FICTITIOUS NAMES

Choosing the name for a professional corporation is a matter of personal preference which must comply with the requirements of local law.

In general, there is no prohibition on the use of an individual's name in the name of a professional corporation and, in fact, some states even require that the name of the professional corporation include the name of at least one of the incorporators. However, almost all state statutes require that the name of the professional corporation include ''Inc.,'' ''Incorporated,'' ''Company,'' ''P.C.,'' ''P.A.,'' ''A Professional Corporation,'' or some similar designation which will indicate to the general public that the professional practice is not a partnership but is incorporated. Further, some state statutes require that the name of the professional corporation also indicate the type of profession that is practiced, such as Louisiana, which requires that law firm names contain the language ''A Professional Legal Corporation.''[19] Even in those states where the designation of the profession is not required, some professional corporation advisors feel that it is important to designate the profession being practiced. The authors feel that this is not necessary unless including the type of profession practiced will help eliminate possible misunderstanding concerning the activities of the corporation.

Certain state statutes also permit the use of ''fictitious'' or generic names, such as ''Atlanta Medical Clinic, P.C.,'' which do not contain the names of any of the professionals and do not necessarily indicate the type of profession being practiced. Where such names are permitted, consideration should be given to the use of this type of name because it may substantially shorten the corporate name (particularly where all the professionals would like their names to be listed), may avoid potential conflict over the order in which names will be listed, may avoid the necessity of amending the corporate charter when new names must be added, and may create name recognition in the community.

A single corporation may also choose to use a fictitious name where it operates in more than one locality and may choose to operate in the other localities under names which are indigenous to those localities. Thus, "Atlanta Medical Clinic, P.C." could also operate in Macon, Georgia, and be called "Macon Medical Clinic, P.C." The use of another name by an existing professional corporation is normally called a "trade name" and is generally permitted for professional corporations (because the use of trade names is permitted for business corporations). On the other hand, most professional corporation statutes do not address the question of whether a permitted trade name must also include the "P.C.," etc. designation. Prudence would, of course, dictate that the trade name should include such a designation and the Secretary of State of the State of Georgia has taken that informal position.

[8.08] MULTI-STATE PRACTICE

Every state has statutes restricting corporations organized in other states ("foreign corporations") from doing business in that state unless the particular foreign corporation is "qualified" to do business in that state. Unfortunately, most of the professional corporation statutes were drafted in the late 1960's and do not specifically address the question of multi-state practice, probably because it was not prevalent at that time. The potential danger envisaged is that, where a state permits a professional corporation to do business in that state after simply "qualifying" with the Secretary of State, it is thought that "qualification" may authorize persons who have not been admitted to practice the profession in that state to engage in the practice of the profession.

Those states that have addressed this question have provided that foreign professional corporations may not be authorized to do business in the state unless all of the shareholders of the corporation are licensed professionals in that state. Further, Section 19 of the Model Professional Corporations Act (which is contained in its entirety in Exhibit 2 of this chapter) also contains this requirement. Although the Model Professional Corporation Act has not been adopted on a wide-spread basis, the authors anticipate that all state statutes will eventually be amended to provide similar provisions or that existing state statutes will be interpreted to require all shareholders of a foreign professional corporation to be admitted to practice the profession in that state. Even without state corporate law requirements, the requirements of each profession restrict the unauthorized practice of a profession in a state in which the professional is not licensed. For example, the letterhead of a law firm must specifically indicate those persons who are not authorized to practice law in the state.

Where a professional moves from one state to another and establishes his practice in his new state of residence, the existing professional corporation may be established in the new state through a simple "domestication." A domestication may occur tax-free by the formation of a new professional corporation in the new state of residence and the old professional corporation may be merged into the new professional corporation under Sections 368(a)(1)(C) or (F) of the Code.[20]

The multi-state practice problem may be avoided by the formation of a partnership in the other state. Most states do not restrict a professional partnership to only those persons who are licensed to practice a profession in that state. Rather, the profession may only be practiced through professionals licensed in that state and any use of the partnership name must indicate those professionals who are not licensed in that state. Consequently, it is possible for all of the shareholders of a professional corporation in State A to form a partnership with individuals licensed to practice in State B. It may also be possible to avoid the multi-state practice problem by the use of an unincorporated association (which is taxable as a corporation for federal tax purposes) in those states where not all of the shareholder professionals are licensed to practice.

Multi-state practice may also produce complicated state income tax problems. Some state income tax laws will require an allocation of a foreign corporation's or partnership's income to that state for income tax purposes where a portion of the income of that corporation or partnership is generated from that state. Such allocations are sometimes difficult and, when a multi-state practice is undertaken, state income tax laws should be examined.[21]

[8.09] MODEL PROFESSIONAL CORPORATION ACT

Even though all states have adopted professional corporation acts of one form or another, the requirements under the the acts vary widely and some of the acts, are unfortunately, deficient in certain respects. To provide a guide and hopefully to engender uniformity, the Committee on Professional Laws of the Corporation, Banking, and Business Section of the American Bar Association has issued a proposed professional corporation supplement to the Model Business Corporation Act, which was adopted as a model act by the Corporation Laws Committee of the Section of Corporation, Banking and Business Law in 1977. Included in this chapter as Exhibit 2 is a copy of this Act with the comments made by the Committee.

[8.10] ACCOUNTS RECEIVABLE

Because accounts receivable normally constitute the largest source of funds and the largest asset of a professional practice, it is usually necessary to transfer accounts receivable to a new professional corporation. While at one time there were severe doubts regarding whether the assignment of accounts receivable to a new professional corporation in a Section 351 transfer created the immediate recognition of gain, these problems have now all but been eliminated. See sections [5.02] and [5.03], *supra*. Consequently, all work in process, all work completed, but not billed, and all accounts receivable should generally be transferred to the new professional corporation in order to provide sufficient working capital during the months following incorporation.

As a practical matter, it is simpler to transfer all accounts receivable to the new professional corporation because the bookkeeping and collection ability of the professional partnership will vanish when the employees of the partnership become employees of the professional corporation. Further, if unbilled receivables or work in process are not transferred to the new professional corporation, there must be some way to distinguish the amount of work which has been generated in the partnership and the amount of compensation which must be paid to the partnership when the fees are collected. In the event that the partnership does retain accounts receivable which will, in all likelihood, be collected by the professional corporation, the corporation should charge the partnership a fee for collecting these receivables. See section [6.03], *supra*, containing the minutes of the initial meeting of the Board of Directors where a fee agreement is discussed.

[8.11] TAX PLANNING POSSIBILITIES WITHIN THE PROFESSIONAL CORPORATION

Other than the choice of employee fringe benefits, the choice of retirement plans, and the choice of fiscal year, which are described in other sections of the Desk Book, there are other tax planning opportunities which occur in the normal course of operating a professional corporation. The primary tax planning areas are year-end planning and the accumulation of cash surplus.

(1) Year-End Planning

The year-end goal for most professionals is to have sufficient earnings to fund the corporation's qualified retirement plans and then to pay out any remaining cash as bonuses or additional salary to the professionals, thus reducing the taxable income of the corporation to a very low figure. Achieving this goal sometimes calls for some hectic planning during the last several days of the corporate year because bonuses paid to employees of professional corporations, which are on a cash basis of accounting (as most are), must actually be paid prior to the end of the fiscal year in order to be deductible in that year. Reducing the taxable income of the corporation requires bonuses to be paid on the last day of the taxable year after receipts for that day have been received and after other expenses have been paid. However, it should be remembered that the payment of retirement plan contributions may be postponed until the time for filing the corporation's federal income tax return under Section 404(a)(6), and, consequently, the retirement plan contributions may be considered a "fudge" figure which can be used to reduce taxable income if the last-minute planning is not totally effective.

The year-end planning to reduce taxable income, although hectic, is possible where sufficient cash flow exists in the corporation. On the other hand, the problem usually encountered at the end of the fiscal year is a cash flow shortage so that the cash on hand is an amount less than the anticipated taxable income of the corporation. Thus, even if all the cash is paid as compensation, the corporation will still have taxable income. This problem occurs in most professional corporations because during the year expenditures are made which are not tax deductible. For example, expenditures for the payment of premiums on key man or split dollar life insurance are not deductible to the corporation but reduce the cash flow. Also, the repayment of corporate loans will not produce a tax deduction, although it reduces cash flow, and the purchase of equipment reduces cash flow (even though it does provide some tax deduction through depreciation).

Since it is always desirable for a professional corporation to have some taxable income, the attorney and accountant, together with the professionals, should prepare cash flow projections. Below is an example of projections which are based on a professional corporation with a fiscal year ended April 30, 1981. Because of the substantial expenditures for life insurance premiums and repayment of loans, there is insufficient cash flow in the corporation. Also, the payment of the pension plan contribution for the year ending April 30, 1980, in July of 1980 reduces fiscal year 1981 cash flow without providing a current tax deduction (because the tax deduction was taken in the year ended April 30, 1980).

PROJECTIONS AS OF APRIL 18, 1981

Taxable Income Projection

Net corporate income as of 3/31/81	$ 23,900
Add back: officer's life insurance	27,350
: note principal paid	40,000
: pension plan contribution for 4/30/80	11,900
Taxable income at 3/31/81	$103,150
Plus cash balance increase since 3/31/81 (Equates to net income 4/1/81 through 4/18/81)	21,700
Less salaries through April 30, 1981	(34,000)
Less deductible insurance premiums now due	(2,000)

Less balance due pension plan—
Need not be paid by 4/30/81
Must be paid before 7/15/81   (20,800)

Projected taxable income for fiscal
year-end 4/30/81 $ 68,050

Cash Projection

Cash balance checking and savings
4/18/81 $ 48,500

Less 4/30/81 salaries   (34,000)

Less insurance premiums due   (2,000)

Projected cash balance 4/30/81 $ 12,500

Collections for the remainder of April, 1981, are not considered since any
collections will increase taxable income, but the increase will be
offset by additional bonuses.

Cash balance is less than taxable income because the following nondeductible items were paid during the year:

$40,000	Note principal paid
$27,350	Life insurance premium
$11,900	Pension plan contributions for year ending 4/30/80 paid July, 1980.

The expenditures during the year for repayment of notes, life insurance
premiums, and the previous year's pension plan contribution make it virtually
impossible to avoid creating some taxable income in the fiscal year ended April 30,
1981, in the above example. If a projected cash balance of $12,500 as of April 30,
1981, is used to fund a portion of the pension plan contribution due for the year, a
projected taxable income for the fiscal year ended April 30, 1981, will be $68,050.
There are several possible steps which could be taken by the corporation to reduce
taxable income. First, the corporation could postpone payment of the pension plan
contribution until after the end of the fiscal year (as occurred last year) and the cash
on hand could be used to pay compensation and bonuses, thus reducing taxable
income to $55,550. Second, this same procedure could be followed, but the
professional corporation could also borrow $25,000 and pay this amount out as
additional compensation or bonuses. Deferring retirement plan contributions and
borrowing to pay compensation are not always the best courses of action, but they
do reduce taxable income. This example illustrates the "robbing Peter to pay Paul"
principle. Once this occurs, the problem will simply continue from year to year
until the corporation no longer defers retirement plan contributions or borrows, in
which event the corporation will report increased taxable income.

(2) Accumulation of Cash Surplus

Although the goal of most professionals is to deplete the professional corporation of cash at the end of each taxable year, it is very important for a professional corporation to retain a sufficient amount of working capital in the form of a cash surplus to provide for those periods in which income may, for some reason, be reduced. The authors feel that a professional corporation should retain a sufficient cash surplus to operate the corporation for two months (including all expenses and compensation payments, or $50,000 whichever is larger). With the rather uncertain economy that the country has faced in the last several years, it is possible for the collection of accounts receivable to slow drastically for several months, placing the corporation in a cash bind. It is also possible for one or more of the professionals to be out of work for several months due to sickness or injury and this should also be protected against by the retention of cash. The professionals, although they will not be entitled to receive the cash surplus held in the corporation, should understand that a cash surplus may be retained at very attractive tax rates and invested in an almost tax-free fashion. It is not necessary to accumulate this surplus in one taxable year and it may be accumulated over a number of years at the lowest corporate tax bracket of 17% (on the first $25,000 of taxable income in 1981, 16% in 1982, and 15% in 1983). Further, the cash surplus in the corporation may be invested in capital stock of other corporations which will provide the possibility of appreciation and, if such stocks pay dividends, will provide the possibility of excluding most of those dividends from taxation. Under the dividends-received deduction of Section 243 of the Code, only 15% of intercorporate dividends is subject to tax. Thus, if a professional corporation receives $1,000 in dividends from an investment in General Motors stock and the professional corporation is in the 17% bracket, the effective tax rate on this $1,000 in dividends will be 2.55% or $25.50.

It should be remembered that the corporate surtax exemption is limited for groups of controlled corporations as defined in Section 1563 of the Code. Where groups of corporations are "controlled" by 5 or fewer shareholders, only one surtax exemption is allowed for the entire group. Professionals should recognize that the controlled group rules are mechanical and may apply to totally unrelated businesses, e.g., a car wash and a medical practice.

[8.12] DOCUMENTATION

It is difficult to estimate the importance of maintaining the integrity of a professional corporation once it has been formed. Almost all professional corporations should be considered separate entities, apart from the professionals, upon incorporation, simply because of the documents which must be filed with public authorities, such as the State Corporate Commissioner. However, once the professional corporation commences business, the professionals often begin to disregard the formal status of the professional corporation as an entity. It is such disregard that often gives rise to possible attacks by the Service, as more completely discussed in the following chapter. One of the principal purposes of this Desk Book is to describe the reasons for, and the methods of, documenting the operation of a professional corporation after it has been established. If the recommendations contained in this Desk Book are followed, it will be very difficult (although not impossible) for the Service to disregard the professional corporation.

When the formal corporate documents, such as employment agreements and stock retirement agreements, are executed, a sufficient number of copies should be executed (these may be photocopies and need not be originals, as long as the document contains a provision which states that it will be executed in multiple counterparts), one executed copy should be given to each professional and an executed copy should be retained by the corporation for its minute book. Also, once during every year, usually immediately prior to the end of the year, a formal meeting of the shareholders and directors should be held. A notice of the meeting, as prescribed in the bylaws, should be given to all shareholders and directors of the corporation. The shareholders and directors may meet either jointly or in separate meetings, and, where all of the shareholders are also directors, it is often more convenient to hold a joint meeting. At the annual meeting, the shareholders and directors should take the following action:

Shareholders:

(1) Review the financial report of the corporation for the fiscal year.

(2) Read and approve all prior minutes and resolutions of the shareholders since and including the last annual meeting of the shareholders.

(3) Discuss the actions of the directors of the corporation during the fiscal year and ratify and approve such acts.

(4) Elect directors of the corporation for the coming fiscal year.

(5) If necessary, agree to the value of the corporation for purposes of the corporation's stock retirement agreement.

Directors:

(1) Review the operations of the corporation for the fiscal year and, particularly, the acts of the officers and employees of the corporation.

(2) Discuss and award bonuses and salary increases to the officers of the corporation.

(3) Discuss and determine the contributions which should be made to the corporation's qualified retirement plans.

(4) Discuss and pass resolutions adopting or modifying existing or additional employee benefits.

(5) Discuss the corporation's need to accumulate income in order to finance expansion, including an indication of the reasons that such accumulation will not run afoul of the rules regarding accumulated earnings under Section 453 of the Code.

(6) Read and approve all minutes and resolutions of the board since and including those of the last annual meeting.

(7) Review the actions of the officers during the fiscal year and ratify and approve such acts.

(8) Elect officers for the ensuing fiscal year.

(9) Discuss and declare a dividend to the stockholders.

(10) Review and agree to extend or call in any loans to officers. Review the expenses incurred by the officers on behalf of the corporation.

(11) Review the possible issuance of any shares of stock to any existing or new shareholder and, if necessary, establish a value for the stock of the corporation under the stock retirement agreement.

A copy of basic annual minutes for a professional corporation is included in this chapter as Exhibit 3. Also included, as Exhibits 4 and 5, respectively, are Annual Meeting and Mid-year Meeting Checklists, which can be used as a guide in reviewing matters at the meeting and in preparing the minutes. The actions taken at any meeting of any executive committee of the board of directors and at any interim or monthly meeting of the board of directors should also be contained in minutes of those meetings.

It is not necessary, in most states, for directors and shareholders actually to hold a meeting in order to make a decision on certain matters. Most state laws permit shareholders and directors to act without a meeting by "unanimous consent" and this is, in fact, the manner in which many actions of professional corporations are taken because of the difficulty in having all professionals present at any one time. An action by unanimous consent is taken by preparing a resolution and having that resolution signed by all of the shareholders or directors. A form of Consent Resolution is included in this chapter as Exhibit 6.

The secretary of the professional corporation is normally entrusted with maintaining the corporate records and minute book. It is very important to keep the corporate minute book organized and up-to-date because usually the first item requested by an examining IRS agent is the corporate minute book. A minute book that is a disorganized mass of documents creates a very unfavorable impression upon an examining agent.

Questions frequently arise regarding the length of time that medical and other business records should be maintained by a professional practice. The authors' experience has shown that records should be maintained for the periods indicated below.

(1) Client Medical Records

Under federal law and under most state laws, physicians and other professionals are not required to maintain records of their patients or clients for any particular period of time. Thus, the decision of how long to maintain records is up to each professional. Although actions for malpractice normally have a very short duration under most state statutes (2-3 years), the statute of limitations may be tolled (suspended) during the period in which the malpractice could not be discovered or during a patient's disability (because he is an infant, an idiot, insane, or in prison). Consequently, actions for malpractice may occur many years following the event. Also, in the medical field, drugs once thought safe are sometimes later found to be unsafe, and it would be helpful for a physician to be in a position to review his files and determine which patient had received the particular drug. Consequently, the authors feel that professional records regarding patients and clients should be maintained for an indefinite period of time, if space permits. Patient and client records may be cataloged and placed in storage boxes and sent to a local business records storage warehouse. Medical groups should not rely on local hospitals to retain records for them and should maintain independent records.

(2) Records Required by the Internal Revenue Service

Section 6001 of the Code requires every person liable for income tax or the collection thereof to keep such records as the Secretary of the Treasury may prescribe. Regulations §1.6001-1(a) requires that all persons subject to income tax or any person required to file an information return with respect to income must keep permanent books of account or records, including inventories, "as are sufficient to establish the amount of gross income, deductions, credits, or other matters required to be shown by such tax or information return." Regulations §1.6001-1(e) also requires that such records be maintained "so long as the contents thereof may become material in the administration of any Internal Revenue Law." Willful failure to keep the required records is a misdemeanor, punishable by not more than a $10,000 fine or a year imprisionment or both under Section 7203 of the Code.

Although, generally, the Service has three years after a return has been filed in which to assess the tax under Section 6501(a), there is also a six-year statute of limitations under Section 6501(e) if the taxpayer has made a substantial omission from the return. Further, under Section 6501(c)(1), (2) and (3), an assessment of tax may be made at any time if there is a false or fraudulent return with the intent to evade tax or if no return is filed. The statute of limitations may also be extended by agreement between the taxpayer and the Service.[22]

Because the Service has six years after assessment in which to collect the taxes under Section 6502(a) and the taxpayer has the right to file a claim for refund within two years from the time the tax is paid under Section 6511(a) of the Code, it is obvious that the records of a taxpayer may be "material in the administration" of the Internal Revenue Laws for quite some time. For example, it is theoretically possible that the Service could wait another six years from the date a return is filed to assess the tax due to the "substantial omission of items" and then wait another six years to collect the tax; and, two years after that date, the taxpayer could file a claim for refund. Without records, the taxpayer would, obviously, have a difficult time supporting his claim for a refund which would occur 14 years after the initial return was filed. This is, of course, an extreme example, but it demonstrates the need to retain records beyond the normal assessment period.

Regulations §31.6001-1(e)(2) provides that all persons required to retain records with respect to the withholding of income taxes for employees, Social Security tax, and federal unemployment tax must retain those records for at least four years after the due date of the return for which the records relate, or the date such tax is paid, whichever is later. Therefore, all such records on employees should be maintained for at least four years.

The authors recommend that conservative practice dictates that business records should be maintained for a period of 15 years.

(3) Records Required by State and Local Governments

Various states and municipalities have separate requirements relating to income tax, sales tax and unemployment insurance, which should be followed. The retention of such records should, however, correspond to the periods such records are maintained for federal tax purposes.

(4) Tax Returns

There are, generally, no provisions requiring the retention by an individual of his tax returns. Prudent practice would, however, dictate that such returns be maintained indefinitely.

(5) Checks

Checks relating to the professional practice are part of its business records and, under Paragraph (2) above should be maintained for at least 15 years.

EXHIBIT 1

MEMORANDUM

TO:

FROM: LAMON, ELROD & HARKLEROAD, P.C.

DATE:

RE: INTERNAL CORPORATE OBLIGATIONS

In connection with the incorporation of your [medical] practice, the following list represents changes which must be made at the time of or immediately following incorporation:

1. All stationery and bills should be revised to reflect the corporate name. The name of the professional corporation may be typed or stamped on existing

stationery and bills and they may be used in this manner until your existing supply is exhausted.

2. All business cards, the business sign on the corporation's offices, and any listing in the building directory should be changed to reflect the corporate name.

3. New bank accounts should be opened in the name of the corporation on the day of incorporation.

4. The listing in the telephone directory and all professional directories should be revised to reflect the corporate name. If it is not possible to accomplish this until the next edition of the directory is issued, this will be acceptable. All utility companies and suppliers should be notified of the date of incorporation and billing should be shifted to the corporation on that date. Utility company and supplier deposits should also be shifted to the name of the corporation.

5. All contractual arrangements relating to the [medical] practice should be assigned to and re-executed in the name of the corporation, including bank loans previously made to the professional practice that are transferred to the corporation. In the future, all loans for the professional practice should be made directly to and in the name of the corporation, even if the professionals must personally guarantee those loans. Further, all leases for office space and equipment and all contracts with institutions and agencies should now be in the name of the corporation.

6. Your malpractice insurance carrier and all other insurance carriers should be notified of the change, and policies should be reissued or endorsed in the name of the corporation. The personal policies of life insurance for directors and officers will remain in their own names at this time.

You should also contact your general insurance carrier regarding an "ERISA" bond if a qualified retirement plan is to be established. This is a simple fidelity bond for the fiduciaries of retirement plans and is generally obtainable for a minimum fee as a rider to your existing fidelity bond.

7. Notify all employees of incorporation.

8. Check with third-party reimbursing agencies (such as Blue Cross/Blue Shield) to determine if they will require any action on your part to shift payment for outstanding bills to the corporation.

9. The professional employees of the corporation will, now, be covered by workmen's compensation and you should advise the insurance agent handling your workmen's compensation insurance to shift the insurance to the corporation. Also, the workmen's compensation experience rating from the former professional practice should be transferred to the professional corporation.

10. If it is at all possible, you should instruct your receptionist to use the corporate name when answering the telephone.

11. We have filed a Form SS-4, application for employer identification number. When the number arrives several weeks from now, please advise us and your accountant. Have your accountant file for a state employer identification number, if necessary.

12. Arrange to have the benefits of the non-owner employees under the H.R. 10 plan paid to them so that the plan may be frozen.

13. Your accountant should arrange for the following:

   A. Filing state unemployment corporation reports.

   B. State sales tax forms, if necessary.

   C. Federal and state income tax withholding.

   D. Change to corporate books and records. The same ledger cards may be maintained on patients, but it is a good idea to red-line the cards or otherwise indicate when the corporation took over. New general ledger accounts should also be commenced.

   E. Prepare a detailed list of receivables to be transferred to the corporation.

   F. File final tax returns for the predecessor practice, including sales, FICA, FUTA, state unemployment taxes, income tax withholding, and workmen's compensation.

14. Change occupational licenses, if required.

15. Arrange for some means of notifying patients of incorporation, such as announcements or a small sign placed in the office. If patients fill out a data sheet on their first visit, we suggest that the data sheet form be revised to indicate that the medical practice is a professional corporation.

16. All employees should fill out a new Form W-4 authorizing federal income tax withholding.

17. Obtain new sales tax number and other special numbers or licenses.

The above changes should be accomplished as soon as possible after incorporation. It may take several weeks to accomplish some of these changes and that is perfectly acceptable as long as the corporation is making a good faith effort to do so.

EXHIBIT 2

PROFESSIONAL CORPORATION SUPPLEMENT TO THE MODEL BUSINESS CORPORATION ACT*

TABLE OF CONTENTS

*©Professional Practice Guide, Englewood Cliffs, N.J., Prentice-Hall, Inc., 1978.

CROSS-REFERENCE TABLE

Model Professional Corporation Act	Related Sections of Model Business Corporation Act
Section 1	Section 1
Section 2	Section 2
Section 3	Section 3
Section 4	None
Section 5	Section 4
Section 6	None
Section 7	Section 6
Section 8	Section 8, 108
Section 9	Section 15, 20, 23, 24
Section 10	Section 81
Section 11	Section 25
Section 12	None
Section 13	Section 33, 34
Section 14	Section 35, 50
Section 15	Section 59, 61
Section 16	Section 71, 72, 77
Section 17	None
Section 18	Section 94, 95
Section 19	Section 106

_____*_____ PROFESSIONAL CORPORATION ACT

SECTION 1. SHORT TITLE

This Act shall be known and may be cited as the "_____ Professional Corporation Act."

Comment

This model professional corporation act is designed as a supplement to the Model Business Corporation Act. Section 27 provides that the state's business corporation act shall apply to professional corporations except to the extent its provisions are inconsistent with the supplemental act. Accordingly, the supplement must be read in conjunction with the Model Business Corporation Act which it closely parallels in structure and semantics. With appropriate modifications, however, this model act may readily be adapted for use as a supplement to other business corporation acts.

SECTION 2. DEFINITIONS

As used in this Act, unless the context otherwise requires, the term:

(1) "Professional service" means any service which may lawfully be rendered only by persons licensed under the provisions of a licensing law of this State and may not lawfully be rendered by a corporation organized under the _____ Business Corporation Act.

(2) "Licensing authority" means the officer, board, agency, court or other authority in this State which has the power to issue a license or other legal authorization to render a professional service.

(3) "Professional corporation" or "domestic professional corporation" means a corporation for profit subject to the provisions of this Act, except a foreign professional corporation.

(4) "Foreign professional corporation" means a corporation for profit or-

_____

*Supply name of State as required throughout the act.

158

ganized for the purpose of rendering professional services under a law other than the law of this State.

(5) "Qualified person" means a natural person, general partnership, or professional corporation[a] which is eligible under this Act to own shares issued by a professional corporation.

(6) "Disqualified person" means any natural person, corporation, partnership, fiduciary, trust, association, government agency, or other entity which for any reason is or becomes ineligible under this Act to own shares issued by a professional corporation.

Comment

Paragraph (1). The definition of "professional service" limits and describes the purposes for which corporations may be organized under Section 3.

As a general proposition, corporations may not be formed under business corporation acts for the purpose of practicing a profession. In the absence of any statutory definition of the word "profession," the courts have held that, although a licensing requirement is characteristic of the professions, all licensed services are not necessarily professional services which may not be rendered by corporations. Accordingly, the determination as to whether particular licensed services may be rendered by corporations has been made on a case by case basis based upon construction of the state business corporation law or the applicable licensing law.[b]

Some of the existing state statutes under which professional persons are permitted to incorporate cover all licensed services. Statutes of this type are not restricted to persons who are prohibited from incorporating under the business corporation law. Other existing state statutes limit those who may incorporate to specific professions described in a single statute or in a series of similar statutes each applicable to one profession. The definition of "professional service" in paragraph (1) has the effect of restricting the use of the act to the practice of the professions. Rather than listing designated professions, however, the model act follows the precedent set by many existing state statutes of defining professional services as those licensed services which may not be rendered by a corporation organized under the business corporation law.

Paragraph (2). See Section 26 with respect to jurisdiction of the licensing authority over professional corporations.

Paragraphs (5) and (6). See comment following Section 9.

SECTION 3. PURPOSES

(a) Except as hereinafter provided in this section professional corporations may be organized under this Act only for the purpose of rendering professional services and services ancillary thereto within a single profession.

(b) A professional corporation may be incorporated for the purpose of rendering professional services within two or more professions and for any purpose or purposes for which corporations may be organized under the _____ Business Corporation Act to the extent that such combination of

---

[a] Delete "professional corporation" if alternate 2 or 3 of Section 11(d) is adopted.

[b] Model Bus. Corp. Act Ann. 2d, Sec. 3, Par. 4.01.

professional purposes or of professional and business purposes is permitted by the licensing laws of this State applicable to such professions and rules or regulations thereunder.

Comment

Apparently most state legislatures have felt that it was necessary to limit the purposes of a professional corporation to the practice of a single profession, and subsection (a) follows the large majority of existing state statutes in this respect. However, the ethical proscriptions of the various professions are not uniform in restricting the activities of a professional group to a single professional field. Some professional groups such as engineers and architects are permitted to carry on joint practice, and in other fields, such as the field of medicine and allied health professions, the extent to which professional practices may be combined is an evolving subject. Accordingly, subsection (b) shifts the responsibility for determining the extent to which two or more professions may combine and the extent to which a professional corporation may engage in business activities to the licensing statutes and regulations governing each profession where variations in public policy and ethical requirements of the various professions may be properly treated.

SECTION 4. PROHIBITED ACTIVITIES

A professional corporation shall not engage in any profession or business other than the profession or professions and businesses permitted by its articles of incorporation, except that a professional corporation may invest its funds in real estate, mortgages, stocks, bonds or any other type of investment.

Comment

Although not normally found in a business corporation law, an express statutory prohibition against ultra vires acts is fairly common in the existing state professional corporation laws. This prohibition provides a basis on which the licensing authority may initiate enforcement action pursuant to Section 18 to prevent a professional corporation from engaging in prohibited activities.

SECTION 5. GENERAL POWERS

A professional corporation shall have the powers enumerated in the _____ Business Corporation Act, except that a professional corporation may be a promoter, general partner, member, associate, or manager only of a partnership, joint venture, trust or other enterprise engaged only in rendering professional services or carrying on business permitted by the articles of incorporation of the corporation.

Comment

Under existing statutes professional corporations generally have all the powers of business corporations. The model act restricts only the power to participate in partnerships and similar enterprises engaged in activities not permitted to the professional corporation. Investment in limited partnerships as a limited partner would not be prohibited by the model act.

SECTION 6. RENDERING PROFESSIONAL SERVICES

A professional corporation, domestic or foreign, may render professional services in this State only through natural persons permitted to render such services in this State; but nothing in this Act shall be construed to require that any person who is employed by a professional corporation be licensed to perform services for which no license is otherwise required or to prohibit the rendering of professional services by a licensed natural person acting in his individual capacity, notwithstanding such person may be a shareholder, director, officer, employee or agent of a professional corporation, domestic or foreign.

Comment

A statement similar to the first clause of Section 6 to make it clear that unlicensed employees of professional corporations are not authorized to render professional services is included in the statutes of all states. The second clause which is also common in existing statutes is intended to insure that the use of para-professionals and other assistants customarily employed by professionals will not be inhibited by the first clause and also to recognize that a licensed employee of a professional corporation may render services in his individual capacity rather than as an employee of the corporation depending upon the circumstances of his employment. For example, an employee of a professional corporation may render professional services in his individual capacity in states in which the professional corporation may not be admitted as a foreign corporation.

SECTION 7. RIGHT OF CORPORATION TO ACQUIRE ITS OWN SHARES

A professional corporation may purchase its own shares from a disqualified person without regard to the availability of capital or surplus for such purchase; however, no purchase of or payment for its own shares shall be made at a time when the corporation is insolvent or when such purchase or payment would make it insolvent.

Comment

Nearly all professional corporation statutes require that shareholders be licensed professional persons, and to implement this requirement most statutes require that the corporation repurchase shares which have become the property of unlicensed persons through operation of law. The usual business corporation law restriction against impairment of capital by purchase of the corporation's own shares may conflict with this statutory requirement for the purchase of shares of a professional corporation. Section 7 of the model act resolves the conflict by removing the Model Business Corporation Act limitation on purchase of shares to the extent of available earned surplus or capital surplus while retaining the insolvency test of Section 6 of the Model Business Corporation Act. Section 10(a) of the professional corporation supplement requires the corporation to repurchase shares ''to the extent of funds which may be legally made available for such purchase.'' Thus the requirement of Section 10 that the professional corporation repurchase the shares of a disqualified person will be subject to the insolvency restriction against repurchase but will not be subject to the capital and surplus restriction.

SECTION 8. CORPORATE NAME

The name of a domestic professional corporation or of a foreign professional corporation authorized to transact business in this State:

(1) Shall contain the words ''professional corporation'' or the abbreviation ''P.C.'';

(2) Shall not contain any word or phrase which indicates or implies that it is organized for any purpose other than the purposes contained in its articles of incorporation;

(3) Shall not be the same as, or deceptively similar to, the name of any domestic corporation existing under the laws of this State or any foreign corporation authorized to transact business in this State, or a name the exclusive right to which is, at the time, reserved in the manner provided in the _____ Business Corporation Act, or the name of a corporation which has in effect a registration of its corporate name as provided in the _____ Business Corporation Act; except that this provision shall not apply if:

    (i) such similarity results from the use in the corporate name of personal names of its shareholders or former shareholders or of natural persons who were associated with a predecessor entity; or

    (ii) the applicant files with the Secretary of State either of the following: (A) the written consent of such other corporation or holder of a reserved or registered name to use the same or deceptively similar name and one or more words are added to make such name distinguishable from such other name, or (B) a certified copy of a final decree of a court of competent jurisdiction establishing the prior right of the applicant to the use of such name in this State; and

(4) shall otherwise conform to any rule promulgated by a licensing authority having jurisdiction of a professional service described in the articles of incorporation of such corporation.

Comment

Existing state statutes vary in the selection of terms required in the corporate name as corporate designators. To encourage uniformity and avoid confusion the model act approves and requires only the term ''professional corporation'' or its abbreviation. The Model Business Corporation Act corporate name provision is further modified in paragraph (3) (i) to permit similarity of names if the similarity results from the use of personal names of persons associated with the organization. Paragraph (4) authorizes the licensing authority to impose by rule additional requirements appropriate to a particular profession.

SECTION 9. ISSUANCE AND TRANSFER OF
SHARES; SHARE CERTIFICATES

(a) A professional corporation may issue shares, fractional shares, and rights or options to purchase shares only to:

(1) natural persons who are authorized by law in this State or in any other state or territory of the United States or the District of Columbia to render a professional service permitted by the articles of incorporation of the corporation;

(2) general partnerships in which all the partners are qualified persons with respect to such professional corporation and in which at least one partner is authorized by law in this State to render a professional service permitted by the articles of incorporation of the corporation; and

(3) professional corporations, domestic or foreign, authorized by law in this State to render a professional service permitted by the articles of incorporation of the corporation.[c]

(b) Where deemed necessary by the licensing authority for any profession in order to prevent violations of the ethical standards of such profession, the licensing authority may by rule further restrict, condition, or abridge the authority of professional corporations to issue shares but no such rule shall, of itself, have the effect of causing a shareholder of a professional corporations at the time such rule becomes effective to become a disqualified person. All shares issued in violation of this section or any rule hereunder shall be void.

(c) A shareholder of a professional corporation may transfer or pledge shares, fractional shares, and rights or options to purchase shares of the corporation only to natural persons, general partnerships and professional corporation[d] qualified hereunder to hold shares issued directly to them by such professional corporation. Any transfer of shares in violation of this provision shall be void; however, nothing herein contained shall prohibit the transfer of shares of a professional corporation by operation of law or court decree.

(d) Every certificate representing shares of a professional corporation shall state conspicuously upon face that the shares represented thereby are subject to restrictions on transfer imposed by this Act and are subject to such further restrictions on transfer as may be imposed by the licensing authority from time to time pursuant to this Act.

Comment

The model act departs from existing statutes in permitting shares of a professional corporation to be issued to persons licensed outside the state of incorporation and to partnerships and other professional corporations authorized to render a professional service permitted by the articles of incorporation of the corporation.

[c]Delete paragraph (3) of subsection (a) if alternate 2 or 3 of Section 11(d) is adopted.
[d]Delete "professional corporations" if alternate 2 or 3 of Section 11(d) is adopted.

Pennsylvania also permits a professional corporation to issue shares to persons licensed in another state, but existing statutes generally restrict shareholders to natural persons. If shareholders are not liable for debts of the corporation, however, there is no policy reason to prohibit the issuance of shares to another corporation which is subject to the same professional c orporation requirements, and under Section 9 of the model act professional corporations may be given the same flexibility in planning the corporate structure as business corporations. If shareholders are personally liable for the performance of professional services rendered on behalf of the corporation, however, as they may be under either alternate 2 or 3 of Section 11 (d), then the holding company device may be used to avoid personal liability, and accordingly, paragraph (3) of subsection (a) should be deleted if alternate 2 or 3 of Section 11 (d) is adopted.

Section 9 of the model act is applicable to all classes of shares issued by a professional corporation. No qualifications are imposed by the model act (or by existing state statutes) on holders of debt securities. It is unlikely that convertible debt will be issued by a professional corporation, since the corporation will not have the power to issue its shares upon conversion if the holder is not a qualified person at the time the shares are to be issued.

SECTION 10. DEATH OR DISQUALIFICATION OF A SHAREHOLDER

(a) Upon the death of a shareholder of a professional corporation or if a shareholder of a professional corporation becomes a disqualified person or if shares of a professional corporation are transferred by operation of law or court decree to a disqualified person, the shares of such deceased shareholder or of such disqualified person may be transferred to a qualified person and, if not so transferred, shall be purchased or redeemed by the corporation to the extent of funds which may be legally made available for such purchase.

(b) If the price for such shares is not fixed by the articles of incorporation or bylaws of the corporation or by private agreement, the corporation, within six months after such death or thirty days after such disqualification or transfer, as the case maybe, shall make a written offer to pay for such shares at a specified price deemed by such corporation to be the fair value thereof as of the date of such death, disqualification or transfer. Such offer shall be given to the executor or administrator of the estate of a deceased shareholder or to the disqualified shareholder or transferee and shall be accompanied by a balance sheet of the corporation, as of the latest available date and not more than twelve months prior to the making of such offer, and a profit and loss statement of such corporation for the twelve months' period ended on the date of such balance sheet.

(c) If within thirty days after the date of such written offer from the corporation the fair value of such shares is agreed upon between such disqualified person and the corporation, payment therefor shall be made within sixty days, or such other period as the parties may fix by agreement, after the date of such offer, upon surrender of the certificate or certificates representing such shares. Upon payment of the agreed value the disqualified persons shall cease to have any interest in such shares.

(d) If within such period of thirty days the disqualified person and the corporation do not so agree, then the corporation, within thirty days after receipt of written demand from the disqualified person given within sixty days after the date of the corporation's written offer shall, or at its election at any time within such period of sixty days may, file a petition in any court of competent jurisdiction in the county in this State where the registered office of the corporation is located requesting that the fair value of such shares be found and determined. If the corporation shall fail to institute the proceeding as herein provided, the disqualified person may do so within sixty days after delivery of such written demand to the corporation. The disqualified person, wherever residing, shall be made a party to the proceeding as an action against his shares quasi in rem. A copy of the petition shall be served on the disqualified person, if a resident of this State, and shall be served by registered or certified mail on the disqualified person, if a non-resident. Service on non-residents shall also be made by publication as provided by law. The jurisdiction of the court shall be plenary and exclusive. The disqualified person shall be entitled to judgment against the corporation for the amount of the fair value of his shares as of the date of death, disqualification or transfer upon surrender to the corporation of the certificate or certificates representing such shares. The court may, at its discretion, order that the judgment be paid in such installments as the court may determine. The court may, if it so elects, appoint one or more persons as appraisers to receive evidence and recommend a decision on the question of fair value. The appraisers shall have such power and authority as shall be specified in the order of their appointment or an amendment thereof.

(e) The judgment shall include an allowance for interest at such rate as the court may find to be fair and equitable in all the circumstances, from the date of death, disqualification or transfer.

(f) The cost and expenses of any such proceeding shall be determined by the court and shall be assessed against the corporation, but all or any part of such costs and expenses may be apportioned and assessed as the court may deem equitable against the disqualified person if the court shall find that the action of such disqualified person in failing to accept such offer was arbitrary or vexatious or not in good faith. Such expenses shall include reasonable compensation for and reasonable expenses of the appraisers, but shall exclude the fees and expenses of counsel for and experts employed by any party; but if the fair value of the shares as determined materially exceeds the amount which the corporation offered to pay therefor, or if no offer was made, the court in its discretion may award to the disqualified person such sum as the court may determine to be reasonable compensation to any expert or experts employed by the disqualified person in the proceeding.

(g) If a purchase, redemption, or transfer of the shares of a deceased or disqualified shareholder or of a transferee who is a disqualified person is not completed within ten months after the death of the deceased shareholder or five months after the disqualification or transfer, as the case may be, the corporation shall forthwith cancel the shares on its books and the disqualified person shall have no further interest as a shareholder in the corporation other than his right to payment for such shares under this section.

(h) Shares acquired by a corporation pursuant to payment of the agreed value therefor or to payment of the judgment entered therefor, as in this section provided, may be held and disposed of by such corporation as in the case of other treasury shares.

(i) This section shall not be deemed to require the purchase of shares of a disqualified person where the period of such disqualification is for less than five months from the date of disqualification or transfer.

(j) Any provision regarding purchase, redemption or transfer of shares of a professional corporation contained in the articles of incorporation, bylaws or any private agreement shall be specifically enforceable in the courts of this State.

(k) Nothing herein contained shall prevent or relieve a professional corporation from paying pension benefits or other deferred compensation for services rendered to or on behalf of a former shareholder as otherwise permitted by law.

Comment

Existing state statutes generally require that the shares of a deceased or disqualified shareholder be transferred to a qualified shareholder or purchased by the corporation within a specified period of time following the shareholder's death or disqualification. The model act requires payment of fair value for such shares if the corporation does not establish an alternative method, and the procedure for determining fair value set forth in subsections (b) through (f) parallels the procedure set forth in Section 81 of the Model Business Corporation Act with respect to the determination of rights of dissenting shareholders. Shares of a deceased or disqualified shareholder that have not been transferred or purchased within the time limits specified in subsection (g) are cancelled, and the shareholder's interest becomes a creditor's claim under this section.

One of the troublesome aspects of the requirement that a shareholder of a professional corporation be licensed to practice the profession is the disposition of the corporation entity of a deceased sole practitioner. Under Section 33 of the Model Business Corporation Act the executor of the estate of a sole practitioner may vote the decedent's shares in his professional corporation. See comment following Section 13. Accordingly, if the shares of a deceased shareholder are not transferred, the executor may vote the shares to dissolve the corporation or to amend the articles of incorporation to change its purposes to those of a business corporation. If the executor elects to dissolve, a licensed member of the profession must act as director and president during the winding up of the corporation's affairs. If the executor elects to amend the articles, he may do so himself by signing and filing articles of amendment pursuant to Section 15.

See comment following Section 7 concerning the effect of statutory restrictions against purchases by a corporation of its own shares resulting in impairment of capital or insolvency. To further reduce the possibility of conflict between the insolvency restriction of Section 7 and the requirement for purchase of shares under Section 10 in the event of a judicial determination of fair value, the court is expressly authorized in subsection (d) to order that the judgment be paid in installments.

SECTION 11. RESPONSIBILITY FOR PROFESSIONAL SERVICES

(a) Any reference to a corporation in this section shall include both domestic and foreign corporations.

(b) Every individual who renders professional services as an employee of a professional corporation shall be liable for any negligent or wrongful act or omission in which he personally participates to the same extent as if he rendered such services as a sole practitioner. An employee of a professional corporation shall not be liable for the conduct of other employees unless he is at fault in appointing, supervising, or cooperating with them.

(c) Every corporation whose employees perform professional services within the scope of their employment or of their apparent authority to act for the corporation shall be liable to the same extent as its employees.

(d) (Alternate 1) Except as otherwise provided by statute, the personal liability of a shareholder of a professional corporation shall be no greater in any respect than that of a shareholder of a corporation organized under the _____ Business Corporation Act.

(e) (Alternate 2) Except as otherwise provided by statute, if any corporation is liable under the provisions of subsection (c) of this section, every shareholder of the corporation shall be liable to the same extent as though he were a partner in a partnership and the services giving rise to liability had been rendered on behalf of the partnership.

(f) (Alternate 3) (1) Except as otherwise provided by statute, if any corporation is liable under the provisions of subsection (c) of this section, every shareholder of that corporation shall be liable to the same extent as though he were a partner in a partnership and the services giving rise to liability had been rendered on behalf of the partnership, unless the corporation has provided security for professional responsibility as provided in paragraph (2) of this subsection and the liability is satisfied to the extent contemplated by the insurance or bond which effectuates the security.

(2) A professional corporation, domestic or foreign, may provide security for professional responsibility by procuring insurance or a surety bond issued by an insurance company, or a combination thereof, as the corporation may elect. The minimum amount of security and requirements as to the form and coverage provided by the insurance policy or surety bond may be established for each profession by the licensing authority for the profession, and the minimum amount may be set to vary with the number of shareholders, the type of practice, or other variables deemed appropriate by the licensing authority. If no effective determination by the licensing authority is in effect, the minimum amount of professional responsibility security for the professional corporation shall be the product of ____*____ dollars multiplied by the number of shareholders of the professional corporation.

---

*A minimum amount to be determined by the state legislature.

Comment

Although all existing state statutes include some provision concerning professional liability or professional responsibility, most statutes are silent as to the vicarious liability of shareholders, leaving this question to be determined by the business corporation law. Several statutes clearly provide that shareholder liability is limited as in a business corporation. A few expressly state that shareholders shall be jointly and severally liable for debts of the corporation. And a few, either by statute or rule of practice, condition limited liability for some professions on maintenance of professional liability insurance. A majority of the statutes contain simply a provision to the effect that the statute does not modify any law applicable to the relationship between a person furnishing professional services and a person receiving such services including liability arising out of such professional services. Although one commentator has suggested that this statutory provision preserves the mutual agency and unlimited liability of partnerships,[e] Federal district courts in Ohio and Florida have held, in the context of cases involving the status of a professional corporation for Federal income tax purposes, that shareholders have limited liability under statutes of this type.[f] Accordingly, it seems that shareholders of professional corporations have limited liability under existing statutes in most states.

Section 11 of the model act states affirmatively the rules for liability of the professional corporation, its employees, and its shareholders resulting from negligence in the performance of professional services. Consistent with the common law doctrine of respondeat superior, subsection (b) limits liability of a professional employee to his personal negligence, and subsection (c) imposes liability on the corporation for conduct of professional employees within the scope of their employment or of their apparent authority.

Three alternative provisions as to liability of shareholders are proposed in subsection (d): limited liability as in a business corporation, vicarious personal liability as in a partnership, and personal liability limited in amount conditioned upon financial responsibility in the form of insurance or a surety bond. Alternate 3 would permit the licensing authority for each profession to establish the minimum amount of security required as a condition for limiting liability of shareholders and to impose requirements as to the coverage provided by the policy or bond representing the security. The minimum amount of security designated in alternate 3 would apply to any profession only if no minimum has been fixed by the licensing authority for the profession, but no attempt is made in the model act to specify minimum coverage requirements. Each alternate recognizes by the introductory phrase, "Except as otherwise provided by statute," that more specific rules as to shareholder liability may be enacted with respect to a particular profession or professions, but the formulation of statutory requirements as to either the minimum amount of security or coverage for particular professions is beyond the scope of this model act.

---

[e] Bittker, *Professional Associations and Federal Income Taxation: Some Comments and Questions*, 17 TAX LAW REVIEW 1.

[f] O'Neill v. United States, 281 F. Supp. 359; Kurzner v. United States, 286 F. Supp. 839.

Limited liability of shareholders has historically been considered by the courts and by the Internal Revenue Service as one of several characteristics that distinguish the corporation from the partnership. It should be noted, therefore, that the choice of alternates in subsection (d) may affect the tax status of professional corporations formed pursuant to the act.

SECTION 12. PROFESSIONAL RELATIONSHIPS PRIVILEGED COMMUNICATIONS

(a) The relationship between an individual performing professional services as employee of a professional corporation, domestic or foreign, and a client or patient shall be the same as if the individual performed such services as a sole practitioner.

(b) The relationship between a professional corporation, domestic or foreign, performing professional services and the client or patient shall be the same as between the client or patient and the individual performing the services.

(c) Any privilege applicable to communications between a person rendering professional services and the person receiving such services recognized under the laws of this State, whether statutory or deriving from common law, shall remain inviolate and shall extend to a professional corporation, domestic or foreign, and its employees in all cases in which it shall be applicable to communications between a natural person rendering professional services on behalf of the corporation and the person receiving such services.

Comment

Many existing state statutes contain provisions similar to Section 12 which makes it clear that any relationship of confidence that exists between a professional person and his client or patient is preserved and extends to the professional corporation and also that any privilege applicable to communications with a professional person is preserved and extends to the professional corporation.

SECTION 13. VOTING OF SHARES

No proxy for shares of a professional corporation shall be valid unless it shall be given to a qualified person. A voting trust with respect to shares of a professional corporation shall not be valid [unless all the trustees and beneficiaries thereof are qualified persons, except that a voting trust may be validly continued for a period of ten months after the death of a deceased beneficiary or for a period of five months after a beneficiary has become a disqualified person].[g]

Comment

Section 13 of the model act requires that the holder of a proxy and the parties to a voting trust agreement be qualified to own shares in the corporation. If shareholders may be personally liable for the performance of professional services rendered on behalf of the corporation, voting trusts should be prohibited to prevent their use to avoid personal liability. See comment following Section 9. With regard

---

[g] Delete the bracketed clause if alternate 2 or 3 of Section 11(d) is adopted.

to other types of agreements regarding voting of shares. Section 34 of the Model Business Corporation Act providing that agreements among shareholders regarding voting shall be valid and enforceable is unchanged by the professional corporation supplement.

Pursuant to Section 33 of the Model Business Corporation Act the shares of a professional corporation held by an administrator, executor, guardian or conservator may be voted without a transfer of such shares, and shares held by a receiver may be voted by the receiver without transfer if such authority is contained in the order of a court by which the receiver was appointed. Upon the death or insolvency of a major shareholder, it may be necessary to dissolve the corporation or amend its articles by changing its purposes to those of a business corporation. The interest of the shareholder's estate will be protected by permitting the holder of his shares to vote on such proposals. In view of the requirement of Section 14 that one-half the directors and the principal officers of a corporation be qualified shareholders, there is no significant risk that an unqualified person may exercise control over the professional practice of the corporation during the period that shares of the corporation may be owned by the estate or receiver of a shareholder under Section 10. Accordingly, the model act does not modify the provisions of the Model Business Corporation Act regarding voting by administrators and receivers.

SECTION 14. DIRECTORS AND OFFICERS

Not less that one-half the directors of a professional corporation and all the officers other than the secretary and the treasurer shall be qualified persons with respect to the corporation.

Comment

Section 14 requires that not less than one-half the directors and the officers other than the secretary and treasurer of a professional corporation be licensed professionals. The professional corporation statutes of many states require that all directors be licensed while others require less than all. Most existing statutes also prohibit unlicensed persons from serving as officers with variations as to whether all or only certain designated offices are subject to the requirement.

SECTION 15. AMENDMENTS TO ARTICLES
OF INCORPORATION

An administrator, executor, guardian, conservator, or receiver of the estate of a shareholder of a professional corporation who holds all of the outstanding shares of the corporation may amend the articles of incorporation by signing a written consent to such amendment. Articles of amendment so adopted shall be executed in duplicate by the corporation by such administrator, executor, guardian, conservator, or receiver and by the secretary or assistant secretary of the corporation and verified by one of the persons signing such articles, and shall set forth:

(1) the name of the corporation;

(2) the amendments so adopted;

(3) the date of adoption of the amendment by the administrator, executor, guardian, conservator, or receiver;

(4) the number of shares outstanding; and

(5) the number of shares held by the administrator, executor, guardian, conservator, or receiver.

Comment

Section 15 enables the professional corporation of the sole practitioner to continue in existence following the death of its shareholders and simplifies the procedure for amendment of articles set forth in the Model Business Corporation Act. Without some modification of the Model Business Corporation Act procedure, the executor of the deceased shareholder's estate would be required to find another member of the profession to serve as director and president for the purpose of adopting and filing articles of amendment.

SECTION 16. MERGER AND CONSOLIDATION

(a) A professional corporation may merge or consolidate with another corporation, domestic or foreign, only if every shareholder of each corporation is qualified to be a shareholder of the surviving or new corporation.

(b) Upon the merger or consolidation of a professional corporation, if the surviving or new corporation, as the case may be, is to render professional services in this state, it shall comply with the provisions of this Act.

Comment

Section 16 permits mergers and consolidations among professional corporations and business corporations to the extent that professional and business purposes may be combined under Section 3. Many existing professional corporation statutes limit mergers and consolidations to domestic professional corporations incorporated for the purpose of rendering the same professional service. Such a limitation would be inconsistent with Section 3 of this Act permitting a broader statement of purposes and Section 19 providing for admission of foreign professional corporations.

SECTION 17. TERMINATION OF PROFESSIONAL ACTIVITIES

If a professional corporation shall cease to render professional services, it shall amend its articles of incorporation to delete from its stated purposes the rendering of professional services and to conform to the requirements of the _____ Business Corporation Act regarding its corporate name. The corporation may then continue in existence as a corporation under the _____ Business Corporation Act and shall no longer be subject to the provisions of this Act.

Comment

Section 17 resolves any question as to the power of a professional corporation to continue in existence under the business corporation act after it has ceased to render professional services and avoids the forced dissolution of a corporation whose shareholders have died or become disqualified. See Comment following

Section 10. A corporation which has ceased to render professional services and does not dissolve is required to amend it articles to comply with the business corporation law.

SECTION 18. INVOLUNTARY DISSOLUTION

A professional corporation may be dissolved involuntarily by a decree of the _____ Court in an action filed by the Attorney General when it is established that the corporation has failed to comply with any provision of this Act applicable to it within sixty days after receipt of written notice of noncompliance. Each licensing authority in this State and the Secretary of State shall certify to the Attorney General, from time to time, the names of all corporations which have given cause for dissolution as provided in this Act, together with the facts pertinent thereto. Whenever the Secretary of State or any licensing authority shall certify the name of a corporation to the Attorney General as having given any cause for dissolution, the Secretary of State or such licensing authority, as the case may be, shall concurrently mail to the corporation at its registered office a notice that such certification has been made. Upon the receipt of such certification, the Attorney General shall file an action in the name of the State against such corporation for its dissolution.

Comment

The Attorney General is authorized to enforce the requirements of the professional corporation act by bringing an action for involuntary dissolution on the grounds of failure of the corporation to comply with any provision of the act. Either the licensing authority or the Secretary of State may initiate such proceedings by certifying the grounds for dissolution to the Attorney General. See Section 24.

SECTION 19. ADMISSION OF FOREIGN PROFESSIONAL CORPORATIONS

(a) A foreign professional corporation shall be entitled to procure a certificate of authority to transact business in this State only if:

(1) the name of the corporation meets the requirements of this Act;
(2) the corporation is organized only for purposes for which a professional corporation organized under this Act may be organized; and
(3) all the shareholders, not less than one-half the directors, and all the officers other than the secretary and treasurer of the corporation are qualified persons with respect to the corporation.

(b) No foreign professional corporation shall be required to obtain a certificate of authority to transact business in this State unless it shall maintain an office in this State for the conduct of business or professional practice.

Comment

Many small as well as large professional practices are conducted in more than one state by individuals licensed to practice in more than one state or by partnerships whose members are licensed to practice in various states. A serious defect in

172

many existing state statutes is the absence of any provision concerning foreign professional corporations, although several statutes do specifically provide for admission of foreign professional corporations.

Under the foreign corporation provisions of state business corporation laws, foreign corporations are generally admitted with few if any restrictions other than restrictions as to the use of corporate names. In order to prevent a professional corporation from avoiding the professional corporation laws of the state in which it carries on its practice by incorporating in a state with more lenient professional corporation requirements, Section 19 requires that foreign corporations comply with the domestic state law requirements concerning corporate purposes and qualification of shareholders, directors and officers. Under Section 6 a foreign corporation may render professional services only through persons permitted to render such services in the state. Section 11 concerning responsibility for professional services and security for professional responsibility is applicable to foreign corporations as well as domestic corporations; and foreign corporations are subject to regulation by the licensing authority to the same extent as domestic corporations under Section 26.

Section 19(b) requires that a professional corporation obtain a certificate of authority only if the corporation maintains an office in the state. This provision would permit foreign professional corporations greater freedom in rendering professional services in the state without complying with foreign corporation law requirements than is permitted in the case of business corporations.

SECTION 20. APPLICATION FOR CERTIFICATE
OF AUTHORITY

The application of a foreign professional corporation for a certificate of authority for the purpose of rendering professional services shall include a statement that all the shareholders, not less than one-half the directors, and all the officers other than the secretary and treasurer are licensed in one or more states or territories of the United States or the District of Columbia to render a professional service described in the statement of purposes of the corporation.

Comment

The requirements of the Model Business Corporation Act regarding the application by a foreign corporation for a certificate of authority are modified to be consistent with the additional requirements for admission under Section 19.

SECTION 21. REVOCATION OF CERTIFICATE
OF AUTHORITY

The certificate of authority of a foreign professional corporation may be revoked by the Secretary of State if the corporation fails to comply with any provision of this Act applicable to it. Each licensing authority in this State shall certify to the Secretary of State, from time to time, the names of all foreign professional corporations which have given cause for revocation as provided in this Act, together with the facts pertinent thereto. Whenever a licensing authority shall certify the name of a corporation to the Secretary of State as having given cause for dissolution, the licensing authority shall concurrently mail to the corporation at its registered office in this State a notice that such certification has been made. No certificate of authority of a foreign professional corporation shall be revoked by the Secretary of State unless he shall have given the corporation not less than sixty days' notice thereof and the corporation shall fail prior to revocation to correct such noncompliance.

Comment

The Model Business Corporation Act procedures for revocation of the certificate of authority of a foreign professional corporation are modified to permit the Secretary of State to revoke the certificate of authority of a foreign corporation for failure to comply with applicable requirements of the professional corporation act and to authorize the licensing authority to certify to the Secretary of State grounds for revocation of the certificate of authority of a foreign professional corporation.

SECTION 22. ANNUAL REPORT OF DOMESTIC AND FOREIGN PROFESSIONAL CORPORATIONS

(a) The annual report of each domestic professional corporation, and each foreign professional corporation authorized to transact business in this State, filed with the Secretary of State pursuant to the _____ Business Corporation Act shall include a statement that all the shareholders, not less than one-half the directors, and all the officers other than the secretary and treasurer of the corporation are qualified persons with respect to the corporation.

(b) Financial information contained in the annual report of a professional corporation, other than the amount of state capital of the corporation, shall not be open to public inspection nor shall the licensing authority disclose any facts or information obtained therefrom except insofar as its official duty may require the same to be made public or in the event such information is required for evidence in any criminal proceedings or in any other action by this State.

Comment

The Model Business Corporation Act requirements for filing an annual report with the Secretary of State are modified to include a statement showing compliance with the requirement of Section 19 as to qualification of shareholders, directors and officers and to provide that financial information shall be confidential.

SECTION 23. ANNUAL STATEMENT OF QUALIFICATIONS OF DOMESTIC AND FOREIGN PROFESSIONAL CORPORATIONS

(a) Each domestic professional corporation, and each foreign professional corporation, authorized to transact business in this State, shall file annually before March 1 with each licensing authority having jurisdiction over a professional service of a type described in its articles of incorporation a statement of qualification setting forth the names and respective addresses of the directors and officers of the corporation and such additional information as the licensing authority may by rule prescribe as appropriate in determining whether such corporation is complying with the provisions of this Act and rules promulgated hereunder.

(b) The licensing authority shall charge and collect a fee of _____ dollars for filing a statement of qualification pursuant to this Act.

Comment

Many existing professional corporation statutes require the filing of an annual report with the Secretary of State or licensing authority setting forth the names and addresses of all shareholders of the corporation. The model act requires that a professional corporation file an annual statement with the licensing authority setting forth the names and addresses of directors and officers and authorizes the licensing authority to require additional information which might include names and addresses of shareholders.

SECTION 24. INTERROGATORIES BY LICENSING AUTHORITY

(a) Each licensing authority of this State may propound to any professional corporation, domestic or foreign, organized to practice a profession within the jurisdiction of such licensing authority, and to any officer or director thereof, such interrogatories as may be reasonably necessary and proper to enable the licensing authority to ascertain whether such corporation has complied with all the provisions of this Act applicable to such corporation. Such interrogatories shall be answered within thirty days after the mailing thereof, or within such additional time as shall be fixed by the licensing authority, and the answers thereto shall be full and complete and shall be made in writing and under oath. If such interrogatories be directed to an individual they shall be answered by him, and if directed to a corporation they shall be answered by the president, vice president, secretary or assistant secretary thereof. The licensing authority shall certify to the Attorney General, for such action as the Attorney General may deem appropriate, all interrogatories and answers thereto which disclose a violation of any of the provisions of this Act.

(b) Interrogatories propounded by a licensing authority and the answers thereto shall not be open to public inspection nor shall the licensing authority disclose any facts or information obtained therefrom except insofar as its official duty may require the same to be made public or in the event such interrogatories or the answers thereto are required for evidence in any criminal proceedings or in any other action by this State.

Comment

Section 24 establishes a procedure for enforcement by the licensing authority similar to the procedure set forth in Section 137 of the Model Business Corporation Act for enforcement by the Secretary of State but provides that the answers to interrogatories propounded by a licensing authority shall be confidential. See comment following Section 18.

SECTION 25. PENALTIES

(a) Each professional corporation, domestic or foreign, that fails or refuses to answer truthfully within the time prescribed by this Act interrogatories propounded in accordance with the provisions of this Act by the licensing authority

175

having jurisdiction of a type of professional service described in the articles of incorporation of such corporation, shall be deemed to be guilty of a misdemeanor and upon conviction thereof may be fined in any amount not exceeding five hundred dollars.

(b) Each officer and director of a professional corporation, domestic or foreign, who fails or refuses within the time prescribed by this Act to answer truthfully and fully interrogatories propounded to him in accordance with the provisions of this Act by the licensing authority having jurisdication of a type of professional service described in the articles of incorporation of such corporation, or who signs any articles, statement, report, application or other document filed with such licensing authority which is known to such officer or director to be false in any material respect, shall be deemed to be guilty of a misdemeanor, and upon conviction thereof may be fined in any amount not exceeding _____ dollars.

Comment

Section 25 imposes penalties for failure to answer interrogatories propounded by the licensing authority which are the same as the penalties imposed by Sections 135 and 136 of the Model Business Corporation Act for failure to answer interrogatories propounded by the Secretary of State.

SECTION 26. REGULATION OF PROFESSIONAL CORPORATIONS

No professional corporation, domestic or foreign, shall begin to render professional services in this State until it has filed a copy of its articles of incorporation with each licensing authority having jurisdiction of a type of professional service described in its articles of incorporation. Each licensing authority in this State is hereby authorized to promulgate rules in accordance with the provisions of this Act which specifically provide for the issuance of rules to the extent consistent with the public interest or required by the public health or welfare or by generally recognized standards of professional conduct. Nothing in this Act shall restrict or limit in any manner the authority or duty of a licensing authority with respect to natural persons rendering a professional service within the jurisdiction of the licensing authority, or any law, rule or regulation pertaining to standards of professional conduct.

Comment

Section 26 requires that a professional corporation register with the appropriate licensing authority by filing a copy of its articles of incorporation with the licensing authority and authorizes the licensing authority to promulgate rules pursuant to the act. Similar provisions appear in a number of existing statues, and the further statement reaffirming the authority of the licensing authority with respect to licensed professionals is common to many statutes.

SECTION 27. APPLICATION OF BUSINESS CORPORATION ACT

The provisions of the _____ Business Corporation Act shall apply to professional corporations, domestic and foreign, except to the extent such provisions are inconsistent with the provisions of this Act.

Comment

See comment following Section 1.

SECTION 28. APPLICATION TO EXISTING CORPORATIONS

(a) The provisions of this Act shall apply to all existing corporations organized under any general act of this State which is repealed by this Act. Every such existing corporation which shall be required to amend its corporate name or purposes to comply with this Act shall deliver duly executed duplicate originals of articles of amendment or restated articles of incorporation containing such amendments to the Secretary of State within ninety days after the effective date of this Act.

(b) Any corporation organized under any act of this State which is not repealed hereby may become subject to the provisions of this Act by delivering to the Secretary of State duly executed duplicate originals of articles of amendment or restated articles of incorporation stating that the corporation elects to become subject to this Act and containing such amendment of its corporate name or purposes as may be required to comply with this Act.

(c) The provisions of this Act shall not apply to any corporation now in existence or hereafter organized under any act of this State which is not repealed hereby unless such corporation voluntarily becomes subject to this Act as herein provided, and nothing contained in this Act shall alter or affect any existing or future right or privilege permitting or not prohibiting performance of professional services through the use of any other form of business organization.

Comment

While most states have adopted a single general professional corporation law applicable to all covered professions, several states have adopted a series of professional corporation laws applicable to individual professions. Section 28 of the model act sets forth procedures with respect to existing corporations which include mandatory provisions applicable to corporations incorporated under a repealed act and also provisions for voluntary compliance with this act by corporations organized under acts which may not be repealed.

SECTION 29. RESERVATION OF POWER

The ___*___ shall at all times have power to prescribe such regulations, provisions and limitations as it may deem advisable, which regulations, provisions and limitations shall be binding upon any and all corporations subject to the provisions of this Act, and the _____ shall have power to amend, repeal or modify this Act at pleasure.

Comment

See Model Business Corporation Act Section 149.

SECTION 30. EFFECT OF REPEAL OF PRIOR ACTS

The repeal of a prior act by this Act shall not affect any right accrued or

---

*Insert name of legislative body.

established, or any liability or penalty incurred, under the provisions of such act, prior to the repeal thereof.

Comment

See Model Business Corporation Act Section 150.

SECTION 31. EFFECT OF INVALIDITY OF PART OF THIS ACT

If a court of competent jurisdiction shall adjudge to be invalid or unconstitutional any clause, sentence, paragraph, section or part of this Act, such judgment or decree shall not affect, impair, invalidate or nullify the remainder of this Act, but the effect thereof shall be confined to the clause, sentence, paragraph, section or part of this Act so adjudged to be invalid or unconstitutional.

Comment

See Model Business Corporation Act Section 151.

SECTION 32. REPEAL OF PRIOR ACTS

(Insert appropriate provisions)

* * * * *

Blue Sky Law Exemption

In most states the interest of a partner in a professional partnership is exempted by definition or otherwise from the application of the state securities law. A few states have exempted shares of a professional corporation, but many states have ignored this problem in enacting professional corporation laws. Because the ''one subject'' requirement of state constitutions may prohibit amendment of the state securities law in a professional corporation act, the model act does not create a securities law exemption for shares of professional corporations. It is recommended, however, that shares of professional corporations be exempted from the state securities law by appropriate amendment of that law.

Comment on the foregoing proposed Professional Corporation Supplement and Comments is invited and should be forwarded prior to March 15, 1977 to John P. Austin, 2700 Crocker Plaza, San Francisco, California 94104.

John P. Austin, Chairman
Committee on Corporate Laws

August 16, 1976
San Francisco, California

EXHIBIT 3

MINUTES OF A JOINT ANNUAL MEETING
OF THE SHAREHOLDERS AND
DIRECTORS OF XYZ, P.C.

A joint meeting of the Shareholders and Directors of XYZ,P.C. for the fiscal year ended September 30, 1978, was held at the offices of the Professional

Corporation in _____

on _____, at _____ p.m. All the Shareholders and all of the Directors of the Corporation were present at the meeting. Also present at the meeting at the invitation of the Directors and Shareholders were _____. Dr. _____ acted as the Chairman of the meeting and Mr. _____ acted as the Secretary. Dr. _____ noted that a quorum was present and opened the meeting for the business.

The first item of business to come before the meeting was the presentation of a tentative financial report for the fiscal year ending September 30, 1978, by Mr. _____. He stated that he anticipated that the Corporation would have an excellent year and that there should be sufficient funds remaining at the end of the year to permit the maximum contribution to the Corporation's Profit Sharing Plan. Mr. _____ stated that the excellent year which the Corporation had was due primarily to the hard work and diligence of the professional employees of the Corporation and, upon motion duly made and seconded, it was unanimously:

RESOLVED, that due to the hard work and diligence of Dr. _____ during the fiscal year ended September 30, 1978, the Board of Directors does hereby grant to him a bonus of $7,500 for such year and, further, does hereby direct the proper officers of the Corporation to set this amount up on the books of the Corporation as a liability and to pay such amount to Dr. _____ no later than two and one-half months after the close of the Corporation's year end; and

FURTHER RESOLVED, that due to the hard work and diligence of Dr. _____ his salary for the fiscal year beginning October 1, 1978, shall be increased to $135,000.

The Board of Directors also instructed the appropriate officers of the Corporation to execute an amendment to Dr. _____'s Employment Agreement to reflect this increase in salary.

Mr. _____ then stated that it was necessary to figure the contributions to the Corporation's qualified retirement plans. He stated that from the books of the Corporation it was evident that the Corporation had already satisfied its liability to the Pension Plan but that the contribution to the Profit Sharing Plan still remained. After examining the books, Mr. _____ stated that there would be sufficient funds available to pay the maximum contribution to the Profit Sharing Plan for this year and, upon motion duly made and seconded, it was unanimously:

RESOLVED, that the Board of Directors of XYZ, P.C. does hereby direct the appropriate officers of the Corporation to make the maximum contributions to the Profit Sharing Plan permitted under the Plan ($20,642.80), and it is further directed that this contribution shall be accrued on the books of the Corporation as a liability for the year ended September 30, 1978, and shall be paid on account thereof, and it is further directed that the foregoing contribution to the Profit Sharing Plan shall be paid on or before the due date for filing the Corporation's federal income tax return (plus extensions thereof), and it is further directed that the establishment of this contribution shall be communicated to the participants in the Plan.

Dr. _____ then made a report regarding office operations and stated that everything was running smoothly but that his nurse, _____, had recently left the employ of the Corporation.

The next item of business to come before the meeting was the reading and approval of the Minutes of the prior meeting of the Board of Directors and Shareholders held on September 15, 1977. These minutes were then presented to the Board and to the Shareholders by Mr. _____ and, upon motion duly made and seconded, it was unanimously:

RESOLVED, that the Minutes of the joint meeting of the Board of Direct ors and of the Shareholders of the Corporation held on September 15, 1977, be and they hereby are, approved as read and the secretary of the meeting is instructed to place them in the Corporation's Minute Book.

A discussion then ensued with regard to the actions of the officers and directors of the Corporation for the preceding year and, upon motion duly made and seconded, it was unanimously:

RESOLVED, that all purchases, contracts, contributions, compensations, acts, proceedings, elections, and appointments by the officers and directors of the Corporation since the Corporation's last annual meeting held on September 15, 1977, be, and they hereby are, approved and ratified.

Dr. _____ then moved that the meeting proceed with the election of officers for the ensuing year. The motion was duly seconded and carried. The names of the following individuals were placed in nomination for the offices set opposite their names:

_____	President and Treasurer
_____	Vice President
_____	Secretary

A ballot was then taken and Dr. _____ announced that as a result of the vote, each of the above-named candidates had been duly elected to his respective office for the ensuing year.

Mr. _____ then stated that the next item of business was the election of directors of the Corporation for the ensuing year and, upon motion duly made and seconded, it was unanimously:

RESOLVED, that the present sole director of the Corporation, Dr. _____, shall be elected to serve as the sole director of the Corporation for the fiscal year beginning October 1, 1978, and Dr. _____ shall serve in such capacity until a successor shall be duly elected and shall qualify.

The next order of business to come before the meeting concerned the declaration of a dividend on the common stock of the Corporation. Mr. _____ stated that he felt that, because the Corporation would have a tax profit for this year, the Corporation could continue its policy of paying a dividend of ten cents per share to holders of the Corporation's common stock. Then, upon motion duly made and seconded, it was unanimously:

> RESOLVED, that a dividend of ten cents per share be paid on the outstanding common stock of the Corporation to Shareholders of record as of September 30, 1978, with payment to be made no later than December 31, 1978.

There being no further business to come before the meeting, the meeting was, upon motion duly made, seconded, and unanimously adopted, adjourned.

Respectfully submitted by the Secretary of the meeting and approved by the Chairman of the meeting this _____ day of _____, 1978.

_____
Secretary of the Meeting

_____
Chairman of the Meeting

EXHIBIT 4

ANNUAL MEETING CHECKLIST

NAME OF CORPORATION: _____

DIRECTORS' MEETING

PERSONS PRESENT: _____
_____
_____
_____
_____
_____
_____

CHAIRMAN: _____
SECRETARY: _____
QUORUM: _____
DATE & TIME: _____
LOCATION: _____
FISCAL YEAR ENDED: _____

REPORT ON OPERATIONS:

    (A) Accountant's Report on Financial Position

        Gross Revenues Current Year:
        Gross Revenues Previous Year:
        Profit/Loss Current Year:

Profit/Loss Previous Year:
Cash Position Current Year:
Cash Position Previous Year:
A/R Current Year:
A/R Previous Year:

Attach balance sheet and income statement to minutes as exhibit.

(B) Review Overhead Expenses

(C) Review Total Annual Compensation to Shareholder Employees

(D) Review Dividends, _____ Per Share Payable _____ to Shareholders of Record as of _____ .

Reason for failing to declare or reducing dividends: _____

_____

(E) Personal Holding Company or Accumulated Earnings Tax Problems?

(F) Review of Capital Expenditures (those made during year and anticipated during next year): _____

_____

_____

_____

_____

(G) Loans:

From Banks and Financial Institutions: Review
Payment To Employees: Appropriate Board Action
and Documentation?

(H) Reimbursable Employee Expenses:

Approval by Board: _____
Substantiation Sufficient: _____

(I) Automobile:

Review Potential Personal Use

(J) Audits:

Have Corporation or Shareholders Received IRS Audit Notice? _____

(K) Fees:
Should Fees be Increased?
Consider Possible Imposition of Wage and Price Controls.

ELECTIONS:

(A) Election of Officers: Compensation

		Current	New	Bonus
President:	_____	_____	_____	_____
V.P.'s:	_____	_____	_____	_____
	_____	_____	_____	_____

Secretary: _____   _____ _____ _____
Treasurer: _____   _____ _____ _____

Review Possible Use of Incentive Compensation and Possible Wage and Price
Controls: _____

Compensation for Non-Officer Employees:

NAME	CURRENT	NEW	BONUS
_____	_____	_____	_____
_____	_____	_____	_____
_____	_____	_____	_____
_____	_____	_____	_____

EMPLOYEE BENEFIT PLANS:

   (A) Review Retirement Plans
      — Review Contributions:
         Profit Sharing: _____
         Money Purchase Pension: _____
         Defined Benefit Pension: _____
      — Section 404(a)(6) Resolutions
      — Possible Amendments
      — Investment Performance/Proper Investment Mix
      — Possible Controlled Group Problems
      — Possible Discrimination in Operation-Participation, etc.
        — Review Status of Part-Time Employees and Independent Con-
          tractors
        — Errors in Administration
      — Loans to Participants
      — Participant Earmarking
      — Qualified Survivor Annuity Notice
      — Beneficiary Designation Forms
      — ERISA Bonds—Review 10%
      — Furnish Allocation Information to Plan Administrator
      — Who Prepares Form 5500, SSA, 1099 and W2-P
      — Report of Actuary/Plan Administrator/Trustee
      — Last Audit of Plan by IRS
   (B) Review Health and Medical Reimbursement Plan

MINUTES & BYLAWS
   (A) Is Minute Book Up-To-Date?
   (B) Reading and Approval of Prior Minutes
   (C) Any Amendments of Bylaws Required?

APPROVAL OF ACTS OF OFFICERS FOR PRIOR YEARS: _____

STOCK RECORDS:
   (A) Stock Sales and/or Redemptions: _____

   _____

   _____

   (B) Stock Retirement Agreement: (set value, etc.)

   _____

   _____

   _____

INSURANCE:
   — Fidelity Bonds
   — Fire & Theft
   — Malpractice
   — Life (Group Term and/or Split Dollar)
   — Use of Excess §79 Coverage
   — Proper Reporting of P.S. 58 Cost on §79 and Split Dollar Insurance
   — Disability
   — Health & Accident
   — Umbrella Coverage: Business _____
                         Personal _____
   — Automobile Coverage

CONTRACTS:
   — Leases (For office space, equipment, etc.)-increased rental?
   — Agreements with Hospitals, etc.
   — Other

REVIEW OF RETAINER RELATIONSHIP: _____

NEXT MEETING: _____

SHAREHOLDERS' MEETING

PERSONS PRESENT: _____

   _____

   _____

   _____

   _____

CHAIRMAN: _____
SECRETARY: _____
QUORUM: _____
          PROXIES? _____
DATE & TIME: _____
LOCATION: _____
F.Y.E.: _____

READING AND APPROVAL OF PRIOR MINUTES

ELECTION OF DIRECTORS: _____
                       _____
                       _____
                       _____

APPROVAL OF ACTS OF DIRECTORS FOR PRIOR YEAR

ESTATE PLANNING FOR SHAREHOLDERS

NEXT MEETING: _____
              _____
              _____

INCOME TAX PLANNING FOR SHAREHOLDERS

EXHIBIT 5

CHECKLIST

MID-YEAR MEETING OF DIRECTORS

NAME OF CORPORATION: _____
PERSONS PRESENT: _____
                 _____
                 _____
                 _____
                 _____
                 _____
                 _____
                 _____

CHAIRMAN: _____
SECRETARY: _____
QUORUM: _____
DATE & TIME: _____
LOCATION: _____

REPORT ON OPERATIONS:
   (A) Accountant's Report on Financial Position for First Six Months.

       Gross Revenues Current Year: _____
       Gross Revenues Previous Year: _____
       Profit/Loss Current Year: _____
       Profit/Loss Previous Year: _____
       Cash Position Current Year: _____
       Cash Position Previous Year: _____
       A/R Current Year: _____
       A/R Previous Year: _____

   (B) Review Expected Expenditures for Next Six Months

   (C) Review Salaries and Potential Bonuses

(D) Review Fees

(E) Office Personnel

Mid-Year Tax Planning for Directors: _____

_____

_____

_____

EXHIBIT 6

UNANIMOUS CONSENT OF THE BOARD OF DIRECTORS
OF XYZ: P.C. IN LIEU OF A MEETING

We, the undersigned, constituting all of the Members of the Board of Directors of XYZ, P.C., do unanimously consent to, ratify, approve, and adopt under Section 22-710 of the Georgia Business Corporation Code, the following statements and resolutions.

WHEREAS, . . . and

WHEREAS, ...

NOW, THEREFORE, be it:

RESOLVED, that . . . . and

FURTHER RESOLVED, that . . . and

FINALLY RESOLVED, that . . . .

Unanimously consented to, adopted, approved, and ratified this _____ day of _____, 19____.

(List Lines for signatures)

NOTES TO CHAPTER 8

1. See *Holder,* Chapter 6, Note 3, *supra.*

2. 29 Ohio St. 2d xxix.

3. Arizona, Colorado, Oregon, Wisconsin.

4. Letter Ruling 8003010.

5. Treas. Regs. §1.446-1(c)(1)(i).

6. Section 166(c) of the Code.

7. Rev. Rul. 76-28, 1976-1 C.B. 106.

8. Rev. Rul. 74-70, 1974-1 C.B. 116.

9. 1975-1 C.B. 131.

10. See Worthy, Chapter 5, note 7, *supra.*

11. See, generally, O'Neill, "Professional Service Corporation: Coping with Professional Problems," 31 *J. Taxation* 94 (1969); Thies, "Professional Service Organizations: A Comment," 24 *Tax Law Review* 291 (1969); Hobbett, "The Corporate Entity: When Will It Be Recognized For Federal Tax Purposes?" 30 *J. Taxation* 74 (1969).

12. 1972-1 C.B. 105.

13. 1975-1 C.B. 169.

14. Levinson, "What it Costs to Incorporate a Practice," *Medical Economics*, September 14, 1970, p.99.

15. Tax Management Portfolio, No. 334, p. A10.

16. Section 195 of the Code also permits the 60-month amortization of pre-incorporation expenses, but does not prohibit the deductibility of expenses otherwise deductible under other Sections of the Code, such as tax advice under Section 212.

17. *Meldrum & Fewsmith, Inc.,* 20 T.C. 790 (1953); *Vanderbilt,* 16 T.C.M. 1081, ¶57,235 P-H Memo T.C. (1957); Wegher, "Deductibility of Fees For Professional Services Accountant or Attorney: Divorce and Separation; Estate Planning; Tax Advice; Title Matters, etc.," 34 *N.Y.U. Inst. Fed. Tax* 163, 169, 171 (1976).

18. For a general discussion of the fees relating to incorporation see:

    Gorlick, "How to Hold Your Legal Expenses to a Minimum", *Medical Economics*, July 10, 1978, page 114.

    Warren and Dunkle, "Professional Corporations—Organization and Operation," BNA Tax Management Portfolio, No. 334, p. A10.

    Kalish and Lewis, "Professional Corporations Revisited (After The Employee Retirement Income Security Act of 1974)," Vol. 28, No. 3 *Tax Lawyer*, p. 493.

    Levinson, "What it Costs to Incorporate a Practice," *Medical Economics*, September 14, 1970, page 99.

19. La. Statutes Ann §12:803.

20. See Letter Rulings 7720005, 7724006, 7730099, 7838015, 7840024, 7903081, 7935056, 7902074, 7925070, 7911049, and 7926080.

21. For a future discussion see Eaton, chapter 7, *supra*, note 1, §9.05.

22. Section 6501(c)(4) of the Code.

REFERENCES FOR PART I

Baker, "Incorporation of the Firm," 26 *Tax Lawyer* 77(1972).

Battle, "The Use of Corporations by Persons Who Perform Services to Gain Tax Advantages," 57 *Taxes* 798 (1979).

Capouano, "Tax Advantages and Disadvantages of Professional Corporations," *A.B.A.J.* 758 (1972).

Dougherty, "Planning Considerations in Establishing the Professional Corporation: Economic Problems of Large Professional Groups; Use of Partial Incorporation or Multiple Corporation," 32 N.Y.C. Inst. on Fed. Tax. 835 (1974).

Grayck, "Tax Qualified Retirement Plans For Professional Practitioners: A Comparison of the Self Employed Individuals Tax Requirements Act of 1962 and the Professional Association," 63 *Colum. L. Rev.* 415 (1962).

Haddleton, "Kintner Regs. Now Block Professional Corporations; Final H.R. 10 Regulations Analyzed," 20 *J. Taxation* 74 (1964).

Kalish and Lewis, "Professional Corporations Revisited (After The Employee Retirement Income Security act of 1974)," 28 *Tax Lawyer*, 495 (1975).

Lamon, "Current Survey of Professional Corporations," *Law Notes*, October, 1971, Vol. 8, Page 1.

Levinson, "What Incorporation is Doing For Doctors," *Medical Economics,* May 24, 1971, at 83.

Siegel, "The Utility of the Professional Corporation: A Rejoinder," Vol. 29 *Tax Lawyer*, p. 265.

Warren and Dunkle, "Professional Corporations—Organization and Operation," BNA Tax Management Portfolio No. 334.

Zalusky, "Comparison of a Professional Corporation With an Unincorporated Practice After ERISA," 34 NYU Inst. Fed Tax 1335 (1976).

PART II

OPERATING TECHNIQUES

CHAPTER 9

Special Tax Problems to Avoid in Operating Professional Corporations

**[9.01]   CORPORATENESS—EARNER OF INCOME
AND SECTION 482 PROBLEMS**

After incorporation, care should be taken to assure that a professional corporation is operated in a manner substantially similar to that employed by business corporations. A professional corporation faces all of the potential hazards and problems which may be encountered by a business corporation, and some of these hazards and problems may be substantially greater. This is particularly true with regard to the question of whether the corporation or the shareholders are actually the earners of the income produced by the professional activity.

The "Earner of Income" question has been one which has plagued service and professional corporations for years. The context in which this issue arises is that of a corporation used to promote the services of an individual, either professional, literary, artistic or otherwise, and in which the corporation, although legally incorporated and validly existing under state law, is more or less disregarded during the actual performance of the particular service. The real issue raised in this situation is whether the income generated will be taxable to the individual or to the corporation. Even with the abandonment of the Kintner Regulations (which are discussed in the Introduction), this issue continues to maintain substantial vitality today. Further, the arguments used by the Service to reach the conclusion that the individual, rather than the professional corporation, is taxable on the income earned through the performance of the services, is not dissimilar from that used under state law to argue that the corporate veil should be pierced and that shareholders should be liable for corporate debts.

If the Service succeeds in an assignment of income contention, the benefits of a professional corporation will be eliminated. The devastating results can be:

(1) The corporation will be considered not to exist, and all income will bypass the corporation and be taxed directly to the professionals.

(2) Income which remains in corporate solution will be considered either a loan by the professionals to the corporation or a contribution to capital. Such loans should, however, be returnable to the professionals without incurring federal income tax. That is, loans could be repaid by the corporation without creating taxable income to the professionals and, even if the funds are considered to be contributions to capital, they could be returned in liquidation without producing a tax.

(3) Since all income is considered taxable to the professionals, the corporation will have no taxable income and, consequently, no current or accumulated earnings or profits from which retirement plan benefits could be paid.

Therefore, if the Service is successful in an assignment of income contention, the professionals will normally have been in a better position had they never incorporated. There are several methods in which the Service has, in the past, attempted to impose such a result. These include the "sham corporation" doctrine under which the corporate status of the professional corporation is ignored, the "assignment of income" doctrine under which the corporate status is recognized but the income is taxed directly to the professionals, and the reallocation of income and deductions under Section 482 in order to correctly reflect income.

(1) Sham Corporations

The sham corporation doctrine was one of the first arguments employed by the Service against service and professional corporations. The early cases involve actors, artists, and other professional entertainers (since most other professionals were, until recently, prohibited from incorporating by state ethical and legal requirements). In these cases the Service argued that the corporation was not a separate legal entity. For example, in *Fontaine Fox*[1], the Service contended that a cartoonist, who had transferred his copyrights and contracts to a service corporation, should be personally taxable on the income generated by his efforts. However, since the corporation was an active, operating entity which had contracts with the cartoonist and with third parties, the court held that the existence of the corporation should be recognized. The other leading early case involved the actor Charles Laughton.[2] Mr. Laughton's service corporation "loaned" him to various engagements, and the court found that the corporation observed the appropriate formalities and was a validly existing corporation for tax purposes.

The Service continued to rely heavily on the sham corporation argument until the *Moline Properties* case[3] in which the Supreme Court held that a corporation is not a sham if it is organized for a legitimate business purpose and is engaged in a substantial business activity.[4] After the holding in the *Moline Properties* case, it was generally felt that the sham corporation doctrine had been eliminated and could not be applied to service corporations.

Although the sham corporation doctrine will, now, only be applied by the Service in egregious cases, it does have some vitality in the professional corporation context. For example, in *Floyd Patterson*,[5] the Service sought to impose the sham corporation doctrine. In that case, Floyd Patterson, the famous boxer, formed a service corporation owned by himself and his manager. The corporation was formed to receive ancillary income, such as royalties generated by television rights, and income from television and movie appearances. However, not all income was paid to the corporation; some was paid directly to Mr. Patterson. The corporation held no corporate meetings except the initial meeting, owned no equipment, and shared an office with Mr. Patterson. The court found that the corporation was formed for a business purpose, but it did not conduct business activities, since it had not entered into contracts and performed no function with respect to Mr. Patterson's appearances. The court also noted that some income was paid directly to Mr. Patterson and that there was a general commingling of funds. Consequently, the court did not recognize the corporation as a separate legal entity.

In another case involving another famous boxer, Ingmar Johansson,[6] the court refused to recognize the existence of a corporation formed to avoid taxes based on the Swedish Tax Treaty. Ingmar Johansson was a non-resident alien who attempted to avoid income tax derived from personal services performed in the United States by applying the treaty between the United States and Sweden. That treaty provided that no income tax would be imposed if the services were performed by a resident Swedish corporation. Mr. Johansson formed a Swedish corporation, of which he was the sole employee and sole source of revenues. Also, in *U.S. v. Empey*,[7] the Service sought to apply the sham transaction doctrine to a group of attorneys who formed a professional corporation in Colorado. The court followed *Kintner* and held that the Kintner Regulations were invalid.

As previously mentioned, the Service has continued to apply the sham corporation doctrine in egregious cases. For example, in *Kimbrell v. Commissioner*,[8] the Fifth Circuit, in affirming the Tax Court, held that a corporation established by the Director of Finance of the State of Alabama was a sham. In following the *Moline Properties* test, the court noted that the corporation which the Director of Finance and two friends formed to receive "commissions" did not engage in business activity and was a mere depository for the commissions received. The corporation offered no services in return for the commissions. However, in several recent cases, there has been an interesting reversal of roles. In *Phillip W. Kessler*,[9] an architect formed a corporation which did not file federal income tax returns. The architect reported the corporation's income and deducted its expenses on his own individual tax return. The taxpayer argued that the corporation was not an active corporation, but the Service argued and the court held, following the tests set forth in *Moline Properties*, that the corporation should be considered for tax purposes since it did conduct a business activity, paid employees, and had a bank account. [10]

Although the sham transaction doctrine has not seen extensive use by the Service in recent years, professional corporation advisors should not consider it to be totally defunct. It will be applied in egregious cases. [11]

(2) Assignment of Income

(a) *General Description*

Where a professional corporation is recognized as a separate taxable entity and not a mere sham, the Service has, in its attacks, generally narrowed the issue to whether the corporation has been given sufficient substance and control over the professional income so that the corporation, and not the individual professionals, can be considered a true earner of the income. Section 61 of the Code provides that, unless otherwise excluded by law, gross income means all income from whatever source derived, including, but not limited to, compensation for services, including fees, commissions, and similar items. It has long been established that income must be taxed to the person who earned it, irrespective of whether he actually received it or assigned the rights to receive it to some other person. The leading assignment of income case is *Lucas v. Earl*[12] in which the Supreme Court held that all income would be taxed to the husband where the husband and wife entered into an agreement under which all earnings would be held as joint tenants with right of survivorship. Consequently, even though the husband was required to transfer half of his earnings to his spouse, he was taxed on all of the income. [13]

Where a professional corporation is involved, the issue is complicated by the fact that the corporation can only act through the professionals who are its controlling shareholders. Nonetheless, so long as the corporation itself earns the income, the corporation will be taxed. [14] But, where the shareholders, in fact, act on their own behalf rather than for the corporation, they, not the corporation, will bear the burden of the tax. The *Laughton* and *Fox* cases, [15] which were sham corporation cases, also address the assignment of income question and the court held, in both cases, that no assignment of income occurred. Notwithstanding the Service's loss in *Laughton* and *Fox*, it has continued to argue the assignment of income doctrine in the professional corporation area and, in some cases, has succeeded. The basic issue to be determined in an assignment of income case is whether the corporation or the shareholder-employees have control over the income-producing activity. When it is apparent that the shareholders, to the exclusion of the professional corporation, have such control, the Service will generally contend that an assignment of income has occurred. In determining whether an assignment of income has, in fact occurred, the following factors should be examined:

(1) Is the professional corporation validly incorporated and is it operated as a bona fide corporation?

(2) Do contracts exist between the professional corporation and other entities and patients/clients? Do the patients/clients of the professional corporation have the right to demand the services of a particular individual?

(3) If, prior to the incorporation of the professional corporation, such contracts existed in the name of the individual, have they been validly assigned to the professional corporation?

(4) Does the professional corporation have employment agreements with its professional employees and are the professional employees required to spend their entire professional time in the service of the professional corporation?

Obviously, where the corporation has been totally disregarded, the Service may either apply the sham corporation doctrine or the assignment of income doctrine. In recent years, however, the Service has generally relied on the assignment of income doctrine as its main weapon of attack.

The leading assignment of income case in the professional corporation area has, for years, been *Jerome J. Roubik*.[16] In *Roubik*, four radiologists, who had previously been engaged separately in the practice of radiology, formed a professional service corporation that was validly incorporated under state law. Each radiologist entered into an employment contract with the corporation. Subsequent to the incorporation of the professional corporation, each radiologist continued to engage separately in his individual professional practice with some of the professionals practicing at different physical locations. The professional corporation did not enter into any arrangements to provide the services of its employees to any of the institutions or doctors for whom the radiologists provided services. The professional corporation also did not own any equipment or incur any debts for rent, office or medical supplies, services or salaries, other than the salaries of the radiologists. The only shared expense was a $45 per month cost for record-keeping of the income received and expenses paid by the professional corporation.

The Service contended that the radiologists in *Roubik* surrendered control over their services to the professional corporation in form only. The Tax Court agreed with the Service and held that the issue was whether the radiologists' business was actually carried on by the professional corporation or whether it was carried on outside the professional corporation by the individuals. In concluding that the professional corporation had nothing to do with earning the income, the Tax Court's opinion was based on the following facts:

(1) The maintenance of income and expense records for tax purposes was the only real business activity of the professional corporation.

(2) The professional corporation did not assign any of the radiologists to the various places of employment and the radiologists continued to perform the services for the hospitals to whom they were contractually obligated.

(3) The mere fact that the radiologists occasionally covered for each other as a matter of convenience did not mean that they had relinquished direction and control over the activities to the professional corporation as their employer.

(4) The corporation was not, as a practical matter, given the right to direct any of its employees in their professional activities.

(5) The professional corporation did not actually control the quality of the radiologists' work or otherwise interfere in the conduct of their separate practices.

Since *Roubik*, the Service has continued to rely on the assignment of income doctrine. A number of interesting cases have been tried in this area and these are listed in the following section (b). However, the most enlightening and important assignment of income case in the service corporation area is *Foglesong v. Commissioner*.[17] In *Foglesong*, the Seventh Circuit Court of Appeals reversed the Tax Court's holding that the shareholders were taxable on the income generated through their personal services. Mr. Foglesong was a successful sales representative for several manufacturing companies. In 1966, he incorporated his business and following that day commissions were paid to the new corporation. Although all commissions were paid to the corporation, it was not until some years later that written agreements were entered into between the corporation and the manufacturers. The corporation complied with generally acceptable corporate formalities, and Mr. Foglesong was paid compensation under a regular (unwritten) salary arrangement.

The Tax Court decision in *Foglesong* found that the corporation was not a sham, but determined that Mr. Foglesong was the true earner of the income because he held the control over virtually all of the earnings and that the "tax avoidance" sought by Mr. Foglesong outweighed any genuine business concern which Mr. Foglesong might have had for establishing the corporation, such as obtaining limited liability. The Tax Court noted that Mr. Foglesong, after incorporation, continued to conduct his business in a manner which was identical to his actions before incorporation. The Seventh Circuit Court of Appeals agreed that Mr. Foglesong's main aim was tax avoidance, but reversed the holding of the Tax Court. Although Mr. Foglesong did not have a written employment agreement with his corporation, the Seventh Circuit felt that the corporation was operated with sufficient formalities and could not be ignored. *Foglesong* should, however, not be viewed as an absolute victory for the incorporated professional because the Seventh Circuit did remand the case to the Tax Court for reconsideration under Section 482 of the Code.

At the time *Foglesong* was on appeal to the Seventh Circuit, the Service issued a Technical Advice Memorandum in another pending audit,[18] which applies the assignment of income doctrine to a professional corporation. In the Technical Advice, a physician, who was a general partner in a medical partnership, formed a wholly owned professional corporation which was to continue, in his stead, as a partner in the professional partnership. The physician continued to perform the same medical services that he had performed as a partner prior to the creation of the professional partnership. The Technical Advice concluded that the physician formed and used the professional corporation primarily for tax avoidance rather than for legitimate business purposes . The factors which indicated to the National Office of the Service that the physician retained control over the ability to earn the income from his medical practice were:

(1) No written partnership agreement existed to indicate that the professional corporation, rather than the physician, was a partner in the partnership.

(2) The physician did not assign his interest in the partnership to the professional corporation.

(3) The physician did not enter into either an employment contract or a convenant not to compete with the professional corporation. Consequently, the physician had complete control over the professional corporation's financial fate and could have set up a separate business and ceased working for the professional corporation altogether, without any recourse by the professional corporation.

(4) The professional corporation did not hire any professional or non-professional employees other than the physician.

(5) Insurance policies were not changed to provide coverage for the professional corporation.

(6) The professional corporation did not incur any significant indebtedness other than that for retirement plan costs.

(7) The professional corporation did not distribute all of its remaining income (after expenses) to the physician either as taxable salary or dividends. Instead, the professional corporation made a substantial loan to the physician and retained the remaining earnings in cash.

These facts indicated that the physician retained control over the earnings of the professional corporation and simply used the corporation for shifting income to the lowest available tax bracket.

(b) Other Important Assignment of Income Cases and Rulings

(1) *Richard Rubin*.[19] Mr. Rubin negotiated a management contract with one of his controlled corporations. Thereafter, Mr. Rubin formed a management company, and a management contract was then entered into between the new management company and the existing controlled company. After the establishment of this contract, Mr. Rubin continued to perform services for others and was not an employee of the management company. When the existing controlled company was eventually sold, the management contract was terminated without further consideration. The original Tax Court opinion held that Mr. Rubin, and not the management company, controlled the provision of services. The Second Circuit reversed and remanded to the Tax Court for consideration of the applicability of Section 482 of the Code.

(2) *American Savings Bank*.[20] The taxpayers formed a partnership to sell title insurance to their controlled bank. The partnership contracted with various life insurance companies to sell policies. Various bank employees, other than the taxpayers, usually were involved in the sale of the insurance policies. The taxpayers then formed a corporation and assigned the contracts to sell insurance to the new corporation, which entered into a management agreement with the bank. The services were rendered by the taxpayers and management fees were paid to the new service corporation, but the corporation never paid a salary to the taxpayers and no employment agreements were executed. The court held that the corporation was not a sham, but that the taxpayers continued to control the earnings of the income and, consequently, the income should be taxable to them.

(3) *Irwin V. Jones*.[21] An individual who was employed as a court reporter established a corporation. The corporation did not, however, assume the loans for the rental of the equipment necessary for use in court reporting and no employment agreement with the individual was executed. Also, under state law, court transcripts had to be personally prepared by the individual. The court held that the individual was taxable on the income.

(4) *McIver*.[22] A real estate broker incorporated his brokerage business but could not transfer his broker's license to the corporation because the corporation could not legally sell property under state law. The court held that the income was taxable to the individual.

(5) *The Estate of Nathaniel Cole*.[23] "Nat" Cole, the late famous singer, owned 50% of a corporation which arranged for his foreign tours. Mr. Cole received a weekly salary and the corporation supplied the orchestra, transportation, and other expenses. The corporation bore the risk of loss and the Tax Court ruled that the corporation was not a sham. The Tax Court also noted that whether the corporation made a profit depended upon the corporation's promotional and managerial efforts and, consequently, the income generated was not controlled by Mr. Cole. The court held that the corporation was taxable on the personal service income generated by Mr. Cole.

(6) *Jack E. Morrison*.[24] The taxpayer purchased a portion of a corporation owned by an insurance agent. The only function of the corporation was to receive commissions earned by the insurance agent from insuring the taxpayer's business and others referred to the agent by the taxpayer. The only records of the corporation were a checkbook and a deposit book. The corporation also owned some real estate and had no employees. The court held that the commissions were earned by the individual and not by the corporation, since the corporation was not licensed to sell or otherwise solicit insurance and no relationship existed between the companies that sold insurance and the corporation. Also, the individual did not hold himself out as an employee of the corporation.

(7) *Benjamin Gettler*.[25] Two lawyers incorporated with a non-lawyer in a labor relations consulting business. Because the lawyers were not entitled under

local ethics rules to participate in a partnership with a non-lawyer, the venture had a business purpose and the court ruled that the income was taxable to the corporation.

(8) *Epperson v. U.S.* [26] A jury verdict held that the true earner of the income was a professional corporation and not the physician employee.

(9) *Edwin Davis.* [27] The taxpayer, an orthopedic surgeon, incorporated his X-ray facilities and his physical therapy facilities into two corporations. The stock in these two corporations was issued to the taxpayer who then gave 90% of the stock to his three children. Both of the corporations were Subchapter S corporations. Each corporation employed its own employees, owned its own equipment, paid its own expenses, and kept its own records. The taxpayer did not render any services to either corporation except as an officer and director, hiring employees, and setting fees. The corporations generally had separate billings. The Tax Court held that the taxpayer had other reasons besides tax motives for forming the corporations (i.e., limitation of liability, personnel problems, etc.) and the income generated by the corporations was taxable to the corporations and not the physician.

(10) *Russell A. Bufalieno.* [28] Amounts paid to a partnership with respect to personal services of a partner constitute income to the partnership and not the partner. The activities of the partner were incident to the partnership's business activity.

(11) Rev. Rul. 76-479. [29] Fees derived from teaching cases were not includable in the gross incomes of the physicians who rendered the services where the physicians on the medical staff of a nonprofit hospital were required to be members of its nonprofit research and educational foundation and to assign all income from the teaching cases to the foundation.

(12) Letter Ruling 7849073. A professional medical corporation was formed so department members could engage in the private practice of medicine as a group, without the problems of group liability and so that the chairman of the university medical department could control the private practice. All physicians employed by the corporation were faculty members of the department and, therefore, university employees. The hospital was a teaching hospital for the university medical school and each faculty member was under a contract with the corporation under which he agreed to perform services at the corporation's direction in return for which he would be paid a salary and other benefits. The corporation operated only at the hospital and faculty members were permitted to engage in unlimited private practice and keep all income earned therefrom, but all private work at the hospital had to be performed through the corporation. All contracts for services performed at the hospital were between the corporation and the various patients. The doctors received no direct payments from patients and the corporation was responsible for all billings and collections. The Service held that the physicians employed by the corporation and serving patients at the hospital were acting as the corporation's agents and, consequently, fees generated by their services were income to the corporation and not to them. Also see Letter Rulings 8042128 and 8042132.

(c) *Conclusion*

As with the sham corporation doctrine, in recent years the assignment of income doctrine has generally been imposed by the courts only in egregious cases. This is evident from cases such as *Roubik* and *Rubin* (and Letter Ruling 8031028), where the doctrine has been imposed, and in cases such as *Foglesong*, where the doctrine has not. It is interesting to note that, where the doctrine has not been imposed, some courts have indicated that Section 482 would be reviewed by the Service for its applicability.

(3) Section 482 of the Code

In addition to the sham corporation doctrine and the assignment of income doctrine, the Service has recently sought to allocate income from a personal service corporation to the controlling shareholders under Section 482 of the Code. The Service has been successful in several cases and, as illustrated in *Foglesong* discussed in the previous section, the courts apparently feel that the issue of whether personal service income should be taxed to a professional corporation or the professional himself is more properly addressed under the provisions of Section 482.

Section 482 of the Code provides statutory authority for the Commissioner of Internal Revenue to distribute, apportion, or allocate gross income, deductions, credits, or allowances between two or more organizations, trades, or businesses which are owned or controlled by the same interests. In order for the Commissioner to employ the provisions of Section 482 of the Code, he must determine that doing so is necessary in order to prevent the evasion of taxes or to reflect clearly the income of such trades or businesses. The Commissioner is authorized to use the provisions of Section 482 at his own discretion and its application is not limited to corporations, but may be applied to individuals and partnerships as well. Although Section 482 should provide a very effective weapon in the hands of the Commissioner, the Commissioner must overcome the technical requirement of finding "two or more trades or business" in order to apply Section 482 in the professional corporation context.

The initial application of Section 482 to service corporations occurred in two well-known cases, *Pauline W. Ach*[30] and *Borge v. Commissioner*,[31] both of which produced victories for the Service.

Pauline Ach, the sole proprietor of a profitable dress business, felt that she had discovered a way in which the profits from her dress business could be offset against the operating losses produced by a family corporation which had formerly been owned by her son. Accordingly, Mrs. Ach sold her profitable dress business to the family corporation and she became an officer of the corporation. The only business of the corporation was her dress business and there were no contracts between Mrs. Ach and the corporation and no covenant against competition. Also, the sale of the dress business to the family corporation appeared not to be at arm's-length because the business was sold for a non-interest-bearing note. In its opinion, the Tax Court noted that it could not ignore the separate corporate existence of the family corporation. However, the court also noted that there were two separate trades or businesses and that when Mrs. Ach sold the "naked assets" of her proprietorship to the corporation she did not cease that trade or business because she did not transfer any intangibles to the corporation and did not enter into an employment agreement with it. Consequently, the Tax Court allocated 70% of the profits generated by the corporation to Mrs. Ach (i.e., 70% of the profits of the corporation were attributable to her personal services and 30% were attributable to the efforts of other employees in the capital invested in the business).

Borge, which involved the famous piano player, is often considered to be the classic Section 482 case. Victor Borge had incurred substantial losses in the operation of a poultry business, so he transferred the poultry business to a new wholly owned corporation and, at the same time, entered into an entertainment contract with the new corporation to provide various entertainment services. Victor Borge hoped that, in this way, the income generated from the entertainment services would be offset by the net operating losses previously created by the poultry business. The Tax Court found that Mr. Borge was engaged in two separate trades or businesses, poultry and entertainment, and that he continued to be separately engaged in the entertainment business. Consequently, a portion of the entertainment income generated by the corporation was allocated to Mr. Borge (however, some of the entertainment income was specifically allocated to the new corporation because of its activities in furnishing his entertainment services).

The application of Section 482 in *Ach* and *Borge*, if not totally acceptable, at least has an obvious foundation. In both cases, individuals sought to offset the profits generated by one trade or business against losses generated by another. The Service has long felt that the losses of one trade or business should not be used to offset those of a second trade or business. However, *Ach* and *Borge* do not provide a precise rationale for applying Section 482 to the professional service corporation where the individual and the corporation are engaged in the same trade or business. Generally, it has been held that merely being an employee of a corporation should not constitute an independent trade or business sufficient to warrant the application of Section 482.[32] Consequently, unless the professional can be said to be in the independent business of providing his professional services, separate and apart from the professional corporation, the Service will have difficulty in applying Section 482. Thus, the same factors which have been present in the application of the sham corporation doctrine and the assignment of income doctrine will also have an impact on the application of Section 482. Where the professional is employed solely by the professional corporation and he is prohibited from establishing an independent practice and operates under an employment agreement which prohibits competition, it will be substantially more difficult for the Service to apply Section 482. It is interesting to note that in *Borge* the court did not comment on the alternative principle urged by the Government in a footnote to its brief that the services of Mr. Borge, alone, should constitute a separate trade or business.

An example of a court's difficulty in determining whether a second trade or business exists occurred in the Tax Court's consideration of *Rubin* on remand, i.e., *Rubin II*.[33] On remand from the Second Circuit, the Tax Court reconsidered *Rubin* and held that Section 482 applied and that income earned by the corporation would be allocated to the individual shareholder-employee. The court did, however, struggle with the concept of finding a second trade or business and did not decide whether employee status constitutes, in and of itself, a separate trade or business. The court simply held that, where the facts show that a shareholder operated an independent business and merely assigned to the corporation a portion of the income therefrom, the business activity of the shareholder may constitute a separate trade or business to which the corporate income may be allocated under Section 482. In *Rubin*, however, the taxpayer clearly had a separate trade or business beyond the corporation's trade or business.

There have been a number of other important service corporation cases in which Section 482 has been applied:

(1) *Irwin V. Jones*.[34] Section 482 applied because the taxpayer maintained an independent business separate and apart from that of the corporation.

(2) *Glen A. Jordan*.[35] Taxpayer continued to perform services independent from that of the corporation. Therefore Section 482 applied.

(3) *Garland Wilson, Jr.*[36] Individual taxpayers negotiated with a meat-packing company to provide consulting services. They then formed a management company and the management company and the meatpacking company entered into a service contract. The contract stated that it was not to be construed as requiring services of any particular person; however, the meatpacking company had the right to terminate the contract if the corporation did not provide competent personnel. The taxpayers then gave the stock in the corporation to their children and received no salary for their services except for a small consulting fee. In determining whether separate trades or businesses existed under Section 482, the court stated that it must be determined whether:

    a. The third party was looking for services of individuals or of the corporation in general (*Rubin*), or

    b. The individuals actually performed the services (*Borge*).

The court determined that the meatpacking company was actually seeking the services of the individuals (noting that the contract was originally negotiated with the individuals) and the meatpacking company had veto power over who provided the services. Consequently, Section 482 was held to be applicable.

(4) *McGuire v. U.S.*[37] The famous singing McGuire Sisters formed corporations to receive entertainment income and invest such income in real estate (although no real estate was ever purchased). The jury found that:

    a. The corporations were not engaged in a valid business activity.

    b. The McGuire Sisters did not have a good faith intention (at the time of forming the corporations) that the corporations would ultimately engage in business activities.

    c. The Service was not arbitrary and capricious in allocating income to the McGuire Sisters under Section 482.

(4) Conclusion

The use of the sham corporation doctrine and the assignment of income doctrine have, generally, been relegated by the courts to those situations involving egregious circumstances, such as those set forth in Letter Ruling 8031028 where the existence of the corporation is ignored by the professional. Consequently, establishing a properly incorporated professional corporation where the professionals are required to work for the professional corporation full-time under employment agreements which prohibit competition, where the professional corporation establishes appropriate contracts with hospitals and other parties to whom it renders services, and where the corporation observes appropriate corporate formalities, should limit the applicability of the sham corporation doctrine and the assignment of income doctrine.

However, the exact parameters of Section 482 in the professional corporation setting have not been determined. Obviously, where there are two distinct trades or businesses or where the individual operates a separate professional practice, apart from that of the professional corporation, the principles of *Ach*, *Borge*, and *Rubin* will be applied to allocate income to the professional. On the other hand, if the Service asserts that simply being an employee will be considered a separate trade or business, even though the employee and the professional corporation are involved in one integrated business and the employee does not perform outside activities, the applicability of Section 482 could be expanded. Such an expansion would be, however, a departure from the long-standing position of the Service that properly operated professional corporations are not subject to attack.[38] In fact, such an expansion would surely jeopardize the existence of one-man professional corporations. Consequently, the authors feel that the applicability of Section 482 should properly be limited only to those situations where there are two separate trades or businesses (such as *Ach* and *Borge*) or where the professional practices his profession both inside and outside of the professional corporations.

[9.02] PERSONAL HOLDING COMPANIES—SECTION 541

The personal holding company provisions contained in Sections 541-565 of the Code were designed to prohibit individual taxpayers from capturing passive income in a corporation and thereby obtaining lower corporate tax rates on that income. Although for a number of years tax practitioners felt that the personal holding company provisions presented an unsurmountable problem for professional corporations, the personal holding company provisions can, generally, be avoided with proper attention, even in one-man professional corporations.

Section 541 of the Code, provides a confiscatory 70% (which rate is reduced to 50% under ERTA for taxable years beginning after December 31, 1981) tax on all "undistributed personal holding company income," and Section 542 provides that a personal holding company is defined as any corporation of which:

  i. At least 60% of its adjusted ordinary gross income (as defined in Section 543(b)(2) of the Code) for the taxable year is personal holding company income (as defined in Section 543(a) of the Code), and

  ii. At any time during the last half of the taxable year, more than 50% in value of the outstanding stock of the corporation is owned, directly or indirectly, by or for not more than five individuals. This test is an entirely mechanical test and no consideration whatsoever is given to the intent of the taxpayer. If the test is met, the corporation will be considered a personal holding company.

The 50% of ownership test is a relatively easy test to avoid in large professional corporations which are, consequently, excluded from the applicability of the personal holding company provisions. On the other hand, smaller professional corporations must determine whether any of the income received by the professional corporation is considered to be "personal holding company income" under Section 543 of the Code.

Section 543 defines personal holding company income to consist of a number of types of passive income such as dividends, rents, royalties, and, most importantly for professionals, income from personal service contracts. Section 543(a)(7) of the Code defines amounts received from personal service contracts as:

(A) Amounts received under a contract under which the corporation is to furnish personal services; if some person other than the corporation has the right to designate (by name or by description) the individual who is to perform the services, or if the individual who is to perform the services is designated (by name or by description) in the contract; and

(B) Amounts received from the sale or other disposition of such a contract.

This paragraph shall apply with respect to amounts received for services under a particular contract only if at some time during the past taxable year 25% or more in value of the outstanding stock of the corporation is owned, directly or indirectly, by or for the individual who has performed, is to perform, or may be disignated (by name or by description), as the one to perform, such services. [39]

Section 543(a)(7) and the Regulations thereunder are sometimes referred to as the incorporated talent provisions. This Section and the Regulations provide particular problems for entertainers and other celebrities who attempt to operate through professional corporations and where, obviously, it is their services which are sought.[40] On the other hand, individuals who perform professional services which are of a general nature (law, accounting, medicine, etc.) which may be performed by any competent professional retained by the corporation, are much less likely to encounter problems under the personal holding company provisions.[41]

The controlling factor in determining whether a corporation has income under a personal service contract which constitutes personal holding company income is whether the person engaging those services has the right to designate the individuals who may perform them. For example, in Rev. Rul. 59-172[42] insurance commissions received by an incorporated insurance agency from the insurance policies written by its two shareholder/officers did not constitute personal holding company income since the officers were not named or designated in the contracts with the various insurance companies and the insurance companies did not have the right to designate any particular individual in the contracts. Further, the Tax Court has held that a mere expectation that a certain individual will perform services is not sufficient to create personal holding company income, and the Service has acquiesced in the case.[43] Also, in *Foglesong*[44] the Service sought to impose the personal holding company provisions on income received by a corporation which was acting as a manufacturer's representative. However, because the manufacturers with whom the corporation dealt did not have the right to designate specific individuals, the Tax Court did not apply the personal holding company provisions.

In 1975, the Service issued Rev. Rul. 75-67,[45] which discussed the application of the personal holding company rules to a one-man professional corporation. Many tax practitioners felt that this Revenue Ruling has foreclosed any future problems with the personal holding company provisions, but the holding of the Ruling is not as broad as some might think and continued care should be taken to avoid the pitfalls of the personal holding company provisions. In Rev. Rul. 75-67, a doctor, specializing in a certain area of medicine, owned 80% of the outstanding stock of a professional corporation. He was the only officer of the corporation who was active in the production of income for the corporation and the only physician employed by the corporation. His services were performed for the professional corporation under an employment agreement and the corporation furnished to him appropriate equipment and office space and also employed appropriate staff personnel. The Ruling noted that, in dealing with a professional service corporation providing medical services, an individual will customarily solicit and expect to receive the services of a particular physician, and the individual will usually be treated by the physician sought. The Service ruled, however, that the creation of a physician-patient relationship in such a context does not constitute a "designation" of the individual who is to perform the services within the meaning of Section 543(a)(7). On the other hand, if the physician or the professional service corporation contracts with the patient that the physician personally will perform particular services for the patient and he has no right to substitute another physician to perform such services, there will be a designation of that physician as the individual to perform the services. The designation may be either oral or written.[46]

Rev. Rul. 75-67 is not, however, the cure-all which it may initially appear to be. The Ruling states that if the services which are to be performed by the physician "are so unique as to preclude substitution of another physician to perform such services, there is also a designation" and the Ruling is conditioned upon the services of the physician not being so unique. Consequently, in situations involving entertainers or highly specialized and well-known professionals, such as a cardiac surgeon with a world-wide reputation for heart transplants, the Service may, under the provisions of Rev. Rul. 75-67, take the position that a "designation" has been made even though there is no written agreement to that effect. To date, there are no existing cases in which the Service has taken such a position, but professional corporation advisors should always consider the possibility that the Service will do so.[47]

There continues to be activity in the personal holding company area as it relates to professional and service corporations.[48] Accordingly, the following steps should be taken by professional corporation advisors to lessen the possibility that some examining agent will attempt to impose the personal holding company provisions:

(1) All contracts with third parties, such as hospitals and other institutions, should be drafted so as to avoid designating any particular individual to perform services. Further, where an individual previously has established such a contract with a third party and, subsequently, incorporates, it would be preferable to execute a new agreement with the third party in the name of the professional corporation, as opposed to assigning the existing contract (obviously with the permission of the third party) to the new professional corporation. Even though a third-party institution may agree to provisions which provide that the professional corporation, and not a particular individual, will provide the services required under the contract, it is possible that such institutions will require that a certain individual maintain his status as president of the corporation or maintain another position, such as being chief of surgery, or the third-party institution will have the right to terminate the agreement. Such a provision in the contract should not operate to characterize the contract as one for designated personal services under Section 543(a)(7).

(2) Patients or clients should not be permitted to designate a particular professional who will treat them and any retainer or engagement agreements should specify that the professional corporation will provide the services.

(3) The organizational documents and the employment agreements of the professionals should provide that the board of directors or the president of the corporation will have the authority to determine the assignment of work and to designate those individuals who will be involved in each particular project.

As a practical matter, however, the imposition of the personal holding company tax in most professional corporations will be an academic question. Since most professional corporations retain little or no taxable income, any personal holding company tax imposed, even at 70% rates, should be minor. Nevertheless, professional corporation advisors should monitor all contracts and engagement agreements entered into by the professional corporation to assure that a particular professional is not "designated" and care should be taken to avoid a *de facto* designation (because the services of a particular professional may be so unique as to preclude substitution).

[9.03] ACQUISITIONS MADE TO EVADE OR AVOID INCOME TAX—SECTION 269

Section 269 of the Code provides, in part, that if any person or persons acquire, directly or indirectly, control of a corporation and if the principal purpose for which such acquisition was made is the evasion or avoidance of federal income tax by securing the benefits of a deduction, credit, or other allowance which such person would not otherwise enjoy, then the Secretary of the Treasury or his delegate may disallow such deduction, credit, or other allowance.

In order to disallow a deduction or credit, it must be found that the principal purpose of a taxpayer in acquiring control of a corporation is the evasion or avoidance of income tax. In reaching such a finding, it is necessary to examine the legislative intent behind the creation of a particular benefit to determine whether its allowance under the particular facts involved would be inconsistent with the scheme Congress was attempting to encourage in enacting the provisions. Section 269 has been applied primarily to disregard the acquisition of companies in order to utilize expiring net operating losses and to gain multiple surtax exemptions.[49]

As is apparent from the legislative history of Section 269, the scope of Section 269 is very broad. However, Section 269 has generally not posed a substantial problem to the formation and operation of bona fide professional corporations, and the explicit recognition of the use of professional corporations in 1970 in Technical Information Release No. 1019[50] should be sufficient indication that the Service will not attempt to apply Section 269 on a wholesale basis to new and existing professional corporations. If the Service were to attempt to so expand the scope of Section 269, it could be argued that, because the formation of a professional corporation permits the use of many employee benefits which are not available to proprietorships, Section 269 should apply to disallow these benefits. If such a position were upheld, all professional corporations would presumably be disregarded. The authors, however, believe that the failure of the Service to apply Section 269 to professional corporations, except in certain egregious cases, should foreclose the ability of the Service to contend that Section 269 should be applicable on a wholesale basis to disallow the benefits obtainable through professional corporations.

The former Chief Counsel, K. Martin Worthy, in his much cited article[51] recognized the obtacles to applying Section 269 to professional corporations.

Further, assuming that a professional corporation was organized for the purpose of obtaining certain employee benefits, such as qualified retirement plans, there is a substantial question whether such a purpose would constitute "evasion or a-voidance" of income taxes under Section 269. For example, In I.T. 3757,[52] the Service ruled that the creation of a new corporation for the purpose of obtaining the benefits of the Western Hemisphere Trade Corporation provisions of the Code[53] did not constitute tax avoidance under Section 269. Similarly, in Rev. Rul. 76-363,[54] the Service held that, although the principal purpose in creating a Subchapter S corporation was to secure the benefit of exemption from corporate income tax, Section 269 did not apply to disallow any deduction, credit, or other allowance resulting from an election by a corporation to be taxed under Subchapter S.

It should be noted, however, that the Service has applied Section 269 to cases involving professionals. For example, in the *Victor Borge* case[55] the Service successfully applied Section 269 to disallow deductions created by Mr. Borge's poultry business which he attempted to offset against his entertainment income. The *Borge* case does, however, fit within the envisioned scope of Section 269 (the use of net operating losses of one trade or business against those of another) and should not constitute authority under which the Service could disallow tax benefits for a validly incorporated professional corporation.

However, a new National Office Technical Advice Memorandum may indicate that the Service will attempt to take a more aggressive view with regard to the application of Section 269.[56] In the Technical Advice Memorandum, a business was conducted through a partnership and a service corporation was formed to perform the sales and customer relations function of the partnership's business. The service corporation was paid a commission and had relatively few employees. The partnership and the service corporation were owned by the same family and the service corporation adopted a medical expense reimbursement plan and a money purchase pension plan for its employees. The Service sought to apply Section 269 of the Code and the Technical Advice examined the legislative history of qualified retirement plans in order to determine whether Section 269 should apply. The Technical Advice stated that it is clear that conducting a business in corporate form to take advantage of certain benefits provided to corporations under the Code does not necessarily indicate attempted tax avoidance to which Section 269 would apply. The Technical Advice further stated:

> However, if it can be concluded from an examination of all the facts and circumstances that the principal purpose behind the formation of a corpo-ration was to take advantage of a benefit provided for in the Code that would not otherwise have been available, and the allowance of the benefit under the circumstances would be inconsistent with the legislative scheme behind its creation, then Section 269 of the Code can be applied to disallow that benefit.

The clear implication of this language is that, if the Service were to conclude that qualified retirement plans were, for example, intended only for regular business corporations and not for professional corporations, Section 269 would operate to disallow any deductions produced by them. To the knowledge of the authors there is nothing in the legislative history of ERISA that would disallow the benefits of qualified retirement plans to professional corporations and, in certain instances, specific reference is made to the use of qualified retirement plans by professional corporations. Consequently, the establishment of qualified retirement plans by professional corporations should not be attacked by the Service under Section 269. Further, Section 269 should not be available to disallow deductions for contributions to other corporate employee benefit plans and arrangements.[57]

Although Section 269 should not be available to the Service to disallow deductions for corporate employee benefits taken by bona fide professional corporations, care should be taken to avoid the implication that the professional corporation (or the benefits provided for it) has been established in order to minimize the personal tax burden of the professionals and permit benefits which would otherwise not be available to them in a proprietorship or a partnership. For example, the incorporation documents should stress the nontax reasons for incorporating the professional practice, such as the limitational collateral malpractice liability.[58] Such a business purpose has been recognized by the courts.[59] Other courts have not been disturbed by the fact that tax savings could have been one of the motivating factors for the formation of a professional corporation. In *Wallace v. U.S.*,[60] the court stated, ''It is clear that Arkansas adopted the statutes which have been mentioned for the express purpose of permitting professional people, such as doctors, lawyers, and dentists to practice within the framework of corporations so as to gain the tax benefits which have been outlined.'' Further, any corporate action adopting specific employee benefits should recognize the explicit business purposes of adopting such benefits, such as creation of employee morale and retention of employees by providing benefits.

[9.04] ACCUMULATED EARNINGS TAX— SECTIONS 531-537

Sections 531-537 of the Code impose a penalty upon corporations which accumulate excess earnings. The accumulated earnings provisions are intended to prohibit the indefinite accumulation of earnings and, thus, to require corporations to pay dividends to shareholders. As with the penalty provisions of the personal holding company rules, the provisions relating to the accumulated earnings tax also apply to professional corporations. However, contrary to the mechanical test under the personal holding company rules, the imposition of the accumulated earnings tax is subject to the existence of the following two conditions:

(1) There must be an intent to avoid the income tax on the part of the shareholders of the corporation, and

(2) There must be an intent to accumulate earnings and profits during the taxable year.

Under Section 534, the burden of proof is normally on the government but can be shifted to the taxpayer.

Section 531 of the Code imposes a tax, in addition to the regular corporate income taxes, on all accumulated earnings equal to the sum of 27½% of the accumulated taxable income, not in excess of $100,000, plus 38½% of the accumulated taxable income in excess of $100,000.

Numerous cases have set forth complicated tests for determining whether accumulated earnings exist. Professional corporation advisors should be aware of a recent Supreme Court case[61] in which the Court held that securities held by a corporation must be included at their fair market value (i.e., unrealized appreciation is taken into account) for purposes of determining accumulated earnings. However, as long as accumulated earnings do not exceed the accumulated earnings credit provided under Section 535(c)(2) of $150,000 or can be shown to be held for the reasonable business needs of the corporation, the accumulated earnings provisions should not pose an insurmountable problem for professional corporations.[62] It should be recognized that ERTA increased the accumulated earnings credit to $250,000, but that corporations, the principal function of which is the performance of services in the field of health, law, engineering, architecture, accounting, actuarial science, performing arts, or consulting, are limited to the existing $150,000 credit.

The $150,000 accumulated earnings credit provided under Section 535(c)(2) should be recognized as the upper limit on accumulated earnings for professional corporations (unless unusual business needs otherwise dictate). The authors feel that it is often difficult to justify accumulated earnings in a professional corporation in excess of $150,000 where the corporation has no liabilities or expansion plans. The dividends received deduction provided under Section 243 (discussed at section [8.11](2), *supra*) does provide an excellent means for the professional corporation to invest accumulated earnings at an almost tax-exempt rate, and the authors generally favor the accumulation of some earnings by professional corporations in order to meet working capital needs. A professional corporation, like all business corporations, has a justified and ongoing need for the retention of working capital and the $150,000 credit should be utilized to the extent possible to accumulate earnings.

To the extent that earnings are accumulated by a professional corporation in excess of $150,000 credit, care should be taken to insure that such accumulation is for "the reasonable needs of the business" as provided in Section 537 of the Code. Such "reasonable needs" include anticipated business needs so long as there is "reasonable anticipation (and not some uncertain need)." For this reason it is very important that corporate records specify the reasons for any accumulation in excess of $150,000. Reasonable business needs of a corporation include the following:[63]

(1) Plans for the acquisition of buildings or equipment. However, an absence of specificity in the plans or a delay of more than ten years may, while the corporation's assets are liquid, void such needs.[64]
(2) Debt retirements.
(3) Acquisition of a business through the purchase of stock or assets.
(4) Working capital.
(5) Premiums on key man life insurance.
(6) Redemption of a deceased shareholder's stock under Section 303.

Normally, accumulations for purposes of funding deferred compensation and retirement agreements for employees of the corporation should also be considered reasonable business needs. However, where abnormally large key man life insurance policies are used to fund such obligations, problems may arise. It is important, however, to distinguish between a "corporate" purpose and a "shareholder" purpose when accumulating earnings to fund such deferred compensation agreements. Similar problems arise with regard to the retention of earnings to fund stock retirement agreements which may not fall under Section 303 of the Code. See, however, *Emeloid Company, Inc.*,[65] where the court held that insuring against the loss of a key man was a business purpose even though after the insurance was taken out an agreement was executed providing for the proceeds to be used for the purpose of purchasing stock from the estate of the deceased shareholder. Also see *Brumer, Moss & Cohen, P.A. v. U.S.*,[66] where a law firm engaged in litigation argued the following business reasons for accumulating profits: to acquire new offices, to fund a stock retirement agreement, and to provide working capital. The jury determined that the accumulations ($52,000 in 1969 and $2,000 in 1970) were reasonable, even though it also found that the avoidance of income tax by the shareholders motivated the 1970 accumulation. The following are not recognized and acceptable reasons for accumulating earnings:

(1) Loans to shareholders and expenditures for their benefit.
(2) Loans to related parties which have no reasonable relation to the corporation's business.
(3) Loans to related corporations.
(4) Investments unrelated to the business enterprise.
(5) Accumulations for unrealistic hazards.

The accumulated earnings tax may also have an impact on the use of partnerships of professional corporations (see Chapter 19, *infra*). However, where the related corporations are not mere holding companies and where multiple surtax exemptions are permitted uunder Section 1561, separate $150,000 accumulated earnings tax credits should also be available.[67]

[9.05]   COLLAPSIBLE CORPORATIONS—SECTION 341

(1)   General Description of the Rules

The collapsible corporation provisions were instituted to prohibit taxpayers from converting what would normally be ordinary income into capital gain. The archetype collapsible corporation is that established by a movie producer to produce one film. After the production of the film, but prior to its release and the receipt of any royalty income, the corporation is dissolved and the shareholders realize capital gain in the amount of the difference between the value of the film and their adjusted basis in their stock. After the receipt of the capital gain, the shareholders can then dispose of the film without recognizing any gain due to the step-up in basis on the liquidation. The provisions of Section 341 of the Code, which contain the collapsible corporation provisions, are some of the most complex provisions in the Code and they are also some of the most far-reaching. It is safe to say that the collapsible corporation provisions must always be considered in corporate planning, including the dissolution or sale of stock of a professional corporation.

Section 341(a) of the Code provides that gain from the sale or exchange of stock of a collapsible corporation will be treated as ordinary income. A collapsible corporation is defined in Section 341(b) of the Code as a corporation formed or availed of principally for the manufacture, construction, or production of property or for the purchase of property which qualifies as a "Section 341 asset" with a view to:

(1) The sale or exchange of stock by its shareholders (whether in liquidation or otherwise), or a distribution to its shareholders, before the realization by the corporation of a substantial part of the taxable income to be derived from such property, and

(2) The realization by such shareholders of a gain attributable to such property.

Section 341(b)(3) defines "Section 341 assets" as any property held for less than three years which constitutes inventory, unrealized receivables or fees, and all property described in Section 1231(b) (depreciable equipment and real property used in a trade or business). Under Section 341(b)(4), unrealized receivables include any rights to income for services which have not been previously included by the corporation as taxable income. Although Section 341(b) refers to Section 341 assets that are "purchased," the term "purchased" clearly applies to the internal generation of accounts receivable as well as the purchase of accounts receivable from a third party. Thus, in determining whether a professional corporation is a collapsible corporation under Section 341(b), both the equipment of the corporation and the accounts receivable of the corporation will qualify as Section 341 assets if held for less than three years.

A presumption is created under Section 341(c) that a corporation shall, unless evidence is presented to the contrary, be deemed to be a collapsible corporation if at the time of the sale or exchange, or the distribution, the fair market value of the Section 341 assets equals:

(1) At least 50% of the fair market value of the total assets of the corporation, and

(2) At least 120% of the adjusted basis of the Section 341 assets.

Although it may be that professional corporations will rarely fall within the collapsible corporation provisions,[68] in some professional corporations it will be difficult to rebut the Section 341(c) presumption. A professional could, obviously, argue that he did not have the requisite "view" required by Section 341(b)(1), but the regulations state that the "view" need only exist at any time during the manufacture, production, construction, or purchase " of the property.[69]

There are a number of limitations on the application of the collapsible corporation provisions, which are as follows:

(1) The collapsible corporation provisions only apply where a stockholder owns, directly or indirectly, more than 5% in value of the outstanding stock of the corporation. Section 341(d)(1).

(2) Section 341 will not apply unless more than 70% of the gain recognized during the taxable year is attributable to Section 341 assets. Section 341(d)(2).

(3) Section 341 will not apply if the gain is realized after the expiration of three years following the completion of such manufacture, construction, production or purchase. Section 341(d)(3).

(4) Section 341 will not apply to certain types of liquidations and sales of stock where gain can be attributable to assets which would have produced capital gain and the net unrealized appreciation in these assets does not exceed 15% of the corporation's net worth. See Section 341(e).

(5) The corporation can make an election under Section 341(f) and agree that, if it disposes of any of its "Subsection (f) assets" at any time after the sale or exchange or other disposition, it will recognize a gain on the disposition notwithstanding other nonrecognitions of the Code. Section 341(f)(4) defines a "Subsection (f) asset" as any asset existing at the time of the sale or distribution which is not a capital asset to the corporation. This section also provides that unrealized receivables or fees will be treated as property which is not a capital asset.

(2) Application to Professional Corporations

The application of the collapsible corporation provisions to a professional corporation can be illustrated by the following example:

Doctor X intends to sell 50% of the stock of his professional corporation to a new shareholder. The selling price will equal 50% of the book value of the corporation on the date of sale, and the corporation will have the following assets:

Assets	Fair Market Value
Cash	$ 50,000
Accounts Receivable	150,000
Note Receivable	20,000
Equipment	50,000
Total Assets	270,000
Accounts Payable	(20,000)
Net Assets	$250,000)

Doctor X's basis in his stock is zero and most of the equipment has been held for three years or longer; however, all of the accounts receivable have been held for less than three years and the corporation uses a cash method of accounting; the receivables, consequently, have a zero basis.

Section 341(a) will not apply to the sale of stock so long as the portion of the gain recognized that is attributable to unrealized receivables or Section 1231(b) assets held for less than three years does not exceed 70% of the total gain on the sale. In other words, the fair market value of both the accounts receivable and the equipment (assuming the equipment has been held for less than three years) cannot exceed 70% of the total fair market value of the assets of the corporation at the time of the sale. If this condition is not met, the entire gain realized on the sale will be treated as ordinary income unless the corporation makes an election under Section 341(f) prior to the sale. This result is based on the following:

(1) In determining whether the corporation is a collapsible corporation under Section 341(b), both the equipment and the accounts receivable qualify as Section 341 assets if held less than three years as of the date of the sale.

(2) It would be difficult for Doctor X to rebut the Section 341(c) presumption. He could argue that he did not have the requisite "view" required by Section 341(b)(1), but the Regulations state that the "view" need only exist at "any time during the manufacture, production, construction or purchase" of the property. Since Doctor X will have planned the sale of the stock for some time during which he was producing some of the accounts receivable, the Service may take the position that a "view" did exist.

(3) Of the exemptions provided in Section 341(d), only the exemption provided in Section 341(d)(2) will be available. Regulations §1.341-4(c)(2) states that the gain attributable to Section 341 assets will equal the excess of the shareholder's recognized gain on the sale of the stock over the recognized gain which the shareholder would have had if the Section 341 assets had not been produced by the corporation.

If the Section 1231(b) assets have been held for three years or more as of the date of sale, it is only necessary to determine the portion of the gain attributable to the accounts receivable. Using the asset projections above. Section 341 would not apply to the transaction since the accounts receivable constitute only 55% of the fair market value of the assets. However, if the equipment does not meet the three-year rule, it will also be considered Section 341 property, and conceivably could push the total gain attributable to Section 341 assets over 70%.

Thus, it will be extremely important to evaluate the asset mix prior to the sale in order to assure the transaction will pass the 70% test. If the equipment has been held for more than three years, there should be no problem. On the other hand, if some of the equipment does not meet the three-year test and the accounts receivable are unusually high, the corporation may find it necessary to adjust the asset mix prior to the sale. For example, it could postpone the sale until the accounts receivable are down to normal levels, or it could delay current billings.[70] Another possibility would be to sell the equipment at book value rather than fair market value, thereby reducing the portion of the gain attributable to Section 1231(b) property. Doctor X might also attempt to allocate a portion of the selling price to goodwill. Since goodwill is not a collapsible asset, this would increase the portion of gain attributable to noncollapsible assets. These measures will help insure that the gain attributable to Section 341 assets does not exceed 70% of the total gain realized.

If the corporation were forced to execute a Section 341(f) election, it would not present a problem for Doctor X or the corporation with regard to the accounts receivable. Most of the receivables would be collected and taken into income by the corporation within a short time after the sale of stock. However, the equipment may be held by the corporation until dissolution. By virtue of having filed the Section 341(f) election, the corporation would be forced to recognize gain in connection with what would otherwise be a nontaxable distribution in liquidation. This negative aspect of the Section 341(f) election may make it an undesirable alternative if the Section 341(d)(2) amnesty is not available. The incoming stockholder may also object to the election, although his consent is not required.

A Section 341(f) election becomes irrevocable as soon as any shareholder has effected a sale of his stock during the six-month period beginning when the election is filed. It should be recognized that the election is not available to the corporation if Doctor X (or any person related to him within the meaning of Section 341(e)(8)(A)) at any time during the five-year period preceding the sale of the stock sold the stock of any other corporation which had made a Section 341(f) election.

If it appears that the sale will not qualify under Section 341(d)(2) and Doctor X is unwilling to elect under Section 341(f), the transaction must be restructured. At that point, the parties could agree that the existing accounts receivable will be paid out to Doctor X as additional salary when they are collected by the corporation. This means the selling price of the shares will be determined without regard to the accounts receivable. As a result, the collapsible corporation problem will be eliminated and the reduced selling price will make it easier for the new shareholder to finance the acquisition. Under this arrangement, however, there is no opportunity to convert ordinary income into long-term capital gain.

(3) Conclusion

The above example illustrates that, although many practitioners feel that the collapsible corporation provisions should not present a problem for professional corporations, the problem does exist. Unless the professional corporation uses the accrual method of accounting (which most do not), the accounts receivable and possibly work in progress will be considered Section 341 assets and may produce a collapsible corporation problem if, upon the sale of stock to a new stockholder, the 341 assets are part of the sale. On the other hand, many professionals simply sell an interest in the hard assets of the corporation and handle the accounts receivable under employment or deferred compensation agreements. (See Section [11.01], *infra*.) It is noteworthy to review the former Chief Counsel's comments (in 1970) on the collapsible corporation provisions which are as follows:

> These provisions are complex, and it may be that professional corporations would rarely fall within them. I would point out, however, that one of the types of property which, when owned by a corporation, can serve to bring the collapsible corporations into operation, is unrealized receivables or fees. As I had mentioned before, this is a type of asset which professional organizations, and particularly a law firm, is likely to possess.[71]

In any event, if the collapsible corporation provisions are imposed, they will probably not provide a more damaging result than that provided under Section 751 and the collapsible partnership provisions of Subchapter K of the Code. Further, professional corporations should normally not incur substantial penalties by making a Section 341(f) consent in order to avoid current tax on accounts receivable. In addition, where a professional corporation is dissolved with existing accounts receivable, it is likely that the receivables will be recognized upon the dissolution.[72]

NOTES TO CHAPTER 9

1. 37 B.T.A. 271 (1937).

2. *Charles Laughton*, 40 B.T.A. 101 (1939).

3. *Moline Properties, Inc. v. Commissioner*, 319 U.S. 436 (1943).

4. Also see *National Carbide Corporation v. Commissioner*, 336 U.S. 441 (1949).

5. 1966-239 T.C. Memo, *aff'd*, 22 A.F.T.R. 2d 5810 (2d Cir. 1968).

6. *Johansson v. U.S.*, 336 F.2d 890 (5th Cir. 1964).

7. *U.S. v. Emprey*, 406 F.2d 157 (10th Cir. 1969).

8. *Kimbrell v. Commissioner*, 371 F.2d 897 (5th Cir. 1967).

9. *Philip W. Kessler*, 36 T.C.M. 514 ¶77,117 P-H Memo T.C. (1977).

10. Also see *Preferred Properties, Inc.*, 1976-18 Tax Court Memo.

11. For a general discussion see, Kronovet, "Straw Corporations, When Will They be Recognized; What Can and Should be Done," *J. Taxation* 54(1973), and Fischer, "Classification under Section 7701—the Past, Present, and Prospects for the Future," 30 *Tax Lawyer* 627 (1977). See *McGee v. U.S.*, 47 A.F.T.R. 2d 81-910 (D.C. Neb. 1981), physician's professional corporation and not physician earned the income where corporation was validly incorporated and not a sham.

12. 281 U.S. 111(1929).

13. Also see Lyon and Eustice, "Assignment of Income, Fruit of the Tree as Irrigated by P.G. Lake," *Tax Law Review* 393 (1962).

14. *Ronan State Bank*, 62 T.C. 27(1974).

15. *supra* Notes 1 and 2.

16. 53 T.C. 365(1969).

17. 1976-294 T.C.M. 45, ¶76,294 P-H Memo T.C., 621 F.2d 865 (7th Cir. 1980).

18. Letter Ruling 8031028.

19. 51 T.C. 251 (1968), reversed and remanded, 429 F.2d 650 (2d. Cir. 1970), on remand 56 T.C. 1155 (1971), *aff'd per curiam*, 460 F.2d 1216 (2d Cir. 1972).

20. 56 T.C. 828(1971).

21. 64 T.C. 1066 (1975).

22. 36 T.C.M. 719, ¶77,174 P-H Memo T.C. (1977).

23. 1973-74 T.C. Memo.

24. 54 T.C. 758 (1970).

25. 34 T.C.M. 442, ¶75,087 P-H Memo T.C. (1975).

26. 33 A.F.T.R. 2d 74-714, *aff'd*, 490 F.2d 98 (7th Cir. 1973).

27. 64 T.C. 1034 (1975).

28. 35 T.C.M. 494, ¶76,110 P-H Memo T.C. (1976).

29. 1976-2 C.B. 20.

30. 42 T.C. 114 (1964), *aff'd*, 358 F.2d 342 (6th Cir. 1966).

31. T.C.M. 1967-173, *aff'd*, 405 F.2d 673 (1968) *cert. denied sub nom. Danica Enterprises v. Commissioner*, 395 U.S. 933 (1969).

32. See *Whipple v. Commissioner*, 373 U.S. 193 (1963).

33. Note 19, *supra*.

34. Note 21, *supra*.

35. 60 T.C. 872 (1973).

36. 530 F.2d 772 (8th Cir. 1976).

37. 69-1 U.S.T.C. ¶9279, 23 AFTR 2d 69-800 (S.D.N.Y. 1969), *aff'd per curiam*, 1971-1 U.S.T.C. ¶9304, 27 AFTR 2d 71-655 (2d Cir. 1971).

38. Worthy, *supra*, Chapter 5, note 7, at 90. Also see: Kauder, "The Service

Corporation as the Taxpayer's Alter Ego: Variations on the Borge Theme,'' 28 *NYU Inst. Fed. Tax* 1109 (1970); and Egerton, ''Reallocation of Income: A New Threat To Professional Corporation?,'' 58 A.B.A.J. 979 (1972). (1972).

McFadden, ''Section 482 and the Professional Corporation: The Foglesong Case,'' 8 *J. Corp. Tax* 35 (1981).

Erbacher, ''Are Courts Making It Harder To Overturn An IRS Allocation Under Section 482?'' 16 *J. Taxation* 286 (1977).

Schwartz ''Meeting a Tax On The Professional Corporation Organizational Problems; Section 482; Reasonable Compensation; Retirements and Liquidations, ''32 *NYU Inst. Fed. Tax.* 859 (1974).

Reimer, ''Professional Corporations: An Analysis,'' 62 *Mass. L.Q.* 151 (1977).

Sacher, ''Is A Partnership Of P.A.'s the Solution To Problems Of Professional Associations?'' 44 *J. Taxation*, 236 (1976).

Battle, ''The Use Of Corporations By Persons Who Perform Services To Gain Tax Advantages,'' see references at end of Part I. However, see the Technical Advice reported as Letter Ruling 8122011 in which the National Office held that status as an employee can be a separate trade or business for purposes of Section 482.

39. Treas. Regs. §1.543-1(b)(8).

40. See example 1 under the Regulations.

41. See example 3 under the Regulations.

42. 1959-1 C.B. 144.

43. *S.O. Claggett*, 44 T.C. 503 (1965), *acq.* 1966-2 C.B. 4.

44. Note 17, *supra*.

45. 1975-1 C.B. 169.

46. See Rev. Rul. 69-299, 1969-1 C.B. 165. Also see Rev. Rul. 75-249, 1975-1 C.B. 171, involving a musician, and Rev. Rul. 75-250, 1975-1 C.B. 172, involving services rendered by an accountant, and Letter Rulings 7733052, 8130049.

47. Worthy, *surpa*, Chapter 5 note 7 at 92:
''This provision will present no problem in cases where a client retains the professional firm as such, and the firm chooses a particular person who will perform services for the client. In many cases, however, a client does have some say in choosing which lawyer in the firm will handle his problem. Obviously, in applying the personal holding company provisions to this type of situation, the question will arise of just what constitutes a ''designation'' for Code purposes. In most of the cases to date where the personal holding company provisions have been applied, the designation has been effected in a written contract, and of course, law firms often do not have written contracts with their clients ... [I]t seems questionable whether the mere fact that a designation is not in writing should render the statute inapplicable. This is an

area where the law may be further developed with the advent of professional corporations."

48. *Thomas P. Byrnes, Inc.*, 73 T.C. No. 36 (December 4, 1979)—Personal Holding Company tax not imposed on service commissions from manufacturing corporations; commissions were not personal holding company income. Manufacturing corporation did not designate service corporation president as person to perform services required by sales representation agreements entered into with service corporation.

Letter Ruling 8003010—Partnership agreement was not contract for professional corporation to provide the specific services of sole shareholder. Other doctors were freely substituted in performance of corporation's obligation to partnership and agreement did not specify who must provide actual services.

Letter Ruling 7934092—A proposes to incorporate his business and transfer assets to M. M will engage in providing engineering consulting services and A will be sole shareholder and employee. M will enter employment contract with N for a period of five years and N will not have right to specify which employee of M will render services. Internal Revenue Service ruled that income earned under contract will not be personal holding company income.

Letter Ruling 7915042—A has been practicing medicine with approximately 25 other doctors. A contemplates formation of professional medical corporation formed pursuant to Louisiana law, with A as sole stockholder. A will enter into employment agreement with corporation which will provide for payment of salary in exchange for exclusive services. Corporation's income will consist of its share of partnership profits and a small amount of investment income not exceeding 50% of gross revenues. As long as A does not perform services that are so unique as to preclude substitution of another physician, there is no physician-patient contract which will constitute contract for personal services under Section 543. The corporation will be treated as corporation for federal tax purposes, and income from distributions of partnership profits will not be personal holding company income. This follows *Revenue Ruling 75-67*, 1975-1 C.B. 169.

Letter Ruling 7909095—Corporation is a consulting firm that provides, among its services, the placing of life and health insurance for its clients. Several of Corporation's employees are agents of insurance companies, but are required by contract to remit all insurance sales commissions to the corporation. Employees are paid on a straight salary basis. Corporation will be treated as a corporation for federal income tax purposes. Because designation within the meaning of Section 543(a)(7) does not exist, insurance premiums assigned to the corporation are not personal holding company income. Also, income is that of corporation and not of assign or employee.

Letter Ruling 7819025—No personal services designation, and therefore, no personal holding company income, if corporation does not agree to perform services that are so unique as to preclude substitution of another doctor. Similar to Revenue Ruling 75-250, 1975-1 C.B. 172 (C.P.A. as sole shareholder but not only employee) and Letter Ruling 7733052 (Computer Programmer who will be the only corporate employee).

49. See *Coastal Oil Storage Co. v. Commissioner*, 242 F. 2d 396 (4th Cir. 1957) where the court stated "that the Section [now Section 269 of the 1954 Code] was intended to reach such schemes for tax evasion or avoidance by the splitting up of business enterpise clearly appears in House Report No. 871, 78th Congress, the First Session, Page 49, where it is said: the crux of the devices which have come to the attention of our Committee has been some form of acquisition on or after the effective day of the Second Revenue Act of 1940, but the devices take many forms. Thus, the acquisition may be an acquisition of the share of a corporation or it may be an acquisition which follows by operation of law in the case of a corporation resulting from a statutory merger or consolidation. The person or persons making the acquisitions likewise vary as do the forms or methods of utilization under which tax avoidance is sought. Likewise, the tax benefit sought may be one or more of several deductions or credits, including the utilization of excess profits credits, carryovers and carrybacks, of losses or unused excess profits credits, and anticipated expense or other deductions'. In light of these considerations, the Section has not confined itself to a description of any particular methods for carrying out such tax avoidance schemes, but has included within its scope these devices in whatever form they may appear. For similar reasons, the scope of the terms used in the Section is to be found in the objective of the Section, namely to prevent the tax liability from being reduced through the distortion or perversion effective through tax avoidance devices... ."

50. See the description of the history of professional corporations following Chapter 19.

51. See Worthy, Note 7 in Chapter 5, *supra*.

52. 1945 C.B. 200.

53. Sections 921 and 922 of the Code.

54. 1976-2 C.B. 90.

55. Note 31, *supra*.

56. *Letter Ruling 7939003*. A National Office Technical Advice Memorandum is a written opinion of the National Office regarding a particular issue under audit. Often, where an issue may not be resolved at the District Level, the District Director and the taxpayer agree to a stipulated set of facts and submit these facts to th National Office with the request that the National Office issue Technical Advice with regard to the proper determination of the issue involved.

57. The Service can reach much the same result provided under Section 269 through various other ways, such as the sham corporation doctrine and the assignment of income doctrine. See section [9.01] *supra*. Also, see *Edward D. Smithback*, 28 T.C.M. 709, 711, ¶69,136 P-H Memo T.C. (1969), where the court said with regard to any medical reimbursement plan, "We under-

stand that the genesis and the primary purpose of the plan—indeed, of incorporating Edward's business—to have been the avoidance of Federal taxation, a purpose which obviously has to benefit Edward in his capacity as owner of the business rather than as an employee.''

58. See section [6.03], *supra*.

59. See *Holder,* Chapter 6, Note 3 *supra*. However, see *Kline v. Kline,* Mich. App., 305 N.W. 2d 297 (3/17/81), where the Michigan Court of Appeals ignored the existence of a professional corporation in a wife's attempt to enforce a support obligation.

60. 294 F. Supp. 1225 (D.C. Ark. 1968), gov't appeal to 8th Cir. dismissed 9/2/69.

61. *Ivan Allen Co. v. Commissioner*, 422 U.S. 617 (1975).

62. The proposed *Tax Reduction Act of 1980* (specifically Section 221 of H.R. 5829) would increase the minimum accumulated earning credit to $250,000. However, this increase would not apply to certain service corporations specified in the Act whose principal businesses consist of ''the performance of services in the field of health, law, engineering, architecture, accounting, actuarial science, performing arts, or consulting.'' The present minimum credit of $150,000 would apply to these corporations.

63. See Worthy, *supra*, Chapter 5, Note 7, at 92:
"It would seem relatively unusual for a professional corporation to have a business need to accumulate more than $100,000 [now $150,000] of earnings, although such a need might exist in the case of a corporation which owned or planned to acquire its own building or in the case of a medical corporation which is required to maintain a heavy investment in equipment. In any event, the existence of the accumulated earnings tax is something which the professional corporation and its shareholders should be aware of when making a decision as to distribution of income.''

64. See *American Metal Products Corporation*, 287 F.2d 860 (8th Cir. 1961).

65. 189 F.2d 230 (3rd Cir. 1951).

66. 37 A.F.T.R. 2d 76-802 (S.D. Fla. 1975); Also see Fromberg and Weinstein, ''Professional Corporations Face New IRS Attack if Earnings Accumulate in the Corporation,'' *Taxation For Lawyers* 118 (1976).

67. See *Lake Textile Company, Inc., 28 T.C.M. 246, ¶69,044 P-H Memo T.C. (1969).

68. Worthy, *supra*, Chapter 5, Note 7, at 92.

69. Treas. Regs. §1.341-2(a)(3).

70. Note however that Treas. Regs. §1.341-2(b)(4) defines the terms ''unrealized receivables'' and ''fees'' so broadly that these terms could include unbilled work in process: ''any rights (contractual or otherwise) to payment for ... services rendered or to be rendered, to the extent such rights have not been included in the income of the corporation under the method of accounting used by it.''

71. Worthy, *supra*, Chapter 5, note 7, at 92.

72. For a general discussion of this topic see: Alexander, ''Some Tax Problems of a Professional Association,'' 13 *Western Reserve Law Review* 221 (1962); Rosenzweig ''Selling or liquidating a Service Business—Special Problems'' 26th *NYU Inst. Fed. Tax* 1001 (1968); Schwartz, ''Meeting Attacks on the Professional Corporation: Organization Problems; Section 482; Reasonable Compensation; Retirements and Liquidations,'' 32 *NYU Inst. Fed. Tax.* 859, at 876 (1974); Eaton, *supra*, Chapter 7 note 1, §6.07.

CHAPTER **10**

Dealing with Employees, Other Professional Corporations, and Institutions—Employment Agreements Generally

[10.01] EMPLOYMENT AGREEMENTS

Employment agreements for the professional employees of a professional corporation, both shareholder and nonshareholder, are indispensable. Employment agreements for professionals serve a number of functions, such as reducing the possibility of an attack on the "corporateness" of the corporation, reducing the possibility that compensation paid to shareholder-employees will be declared unreasonable, facilitating a professional's deduction of business expenses on his own return, avoiding the personal holding company tax, avoiding disputes among shareholders regarding salaries, bonuses, vacation and termination pay, insulating the professionals against wage freezes, and providing certain other benefits, such as the $5,000 death benefit under Section 101(b) of the Code. Employment agreements for shareholders and nonshareholders are usually drafted somewhat differently. The provisions contained in an employment agreement for a shareholder-employee generally correspond to provisions which would be contained in a partnership agreement. On the other hand, the provisions of a nonshareholder employment agreement simply relate to the fact of employment.

Contained below in this section are shareholder and nonshareholder employment agreements. Each section of these agreements is followed by comments relating to the appropriateness of the section.

(1) Employment Agreements for Shareholder Employees

STATE OF GEORGIA

COUNTY OF _____

EMPLOYMENT AGREEMENT

THIS AGREEMENT, made and entered into this _____ day of _____, 19_____, by and between _____, a Georgia professional corporation, hereinafter referred to as "EMPLOYER", and _____, M.D., a resident of said State and County, hereinafter referred to as "EMPLOYEE",

WHEREAS, the EMPLOYER is a professional corporation rendering professional services in the State of Georgia through its employees who are duly licensed to practice medicine in that state; and

WHEREAS, the EMPLOYEE is a physician duly licensed to practice medicine in the State of Georgia; and

WHEREAS, the EMPLOYER desires to employ the EMPLOYEE and the EMPLOYEE desires to become employed by the EMPLOYER, all on the terms and conditions hereinafter set forth;

NOW, THEREFORE, the parties, for and in consideration of the mutual and reciprocal covenants and agreements hereinafter contained, do contract and agree as follows, to-wit:

1. Purpose and Employment. The purpose of this Agreement is to define the relationship between the EMPLOYER as an employer and EMPLOYEE as an employee of the EMPLOYER. EMPLOYER hereby employs EMPLOYEE, and EMPLOYEE hereby accepts employment by EMPLOYER upon all of the terms and conditions as are hereinafter set forth.

2. Duties. EMPLOYEE agrees to practice his medical specialty solely as an employee of the EMPLOYER and, except as hereinafter provided, shall devote his entire professional time to the affairs of the EMPLOYER. In addition, EMPLOYEE agrees to devote all necessary time and his best efforts in the performance of his duties as a doctor of medicine for the EMPLOYER and to perform such other duties as are assigned to him from time to time by the board of directors of EMPLOYER (the "Board of Directors"). EMPLOYEE shall be free to exercise his own judgment regarding the treatment of any particular patient, however, EMPLOYEE agrees to observe and comply with the rules and regulations of EMPLOYER as adopted from time to time by the Board of Directors. EMPLOYEE specifically agrees that the Board of Directors shall have the sole right to designate and assign patients to EMPLOYEE for treatment and that the Board of Directors shall determine the fee to be charged by EMPLOYER for the professional services rendered by EMPLOYEE hereunder. Further, the Board of Directors shall have the final authority over acceptance or refusal of any person for

whom professional services may be rendered. EMPLOYEE shall also keep and maintain (or cause to be kept and maintained) appropriate records relating to all professional services rendered by him hereunder and he shall also prepare and attend to all billing, reports, claims, and correspondence required in connection with his services rendered hereunder.

Comment:

Paragraphs 1 and 2 are standard paragraphs which establish the relationship of employee and employer. There is substantial latitude in drafting these paragraphs, and they may also include such matters as the specific assignments to be given to the employee, or the fact that the employee will be elected as a director or officer of the corporation. Such additional considerations are, however, not essential to the proper operation of these paragraphs. The requirements that the employee shall follow the rules and regulations of the Board of Directors will permit the implementation of rules relating to the activities of the employee. Also, if it is felt that an agreement must be reached regarding the election of officers and directors, it may be advisable to prepare a shareholders' agreement such as that described in section [6.05], *supra*.

The establishment of the employee-employer relationship in these paragraphs is essential to assure the integrity of the corporate status and to avoid personal holding company problems. As indicated under Rev. Rul. 75-67,[1] the Board of Directors should have the ability to determine which patients will be seen by the corporation, which patients will be seen by the employee, and what will be charged for the employee's services. Care should be taken, however, not to impinge upon the employee's professional judgment.

In community property states, it is probably advisable to require the spouse of the professional to accept and approve the employment agreement by signing a separate acceptance and approval which should be attached to the employment agreement.

3. <u>Term.</u> The term of employment under this Agreement shall be for the year beginning _____ and ending _____, and for each successive year thereafter unless and until terminated as hereinafter provided.

Comment:

Every employment agreement should have a specified term, but the agreement should also be self-renewing. This will eliminate the necessity for the annual execution of new employment agreements.

4. <u>Compensation.</u> For all the services to be rendered by EMPLOYEE in any capacity hereunder, including services as an officer, member of the EMPLOYER's Board of Directors, or any other duties assigned to him by the Board of Directors, EMPLOYER shall pay EMPLOYEE a monthly salary of $_____, payable at the end of each month during the term of this Agreement. All compensation paid to EMPLOYEE shall be subject to customary withholding and employment taxes. If the EMPLOYER does not have adequate funds from

operations to pay the full salary, any monthly salary payment may be deferred until funds are available to make such payment and any unpaid obligation as of the end of a fiscal year shall be canceled.

The EMPLOYER and EMPLOYEE may, from time to time, reflect increases or decreases in the above monthly salary as may be mutually agreed upon by entering any such change upon the "Schedule of Compensation," attached hereto as Exhibit "A" and made a part hereof. If a change in compensation is entered on said Schedule and duly signed by the proper officers of EMPLOYER and by EMPLOYEE, said entry shall constitute an amendment to this Employment Agreement as of the date of said entry and shall supersede the monthly salary provided for in the immediately preceding paragraph of this Agreement and any other change or changes previously entered on said Schedule.

Comment

This section of the employment agreement is structured so that all compensation payable to the employee will be paid to him as salary. In closely held corporations, it is usually best to avoid the use of a discretionary bonus, which is paid at the end of the year in order to reduce taxable income. A similar rule should generally apply to professional corporations, although, historically, professional corporations have not encountered a significant problem with reasonable compensation issues, at least where the compensation paid does not exceed billings. See Chapter 13, *infra*. Unless a specified contractual bonus arrangement will be employed, as is discussed in the paragraphs below, the authors feel that discretionary bonuses should be avoided and that employment agreements should be structured so that all compensation paid will be in the form of salaries. In order to establish such a compensation mechanism, it will be necessary for the board of directors of a professional corporation to place the compensation of each professional at a level which will equal the professional's anticipated total annual compensation. Then, the board may permit the professional to receive monthly salary payments at this level, or at a lower level, if the cash flow of the corporation so dictates. Further, in the event that the cash flow of the corporation is not sufficient to meet the entire salary, the agreement provides that any unpaid salary will be canceled at the end of the year. This should eliminate any constructive receipt problems.[2] Such a compensation arrangement, because it is based on anticipated total compensation, should also eliminate the necessity of discretionary bonuses.

Employment agreements should also be drafted to that compensation may be increased or decreased on a schedule to that agreement without the necessity of redrafting the agreement. The form agreement provides for such a schedule.

The above compensation clause may be easily modified in order to address the "bunching" problem which may occur upon the incorporation of a fiscal year partnership. First, the compensation clause may provide for a two-step salary level: a small salary for the first six months of employment and an increased salary for the remainder. Also, the agreement could provide that the corporation's liability for any unpaid salary at the end of any fiscal year will not be canceled but will be "carried over to the following year." Such language should provide flexibility in determining when the bunched income will be recognized.

In some professional groups, it is impossible to provide a stated salary which will be accepted by all of the professionals. For this reason, many professional groups employ "production" formulae. Such production formulae should, however, not be considered to interfere with the integrity of the corporation because it is not unreasonable for the professionals to expect that their compensation will be based on their efforts. In reviewing production formulae, the professional corporation advisor should realize that the "collections" of a professional corporation will not approach the "billings" because of the uncollectable factor. Therefore, production formulae should be based on collections or take into account a standard uncollectable factor based on billings.

Similarly, many production formulae adjust compensation based on all of the fringe benefits received by the professionals, such as accident, health, and life insurance, retirement plan contributions, etc. It is possible that a production formula which takes such fringe benefits into account will be considered a *de facto* cafeteria plan or a cash or deferred plan. Special provisions were provided under the Revenue Act of 1978 to deal with cafeteria and cash or deferred plans, and, if a productivity formula is considered to be one of such plans, it will probably not comply with the nondiscrimination rules, creating an enormous and unforeseen tax liability. See, generally, sections [14.04] and [15.02], *infra*. However, if the corporation has properly adopted its employee benefit "plans," the reference to such benefit plans in a production formula should not constitute a cafeteria or cash or deferred plan, but should be considered only a method of deducting from each professional the proportion of the overhead of the corporation which is allocable to him.

The authors have encountered a number of production formulae which have been successful in assuaging professional egos. However, the authors would also like to point out that productivity formulae are sometimes not beneficial. For example, productivity formulae tend to isolate the professionals so that each professional considers his practice independent of that of the corporation and the other professionals. This militates against the theory of a group practice and, in some instances, leads to the breakup of the group. On the other hand, the use of a productivity formula may tend to hold a diverse group together because each professional does not feel that he is being required to support other, less hard-working professionals. The effectiveness of a production formula will depend on the particular personalities involved.

The following are examples of production formulae which have been employed by professional medical groups:

(1) *The Pure Production Formula*. This is probably the simplest formula in theory, but probably the most difficult to implement. Under this formula, the professional corporation will isolate each professional's billings, collections and

expenses. The net amount available, after expenses are deducted from collections, is used to provide the employee benefits and compensation of each professional. As a practical matter, such an absolute collection formula is difficult to implement without keeping a separate set of books for each professional. Since most professional corporations maintain only one set of books, it is possible to keep track of a professional's billings, but usually impossible to keep track of a professional's collections. For this reason, many total production formulae are based upon a professional's percentage of the total collections of the practice (total collections multiplied by a fraction, the numerator of which is the professional's total billings and the denominator of which is the total billings of all the professionals). Then the expenses attributable to that professional are subtracted. Determining the exact dollar value of the expenses to be subtracted is also difficult. For example, the common professional expenses, such as rent, staff salaries, and medical supplies are difficult to allocate to a particular professional and they are often prorated to each professional based on his percentage of billings to the total billings. The particular expenses which can be allocated to a professional (such as cost of insurance and retirement plan contributions) are so allocated.

(2) *Flat Percentage of Billings*. Where a professional corporation has a stable practice, the approximate annual cost of running the corporation and providing employee benefits (other than compensation and benefits for professionals) may be anticipated. In this situation, a straightforward method of determining compensation is to provide for each professional a flat percentage of his billings, which will be used for providing his compensation and fringe benefits. Since, in most professional corporations, actual nonprofessional overhead expenses run between 30% and 40% of collections and uncollectable accounts run between 5% and 15% of billings, it is likely that such a flat percentage will be between 55% and 70% of billings, depending upon the particular paractice. In some practices which employ the flat percentage method, certain professionals often feel that their portion of the overhead is not as high as that of other professionals and that, as their productivity increases, their percentage share of the overhead decreases. This is particularly true where a professional corporation employs different types of professionals, such as internists and surgeons. Typically, the overhead expenses related to a surgical practice, including scrub nurse, etc., will be higher than those of an office-based internal medicine practice. In such situations, the authors have seen the following flat percentages used:

Gross Billings of Employee for Employment Year	Percentage to be Paid Employee as Total Compensation
$1 through $100,000	60%
$100,001 through $200,000	65%
$200,001 through $250,000	70%
$250,001 through $300,000	80%
Over $300,000	85%

(3) *Division of Net Profit Based on Various Factors.* Some professional corporations divide the net profit based on various factors in addition to productivity, such as longevity and the extent to which one professional is on call. For example, one such formula begins with gross collections and subtracts common overhead expenses such as staff salaries, rent, malpractice insurance, etc. The net income so obtained is divided among the professionals and is used to provide compensation and fringe benefits. The net income is divided as follows:

(i) Eighty percent of the net income is divided based on productivity. A professional's portion is based on his percentage of billings to the total billings of the professional corporation.

(ii) Ten percent of the net income is divided based on nights and weekends on call, with the formula being a professional's nights and weekends on call over all professionals' nights and weekends on call.

(iii) The remaining 10% of the net income is divided based on longevity, with the formula being a professional's years of service with the professional corporation, divided by all years of service with the professional corporation of all professionals.

Of course, any number of other factors could be used in computing the allocation.

(4) *Base Compensation with Production Bonus.* Under this method, the computation is far more complicated. The first step in the formula is to determine collections for the fiscal year and subtract common operating overhead and base salaries for the professionals. The figure obtained is the net income available for fringe benefits and additional compensation distributions, which is then prorated based upon each professional's percentage of collections, if it is obtainable, and if not, each professional's percentage of billings. An example of the computation of this formula follows:

$1,200,000	Collections for FYE 4/30/81
(300,000)	Less common operating overhead, excluding salaries and fringe benefits for Dr. X and Dr. Y (retirement plan contributions per the actuarial report, life, health and disability insurance, auto and lease expenses, travel and entertainment, and dues and professional meeting expenses) for Drs. X and Y.
	less base salaries:
(100,000)	Dr. X
(100,000)	Dr. Y
$ 700,000	Net available for fringe benefits and additional compensation distributions.

Division of Net Per Production
Assuming 42% for Dr. Y and 58%
for Dr. X

	Dr. Y (42%)	Dr. X (58%)
Allocation of net available	$294,000	$406,000
Less cost of fringe benefits for Drs. X and Y	(100,000)	(125,000)
Amount available for distribution as additional compensation	194,000	281,000

Recapitulation

	Dr. Y	Dr. X
Base Salary	$100,000	$100,000
Fringe Benefits	100,000	125,000
Additional Compensation	194,000	281,000
Total Compensation	$394,000	$506,000

This formula approximates a ''pure production'' formula, but it does provide a base salary (on which production is not computed) in order to reflect the ''value'' of the professional's presence with the professional corporation. Obviously, to the extent that the base salary is increased, the production aspect of this formula is reduced. In fact, some professional corporations use a ''bonus pool'' approach. Based on the above example (using the salaries of $200,000 each which were actually paid to Dr. X and Dr. Y), the bonus pool method would provide the following bonuses:

Bonus Pool Formula

Total Collections	$1,200,000
Less:	
Common Overhead	(300,000)
Salaries Actually Paid for Dr. X and Dr. Y	(400,000)
Fringe Benefits for Dr. X and Dr. Y	(225,000)
Bonus Pool	$ 275,000

Division of Bonus Pool Based on Production:

$$Dr.\ X = \$275,000 \times 58\% = \$159,500$$

$$Dr.\ Y = \$275,000 \times 42\% = \$115,500$$

Recapitulation

	Dr. X	Dr. Y
Actual Salary	$200,000	$200,000
Fringe Benefits	100,000	125,000
Bonus	115,500	159,500
Total Compensation	$415,500	$484,500

Obviously, the "bonus pool" formula reduces further the compensation which Dr. X receives.

(5) *Bonus Based on Low Man's Production.* In some professional corporations where the professionals are performing approximately the same amount of work, it is felt desirable to provide a small incentive for additional production. In such a situation, a production formula can be established so that each professional receives a bonus equal to a stated percentage of his collections (or billings) in excess of that of the lowest professional. Depending upon the salaries granted to the professionals, this percentage could run from 5% to 30% and does appear to give a moderate incentive for production without coverting the compensation process into a pure production formula.

It is also possible, of course, for professional corporations to provide in the employment agreements of the professionals that a bonus pool will be determined by the board of directors and that each professional will have a contractual right to a stated percentage of that bonus pool.

If a production formula is not chosen, the authors recommend using such a contractual bonus formula in employment agreements as opposed to implementing discretionary bonuses.

Each profession generally compensates professionals based on the particular aspects of that profession. However, the authors' experience has shown that, as a general rule, the various types of professional corporations compensate professional employees in approximately the same fashion. For example, medical groups generally compensate nonshareholder professional employees on a stated salary basis with a small discretionary annual bonus. This continues for a period of two to four years, after which the professional employee becomes a shareholder in the corporation (a more or less "equal" partner) and is compensated on the same basis as the other shareholder-employees of the corporation. On the other hand, legal and accounting firms tend to compensate both nonshareholder and shareholder professional employees based upon a prearranged salary structure which provides that employees will earn a certain salary based upon their particular position in the firm, i.e., fifth-year shareholder. This is particularly true in larger accounting and law firms. However, some smaller accounting and law firms grant bonuses based upon production in an attempt to encourage the professionals to garner new business. For example, many accounting and law firms use formulae such as the well-known Hale & Dorr formula, which grants credit for both bringing the particular client to the firm and performing the work for the client. Such a production formula is more important in a law or accounting practice (than in a medical practice) where the clients of the firm usually produce recurring fees.

The following is a bonus formula used in professional law corporations which has been circulated among members of the Professional Service Corporations Committee of the Tax Section of the American Bar Association.

Bonus mentioned in paragraph _____ shall be _____% of Adjusted Net Income.

"Adjusted Net Income" shall mean the net income of the Corporation for its fiscal year in question calculated on the cash basis in accordance with generally accepted accounting practices, consistently applied, by the Corporation's auditors for federal income tax purposes; provided, however, that in computing such net income for purposes of this Agreement—

1. There shall be no recognition or inclusion of (i) gains or losses resulting from the sale or exchange of capital assets or assets subject to allowance for depreciation, obsolescence or amortization, other than office equipment, all within the meaning of the Code, or (ii) proceeds of any fire or casualty insurance or any insurance carried by the Corporation upon the life of any individual, except in the fiscal year or years and to the extent, if any, that post-death payments to such individual or his estate or beneficiary are made under paragraph ____ of this Agreement and are deducted (under (2) below or otherwise) in computing Adjusted Net Income.

2. There shall be no deduction or provision for income, excess profits, or similar taxes imposed by the United States or any state or foreign country, or any political subdivision thereof, which are paid or accrued with respect to the fiscal year in question or any other fiscal year.

3. The following shall be deducted:

a. Amounts paid or payable by the Corporation for the fiscal year in question under any defined contribution or defined benefit plan which the Corporation regards as qualified for purposes of Section 401 of the Code or under any other fringe benefit program comprehended by paragraph ____ of this Agreement (thus including insurance payments, if any);

b. Amounts, if any, paid by the Corporation to _____ and _____, except to the extent, if any, that they are the purchase price of capital stock of the Corporation;

c. Salaries paid or payable by the Corporation to lawyer employees (including the Employee) with respect to the fiscal year in question; and

d. An arbitrary amount (for working capital, stock redemption, or otherwise) which the Board, in its discretion (after consultation with the Corporation's auditors), shall decide to subtract in computing Adjusted Net

Income with respect to all lawyers who have written employment agreemens with the Corporation, not merely with respect to the Employee.

The following is another common bonus formula used by professional corporations:

(1) For purposes of this Schedule A—

(a) ''Allocated,'' where used with reference to a client, means that such client, in accordance with the Corporation's custom, is regarded as ''belonging'' to the Employee. In instances of a dispute as to the application of this definition, a good faith determination by the Board of Directors shall be conclusive; provided, however that—

(i) If a client comes to the Corporation by reason of a neutral source, such as a listing in the Martindale-Hubbell Law Directory, such client shall be Allocated to the Corporation.

(ii) If a client is inherited by the Corporation from a lawyer (to whom such client was Allocated) who was formerly employed by the Corporation, such client shall be Allocated to the Corporation unless he is directed to (or without solicitation chooses) a particular lawyer employed by the Corporation.

(iii) If a client comes initially to two or more lawyers employed by the Corporation, he shall be treated as a joint client of such lawyers.

(iv) If a client who is Allocated to one lawyer employed by the Corporation refers a new client to another lawyer employed by the Corporation, the new client shall be Allocated to the latter lawyer, if such lawyer is an Officer.

(v) If a client is Allocated in whole or in part to a lawyer employed by the Corporation who is not an Officer, he shall for purposes of this Exhibit A, be Allocated to that extent as in (i) above.

(vi) The fact that certain work for a client is assigned by the Board of Directors to a particular lawyer or other employee pursuant to Article ____, Section ____, of the Bylaws of the Corporation shall be irrelevant for purposes of determining to whom the client is Allocated.

(b) ''Fees Received'' means the fees (less direct expenses of collection) actually received from a client by the Corporation during its fiscal year in question for services rendered or to be rendered or as a retainer, provided that no such amount shall be included in the bonus computation for more than one fiscal year.

(c) ''Overhead'' means and include the overhead costs and expenses of the Corporation for the fiscal year in question, determined by the Corporation's outside accountant promptly after each fiscal year end in accordance with the Corporation's customary practice, and shall be expressed as a percentage of the aggregate Fees Received by the Corporation during said fiscal year. In computing Overhead, said accountant shall include as Overhead whatever additional amount (intended as an addition to working capital) shall be reasonably determined by the Board of Directors. On the other hand, Overhead shall be credited with (i.e., reduced by) Fees Received for certain work performed to the extent provided in paragraph 3 below. For purposes of determining monthly or other draws under paragraph 2(b) of the Agreement to which this Schedule A is attached (and similar provisions of employment agreement with other Officers), the President may in his discretion make an estimated computation of Overhead for the period in question, subject nevertheless to year-end adjustment as above set forth.

(d) ''Officer means an employee of the Corporation who is an officer or director of the Corporation at the time in question.

(2) The bonus for a particular fiscal year shall be computed as follows:

(a) Add 1 % of Fees Received to the extent attributable to clients allocated solely to the Employee.

(b) Add an appropriate portion of 15% of Fees Received to the extent attributable to clients Allocated partly to the Employee and partly to one or more other persons.

(c) Add 45% of Fees Received to the extent attributable to services rendered by the Employee.

(d) Add or subtract an amount appropriate to spread among the Employee and all other Officers (proportionate to their total salaries and bonuses for the fiscal year in question) the excess or shortage, as the case may be, in the Corporation's Overhead account, assuming that the amount credited to the Overhead account for said fiscal year was 40% of Fees Received.

(e) Subtract from the net amount determined under (a), (b), (c) and (d) above the Employee's salary for the fiscal year in question together with his Disability Benefit and sick leave payments, if any, received for such year to the extent not defrayed by insurance.

(f) Make such other adjustments as the Employee and all the other Officers shall mutually agree.

(3) Notwithstanding paragraphs (1) and (2) above—

(a) If services are rendered to a client by an associate (non-Officer) lawyer, all Fees Received for such services shall be allotted (credited) to the Overhead account of the Corporation, except for the 15% credited to the one or more originating Officers as provided in (2)(a) and (b) above.

(b) If a client is Allocated to the Corporation, the 15% of Fees Received from said client, mentioned in (2)(a) and (b) above, shall be allotted (credited) to the Overhead account of the Corporation.

Many employment agreements for shareholder-employees contain ''Oswald'' clauses, which require the return to the corporation of any disallowed ''unreasonable'' compensation:

It is understood and agreed, however, that in the event a deduction shall be disallowed for federal and/or state income tax purposes of all or any part of the compensation provided for in this Paragraph 4 and EMPLOYER shall be required to pay a deficiency on account of such disallowance, EMPLOYEE shall refund to the EMPLOYER an amount equal to the disallowed portion of such compensation. Such disallowed amount shall be paid to EMPLOYER within one (1) year after the date on which EMPLOYER paid the deficiency with respect to such compensation. It is further understood that the EMPLOYER shall not be required to legally defend any proposed disallowance by the Internal Revenue Service and the amount required to be reimbursed by EMPLOYEE shall be the amount, as finally determined by agreement or otherwise, actually allowed as a deduction. EMPLOYEE shall be obligated to make such repayments only if the amounts so repaid to the EMPLOYER will be deductible or excludable from the gross income of EMPLOYEE under the Internal Revenue Code of 1954, as amended, and is such repayment is determined not to be deductible or excludable by EMPLOYEE, such repayment shall be refunded by the EMPLOYER to EMPLOYEE within 90 days from the date of such determination.

Comment:

The "Oswald" clause takes its name from the well-known case of *Vincent Oswald v. Commissioner*.[3] The holding of the *Oswald* case provides that, where compensation is deemed to be unreasonable, the shareholder may repay the compensation to the corporation and take a deduction therefor. Several cases following *Oswald* have upheld its theory but have specifically stated that the obligation to repay the unreasonable compensation must be in place prior to the payment of the compensation to the shareholder.[4]

Many commentators feel that the use of an "Oswald" provision lessens the possibility that the Service will seek to declare unreasonable a portion of the compensation paid to a shareholder in a closely held company. Recently, the efficacy of "Oswald " clauses has been questioned, and in a recent case, *Castle Ford, Inc.*,[5] the Tax Court opinion stated, in *dictum*, that the use of an "Oswald" clause in an employment agreement may be an indication that the shareholders felt that the compensation paid was unreasonable. To date, there have been no cases decided solely on the basis of the statement in *Castle Ford*,[6] and the authors question the correctness of the *Castle Ford* statement and anticipate that it will not become the general rule. For this reason, the authors still favor the use of "Oswald" clauses in employment agreements for shareholder professionals.

Since the "Oswald" clause must be in effect prior to the time at which the compensation is paid, the "Oswald" clause must appear in the employment agreement or some other binding corporate document. Because of the position taken in *Castle Ford*, some tax attorneys have favored placing the "Oswald" clause in the bylaws of the professional corporation, so as to have it in place but not readily available to an examining agent, who will more than likely read the employment agreements but possibly bypass the rather lengthy bylaws. The authors feel that it is acceptable to place the "Oswald" clause in either the bylaws or the employment agreement.

One of the most important considerations in determining whether an "Oswald" clause should be used is whether the professionals feel that they will be in a position, as a practical matter, to repay to the corporation the unreasonable portion of the compensation. It should be noted that the "Oswald" clause appearing above is contingent upon the shareholders' obtaining a deduction for the repayment. The repayment should, however, not place any long-term financial stress upon the professionals because the repaid funds will be available in the professional corporation and may be repaid in later years when, hopefully, compensation has been established at a "reasonable" level.

5. Working Facilities. EMPLOYEE shall be provided with an office, stenographic and technical help, and such other facilities and services suitable to his pos ion and adequate for the performance of his duties.

6. Expenses. EMPLOYEE is encouraged and is expected, from time to time, to incur reasonable expenses for promoting the business of EMPLOYER, including expenses for civic club membership and participation, entertainment, travel and similar items. The cost of such activities shall be at the sole expense of EMPLOYEE unless EMPLOYER shall determine that such activities of EMPLOYEE should be authorized as an expense of EMPLOYER. Should any such expense of EMPLOYEE be so authorized, EMPLOYEE shall be reimbursed therefor upon his presenting to EMPLOYER an itemized expense voucher. EMPLOYER shall, however, bear the cost of dues for the professional societies and associations of which EMPLOYEE is a member.

EMPLOYEE shall have, maintain, and use as necessary, an automobile, home telephone, and such other facilities and equipment as are necessary in connection with EMPLOYEE'S performance of duties under this Agreement, all of which shall be at the EMPLOYEE'S expense, except as such may be furnished from time to time by EMPLOYER at its expense. EMPLOYEE shall also, at his own expense, carry public liability insurance coverage protecting himself against claims arising out of the use of such automobile (or any other motor vehicle) in the course of his employment hereunder, in such amounts as the Board of Directors may, from time to time, reasonably request.

In the event that any funds are drawn by EMPLOYEE for entertainment and travel expenses on behalf of EMPLOYER and any portions of such funds are unexpended and retained by EMPLOYEE, then such funds shall be considered compensation in addition to the salary hereinbefore described. Should any travel and entertainment expenses as drawn by EMPLOYEE be held nondeductible as travel and entertainment expenses to EMPLOYER by the Internal Revenue Service, then such nondeductible travel and entertainment expenses shall be considered additional compensation to EMPLOYEE and the provisions of Paragraph 4 relating to the repayment of compensation to EMPLOYER shall apply to such expenses which are treated as compensation, as if they had been paid under Paragraph 4.

Comment:

Paragraphs 5 and 6 are placed in the employment agreement to define further the employee status of the employee. Under paragraph 5, the employee is assured that the employer will provide appropriate facilities for him to perform his duties, and the first paragraph of paragraph 6 is placed in the agreement to facilitate the employee's deduction of his individual business expenses. Without such a provision in the employment agreement, it is possible for the Service to take the position that, since the employer determined that such expenses did not further its business (or, presumably, it would have reimbursed the employee for these expenses), they are not deductible to the employee. It is also advisable to have the approval of board of directors for any expenses incurred by the employee.[7]

The amount of an employee's business expenses which will be reimbursed is an area of concern because some professionals worry that their fellow professionals will take too much liberty with the corporate pocket book. For this reason, the amount of business expenses which the employer will pay is usually limited only to those expenses which have been specifically approved by the Board of Directors. The employment agreement should, however, specifically provide that the employer will pay for any business expenses common to all professionals, such as the dues for professional societies and associations, although sometimes it is advisable to place a limit on the number of such societies and associations.

The handling of automobiles in a professional corporation is also a point of much discussion. The second paragraph of paragraph 6 above provides flexibility in that it requires the employee to have and maintain an automobile, unless one is provided by the corporation. This permits the board of directors to reach its decision on automobiles independently.

The third paragraph of paragraph 6 provides an ''Oswald'' provision relating to employee business expenses. The use of such a clause will depend upon the criteria discussed in the comment to paragraph 4, *supra*.

> 7. <u>Case Records and Histories</u>. All case records, case histories, X-ray films, or personal and regular files concerning patients of the EMPLOYER or patients consulted, interviewed or treated and cared for by EMPLOYEE shall belong to and remain the property of EMPLOYER; however, upon termination of this Agreement, EMPLOYEE shall have the privilege, within ninety (90) days after such termination, of reproducing at his own expense any of such patients' records so treated or cared for by him during his employment by EMPLOYER.

Comment:

All employment agreements with professional employees should contain a paragraph comparable to paragraph 7 which indicates the professional corporation's right to client files *vis-a-vis* the professional employee. As a practical matter, however, the medical records of patients and the records of clients of accounting and legal professional corporations do, generally, as an ethical matter, belong to the patient or client. Where a patient demands his record, he may obtain it.

> 8. <u>Meetings and Postgraduate Courses</u>. EMPLOYEE is encouraged and is expected, from time to time, to attend scientific meetings, professional conventions, and postgraduate courses in his field of medicine. The cost of tuition and registration for attending such activities shall be paid for by the EMPLOYER; however, any other costs incurred by EMPLOYEE in connection with such activities shall be the sole expense of EMPLOYEE unless EMPLOYER shall determine that the full cost of EMPLOYEE'S attendance should be authorized as an expense of EMPLOYER. Should such full expenses of attendance be so

authorized, EMPLOYEE shall be reimbursed therefor upon his presenting to EMPLOYER an itemized expense voucher.

Comment:

Paragraph 8 is placed in the employment agreement for much the same reasons as paragraphs 5 and 6. It informs the professional employee that the amount which the professional corporation will advance toward his attendance at professional meetings and seminars is limited, unless he can persuade the corporation that his attendance at such meetings is necessary. Generally, the largest portion of the cost of attending professional meetings is not the tuition and registration, but the airfare and lodging expenses. Some professional corporations prefer to limit attendance to one or two special meetings, such as the annual American Bar Association convention. Other professional corporations prefer to limit the amount of reimbursement and such an alternate provision would be as follows:

EMPLOYEE shall be reimbursed for one (1) major (outside the State of Georgia) and one (1) minor (inside the State of Georgia) professional meeting each fiscal year, in the following manner: (a) living expenses of one hundred dollars ($100) a day for a maximum of seven (7) days, and (b) first class round-trip air fare to any destination within the continental United States (excluding Alaska, with first class round-trip air fare paid to Seattle, Washington, for destinations outside the continental United States).

9. <u>Vacation</u>. EMPLOYEE shall be entitled to _____ (____) weeks of vacation with pay plus an additional _____ (____) days with pay for attendance at professional meetings (or such greater length of time as may be approved from time to time by EMPLOYER) during each fiscal year of EMPLOYER, such vacation to be taken by EMPLOYEE at such time or times as shall be approved by EMPLOYER. In addition, EMPLOYER shall be entitled to such holidays as the EMPLOYER may approve. Unused holidays and days of vacation may not be carried over from one fiscal year to another, and additional income will not be given for vacation time or holidays not taken during any year.

Notwithstanding the foregoing, in the event this Agreement is terminated for any reason under Paragraph 10 hereof, EMPLOYEE shall be entitled to be paid for vacation accrued but not taken (such accrual shall occur at the rate of two and one-half (2½) days per month); provided, however, that EMPLOYEE shall only be entitled to vacation pay for a month if EMPLOYEE is employed for the entire month and vacation shall not accrue for any month during the termination notice period described in Paragraph 10 hereof). Said payment shall be made in a lump sum upon the date of termination.

Comment:

The establishment of a vacation is not only standard in employment areements (both professional and otherwise), but it also helps to eliminate misunderstandings regarding the amount of vacation and professional meeting time which may be taken. Normally, unused holidays and days of vacation may not be carried over and additional compensation is not given for them.

10. <u>Outside Professional Activities</u>. EMPLOYEE may not keep as his own any fees or other honorariums he receives for rendering professional services or engaging in any other professional activities during his off days or any other time; it being clearly understood that EMPLOYEE shall be considered an employee of the EMPLOYER at all times that he is rendering professional services or engaging in any professional activities and all fees or honorariums for said services or activities shall be paid to and be the property of the EMPLOYER.

Comment:

While some professionals may feel that they should be entitled to retain honorariums and other fees which they receive, the authors recommend that a paragraph such as paragraph 10 above should appear in the employment agreement and that the professional should not be permitted to receive outside fees. A provision such as paragraph 10 above further strengthens the independent integrity of the professional corporation and buttresses the argument that the professional is an employee of the corporation at all times during which he is practicing his profession. In the alternative, a provision such as the following may be employed, which gives the board of directors the final authority over whether the professional may retain outside fees.

10. <u>Outside Professional Activities</u>. Anything in this Agreement to the contrary notwithstanding, EMPLOYEE may keep as his own any fees or other honorariums received by him for those professional services or other professional activities which are approved by the Board of Directors and performed by EMPLOYEE on his off days or during such other time or times as shall not interfere with his duties hereunder on behalf of EMPLOYER.

11. <u>Sickness and Total Disability</u>. EMPLOYEE shall be entitled to sixty (60) calendar days sick leave in each fiscal year of EMPLOYER because of sickness or accident (not resulting in EMPLOYEE becoming ''totally disabled'', as that term is hereinafter defined) without any adjustment in his salary. Unused sick leave may neither be carried over from one fiscal year to another nor used for additional vacation.

Should EMPLOYEE become totally disabled as a result of sickness or accident and unable to attend to his duties prescribed in this Agreement, his salary shall be reduced in accordance with the following schedule during the continuance of such disability and for a period not exceeding twelve (12) months for each continuous disability.

TOTAL DISABILITY BENEFIT SCHEDULE

Months Totally Disabled	Amount of Employee's Salary
1-3	100%
4-6	75%
7-9	50%
10-12	25%

Should such total disability continue for a period of twelve (12) months, this Agreement shall, at the end of such 12-month period, be automatically terminated; however, EMPLOYER shall continue EMPLOYEE'S personal and his dependents' hospital, major medical, and group term life insurance for a period of twelve (12) months from the date of the inception of the total disability or EMPLOYEE'S death, whichever shall occur first. If, however, prior to the end of such 12-month period, EMPLOYEE'S total disability shall have ceased and he shall have commenced to perform his duties hereunder, this Agreement shall continue in full force and effect and EMPLOYEE shall be entitled to resume his employment hereunder and to thereafter receive his full compensation as though he had not been disabled; provided, however, unless EMPLOYEE shall perform his duties hereunder for a continuous period of at least sixty (60) days following a period of total disability before EMPLOYEE again becomes totally disabled, he shall not be entitled to start a new 12-month period of total disability. In such event the running of the original 12-month period of total disability shall cease during the time of EMPLOYEE'S performance of his duties following his original period of total disability before becoming totally disabled again.

In the event EMPLOYEE becomes totally disabled, he shall not be entitled to sixty (60) days sick leave at full salary during such period of total disability in addition to the disability benefits under the Total Disability Benefit Schedule, it being clearly understood that EMPLOYEE, if totally disabled, shall receive only such benefits for such period of time as provided for in said Total Disability Benefit Schedule.

EMPLOYEE and EMPLOYER agree that payments under this Paragraph 11 shall be considered compensation deductible by EMPLOYER and includable by EMPLOYEE as income for federal income tax purposes.

For purposes of this Agreement, the term "totally disabled" or "total disability" shall mean the EMPLOYEE's inability to engage in the practice of his profession on a substantially full-time basis by reason of any medically determinable physical or mental impairment which can be expected to result in death or which has lasted or can be expected to last for a continuous period of not less than 12 months; provided, however, that total disability shall not exist unless the Board of Directors determines (prospectively or retroactively), on the basis of such proof as may reasonably require, that total disability exists; and further provided, however, that total disability shall not be deemed to exist if the EMPLOYEE'S employment hereunder has terminated prior to the time he became totally disabled.

Comments:

This provision relating to sickness and total disability is provided because, when an employee becomes very sick or totally disabled, the other professionals in the corporation usually desire to make his transition to disability status as easy as possible. Consequently, provisions such as paragraph 11 are normally drafted in favor of the sick or disabled employee and not the corporation. Even though Section 505 of the Tax Reform Act of 1976 has made wage continuation (sick pay) plans virtually useless for tax purposes (see section [14.06]), it is preferable to provide a provision such as paragraph 11 so that the amounts paid will be considered deductible compensation.

Further, the amounts which will be paid under the total disability benefit schedule should be based upon the agreement of the professionals. In most instances full compensation is continued for a period at least as long as the waiting period under the disability policies maintained by the professional (usually 90 days but in some events 180 days).

12. Professional Liability Insurance. During the term of this Agreement, the EMPLOYER shall obtain and maintain in full force and effect a policy or policies of professional malpractice insurance insuring the EMPLOYER and the EMPLOYEE against any and all liabilities from or attributable to any acts or omissions of the EMPLOYEE in the course of his employment by the EMPLOYER in the same amounts as provided for other professional employees of the EMPLOYER.

In the event that EMPLOYEE has been employed by EMPLOYER for a period of ten (10) years, EMPLOYER agrees, upon the death, disability, or termination of employment of EMPLOYEE, to obtain and maintain in full force and effect a policy or policies of professional malpractice insurance insuring EMPLOYER and EMPLOYEE against any and all liabilities from or attributable to acts or omissions of the EMPLOYEE during the course of his employment by EMPLOYER.

Comment:

It is typical to provide a provision such as paragraph 12, which indicates to the professional employee that malpractice insurance will be maintained by the professional corporation for him. Several years ago, commercial insurance companies shifted from a "claims incurred" to a "claims made" basis for underwriting professional liability insurance coverage. Under the old "claims incurred" approach, if a professional had malpractice insurance coverage for a year, that coverage would protect him in the future in the event that claims were made later due to events which occurred in that year. Under the new "claims made" basis of underwriting, malpractice insurance coverage is simply a year-to-year contract insuring only claims actually made during that year, whether or not the potential malpractice occurred in that year. Consequently, when a shareholder dies, becomes disabled, or retires, the professional corporation should consider continued malpractice coverage in order to protect the shareholder (or his estate) and the corporation. At the present time, insurance companies are offering such "tail" coverage, and it is usually obtainable through the purchase of a single premium policy.

13. Medical, Disability and Life Insurance. EMPLOYER agrees to provide basic hospital, major medical, and group term life insurance for EMPLOYEE during the term of this Agreement. EMPLOYER also agrees to include EMPLOYEE in the Health and Medical Reimbursement Plan of EMPLOYER and to provide for EMPLOYEE disability insurance not to exceed _____ ($____) per month.

Comment:

This provision is contained in the Agreement in order to assure the professional employee of the employee benefits he will receive. Such a provision should also aid in establishing the "plan" status of the benefits because the employer is contractually bound to provide them.

14. <u>Termination of Employment</u>. EMPLOYER may terminate this Agreement without cause and at any time (except during a period when EMPLOYEE is totally disabled) upon thirty (30) days written notice to EMPLOYEE, and EMPLOYER shall only be obligated to continue to pay EMPLOYEE the salary due him under this Agreement up to the date of termination, plus EMPLOYEE'S current monthly salary for a period of _____ (___) months following the date of EMPLOYEE'S termination which shall be in lieu of any claims EMPLOYEE may have with respect to accounts receivable generated by EMPLOYEE while an employee hereunder.

EMPLOYEE may terminate this Agreement at any time upon thirty (30) days written notice to EMPLOYER and EMPLOYER shall be obligated only to continue to pay EMPLOYEE his said salary up to the date of termination. Upon such voluntary termination, EMPLOYEE hereby transfers to EMPLOYER any rights he may have in all accounts receivable generated by him while an employee of EMPLOYER and waives all claims he may have with respect to such receivables and termination pay hereunder.

If EMPLOYEE shall retire on or after reaching the age of sixty (60) years, EMPLOYEE shall receive his current salary for a period of _____ (___) months following the date of his retirement which shall be in lieu of any claims he might have with respect to accounts receivable generated by him while an employee of EMPLOYER.

Following any notice of termination of employment hereunder, whether given by EMPLOYER or EMPLOYEE, EMPLOYEE shall fully cooperate with EMPLOYER in all matters relating to the winding up of his pending work on behalf of the EMPLOYER and the orderly transfer of such work to the other professional employees of EMPLOYER. On or after the giving of notice of termination hereunder and during any notice period, EMPLOYER shall be entitled to such full-time or part-time services of EMPLOYEE as EMPLOYER may reasonably require and EMPLOYER shall specifically have the right to terminate the active services of EMPLOYEE at the time such notice is given and to pay to EMPLOYEE the compensation due to him under Paragraph 4 of this Agreement for the duration of the notice period.

Comment:

Other than the provisions providing compensation, the provisions relating to the termination of a professional's employment are probably the most important provisions of his employment agreement. Many employment agreements for professionals go to great lengths to describe the manner in which a professional's employment may be terminated and provide different periods of notice for termination "with cause" and termination "without cause." Further, some employment agreements provide that an employee's employment agreement may not be unilaterally terminated by the corporation except for cause. The authors feel that termination for "cause" provisions, no matter how accurately drafted, give rise to possible acrimony and potential law suits. Further, professionals have proven that, if they chose not to work together, they will not work together, regardless of the terms of their employment agreements. For these reasons, the authors feel that the provisions relating to termination of employment of a professional should provide that the professional or the corporation may terminate the agreement upon 30 or 60 days' notice. The termination clause should further provide that, during the pendency of the notice period, the corporation may, at its option, suspend the employee from active service with the corporation.

Other than the factors which may cause termination, the second most important question to be addressed in a termination provision is the amount of compensation that should be paid to the terminated employee. The authors have found that the amounts paid to terminated employees differ, generally, based upon the type of profession. A professional corporation which operates on a cash basis will have two major assets: the accounts receivable (including work in process) and the book value of the corporation's other assets. As a general matter, most professional corporations handle the payment to a stockholder for these two assets by providing for the repurchase of a stockholder's stock under a variety of stock retirement agreements and by providing payment to the stockholder for his share of the existing accounts receivable and work in process through salary continuation in the employment agreement.

In professional medical practices, the amount of salary continuation usually equals the estimated accounts receivable which the professional has on the corporation's books. Since, in professional medical practices, collections lag behind billings by three to six months, it is common for a professional medical practice to provide a salary continuation for three to six months. On the other hand, in law and accounting firms, the salary continuation is normally based on a percentage of the employee's normal annual compensation (or the average compensation for the last five years). Some law and accounting firms also provide for the phase-in of such payments (sometimes over a period of ten years) so that the lawyer or accountant must be an employee of the corporation for ten years in order to receive the full salary continuation. While some employment agreements provide that the amount of salary continuation paid to a professional employee should be reduced by the amount due to him under the corporation's qualified retirement plans, the authors do not feel that such a reduction is justified. The benefits payable to the professional employee under the qualified retirement plans of the professional corporation merely represent previously deferred salary and have no relationship to the amount of work outstanding at the time of the employee's termination.

Once the amount to be paid to the terminating employee has been established, it should be determined whether that amount should be reduced due to the type of termination. For example, if the professional employee's employment is involuntarily terminated by the professional corporation he should probably receive the full amount of his termination pay (see the provisions above in paragraph 12). On the other hand, it is felt by some that the amount due to a professional employee should be reduced where his employment is terminated for cause. As mentioned above, the authors feel that the reduction of the amount paid to a professional employee due to his termination for ''cause'' may provoke disputes (''cause'' is often defined as occurring if the professional is expelled, suspended, or otherwise disciplined by the final action of any professional or scientific organization, if he resigns from any professional or scientific organization under the threat of disciplinary action, if he is convicted of any offense punishable as a felony or involving turpitude or immoral conduct, or he is disqualified from practicing his profession). However, such provisions are widely used in the employment agreements of professionals.

On the other hand, many employment agreements for professionals provide for a reduction in termination pay where the professional, himself, voluntarily terminates his employment with the professional corporation. Paragraph 14 of the form so provides. The assumption in such a provision is that the professional has terminated his employment with the corporation in order to continue his profession in competition with the corporation. However, it is possible that the professional could continue to practice his profession in such a manner so as not to compete unduly with the corporation, such as moving to another state or joining the faculty of a local professional school where his private practice would be severely restricted. In such an event, it is not uncommon for employment agreements to provide that the amounts due to the professional following such a termination of employment will not be reduced.

There are various other matters which must be addressed when a professional leaves a professional corporation, such as the disposition of insurance policies, the name of the corporation, the telephone number of the corporation, the corporation's library, the corporation's equipment, secretaries, and clients. In the authors' experience, it is normally best not to attempt to provide explicitly in the employment agreement for the handling of these matters. If it is felt that these matters should be addressed, a separate shareholder's agreement, similar to that provided in section [6.05], *supra*, should be implemented.

15. <u>Death Benefit</u>. In the event of EMPLOYEE'S death during the term of this Agreement, this Agreement shall terminate immediately and EMPLOYEE'S estate shall be entitled to receive the salary due EMPLOYEE through the last day of the calendar month in which his death shall have occurred. In addition, EMPLOYEE'S estate shall be entitled to receive terminal pay in an amount equal to EMPLOYEE'S last _____ (__) months' salary paid under this Agreement (reduced by any amounts paid upon the disability of EMPLOYEE as provided for in Paragraph 11), such terminal pay to be paid to EMPLOYEE'S estate in twelve (12) equal monthly installments beginning on the first day of the month next

following the month during which his death occurs. The method of payment shall be at the discretion of the Board of Directors of EMPLOYER. Terminal pay as herein provided for in this paragraph shall be in addition to amounts otherwise receivable by EMPLOYEE or his estate under this or any other agreements with EMPLOYER and shall be in lieu of any claims EMPLOYEE'S estate may have with respect to accounts receivable generated by EMPLOYEE while an employee of EMPLOYER.

In addition, within ninety (90) days after the date of EMPLOYEE'S death, EMPLOYER will pay, by reason of the death of EMPLOYEE, the sum of $5,000.00 to EMPLOYEE'S wife, if she be then living, and if EMPLOYEE'S wife be not then living, said sum shall be paid to EMPLOYEE'S estate.

Comment:

The initial death benefit provided under paragraph 15 above is comparable to the salary continuation which is payable on the termination of an employee and is intended to compensate the employee's estate for his share of the receivables and work in process of the corporation. Paragraph 15 also provides a standard tax-free death benefit under Section 101(b) of the Code.

16. <u>Competition</u>. Upon termination of this Agreement, EMPLOYEE agrees that he will not, for a period of one year, practice _____ in _____ County, Georgia, or any county of the State of Georgia which is contiguous to any boundary of _____ County.

If any court shall determine that the duration or geographical limit of any restriction contained in this paragraph is unenforceable, it is the intention of the parties that the restrictions set forth herein will not be thereby terminated but shall be deemed reduced to the extent required to render them valid and enforceable.

Comment:

In discussing with professionals the possible use of restrictive covenants, the authors often hear the remark "restrictive convenants do not apply to professionals," and the professionals are very surprised to learn that restrictive covenants do, in fact, apply to professionals. Under most state laws, there are three requirements which must be met in order to have a binding restrictive covenant (even for professionals), and they are:

(1) The duration of the restriction must be reasonable,
(2) The territorial restriction of the covenant must be reasonable, and
(3) The restrictions in the covenant must, in general, be reasonable.

Most states take a different view toward restrictions imposed upon individuals selling their businesses (shareholder-employees) than with regard to restrictions which may be placed on mere employees. As a general rule, courts permit more restrictions to be imposed on shareholder-employees. For example, some states permit a restrictive covenant to have an unlimited duration when applied to shareholder-employees and to cover a much broader territory. However, the authors recommend that, in preparing a restrictive covenant for use in a professional corporation, the attorney should be aware that the covenant may, at a later date, be the subject of litigation and that it is best for the covenant to be less restrictive and enforceable than more restrictive and unenforceable. In fact, most state courts have refused to ''blue pencil'' restrictive covenants and reduce the restrictions to a point where they will be enforceable. Consequently, if any portion of a restrictive covenant is invalid, it is possible for the entire covenant to fail. Some courts are, however, responding to provisions such as that contained in paragraph 16 above and conform to the parties' intent that the covenant be enforceable even if the restrictions must be reduced. Attorneys drafting restrictive covenants must also be aware that legal malpractice cases have been instituted against attorneys who have drafted restrictive covenants which have not been held to be enforceable.

It has been the authors' experience that restrictive covenants with the duration of one year to 18 months will generally be held to be enforceable and to provide a sufficient incentive to the terminating professional to move his practice beyond the territorial restriction. Also, restrictive covenants relating to a certain city or its metropolitan area (and generally covenants with a radius of less than 25 miles) are usually enforceable.

In considering the use of restrictive covenants, there are also various ethical considerations. For example, the American Bar Association's D.R. 2-108(A) provides ''a lawyer shall not be a party to or participate in a partnership or employment agreement with another lawyer which restricts the right of a lawyer to practice law after the termination of a relationship created by the agreement, except as a condition to payment of retirement benefits.'' This position has been upheld in a number of formal and informal opinions by the ABA.[8]

> 17. Disclosure of Information. EMPLOYEE shall not, during or after the term of this Agreement, disclose any information relating to EMPLOYER, its officers, its employees, clients, or patients, including information regarding the affairs or operations of EMPLOYER, without obtaining the prior written consent of EMPLOYER.

Comment:

Some professionals feel that such a restriction on the disclosure of confidential information is necessary. Generally, ethical restraints will prohibit a professional from disclosing client information to others, but it may also be advisable to prohibit the professional from disclosing the financial information of shareholder-employees with whom he was previously associated. If such a clause is used, it should be placed in a separate paragraph and not included along with the covenant not to compete. If such a clause is placed in the same paragraph as the covenant not to compete, some courts have considered this restriction along with the covenant not to compete and, if the covenant not to compete fails to be upheld, this restriction will also be denied.

18. Indemnification of Employer. EMPLOYEE hereby agrees to indemnify, defend, and hold harmless the EMPLOYER, and its officers, directors, shareholders, employees, and agents, from any claim, loss, damage, cost, expense or liability arising out of or relating to the services performed by them at the request of EMPLOYEE or to the performance or nonperformance by EMPLOYEE of any services to be performed or provided by him under this Agreement. EMPLOYEE shall not, however, be required to make any reimbursement to the EMPLOYER or its officers, directors, shareholders, employees, or agents for any claims, losses, damages, costs or expenses which are reimbursed by insurance or otherwise.

Comment:

Since many states provide for a restriction on collateral liability, many professionals feel that a provision such as paragraph 18 above is necessary only to protect the corporation (and its assets) from the negligent acts of the professional employees. Such protection will be available, however, only to the extent that the professional has funds, and any judgment against the professional large enough to exceed the insurance coverage carried by the corporation and the professional will, more than likely, also bankrupt the professional.

19. Arbitration. Except as herein otherwise provided, any claim or controversy arising out of or relating to this agreement or any breach hereof shall, upon the request of either the EMPLOYER or EMPLOYEE, be submitted to and settled by arbitration in _____ in accordance with the rules of the American Arbitration Association then in effect. Any decision made pursuant to such arbitration shall be binding and conclusive upon the EMPLOYER and the EMPLOYEE.

Comment:

Arbitration of certain aspects of agreements among professionals may be unethical, unless the arbitrators are lawyers. It appears, however, that the rules and practices of the American Arbitration Association take this into account. Some attorneys feel that the use of arbitration is preferable to the litigation of matters contained in an employment agreement. However, if matters which require the judgment of either of the parties are removed from the employment agreement, such as determining when employment terminates for "cause," the risk of litigation is reduced. If employment agreements can be so drafted, the authors recommend against the use of arbitration because it may unduly postpone the final conclusion of the matters under dispute.

20. Waiver of Breach or Violation not Deemed Continuing. The waiver by either party of a breach or violation of any provision of this Agreement shall not operate as, or be construed to be, a waiver of any subsequent breach hereof.

21. Notices. Any and all notices required or permitted to be given under this Agreement will be sufficient if furnished in writing, sent by registered mail to his last known residence in case of EMPLOYEE or to its principal office in _____, Georgia, in the case of the EMPLOYER.

22. <u>Authority</u>. The provisions of this Agreement required to be approved by the Board of Directors of EMPLOYER have been so approved and authorized.

23. <u>Governing Law</u>. This Agreement shall be interpreted, construed and governed according to the laws of the State of Georgia.

24. <u>Paragraph Headings</u>. The paragraph headings contained in this Agreement are for convenience only and shall in no manner be construed as a part of this Agreement.

25. <u>Counterparts</u>. This Agreement is executed in multiple counterparts, each of which shall be deemed an original and together shall constitute one and the same agreement, with one counterpart being delivered to each party hereto.

Comments:

The above are standard "boilerplate" and should be contained in any agreement between a professional corporation and its shareholders.

IN WITNESS WHEREOF, EMPLOYER has caused this Agreement to be executed by its duly authorized officers and its seal to be hereunto affixed, and EMPLOYEE has hereunto set his hand and seal, all being done in duplicate originals with one original being delivered to each party on the day and year first above written.

(CORPORATE SEAL)   EMPLOYER:

_____

ATTEST:

By _____   By _____
  Secretary   President

            EMPLOYEE:

            _____ (SEAL)
               M.D.

EXHIBIT "A"

SCHEDULE OF COMPENSATION

The undersigned hereby agree that the monthly salary due EMPLOYEE under paragraph 4 of the foregoing Employment Agreement shall be $____ per month beginning _____, 19___, and for each successive month thereafter unless hereafter changed by mutual agreement.

This ____ day of _____, 19___.

(CORPORATE SEAL)   EMPLOYER:

ATTEST: _____

_____

Secretary

                                         By: _____
                                              President

                                         EMPLOYER:

                                         _____ (SEAL)
                                                   M.D.

(2) Employment Agreements for Nonshareholder-Employees

In considering the employment of a nonshareholder professional employee, the professional corporation should not only consider the terms of the employment agreement for this employee, but, more importantly, the impact of the addition of another professional to the staff of the corporation. The immediate question to be asked is "When should we hire another professional?"

It has been the authors' experience that professional groups of all types generally wait too long, until work has expanded beyond the point where an additional professional is needed, before they begin the process of interviewing prospective employees. This is not to say that professional groups should hire professional employees in anticipation of work, but in the authors' experience it is a very difficult and time-consuming task to find the right professional employee and it is almost impossible to hire the right man or woman on short notice. For this reason, those professionals charged with the management of the corporation should keep a close eye on the volume being produced by the corporation and the need to supplement the professional staff. It should be remembered, however, that it is much easier to suffer through months of increased work load due to professional staff shortages than it is to hire the wrong professional and then agonize for several months prior to terminating the relationship. Consequently, the first rule of hiring for professional practices is to take your time and hire the right person.

In discussing salary with the prospective professional, a professional corporation should realize that the actual out-of-pocket costs to the corporation to employ a professional may approximate twice the professional's annual salary. Consequently, the corporation should review very closely the compensation and benefits which will be provided to the proposed employee and should attempt to relay these benefits to the prospective employee. Many professional groups find that it is advantageous to have the corporation's lawyer or accountant meet with the prospective employee and discuss compensation and other employee benefits. If this is done, it is often advisable to present a memorandum to the employee outlining the employee benefits, cost to the corporation, and general employment rules relating to tne pospective employee's status as a nonshareholder in the professional corporation. A copy of such a memorandum is included in this section as Exhibit 1.

Generally, nonshareholder employees should be informed that their first year of employment will be a probationary year, after which their performance will be reviewed. Even after the initial year, the professional corporation should take steps to review and assess the performance of nonshareholder employees on an annual basis and to inform the employees of the results of that review. Also, it is usually advantageous to provide staged increases in compensation and employee benefits for the nonshareholder professional employees. If an employee's performance has been satisfactory, in lieu of increasing compensation, the corporation may grant increases in disability insurance, group term life insurance, or other fringe benefits which may be just as (or more) important than direct compensation.

Even though employment agreements for nonshareholder professional employees are not absolutely necessary in order to establish the independent integrity of the professional corporation, such agreements should be used. Employment agreements for nonprofessional employees need not be nearly as complicated as those of the shareholders because there is no need to cover matters such as the continuation of compensation upon termination of employment. The employment agreement of a nonshareholder professional employee should describe his rights and duties *vis-a-vis* the corporation. Contained below is a form of employment agreement for a nonshareholder professional employee. Some of the provisions of this agreement are similar or identical to those contained in the shareholder employment agreement contained in section [10.01](1), *supra*.

STATE OF GEORGIA

COUNTY OF _____

EMPLOYMENT AGREEMENT

THIS AGREEMENT, made and entered into this _____ day of _____ 19____, by and between _____, a Georgia professional corporation, hereinafter referred to as "EMPLOYER", and _____, a resident of said State and County, hereinafter referred to as "EMPLOYEE",

WHEREAS, the EMPLOYER is a professional corporation rendering professional services in the State of Georgia through its employees who are duly licensed to practice medicine in that state; and

WHEREAS, the EMPLOYEE is a physician duly licensed to practice medicine in the State of Georgia; and

WHEREAS, the EMPLOYER desires to employ the EMPLOYEE and the Employee desires to become employed by the EMPLOYER, all on the terms and conditions hereinafter set forth;

NOW, THEREFORE, the parties, for and in consideration of the mutual and reciprocal covenants and agreements hereinafter contained, do contract and agree as follows, to-wit:

1. Purpose and Employment. The purpose of this Agreement is to define the relationship between the EMPLOYER as an employer and EMPLOYEE as an employee of the EMPLOYER. EMPLOYER hereby employs EMPLOYEE, and EMPLOYEE hereby accepts employment by EMPLOYER upon all of the terms and conditions as are hereinafter set forth.

2. Duties. EMPLOYEE agrees to practice his medical specialty solely as an employee of the EMPLOYER and, except as hereinafter provided, shall devote his entire professional time to the affairs of the EMPLOYER. In addition, EMPLOYEE agrees to devote all necessary time and his best efforts in the performance of his duties as a doctor of medicine for the EMPLOYER and to perform such other duties as are assigned to him from time to time by the board of directors of EMPLOYER (the ''Board of Directors''). EMPLOYEE will hold out and represent himself as being employed by, and as a doctor practicing medicine for, EMPLOYER. EMPLOYEE shall be free to exercise his own judgment regarding the treatment of any particular patient; however, EMPLOYEE agrees to observe and comply with the rules and regulations of EMPLOYER as adopted from time to time by the Board of Directors. EMPLOYEE specifically agrees that the Board of Directors shall have the sole right to designate and assign patients to EMPLOYEE for treatment and that the Board of Directors shall determine the fee to be charged by EMPLOYER for the professional services rendered by EMPLOYEE hereunder. Further, the Board of Directiors shall have the final authority over acceptance or refusal of any person for whom professional services may be rendered.

3. Term. The term of employment under this Agreement shall be for one (1) year beginning _____ and ending _____, and for each successive year thereafter unless and until terminated as hereinafter provided.

4. Regular Compensation. For all the services to be rendered by EMPLOYEE in any capacity hereunder, including any duties assigned to him by the Board of Directors, EMPLOYER shall pay EMPLOYEE a monthly salary of $_____, payable at the end of each month during the term of this Agreement. If the EMPLOYER does not have adequate funds from operations to pay the full salary, any unpaid obligation as of the end of a fiscal year shall be carried over to the following year.

Comment:

It is normally best to provide for a stated salary for nonshareholder employees during their first and remaining years as nonshareholders. As a practical matter, a nonshareholder professional will generally prefer a stated salary, because, as he begins his practice, he will not have established a sufficient number of clients/patients to make a production formula more attractive. Even if a nonshareholder professional does have an established practice, it is usually best to establish a fixed salary, at least for the first year. The authors have found that production formulae for nonshareholder professionals tend to make them feel more like independent practitioners and may weaken the entity concept which most group practices attempt to foster.

It is normally advisable to provide no bonus or a discretionary bonus for the nonshareholder professional employee after his first year of employment (in lieu of a contractual bonus arrangement). During a nonshareholder's second year of employment, it is acceptable to grant a contractual bonus arrangement. Contractual bonus arrangements for nonshareholder professionals are normally based on production. A common formula provides a bonus based on production in excess of a stated percentage of the professional's salary. Such a contractual bonus arrangement could be structured as follows:

> Within thirty (30) days after the end of each Employment Year under this Agreement (beginning January 1 and ending December 31) and after the termination of employment during the term of this Agreement, EMPLOYEE shall be paid incentive compensation equal to _____ percent of EMPLOYEE'S gross fees collected by EMPLOYER during the Employment Year or during the period ending on the date of termination of this Agreement, in excess of twice EMPLOYEE'S total monthly salary during such period. The first such period for which incentive compensation will be paid shall be the period beginning _____ and ending _____. For purposes of this Agreement, the term "EMPLOYEE'S gross fees collected by EMPLOYER" shall mean the total fees collected by EMPLOYER on account of EMPLOYEE'S services, as shown on the books of EMPLOYER.

Many nonshareholder professionals feel that the percentage in such a bonus formula should be 50%. The authors feel, however, that 50% is too large and that the bonus range should be somewhere between 25% and 40%. Unless the bonus is computed on collections in excess of twice the salary (plus possibly the employee's allocations under the corporation's retirement plans) the corporation may be in a negative cash position due to the additional overhead costs the professional employee creates. Including the retirement plan contributions in the bonus formula does portray a more accurate picture, particularly if the vesting schedule in the retirement plans is short.

5. <u>Working Facilities and Expenses</u>. EMPLOYEE shall be provided with an office, stenographic and technical help, and such other facilities and services suitable to his position and adequate for the performance of his duties.

EMPLOYEE is encouraged and is expected, from time to time, to incur reasonable expenses for promoting the business of EMPLOYER including expenses for civic club membership and participation, entertainment, travel and similar items. The cost of such activities shall be at the sole expense of EMPLOYEE unless EMPLOYER shall determine that such activities of EMPLOYEE should be authorized as an expense of EMPLOYER. Should any such expense of EMPLOYEE be so authorized, EMPLOYEE shall be reimbursed therefor upon his presenting to EMPLOYER an itemized expense voucher. EMPLOYER shall, however, pay the yearly dues for the professional organizations of which EMPLOYEE is a member.

Comment:

The nonshareholder professional employee should be advised regarding those expenses for which the professional corporation will provide reimbursement.

6. <u>Case Records and Histories</u>. All case records, case histories, X-ray films, or personal and regular files concerning patients of the EMPLOYER or patients consulted, interviewed or treated and cared for by EMPLOYEE shall belong to and remain the property of EMPLOYER; however, upon request EMPLOYEE may at his own expense make copies of any of such records for his own use.

7. <u>Meetings and Postgraduate Courses</u>. EMPLOYEE is encouraged and is expected, from time to time, to attend scientific meetings, professional conventions, and postgraduate courses in his field of medicine. The cost of tuition and registration for attending such activities shall be paid for by the EMPLOYER; however, any other costs incurred by EMPLOYEE in connection with such activities shall be the sole expense of EMPLOYEE unless EMPLOYER shall determine that the full cost of EMPLOYEE'S attendance should be authorized as an expense of EMPLOYER. Should such full expenses of attendance be so authorized, EMPLOYEE shall be reimbursed therefor upon his presenting to EMPLOYER an itemized expense voucher.

8. <u>Vacation</u>. EMPLOYEE shall be entitled to _____ (___) weeks of vacation with pay, plus an additional _____ (___) weeks with pay for attendance at professional meetings (or such greater length of time as may be approved from time to time by the EMPLOYER) during each fiscal year of EMPLOYER, such vacation to be taken by EMPLOYEE at such time or times as shall be approved by the EMPLOYER. In addition, EMPLOYEE shall be entitled to such holidays as the EMPLOYER may approve and to one (1) day per month sick leave, contingent upon the sickness of EMPLOYEE or a near relative. Unused holidays and days of vacation and sick leave may not be carried over from one fiscal year to another and no additional salary will be given for vacation time or holidays or sick leave not taken during any year.

Notwithstanding the foregoing, in the event this Agreement is terminated for any reason under Paragraph 10 hereof, EMPLOYEE shall be entitled to be paid for vacation accrued but not taken (such accrual shall occur at the rate of two and one-half (2½) days per month); provided, however, that EMPLOYEE shall only be entitled to vacation pay for a month if EMPLOYEE is employed for the entire month and vacation shall not accrue for any month during the termination notice period described in Paragraph 10 hereof). Said payment shall be made in lump sum upon the date of termination.

Comment:

It is advisable to provide a specified amount of sick leave per year until the nonshareholder professional's work habits become known.

9. <u>Outside Professional Activities</u>. EMPLOYEE agrees to treat and render services to all patients assigned to him by EMPLOYER and may not keep as his

own fees or other honorariums he receives for rendering professional services or engaging in any other professional activities during his off days or any other time; it being clearly understood that EMPLOYEE shall be considered an employee of the EMPLOYER at all times that he is rendering profesional services or engaging in any professional activities and all fees or honorariums for said services or activities shall be paid to and be the property of the EMPLOYER.

Comment:

It is almost always advisable that nonshareholder professional employees not be permitted to receive any outside fees. Permitting them to do so may reduce their allegiance to the corporation, or so many advisors feel.

10. Termination of Employment. EMPLOYER may terminate this Agreement, without cause and at any time, upon thirty (30) days written notice to EMPLOYEE, and EMPLOYER shall only be obligated to continue to pay EMPLOYEE the salary due him under this Agreement up to the date of termination or up to the date on which EMPLOYEE voluntarily ceases active employment with EMPLOYER, whichever is earlier.

EMPLOYEE may terminate this Agreement at any time upon thirty (30) days written notice to EMPLOYER and EMPLOYER shall be obligated only to continue to pay EMPLOYEE his said salary up to the date of termination.

In the event of EMPLOYEE'S death during the term of this Agreement. this Agreement shall terminate immediately, and EMPLOYEE'S estate shall be entitled to receive the salary due EMPLOYEE through the last day of the calendar month in which his death shall have occurred.

Following any notice of termination under this paragraph, EMPLOYEE shall fully cooperate with EMPLOYER in all matters relating to the winding up of EMPLOYEE'S work on behalf of EMPLOYER and the orderly transfer of any such pending work to other professional employees of EMPLOYER. EMPLOYER shall be entitled to such full-time or part-time services of EMPLOYEE as EMPLOYER may reasonably require during any part of the notice termination period and EMPLOYER shall have the specific right to prohibit EMPLOYEE from the continued active performance of services for the EMPLOYER and to pay EMPLOYEE the compensation due to him for the remainder of the notice period.

Comments:

The provisions relating to the termination of a nonshareholder professional's employment agreement should permit termination by either party on relatively short notice, 30 or 60 days. Further, it is customary that upon termination the employee will not receive any amount to compensate him for the accounts receivable which are remaining on the books of the corporation due to his services because it is generally felt that the employee received compensation during the first three to four months of employment when he was building up these receivables and actually collected no fees. In the event that a contractual bonus formula is used, the termination provision should reference the bonus formula, either providing that no bonus will be payable or that the terminated employee will receive a pro rata portion of the bonus. Further, employment agreements for nonshareholder professionals normally do not provide for the $5,000 death benefit as is provided in the shareholder agreement previously described in this section. Such a benefit may, however, be added as the nonshareholder progresses toward shareholder status.

11. Professional Liability Insurance. The EMPLOYER shall obtain and maintain in full force and effect a policy or policies of professional malpractice insurance insuring the EMPLOYER and the EMPLOYEE against any and all liabilities from or attributable to any acts or omissions of the EMPLOYEE in the course of his employment by the EMPLOYER in the same amounts as provided for other professional employees of the EMPLOYER.

12. Medical and Disability Insurance. EMPLOYER agrees to provide basic hospital and major medical insurance for EMPLOYEE during the term of this Agreement. EMPLOYER also agrees to provide for EMPLOYEE disability insurance covering total and permanent disability in an amount not to exceed _____ per month. The EMPLOYEE may acquire disability insurance in a larger amount than that provided by EMPLOYER, but shall be required to pay any additional permium occasioned thereby.

13. Purchase of Stock. It is the intention of EMPLOYER, but EMPLOYER is not required, to sell EMPLOYEE a stock interest in EMPLOYER upon the completion of _____ (___) full years of employment. The purchase price of such stock sold to EMPLOYEE shall be determined in accordance with a formula prepared by the independent certified public accountants then regularly auditing the accounts of EMPLOYER, which shall be the formula adopted by the EMPLOYER for its Stock Retirement Agreement.

Comment:

Nonshareholder professionals are often very concerned regarding the length of time before they will be considered for shareholder status. It is advisable not to enter into any binding commitment to sell stock to a nonshareholder professional at any time in the future. However, in order to assuage the desires of the nonshareholder professionals, it is often advisable to place some type of precatory language in the employment agreement to state the intention of the parties.

14. Competition. Upon termination of this Agreement, EMPLOYEE agrees that he will not, for a period of one year, practice _____ in _____ County, Georgia, or in any county of the State of Georgia which is contiguous to any boundary of _____ County.

If any court shall determine that the duration or geographical limits of any restriction contained in this paragraph is unenforceable, it is the intention of the EMPLOYEE and EMPLOYER that the restrictions set forth herein shall not thereby be terminated but shall be deemed amended and revised to the extent required to render them valid and enforceable.

Comment:

The comment relating to paragraph 16 of the shareholder employment agreement is applicable here. Further, it should be recognized that under most state laws the restrictions which may be imposed upon nonshareholder employees are limited.

15. <u>Disclsoure of Information</u>. EMPLOYEE shall not, during or after the term of this Agreement, disclose any information relating to EMPLOYER, its officers, its employees, clients, or patients, including information regarding the affairs or operations of EMPLOYER, without obtaining the prior written consent of EMPLOYER.

16. <u>Indemnification of EMPLOYER</u>. EMPLOYEE hereby agrees to indemnify, defend, and hold harmless the EMPLOYER, and its officers, directors, shareholders, employees, and agents, from any claim, loss, damage, cost, expense or liability arising out of or relating to the services performed by them at the request of EMPLOYEE or to the performance or nonperformance by EMPLOYEE of any services to be performed or provided by him under this Agreement. EMPLOYEE shall not, however, be required to make any reimbursement to the Corporation or its officers, directors, shareholders, employees, or agents for any losses, claims, damages, costs or expenses which are reimbursed by insurance or otherwise.

17. <u>Waiver of Breach or Violation not Deemed Continuing</u>. The waiver by either party of a breach or violation of any provision of this Agreement shall not operate as or be construed to be a waiver of any subsequent breach hereof.

18. <u>Notices</u>. Any and all notices required or permitted to be given under this Agreement will be sufficient if furnished in writing, sent by registered mail to his last known residence in the case of EMPLOYEE or to its principal office in _____, Georgia, in the case of the EMPLOYER.

19. <u>Authority</u>. The provisions of this Agreement required to be approved by the Board of Directors of EMPLOYER have been so approved and authorized.

20. <u>Governing Law</u>. This Agreement shall be interpreted, construed and governed according to the laws of the State of Georgia.

21. <u>Paragraph Headings</u>. The paragraph headings contained in this Agreement are for convenience only and shall be in no manner be construed as a part of this Agreement.

22. <u>Entire Agreement</u>. This Agreement supersedes all prior discussions and agreements between EMPLOYER, or any of its officers, directors, employees, or agents, and EMPLOYEE with respect to all matters relating to the employment by EMPLOYER of EMPLOYEE and all other matters contained herein, and this Agreement constitutes the sole and entire agreement with respect thereto. Any representation, inducement, promise or agreement, whether oral or written, between EMPLOYER, or any of its officers, directors, employees, or agents, and EMPLOYEE which is not embodied herein shall be of no force or effect.

23. <u>Counterparts</u>. This Agreement is executed in multiple counterparts, each of which shall be deemed an original and together shall constitute one and the same agreement, with one counterpart being delivered to each party thereto.

IN WITNESS WHEREOF, EMPLOYER has caused this Agreement to be executed by its duly authorized officers and its seal to be hereunto affixed, and EMPLOYEE has hereunto set his hand and seal, all being done in duplicate originals with one original being delivered to each party on the day and year first above written.

(CORPORATE SEAL)   EMPLOYER:

ATTEST:

                                      By: _____

_____

Secretary   President

EMPLOYEE:

_____ (SEAL)

EXHIBIT 1

MEMORANDUM

TO:

FROM:

DATE:

RE: DIRECT VALUE AND COSTS OF EMPLOYMENT

You have asked us to summarize the direct value to the prospective employee of the compensation package which the Corporation will be offering to him, together with an estimate of the out-of-pocket costs to the Corporation of his employment. The figures listed below are estimates which have been prepared with the assistance of the office manager and the Corporation's accountant. The estimates below are conservative and, consequently, we would anticipate that costs may increase, not decrease. Also, in computing the direct value of the compensation package to the prospective employee, the cost of certain items (such as insurance) has been doubled to reflect the effective tax-free benefit.

Direct Value of Compensation Package

Salary	$ 50,000
Pension Plan Contribution (approximate, participation commences after three years of service)	7,200
Group Medical Insurance—$600 × 2	1,200
Group Disability Insurance—$600 × 2	1,200

Group Term Life Insurance	200
($25,000 in coverage)—$100 × 2	200
Parking—$150 × 2	300
Auto Lease—$250 per month × 2	6,000
Auto Insurance, Tax, Expenses—$2,000 × 2	4,000
Malpractice Insurance	7,200
Professional Dues	850
Business License	150
Professional Travel	500
Total Value to Employee	$ 78,800

Cost to Corporation

Salary	50,000
Pension Plan	7,200
Group Medical	600
Group Disability	600
Group Term Life	100
Parking	150
Auto Lease and Expenses	5,000
Malpractice Insurance	7,200
Salary and Expenses for Secretary	14,000
Professional Dues	850
Business License	150
Social Security	1,600
Increased Overhead	1,500
Professional Travel	500
Total Cost to Corporation	$ 89,450

The first year of employment will be a trial year. After the first year, performance will be reviewed and, if the Corporation and the new employee elect to continue the employment relationship, he will be given a three-year employment contract, with the anticipation that the new employee will become a shareholder of the Corporation upon the expiration of the contract. Upon becoming a shareholder of the Corporation, the new employee will participate in the compensation formula for the shareholders, which provides a base salary with bonuses based on production.

During the one-year trial period, the new employee will, in addition to the benefits described above, be entitled to three weeks paid vacation and one week off (with pay) for attendance at professional meetings. He will not be entitled to a specific bonus for the trial year, but a discretionary bonus may be awarded to him based on performance.

After the one-year trial period, the new employee's benefits will be adjusted as follows:

1. Salary will be increased to reflect performance and consideration will be given to establishing a bonus formula based upon production.
2. An additional week of paid vacation will be granted for each year of employment, up to a maximum of six weeks of vacation.
3. Group term life insurance coverage will be increased to $50,000.
4. After three years of employment, the new employee's benefits in the pension plan will become fully vested.

[10.02] AGREEMENTS WITH INDEPENDENT CONTRACTORS

Under the federal income tax laws, an independent contractor is treated as his own employer. In order to attain the status of an independent contractor, it is necessary that the independent contractor be subject to the direction of those who employ him only as to the results to be achieved and not as to the manner and method of achieving those results. Consequently, it is impossible for many individuals who must operate under the direct supervision of others, such as nurses and physicians' assistants, to reach the status of independent contractors. On the other hand, professionals may hire themselves out solely to obtain certain results and, consequently, obtain independent contractor status. For a general discussion of the independent contractor issue, see section [10.04], *infra*.

It is customary that professional corporations retain the services of professionals as independent contractors in the following situations:

1. Where a professional with an existing practice wishes to become affiliated with a professional corporation on a trial basis, or
2. Where an established practice has excess work, which must be handled and, for one reason or another desires to become affiliated with another professional or professional corporation to alleviate this problem.

Probably the most important aspect of independent contractor status is that the independent contractor (and any persons employed by him) will not be considered employees of the professional corporation which engages him and, consequently, will not be covered by the employee benefits maintained by the professional corporation. It appears that this is, often, the reason why many professionals prefer independent contractor status, i.e., so that they may establish their own employee benefit plans. In fact, the situation where one professional, or his professional corporation, becomes an independent contractor of another professional, or his professional corporation, closely resembles a partnership of professional corporations, which is more completely discussed in Chapter 19, *infra*.

A properly drafted agreement retaining an independent contractor, which is usually known as a ''practice agreement,'' will contain many provisions that are comparable to those in an employment agreement with a shareholder employee. However, in drafting a practice agreement with an independent contractor, specific emphasis should be placed on the following aspects:

(1) *Duties*. The agreement should specifically provide the duties the professional is expected to render and that he will render those duties as an independent contractor. It is particularly important to assure that the independent contractor is not entitled to participate in the employee benefit plans of the professional corporation and that the professional corporation will not be responsible for the federal and state income, Social Security, and unemployment tax withholding for the independent contractor or his employees. The agreement should also specifically state that the independent contractor will be responsible for these taxes and that he disclaims any interest in the employee benefit plans of the professional corporation.

(2) *Compensation*. Normally, the compensation paid to an independent contractor will be based on a percentage of production, and this percentage will vary depending upon the expenses which each party will be required to pay and the facilities provided by the professional corporation. Further; the professional corporation should be compensated for performing billing and collection services for the independent contractor. One of the larger expense items for some professionals, particularly surgeons, is the medical malpractice insurance premium, and the independent contractor should almost always carry his own malpractice insurance and should be required to furnish proof of the existence of such insurance to the professional corporation.

(3) *Outside Services*. While it is not necessary, in order to substantiate the integrity of the professional corporation, to require the independent contractor to remit all outside professional fees to the professional corporation, professional corporations customarily require independent contractors to do so. Requiring the independent contractor to remit all outside professional fees to the professional corporation will permit the professional corporation to receive its collection percentage. The agreement might also contain a provision requiring the independent contractor to devote his entire professional time to the business of the professional corporation.

(4) *Termination*. The agreement should provide for termination by either party on 30 or 60 days' notice, with a continuation of compensation to the independent contractor based on the production formula contained in the agreement.

(5) *Disclosure of Information*. The agreement should restrain the independent contractor from disclosing information obtained in his association with the professional corporation.

(6) *Indemnification*. The agreement should also require the independent contractor to indemnify, defend, and hold harmless the professional corporation

and its employees from losses due to the negligence of the independent contractor or his employees.

(7) *Competition.* Most agreements with independent contractors do not contain provisions limiting competition after the agreement is terminated (simply because most independent contractors feel that the professional corporation has no right to such a restriction and they will not enter into agreements which contain them). If restrictive covenants are used, one comparable to paragraph 14 in the employment agreement for nonshareholder employees, section [10.01], *supra,* would be appropriate.

The following is a form of Practice Agreement which may be used with independent contractors.

PRACTICE AGREEMENT

THIS AGREEMENT, made as of this ____ day of _____, 19____, by and between _____ (hereinafter referred to as "Corporation") and _____ (hereinafter referred to as "Physician".

W I T N E S S E T H:

WHEREAS, Corporation is engaged in the business of conducting a professional medical practice specializing in _____ in the city of _____ _____, _____; and

WHEREAS, Physician is a doctor licensed to practice medicine in the State of _____; and

WHEREAS, Physician desires to practice medicine through Corporation and Corporation desires to obtain the services of Physician as an independent contractor all on the terms and conditions hereinafter set forth;

NOW, THEREFORE, for and in consideration of the promises, covenants, and agreements hereinafter set forth, the parties hereto agree as follows:

1. Engagement as Independent Contractor. The Corporation hereby engages Physician as an independent contractor to perform medical services for Corporation, and Physician hereby accepts said engagement for the term hereof with the respective duties, responsibilities, and obligations hereinafter set forth.

2. Duties. Physician, as an independent contractor, agrees to practice his medical specialty through Corporation. Physician also agrees to make himself available to provide medical services to Corporation during such reasonable hours and at such times as Corporation may from time to time request. Physician also agrees to perform such other reasonable tasks and services as the Corporation may from time to time request.

In performing services under this Agreement, Physician covenants and agrees that he: (i) shall use diligent efforts and professional skills and judgment, (ii) shall render care to patients in accordance with and in a manner consistent with customary and recognized standards of the medical profession, (iii) shall conduct himself in a manner consistent with the Principles of Medical Ethics of the American Medical Association, and (iv) shall comply with the Bylaws, rules and regulations of the Corporation.

3. Facilities. While this Agreement is in effect, Corporation will make available to Physician as an independent contractor adequate physical facilities, as well as equipment and supplies, which Corporation deems reasonably necessary to the practice of medicine. Corporation also agrees to provide the services of such medical technicians, nurses, and nonprofessional personnel, but not including secretarial staff and photocopying facilities, as the Corporation shall deem reasonably necessary for the conduct of its business.

4. Compensation. Physician shall receive as compensation for all services provided or caused to be provided by him as an independent contractor under this Agreement seventy percent (70%) of the gross collections of Corporation that are produced by the efforts of Physician in connection with Corporation's business. Said compensation shall be paid monthly, not later than ten (10) days following the end of each month, and shall be based on the gross collections produced by the efforts of Physician and received by Corporation during that month. The ''gross collections'' produced by the efforts of Physician shall be conclusively presumed to be his collections as appearing on the books of account of Corporation.

5. Records, Billing, etc. During the time that this Agreement is in effect and for as long thereafter as is necessary to collect amounts for the services rendered by Physician:

(a) The parties agree that Corporation will bill and collect all fees relating to services rendered by Physician pursuant to this Agreement and shall be entitled to retain thirty percent (30%) of all such amounts collected on account of Physician's services in consideration of Corporation's services provided hereunder. Physician shall cooperate with Corporation in the collection of the charges for his services hereunder.

(b) Physician shall be responsible for and shall provide all services and expenses not provided by Corporation necessary for the practice of medicine, including but not limited to medical malpractice insurance, professional society dues, travel and entertainment expenses, telephone and answering service, stationery, stamps, photocopies, and stenographic assistance. During the term of this Agreement, Physician shall obtain and maintain a policy or policies of: (1) medical malpractice insurance having a face amount of not less than $1,000,000 for each occurrence and $3,000,000 annual aggregate, and (2) motor vehicle liability insurance having a face amount of not less than $100,000 for each occurrence and $300,000 annual aggregate. Within thirty (30) days after the execution of this Agreement, Physician shall furnish appropriate evidence of the existence of such insurance to Corporation.

(c) Physician's charges for professional services rendered shall be established from time to time by Corporation.

6. Term. The term of this Agreement shall be for the year beginning _____ and ending _____.

7. <u>Case Records and Histories</u>. All case records, case histories, X-ray films, or personal and regular files concerning patients of Corporation or patients consulted, interviewed or treated and cared for by Physician during the term of this Agreement shall belong to and remain the property of Corporation; however, upon termination of this Agreement, Physician shall have the privilege, within 90 days after such termination, of reproducing at his own expense any of such patients' records so treated or cared for by him during the term of this Agreement.

8. <u>Independent Contractor Status</u>. In consideration of this Agreement, Physician acknowledges, recognizes and defines himself as being an independent contractor of the Corporation and not an employee of the Corporation, and further acknowledges, agrees and defines any persons employed or otherwise retained by him to be employed or otherwise retained by him in his capacity as an independent contractor to the Corporation, and acknowledges and agrees that such persons are not employees of the Corporation. Physician agrees that he alone has the responsibility of paying such persons employed or retained by him, making deductions required by law, reporting compensation of such employees as required by law, and generally determining any and all appropriate forms of compensation and fringe benefits for them. Physician, individually and as an independent contractor, hereby specifically waives any claim of rights or benefits, whether present or future, under the Corporation's retirement plans, fringe benefits afforded employees of the Corporation, or the payment of Social Security taxes by the Corporation, Workmen's Compensation or Unemployment Compensation or like benefits normally afforded employees of the Corporation; provided, further, that Physician, in his capacity as independent contractor, shall obtain and give to the Corporation, waivers from all persons employed or otherwise retained by him, including himself, individually acknowledging that they are not employees of the Corporation and acknowledging further that they waive any claim of rights or benefits normally afforded employees of the Corporation. Physician hereby agrees to indemnify and hold the Corporation harmless from such claims by any such employees or such persons otherwise retained.

As an independent contractor, Physician acknowledges that he has no control over the employees of Corporation. Nothing herein shall be construed as giving Corporation control over, or the right to control, the professional judgment, treatment, or actions of Physician with respect to the professional services rendered hereunder.

9. <u>Physician's Warranties</u>. Physician represents and warrants to Corporation that: (a) he is duly licensed to practice medicine in the State of _____; (b) he has all customary narcotics and controlled substances numbers and licenses; (c) his license to practice medicine in any state has never been suspended or revoked; and (d) he has never been denied membership or re-appointment of membership on the medical staff of any hospital, and no hospital medical staff membership or clinical privileges have ever been suspended, curtailed, or revoked.

10. <u>Vacation and Other Absences</u>. At such times as Corporation and Physician shall mutually agree, Physician shall be entitled temporarily to cease rendering services under this Agreement for such period of time as Corporation and Physician shall mutually agree.

11. <u>Outside Professional Activities</u>. During the term of this Agreement, Physician may not keep as his own any fees or other honorariums he receives for rendering professional services or engaging in any other professional activities during his off days or any other time; it being clearly understood that all fees or honorariums for the professional services of Physician rendered during the term of this Agreement shall be paid to Corporation, shall be subject to this Agreement, and shall be considered to be part of the gross collections produced by the efforts of Physician.

12. <u>Exclusive Nature of Agreement</u>. During the term of this Agreement, Physician shall devote his entire professional time to the business of Corporation. Physician shall not, directly or indirectly, engage in any other business or occupation, whether full-time, part-time or otherwise, detrimental to his required active participation in Corporation's business; provided, however, that nothing herein contained shall prohibit the activity of Physician in investing or trading in stocks, bonds, commodities, securities, real estate or other forms of investment, or in any venture that does not require his active participation.

13. <u>Termination of Agreement</u>. Corporation or Physician may terminate this Agreement without cause and at any time upon thirty (30) days written notice, in which event Corporation shall only be obligated to continue to pay Physician the amounts due him under Paragraph 4 of this Agreement.

Upon termination of this Agreement, Corporation shall continue to collect the amounts billed on account of the efforts of Physician.

14. <u>Possible Future Employment by Corporation</u>. After the expiration of the term of this Agreement, Corporation intends, but is not contractually bound, to sell a stock interest in Corporation to Physician, at which time Physician will become an employee of Corporation. If Physician does, in fact, become a shareholder and employee of Corporation upon termination of this Agreement, the specific provisions of Physician's employment shall be mutually agreed upon at that time by Corporation and Physician.

15. <u>Assignments</u>. The rights and obligations of Physician under this Agreement, as an independent contractor, relate to specialized personal services rendered by Physician and may not be assigned by him.

Corporation may assign its rights and obligations under this Agreement to any legal entity or individual that acquires or otherwise continues the practice of medicine currently conducted by it.

16. <u>Disclosure of Information</u>. Physician shall not, during or after the term of this Agreement, disclose any information relating to the Corporation, its officers, employees, clients or patients, including information regarding the affairs or operations of the Corporation, without obtaining the prior written consent of the Corporation.

17. <u>Indemnification of Corporation</u>. Physician hereby agrees to indemnify, defend, and hold harmless the Corporation, and its officers, directors, shareholders, employees, and agents, from any claim, loss, damage, cost, expense or liability arising out of or related to the performance or nonperformance by him of any services to be performed or provided by him under this Agreement, except as may be reimbursed by insurance or otherwise.

18. Satellite Facilities and Branch Offices. This Agreement covers only the services provided by Physician in connection with Corporation's present operations on _____. The services to be provided by Physician at other facilities that may be established by Corporation shall be agreed upon by Physician and Corporation at the time Corporation desires such services.

19. Waiver of Breach or Violation not Deemed Continuing. The waiver by either party of a breach or violation of any provision of this Agreement shall not operate as or be construed to be a waiver of any subsequent breach hereof.

20. Notices. Any and all notices required or permitted to be given under this Agreement will be sufficient if furnished in writing, sent by registered mail to his last known residence in case of Physician or to its principal office at _____, in the case of the Corporation.

21. Governing Law. This Agreement shall be interpreted, construed and governed according to the laws of the State of _____.

22. Paragraph Headings. The paragraph headings contained in this Agreement are for convenience only and shall in no manner be construed as a part of this Agreement.

23. Entire Agreement. This Agreement supersedes all prior discussions and agreements between Corporation, or any of its officers, directors, employees, or agents, and Physician with respect to all matters contained herein, and this Agreement constitutes the sole and entire agreement with respect thereto. Any representation, inducement, promise or agreement, whether oral or written, between Corporation, or any of its officers, directors, employees, or agents, and Physician that is not embodied herein shall be of no force or effect.

24. Counterparts. This Agreement is executed in multiple counterparts, each of which shall be deemed an original and together shall constitute one and the same agreement, with one counterpart being delivered to each party hereto.

IN WITNESS WHEREOF, Corporation has caused this Agreement to be executed by its duly authorized officers, and Physician has hereunto set his hand and seal, all being done in duplicate originals with one original being delivered to each party on the day and year first above written.

CORPORATION

_____

ATTEST:

_____   By: _____
Secretary   President

INDEPENDENT CONTRACTOR

_____   _____ (SEAL)
Witness

CERTIFICATION OF
EMPLOYEE STATUS

I hereby acknowledge that I am employed by Dr. A, and, as such, am entitled only to the employee benefits provided by him. I understand that, by virtue of Dr. A's relationship with XYZ, P.C., a professional medical corporation, I am not, nor do I consider myself, an employee of said Corporation. Further, I hereby waive any claim or rights or benefits normally afforded employees of said Corporation.

_____

Date: _____

[10.03] AGREEMENTS WITH OTHER PROFESSIONAL CORPORATIONS

(1) Joint Venture Agreements

Professional corporations sometimes enter into joint ventures whereby the two professional corporations share space, equipment and utilities to the common goal of the practice of the professional. The provisions which will exist in such an agreement will be similar to both employment agreements for shareholders and practice agreements for independent contractors. In other words, the agreement should specifically state that the two professional corporations are separate legal entities. On the other hand, the two corporations are sharing in the profits generated from the business, and this must be provided for upon termination. Potential problems may arise with regard to the nondiscrimination rules under Section 414(m) for qualified retirement plans of "affiliated service corporations." This aspect of the relationship should be specifically addressed in the joint venture agreement. For a detailed discussion of this issue, see section [19.03], *infra*.

The following is a form of joint venture agreement which may be used between two professional corporations.

JOINT VENTURE AGREEMENT

THIS AGREEMENT, made as of this _____ day of _____, 19_____, by and between _____, a Georgia professional corporation" (hereinafter referred to as "Corporation"), and _____, a Georgia professional corporation (hereinafter referred to as "P.C.").

W I T N E S S E T H:

WHEREAS, Corporation is engaged in the business of conducting a professional medical practice specializing in _____ in _____, Georgia; and

WHEREAS, P.C. is also engaged in the business of conducting a professional medical practice in _____, Georgia; and

266

WHEREAS, from _____, 19__, through _____, 19__, the professional employee of P.C., _____, M.D., (the "Professional Employee"), practiced medicine as an employee of Corporation, but, for various reasons, on _____, 19__, _____M.D., resigned as an employee of Corporation and separately incorporated his medical practice in P.C.; and

WHEREAS, P.C. desires to practice medicine through Corporation and Corporation desires to obtain the services of P.C. as an independent contractor all on the terms and conditions hereinafter set forth;

NOW, THEREFORE, for and in consideration of the promises, covenants, and agreements hereinafter set forth, the parties hereto agree as follows:

1. Engagement as Independent Contractor. Corporation hereby engages P.C. as an independent contractor to perform medical services for Corporation, and P.C. hereby accepts said engagement for the term hereof with the respective duties, responsibilities, and obligations hereinafter set forth. P.C. shall furnish said services by and through qualified physicians, duly licensed to practice medicine in the State of Georgia.

2. Duties. P.C., as an independent contractor, agrees to practice its medical specialty of _____ through Corporation. P.C. also agrees to provide medical services to Corporation during such reasonable hours and at such times as Corporation may from time to time reasonably request. P.C. also agrees to perform such other reasonable tasks and services as Corporation may from time to time request.

In performing services under this Agreement, P.C. covenants and agrees that its employees: (i) shall use diligent efforts and professional skills and judgment, (ii) shall render care to patients in accordance with and in a manner consistent with customary and recognized standards of the medical profession, and (iii) shall conduct themselves in a manner consistent with the Principles of Medical Ethics of the American Medical Association.

3. Facilities. While this Agreement is in effect, Corporation will make available to P.C. as an independent contractor adequate physical facilities, as well as equipment, supplies, medical technicians, office nurses, and non-professional personnel, including the availability of reception, transcription, bookkeeping, and billing services, which Corporation and P.C. deem reasonably necessary for the practice of medicine. P.C. also agrees to make its medical equipment available for use in the medical practice of Corporation.

4. Compensation. P.C. shall receive as compensation for all services provided by it as an independent contractor under this Agreement, one-forth (¼) of the gross revenues of Corporation reduced by one-forth (¼) of the common expenses of conducting the medical practice of Corporation. Said compensation shall be paid monthly, not later than twenty (20) days following the end of each month, and shall be based on the gross revenues received and expenses incurred by Corporation during that month. The "gross revenues" of Corporation shall be conclusively presumed to be the revenues received by Corporation as appearing on the books of account of Corporation, including proceeds of key man life insurance policies payable to Corporation. The "common expenses of conducting the medical practice of Corporation" shall be those expenses incurred by Corporation

for the common benefit of Corporation and P.C. The "common expenses" shall include, but shall not be limited to, employment and withholding taxes, workmen's compensation and employment compensation benefits, salaries, insurance benefits, and other expenses incurred for nurses and staff persons, bank charges, billing and collection expenses, dues and subscriptions, promotion, equipment rental, general office insurance, supplies, postage, printing, repairs and maintenance, taxes, licenses, rent, telephone, key man life insurance premiums, and other miscellaneous office and practice expenses. Such "common expenses" shall, however, not include legal fees, medical reimbursement, malpractice, life (excluding key man insurance), medical and disability insurance, salaries, employment and withholding taxes, automobile allowances and expenses, personal telephone calls and other compensation, fringe benefits and expenses to the extent they inure solely to the benefit of Corporation or its physician-employees. In addition, such common expenses shall not include depreciation of the assets of Corporation or contributions to its qualified retirement plans. Corporation and P.C. shall agree upon the allocation of common expenses on the date of this Agreement and on each subsequent anniversary hereof.

5. <u>Billing and Fees</u>. During the time that this Agreement is in effect:

(a) The parties agree that Corporation will bill and collect all fees relating to services rendered by P.C. pursuant to this Agreement; and

(b) P.C.'s charges for professional services rendered shall be established from time to time by Corporation and P.C.

6. <u>Term</u>. The term of this Agreement shall be for the year beginning _____, 19___, and ending _____, 19___, and for each successive year thereafter unless and until terminated as provided herein. Each 12-month period beginning _____ and ending _____ shall be referred to hereunder as a "Contract Year".

7. <u>Case Records and Histories</u>. All case records, case histories, X-ray films, and regular files concerning patients of Corporation or patients consulted, interviewed or treated and cared for by P.C. during the term of this Agreement shall belong to and remain the property of Corporation; however, upon termination of this Agreement, P.C. shall have the privilege, within 90 days after such termination, of reproducing at its own expense, the records of any patients for whom it or its Professional Employee rendered services.

8. <u>Independent Contractor Status</u>. In consideration of this Agreement, P.C. acknowledges, recognizes and defines itself as being an independent contractor of Corporation and not an employee of Corporation, and further acknowledges, agrees and defines any persons employed or otherwise retained by it to be employed or otherwise retained by it in its capacity as an independent contractor to Corporation, and acknowledges and agrees that such persons are not employees of Corporation. P.C. agrees that it, alone, has the responsibility of paying such persons employed or retained by it, making deductions required by law, reporting compensation of such employees as required by law, and generally determining any and all appropriate forms of compensation and fringe benefits for them. P.C., as an independent contractor, hereby specifically waives any claim of rights or benefits, whether present or future, under Corporation's retirement plans, fringe

benefits afforded employees of Corporation, or the payment of Social Security taxes by Corporation, workmen's compensation or unemployment compensation or like benefits normally afforded employees of Corporation.

Nothing herein shall be construed as giving Corporation control over, or the right to control, the professional judgment, treatment, or actions of the employees of P.C. with respect to the professional services rendered hereunder.

9. <u>Vacation and Other Absences</u>. P.C. shall be entitled to twenty (20) working days per Contract Year with pay during which services are not required hereunder. There shall be no carryover of any unused portion of such time from one Contract Year to another. In determining working days for purposes of this Section 9, Saturdays, Sundays and holidays on which Corporation's office is closed shall not be counted. If for any reason this Agreement is terminated during a Contract Year, the number of working days to which P.C. is entitled in this Section 9 shall be multiplied by a fraction, the denominator of which shall be 365 and the numerator of which shall be the number of calendar days in the Contract Year prior to the date of such termination.

10. <u>Outside Professional Activities</u>. During the term of this Agreement, neither P.C. nor its Professional Employee may keep as their own any fees or other honorariums they receive for rendering professional services or engaging in any other professional activities during off days or any other time; it being clearly understood that all fees for the professional services of P.C. and the Professional Employee rendered during the term of this Agreement shall be paid to Corporation, shall be subject to this Agreement, and shall be considered to be part of the gross revenues of Corporation. However, income paid to Professional Employee for teaching, lectures, writing of treatises and articles, and reimbursements for charitable and professional activities shall belong solely to him, when such activities have been approved by Corporation.

11. <u>Exclusive Nature of Agreement</u>. During the term of this Agreement, P.C. and its Professional Employee shall devote their entire professional time to the business of Corporation. Neither P.C. nor its Professional Employee shall, directly or indirectly, engage in any other business or occupation, whether full-time, part-time or otherwise, detrimental to their required active participation in Corporation's business; provided, however, that nothing herein contained shall prohibit them from investing or trading in stocks, bonds, commodities, securities, real estate or other forms of investment, or in any venture that does not require their active participation.

12. <u>Qualified Retirement Plans</u>. Corporation and P.C. agree that, for purposes of determining participation in their qualified retirement plans, the non-physician employees of Corporation shall be considered full-time employees of P.C. to the extent of one-fourth (¼) of their compensation and full-time employees of Corporation to the extent of three-fourths (¾) of their compensation. Consequently, the nonphysician employees of Corporation shall be entitled to participate in both the qualified retirement plans of Corporation and P.C. as provided under the terms of those plans. Although the nonphysician employees of Corporation will be considered employees of P.C. for this limited purpose, the ultimate

decision regarding the employment of such employees will rest with Corporation and Corporation shall be solely responsible for all federal and state withholding and employment taxes on its nonphysician employees.

If, in order to maintain the qualified status of Corporation's retirement plans, the nonphysician employees of Corporation must not be considered participants in P.C.'s qualified retirement plans but, rather, participants in Corporation's qualified retirement plans to the full extent of their compensation, then for purposes of figuring the compensation due to P.C. under Section 4 hereof, P.C.'s compensation shall be reduced annually by one-fourth (¼) of Corporation's contributions to its qualified retirement plans that are made on account of and allocated to its nonphysician employees. However, in determining this reduction, P.C. shall receive a credit for one-fourth (¼) of the annual forfeitures occurring in the accounts of nonphysician employee participants in Corporation's qualified retirement plans, which are allocated to the accounts of Corporation's physician employees and which do not reduce Corporation's contributions.

If, in order to maintain the qualified status of Corporation's retirement plans, the nonphysician employees of Corporation must be considered participants in P.C.'s and Corporation's plans on a basis different from those described above, a proper adjustment in the compensation due to P.C. under Section 4 shall be made in the same manner as the adjustment described in the second paragraph of this Section.

13. Disability Compensation Continuation.

(a) If, as a result of illness or physical or mental incapacity, the Professional Employee of P.C. is unable to provide services during normal hours and perform normal duties, then, in lieu of the compensation provided in Section 4, compensation shall be paid to P.C. as follows:

(i) During the first eight (8) weeks of continuous disability, Corporation agrees to pay P.C. the disability compensation as set forth in Subsection (e) below.

(ii) If the Professional Employee's uninterrupted disability continues thereafter, Corporation agrees during the next twenty (20) weeks of such continuous disability to pay P.C. the greater of: (a) fifty percent (50%) of P.C.'s disability compensation as set forth in Subsection (e) below, or (b) P.C.'s normal compensation as set forth in Subsection (e) below multiplied by a fraction, the denominator of which shall be P.C.'s regular hours of service and the numerator of which shall be P.C.'s reduced hours of service.

(iii) After twenty-eight (28) weeks of continuous disability, no further compensation shall be paid by Corporation to P.C. hereunder unless P.C. is performing some services, in which event Corporation shall pay P.C. the normal compensation as set forth in Subsection (e) below multiplied by a fraction, the denominator of which shall be P.C.'s regular hours of service and the numerator of which shall be P.C.'s reduced hours of service.

(b) If the Professional Employee becomes disabled within one (1) year after the end of any previous period of disability (regardless of the similarity or difference of causes of disability), then such subsequent period of disability shall be deemed to be a continuation of the prior period of disability.

(c) For purposes of this Agreement, normal hours of service and reduced hours of service for purposes of this Section 13 shall be determined by the mutual agreement of Corporation and P.C.

(d) Anything herein to the contrary notwithstanding, accrued but unused vacation time of P.C. shall be applied toward a period of total disability, except for the first two (2) weeks of such total disability, and any such application of vacation time shall toll the running of the weekly periods set forth in Subsection (a) above. For purposes of this Subsection (d), a week of total disability shall mean a wcck in which P.C. devotes less than fitteen (15) hours to its duties hereunder.

(e) As used in this Agreement and terms P.C.'s ''disability compensation'' and ''normal compensation'' shall be determined annually by the mutual agreement of Corporation and P.C.

14. Deferred Compensation. Upon the termination of this Agreement, Corporation shall pay to P.C., as deferred compensation for services rendered during the term of this Agreement, an amount determined as follows:

(a) The accounts receivable of Corporation shall be determined as of the last day of the calendar month immediately preceding the effective date of termination of this Agreement. For purposes of this determination, accounts receivable which have been on Corporation's books less than three months as of the valuation date shall be valued at ninety-five percent (95%) of their face, and accounts receivable which have been on Corporation's books for three (3) months or more shall be valued at fifty percent (50%) of their face; provided, that accounts receivable which have been on Corporation's books for six (6) months or more shall be totally excluded from such valuation.

(b) The result of the computations of Subsection (a) above shall be divided by four.

(c) The amount thus determined shall be paid by Corporation to P.C. no later than six (6) months after the effective date of the termination hereunder.

(d) Anything in this Agreement to the contrary notwithstanding, and except as provided in (i) below, any payments made to P.C. during a period of disability as provided in Section 13 above shall be subtracted from the amount of deferred compensation payable to P.C. pursuant to this Section 14. If the amounts paid during such period of disability are greater than the amount payable to P.C. pursuant to this Section 14, then the excess shall be applied to reduce any sums payable to P.C. pursuant to Section 15 below. The provisions of this Subsection (d) shall not apply if the period of disability ended more than one year prior to the effective date of termination.

(i) Payments made to P.C. during any period of disability which are attributable to services actually performed by P.C. during such period of disability shall not be subtracted from the amount of deferred compensation payable to P.C. pursuant to this Section 14. To make such determination, amounts paid to P.C. which are attributable to services actually performed by P.C. shall be deemed to be P.C.'s normal compensation multiplied by a fraction, the denominator of which shall be P.C.'s regular hours of service and the numerator of which shall be P.C.'s reduced hours of service, making appropriate calculations on a weekly basis for payments made to P.C. during the period of disability.

15. Additional Deferred Compensation. Subject to the provisions of this Section 15, if this Agreement is terminated, Corporation shall pay to P.C. as additional deferred compensation twenty-five percent (25%; of P.C.'s average annual compensation from Corporation for the three (3) Contract Years ending on the last day of the Contract Year immediately preceding the effective date of the termination; provided, that is such termination occurs prior to _____, 19___, the number of Contract Years, if less then three (3), shall be used for purposes of the calculation required under this Section 15.

(a) The computations required by this Section 15 shall be made by Corporation's accountants, in accordance with accounting principles consistently applied.

(b) Payment of additional deferred compensation pursuant to this Section 15 shall be made as follows:

(i) If due to P.C.'s voluntary termination of this Agreement hereunder [as set forth in Section 16(a)], or if due to P.C.'s disqualification [as provided in Section 16 (c)], or if due to termination by Corporation for cause [as provided in Section 16(e) below], any additional deferred compensation to be paid to P.C. hereunder shall be paid in twenty-four (24) equal monthly installments (without interest), such installments to commence not later than three (3) months after the effective date of P.C.'s termination of this Agreement.

(ii) If due to any reason other than those set forth in Subsection (i) above, any additional deferred compensation to be paid to P.C. hereunder shall be paid in full not later than three (3) months after the effective date of the termination.

(c) In consideration of the right to receive additional deferred compensation hereunder, P.C. and its Professional Employee agree that neither of them will enter into the private practice of general _____ medicine within a one hundred (100) mile radius of Corporation's principal office at any time within three (3) years following the effective date of the termination hereunder. If either P.C. or its Professional Employee elects, at any time during such three (3) year period, to enter into the private practice of general _____ medicine within a one hundred (100) mile radius of Corporation's principal office, and payments of additional deferred compensation have already been made pursuant to this Section 15, P.C. agrees that it shall forthwith repay to Corporation the amounts received pursuant to this Section 15 (and in the event P.C. is unable to do so, the Professional Employee agrees to repay such amounts). The private practice of general _____ medicine includes partnership or clinic private practice and includes private practice whether it is the sole proprietor, partner or through a corporation or professional association, but shall not include services rendered primarily as a hospital inpatient physician.

16. Termination. This Agreement, or any extension or renewal hereof, may be terminated as follows:

(a) Withdrawal. P.C. shall have the right to terminate this Agreement at any time by giving three (3) months' written notice. The effective date of termination shall be the date that P.C. ceases to perform services pursuant to said notice.

(b) Disability. If the Professional Employee is disabled, as provided in Section 13 of this Agreement, for a period of fifty-two (52) weeks during any one hundred-four (104) week period, this Agreement shall be terminated effective at the end of such fifty-two (52) week period; provided, however, that for purposes of this Subsection (b) only, if P.C. devotes at least fifteen (15) hours during any week to its duties hereunder, such week shall be counted as two-thirds (⅔) of a week in determining whether the Professional Employee has been disabled for a period of fifty-two (52) weeks. For purposes of this Subsection (b), the application of vacation time to a period of disability, as provided in Subsection (d) of Section 13, shall not be deemed a period of disability.

(c) Disqualification. If the Professional Employee's right to practice medicine in the specialty of _____ is suspended or revoked, this Agreement shall be terminated effective as of the date of such suspension or revocation.

(d) Death. Upon the death of the Professional Employee, this Agreement shall be deemed automatically terminated as of such date.

(e) Termination by Corporation For Cause. Corporation may terminate this Agreement "for cause" upon immediate written notice to P.C. As used in the preceding sentence, "for cause" shall mean gross, willful and continuous failure of P.C. to comply with the terms and provisions of this Agreement; P.C.'s continuous failure to perform competently its medical duties; or the Professional Employee's conviction of a crime involving moral turpitude. The effective date of termination for cause shall be the date that notice is given, unless such notice sets forth a later date.

Should more than one of the foregoing events be applicable, the effective date of the first occurring event shall control the method of termination. In the event of termination hereunder, P.C. shall continue to perform its regular duties and Corporation shall continue to pay compensation through the effective date of termination. In lieu of the foregoing and at the option of Corporation, upon notice of termination, Corporation may immediately suspend P.C. from further services hereunder and continue to pay the normal compensation to P.C. through the date which would have been the effective date of termination.

17. Additional Death Benefits. Notwithstanding anything contained in this Agreement, Corporation shall pay to P.C. an additional benefit upon the death of the Professional Employee equal to the excess, if any, of (a) over (b):

(a) The proceeds of any key man insurance policy maintained by Corporation on the life of the Professional Employee, which proceeds are payable to Corporation;

(b) The amounts previously paid, or to become payable, to P.C. under Sections 14 and 15 of this Agreement.

Such additional death benefit shall be paid to P.C. immediately after the receipt by Corporation of said insurance proceeds. Further, the amount of key man life insurance maintained by Corporation on its physician-employees and on the Professional Employee shall be established from time to time by Corporation and P.C.

18. Additional Physician-Employees. Corporation may hire additional physician-employees provided it has the consent of P.C. and P.C. may hire additional physician-employees provided it has the consent of Corporation.

19. Change in Number of Physician-Employees. In the event that there is a change in the number of physician employees of Corporation or P.C., appropriate adjustments shall be made in this Agreement. Also, in the event that the number of active physician-employees of Corporation shall decrease due to disability (for more than two weeks), death, or other termination of employment, an immediate downward adjustment in the amounts due Corporation under Section 4 of this Agreement shall be made as of the date of such disability, death, or termination and the Disability Salary Continuation, the Deferred Compensation, and the Additional Deferred Compensation (as those terms are defined in Sections 9, 12, and 13 of the Employment Agreements of the physician-employees of Corporation) and payments pursuant to Paragraph 20(d) of the Corporate Shareholders' Agreement attached hereto as "Exhibit A" shall be considered a common expense of conducting the medical practice of Corporation under Section 4 of this Agreement.

20. Amendment of Agreements. The terms of this Agreement and the Shareholders' Agreement and Employment Agreements of the physician-employees of Corporation (copies of which are attached hereto as "Exhibit B" shall, during the period in which this Agreement is in effect, in all material respects, be identical to their present forms, and such Agreements shall not be amended without the mutual consent of Corporation and P.C.

21. Assignments. The rights and obligations provided under this Agreement are not assignable; provided that Corporation and P.C. may assign their rights and obligations under this Agreement to any legal entity or individual that acquires or otherwise continues the practice of medicine currently conducted by them.

22. Nature of Agreement. This Agreement contains the terms under which Corporation and P.C. jointly agree to practice medicine and share office space, expenses, and employees, and the relationship between Corporation and P.C. shall not be deemed to be a partnership.

23. Waiver of Breach or Violation not Deemed Continuing. The waiver by either party of a breach or violation of any provision of this Agreement shall not operate as or be construed to be a waiver of any subsequent breach hereof.

24. Notices. Any and all notices required or permitted to be given under this Agreement will be sufficient if furnished in writing, sent by registered mail to Professional Employee's last known residence in case of P.C. or to its principal office at _____, _____, Georgia, in the case of the Corporation.

25. Governing Law. This Agreement shall be interpreted, construed and governed according to the laws of the State of Georgia.

26. Paragraph Headings. The paragraph headings contained in this Agreement are for convenience only and shall in no manner be construed as a part of this Agreement.

27. Entire Agreement. This Agreement supersedes all prior discussions and agreements between Corporation, or any of its officers, directors, employees, or

agents, and P.C. with respect to all matters contained herein, and this Agreement constitutes the sole and entire agreement with respect thereto. Any representation, inducement, promise or agreement, whether oral or written, between Corporation, or any of its officers, directors, employees, or agents, and P.C. that is not embodied herein shall be of no force or effect.

28. Counterparts. This Agreement is executed in multiple counterparts, each of which shall be deemed an original and together shall constitute one and the same agreement, with one counterpart being delivered to each party hereto.

IN WITNESS WHEREOF, Corporation and P.C. hereunto caused this Agreement to be executed by their duly authorized officers all being done in duplicate originals with one original being delivered to each party on the day and year first above written.

(CORPORATE SEAL)   CORPORATION

ATTEST:

_____   By: _____
Secretary   President

(CORPORATE SEAL)   P.C.

ATTEST:

_____   By: _____
Secretary   President

(2) Partnerships of Professional Corporations

In order to obtain benefits which are available through incorporation, often one or more of the professionals in a professional partnership will incorporate, and the professional corporations will become partners in the partnership. Various aspects of such a partnership are discussed in Chapter 19, *infra*. The following is a form of partnership agreement in which some of the partners are professional corporations:

PARTNERSHIP AGREEMENT

STATE OF GEORGIA

COUNTY OF FULTON

_____, Attorney at Law, P.C., _____, _____, _____, Attorney at Law, P.C., _____, _____, _____, _____, _____, _____, _____, _____, and _____ enter into these ARTICLES OF PARTNERSHIP, to-wit:

ARTICLE ONE

The parties hereto constitute themselves a partnership, beginning _____, 19____, to engage in the practice of law under the name and style of:

_____

with offices located at _____, Georgia, and _____, Georgia. The parties recognize that certain partners are professional corporations, and the partners which are professional corporations agree to cause their employees to act in a manner consistent with the terms of this Agreement. The partners who are individuals are sometimes referred to herein as the "individual partners," the partners which are professional corporations are sometimes referred to herein as the "corporate partners," and the individual partners and the corporate partners are sometimes collectively referred to herein as the "partners."

ARTICLE TWO

(a) All partners agree to devote their entire time, attention and best efforts to the firm and its business through the life of this Agreement and each partner shall have an automobile available for use in discharging the business of the firm. Each individual partner and each corporate partner further agrees to conduct themselves (and, in the case of corporate partners, their employees), personally and in partnership affairs, so as not to reflect discredit on the partnership.

(b) The business affairs of the partnership shall be managed by the partners and decisions shall be made by a vote of the partners holding a voting interest in the firm. Voting interest is defined as the percentage of ownerhip held by a partner in the firm. Except as otherwise provided herein, decisions which may obligate the partnership beyond routine and ordinary matters or which might effect a substantial change in the method of business operations shall be subject to the approval of a majority of the voting interest in the firm. The extending of an invitation to one not a partner in this firm to become a partner shall be by not less than two-thirds majority of the voting interest.

(c) To assist in conducting the business affairs of the partnership there shall be an Administrative Partner, Financial Partner and a Hiring Committee, who shall be elected by the partnership. The Administrative Partner shall serve for a period of one year, beginning on _____ of each year, and shall, among other things, be responsible for implementing the decisions of the partnership. The Financial Partner shall serve for a period of four months, beginning on _____ of each year and shall be responsible for supervising the financial tranactions of the firm. The Hiring Committee shall consist of _____ (___) partners, which may not include the Administrative Partner, and shall serve for a period of one year, beginning on _____. This Committee shall be responsible for conducting the functions incident to the acquisition of new personnel.

ARTICLE THREE

The partnership shall maintain complete and accurate books and records showing the status of the partnership at all times and it shall maintain in the name of the partnership an account in _____ Bank or such other bank as the partnership from time to time shall select. Checks on partnership deposits shall be signed in the partnership name by one or more of the individual partners or the president of a corporate partner. The voting partners of the partnership shall be liable for any and all debts and obligations incurred by or on behalf of the partnership to the extent of the ownership interest and the owner partners shall own all of the assets of the firm and all proceeds from the practice of law shall be deposited in the partnership account. After all debts and obligations of the partnership have been paid, the partners shall share in the profits as more specifically hereinafter set forth.

ARTICLE FOUR

The value of the capital account of the partnership shall be whatever the partnership from time to time may determine, it being understood that the partnership will commence its business on _____, 19___, with a capital account evaluation of _____ DOLLARS, which is comprised of leasehold improvements and furniture and fixtures and each partner shall be expected as soon as possible after execution of this Agreement to bear his percentage of that amount.

ARTICLE FIVE

The retirement of a partner or the death of an individual partner or the dissolution of a corporate partner shall not require a dissolution of the firm and the liquidation of its business, but the business shall be continued by the survivors at their option, without interruption, subject to the conditions hereafter set forth.

ARTICLE SIX

(a) Upon the death of an individual partner or upon the dissolution of a corporate partner following the death of its president, the Estate or designated beneficiary of such deceased individual partner or the stockholders of such dissolved corporate partner, respectively, shall be paid:

(1) within fifteen (15) days thereafter that percentage which such partner held in the partnership at the time of such death or dissolution of any undisbursed net fees in the account of the partnership; and

(2) within not more than sixty (60) days, such partner's then percentage of the capital and capital assets of the partnership and such additional sums as apply to such partner under subsection (b) of this Article.

(b) If such partner has been a partner of this firm or its predecessor firm for a period of not less than five (5) years immediately preceding such death or dissolution, then such individual partner's Estate or the stockholders of such corporate partner shall be entitled to an amount equivalent to such partner's earnings from the partnership for the twelve (12) month period immediately preceding the death of such individual partner or the death of the president of such corporate partner or such partner's percentage of the partnership profits for a period of twelve (12) months following such death with the option to be exercised by the individual partner's Estate or the corporate partner's stockholders. If the former option is exercised, the payment will be made within sixty (60) days.

In the event that such partner has been a partner of this firm for a period less than five (5) years, but not less than four (4) years, then the amount provided by this subsection will be computed on an eighty (80) percent basis with the Estate or stockholders having the same option.

In the event that such partner has been a partner of this firm for a period less than four (4) years, but not less than three (3) years, then the amount provided by this subsection will be computed on the basis of sixty (60) percent with the Estate or stockholders having the same option.

In the event that such partner has been a partner of this firm for a period less than three (3) years, but not less than two (2) years, then the amount provided by this subsection will be computed on the basis of forty (40) percent with the Estate or stockholders having the same option.

In the event that such partner has been a partner of this firm for a period less than two (2) years, but not less than one (1) year, then the amount provided by this subsection will be computed on the basis of twenty (20) percent with the Estate or stockholders having the same option.

In the event that such partner has been a partner of this firm for a period less than one (1) year, then the amount provided by this subsection shall be ten (10) percent of such partner's earnings during the time he was a partner.

For purposes of computing the time that any corporate partner has been a partner of this firm or its predecessor firm hereunder, there shall also be included that period of time during which the president of a corporate partner was a partner in this firm or its predecessor firm.

(c) Upon the withdrawal of a partner from this firm, such withdrawing partner shall be entitled to his then percentage of the undisbursed fees of the partnership, which shall be computed and paid immediately and also such partner shall be entitled to his then percentage of the capital assets of the firm, which shall be due and payable within sixty (60) days of the effective date of such partner's withdrawal or retirement. These balances when computed and paid shall cover and represent the withdrawing partner's entire interest in the partnership and all net assets, tangible or intangible, of the firm, including, but not limited to files, law business and any other assets of the firm.

(d) The membership of any partner may be terminated at any time upon a unanimous vote in favor thereof by all other partners holding a voting interest in the partnership. In the event this occurs, such terminated partner shall be entitled to his then percentage of any undisbursed fees in the partnership account, which shall be due and payable immediately, and, additionally, such partner shall be entitled to his paid percentage of the capital assets of the partnership, which shall be due and payable within thirty (30) days of the termination date. The payment of these amounts shall cover and represent the terminated partner's entire interest in the partnership and all net assets, tangible or intangible, of the firm, including but not limited to files, law business and any other asset of the firm.

(e) In the event of either temporary or permanent disability rendering an individual partner incapable of performing his duties as a partner of this firm or in the event of the temporary or permanent disability of the president of a corporate partner rendering a corporate partner incapable of performing its duties as a partner of this firm, then the firm shall for a period of ninety (90) days following the commencement of such disability, pay such afflicted individual partner or such corporate partner for that period of time the sums which such partner would otherwise have drawn had such incapacity not occurred. Any additional sums which such afflicted individual or corporate partner may draw beyond the ninety (90) day period shall be decided by a majority vote of the voting interest in the partnership of the remaining partners.

(f) The partners by a majority vote of the voting interest in the partnership may elect to fund all or part of the contingent obligations arising as the result of the death or retirement of a partner by obtaining appropriate insurance and in the event such is done, the premiums will be paid by the partnership and the proceeds of said policy or policies shall be applied toward the discharge of the liability of the partnership for those sums for which the partnership may otherwise be liable under Subsection (b) of this Article. In the event that the proceeds are insufficient to extinguish all of the liability of the partnership, then the partnership shall be obligated for the balance. In the event that the proceeds of the policy exceed the liability of the partnership, then such excess proceeds shall be the property of the partnership.

ARTICLE SEVEN

During the year 19___, a concerted effort will be made by the partnership to formulate an appropriate retirement plan for partners. It is anticipated that such plan will become part of the next partnership agreement.

ARTICLE EIGHT

Effective at the commencement of this partnership on _____, 19___, the participation in the partnership and its earnings shall be as follows:

_____   _____ percent

_____   _____ percent

_____   _____ percent

_____   _____ percent

ARTICLE NINE

All provisions of this Agreement apply to all partners except that Articles Four, Six and Seven shall have no applicability to _____, who shall hold no voting interest nor ownership in the partnership and whose earnings shall be computed as follows:

(a) $3,333.33 per month; and also

(b) Fifty (50%) percent of the net profit of the satellite office.

ARTICLE TEN

This Agreement shall continue in force from _____, 19____, for the remainder of the calendar year and thereafter from year to year, unless superseded or modified by written agreement. Each partner to this Agreement, both individually and as a member of the partnership as presently formed, agrees to be bound to each of the other partners to this Agreement so long as he is engaged in the active practice of law as a partner of this firm to fulfill the provisions of this Agreement.

IN WITNESS WHEREOF, the parties have hereunto set their hands and seals, this____ day of____ , 19___ .

(CORPORATE SEAL)   _____, ATTORNEY
                                            AT LAW, P.C.

ATTEST:

BY: _____   By: _____
     Secretary   President

                               _____ (SEAL)
                               _____

                               _____ (SEAL)
                               _____

(CORPORATE SEAL)   _____, ATTORNEY
                                            AT LAW, P.C.

ATTEST:

By: _____   By: _____
     Secretary   President

[10.04]   AGREEMENTS WITH INSTITUTIONS

Very often, professionals have agreements with institutions to provide professional services and these agreements are usually executed in the name of the professional corporation. Such agreements often involve the provision by physicians of medical services to hospitals. In reviewing these agreements, there are a number of tax and practical aspects which must be considered. Such agreements are, however, subject to negotiation and, consequently, it is not always possible to obtain all of the desired provisions.

(1)   Execution of the Agreement

The agreement should be executed in the name of the professional corporation and not in the name of the individual professionals. Further, where possible, the agreement should provide that the professional services to be rendered will be provided by the professional corporation and not by any particular, named professional. Also, the agreement should provide that the professional corporation may employ and designate the physician who will perform the professional services.

(2) Compensation

The manner in which compensation is computed is, obviously, one of the important aspects of the agreement. In many agreements where the professional served as a director of the institution or the head of one of its departments, the agreement may call for a flat fee. Where the professional runs a department and sees private patients/clients, it is likely that the professional will have the responsibility for billing and collecting his own fees. It is usual for the institution to agree to undertake this function for a charge of between 5% and 10%. If the professional permits the institution to undertake this function, the agreement should specifically provide that the professional may review the collection procedures of the institution and outstanding accounts receivable will not be written off until the professional has specifically agreed.

(3) Facilities Provided

The agreement should specifically state what facilities, such as office space and staff, will be provided by the institution.

(4) Duties

To the extent possible, the agreement should state that the professional corporation will have exclusive control over the department or area covered by the agreement and will state only the end result to be achieved, such as running the department. The agreement should state that there are no specific hours during which the professional corporation must have employees on duty and that the professional corporation will have absolute control over the employment (and termination of employment) of the professionals employed in that department. If the staff personnel are also employed by the professional corporation, the agreement should also state that they may be employed and discharged by the professional corporation, although it is probable that the professional corporation and its professional employees will be charged with the responsibility of following institution rules and regulations. The agreement should specifically state that the sole control of the professional services to be rendered and the professional judgment are under the control of the professional corporation.

(5) Termination

Probably the most important provision of the agreement is that which describes the institution's ability to terminate the services of the professional corporation. In most agreements, the services of the professional corporation may be terminated upon 60, 90, or 180 days' notice, with or without cause. The advisors for the professional corporation should attempt to obtain in the agreement provisions stating that the agreement may only be terminated by the institution for stated reasons, which should be specifically defined. This is, generally, a very difficult provision to obtain on behalf of a professional corporation, particularly with institutions such as proprietary hospitals. In the alternative, it is advisable to obtain provisions stating that the agreement may only be terminated upon a majority vote of the board of directors or trustees of the institution or the unanimous vote of the professional staff.

The authors cannot over-emphasize the importance of the termination provision; the professional lives of those involved may be shattered should the institution simply terminate the contract with the professional corporation and enter into a new contract with one of the nonshareholder professional employees of that corporation. Without restrictions on the ability of the institution to terminate the agreement, the professional corporation (and the professional shareholders) should realize that they are simply tenants at will.

(6) Status as Independent Contractor

There are three sets of Regulations dealing with the question of whether an individual will be considered an independent contractor[9] and the determination is a factual one, i.e., does the institution control only the end result to be achieved and not the manner of achieving the end result? At the present time, the Service's employment tax program has designated several areas of known or probable noncompliance with the employment tax provisions, and one of these areas is that of physicians employed by hospitals.[10] Most of the rulings and cases in this area deal with the question of whether individual physicians are employees or independent contractors of hospitals where they are employed by hospitals to run a particular department. However, the general rules applicable to individual physicians should also be applicable in determining whether professional corporations are, themselves, independent contractors of institutions or whether the professional corporation should be ignored and the professional should be considered a direct employee of the institution.

In determining whether the proper control and supervision required under the Regulations exists, the Service has developed a list of 20 factors.[11] Since many of these factors are not applicable in the professional corporation setting, the four factors set forth in Rev. Rul. 66-274[12] should provide a guide. That ruling involved the question of whether a physician who performs services as the director of a hospital's department of pathology should be considered an employee of the hospital for federal income and withholding tax purposes. The criteria analyzed in that ruling are as follows:

(1) The degree to which the physician became integrated into the operating organization of the hospital,

(2) The nature, regularity, and continuity of his work for the hospital,

(3) The authority vested in or reserved by the hospital to require the physician to comply with its general policies, and

(4) The degree to which the physician was viewed as, and received the rights and privileges of, an employee of the hospital.

A professional corporation should generally be able to achieve classification as an independent contractor where the agreement with the institution contains the following:

(1) The compensation paid to the professional corporation is based upon the earnings produced by it.

(2) The professional corporation is responsible for the hiring (and termination) of professional employees to perform the duties assigned to the professional corporation under the agreement.

(3) The professional corporation is required to perform duties at all times, even during those times when the professional employees of the professional corporation are unavailable.

(4) The professional corporation is responsible for the expenses and employee benefits of its own professional employees.

(5) The professional corporation may maintain an independent practice outside the institution.

(6) The professional corporation has the right to designate its own rules and policies which must be followed by its professional employees.

(7) The intent of the parties is to establish independent contractor status.

If these factors exist, the professional employees will generally be considered employees of the professional corporation and the professional corporation will generally be considered as an independent contractor of the institution.

In structuring agreements intended to create an independent contractor relationship, professional corporation advisors should be aware that the Service is making an attempt to impose mandatory withholding on service providers. However, Section 530 of the Revenue Act of 1978 suspends any attempt by the Service to apply new rules (before June 3, 1982) to new and existing independent contractor relationships as long as there is a reasonable basis for not treating the physician (or professional corporation) as an employee. The proposed amendments to clarify the independent contractor rules (the latest being Senate Bill 5.8, submitted on January 5, 1981 which will provide certain safe harbors) should not affect properly structured relationships between professionals and professional corporations and between professional corporations and institutions. Until this issue is resolved, care should be taken to assure that written agreements are established, the federal income tax reporting is consistent with independent contractor status, and there is compliance with existing case law and rulings.[13]

The following is a form of operating (independent contractor) agreement between a physician and a proprietary hospital.

OPERATING AGREEMENT

BETWEEN

XYZ MEDICAL CORPORATION

AND

RICHARD ROE, M.D., P.C.

THIS AGREEMENT made this _____ day of _____, 19___, by and between XYZ MEDICAL CORPORATION ("Corporation"), a Georgia corporation, and RICHARD ROE, M.D., P.C. ("P.C."), a Georgia corporation.

WHEREAS, Corporation operates a hospital, ABC Hospital ("Hospital"), in Atlanta, Georgia; and

WHEREAS, Corporation desires to engage P.C. to perform services for Corporation and to operate and be the exclusive director of the _____ Department of the Hospital (the "Program"); and

WHEREAS, P.C. desires to perform such services, all on the terms and conditions specified in this Agreement;

NOW, THEREFORE, in consideration of the mutual covenants herein contained, the parties hereto agree as follows:

1. <u>Services to be Provided by P.C.</u> P.C. agrees to provide the following services in the specialty of _____ to Corporation ad to Hospital patients:

(a) P.C. shall operate and shall be the exclusive director of the Program established at Hospital.

(b) The services provided byP.C. hereunder shall be in conformance with Hospital policies and procedures established from time to time by Hospital, applicable standards of the Joint Commission on Accreditation of Hospitals ("JCAH"), and federal, state and local laws and regulations governing the provision of professional medical services. Periodic medical reviews shall be conducted by P.C. to ensure compliance with the foregoing and quality assurance and medical audit programs of the Hospital and its staff.

(c) P.C. shall be available at reasonable times for consultation with individual members of the medical staff of the Hospital (and physicians consulting with such staff members), committees of the medical staff and nursing and administrative employees of the Hospital. P.C. shall participate actively in the affairs of the medical staff of the Hospital, shall participate for reasonable periods of time in educational and teaching functions and programs of the Hospital and the medical staff, and shall perform such tasks and provide such reasonable services as the medical staff, or any committee thereof, may from time to time request.

(d) P.C. shall assist Hospital in the training of personnel involved in the Program.

2. Employment of Physicians by P.C. In order to provide for Corporation the services described in Section 1, P.C. shall provide the services of physicians as may be necessary to perform P.C.'s obligations under Section 1. Physicians who provide coverage on behalf of P.C. shall be employees of P.C. and approved by Corporation. P.C. shall be responsible for recruiting, contracting, scheduling, compensating and supervising all such physicians. Physicians employed by P.C. shall meet the license, certification and membership requirements which P.C. warrants in Section 4 and shall have and maintain professional insurance in a type and amount equivalent to that which P.C. is required to have and maintain under Section 3.

3. P.C.'s Insurance. P.C. shall obtain and maintain professional malpractice insurance in the amount of not less than $250,000 for each occurrence and $1,000,000 annual aggregate. P.C. shall, within five (5) days after execution of this Agreement, furnish appropriate evidence to Corporation of the existence of such insurance and, thereafter, P.C. shall immediately notify Corporation in the event that such insurance is no longer in force.

4. P.C.'s Warranties. P.C. represents and warrants to Corporation that any physician employed by it to perform services under this Agreement: (a) is duly licensed to practice medicine in the state of Georgia; (b) is a member of the active medical staff of Hospital, with clinical privileges in its Department of _____ sufficient to permit the physician to perform all services required under Section 1; and (c) has all customary narcotics and controlled substances numbers and licenses. P.C. further represents and warrants to Corporation that, with regard to any of the physicians employed by it to perform services under this Agreement, such physician's license to practice medicine in any state has never been suspended or revoked.

5. Supporting Facilities and Services. Corporation shall provide to P.C., for the benefit of patients, a suitably equipped _____ Department, served by an adequate number of employees, as determined by the mutural agreement of Corporation and P.C.

(a) Employees. All nonprofessional employees serving in the Program shall be hired and employed by the Hospital, shall be employees of the Hospital, shall be required to comply with all rules and regulations established by the administration of the Hospital, and shall work for compensation rates established by Hospital. The discharge or transfer of employees shall be the sole responsibility of the Hospital, after such consultation with P.C. as it deems necessary. P.C. shall not alter or vary Hospital policies and procedures with respect of personnel in any way. The number of employees assigned to the Program shall be determined by the mutual agreement of Corporation and P.C.

(b) Facilities. Corporation shall furnish such equipment and apparatus as is mutually agreed upon by Corporation and P.C. for the operation of the Program and Corporation shall keep the same in good repair. Additional equipment shall be obtained by Corporation from time to time if deemed necessary or desirable by Corporation and P.C. Supplies for the Program shall be purchased by Corporation; and the type of services and the facilities maintained shall be determined by the mutual agreement of the Corporation and P.C.

6. Financial Matters.

(a) Fees for P.C.'s Services. Each patient at the Hospital receiving services from P.C. shall be billed for such services. P.C.'s charges for the professional component of services performed or procedures performed by P.C. shall be established by P.C. Such charges shall be reasonable and customary in the Atlanta, Georgia, community and, consistent with such standards, shall be subject to the approval of Corporation. P.C.'s charges shall be reviewed annually by Corporation to determine if such charges are reasonable and customary. P.C. agrees and understands that charges for supplies and other nonprofessional components of services shall be established by Corporation.

(b) Billing Procedures. On a daily basis, P.C. shall accurately record professional services rendered and the charges therefor on forms provided by it. Corporation shall process such charges and shall post such charges on the patient's account. Such charges shall be designated on each patient's account as P.C.'s professional fee, and bills and statements relating thereto shall be rendered by Corporation.

(c) Payments to P.C. of Professional Fees. On or before the tenth day of each month during the term of this Agreement, Corporation shall pay to P.C. an amount equal to the aggregate fees charged by P.C. for professional services rendered to Hospital patients during the immediately preceding month, less 15% of said amount to be retained by Corporation to cover bad debts, billing and collection expenses, and other indirect and overhead expenses relating thereto. With regard to services to patients for which payment is received under Medicare or Medicaid or Blue Cross/Blue Shield, "fees charged," for purposes of determining payments hereunder, shall not be in excess of the amounts actually reimbursable under such programs.

7. Responsibilities of P.C.

(a) Nothing herein shall be construed as giving Corporation or Hospital control over, or the right to control, the professional judgment, treatment or actions of physicians employed by P.C. with respect to professional services rendered by them hereunder, and P.C. shall at all times act as and be deemed to be an independent contractor. The interest and responsibility of Corporation and Hospital are to ensure that the Program is operated, and the services rendered are performed, in a competent and satisfactory manner. Physicians employed by P.C. are not and shall not be considered employees, agents or servants of the Corporation; instead, they shall be considered employees of P.C.

(b) In performing services under this Agreement, P.C. covenants and agrees that the physicians employed by it, (i) shall use diligent efforts and professional skill and judgment, (ii) shall perform professional and supervisory services and shall render care to patients in accordance with and in a manner consistent with customary and recognized standards of the medical profession, (iii) shall conduct themselves in a manner consistent with the Principles of Medical Ethics of the American Medical Association, and (iv) shall comply with the bylaws, rules and regulations of the medical staff of the Hospital.

(c) P.C. shall promptly notify Hospital if any equipment in the Program is defective, inoperative or in disrepair and if any employee of Hospital in the Program, to the best judgment of the physicians employed by P.C., is incompetent, inadequately trained or absent without proper excuse.

(d) P.C. shall cause the physicians employed by it to attend continuing educational programs in the specialty of _____.

(e) P.C. shall not disclose information relating to the business affairs or operations of the Corporation to persons other than members of the medical staff, state licensing boards and the Joint Commission on Accreditation of Hospitals, without obtaining the prior written consent of the Corporation. P.C. shall not disclose such information to third-party reimbursement agencies (whether public or private) unless such disclosure is required by applicable law and regulations or the terms and conditions of an applicable contract or agreement for reimbursement.

8. <u>Indemnification</u>. P.C. hereby agrees to idemnify and hold harmless Corporation from and against any claim, loss, damage, cost, expense or liability arising out of or related to the negligent performance or nonperformance by P.C., or any physicians employed by it, to provide coverage on its behalf, of any services (including supervision of Corporation's employees, but only to the extent that the direct responsibility for the actions of such employees of Corporation rests with P.C., or physicians employed by it, at the time of the negligent performance or nonperformance of any act or duty by such employees) to be performed or provided by P.C. under this Agreement, including but not limited to the practice of the profession of medicine. P.C. shall be liable hereunder only to the extent that such losses and liabilities are not covered by Corporation's insurance.

Corporation hereby agrees to indemnify and hold harmless P.C., its shareholders and directors, and any physician employed by it to provide coverage under this Agreement on its behalf, from and against any claim, loss, damage, cost, expense, or liability arising out of or related to: (1) the performance or nonperformance of any act or duty, negligent, tortious or otherwise, by an employee or agent of Corporation over which neither P.C. nor its employees are acting in a direct supervisory capacity at the time of the performance or nonperformance of such act or duty, and (2) Corporation's deliberate breach of one or more of the provisions of this Agreement.

9. <u>Term</u>. The term of this Agreement shall be for three years, commencing on _____, 19____, and this agreement shall be self-renewing for additional three-year terms, unless Corporation or P.C. terminates this Agreement by giving written notice to the other party at least sixty (60) days prior to the last day of any term.

10. <u>Termination</u>. Corporation may terminate this Agreement immediately upon written notice to P.C. in the event that: (a) P.C. is dissolved or files a petition in bankruptcy; (b) P.C. fails to obtain or maintain insurance as provided herein; (c) the license of the president of P.C. to practice medicine in any state is suspended, revoked or terminated, or the State Board of Medical Examiners or other govern-

mental agency having jurisdiction over such physician initiates any proceding or investigation for the purpose of suspending terminating or revoking any such license or for the purpose of considering any of the foregoing; (d) the right or license of the president of P.C. to use or prescribe any controlled substance is suspended, revoked or terminated or any governmental agency having jurisdiction over controlled substances initiates any proceeding or investigation for the purpose of suspending, terminating or revoking any such right or license or for the purpose of considering any of the foregoing; or (e) the membership of the president of P.C. on the active medical staff of the Hospital or such physician's clinical privileges with Hospital are suspended or revoked.

Corporation may also terminate this Agreement upon ten (10) days written notice to P.C. in the event that P.C. fails, after thirty (30) days written notice of default or failure to comply, to provide the professional services required to be provided under this Agreement, or to comply and to maintain compliance with any other provisions of this Agreement.

P.C. may also terminate this Agreement upon thirty (30) days written notice to Corporation.

In the event that this Agreement is terminated under this Section, all obligations of Corporation and P.C. hereunder shall cease upon termination and all outstanding charges and accounts receivable attributable to the operation of the Program shall belong to Corporation; provided, however, that income or compensation under Section 6 shall be payable to P.C. for services through the date of termination; and further provided that this provision shall not constitute an election of remedies by Corporation or P.C., or liquidated damages to the Corporation or P.C., and Corporation and P.C. shall have and retain all rights to damages at law and rights to equitable relief in the event of breach by the other party.

11. Assignment. This is a contract for specialized services and shall not be assigned by P.C. or Corporation in any manner or by operation of law; provided, however, that this restriction against assignment shall not preclude assignment by Corporation or P.C., which assignment may be effected through a merger into, consolidation with, or sale of substantially all of Corporation's or P.C.'s assets to another entity. Subject to the above provisions, this Agreement shall be binding upon and inure to the benefit of the parties hereto and their assigns.

12. Prohibition on Outside Practice. P.C. shall not, except as provided in the following sentence, provide or negotiate similar services to any other hospital, agency or corporation pursuant to this Agreement, during the term of this Agreement. Nothing in this Agreement shall prohibit P.C. from continuing its present activities in the field of _____; its existing program with _____ Hospital, Atlanta, Georgia, or from acting solely as a consultant in the field of _____ to Corporation or others.

13. Modification of Agreement. This Agreement contains the entire understanding of the parties regarding P.C.'s operation of the Program and does not supersede or prohibit any other existing or future relationships which P.C. has or may have with Corporation. This Agreement shall be modified only by an instrument in writing signed on behalf of each party hereto.

14. Governing Law. This Agreement is made in Georgia and shall be construed, interpreted and governed by the laws of such state.

15. Notices. Any notices required or permitted hereunder shall be sufficiently given if sent by registered or certified mail, postage prepaid, or personally delivered, addressed or delivered as follows:

P.C.:	Richard Rowe, M.D., P.C.
	Suite 107
	Atlanta, Georgia
Corporation:	Vice-President Operations
	XYZ Medical Corporation
	Atlanta, Georgia
	Copy to: Administrator
	_____ Hospital
	Atlanta, Georgia

or to such other addresses as shall be furnished in writing by either party to the other party; and any such notice shall be deemed to have been given, if mailed, as of the date mailed, and, if personally delivered, as of the date delivered.

16. No Waiver. No waiver of a breach of any provision of this Agreement shall be construed to be a waiver of any breach of any other provision of this Agreement or of any succeeding breach of the same provision. No delay in acting with regard to any breach of any provision of this Agreement shall be construed to be a waiver of such breach.

17. Rights in Property. All title to supplies, fiscal records (except the personal records of the physicians employed by P.C.) patient charts, patient records, patient information, equipment and furnishings shall remain the sole property of Corporation. P.C. may, however, secure copies of fiscal records and patient charts at its own expense.

18. Exclusive Right to Operate Program. During the term of this Agreement, P.C. shall have the exclusive right to operate, and shall be the sole director of, the Program maintained by Hospital and by any other facility upon which P.C. and Corporation shall agree. All professional services provided in the Program and the professional medical treatment of all patients in the Program shall be under the sole direction of the physicians employed by P.C. Neither Corporation, Hospital, nor any of their employees or agents shall have any right to exercise control over the medical treatment of the patients in the Program.

19. Paragraph Headings. The paragraph headings contained in this Agreement are for convenience only and shall in no manner be construed as a part of this Agreement.

20. Counterparts. This Agreement is executed in multiple counterparts, each of which shall be deemed an original and together shall constitute one and the same agreement.

IN WITNESS WHEREOF, P.C. and Corporation have caused this Agreement to be executed by their duty authorized officers, and their corporate seals to be affixed all being done in duplicate originals with one copy being delivered to each party on the day and year first above written.

(CORPORATE SEAL)   RICHARD ROE, M.D., P.C.

ATTEST:

_____   By: _____
Secretary   President

(CORPORATE SEAL)   XYZ MEDICAL CORPORATION

ATTEST:

_____   By: _____
Secretary

                                         Title: _____

[10.05] LEASES

Any lease entered into by a professional corporation for office space should, obviously, correspond to local law and should be negotiated and reviewed by the attorney representing the professional corporation. In reviewing proposed leases for professional corporations, there are several aspects which should be closely examined to assure that the lease is as favorable to the professional corporation as possible. These aspects are as follows:

(1) Delivery Date

When a professional corporation arranges to move into new offices, the lease will frequently leave open the date on which delivery of possession will occur. In order to avoid interruption of a professional practice, any lease for a professional corporation should provide that delivery will occur on or before a certain date or the professional corporation will be free to terminate the lease (or the landlord can be required to furnish comparable alternate space in the same building or will be liable for stated damages).

(2) Personal Property

Because professional corporations normally own a substantial amount of specialized personal property, any lease entered into should provide that the personal property of the professional corporation will not become "fixtures" and, therefore, the property of the landlord at the expiration of the term of the lease. The lease should also provide that the professional corporation lessee will have a stated period of time, usually 30 days, to remove its personal property after the end of the lease.

(3) Right to Cure Defaults and Reporting of Defective Conditions

Because professionals are so involved in their practices, they sometimes do not notify the landlord regarding certain matters. For this reason, any provision in the lease relating to default by the professional corporation (such as in payment of rent, etc.) should provide that the professional corporation will have a stated period of time (at least five days) to cure any default after notice has been given by the landlord. The lease should further state that the landlord may commence proceedings against the professional corporation due to default (i.e., in paying rent) only if default still exists at the time action is commenced. Also, leases should provide that, if the professional corporation is aware of defects in the premises, the professional corporation will be responsible for notifying the landlord, but the professional corporation will only be liable for damages which occur due to the delay in notification.

(4) Use of the Office as a Professional Office

The lease should specifically state that the office is to be used as a professional office and that the landlord will not unduly interfere with the professional corporation's use of the premises as such. It is possible that the landlord's right to show the premises to prospective tenants prior to the end of the term would give the landlord the right to bring prospective tenants through the premises during business hours. The professional corporation must assure the privacy of its patients/clients.

(5) Assignment

The lease should be assignable with the consent of the landlord, which may not be unreasonably withheld. The lease should further state that the lease may be assigned, without the consent of the landlord, to any legal entity through which the professional corporation practices or to which it transfers its assets.

(6) Destruction

Many leases provide that upon a partial destruction of the premises the rent will abate, based on the percentage of floor space which is destroyed. Such a clause will provide little benefit to a professional medical corporation where, for example, all of the examining rooms are destroyed but the offices and waiting room are not. Consequently, leases for professional corporations should provide that rent will be abated to the extent that the utilization of the entire office space is lessened. Also, the lease should provide that the landlord will, within a period of 45 days after damage or destruction, notify the professional corporation whether the office space will be repaired or demolished.

(7) Indemnification

The lease should specifically provide that the landlord will indemnify, defend and hold harmless the professional corporation from any losses or damages which it suffers due to the negligent (not *gross* negligence) or intentional acts of the landlord's employees or agents. Such a provision will protect the professional corporation in the event that some of its patients/clients are harmed in the professional building due to neglect of workmen and repairmen, etc.

(8) Termination

The lease should provide that upon the professional's death, disability (physical or mental), or removal from the medical staff of the adjacent hospital (if any), the professional corporation will have the right to terminate the lease.

(9) Execution

The lease should be executed in the name of the professional corporation and not in the name of the professionals, unless this is specifically desired because of the manner in which the personal property of the professional corporation is being handled.

Obviously, these aspects and, in fact, all of the terms of any proposed lease between a professional corporation and a third party must be negotiated. The following is a lease typically used by large hospitals. While hospitals, generally, refuse to change their "form," the authors have, in most instances, found that hospitals will permit special stipulations on the above aspects.

PROFESSIONAL BUILDING LEASE

STATE OF GEORGIA

FULTON COUNTY

THIS LEASE, Made as of the _____ day of _____, 19___, by and between _____ Hospital, Inc. ("Landlord"), and _____ ("Tenant").

WITNESSETH

1. Premises. Landlord, for and in consideration of the rents, covenants, agreements and stipulations hereinafter mentioned, reserved, and contained, to be paid, kept and performed by Tenant, has leased and rented, and by these presents does lease and rent unto Tenant, and Tenant hereby agrees to lease and take upon the terms and conditions which hereinafter appear, the following described space in the office building known as _____ (hereinafter called the "Building"), situated in Atlanta, Georgia, at _____. The space hereby leased to and by Tenant (hereinafter called the "Premises") is set forth on

the floor plan attached hereto as Exhibit A and made a part hereof. No easement for light or air is included in the Premises. The Premises hereby leased by Tenant may be used and occupied by Tenant for rendering professional medical services and for no other purposes.

2. Term. The term of this Lease began on the _____ day of _____, 19____, and ends on the last day of _____, 19____.

3. Rental.

(a) Tenant agrees to pay to Landlord at the office of Landlord in Atlanta, Georgia, or at such other place or to such other person or persons as Landlord may from time to time designate in writing, without demand, deduction or setoff, an annual base rental at the rate of $_____ per annum, payable in equal monthly installments in advance on the first day of each calendar month during the term of this lease in the amount of $_____, each. If the term hereof begins on other than the first day of the month, Tenant shall pay to Landlord, on demand, a prorated monthly installment of said annual base rental.

(b) On the first day of the lease year next following the base year and on the first day of each lease year thereafter, the annual base rental as set out above, and the monthly rental payments as computed thereon, shall be adjusted as follows: The annual base rental shall be increased or decreased by an amount equal to the change in operating cost for the Premises.

(c) For the purposes of this Lease:

(i) The term "change in operating cost" means the difference between operating cost for the last calendar year ending prior to the beginning of the lease year for which adjustments is to be made and the operating cost for the base year of operation.

(ii) The term "base year of operation" means calendar year

_____.

(iii) The term "operating cost" means the annual cost to Landlord of operating and maintaining the building during each calendar year as determined by an audit conducted by independent certified public accountants selected by Landlord, and shall include: ad valorem taxes assessed against the building, the underlying land, and Landlord's subleasehold estate in the land; all taxes, including without limitation, sales, license, business or franchise taxes, imposed on the rentals payable hereunder, other than income taxes; janitorial labor and supplies, including lavatory and washroom supplies, gross wages and salaries, including Social Security and insurance payable by Landlord with respect to such wages and salaries, of all persons directly employed by Landlord for, and rendering services connected with, the normal operation, maintenance and repair of the building and the sidewalks, curbs and landscaped areas adjoining the building; allocable management, bookkeeping and administrative office expenses of Landlord related to the operation of the building; management fees paid by Landlord if any; utility expenses, including power, electricity, gas, water and sewage and garbage and rubbish removal; routine servicing and maintenance of elevators and the plumbing, heating, ventilating, air conditioning and electrical systems; window cleaning, gardening and lawn services and security services; insurance premiums for fire, extended coverage and other casualty and liability insurance covering the building and any occurrence therein. Expenditures by Landlord for replacement of the basic components of the building and other capital improvements, as distinguished from expenditures for repairs and maintenance, are excluded from the term "operating cost" as herein defined. Moreover, such term shall not be deemed to include any expense of Landlord for which Landlord receives compensation from a tenant under such tenant's lease.

(d) Landlord agrees to furnish to Tenant, as soon as such statements are available, a statement containing a summary of the operating cost, as above defined, for the base year of operation and each calendar year thereafter. In the event any such statement is not available at the commencement of any lease year, then the monthly rental payments for such lease year shall be made on the basis of the annual rental paid during the preceding lease year until the statement is furnished to Tenant, and on the next rent paying date thereafter, the monthly rental payment then due shall be computed on the basis of the next annual rental, increased or decreased to retroactively adjust the rentals paid during such lease year at the old rate, and all subsequent monthly payments in such lease year shall be at the new rate.

4. <u>Failure to Give Possession</u>. If Landlord is unable to give possession of the premises to Tenant on the date on which the term hereof begins because (a) the premises are not sufficiently completed to render the premises ready for occupancy, or (b) a certificate of occupancy required by any law, ordinance or regulation for the premises has not been received by Landlord or (c) a tenant or occupant remains in possession of the premises, then Landlord shall not be liable for failure to give possession of the premises on the first day of the term hereof. No such failure to give possession of the premises on the first day of the term hereof shall affect the validity of this Lease or extend the term hereof beyond the above stated expiration date of the term; provided, however, Tenant shall not be required to pay rent for the period during which Landlord is so prevented from giving possession of the premises to Tenant.

5. <u>Services</u>.

(a) Landlord agrees to furnish during normal business hours the following: electricity, water and elevator service, and heating and air conditioning service sufficient to reasonably cool or heat the premises. Landlord shall also furnish at such times as Landlord shall designate the general cleaning and janitorial services and security services. As used herein, the term "normal business hours" shall mean the days Monday through Friday, inclusive, legal holidays excepted, during the hours from 8 a.m. to 6 p.m., and Saturdays, except legal holidays, from 8 a.m. to 1 p.m.

(b) Landlord shall not be liable to Tenant in any manner whatsoever, including, but not limited to abatement of rent, for failure to furnish, or delay in furnishing, any service described in subparagraph (a) above, whether or not such failure or delay is caused by repairs, renewals, or improvements, or by any strike, lockout or other labor controversy, or by any accident, or by negligence of Landlord or its employees, or any casualty whatsoever, or by the act or failure to act, or the fault of Tenant or other person whomsoever, and whether the reason therefor or cause thereof is within or without the control of Landlord; nor shall any such failure or delay or failure to act or negligence of Landlord's employees be deemed an actual or constructive eviction of Tenant; nor shall any such event operate to relieve Tenant of the prompt and punctual performance of each of the covenants to be performed by the Tenant hereunder; nor shall Landlord be liable to Tenant for damage to person or property caused by defects in the cooling, heating, electric, water, elevator or other apparatus or systems.

6. Landlord's Repairs. Landlord shall have no duty to Tenant to make any repairs or improvements to the premises except structural repairs necessary for safety and tenant-ability, and then only if not occasioned by any act or neglect of Tenant, its agents, employees or visitors. Landlord and its agents, employees and independent contractors shall have the right to enter the premises at such times as Landlord deems reasonably necessary to inspect and examine same, to make such repairs, additions, alterations and improvements as Landlord desires to make to the building or the premises, to exhibit the premises to prospective purchasers or tenants, and to remove anything from the premises which does not conform to this Lease or the Rules and Regulations of Landlord, as amended. Landlord shall also be allowed to take any and all needed materials into and through the premises that may be required to make such repairs, additions, alternations and improvements, all without being liable to Tenant in any manner whatsoever. During such time as such work is being carried on in or about the premises the rent provided herein shall in no wise abate, and Tenant waives any claim and cause of action against Landlord for damages by reason of loss or interruption to Tenant's business and profits therefrom because of the prosecution of any such work or any part thereof.

7. Tenant's Covenants. Tenant covenants and agrees that Tenant shall:

(a) At its own expense keep the premises in good repair and tenantable condition and replace any and all broken glass in and about the premises with the same quality and size of materials, including all signs thereon, and indemnify Landlord against any loss, damage, or expense to the premises and to the heating, cooling, water or other apparatus and systems and to the electric system, including wires and lights, and to any part of the building, including its fixtures and apurtenances, arising by reason of any failure so to keep the premises in good repair and tenantable condition or due to any act or neglect of Tenant, its employees, agents and visitors.

(b) Make no alterations or additions in or to the premises, nor paint nor place any wall cover on any part thereof, without first obtaining Landlord's written consent. All such alterations and any additions, all fixtures and carpet placed within the improvements by Tenant and all leasehold improvements to the premises made by Landlord or Tenant, whether temporary or permanent in character, except only the movable office furniture and equipment of Tenant, shall be Landlord's property and shall remain upon and in the premises at the termination of this Lease whether by lapse of time or otherwise, all without compensation or payment to Tenant; provided, however, that so long as this Lease remains in effect Tenant shall return for ad valorem taxes all alterations, additions and leasehold improvements made by Tenant and all other property placed within the premises by Tenant, and Tenant shall promptly pay all taxes assessed against any of said improvements and property.

(c) Use the premises for professional medical purposes only and not use the same for any illegal purpose nor violate any statute, regulation, rule or order of any governmental body; nor create or allow to exist any nuisance or trespass; nor do any act in or about the premises or bring anything onto or in the premises or the building containing same which might vitiate or increase the rate of insurance on the premises or the building; nor deface or injure the premises or the building or overload the floor of the premises.

(d) At its sole expense comply with all statutes, regulations, rules, ordinances and orders of any governmental body, department or agency thereof, and abide by and observe the Rules and Regulations printed on this Lease, which are hereby made a part of this Lease, together with such amendments thereto and such rules and regulations for the management of the building as may hereafter, from time to time, be established in writing by Landlord and served upon Tenant.

(e) Report immediately in writing to Landlord any defective condition in or about the premises known to Tenant and a failure to so report shall make Tenant liable to Landlord for any expense of, or damage to, Landlord resulting from such defective condition.

(f) In the use of electricity, not exceed the capacity of existing feeders, risers, circuitry or wiring, which are designed to provide lighting and current for electrical apparatus using 110 volt, 20 AMP circuits. If additional circuitry or wiring is required by Tenant and Landlord approves the installation of the same in writing, such work shall be performed at Tenant's expense by Landlord's electrician or under Landlord's control and supervision and Tenant shall pay Landlord for such additional work as billed.

8. Alterations Required by Law or Regulation. If, because of the nature of Tenant's use or occupancy of the premises, any addition, alteration, change, repair or other work of any nature, structural or otherwise, shall be required or ordered or become necessary at any time during the term because of any law, or governmental regulation now or hereafter in effect, or any order or decree of any court, the entire expense thereof, irrespective of when the same shall be incurred or become due, shall be the sole liability of Tenant, and Landlord will not contribute thereto.

9. Governmental Orders. Except as otherwise provided in paragraph 8 hereof, in the event Landlord, during the term of this Lease, shall be required by any governmental authority, or by the order or decree of any court, to repair, alter, remove, construct, reconstruct, or improve any part or all of the building or the Premises, then such action shall be taken by Landlord at its expense, but such action shall not in any way affect Tenant's obligations under this Lease, and Tenant waives all claim for injury, damage or abatement of rent because of such repair, alteration, removal, construction, reconstruction or improvement; provided, however, that if such action by Landlord shall render the premises wholly untenantable, and if, in Landlord's judgment, such acts cannot be completed within 90 days after notice to Landlord to perform such actions by such governmental authority, then this Lease shall, at the option of Landlord, terminate as of

the date of said notice to Landlord by such governmental authority or court, and in such event Tenant shall immediately surrender the premises and rent shall be apportioned and be paid up to and including the date the premises became wholly untenantable. Notwithstanding the foregoing, Tenant shall be responsible for paying all costs of complying with all requirements of governmental authorities and orders or decrees of courts requiring any action where such requirements, orders or decrees result from the manner in which Tenant uses and occupies the Premises.

10. <u>Destruction of or Damage to the Building or the Premises and Demolition</u>. In the event the building or the Premises are injured or damaged by fire or other casualty or the elements to the extent that, in the judgment of Landlord, the damage to the building or the Premises resulting cannot be repaired within 90 days from the date of such damage, or if the building or any part thereof is so injured or destroyed that Landlord shall decide to demolish, rebuild or reconstruct the building or any part thereof, or if Landlord for any reason decides to demolish rebuild or reconstruct the building or any part thereof, this Lease shall, at the option of Landlord, terminate as of the date of such damage, destruction or decision, and thereupon Tenant shall immediately surrender the Premises to Landlord and pay rent up to the date of such surrender. If the building or the Premises are injured or damaged by fire or other casualty or the elements but, in the judgment of Landlord, can be repaired within 90 days from the date of such damage, Landlord shall repair such damage within a reasonable time. If any event referred to in this paragraph occurs, Landlord shall not be liable to Tenant for inconvenience, annoyance, loss of profits, expenses or other type of injury or damage resulting from the repair of any such damage, or any delay in making such repairs, or from any repair, modification, arranging or rearranging of any portion of the Premises or any part or all of the building or for the termination of this Lease as provided in this paragraph. Tenant assumes the risk of any and all damage from any casualty whatsoever to its improvements to, and equipment and personal property within, the Premises.

11. <u>Condemnation</u>. If the whole of the building or of the Premises be condemned by any legally constituted authority for any public use or purpose, then in either of said events the term hereby granted shall cease from the time possession is taken by such public authority, and rental shall be accounted for as between Landlord and Tenant as of that date, and all rights of Tenant under this Lease shall immediately cease and terminate, and Tenant shall have no right or claim to any part of any award made to or received by Landlord for such taking.

12. <u>Assignment and Subletting</u>. Landlord grants to Tenant under this Lease the right to possess and enjoy the use of the premises but no estate passes out of Landlord and Tenant has only a usufruct not subject to levy or sale. Tenant shall not, without the prior written consent of Landlord endorsed hereon, assign this Lease or any interest hereunder, or sublet the premises or any part thereof, or permit the use of the premises by any party other than Tenant. Consent to any assignment or sublease shall not destroy this provision, and all other assignments or subleases shall be made likewise only upon the prior written consent of

Landlord. Any assignee or sublessee of Tenant, at the option of Landlord, shall become directly liable to Landlord for all obligations of Tenant hereunder, but no sublease or assignment by Tenant shall relieve Tenant of any liability hereunder.

13. <u>Personal Property of Tenant</u>. If Tenant is not in default hereunder, Tenant may, upon expiration of the term hereof, remove from the premises Tenant's movable personal property within the Premises. Upon the expiration or earlier termination of this Lease, Tenant shall surrender the Premises and the keys thereto to Landlord in the same condition as at the beginning of the term of this Lease, ordinary wear and tear only excepted. Such property of Tenant as Tenant fails to remove either from the Premises or the building after the termination of this Lease shall be considered as abandoned by Tenant and may be disposed of by Landlord in any manner whatsoever without accounting to Tenant for same or being liable in any way to Tenant for such disposition.

14. <u>Landlord's Remedies Upon Default</u>. In the event Tenant shall default in the payment, when due, of any installment of rent or other charges or money obligation to be paid by Tenant hereunder (all of which monetary obligations of Tenant shall bear interest at the rate of 8% per annum from the date due until paid) and fails to cure said default within five days after written notice thereof from Landlord; or if Tenant shall default in performing any of the covenants, terms or provisions of this Lease (other than the payment, when due, of any of Tenant's monetary obligations hereunder) or any of the Rules and Regulations now or hereafter established by Landlord to govern the operation of the building, and fails to cure such default within 30 days after written notice thereof from Landlord; or if Tenant is adjudicated a bankrupt; or if a permanent receiver is appointed for Tenant's property; or if, whether voluntarily or involuntarily, Tenant takes advantage of any debtor relief proceedings under any present or future law, whereby the rent or any part thereof, is, or is proposed to be, reduced or payment thereof deferred; or if Tenant makes an assignment for the benefit of creditors; or if Tenant's effects should be levied upon or attached under process against Tenant, not satisfied or dissolved within 10 days after written notice form Landlord to Tenant to obtain satisfaction thereof, then, and in any of said events, Landlord, at its option, may pursue any one or more of the following remedies without any notice or demand whatsoever:

(a) Landlord, at its option, may at once, or at any time thereafter terminate this Lease by written notice to Tenant, whereupon this Lease shall end. Upon such termination by Landlord, Tenant will at once surrender possession of the Premises to Landlord and remove all of Tenant's effects therefrom, and Landlord may forthwith render the Premises and repossess himself thereof, and remove all persons and effects therefrom, using such force as may be necessary, without being guilty of trespass, forcible entry, detainer or other tort.

(b) Landlord may enter upon and take possession of the Premises and expel or remove Tenant and any other person who may be occupying the Premises or any part thereof, without being liable for prosecution or any claim for damages therefor, and, if Landlord so elects, make such alterations and repairs as, in Landlord's judgment, may be necessary to relet the Premises, and any part thereof for such rent and for such period of time and subject to such terms and conditions as Landlord may deem advisable and receive the rent therefor. Upon such reletting, all rent received by Landlord from such reletting shall be applied: first, to the payment of any indebtedness, other than rent, due hereunder from Tenant to Landlord, including interest thereon; second, to the payment of any loss and expenses of such reletting, including brokerage fees, attorneys' fees and the cost of such alterations and repair; third, to the payment of rent due and unpaid hereunder, together with interest thereon as herein provided; the residue, if any, shall be held by Landlord and applied in payment to future rent as the same may become due and payable hereunder. Tenant agrees to pay to Landlord, on demand, any deficiency that may arise by reason of such reletting. Notwithstanding any such reletting without termination, Landlord may at any time thereafter elect to terminate this Lease for such prior default.

(c) In the event Landlord terminates this Lease in accordance with the provisions of this paragraph 14, Landlord may, in addition to any other remedy it may have, recover from Tenant all damages and expenses Landlord may suffer or incur by reason of Tenant's default hereunder, including the cost of recovering the Premises, reasonable attorneys' fees and the worth at the time of such termination of the excess, if any, of the amount of rent and charges equivalent to the rent reserved in this Lease for the remainder of the stated term, all of which sums shall become immediately due and payable by Tenant to Landlord upon demand of Landlord.

(d) Pursuit of any of the foregoing remedies shall not preclude Landlord from pursuing any other remedies herein or at law or in equity provided, nor shall pursuit of any remedy by Landlord constitute a forfeiture or waiver of any rent due to Landlord hereunder or any damages accruing to Landlord by reason of Tenant's violation of any of the covenants and provisions of this Lease.

(e) Tenant hereby appoints as its agent to receive service of all dispossessory or restraint proceedings and notices thereunder and under this Lease the person in charge of the Premises at the time, and if no person is then in charge of the Premises, then such service or notice may be made by attaching the same to the main entrance of the Premises, provided that a copy of any such proceedings or notices shall be mailed to Tenant in the manner set forth in paragraph 23 hereof.

15. Signs. Tenant shall place no signs upon the outside walls or roof of the building or on the walls or doors of the Premises except with the written consent of Landlord, and any and all approved signs placed on the Premises by Tenant shall be installed and maintained in compliance with such rules as Landlord may from time to time prescribe. Tenant shall be liable to Landlord for any damage caused by the installation, use or maintenance of said signs, and Tenant agrees upon removal of said signs to repair all damage incident to such removal.

16. Indemnity.

(a) Tenant does hereby agree to indemnify and save Landlord harmless from and against any and all liability for any injury to or death of any person or persons or damage to property in any way arising out of or connected with the condition, use or occupancy of the Premises, or in any way arising out of the activities of Tenant, its agents, employees, licensees or invitees in the building, and from all costs, expenses and liabilities, including but not limited to reasonable attorneys' fees, incurred by Landlord in connection therewith.

(b) Tenant covenants and agrees that Landlord shall not be liable to Tenant for any injury or death to any person or persons or for damage to any property, to Tenant, or any person claiming through Tenant, arising out of any accident or occurrence in the building, including, without limiting the generality of the foregoing, injury, death or damage caused by the Premises or other portions of the building, being out of repair or caused by any defect in or failure of equipment, pipes, or wiring, or caused by broken glass, or caused by the backing up of drains, or caused by gas, water, steam, electricity, or oil leaking, escaping or flowing into the Premises or caused by fire or smoke or caused by the acts or omissions of other tenants located in the building.

17. Effect of Termination of Lease. No termination of this Lease prior to the normal ending hereof, by lapse of time or otherwise, shall affect Landlord's right to collect rent for the period prior to termination hereof.

18. Holding Over. If Tenant remains in possession of the premises after the expiration of the term hereof, Tenant shall be deemed to be a tenant from month to month, at twice the rental rate in effect at the end of the term hereof, and there shall be no renewal of this Lease by operation of law.

19. Attorney's Fees, Rent Control and Homestead. Tenant hereby waives and renounces for himself and family any and all homestead or exemption rights which he may have under or by virtue of the Constitution and laws of the United States, Georgia, and any other State as against any debt Tenant may owe Landlord under this Lease and, to pay any such debt Tenant may owe Landlord under this Lease, Tenant hereby transfers, conveys and assigns to Landlord all homestead or exemption rights which may be allowed or set apart to Tenant, including such as may be set apart in any bankruptcy proceeding. If any rent or other debt owing by Tenant to Landlord hereunder is collected by or through an attorney at law, Tenant agrees to pay an additional amount equal to fifteen percent (15%) of the principal and interest owing under this Lease as attorney's fees. Landlord and Tenant hereby waive a trial by jury of any issues arising in any action or proceeding in any way connected with this Lease or Tenant's use or occupancy of any part of the building. To the extent permitted by law, Tenant waives the benefits of all existing and future rent control legislation and statutes and similar governmental rules and regulations, whether in time of war or not.

20. No Waiver. No failure or delay of Landlord to exercise any right or power given it herein or to insist upon strict compliance by Tenant of any obligation imposed on it herein and no custom or practice of either party hereto at variance with any term hereof shall constitute a modification hereof or a waiver by Landlord of its right to demand strict compliance with the terms hereof by Tenant. This Lease constitutes and contains the sole and entire agreement of Landlord and Tenant and no prior or contemporaneous oral or written representation or agreement between the parties and affecting the Premises shall have any legal effect. No member, officer, agent, or employee of Landlord has or shall have any authority to

waive any provision of this Lease unless such waiver is expressly made in writing and signed by a member or authorized officer of Landlord.

21. <u>Notices</u>. All notices required or permitted under this Lease from one party to the other should be in writing and shall be sent by registered or certified mail, postage prepaid, and addressed, as to Landlord, at the building and, as to Tenant, at the Premises, or, in the case of notice given by Tenant, personally delivered to Landlord's office at which rent is being paid by Tenant, or, in the case of notices given by Landlord, physically attached to the door at the main entrance to the Premises. All notices mailed in the foregoing manner shall be effective upon receipt or attachment to the door at the main entrance to the Premises, as the case may be.

22. <u>Time of Essence</u>. Time is of the essence of this Lease.

23. <u>Jurisdiction and Severability</u>. This Lease has been executed and de-livered in the State of Georgia and shall be governed by the laws of said State. If any provision of this Lease is or becomes illegal, invalid or unenforceable by reason of present or future laws or rules or regulations of any governmental body or entity, the intention of the parties hereto is that the remaining parts of this Lease shall not be affected thereby unless such provision or provisions, in the sole determination of Landlord, are essential to the rights of Landlord or Tenant, in which event Landlord may terminate this Lease by written notice to Tenant.

24. <u>Death or Disability</u>. It is further agreed that in the event of the death of the Lessee or his disability, whether physical or mental or both, so that he is unable to continue the practice of medicine, during the term of this Lease or any renewals thereof, then Lessee, or his heirs or representatives, hereby is granted the option of canceling this Lease upon sixty (60) days written notice to the Lessor.

25. <u>Definitions</u>. The term "Landlord" as used in this Lease means only the present owner of the aforesaid subleasehold estate in the land on which the building rests and the building, so that in the event of any sale or sales thereof, Landlord, who is a grantor in any such sale, shall be and hereby is entirely relieved of all of the obligations of Landlord hereunder including any obligation for the return to Tenant of any security deposit. The term "Tenant" shall include Tenant's heirs, legal representatives, successors and assigns. The use of the masculine or neuter genders herein shall include the masculine, feminine and neuter and the singular form shall include the plural where the context so requires. The headings of the paragraphs in this Lease are merely descriptive, are intended for reference pur-poses only and do not constitute a part of the terms and provisions of this Lease.

IN WITNESS WHEREOF, the parties herein have hereunto set their hands and seals, in triplicate, the day and year first above written.

_____	_____ (SEAL)
Witness	Tenant
_____	_____ (SEAL)
Witness	Landlord

NOTES TO CHAPTER 10

1. Note 2, Chapter 8, *supra*.

2. See section [16.02].

3. 49 T.C. 645 (1968). Also see section [13.04](7).

4. *John G. Paul*, 67 T.C. 286 (1976); Rev. Rul. 79-311, 1979-2 C.B. 25. Also see Cook, "Deduction for Return of Disallowed Corporate Payments Depends on Prior Agreement", 5 *Taxation for Lawyers* 326 (1976); Riemer, "Shareholder-employee Compensation—How to Minimize Chances of IRS Disallowance," 5 *Taxation for Lawyers* 356 (1976); Tannenbaum, "How to Prevent the IRS From Claiming that an Employee's Compensation is a Disguised Dividend," 4 *Taxation for Lawyers* 288 (1976).

5. 37 T.C.M. 692, ¶78,157 P-H Memo T.C. (1978).

6. See *Steel Contractors,* 37 T.C.M. 1951, ¶78,489 P-H Memo T.C. (1978).

7. See *Leon D. Horowitz,* 38 T.C.M. 108, ¶79,027 P-H Memo T.C. (1979).

8. See Formal Opinion 300 (August, 1961), Informal Opinion 1072 (October 8, 1968), Informal Opinion 1171 (February 4, 1971), Informal Opinion 1301 (March 25, 1975), and Informal Opinion 1417 (June 27, 1978).

9. Treas. Regs. §31.3121(d)-1, §31.3306(i)-1, and §31.340(c)-1.

10. See Internal Revenue Manual—Audit 4621 (April 15, 1977).

11. Internal Revenue Manual—Audit Chapter 4600, Exhibit 4640-1.

12. 1966-2 C.B. 446.

13. Letter Ruling 7904005—Physicians are not hospital employees where permitted to serve others, hire and pay own assistants, and carry own malpractice insurance, not required to observe fixed schedule, not subject to fee rules, not eligible for employee benefits.

    Letter Ruling 7804002—Emergency room doctors are hospital employees where hospital collects and distributes their fees and doctors are guaranteed minimum salary; can't employ assistants; can't practice within 20 miles of hospital; can't admit patients; follow work schedule; observe hospital rules;—Although tenuous control of doctor, is all that is necessary for doctors.

    Letter Ruling 7808061—Professional is employee of P.C. where he is president and sole shareholder, performs minor services, performs P.C. services *and* administrative functions, and is paid regularly 90% of client fees paid to P.C.

    Wendell James, 25 T.C. 1296 (1956) (pathologist held employee where he was paid a salary and hospital had control over services).

    Vincent M. Ravel, 26 T.C.M. 885, ¶67,182 P-H Memo T.C. (1967) (radiologist considered employee of hospital where paid by hospital and hospital controlled his services);

    Azad v. U.S., 388 F.2d 74 (8th Cir. 1968) (radiologist was independent contractor of hospital, no special rules imposed on radiologist, radiologist could work for others, and both parties considered the relationship to be that of an independent contractor).

Robert H. Cowing, 28 T.C.M. 696, ¶69,135 P-H Memo T.C. (1969) (radiologist was employee of hospital, paid by hospital and received employee benefits;

Roger K. Haugen, 30 T.C.M. 1247, ¶71,294 P-H Memo T.C. (1971) (pathologist was employee of hospital; he could not engage in private practice);

Frank Vessy, 33 T.C.M. 697, ¶74,163 P-H Memo T.C. (1974) (Ophthalmologist employed by Veteran's Administration was employee, he kept regular hours and could not accept fees from private practice);

McGee v. U.S., 47 A.F.T.R. 2d 81-910 (D.C. Neb. 1981) (physician in department of hospital was an independent contractor not an employee).

Rev. Rul. 61-178, 1961-1 C.B. 153 (physician worked part-time for a corporation found to be employee where hours and work were established by head physician and he received a monthly salary).

Rev. Rul. 72-203, 1972-1 C.B. 324 (associates of pathologist who is an independent contractor at hospital are considered employees of the pathologist).

Rev. Rul. 73-417, 1973-2 C.B. 333 (pathologist considered employee of hospital where he must work only at hospital and received guaranteed minimum income).

Rev. Rul. 75-41, 1975-1 C.B. 323 (corporation provides secretaries, nurses, dental assistants, etc., to subscribing professionals, corporation is employer and not subscribers where subscribers do not control the nurses, secretaries, dental assistants, etc).

Also see Rev. Rul. 75-35, 1975-1 C.B. 131, and *Ronald C. Packard*, 63 T.C. 621 (1975). Also see Rev. Rul. 84, 1953-1 C.B. 404 and Rev. Rul. 57-21, 1957-1 C.B. 317.

CHAPTER **11**

Shareholder Status and Stock Retirement Agreements

[11.01] SHAREHOLDER STATUS

When the existing shareholders begin to debate whether stock in the professional corporation should be sold to one of the nonshareholder professional employees of the corporation, a number of considerations arise for the existing shareholders, the professional corporation, and the incoming shareholder. These considerations are discussed in this chapter.

(1) When to Sell Stock

As discussed in section [10.01](2), *supra*, relating to nonshareholder employment agreements, it is the exceptional case where a professional is offered stock in a professional corporation at the time of his employment. Unless there has been a long-standing relationship among the professionals, it is usually important to provide at least a one-year trial period before the sale of stock in the professional corporation is discussed. If such a trial period is established, the professional corporation should not become contractually bound to sell stock to the non-shareholder professional employee at the end of the period.

When hiring professionals who do not have prior professional experience, it is almost always advisable to postpone shareholder status for a number of years in order to review the development of the professional. However, the various waiting periods differ with professions. For example, physicians are often offered shareholder status after their third year of practice. The reason for this is that their medical education, including internship and residency, has qualified them to practice medicine and the three-year waiting period is simply a period in which they can become accustomed to the professional corporation and the type of practice which it generates. The legal profession, on the other hand, normally requires five to eight years of "associate status." The feeling of most lawyers is that, upon graduation from law school, most young lawyers have not had the experience which physicians receive in their internship and residency and, consequently, the first three to four years of practice in a law firm equate to an internship or residency. For this reason, the waiting period for most lawyers is several years longer than for most doctors. On the other hand, the waiting period for most accountants is even longer, up to a period of 10 to 11 years. Since accountants are not required to have post-graduate education after college, the waiting period for accountants includes a three-year period which roughly equates to law or graduate school, a three to four-year period equating to internship or residency, and a three-year period as the final stage before becoming a shareholder.

When a professional reaches the stage at which he will be offered stock in the professional corporation, his compensation has increased, usually substantially, but the immediate outlay of funds for the purchase of stock may create a substantial burden. For this reason, some professionals postpone the purchase of stock in the professional corporation if they can achieve the "status" of a shareholder without having to make a cash outlay to purchase stock. For this reason, many professional corporations adopt an "up or out" rule which requires a professional to agree to purchase stock after it is offered to him, although the actual payment for the stock may be on an installment basis. The authors feel that this is an excellent way for professional corporations to obtain from the younger professionals the "commitment" necessary to perpetuate the professional corporation.

(2)   From Whom Should the Stock Be Purchased?

Many attorneys and accountants feel that when stock is offered to a nonshareholder professional, the stock should be offered by the professional corporation. A sale by the professional corporation will not require it to recognize income on the sale since Section 1032 of the Code provides an exemption. Further, since most professional corporations have a relatively thin capital structure (and possibly an insufficient amount of working capital), the sale of stock by the professional corporation will create an infusion of capital which will assist in obtaining the cash surplus recommended in section [8.11], *supra*.

On the other hand, in professional corporations where there is sufficient working capital, the sale of stock by the existing stockholders offers an excellent means for them to "bail out" funds from the corporation at capital gains rates. If stock in the professional corporation is sold to the incoming stockholder by the existing shareholders, the selling shareholders will, normally, receive long-term capital gains treatment, producing a maximum tax of approximately 20%. See Section 1202 of the Code.

(3) How Much Stock Should Be Sold?

In many larger professional corporations, it is customary that each shareholder of the professional corporation own the same number of shares of stock, thus providing each shareholder with an equal voice in the affairs of the corporation. In smaller professional corporations, however, this is generally not the case, and the founders of the professional corporation usually retain voting control of the corporation. Since, absent a shareholder's operating agreement as described in section [6.05], *supra*, the voting control of the corporation determines which professionals will be entitled to continue to use the corporation's name, offices, and telephone number, the ownership of a majority voting interest in the stock of the professional corporation can be extremely important. For this reason, the founders of a professional corporation should avoid the temptation to appease younger professionals by selling them 50% or more of the stock. In a number of one-man corporations, an incoming shareholder will, obviously, desire to purchase a 50% interest. In almost all situations, particularly where the incoming shareholder does not have a substantial professional practice, the authors recommend against the existing shareholder selling more than a 49% interest to the new shareholder.

If the stock which will be sold to the incoming shareholder will be sold from the existing shareholders, there is no difficulty in determining the number of shares to be sold. For example, if two shareholders each own 5,000 of the 10,000 outstanding shares of a professional corporation and they desire to take in a third shareholder as an equal, each existing shareholder will sell 1,667 shares of stock to the incoming shareholder and each existing shareholder will purchase one share from the corporation, so that, after the sale of stock, each of the shareholders will own, 3,334 shares of the stock of the corporation. On the other hand, where stock will be purchased from the professional corporation, it must be realized that the number of shares to be purchased must be "grossed up" because the incoming shareholder must have a certain percentage of the stock after the issuance of the stock to be sold to him. For example, if it is anticipated that an incoming shareholder in a professional corporation with 10,000 shares outstanding (5,000 shares owned by each of two professional shareholders) will own one-third of the outstanding stock of the corporation, as in the example immediately above, the issuance by the corporation of 3,334 shares to the new professional will not provide him with one-third ownership. Rather, he will only own 25% of the corporation (3,334 divided by 13,334). In order to determine the exact number of shares to be sold by a professional corporation to an incoming professional, the following formula must be used:

Formula to determine number of shares which must be purchased from the corporation to acquire a given percentage ownership:

N = Number of shares held by new shareholder before issuance

X = Number of shares to be issued to new shareholder.

A = Percentage of shares that new shareholder is to own after issue.

B = Number of shares outstanding before shares are issued to new shareholder.

$$X = \frac{(AB)-N}{1-A}$$

Under this formula, the new shareholder must purchase 5,000 shares of stock from the professional corporation to be an equal shareholder.

(4)   What Value Should Be Affixed to the Stock?

In order to facilitate the purchase of stock in the professional corporation by incoming shareholders, it is preferable that the value of the professional corporation be kept at a low level. For this reason, the value of the stock in most professional corporations is computed by using only the net book value of the assets (computed on the cash basis) and excluding all accounts receivable and work in process. As previously discussed in section [10.01](1), *supra*, relating to the employment agreements of shareholder employees, shareholders are generally compensated for their share of the accounts receivable and work in process when they die or terminate their employment agreements. For this reason, most stock retirement agreements contemplate a payment for the stock based on its "net book value," and the value normally placed on the stock for purposes of sale to an incoming shareholder is the same value. It is possible, however, for the corporation or the existing shareholders to sell the stock in the professional corporation for a value in excess of or below the net book value.

Stock in a professional corporation is often sold for a value in excess of the net book value because the existing shareholders feel that the accounts receivable on the books of the corporation at the time of the sale "belong to them" and not to the incoming shareholder. Consequently, they feel that the incoming shareholder must be prepared to purchase his pro rata portion of the accounts receivable. This is not an uncommon practice among professional corporations, but it sometimes produces practical difficulties because of the incoming professional's inability to pay the increased purchase price. One method of eliminating the necessity of a large payment by the incoming professional is to provide for the existing professionals deferred compensation equal to the amount of the existing accounts receivable at the time the incoming shareholder purchases stock in the corporation. Such deferred compensation "pays" the existing shareholders for the accounts receivable at the time of the admission of the stockholder. Unless an interest factor is placed on this deferred compensation (so that it will compound), its value will be minimized by the passage of time. Other professionals seek to achieve the same goal by recapitalizing the professional corporation at the time of the entrance of a new shareholder. That is, prior to the time when stock will be sold to the new professional, the professional corporation is recapitalized to create a class of preferred stock which will have a preference on liquidation in an amount equal to the accounts receivable at the time of the admission of the new shareholder. The professional corporation will then be in a position to sell its regular voting common stock to the new professional at the current book value. It should be recognized, however, that any such stock distributed to the existing shareholders of a professional corporation will be "Section 306 stock" and may create ordinary income upon its later transfer. See Section 306 of the Code.

As another alternative to the accounts receivable problem, some professional corporations agree just to "start over." In other words, when the existing accounts receivable are collected, they are used to fund compensation payments to the existing shareholders. Only accounts receivable generated by the professional corporation after the date of the sale of stock to the new shareholder will be used to fund compensation payments to all of the shareholders. This method does compensate the existing shareholders for "their" accounts receivable, but it will generally result in a period of approximately three months during which the incoming shareholder receives very little, or possibly no, compensation.

(5)   How Should Payment for the Stock Be Made?

A major problem which incoming shareholders encounter in purchasing stock in a professional corporation is that the stock must be purchased with after-tax dollars. For this reason, it is customary to permit an incoming shareholder to purchase his stock on an installment basis and professional corporations often sell stock so that any required annual installments may be paid from annual bonuses. Further, it is possible for a professional corporation to issue stock to an incoming shareholder without requiring from him any amount toward the purchase of that stock. If this occurs, the fair market value of that stock will be considered income to the professional at the time of receipt under Section 83 of the Code, as long as there are no substantial restrictions which may cause the stock to be forfeited at a later date. Generally, the requirement that the stock be resold to the corporation under a stock retirement agreement at a specified price is not a restriction which will prevent the stock from being taxable to the professional upon receipt. Section 83 of the Code provides an excellent mechanism for permitting an incoming shareholder to obtain stock at a low cost, yet providing a tax benefit for the corporation. If Section 83 is employed, and the incoming shareholder is given stock with a fair market value of $10,000, the out-of-pocket cost to the shareholder will be approximately $5,000 in taxes due, assuming a 50% marginal tax rate. This is substantially less than would be required if the incoming shareholder were required to pay $10,000 to the professional corporation (i.e., the shareholder would be required to spend $20,000 in pretax funds). It should be recognized, however, that the issuance of stock under Section 83 will not create any additional infusion of cash working capital into the professional corporation from the shareholder, but the professional corporation will receive a deduction for the fair market value of the stock issued to the shareholder, which deduction will create a tax savings.[1]

(6)   How to Effect the Sale

When a professional becomes a shareholder in a professional corporation, there are a number of steps which should be taken. Initially, the shareholder will usually be elected an officer and member of the board of directors of the professional corporation and a new employment agreement (of the shareholder variety, see section [10.01](1), *supra*) will be prepared for him. Further, once the stock is sold to the incoming professional, he must also execute the existing stock retirement agreement, and it is advisable for him to execute stock subscription and stock transfer agreements. See section [7.05], *supra*, for these forms.

The actual issuance of stock to the professional is a relatively simple matter. In the event that stock is to be sold from the professional corporation, a new stock certificate will be issued to the professional. On the other hand, if stock is to be purchased from existing professionals, it is often necessary for them to split their stock certificates in order to create certificates which may be transferred to the incoming shareholder. This splitting and re-issuance of such certificates should, of course, be recorded in the stock transfer books of the professional corporation, and a short stock sales agreement should be prepared. This stock sales agreement is very similar to the stock subscription agreements used upon incorporation and protects the selling shareholder from federal securities laws violations while also acting as a record of the transaction. A copy of a stock sales agreement is contained in section [7.05], *supra*.

(7)   What Should a Prospective Shareholder Look For?

In examining the documents which he will be asked to execute upon becoming a shareholder, the professional employee should specifically be aware of the following:

(a)   *New Employment Agreement*

The new shareholder should determine those points in the shareholder style employment agreement which differ from his existing employment agreement, and he should make specific note of the manner in which his compensation (and any bonuses) will be computed. He should also review the provisions relating to payment of benefits upon termination of employment and should determine whether he will be compensated for his share of the accounts receivable on the books of the corporation at his termination and whether there will be any reduction in those benefits if he voluntarily terminates his employment. Further, he should examine the provisions of any restrictive covenant contained in the employment agreement and determine whether they are acceptable. The incoming professional employee should also obtain from the professional corporation a salary schedule which indicates the compensation and bonuses paid to the other professional employees of the corporation so that he may compare it with the compensation which will be paid to him.

(b) Employee Benefits

The incoming shareholder should also examine the amount of increase which he will receive in his employee benefits, such as vacation, group term life insurance, disability insurance, split dollar insurance, accident and health insurance, and automobile allowances. The new shareholder should also determine if these benefits are comparable to those of the other professional shareholders.

(c) Qualified Retirement Plans

The incoming shareholder should definitely review the benefits provided under the qualified retirement plans and particularly the vesting schedule. He should determine, in the event that he leaves the professional corporation, whether the professional corporation will be otherwise contractually bound to compensate him for any unvested portion of his retirement plan benefits, which would otherwise be forfeitable.

(d) Stock Retirement Agreement

The incoming shareholder should examine the manner in which the value is computed under the stock retirement agreement and whether there will be any diminution in that value in the event that his employment with the professional corporation terminates prior to his death, disability, or reaching normal retirement age. He should also determine whether the agreement contains covenants against competition and whether he will be required, under the stock retirement agreement, to personally guarantee the obligations of the corporation.

(e) Stockholdings

The incoming shareholder should review the percentage of stock ownership of the other shareholders so that he will understand the control of the corporation.

(f) Financial Matters

The incoming shareholder should ask for, receive, and review copies of financial statements of the professional corporation for the last three years and any other significant contractual obligations of the professional corporation, either to shareholders of the corporation or to third parties. He should also determine what, if any, additional obligations of the corporation he will be required to guarantee upon becoming a shareholder.

[11.02] STOCK RETIREMENT AGREEMENT

(1) Should a Professional Corporation Have a Stock Retirement Agreement?

The undeniable answer to this question is "yes." A stock retirement agreement is an indispensable element of a properly administered professional corporation. A properly drafted stock retirement agreement serves a number of important purposes, several of which are:

(1) A stock retirement agreement restricts the ability of shareholders to transfer their shares and assures the remaining shareholders that the shareholders of the corporation will always be individuals acceptable to them. Consequently, a stock retirement agreement avoids disputes between active shareholders and wives, children, and estates of deceased shareholders.

(2) A stock retirement agreement provides a market for stock which is otherwise unmarketable and sets forth a mechanism to enable the stock to be purchased. In this manner, stock retirement agreements protect both the corporation and inactive or deceased shareholders. Without a stock retirement agreement, it might be possible for the corporation to insist on paying an inordinately low price for the stock of a deceased shareholder and, if the estate of the deceased shareholder did not accept the price, to let the estate continue to hold the stock (if permitted under state law).

(3) A stock retirement agreement sets forth the value to be paid for shares which will be repurchased and avoids questions as to the manner in which stock will be valued.

(4) A properly drafted stock retirement agreement will fix the value of shares for federal estate tax purposes.

(5) A stock retirement agreement provides a mechanism to facilitate funding of the purchase of a deceased shareholder's stock, through the use of life insurance, and provides a source of funds for the estate of a deceased shareholder which can be used to pay federal estate taxes.

(6) For Subchapter S corporations, the stock retirement agreement provides a mechanism whereby the Subchapter S election may be protected.

(2) What Type of Stock Retirement Agreement Should Be Used?

There are basically two varieties of stock retirement agreements, those which require the corporation to purchase a deceased or terminated shareholder's stock (otherwise known as entity or redemption agreements) and agreements whereby the remaining shareholders agree, individually, to purchase the stock of other shareholders (known as cross-purchase agreements). Each type of agreement has various advantages and disadvantages, which are as follows:

ASPECT	CROSS-PURCHASE	REDEMPTION
Purchaser:	Surviving shareholders.	Corporation.
Effect on remaining shareholders	Surviving shareholders purchase stock of other shareholders and gain 100% control. Also, surviving shareholders receive a "step up" in the basis of the stock purchased by them from the deceased or terminated shareholders and the basis in that stock will equal its cost.	The corporation purchases the stock and the surviving shareholders continue to have 100% control. The basis in the stock outstanding in the surviving shareholders remains the same.
General restrictions	Limitations on enforceability of contracts and requirements regarding reasonableness of restrictions on transferability of stock under state law.	Same.
Corporate law	Generally, none.	May run afoul of state law prohibition against issuance of redeemable common stock.
Securities law restrictions	Anti-fraud restrictions and resale restrictions.	Same.
Tax implications	Stock purchased by shareholders with after-tax dollars and any insurance premiums paid by shareholders of life insurance to fund the purchase will also be paid with after-tax dollars. However, split dollar insurance may be	Amounts paid by corporation in redemption of stock are not deductible. Also, premiums paid by the corporation for the purchase of life insurance to fund the agreement are not deductible. However, corporate rate may be significantly lower than individual tax rate, thus

ASPECT	CROSS-PURCHASE	REDEMPTION
	used to provide funding. Further, if additional bonuses must be made to shareholders in order to permit the payment of premiums, such bonuses may run afoul of reasonable compensation rules.	providing a tax savings. Cash surrender value of policies maintained by corporation may expose corporation to accumulated earnings tax penalty.
Funding consideration	Proliferation of policies where each shareholder must maintain a policy on the life of every other shareholder. Also, age disparity and percentage ownership disparities may cause younger shareholders to bear inordinate portion of insurance premium. Also, insurance held by a deceased shareholder on the surviving stockholders will pass through decedent's estate. Any transfer of life insurance policies from one shareholder to another will result in "transfer for value" rule under Section 101(2) of the Code being implemented and possible income taxation of proceeds.	No proliferation of policies, corporation need only maintain one policy on each shareholder and corporation pays entire premium so that, in effect, the burden of all policies is on the shareholders equally.
Other considerations	1. Stepped-up basis in decedent's stock is primarily advantageous to other shareholders where	1. Not applicable

313

ASPECT	CROSS-PURCHASE	REDEMPTION
Other considerations	*inter vivos* transfers are contemplated. Advantage deferred indefinitely where stock will be held until death or retirement (such as in professional corporations).	
	2. Insurance policies and proceeds are subject to the creditors of the individual shareholders.	2. Insurance policies and proceeds are subject to the creditors of the corporation.

Because of the ease of implementing and administering a redemption stock retirement agreement, the authors generally recommend that it be used in lieu of a cross-purchase agreement. In professional groups with more than three or four shareholders, the proliferation of insurance policies will usually mandate the use of a redemption agreement as opposed to a cross-purchase agreement, although insurance companies are providing insurance products which will eliminate the number of policies required to be maintained. The form discussed in this chapter is, basically, a redemption agreement but does permit a cross-purchase to take place in the event that the corporation determines not to purchase the stock.

(3) What Provisions Should Be Contained in a Stock Retirement Agreement?

In drafting a stock retirement agreement, the professional and his advisors should consider the following questions:

(a) *Will Redemption Be Mandatory or Optional?*

The shareholders may desire to use a mandatory redemption upon the death, disability or retirement of a shareholder, but provide optional redemption upon the termination of employment of a shareholder prior to retirement. If an optional redemption is used, will the corporation retain a first refusal in the stock at a stated price?

(b) *What Value Will Be Used?*

Will the agreement provide for a value which will be determined every year by the shareholders, the use of the "book" value, a value based on a formula, a value based on an appraisal, or a value based on the "shoot out" approach?

(c) *How Will the Payment of the Purchase Price Be Made?*

Will the purchase price be paid in all cash or in installments? Will the proceeds from any insurance received by the corporation be paid in a lump sum? Will the shareholder or his estate retain a security interest in the stock redeemed, and will the remaining shareholders be required to guarantee the payment of the purchase price?

(d) *How Will the Purchase Price Be Funded?*

Will the corporation purchase key man insurance on the lives of all the shareholders and will the proceeds of the key man insurance be included in the value for purposes of determining the purchase price?

Contained below is a form of redemption stock retirement agreement which contains various options. Each provision of the agreement and the options are followed by comments which describe the applicability of those provisions and options and, where appropriate, indicate further options:

XYZ, P.C.
STOCK RETIREMENT AGREEMENT

This Agreement, made and entered into this _____ day of _____ , 19___ , by and between _____ , _____ , and _____ (hereinafter collectively referred to as the "Stockholders") and _____ (hereinafter referred to as the "Corporation").

W I T N E S S E T H:

WHEREAS, the Corporation is a professional corporation organized and in good standing under the laws of the State of Georgia with its principal place of business in _____ County, Georgia; and

WHEREAS, _____ , _____ , and _____ are the sole Stockholders of the corporation, owning all of the outstanding stock thereof (the "Stock"); and

WHEREAS, the parties to this Agreement believe it is to their mutual best interest to provide for continuity and harmony in the management and policies of the Corporation; and

WHEREAS, therefore, it is their mutual purpose to: (a) provide for the purchase by the Corporation of a deceased Stockholder's Stock; (b) provide for the purchase by the Corporation of a Stockholder's Stock upon a Stockholder's total disability; (c) provide for the purchase by the Corporation of a Stockholder's Stock upon a Stockholder's termination of employment; (d) provide for the purchase of a Stockholder's Stock should such Stockholder desire to sell his Stock; and (e) provide the funds necessary to carry out such purpose.

Comment:

The above "recitals" are standard in most stock retirement agreements and set forth the reasons of the parties for entering into the agreement and the anticipated purpose which the agreement will serve.

NOW, THEREFORE, in consideration of the mutual agreements and covenants contained herein and for other good and valuable consideration, the receipt and sufficiency of which are hereby acknowledged, it is mutually agreed and covenanted by and between the parties to this Agreement as follows:

ARTICLE 1

(Option 1)

PURCHASE UPON DEATH, DISABILITY, OR TERMINATION OF EMPLOYMENT ON OR AFTER ATTAINMENT OF AGE 65

Upon the earlier of a Stockholder's death or disability or upon the termination of a Stockholder's employment on or after the attainment of age sixty-five (65), the Corporation shall have an obligation to purchase, and the Stockholder or his estate shall be obligated to sell all of the Stock then owned by the Stockholder or his estate. The purchase price of such Stock and the terms of sale shall be determined in accordance with the provisions of Articles 3 and 4, respectively, of ths Agreement. For purposes of this Agreement, the term "Disability" shall be defined as the complete inability of a Stockholder to continue to perform the duties incident to his employment with the Corporation as a result of mental or physical illness, sickness, or injury. The determination of whether a Stockholder is disabled shall be made by the Board of Directors of the Corporation and shall be based on competent medical advice, and the determination of the Board of Directors as to the disability of a Stockholder shall be conclusive and binding upon the Corporation and the Stockholders.

Comment:

This option is designed to be used in conjunction with Option 1 of Article 2. This option provides for a mandatory redemption upon the death, disability, or termination of employment after reaching a certain age (usually 60 or 65) for all stockholders. It is normal to require mandatory redemption upon death, disability or retirement because it is important to have an obligation on behalf of the corporation to redeem, and a corresponding obligation on behalf of the shareholder or his estate to offer, the stock for redemption. This assures both parties that there will be a market for the stock. This provision also provides that the determination of the "disability" of the professional employee will be based on the decision of the Board of Directors, which shall be conclusive. It may be advisable to list certain extrinsic factors which would indicate disability or state that the opinion of three competent physicians would be required in order to certify disability. In any event, however, it is important to leave this decision up to the corporation.

316

ARTICLE 1

(Option 2)

PURCHASE BY CORPORATION

Upon the earlier of a Stockholder's death, disability, or termination of employment with the Corporation, either by the Stockholder or by the Corporation for any reason, with or without cause, or if a Stockholder should otherwise desire to sell, transfer or otherwise dispose of any portion or all of his Stock in the Corporation, the Corporation shall have an obligation to purchase and the Stockholder or his estate shall be obligated to sell all of the Stock (or such portion thereof as the case may be) owned by the Stockholder or his estate. The purchase price of such Stock and the terms of sale shall be determined in accordance with the provisions of Articles 2 and 3, respectively, of this Agreement. For purposes of this Agreement, the term "Disability" shall be defined as the complete inability of a Stockholder to continue to perform the duties incident to his employment with the Corporation as a result of mental or physical illness, sickness or injury. [The determination of whether a Stockholder is disabled shall be made by majority vote of a panel of physicians consisting of three (3) physicians, one physician to be chosen by _____, one physician to be chosen by _____, and the third physician to be chosen by agreement of the two physicians chosen by _____ and _____.] or [The determination of whether a Stockholder is disabled shall be made by the Board of Directors of the Corporation and shall be based on competent medical advice, and the determination of the Board of Directors as to the disability of a Stockholder shall be conclusive and binding upon the Corporation and the Stockholders.]

Comment:

This option is comparable to Option 1 but requires redemption by the corporation in all events. A provision of this type is by far the easiest provision to implement and, to some extent, favors the minority shareholders of the professional corporation whose stock may not be redeemed if their employment were terminated prior to reaching retirement age.

With regard to the term "termination of employment," both Options 1 and 2 to Article 1 take the simple approach. It mades no difference whether there has been a voluntary resignation by the employee or whether his employment has been terminated by the employer with or without cause. Strong arguments can be made that different treatment should be afforded to each of the various methods of terminated employment, and this is the reason for the following Option 1 to Article 2.

ARTICLE 2

(Option 1)

TRANSFER OF SHARES NOT OCCASIONED BY
DEATH, DISABILITY, OR RETIREMENT

If a Stockholder's employment with the Corporation is terminated, either by the Stockholder or by the Corporation, for any reason, with or without cause, other than death or disability prior to reaching age sixty-five (65), or if for any reason a Stockholder desires to sell, transfer, or otherwise dispose of any portion or all of his Stock in the Corporation, he shall offer to sell his entire Stock interest in the Corporation (or such portion thereof, as the case may be) to the Corporation at a price and upon the terms determined in accordance with the provisions of Articles 3 and 4, respectively, of this Agreement. Where a Stockholder's employment is so terminated, his offer to sell shall be made to the Corporation in writing within thirty (30) days after his said termination of employment. Any Stock not purchased by the Corporation within thirty (30) days after receipt of such offer in writing shall be offered at the same price and terms to the other Stockholders, each of whom shall have the right, within (10) days after the expiration of the Corporation's option to purchase, to purchase such portion of the remaining Stock offered for sale as the number of shares owned by him on the date the offering Stockholder first offered his Stock to the Corporation shall bear to the total number of shares of stock owned by the Stockholders on such date, excluding the shares of Stock owned by the offering Stockholder or Stockholders; provided, however, that if any remaining Stockholder does not purchase his full proportionate share of the Stock within said ten (10) days, the balance of the Stock may, within five (5) days after the expiration of said ten (10) day period, be purchased by the other remaining Stockholders as they shall agree but, failing agreement, in equal shares. If both the Corporation and the remaining Stockholders fail or refuse to purchase the Stock of the offering Stockholder at the price and upon the terms and within the times aforesaid, then the offering Stockholder shall be at liberty to offer his Stock in the Corporation to any other third party (other than the remaining Stockholders) who is qualified under the laws of the State of Georgia to own such Stock, but the offering Stockholder shall not sell such Stock to any such third party without again offering such Stock first to the Corporation and then to the remaining Stockholders as provided above, allowing the periods provided above in each instance for the acceptance thereof, at such price and terms aforesaid or, at such price and terms offered to any third party. Prior to any sale of Stock by an offering Stockholder to any such third party, the Corporation must have received from its counsel the unqualified opinion of such counsel that the proposed sale will not violate Federal and applicable state securities laws.

Comment:

This option is intended for use when Option 1 to Article 1 is employed. This provision assumes that, where a shareholder terminates his employment prior to his death, becoming disabled, or reaching retirement age, the corporation may or may not desire to purchase his stock. For example, if a younger, minority shareholder of the corporation desires to leave the corporation after several years of practice, the corporation and the remaining shareholders may have a strong desire to inhibit the ability of the departing shareholder to compete with the corportion (this is a definite factor where there is no covenant against competition provided in either the stock retirement agreement or the employment agreement). If the remaining shareholders anticipate that the departing shareholder will be competing with the corporation, they may desire to postpone the redemption in order to avoid "funding" the competing enterprise. Option 1 to Article 2 permits the remaining shareholders and the professional corporation to accomplish this. It should be remembered, however, that it is almost always best to have a "clean break" with a departing shareholder. If the terminated shareholder owns 5% or more of the stock of the professional corporation, most state laws will permit him, upon reasonable notice, to examine the books and records of the professional corporation. While this might not be extraordinarily detrimental to the professional corporation, it may cause some uneasiness among the remaining shareholders.

Option 1 to Article 2 also provides for an alternative mechanism whereby a cross-purchase may be arranged among the shareholders, either proportionately or disproportionately. It is not anticipated that this would normally occur, but it is important to have this option.

This alternative also provides for a first refusal which will remain with the corporation and the remaining stockholders in the event that they initially refuse to repurchase the stock of the departing shareholder. This first refusal not only requires that the departing shareholder re-offer his stock to the professional corporation (and then to the shareholders) but that he re-offer the stock at the price and terms provided in the agreement or at the price and terms at which he is offering the stock to any third party, if such price and terms are lower or more favorable. This provision permits the corporation to repurchase the stock at the lowest price available.

Most state corporate statutes (or in some states, the case law) declare invalid certain restrictions which corporations may impose upon the alienation of its shares. Some state statutes prohibit absolute restrictions upon the *inter vivos* disposition of corporate stock, whereas most state statutes permit restrictions taking the form of a first refusal. Also, most state statutes construe restrictions on alienation very strictly and will often refuse to grant specific performance on such restrictions if the terms of the restrictions are not specifically clear, particularly as to the purchase price.

Most state corporate statutes also prohibit the issuance of "redeemable common stock" and those statutes should be reviewed in order to determine that neither the rights of the corporation to redeem the stock nor the granting of a first refusal will constitute a violation.

ARTICLE 3

(Option 1)

VALUE

Unless and until changed as provided hereinafter, it is agreed that, for the purpose of determining the purchase price to be paid for the Stock of a Stockholder, the value of each share of Stock of the Corporation will be determined by the independent certified public accountants then regularly employed by the Corporation, which value shall be accepted by a two-thirds (⅔) vote of the Stock outstanding and by the Corporation.

As of the date of this Agreement, each of the Stockholders owns the number of shares set opposite his name:

_____   _____

_____   _____

_____   _____

The value of each share of Stock established by the independent certified public accountants employed by the corporation and agreed upon by a two-thirds (⅔) vote of the Stock outstanding and the Corporation represents the fair value of the interest of each Stockholder including his interest in the goodwill of the Corporation. The Stockholders and the Corporation agree to redetermine the value of the Corporation and their respective interests therein within sixty (60) days following the end of each fiscal year. It is understood and agreed between the parties hereto that the value determined and redetermined in each subsequent year in accordance with this Article 3 is the fair value of each share of Stock of the Corporation subject to this Agreement, and that all assets, both tangible and intangible, if any, as well as all liabilities including mortgages, liens or other encumbrances of any kind whatsoever of or upon the assets of the Corporation, if any, have been considered in determining said value. The value so agreed upon by a two-thirds (⅔) vote of the Stock outstanding and the Corporation shall be certified on "Schedule A" attached hereto and made a part of this Agreement and such certification shall take the following form:

The undersigned mutually agree on this _____ day of _____, 19 ____, that for the purposes of this Stock Retirement Agreement, each share of Stock of the Corporation has a value of $_____.

In the event that the value of the Stock of the Corporation is agreed upon by a two-thirds (⅔) vote of the outstanding Stock and the Corporation as provided in the preceding Paragraph, all of the Stockholders agree to be bound by such value, whether or not they agree with such determined value and whether or not they have executed the "Schedule A" referred to in such Paragraph.

If the Stockholders and the Corporation fail to make a redetermination of the value for a particular year, the last previously certified value shall control, except that if the Stockholders and the Corporation have not so redetermined the value within the twelve (12) months immediately preceding an offer to sell or the termination of employment, disability or death of a Stockholder, then the price of each share of Stock shall be the value set forth in the most recent certification, plus or minus the net earnings or losses per share (less cash dividends paid or payable thereon) for each fiscal year (or portion thereof) ended since the date of the most recent certification prior to the date of such offer, disability, termination of employment, or death, as the case may be.

(i) The term "net earnings" or "net losses" shall mean earnings or losses of the Corporation, net after deduction for all taxes or reserve for taxes, as determined in accordance with generally accepted accounting principles consistently followed by the independent certified public accountants then regularly employed by the Corporation. The parties specifically agree that unrealized appreciation and depreciation in the Corporation's assets will not be considered in computing the "net earnings" or "net losses" of the corporation.

(ii) Appropriate adjustment in the price per share shall be made for any stock dividend, stock split, recapitalization or issuance by the Corporation of additional shares, occurring after the date of the most recent certification.

(iii) The purchase price as determined above shall be final and conclusive and shall not be subject to recomputation by reason of events occurring or becoming known subsequent to the certification or to the completion of the profit and loss statements, as the case may be, even though such events and information relate to the business of the Corporation transacted prior thereto.

The Stockholders and the Corporation agree that any financial statement of the Corporation upon which the value of the Stock is determined is not required to be an audited statement; however, if any party to this Agreement shall request that such statement be audited, the Corporation may, in its sole discretion, direct that such statement be audited by the independent certified public accountants then employed by the Corporation, but such requesting party shall bear all of the expenses of conducting such audit.

It is further agreed that, if a purchase of a Stockholder's Stock is made because of the termination of the Stockholder's employment with the Corporation, either by the Stockholder or by the Corporation and irrespective of the reason for or cause of such termination, prior to his death, disability and prior to his attaining age sixty-five (65) or because the Stockholder desires to sell his shares of Stock in the Corporation prior to his attaining age sixty-five (65), the purchase price for such shares shall only be _____ percent (____%) of the value of such shares as determined in accordance with this Article.

Comment:

There are a number of methods of fixing the value of stock of a professional corporation. The method contained in Article 3 above is, by far, the easiest and requires the professionals to agree upon a value once each year, preferably at the annual meeting at which the accountant and attorney are present. The form above requires a two-thirds vote of the shareholders to agree upon a value and further provides that all shareholders will be bound if two-thirds of the shareholders shall agree. There is no reason why the agreement should not provide for a unanimous agreement of all the shareholders, and, in fact, strong arguments can be made that unanimous consent should be required. The above form further provides that, in the event the value of the stock is not redetermined annually, the value will be increased by the net earnings or decreased by the net losses since the last valuation. This is basically a book value approach and it is important to provide in the agreement that the financial statements which will be used by the corporation will not be "audited" statements but that the shareholders themselves may obtain audited statements if they desire to pay the cost.

Another very common method of valuing the stock in a professional corporation is to state in the stock retirement agreement that stock will be computed on its "net book" value by the accountant on an annual basis. Since most professional corporations operate on a cash basis, the value of the stock of the corporation will not include accounts receivable or be reduced by various contingent liabilities. One reason for not using the "net book" value approach is that the shareholders may desire that a number of adjustments be made to the book value to provide a correct reflection of the value of the professional corporation. The authors have, in numerous situations, made adjustments to book value for some or all of the following factors:

(1) Life Insurance. Should the value of the corporation reflect the cash value of the life insurance or the proceeds received upon the death of a professional? A financial statement based on the cash method will normally include as an asset the cash value of the life insurance policy and, without specific omission, the value of the corporation following the date of death of a shareholder should include the value of the proceeds if they have been paid. The general tendency is, however, to omit the value of the proceeds from the value of the stock. It might be advisable, however, to include the value of the proceeds if all of the professionals happen to die in the same six month period. See the comment to Article 5, *infra*, for a complete discussion of the use of life insurance in this stock retirement agreement.

(2) Investment Securities and Real Estate. Should investment securities and real estate be valued at cost or appraised fair market value for purposes of computing the value of the stock?

(3) Accounts Receivable and Work in Process. Should accounts receivable and work in process be included for purposes of valuing the interest of each shareholder? If so, should an amount be deducted for approximated uncollectable accounts and should an amount also be deducted for anticipated corporate income tax on those receivables? Inclusion of accounts receivable in the value of the stock should only occur where the shareholder does not receive payment for his share of the receivables under an employment or deferred compensation agreement.

(4) Fixed Assets. Should fixed assets be valued at depreciated, adjusted basis or at some percentage of cost? A good argument can be made that office equipment and some leasehold improvements should be valued at the higher of their adjusted basis or 50% of cost.

(5) Amounts Due Under Employment Agreements. In computing the value of stock due to a shareholder, should the corporation list as a liability the amounts which become payable to him upon the termination of his employment under his employment agreement?

(6) <u>Deferred Compensation</u>. In valuing the stock of the corporation, should the cash basis value of the corporation be adjusted by liabilities for deferred compensation which will be payable to the other shareholders of the corporation?

(7) <u>Contributions to Qualified Retirement Plans</u>. Should the cash basis book value also be adjusted for accrued (or anticipated) liabilities to qualified retirement plans?

(8) <u>Prepaid Expenses</u>. Should prepaid expenses be prorated, in order to increase the value of the corporation?

(9) <u>Library and Files</u>. Many professionals feel that professional libraries, which have been expensed over the years, should have a significant value and should be included as an asset.

The determination of whether any of the above factors, or any other factors, are used to adjust the book value of stock of a professional corporation is a determination which must be made by the shareholders.

Stock retirement agreements of professional corporations may also provide that the value of the stock will be determined by a stated formula (such as five times annual earnings) or may be arrived at by an independent appraiser. These are both acceptable methods of valuing stock in business corporations, but generally are inapplicable in professional corporations. Also, in two-man professional corporations, where the stock is equally owned, it is often advisable to use a "shoot out" or a "put and call" buy-sell agreement under which one of the shareholders must offer to buy the stock of the other shareholder at a certain price or agree to sell his stock at that same price. This type of provision may also assist in holding the shareholders together. An example of this type of provision follows:

ARTICLE 3

(Option 2)

PUT AND CALL BUY-SELL

3.1 <u>Manner of Offer</u>. Any shareholder, or group of shareholders ("Offeror"), at any time may offer to any other Shareholder or group of Shareholders ("Offeree"), both to sell all the Offeror's Stock and to buy all of the Offeree's Stock. Such offer must be in writing and must contain the following:

(i)   A statement of intention to rely on this paragraph 3.1;

(ii) A statement of the Offeror's determination of the per share value of the stock subject to the offer, which must be identical for each share of stock;

(iii) A statement that a condition to any purchase pursuant to the offer shall be the absolute and unconditional idemnity by the purchaser of the seller against any loss, claim, or damage that the seller may suffer arising out of any guarantee to the seller of any debt of the Corporation for borrowed money;

(iv) A statement that the purchase price of the stock subject to the offer shall be payable in cash at closing; and

(v) A statement that such offer is both an offer to sell all the stock owned by the Offeror and an offer to purchase all of the stock owned by the Offeree.

Such offer shall be irrevocable for a period of 60 days and the Offeree may, on or before such 60th day, either accept the offer to sell or accept the offer to buy (but he may not accept both) and upon such acceptance the Offeror and the Offeree shall be required to sell or to buy, as the case may be. If the Offeree fails to accept either offer within the 60 day period, the offer shall expire. Following the expiration of the offer, the Offeror shall have the right, exercisable on or before the 15th day after the expiration of the 60 day period, either to buy all the stock of the Offeree or to sell all his stock to the Offeree and, if the Offeror exercises such right, the Offeree shall be required to buy or sell, in accordance with the terms of the offer and the provisions of this paragraph.

3.2 Manner of Acceptance. Acceptance by an Offeree of any offer to buy or sell and exercised by an Offeror of the right to buy or sell shall consist of a tender of all documents, duly executed, necessary to convey the stock being sold, with full warranty of title thereto, or a tender of the purchase price in cash, as the case may be.

3.3 Power of Attorney and Release. Shareholder A hereby appoints Shareholders B and C, and Shareholder B hereby appoints Shareholders A and C, and Shareholder C hereby appoints Shareholders A and B as the appointing parties, agents, and attorneys in fact for the purpose of executing and delivering any and all documents necessary to convey the appointing parties' stock pursuant to the provisions of this paragraph, and any conveyance by the person or persons appointed shall be a conveyance of all right, title, or equity in and to the Stock. This power of attorney shall be coupled with an interest and shall not expire upon the incapacity or death of the appointing party.

3.4 Closing. The closing of such purchase and sale shall be held at the time and place and on the date specified by the buyers by written notice to the sellers, which date shall be on or before the 10th day after such right to purchase or sell has been exercised.

3.5 Death or Disability. If death, total disability, or termination of employment precedes the giving of notice under this paragraph 3, the provisions of Article 1 shall control, but otherwise the provisions of this Article 3 shall control.

Comment:

In most professional corporations, the accounts receivable of the professional corporation are specifically excluded in the valuation of the stock. This is because accounts receivable are normally accounted for, and shareholders receive compensation for them under the provisions of their employment or deferred compensation agreements. Accounts receivable are normally handled in this manner in order to provide for a payment to the departing shareholder which will be deductible. In other words, as the accounts receivable are received, the corporation will be required to report them as income and pay tax upon them unless they are paid out to the departing shareholder as compensation. If the accounts receivable are collected by the corporation and, then, the corporation makes a nondeductible payment in redemption of stock to the departing professional, the professional corporation will be out-of-pocket for the additional federal income taxes which it must pay on the accounts receivable unless an appropriate amount is deducted from the amount due to the professional.

Because of this difference in tax treatment, the question often arises, ''Can accounts receivable be excluded from the value of the corporation for tax purposes?'' An agreement can be made that the payment received under the departing employee's employment agreement for accounts receivable should be considered part of the redemption price for his stock and should, consequently, be treated as long-term capital gain. If a stock retirement agreement is improperly drafted, this argument may succeed. For example, in *Ted N. Steffen*,[2] a physician in a professional corporation received $40,000 in return for his stock, pursuant to the corporation's stock retirement agreement. The $40,000 represented the physician's share of the corporation's accounts receivable. The court held that no part of the $40,000 was deductible by the corporation as a salary expense but was actually paid for the redemption of the physician's stock.

Further, many professionals feel that a differentiation should be made (in the amount paid) where a shareholder's employment is terminated (either voluntarily or involuntarily) prior to reaching retirement age. Such a provision, commonly called a ''golden handcuffs'' provision, resembles paragraph 14 in the shareholder employment agreement described above in section [10.01](1). The same comments made in that section also apply here. However, many professional groups prefer to limit the amount which the professional receives (computed on accounts receivable) under the employment agreement, whereas they prefer that no reduction be made in the amount which will be received by the departing shareholder under the stock retirement agreement. The amount due to the departing shareholder under the stock retirement agreement usually represents an interest in the corporation for which he has previously paid and most professionals see the redemption of the stock as simply a return of purchase price which should not be withheld. On the other hand, some professional groups reduce the amount paid to a terminating shareholder only where his employment is terminated voluntarily by him prior to reaching normal retirement age and he enters into competition with the professional corporation.

Stock retirement agreements should be drafted with federal estate taxes in mind and, with proper draftsmanship, the stock retirement agreement can provide both a value which the shareholders have agreed upon and a value which the Service will be bound to accept for federal estate tax purposes. Regulations §20.2031-2(h) provides that a purchase price fixed by an option or agreement to buy stock from a deceased shareholder's estate is binding for federal estate tax purposes even if the purchase price is less than the fair market value when the following requirements are met:

(1) The stock retirement agreement is a ''bona fide'' business agreement and not a device to pass the shares of stock on to the natural objects of the deceased shareholder's bounty for less than adequate and full consideration. In a properly drafted stock retirement agreement for a professional corporation, this is generally not a problem.

(2) The agreement must have restricted the disposition of the decedent's stock during his lifetime. Where the decedent is free to sell or dispose of his stock during his lifetime without regard to the agreement, the full fair market value of the stock (as determined by the Service) will be includable in his estate. Further, the *inter vivos* purchase price should not exceed the price which is applicable on death; a right of first refusal in a stock retirement agreement is sufficient for this purpose. This requirement generally is not a problem in a properly drafted stock retirement agreement.

(3) The agreement must obligate the decedent's estate to sell the shares upon his death. This, also, is generally not a problem in a professional corporation's stock retirement agreement.

(4) The agreement should state a specific price or a method of arriving at a specific price, and this, also, is generally not a problem.[3]

ARTICLE 4

(Option 1)

PAYMENT OF PURCHASE PRICE

(a) <u>Purchase Pursuant to Article 1</u>.

If a Stockholder's Stock is purchased pursuant to the provisions of Article 1, the purchase price shall be evidenced by a negotiable, promissory note executed by the Corporation bearing interest at _____ percent (___%) per annum, calling for _____ (___) consecutive, equal monthly payments payable on the first day of each month, with the first such payment to be made on the date of purchase. Such note shall provide that, upon default in the payment of any installment of interest or principal, all remaining installment payments shall, at the option of the selling Stockholder or any other holder of said note, become immediately due and payable. Said note shall also give the Corporation the option of prepayment in whole or in part at any time. Such note shall be in the form attached hereto as Exhibit ''A''. Upon the sale of his Stock to the Corporation, the Stockholder shall be entitled to retain a security interest in the Stock to secure payment of the Corporation's obligation, which security interest shall be reliquished by the Stockholder upon full payment for all of his Stock to be purchased under this Agreement.

The provisions of this Paragraph (a) shall also apply to the estate of a deceased Stockholder or to the personal representative of any disabled or incapacitated Stockholder.

(b) <u>Purchase Pursuant to Article 2</u>.

If a Stockholder's Stock is purchased pursuant to the provisions of Article 2, the purchase price shall be evidenced by a negotiable, installment promissory note executed by the Corporation or the respective purchasing Stockholders, as the case may be, bearing interest at ___ percent (____%) per annum, calling for _____ (___) consecutive, equal monthly payments payable upon the first day of each month, with the first such payment to be made on the date of purchase. Such note shall provide that, upon default in the payment of any installment of interest or principal, all remaining installment payments shall, at the option of the selling Stockholder or any other holder of said note, become immediately due and payable. Said note shall also give the Corporation or the respective purchasing Stockholders the option of prepayment in whole or in part at any time. Such note shall be in the form attached hereto as Exhibit "A". Upon the sale of his Stock to the Corporation, the Stockholder shall be entitled to retain a security interest in the Stock to secure payment of the Corporation's obligation, which security interest shall be relinquished by the Stockholder upon full payment for all of his Stock to be purchased under this Agreement.

(c) <u>Closing</u>.

(i) <u>Date</u>. The closing of any purchase under Article 1 or 2 of this Agreement shall take place at 1:00 o'clock p.m. on the day provided in this Paragraph (c) at the offices of Lamon, Elrod & Harkleroad, P.C., 229 Peachtree Street, N.E., Suite 2500, Atlanta, Georgia 30043, or at such other time and place as shall be fixed by written agreement of the parties hereto (the "Closing"). In the case of a purchase under Article 1, the Closing of the purchase of the Stock of a Stockholder shall take place on the ninetieth (90th) day after the death, disability or termination of the employment of the Stockholder, or the ninetieth (90th) day after the qualification of a deceased Stockholder's personal representative, whichever is later. In the case of a purchase under Article 2, the Closing shall take place on the first day of the month following the date on which the selling Stockholder's offer was accepted by the Corporation or the respective purchasing Stockholders.

(ii) <u>Delivery at Closing</u>. At the Closing, the selling Stockholder or his personal representative shall deliver to the Corporation or to the purchasing Stockholders, as the case may be, certificates representing all of the stock to be purchased, duly endorsed, free and clear of all liens, claims or encumbrances, with evidence of payment of all transfer taxes and fees, if any. The Corporation or the purchasing Stockholders, as the case may be, shall deliver to the selling Stockholder or his personal representative the payment (by certified or cashier's check) or the promissory note, as provided in Paragraphs (a) and (b) of this Article. In connection with the Closing, the Corporation and all Stockholders and their personal representatives, if any, shall do all things necessary and appropriate to accomplish the purchase and sale.

If the selling Stockholder or his personal representative does not tender the certificates for the shares of Stock to be purchased as provided herein at the Closing, the Corporation shall cause the transfer books of the Corporation to reflect that such shares of Stock have been canceled or transferred, as the case may be, and the Corporation or the purchasing Stockholders, as the case may be, shall tender to the selling Stockholder or his personal representative the payment (by certified or cashier's check) or the promissory note, as provided in Paragraphs (a) and (b) above. After the transfer books of the corporation have been so modified and after such tender of payment has been made (whether or not accepted by the selling Stockholder, his estate, or his personal representative), neither the selling Stockholder, his estate, nor his personal representative shall be considered to own Stock in the Corporation and shall have no rights as a stockholder to the extent of the shares of Stock so canceled or transferred under the terms of this Paragraph.

Each Stockholder hereby appoints the Corporation as his agent and attorney-in-fact for the purpose of executing and delivering any and all documents necessary to convey such Stockholder's Stock pursuant to the provisions of this Paragraph in the event the Stockholder is not present at the Closing, and any conveyance by such agent and attorney-in-fact shall be a conveyance of all of the Stockholder's right, title, and equity in and to the Stock. This power of attorney is coupled with an interest and shall not expire upon the death or incapacity of a Stockholder, nor may this power of attorney be terminated by any Stockholder as long as this Agreement remains in effect.

(d) Stock Purchases Occurring on the Same Date.

If more than one purchase of Stock made pursuant to this Agreement shall occur on the same date, such purchases shall take place at the same time on that date and shall be deemed to have occurred simultaneously.

Comment:

The payment of the purchase price under stock redemption agreements of professional corporations is almost always made on an installment basis, in order to permit the professional corporation to accumulate the appropriate funds. Paragraph (a) of above Article 3 provides such a delay, and a description of the method of payment, including the promissory note, is a definite necessity for any stock retirement agreement of a professional corporation.

The installment method of reporting income will be available to the seller if installment sale treatment is not refused and if deferred payments are received. See Section 453 of the Code.[4]

Some stock retirement agreements for professional corporations provide that the corporation will be required to make an immediate payment of the purchase price in an amount equal to the insurance proceeds obtained by the corporation on key man insurance on the life of the deceased professional employee. Where there is sufficient key man insurance purchased on the lives of the professional employees to fund fully the purchase price, such a provision may be desirable, for it will provide immediate funds to the estate of the deceased shareholder and will eliminate the possibility that, during the installment payment period, the professional corporation may in one way or another misuse the insurance proceeds and be unable to make the installment payments. The possibility that the professional corporation may be unable to make the payments due to misuse may, however, be alleviated by requiring personal guarantees of the remaining shareholders. Since the repeal of the carryover basis provisions originally adopted in the Tax Reform Act of 1976, very little or no capital gain should be recognized by the estate of a deceased shareholder because the estate will receive a "stepped-up" basis in the stock equal to the fair market value at the time of death. See Section 1014 of the Code.

Paragraph (b) of above Article 4 permits the corporation to defer payments longer, at a reduced interest rate in those situations where the stock of a shareholder is redeemed prior to his death, disability, or reaching normal retirement age. In reaching a decision on the appropriate interest rate to be charged, Section 483 of the Code should be taken into consideration. This Section "imputes" interest on certain installment sales where there is no stated interest or the stated interest rate is below 9%. Where this occurs, the Service will, automatically, impute interest into an installment sale transaction at the rate of 10%.[5] This imputed interest does not vary the amount of the proceeds received by the selling shareholder; it simply varies the character of the proceeds, by converting 10% of each payment from long-term capital gain into ordinary income. In order to avoid Section 483, it is generally advisable to have a stated interest rate of at least 9% in all agreements. Generally, agreements entered into prior to increases in the imputed interest rate will be "grandfathered," i.e., will be subject to the imputed interest rates at the time of execution unless material changes are made in the agreements after the imputed interest rates change.[6]

ARTICLE 4

(Option 2)

PAYMENT OF PURCHASE PRICE

(a) Purchase Pursuant to Article 1.

If a Stockholder's Stock is purchased pursuant to the provisions of Article 1, the purchase price of the Stock of a Stockholder shall be evidenced by a negotiable, installment promissory note executed by the Corporation bearing interest at _____ percent (___%) per annum, calling for _____ (___) consecutive, equal monthly payments payable on the first day of each month, with the first such payment to be made on the date of purchase; provided, however, that if such purchase is made because of the termination of the Stockholder's employment with the Corporation, either by the stockholder or the corporation and irrespective of the reason for or the cause of such termination, prior to his death or disability and prior to his attaining age _____ (___) or because the Stockholder desires to sell his shares of Stock in the Corporation prior to his attaining age _____ (___), such installment note shall bear interest at _____ percent (___%) per annum, calling for _____ (___) consecutive, equal monthly payments payable on the first day of each month, with the first such payment to be made on the date of purchase. Such note shall provide that, upon default in the payment of any installment of interest or principal, all remaining installment payments shall, at the option of the selling Stockholder or any other holder of said note, become immediately due and payable. Said note shall also give the Corporation the option of prepayment in whole or in part at any time. Such note shall be in the form attached hereto as Exhibit "A". Upon the sale of his Stock to the Corporation, the Stockholder shall be entitled to retain a security interest in the Stock to secure payment of the Corporation's obligation, which security interest shall be relinquished by the Stockholder upon full payment for all of his Stock to be purchased under this Agreement.

The provisions of this Paragraph (a) shall also apply to the estate of the deceased Stockholder or to the personal representative of any disabled or incapacitated Stockholder.

(b) Closing.

(i) Date. The closing of any purchase under Article 1 of this Agreement shall take place at 1:00 o'clock p.m. of the day provided in this Paragraph (b) at the offices of Lamon, Elrod & Harkleroad, P.C., 229 Peachtree Street, N.E., Suite 2500, Atlanta, Georgia 30043, or at such other time and place as shall be fixed by written agreement of the parties hereto (the "Closing"). The Closing of the purchase of the Stock of a Stockholder shall take place on the ninetieth (90th) day after the death, disability, termination of the Stockholder's employment with the Corporation, or notification by the Stockholder to the Corporation of his desire to sell his Stock, or the ninetieth (90th) day after the qualification of a deceased Stockholder's personal representative, whichever is later.

(ii) Delivery at Closing. At the Closing, the selling Stockholder or his personal representative shall deliver to the Corporation or buying Stockholder certificates representing all of the shares to be purchased, duly endorsed, free and clear of all liens, claims or encumbrances, with evidence of payment of all transfer taxes and fees, if any. The Corporation or buying Stockholder shall deliver to the selling Stockholder or his personal representative the payment (by certified or cashier's check) or the promissory note, as provided in Paragraph (a) of this Article. In connection with the Closing, the Corporation and all Stockholders and their personal representatives, if any, shall do all things necessary and appropriate to accomplish the purchase and sale.

If the selling Stockholder or his personal representative does not tender the certificates for the shares of Stock to be purchased as provided herein at the Closing, the Corporation shall cause the transfer books of the Corporation to reflect that such shares of Stock have been canceled, and the Corporation shall tender to the selling Stockholder or his personal representative the payment (by certified or cashier's check) or promissory note, as provided in Paragraph (a) above. After the transfer books of the Corporation have been so modified and after such tender of payment has been made (whether or not accepted by the selling Stockholder, his estate, or his personal representative), neither the selling Stockholder, his estate nor his personal representative shall be considered to own Stock in the Corporation and shall have no rights as a stockholder to the extent of the shares of Stock so canceled or transferred under the terms of this Paragraph.

(c) Stock Purchases Occurring on the Same Date.

If more than one purchase of Stock made pursuant to this Agreement shall occur on the same date, such purchases shall take place at the same time on that date and shall be deemed to have occurred simultaneously.

Comment:

This option to Article 4 should be used in conjunction with Option 2 to Article 1. The comments contained in Option 1 to Article 4 also apply here.

ARTICLE 5

LIFE INSURANCE

The Corporation shall have the right to purchase insurance on the lives of any or all of the Stockholders to fund its obligations under this Agreement. The Corporation agrees to pay premiums on said insurance policies, if any, and shall provide proof of payment of premiums to any Stockholder who requests such proof. If a premium is not paid within ten (10) days after its due date, the insured shall have the right to pay such premiums and be reimbursed therefor by the Corporation. In the event that the Corporation decides to purchase life insurance on any Stockholder, each Stockholder hereby agrees to cooperate fully by performing all the requirements of the insurer which are necessary conditions precedent to the issuance of life insurance policies. The Corporation shall be the sole owner of the policies issued to it and it may apply any dividends toward the payment of premiums.

If any Stockholder's employment with the Corporation is terminated during his lifetime, and if such Stockholder and the Corporation shall mutually agree, such Stockholder shall have the option of purchasing from the Corporation the insurance policy or policies on his life owned by the Corporation by paying to the Corporation an amount equal to the cash surrender value thereof (or the interpolated terminal reserve value computed by the life insurance company issuing such policy or policies, if greater) on the date of transfer, less any existing indebtedness charged against the policy or policies.

Notwithstanding the provisions of this Agreement, any life insurance company which has issued a policy of life insurance subject to the provisions of this Agreement is hereby authorized to act in accordance with the terms of such policy as if the Agreement did not exist, and the payment or other performance of its contractual obligations required by any such policy shall completely discharge such company from all claims, suits and demands of all persons whomsoever.

If, at any time after the death of a Stockholder, the Corporation shall receive the proceeds from any insurance policy owned by the Corporation on the life of the deceased Stockholder, the Corporation shall immediately use such funds to prepay the installment payments owing to the estate or any beneficiary of the deceased Stockholder, as provided in Article 4.

Comment:

This section provides a mechanism whereby the corporation may purchase "key man" life insurance on the lives of the shareholders. Key man life insurance is more fully described in section [14.02](5), *infra*. Key man insurance may be whole life or term insurance which the corporation purchases on the lives of the shareholders (the corporation is the owner and the beneficiary and pays the premium on the policies). Although the premium is not deductible by the corporation, the proceeds payable under the policy are not taxable income to the corporation.

This paragraph permits the shareholder, with the consent of the corporation, to have the option to purchase the policy from the corporation in the event his employment is terminated. Further, the shareholder has the option of paying the premium in the event that the corporation fails to do so. Some stock retirement agreements specifically provide that the shareholder shall have the unilateral option to purchase the policy at the cash value. In the past, such a requirement has been considered by the Service to be an incident of ownership which would require that the proceeds of the policy be includable in the estate of the deceased shareholder.[7] However, this position was not upheld by the courts and the Service agreed, reluctantly, that no incident of ownership existed.[8] Where the shareholder may only purchase the policy with the consent of the corporation, the problems encountered in Rev. Rul. 79-46 are obviated.

The purchase of life insurance to provide funding under a stock retirement agreement creates the potential of a "tontine" situation, where on the death of one shareholder the surviving shareholders may receive a windfall. A tontine effect may occur where insurance is purchased to fund fully the cost of the stock retirement agreement. Following the untimely death of several shareholders, the remaining shareholders will effectively retain the entire professional corporation at no cost, since the amounts required to be paid to the estates of the deceased shareholders will be entirely funded by life insurance. The tontine effect is heightened further where the death benefit is over-insured. For example, where the value of each shareholder's interest under the stock retirement agreement approximates $50,000, and the corporation maintains a $100,000 key man policy on the life of each shareholder, the remaining shareholders will not only be in a position to purchase the stock of a deceased shareholder but will have an additional windfall of $50,000. For this reason, where the shareholders of a professional corporation feel that more insurance is warranted, consideration should be given to providing insurance in another manner, such as additional group term or group permanent life or split dollar insurance, where the insurance proceeds will be payable directly to the estates of the deceased shareholders or their assignees. Conversely, the value of additional insurance proceeds could be included as an asset of the professional corporation for valuation purposes, assuming that the deceased shareholder will receive some portion of the insurance proceeds.[9]

The ownership of whole life insurance by a professional corporation which will be used to fund the purchase of stock under a stock retirement agreement may also make the professional corporation subject to the accumulated earnings tax where the accumulated cash values are substantial. There are also other problems related to the accumulated earnings tax and the use of life insurance, and these are discussed in section [9.04], *supra*.

ARTICLE 6

TRANSFER IN VIOLATION OF THIS AGREEMENT

The Stockholders may not, either singly or collectively, under any circumstances sell or transfer their Stock in the Corporation other than in accordance with the terms of this Agreement, nor may they pledge, assign, or otherwise encumber their Stock therein.

In the event any Stockholder (hereinafter referred to as the "Offending Stockholder") sells, assigns, transfers, gives, pledges, encumbers, or otherwise disposes of or grants a security interest in any of the Stock owned by him otherwise than in strict accordance with the terms of this Agreement, then, in addition to the right to any other remedies hereunder, including specific performance, the Corporation shall have the option to purchase such Stock from the person, trust, association, company, firm or corporation (the "Transferee") to whom such Stock has been sold, assigned, transferred, given, pledged, encumbered, or otherwise disposed of, for an amount, in cash, equal to the amount paid by such Transferee for such Stock or fifty percent (50%) of the value of such Stock, as set forth in the most recent certification of value set forth as Schedule A attached hereto, whichever is less. The payment of such purchase price shall be by certified or cashier's check at the closing described in the following Paragraph.

The Corporation may exercise the purchase option provided for in this Article by giving written notice to the Transferee of the Offending Stockholder at any time within one year after the Corporation receives actual notice of such sale, assignment, transfer, gift, pledge, encumbrance or other disposition of Stock otherwise than in accordance with the provisions of this Agreement. The closing of any purchase under this Article shall take place at the offices of Lamon, Elrod & Harkleroad, P.C., 229 Peachtree Street, N.E., Suite 2500, Atlanta, Georgia 30043 at 1:00 o'clock p.m. on the thirtieth (30th) day after the Corporation delivers such notice to the Transferee, or at such other time and place as shall be fixed by written agreement of the Corporation and the Transferee. At such closing, the Transferee shall deliver to the Corporation certificates representing the Stock transferred to him by the Offending Stockholder, duly endorsed in blank for transfer, or with duly executed blank stock powers attached, free and clear of all liens, claims or encumbrances, with evidence of payment of all transfer taxes and fees, if any, and accompanied by such further instruments as may be necessary or desirable, in the opinion of counsel for the Corporation, to effect the transfer of such Stock. The Corporation shall deliver to the Transferee or his personal representative the payment (by certified or cashier's check) for the Stock, as provided in this Article. Acceptance by any purchaser, assignee, transferee, donee, pledgee or other party of any of the Stock held by any of the Stockholders shall evidence conclusively the consent of such party to all the terms and provisions hereof, and all such parties agree to do all things necessary and appropriate to accomplish the purchase and sale pursuant to this Article.

If the Transferee or his personal representative does not tender the certificates for the shares of Stock to be purchased as provided herein at such closing, the Corporation shall cause the transfer books of the Corporation to reflect that such shares of Stock have been canceled upon the tender by the Corporation to the Transferee or his personal representative of a certified or cashier's check for the full amount of the purchase price as provided in this Article. After the transfer books have been so modified and after such tender of payment has been made (whether or not accepted by the Transferee or his personal representative), neither the Transferee nor his personal representative shall be considered to own Stock in the Corporation and shall have no rights as a stockholder to the extent of the shares of Stock so canceled under the terms of this Article.

Comment:

Every stock retirement agreement should contain a provision limiting the ability of the shareholders to transfer or dispose of their stock in a manner which is not in accordance with the agreement. Some stock retirement agreements also contain a provision similar to that in the second paragraph of the above Article 6 which specifically provides that the corporation has the right to repurchase the stock transferred in violation of the agreement. Other stock retirement agreements simply provide that such a transfer is void.

ARTICLE 7

EFFECT OF AGREEMENT

This Agreement shall not supersede or constitute a change in any provisions of the Articles of Incorporation or Bylaws of the Corporation, employment agreements, deferred compensation agreements, or other documents and agreements presently in effect, except insofar as they relate to the purchase and sale of Stock. This Agreement does, however, supersede and totally revoke any existing stock retirement or stock purchase agreement between the Corporation and any Stockholder or Stockholders.

Comment:

It is important to provide that all prior agreements, whether oral or written, and all provisions of the corporation's bylaws and articles of incorporation are specifically superseded by the stock retirement agreement and that the stock retirement agreement incorporates all understandings of the parties.

ARTICLE 8

FUTURE STOCKHOLDERS AND ADDITIONAL
STOCK PURCHASES

It is understood and agreed that the provisions of this Agreement shall control the present Stockholders of the Corporation and that future stockholders of the

Corporation shall be required to agree to the provisions stated herein as a condition of their becoming stockholders. The provisions of this Agreement shall also apply to all Stock in the Corporation now owned or hereafter acquired by the Stockholders.

Each certificate evidencing shares of Stock of the Corporation shall bear the following legend on the face of such certificate:

> The shares of stock represented by this certificate (and all transfers thereof) are subject to the terms of a Stock Retirement Agreement dated _____, by and between _____ and its shareholders, a copy of which is on file at the principal offices of the Corporation and is available for inspection during reasonable business hours. No transfer of any share represented by this certificate shall be valid unless made in accordance with such Agreement.

In the event such legend cannot practicably be placed on the face of such certificate, either alone or in conjunction with other legends required by law or by agreement to be placed on the face of such certificate, the legend shall be set out in conspicuous type on the back of the certificate, and notice thereof shall be given in conspicuous type on the front of the certificate.

Comment:

It is also important that all future shareholders of the professional corporation be bound by the agreement and all existing shareholders be bound by the agreement with regard to additional stock which they may purchase. Further, each stock certificate should contain an appropriate legend indicating that the stock is subject to the agreement. Such a legend will place any potential purchaser on notice that the stock is ''restricted'' and that he should review the agreement prior to purchasing the stock. Many state statutes require that stock notices be placed on the ''face'' of the certificate or that an appropriate declaration be placed on the face referring to the full notice on the reverse side.

ARTICLE 9

CORPORATE ACTION AND STOCKHOLDER GUARANTY

If the Corporation is unable to make any purchase required of it under this Agreement, or to fulfill any obligation incurred in connection therewith, because of the provisions of applicable statutes or of its Articles of Incorporation or Bylaws, the Corporation agrees to take such action as may be necessary to permit it to make such purchases and the Stockholders agree that they will also take such action (other than making additional capital contributions to the Corporation or guaranteeing debts of the Corporation) as may be necessary for the Corporation to make such purchases when, as, and if required.

If the Corporation shall, nevertheless, be unable or refuse to purchase all of a Stockholder's Stock or be unable to make payment upon any note given to a Stockholder in the purchase of his Stock, the obligation of the Corporation with respect to the shares of Stock which the Corporation shall be unable or refuses to purchase shall be deeemed assumed by the remaining Stockholders. The obligation of the Corporation to purchase a Stockholder's Stock under this Agreement shall be primary and the aforementioned obligation of the Stockholders shall be secondary and conditional. If the Stockholders are called upon to purchase the Stock of a Stockholder hereunder, each remaining Stockholder shall be obligated to purchase, on the same terms and conditions as would be applicable to a purchase by the Corporation, such portion of the Stock offered for sale as the number of shares owned by him (on the date on which the Corporation's obligation to purchase such Stock arose) shall bear to the total number of shares of Stock owned by the Stockholders on such date, excluding the Stock which the Corporation is obligated to purchase.

Comment:

Most state laws impose restrictions on the ability of a corporation to redeem its stock. The primary restriction imposed by state laws is that corporations may not redeem stock where a redemption would ''impair the capital'' of the corporation, and most states limit the use of corporate assets for redemptions to ''unreserved and unrestricted capital surplus'' or ''current net earnings and capital surplus.'' On the other hand, some states, such as Delaware, simply require that a redemption of stock not impair capital.[10] Further, some states require that a majority vote of the board of directors must occur prior to the redemption. Consequently, it is important to require in a stock retirement agreement that the shareholders will take such corporate action as is necessary in order to permit the corporation to implement the redemption. This normally means action by the board of directors.

It is often necessary in professional corporations to provide that the remaining shareholders in a professional corporation will personally guarantee the debt of the corporation to the surviving shareholder or his estate. This is particularly important where the agreement does not provide that all of the insurance proceeds payable upon the death of a shareholder must be paid in a lump sum. In determining what manner of guarantee to employ, the guarantee may either be absolute or based only upon matters which occur outside the control of the shareholders. Further, the guarantee may be joint and several or each shareholder may only be required to guarantee a pro rata portion of the corporation's debt. The guarantee above is absolute, requiring the shareholders to purchase a pro rata share of the stock of the shareholder. It is probably advisable to use an absolute guarantee because conditional guarantees leave open a significant fact, i.e., has a condition been met? A conditional guarantee follows at the end of this comment. The remaining shareholders can also be required to guarantee the payment of any notes given by the corporation in the redemption of stock.

A significant tax problem arises with the use of shareholder guarantees. If, under the guarantee, the shareholders have the primary obligation to purchase the stock of a deceased shareholder, and the stock is actually purchased by the corporation, the Service will take the position that a constructive dividend has occurred. That is, the corporation will be considered to have distributed a constructive dividend (of the funds required to purchase the stock) to the surviving shareholders who then purchased the stock from the deceased shareholder's estate and contributed the stock to the corporation.[11] Consequently, it is very important that any guarantee under an entity-type stock redemption agreement not contain a provision requiring that the remaining shareholders have primary responsibility for the purchase of the stock. On the other hand, if the agreement provides that the corporation is primarily responsible for the redemption and that the remaining shareholders are only secondarily or conditionally responsible in the event that the corporation defaults, no constructive dividend should be imposed.[12] The above guarantee is drafted in this manner.

The following guarantee imposes a joint and several liability upon the remaining shareholders to fulfill the corporation's primary obligation to purchase the stock, but only in the event that the corporation is unable to purchase the stock due to the actions of the remaining shareholders.

> If, nevertheless, the Corporation is unable to fulfill the obligations incurred in connection with the purchase of a Stockholder's Stock pursuant to this Agreement, the remaining Stockholders shall not, except as hereinafter provided, be personally liable to fulfill the obligations of the Corporation hereunder. The remaining Stockholders shall become jointly and severally liable with respect to such obligations of the Corporation only if the Corporation shall be unable to satisfy such obligations in whole or in part and such inability is attributable, directly or indirectly to events occurring subsequent to the date of purchase including, but not limited to:
>
> (i) The dissolution or liquidation of the Corporation, whether voluntary or involuntary;
>
> (ii) The reorganization or merger of the Corporation;
>
> (iii) The sale, exchange, or other transfer of the assets of the Corporation to any third party or to a remaining Stockholder, if such sale, exchange or transfer was not in the ordinary course of business or if such sale, exchange, or transfer results in a significant contraction of the business activities of the Corporation;
>
> (iv) The payment of unreasonable or excessive compensation to remaining Stockholders, the determination of which shall be governed by the definition of unreasonable compensation provided for in Section 162(a)(1) of the Internal Revenue Code of 1954, and the case law thereunder;
>
> (v) The payment of dividends to the remaining Stockholders;
>
> (vi) Loans or other payments or distributions from the corporation to a Stockholder or any third party;
>
> (vii) Any purchase by the Corporation of its own Stock, if such purchase is accomplished in a manner other than that provided for in this Agreement; or
>
> (viii) The termination of any employment relationship between the Corporation and any remaining Stockholder, if, at any time during the five (5)

years immediately following such termination, the Stockholder engages in activities comparable to those performed by the Stockholder for the Corporation within _____ miles of its principal place of business.

The obligation of the Corporation to fulfill any obligations incurred in connection with a purchase of Stock pursuant to this Agreement shall be primary, and the aforementioned obligation of the Stockholders shall be secondary and conditional. The liability of the Stockholders hereunder shall continue untill all obligations under this Agreement have been satisfied; provided, however, that in no event shall a remaining Stockholder be liable on such obligations, if, at all times subsequent to the date of a purchase of Stock hereunder, he acted in good faith and in a manner he reasonably believed to be in the best interest of the Corporation.

ARTICLE 10

AMENDMENT AND TERMINATION

This Agreement may be altered, amended or terminated at any time only by a written instrument executed by all the parties hereto. This Agreement shall terminate upon the occurrence of any of the following events:

(i) The bankruptcy, receivership or dissolution of the Corporation; or

(ii) The death or disability of all Stockholders within a period of ninety (90) days, in which case the Agreement shall be deemed to have terminated on the day immediately preceding the date on which the first such Stockholder shall have died or become disabled.

The termination of this Agreement as herein provided shall have no effect on any obligation of the parties which arose pursuant to the purchase of Stock under this Agreement prior to its termination under this Article.

Comment:

It is important to provide for the termination of the agreement on the occurrence of certain events. Specifically, the provision above states that the agreement will terminate upon the death or disability of all of the shareholders within a period of 90 days, with the result being that the shareholders will not receive the amounts stated under the agreement, but will simply receive a pro rata share of the funds remaining in the corporation upon its liquidation.

ARTICLE 11

INSTRUCTIONS TO EXECUTOR

Each Stockholder shall execute a will directing his respective executor to perform according to this Agreement and to execute all documents necessary to effectuate the purposes of this Agreement. The failure, however, of any Stockholder to execute such a will shall not affect the rights of any Stockholder or the obligations of his estate, as provided herein.

Comment:

Although the above provision is not absolutely necessary, since the stock retirement agreement will be binding upon the shareholder and his estate, it is advisable for the shareholders to place instructions in their wills for their executors to comply with the agreement.

ARTICLE 12

NOTICES AND OTHER COMMUNICATIONS

Any notice, offer, acceptance of an offer, or other communication provided for or required by this Agreement shall be in writing and shall be deemed to have been given when delivered by hand or when deposited in the United States mail, certified or registered, return receipt requested, postage prepaid, properly addressed to the party to whom such notice or other communication is intended to be given. The proper address of the Corporation shall be:

_____

_____

_____

and in the case of any other party, shall be such address as such other party may have previously furnished in writing to the Corporation or such other party's last known address.

Comment:

This is a typical "boilerplate" provision and normally does not come into play until disputes arise. It is, nevertheless, important that a stock retirement agreement contain such a notice provision.

ARTICLE 13

ENFORCEABILITY

The parties hereto do hereby recognize and acknowledge that it is impossible to measure in money the damages which would result to a party or to the personal representative of a deceased party by reason of a failure of any of the parties to perform any obligations imposed upon him or it under this Agreement. Therefore, if any party or the personal representative of any deceased party should institute an action or proceeding to enforce the provisions hereof, any person against whom such action or proceeding is brought hereby waives the claim or defense that such party or such personal representative has an adequate remedy at law, and such person shall not urge in any action or proceeding the claim or defense that such a remedy at law exists.

Comment:

It is important to give the corporation and the remaining shareholders the right to seek specific performance in order to force the terminated shareholder or the estate of a deceased shareholder to comply with the terms of the agreement.

ARTICLE 14

REPRESENTATIONS AND WARRANTIES

Each Stockholder hereby represents and warrants that he owns his Stock in the Corporation free and clear of all liens, restrictions, pledges, and encumbrances, that he has made no disposition of such Stock which has not been recorded on the books and records of the Corporation, and that he has granted no proxy rights or other voting rights with respect to such Stock. Each Stockholder and the Corporation further represent and warrant that:

(i) No preferred stock, stock options, warrants or other equity interests in the Corporation are outstanding;

(ii) The stock transfer records of the Corporation are accurate and reflect all requests to date for registration of shares of Stock; and

(iii) The Corporation has no outstanding bonds, debentures, or other debt instruments of any type that are convertible into Stock.

Comment:

It is important that the shareholders represent to the corporation that they are the owners of the stock covered by the stock retirement agreement, and, in a like manner, the corporation should represent to the shareholders that there are no other outstanding shares.

ARTICLE 15

TERM

The term of this Agreement shall be for twenty (20) years from the date of execution hereof, unless terminated or extended as provided herein. However, when a new Schedule A to this Agreement is executed, such execution shall constitute the execution of a new Stock Retirement Agreement as modified by said Schedule A and the term of said new Agreement as so modified shall be for twenty (20) years from the date of the execution of said Schedule A.

ARTICLE 16

POWER OF ATTORNEY

Each Stockholder hereby appoints the Corporation as his agent and attorney-in-fact for the purpose of executing and delivering any and all documents necessary to convey such Stockholder's Stock pursuant to the provisions of this Agreement. In the event the Stockholder refuses to comply with the provisions of this Agreement or is not present at the Closing, any conveyance by such agent and attorney-in-fact shall be a conveyance of all of the Stockholder's right, title and equity in and to the Stock. This power of attorney is coupled with an interest and shall not expire upon the death or incapacity of a Stockholder, nor may this power of attorney be terminated by any Stockholder as long as this Agreement remains in effect.

ARTICLE 17

MISCELLANEOUS

(a) Invalid Provisions.

The invalidity or unenforceability of any one or more of the particular provisions of this Agreement shall not affect the enforceability of the other provisions hereof, all of which are inserted conditionally on their being valid in law, and in the event one or more provisions contained herein shall be invalid, this instrument shall be construed as if such invalid provision had not been inserted, and if such invalidity shall be caused by the length of any period of time, the size of any area or the scope of activities set forth in any provision hereof, such period of time, such area or scope or all, shall be considered to be reduced to a period, area, or scope which would cure such invalidity.

(b) Binding Effect.

This Agreement shall be binding upon and inure to the benefit of the parties hereto and their respective heirs, executors, administrators, legal representatives, successors and assigns.

(c) Counterparts.

For the convenience of the parties hereto, any number of counterparts hereof may be executed, and each such executed counterpart shall be deemed to be an original instrument.

(d) Governing Law.

This Agreement shall be interpreted, construed, and enforced in accordance with the laws of the State of Georgia.

(e) Authority.

All provisions, terms and conditions of this Agreement have been duly consented to, ratified, approved, and adopted by the Board of Directors of the Corporation, and appropriate authority has been delegated to the undersigned officers of the Corporation to execute this Agreement.

(f) Article or Paragraph Headings.

The Article and Paragraph headings contained in this Agreement are for convenience only and shall in no manner be construed as a part of this Agreement.

(g) Gender.

Where the context so requires, the masculine gender shall be construed to include the feminine, a corporation, a trust, or other entity, and the singular shall be construed to include the plural and the plural and singular.

(h) Entire Agreement.

This Agreement constitutes the sole and entire agreement of the parties with respect to the matters contained herein, and any representation, inducement, promise, or agreement, whether oral or written, which pertains to such matters and is not embodied herein shall be of no force or effect.

Comment:

These are standard boilerplate provisions which should be included in any stock retirement agreement.

IN WITNESS WHEREOF, the parties hereto have executed this Agreement at _____, in the County of _____, State of Georgia, on the date and year first above written.

(CORPORATE SEAL)

ATTEST: XYZ CORPORATION

By: _____   By: _____
    Secretary   President

                                                   STOCKHOLDERS:

Signed, sealed and sworn   _____
to this ____ day of   Address: _____
_____, 19____   _____

_____   _____

Witness
                                                   Address: _____
                                                            _____

_____   _____

Notary Public
                                                   Address: _____
                                                            _____

SCHEDULE A

VALUATION OF STOCK IN XYZ CORPORATION

The undersigned mutually agree on this ____ day of _____, 19____, that, for the purposes of this Stock Retirement Agreement, each share of Stock of the Corporation has a value of $_____.

(CORPORATE SEAL)   XYZ CORPORATION
ATTEST:

_____   By: _____
Secretary   President

                                                   STOCKHOLDERS:

                                                   _____

                                                   _____

                                                   _____

[11.03] THE DEPARTING SHAREHOLDER WHERE THE CORPORATION STAYS IN EXISTENCE

(1) Tax Impact

Where a shareholder employee terminates his employment and either the corporation or the remaining shareholders purchase his stock, any gain recognized on the sale of the stock will, generally, be treated as long-term capital gain. That is, where a shareholder sells his stock to the other shareholders, either under a cross-purchase agreement or under the option provided in Option 1 to Article 2 in the stock retirement agreement in section [11.02](3), *supra*, the selling shareholder will recognize long-term capital gain to the extent that the amount received exceeds his adjusted basis in the stock.[13]

On the other hand, where the shareholder's entire stock interest is redeemed by the corporation, the redemption will normally be considered a sale under either Section 302 or 303 of the Code.[14] Where a shareholder's entire stock interest is not redeemed by the corporation, the redemption may be treated as a dividend and taxed as such to the extent of the earnings and profits of the professional corporation. In order for a redemption of a shareholder's stock to be considered a sale or exchange producing long-term capital gain, the redemption must meet one of the following four requirements:

(1) All of the shareholder's stock must be redeemed. For purposes of determining a shareholder's interest in a corporation, stock of certain family members and others who own stock in the same professional corporation will be attributed to the shareholder under Section 318 of the Code. This is generally not a problem in professional corporations except where family member professionals are involved. Even then, where a family member has stock redeemed in order to terminate his entire interest in the professional corporation, the family attribution rules may be waived.

(2) The redemption must be a "substantially disproportionate" redemption under Section 302(b)(2) of the Code. A redemption will not be considered "substantially disproportionate" unless after the redemption the shareholder owns less than 50% of the total combined voting power of the stock of the corporation and the percentage of the corporation's voting stock owned (actually and constructively) by him after redemption is less than 80% of the voting stock interest which he owned (actively and constructively) before the redemption. The stock attribution rules of Section 318 of the Code are applied to substantially disproportionate redemptions in determining stock ownership and, consequently, it may be difficult to achieve a substantially disproportionate redemption in a family-owned professional corporation.

However, under Section 302(c)(2) of the Code, the family attribution rules may be waived upon the complete termination of a shareholder's interest if immediately after the redemption and for the next 10 years the selling shareholder has no interest in the corporation other than as a creditor (nor may he be an officer, director, or employee). Also, no part of the stock redeemed can have been acquired by the selling shareholder within the last 10 years from a person whose stock would be attributable to the selling shareholder under Section 318(a) and the selling shareholder cannot, within the past 10 years, have transferred any stock in the corporation to a person whose stock would be attributable to him under section 318(a) unless such person is no longer a shareholder of the corporation or the stock owned by that person is redeemed in the same transaction.

(3) The redemption is "not essentially equivalent to a dividend" under Section 302(b)(1) of the Code. This provision is difficult to meet and should only be used as a last resort and not as a planning tool unless a prior letter ruling from the Service is obtained.

(4) The redemption occurs under Section 303 of the Code. Section 303 of the Code provides for sale treatment upon the partial redemption of stock of a deceased shareholder even though the sale would not, under the rules of Section 302, be considered a sale. In order to come within the provisions of Section 303, the stock included in the decedent's gross estate must exceed 50% of the value of the gross estate reduced by losses, debts and expenses. This requirement may be met by aggregating stock of two or more corporations if the decedent's stockholdings in each corporation were more than 75%.

Since, in most professional corporations, a professional shareholder's entire interest in the corporation will be redeemed upon his death, disability, or termination of employment, the above rules relating to the tax treatment of redemptions will usually not be of significant import. Also, Section 303 will generally not be applicable in the professional corporation setting because the value of the stock of the professional corporation will not constitute 50% of the value of the gross estate (reduced by losses, debts, and expenses).

(2) Settlement Agreement and Release

Even where professional employees terminate their relationship with the professional corporation in an amicable manner, it is best to prepare a short separation agreement which establishes the rights and duties of the corporation and the terminating shareholder with regard to the various matters which will be under consideration at that time (such as the payment of additional compensation under the employment agreement, the amount payable under the stock retirement agreement, the disposition of client/patient files and records, etc.). When a shareholder leaves a professional corporation, it is almost always preferable to have a "clean break" with all amounts due to the departing shareholder paid at the time of the separation. Some consideration should also be given to the operation of the corporation's qualified retirement plans and the possible forfeitures which may occur in the account of the terminating shareholder. In many situations, the vesting schedules used in professional corporation retirement plans are sufficiently long that a shareholder employee's employment may be terminated before he becomes fully vested. In such a situation, most terminated shareholder employees feel that the full amount of the retirement plan account belongs to them, even though the vesting schedule in the retirement plan would provide otherwise. Obviously, the trustee of the plan cannot, without amendment, pay to the terminating professional the entire balance of his retirement plan accounts if such payment violates the vesting schedule. On the other hand, the vesting schedule in the retirement plan could be amended to provide full vesting for the terminated participant (such an amendment would also apply to all other participants). It is also possible for the professional corporation to make an additional payment to the departing shareholder to compensate him for the forfeited amounts. While there is nothing that would prevent such a payment, it is a good policy not to begin such a practice because the qualified plans may be disqualified. See section [15.02](11), *infra*. Further, the size of the retirement funds may make this impossible as a practical matter.

In many cases where a shareholder's employment with the professional corporation is terminated, either by the corporation or by the shareholder, prior to his normal retirement date, it is preferable to terminate his employment immediately and pay the amounts provided under the employment agreement. The form employment agreement provided in section [10.01](1), *supra*, makes provision for this. It is the authors' experience that, only in rare instances, will a shareholder's continued employment after notice of termination has been given be of benefit either to the shareholder or to the corporation. There is often resentment in this situation and, where the shareholder is voluntarily terminating his employment, he often uses the waiting period to consolidate his position and take what business he can away from the existing professional corporation. Below is a form of settlement agreement which can be used upon the termination of a shareholder's employment.

SETTLEMENT AGREEMENT

SETTLEMENT AGREEMENT made and entered into this _____ day of _____, 19__, by and between _____ ("Employee") and _____ ("Corporation"), a Georgia professional corporation.

W I T N E S S E T H:

WHEREAS, Employee has served as an employee of Corporation under an Employment Agreement dated _____ (the "Employment Agreement"); and

WHEREAS, Employee is a shareholder of Corporation owning _____ shares of the common stock thereof; and

WHEREAS, there exists a stock retirement agreement dated _____, between the Corporation and all of its shareholders, including Employee, governing the transfer of shares of stock in the Corporation (the "Stock Retirement Agreement"): and

WHEREAS, Employee is a participant in Corporation's qualified profit sharing plan which was adopted on _____ (the "Profit Sharing Plan"), and money purchase pension plan, which was adopted on _____ (the "Money Purchase Pension Plan"); and

WHEREAS, Employee terminated his employment with Corporation effective _____; and

WHEREAS, the parties have reached agreement upon the amounts due to Employee under the Employment Agreement, the Stock Retirement Agreement, the Money Purchase Pension Plan and the Profit Sharing Plan; and

WHEREAS, Employee and Corporation desire to finally terminate Employee's relationship with Corporation as an employee, shareholder, and retirement plan participant by providing to Employee the agreed amounts due to him under the Employment Agreement, the Stock Retirement Agreement, the Profit Sharing Plan, and the Money Purchase Pension Plan;

NOW, THEREFORE, in consideration of the mutual covenants contained herein, the parties hereto agree as follows:

1. Employment Agreement. The parties agree that Employee has received from Corporation the sum of $_____, as _____ (___) months' termination pay in settlement of his rights under the Employment Agreement. Employee also agrees that from and after _____, 19____, he has not, and will not, hold himself out as an employee of Corporation. Corporation also agrees that from and after _____, 19____, neither it nor its officers will represent to the general public that Employee is an employee of the Corporation.

2. Patient Charts, Records, and X-Rays. Corporation agrees that, from and after the date of this Agreement, Employee shall have access to the charts, records, and X-rays maintained by the Corporation on patients treated by Employee while he was an employee of the Corporation, which charts, records, and X-rays will be made available to Employee at the offices of the Corporation during reasonable business hours upon reasonable advance request.

3. Qualified Retirement Plans. The parties agree that heretofore or contemporaneously with the execution of this Agreement, _____, the trustee of the Plans, has been instructed, at Employee's request, to transfer his entire vested interest in the Money Purchase Pension Plan and the Profit Sharing Plan to _____ to be held for him. The vested amounts due to Employee as determined under the terms of the Plans consist of the following:

Profit Sharing Plan:

$_____, plus earnings to the date of distribution.
Money Purchase Pension Plan:

   a) _____ (insurance policy) No. _____(the "Policy") on Employee's life, plus the cash value thereof as of _____, of $_____.

b) Cash balance of $_____, plus earnings thereon to the date of distribution, but reduced by life insurance premiums paid on the Policy since _____ of $_____ and the unvested portion of the cash value of the Policy of $_____. The parties hereto agree that, because Employee's employment with Corporation terminated on _____, he will not be entitled to participate in the Profit Sharing Plan or the Money Purchase Pension Plan for the Plan years ended _____.

4. <u>Stock Retirement Agreement</u>. The parties agree that, heretofore or contemporaneously with the execution of this agreement, Corporation has paid to Employee the sum of $_____ in exchange for his _____ shares of stock of the Corporation and in settlement of Employee's rights under the Stock Retirement Agreement.

5. <u>General Release</u>. Employee for himself, his heirs, executors, administrators, and assigns, does hereby release, quitclaim, acquit, and forever discharge Corporation and its agents, shareholders, officers, directors, and employees, individually, and all others at interest therewith, and their successors and assigns, of and from any and all actions, causes of action, claims, demands, damages, costs, loss of service, expenses, compensation, covenants, contracts, controversies, agreements, promises, and any and all liabilities of any kind of nature whatsoever, at law and equity or otherwise, which he has ever had, now has, or which he, his heirs, executors, administrators and assigns hereafter can, shall, or may have, on account of, or arising out of, any rights which he may have under the Employment Agreement, the Stock Retirement Agreement, the Profit Sharing Plan, and the Money Purchase Pension Plan.

The terms of this release are contractual and not merely a recital. This release is given voluntarily and is not based on any representations other than those made herein, and Employee agrees that this release may be pled as an absolute and final bar to any and all claims which may be made on account of the matters aforesaid.

6. <u>Entire Agreement</u>. This Agreement contains the entire agreement between the parties hereto, and the parties make no representations other than those contained herein.

IN WITNESS WHEREOF, Corporation has caused this Agreement to be executed by its duly authorized officers and its seal to be hereunto affixed, and Employee has hereunto set his hand and seal, all being done in duplicate originals on the day and year first above written, with one original being delivered to each party.

(CORPORATE SEAL)   CORPORATION

ATTEST:

By: _____   By: _____
    Secretary   President

                                                   EMPLOYEE

_____   _____ (Seal)
Witness

NOTES TO CHAPTER 11

1. See Rev. Rul. 62-217, 1962-2 C.B. 59, and Rev. Rul 69-75, 1969-1 C.B. 56. Under Section 83, the professional corporation will also be required to make appropriate federal income tax withholding on the value of the stock given, and this may create a problem. Treas. Regs. §1.83-6.

2. 69 T.C. 1049 (1978), gov't appeal dismissed *nolle pros* 9/6/78. Also see *Chekow*, 1978-330 T.C.M. (payments were compensation and not for stock, no stock was issued); *Edward A. Ruestow,* 1978-147 TCM (amount determined to be severance pay); *Muscogie Radiology, infra,* Chapter 16, note 1.

3. See, generally, *Estate of John Federick Davis,* 37 T.C.M. 341, ¶78,069 P-H Memo T.C. (1978), Rev. Rul. 78-58 1978-1 C.B. 279. Also see Stechel, "Restricted Buy-Sell Agreements Can Limit Estate Value of a Business Interest," 44 *J. Taxation* 360 (1976).

4. The Installment Sales Revision Act of 1980 has eliminated many of the previous requirements of installment reporting, such as the requirement that not more than 30% of the total selling price could be received in the year of sale. Further, installment reporting is now available on a single, deferred lump sum payment, and the selling price need not be in excess of $1,000.

5. See Treas. Regs. §1.483-1(c)(2). The Treasury Department, from time to time, increases the imputed interest rate, and has proposed increases effective July 1, 1981, so that a 10% rate of interest (compounded semi-annually) will be imposed if a 9% per annum simple interest rate is not provided. See Prop. Treas. Regs. §1.483-1. This Treasury proposal which has increased the imputed interest rates from 6%/7% to 9%/10% has received strong criticism and may eventually be withdrawn. However, ERTA has apparently provided Congressional sanction to these increased rates because ERTA decreased rates only for certain land sales between family members.

6. See, for example, Treas. Regs. §1.483-1(b)(4) and (d)(4).

7. See Rev. Rul. 79-46, 1979-1 C.B. 303.

8. *Estate of John Smith,* 73 T.C. 307 (1979), acq. 1981 Prentice-Hall *Federal Taxes* at ¶55-154. Also see L.R. 8049002.

9. See Appleman, "A New Approach to Buy-and-Sell Agreements," 30 *Taxes* 821 (1952).

10. See Delaware General Corporate Code, Section 160.

11. See Rev. Rul. 69-608, 1969-2 C.B. 43.

12. See Rev. Rul. 69-608 (Situation 5), *id.*

13. Under Section 1001 and Section 1221 of the Code.

14. There are certain reporting requirements for redemptions. See Treas. Regs. §1.6043-1(a) regarding Form 966 and Treas. Regs. §1.6043-2(a) regarding Forms 1096 and 1099L.

CHAPTER **12**

General Business Expenses

[12.01] GENERAL RULES

Section 162 of the Code allows as a deduction all ordinary and necessary expenses paid or incurred during the taxable year in carrying on any trade or business. However, certain items, such as illegal bribes, kickbacks, fines and penalties, are not deductible as business expenses. See Sections 162(c) and (f) of the Code.

In determining whether an item is deductible as a business expense under Section 162 of the Code, the primary questions to be answered are the following:[1]

(1) Does the expense (or a portion of the expense) meet the general requirements for deductibility?
(2) What proof regarding the nature of the expenditure must be maintained by the taxpayer?
(3) When may the deduction be taken?
(4) Who may take the deduction?

(1) General Requirements for Deductibility

The general requirements for the deductibility of expenses are that they must be incurred in carrying on a ''trade, business or profession,'' must be ''ordinary and necessary,'' and must be ''reasonable.''

(a) *Carrying on a Trade or Business*

There is no specific definition of the term ''carrying on a trade or business'' that covers all situations, and, in the past, the courts have struggled to create a single, acceptable definition.[2] For purposes of the incorporated professional, how-ever, this general requirement will be met if the professional is *actively* engaged in carrying on his profession. Thus, this requirement will generally not present a problem unless the professional is using his dormant professional practice as a subterfuge for deducting expenses which would otherwise be personal. This may be a potential problem with retired professionals, see section [12.05], *infra*.

(b) *Ordinary and Necessary Expenses*

Because most professions satisfy the trade or business requirement, the primary test to determine deductibility is whether the expenses are "ordinary and necessary." The delineation of what is an ordinary and necessary business expense is made, not in the Treasury Regulations, but in the case law. The leading case in the area is *Welch v. Helvering*.[3] The court in *Welch* specifically states that the test is two-pronged: the expense must be both "necessary" and "ordinary." In general practice, however, if an expense is considered an ordinary expense, it will also be considered necessary.[4] An ordinary business expense is one which is generally accepted in the industry and which is not a capital expenditure. In order to be necessary, an expenditure need only be appropriate and helpful, not indispensable.

(c) *Reasonableness*

In order to be deductible, business expenses must not only be ordinary and necessary but they must also be reasonable in amount. It has long been recognized that Congress did not intend to allow deductions automatically in unlimited amounts.[5] A distinction must be made between what is reasonable and what is "lavish and excessive."

(2) Proof in Support of Deductions

A taxpayer who claims a deduction for a trade or business expense must be able to prove, if audited by the Service, that the expenditure was actually made and qualifies as a deduction under the above-described rules of Section 162 of the Code. The genesis of this rule of proof is the general principle that deductions are considered a matter of legislative grace and, therefore, taxpayers seeking to take deductions must be able to point to an applicable statute and show in what manner a specific deduction comes within that statute.[6] Disputes most often arise between taxpayers and the Service due to lack of adequate records showing the amount of the deduction claimed and the reason for which the expense was actually incurred. Even though the taxpayer has this burden of proof, the courts have not always refused to grant deductions where a taxpayer is unable to establish all of the necessary facts to sustain the exact amount of the deduction. Approximates or close estimates have been permitted in clear business settings under the so-called "Cohan Rule."[7] In order to obtain deductions based on estimates, it must be shown that the expense was in fact incurred and there is some basis for the approximation.

In addition to the general burden of proof requirement for all deductions, certain deductions, such as entertainment, gift, and travel expenses, are required to pass additional substantiation tests.[8] These substantiation rules are extremely complicated and the professional should consult his advisors concerning them. In general, the amount of the expense, the time and place where incurred, the business purpose for the expense, and the business relationship of the taxpayer to the other individuals involved must be provided. Effective December 31, 1962, the special rules of Section 274(d) in the Code override the Cohan Rule with regard to entertainment, travel, and business gifts.[9]

The following is a general description of what type of substantiation is required under Section 274:

(a) Entertainment Expenses[10]

(1) The amount of each separate expenditure, with certain exceptions for incidental items, such as taxi fares, telephone calls, and tips, which may be aggregated on a daily basis.

(2) The date of the expenditure.

(3) The place of the expenditure, including name and address, and the type of entertainment involved, such as dinner or theater.

(4) The business purpose for the entertainment and the nature of the business discussion or activity conducted.

(5) The business relationship, including the occupation or other information regarding the persons entertained, and a listing of the total number of persons entertained, including nonbusiness guests.

(b) Travel Expenses

(1) The amount of each separate expenditure for travel away from home, i.e., transportation and lodging, with the exception that the daily costs of the meals for the traveler may be aggregated.

(2) The dates of departure and return and a listing of the number of days spent on business.

(3) The names of the cities and towns visited.

(4) The business reason for the travel and the business benefit obtained.

(c) Gift Expenses

(1) The cost to the taxpayer.

(2) The date of the gift.

(3) A description of the gift.

(4) The business purpose for the gift and the nature of the business benefit obtained.

(5) The business relationship between donee and donor, including donee's name and title.

Obviously, the substantiation requirements necessary to meet the burden of proof for normal deductions are considerable, and some might think that the requirements of Section 274 are excessive. In any event, these requirements do exist and will be examined closely by Service agents upon audit. Consequently, professionals and their advisors should take steps to assure that, to the extent possible, the substantiation requirements can be met. Since the Regulations require that the taxpayer must substantiate each element of the expenditure ''by adequate records or by sufficient evidence corroborating his own statement,'' the best method of establishing the expenditure is to retain a statement of the expense plus documentary evidence. The statement of the expense, which should be made at or near the time at which the expenditure is made, may be contained in an account book, a diary, or an expense form. It is always best to make these entries at or soon after the time of the expenditure when the details will be fresh in the mind of the taxpayer. Most credit card charge slips provide, on the reverse side, room for making such notations, and, for this reason, many professional corporation advisors suggest that all professional expenses be paid through the use of credit cards. Even if credit cards are used, it is often advisable to keep a separate account of the reason for the expense through the use of internal corporate expense reporting forms. An appropriate expense reporting form is added as Exhibit 1 at the end of this chapter.

In addition to the statement of the taxpayer regarding the expense, the taxpayer should also maintain documentary evidence, such as receipts, paid bills, and canceled checks, showing the nature of the expenditure. Normally, it is best if the documentary evidence is attached to the statement of the taxpayer (such as the expense form) and then kept in the corporate records.

A note of caution: Care should be taken by the professional and his advisors not to become lax in accounting for business and entertainment expenses. Insufficient records may lead to the disallowance of such expenses (as a normal result of an audit) and possibly raise the question of whether the professional corporation should be recognized as a separate entity.

(3) When Is an Expense Deductible?

The business expenses of a professional corporation will be deductible by the corporation in accordance with the accounting method adopted for the corporation. See section [8.04], *supra*, regarding accounting methods. In general, an expense must be paid (in the case of a cash method taxpayer) or incurred (for an accrual method taxpayer) by the last day of a taxable year in order to be deductible for that year. Since most professional corporations operate on the cash basis, items must actually be paid prior to the end of the year and the items must be paid subject to a legal obligation. When a taxpayer voluntarily assumes the obligation of another or pays an amount for which there exists no legal obligation, a business deduction will generally not be allowed. For example, deposits made by a cash basis professional corporation, which are returnable, are not deductible and prepayments for future expenses, such as interest, are also not deductible by a cash basis taxpayer.[11]

Special rules disallow deductions to accrual basis professional corporations where the accrued expense is not paid within 2½ months following the end of the corporation's fiscal year.[12] Under Section 267(a)(2) of the Code, an accrual corporation which claims deductions for accrued expenses or interest owing to "related" persons may suffer loss of the deductions due to lack of payment within 2½ months following the end of the fiscal year. A deduction which is lost under this section is *permanently* lost and cannot be deducted even in later taxable years when payment is actually made. Section 267(a)(2) was enacted to eliminate a previous tax avoidance method available to accrual basis corporations (accrual of expense payments to cash basis taxpayers who could avoid receipt and thereby postpone taxability). "Related parties" include family members and any individual who owns more than 50%, in value, of a corporation's stock. There are certain rules of contructive ownership under Section 267(c) which attribute stock of family members (to family members) for determining 50% ownership. Section 267 will apply to professional corporations which operate on the accrual method.

(4) Who May Deduct Business Expenses?

In general, a person may deduct his own business expenses, but a person who makes an expenditure on behalf of another is not entitled to a deduction. The courts have generally not considered the payment of another's expenses to be "ordinary" in carrying on one's trade or business. This issue is usually not of major importance for professional corporations, because professional corporations will, generally, pay all of the business expenses related to the professional practice. This issue does arise, however, when the individual professional pays and claims deductions for expenses for his professional practice which are, in fact, not paid by the professional corporation. In the past, the Service has taken the position that corporate officers (professionals) are not entitled to deduct on their personal returns expenses which are normally attributable to the business of the corporation. If a corporate officer is treated as having the separate trade or business of being an employee of the professional corporation, the Service frequently questions whether expenditures claimed as deductions by the officer are those "ordinarily" incurred by an employee. This issue can be resolved, however, by requiring the professional employee, in his employment agreement, to incur certain travel, entertainment, and other professional expenses, on behalf of the professional corporation without reimbursement. Generally, the courts have recognized that a requirement in an employment agreement creates an obligation in the employee to incur business expenses and, consequently, have permitted the deduction by the employee of his expenses.[13]

(5) Practical Considerations

It has long been recognized that a professional person engaged in the conduct of his profession is engaged in a trade or business and is entitled to deduct expenses paid or incurred to maintain that practice, assuming that the expenses are ordinary and necessary.[14] For example, see Regulations §1.162-6, which states:

> A professional man may claim as deductions the cost of supplies used by him in the practice of his profession, expenses paid or accrued in the operation and repair of an automobile used in making professional calls, dues to professional societies and subscriptions to professional journals, rent paid or accrued for office rooms, the cost of the fuel, lights, water, telephone, etc. used in such offices, and the hire of professional assistants. Amounts currently paid or accrued for books, furniture, and professional instruments and equipment, the useful life of which is short, may be deducted.

The problem which most professionals encounter involves not the general business expenses of running a professional practice, but those expenses which can be considered somewhat personal, such as the use of automobiles, entertainment, convention expenses, and long distance telephone tolls. Because the general nature of the expenses of a professional practice does not vary substantially from practice to practice, expenses which have personal attributes are easy for an examining agent to identify. For this reason, many professional corporation advisors follow the so-called "pig theory." That is, that "shoats get fat, pigs get fatter, and hogs get butchered." In other words, the professional corporation should pay for those expenses which are related to the professional practice and the professional should pay for those expenses which are not. By having the professional corporation pay for all personal and professional expenses, the income statement of the professional corporation may set forth what appears to be an abusive situation to an examining agent. If the agent feels that abuse has occurred, he will examine not only abusive expenses, but also all expenses, and may disallow more expenses than he would have had the professional corporation only paid for and deducted the expenses with some business purpose.

On the other hand, some professional corporation advisors follow the "first offer" theory, i.e., that the income tax return for the professional corporation is the first offer made by the taxpayer in negotiating his tax liability and that the Service should respond to it, if it desires, with a counteroffer (i.e., an audit). Under the "first offer" theory, all expenses with any relationship whatsoever to the professional practice (and possibly some without) are deducted on the return in the hope that the return will not be audited and the expenses will, consequently, be deductible. The authors feel that the use of the "first offer" approach should be avoided because it often (and sometimes rightfully so) antagonizes examining revenue agents and causes them to view the examined professional corporation as an abusive situation. It is also possible for the examining agent to impose the 5% negligence penalty under Section 6653(a) of the Code in "first offer" situations. The Code does not provide for the negotiation of a taxpayer's liability.

[12.02] TRANSPORTATION EXPENSES

(1) General Rules

Under Section 162 of the Code, a taxpayer is allowed a deduction for the ordinary and necessary transportation expenses incurred in the pursuit of his trade or business. However, Regulations §1.162-2 excludes from deductible transportation expenses those expenses which are primarily personal in nature. Further, under Regulations §1.162-2(e), commuting expenses are nondeductible. Transportation expenses which are not deductible can be divided into two broad categories: (1) general use of the automobile for personal activities, such as vacations, and (2) commuting expenses.

The use of corporate automobiles on personal trips does not give rise to a business deduction. Whether a trip is primarily related to the corporation's trade or business or is primarily personal in nature depends upon the facts and circumstances of each case. The amount of time during the trip which is spent on personal activity compared to the amount of time spent on activities relating to the trade or business is an important factor in determining whether the trip is primarily personal. If, for example, a taxpayer spends one week at a location for activities which are directly related to his trade or business and subsequently spends an additional five weeks there for a vacation or other personal activities, the trip will be considered primarily personal in nature in the absence of a clear showing to the contrary.[15]

(2) Commuting

The majority of the questions involving transportation expenses involve the commuting expenses. Generally, transportation deductions are considered commuting expenses and are nondeductible if the taxpayer is traveling to his principal place of work from his residence or is returning to his residence from his principal place of work. On the other hand, transportation expenses to and from temporary work sites are deductible as business expenses. Commuting expenses may be expenses for travel within the general area of the business or employment and travel outside such area.

(a) *Travel Outside General Area of Business or Employment*

If an employee is required to work at a temporary location outside the general area which is his principal place of employment, reasonable transportation expenses for daily round trips from his residence to such temporary location are deductible.[16]

(b) *Travel Within General Area of Business or Employment*

The daily commuting expenses of an individual employed on different days at different locations within the same general area of his principal place of employment are not deductible unless he is also working at some other business location during the day. For example, if an employee is required to work part of the same day at each of two different locations, traveling between these two locations represents business travel expenses which are deductible.[17] A question has arisen, however, with regard to initial transportation expenses to a temporary place of work within the general area of employment and transportation expenses for returning to home from a temporary place of work within the general work area. For example, assume that Dr. X travels from home to the hospital to make rounds, then travels to the office to see patients for the majority of the day, and then travels back to the hospital to make rounds prior to returning to home. Under published Revenue Rulings, the first and last trips of the day are considered nondeductible commuting expenses rather than business trips (unless the individual's home is also his principal place of business). The trips from the hospital to the office and from the office to the hospital are considered deductible transportation expenses. Nevertheless, many professionals deduct the full transportation expenses without substantial Service objection because the hospital location is seen as a temporary work place. The cost of commuting would, in addition, be deductible if the physician were required to carry bulky tools and equipment in his automobile because there was no other efficient way to get them to the office.[18]

(c) *Internal Revenue Service Attempt to Modify Existing Rules*

In 1976, the Internal Revenue Service issued Rev. Rul. 76-453,[19] which effectively classifies all expenses incurred in traveling between a taxpayer's residence and a place of work, even a temporary place of work, as nondeductible commuting expenses and treats any reimbursement to the employee by the employer for such expenses as wages. The new ruling will probably result in a much closer examination of transportation expenses by examining agents, in order to disallow deductions for the first and last trip of the day. The general principle of Rev. Rul. 76-453 is illustrated in Example 8 of that ruling which states as follows:

> F, who regularly works in an office located other than in F's residence, has duties that require activities in that office and at various other locations of clients. On any given day, F may (1) go directly from home to the office and return home from the office; (2) go from home to the office, later go to see a client during the day, and then return home; or (3) go from home directly to see a client, later go the office, and then return home. In each situation, F has not incurred any deductible transportation expenses for any of the costs incurred in going from home to the first work location and in returning from the last work location.

If, on the other hand, F had traveled to the office, then to meet a client, then back to the office, and then home, F would be entitled to deduct the cost of the travel om the office to the client's office and back to F's office. An exception to the eneral rule is contained in Example 3 of the Rev. Rul. 76-453, which states as ollows:

> A, a self employed individual, maintains a principal place of work in a downtown office building. In order to attend a business meeting in a distant city, A drives directly from A's residence to an airport, flies to the distant city, and later the same day returns directly to A's residence. Due to the length of time required to make the trip and attend the meeting, it is not reasonable to expect A to stop at the office on the way out of town and on the way back. However, in effect, A is traveling between one work location and another. Transportation costs incurred between work locations are deductible business expenses. Therefore, A should be entitled to deduct the lesser of (1) the expenses incurred in traveling between A's residence and the business meeting and (2) the expenses that would have been incurred if A had traveled between A's office and the business meeting by the same mode or modes of transportation.

> However, because the difference between (1) and (2) is generally *de minimis* compared with the total transportation expenses incurred for the trip, the Service will allow A to deduct the expenses incurred in traveling between A's home and the business meeting.

Based on Rev. Rul. 76-453, it will be preferable for professionals to go by 1e office first before traveling to a client's office and then to return to the office fter the meeting with the client before returning home.

Implementation of Rev. Rul. 76-453 has been suspended. The effective ate of Rev. Rul. 76-453 was suspended indefinitely by Announcement 7-147(IR-1884).[20] Also, the Service cannot issue any ruling or final regulation hanging the tax treatment of such transportation expenses before June 1, 1981.[21] Consequently, the existing rules will continue to apply.[22] However, ERTA did not efer the power of the Treasury Department to issue Regulations changing the tax reatment of transportation expenses and professionals should be aware that regula- ons under Rev. Rul. 76-453 may be forthcoming.

(d) *Tax Cases Reach Divergent Results*

Cases involving ordinary and necessary commuting expenses have been ecided by considering whether the taxpayer is going to the place where he begins vork and is returning from the place where he ceases work.[23] In *Bovington v. Jnited States*,[24] the court held that the nature of a medical doctor's business, when 1e is engaged in the private, general practice of medicine, making house calls and isiting with various medical institutions, precludes an arbitrary application of the ommuter expense rule holding that every time a physician leaves his family and usiness he is "commuting," thus incurring nondeductible personal expenses. The court in *Bovington* allowed the taxpayer to deduct all transportation expenses he incurred in excess of the amount attributable to round trip travel between his home and office. Similarly, in *Norman S. Brandes*[25] the Tax Court disallowed the deduction of certain automobile expenses because of the taxpayer's failure to prove that they were in addition to amounts incurred in normal travel between his primary office and home. The question of whether traveling from home to an initial hospital visit will facilitate the deduction of travel expenses is also questionable where the doctor's office is located adjacent to the hospital.[26]

Other cases have been more restrictive regarding the deductibility of physicians' automobile expenses. The courts have pointed out that a physician's travel from his home directly to his office is a nondeductible commuting expense and found the rule to be no different when the physician travels from his home to a hospital or to another place to practice his profession. *Jasper H. Arnold*[27] and *Richard F. Tyson.*[28] The courts in both cases appear to base their decisions on the rationale that the hospital is one of the physician's regular places of work (i.e., travel expenses to the hospital to handle emergency cases also are nondeductible, personal commuting expenses).[29] However, these cases do allow a deduction by a physician for automobile expenses incurred on travel between his office and the hospital where he regularly works.

In summary, the cases appear to indicate and the Service would contend that, when a physician is engaged in activities which require his presence at his office as well as at hospitals, nursing homes, and similar locations, the amount which he may deduct for using his automobile is limited to the expenses incurred in traveling from his office to the other work sites and back. However, an argument can be made under *Bovington* that an arbitrary application of the commuter expense rule should not be applied and that all expenses other than those incurred in normal travel between the office and residence are non-personal expenses and are, therefore, deductible.[30]

(3) Who Should Own the Cars; the P.C. or the Professionals?

Professional corporation advisors often differ on whether professional automobiles should be purchased by the professional corporation or whether they should be purchased by the individuals, with the professional corporation possibly paying maintenance charges. Although there are very real, formal differences in the manner in which professional automobiles are owned, the authors see very little substantive differences which are quantifiable from a tax point of view. That is, if the use of the car owned by the corporation is fully deductible, the use of the car owned by the individual should, likewise, be fully deductible. Further, the investment tax credit provided under Section 46 of the Code is available for the automobile, whether owned by the corporation or the professional. On the other hand, some accountants feel that it is best to keep individual returns ''clean'' and place as many business deductions as possible on the professional corporation's return. However, substantial amounts of business entertainment and automobile expenses are readily apparent when listed in an income and expense statement of a professional corporation. The primary factor in deciding whether automobiles should be owned by the professional corporation is the personalities of the various professionals involved. Automobiles can very easily become a source of animosity which shatters the equilibrium of the corporation, because some individuals prefer to drive "clunkers" while others prefer to drive the latest models. For this reason, the authors often recommend that automobiles be purchased outside the professional corporation unless the professionals can agree to specific terms for handling the automobiles within the corporation.

(a) *Ownership of Automobiles by the Professional Corporation*

Where an agreement has been made to require the professional corporation to own the automobiles, the question arises regarding what type of cars should be purchased. There are several different alternatives. The professional corporation can buy the same car for each professional (this is very seldom done because professionals usually cannot come to a consensus). On the other hand, each professional will be allowed to pick his car, with the purchase price of the car being limited to a specific maximum dollar amount or a specific percentage of his salary. It is possible for problems with constructive dividends to arise if the purchase price of an automobile is over the basic maximum and, consequently, the maximum should be set high enough to permit individuals to purchase the desired vehicles. On the other hand, it is very difficult to compensate the professional whose automobile costs less than the allowed amount.

Because it is almost inevitable that some personal use of corporate-owned automobiles will occur, most professional advisors suggest that some accommodation be made for possible personal use by the professional. Some advisors recommend that a fixed dollar amount per month or a certain percentage of the total cost of operating and maintaining the vehicle be supplied by the corporation as the cost of personal use. The professional may be required to reimburse the corporation for this amount, or the amount may be included in the income of the professional. Including the cost of personal use in the income of the professional will cost the professional less out-of-pocket dollars. That is, if the personal use of the automobile is determined to be $600 per year and that amount is required to be included in the income of the professional, the tax cost of that income will be $300 (assuming a 50% rate). However, if the professional is required to reimburse the corporation in an amount equal to $600, he must do so with after-tax dollars, with an effective cost of $1,200 (at the 50% rate, $1,200 of income equals $600 in tax with $600 remaining to reimburse to the corporation). The authors feel that either method is acceptable but that, where the personal use component is included in the income of the professional, there is a possible argument to be made by the Service that the amounts included in income are not compensation but are constructive dividends. Such an argument can be countered by a specific provision in the professional's employment agreement stating that such amounts are compensation or by the annual adoption of a resolution of the board of directors to the same effect.

(b) *Personal Ownership of the Automobiles*

Where the individual professionals own the automobiles, questions arise with regard to the deduction of expenses and the amount of reimbursement, if any.

In computing deductions, the professional may compute the entire expense of owning the automobile, including depreciation, insurance, taxes, gasoline, and tires, and deducting those expenses on his personal return as a business expense. Obviously, only the expenses which relate to the business use of the automobile may be deducted and, generally, a proration of expenses is required. Although there is no specific rule with regard to the method of prorating business and nonbusiness use, the authors feel that any proration based on other than mileage or months of use will be subject to scrutiny by the Service. Of course, expenses may not be deducted by the professional to the extent they are reimbursed. In an attempt to facilitate the proration of expenses, most professionals use one car as the "business car" and one car as the "family car." However, depending upon the value of the automobiles in question, it may be advantageous to use both cars, partially, for business use. For instance, if the family car has a higher purchase price, it is possible to generate a larger depreciation deduction by depreciating 50% of the purchase price of both the family and business cars as opposed to 100% of the purchase price of the lesser-valued business car.

A professional may, however, choose not to deduct the total amount of actual business expenses and use the optional method provided by the Service. Normally, the choice of the optional method should be made only after a calculation of the deductions which would be provided by the use of the actual expense method. Under the optional method for usage after 1979,[31] a taxpayer may deduct $.20 per mile for the first 15,000 miles of use in any year and $.11 per mile for any excess use. Of course, miles for which the professional is reimbursed (at the full rate) may not be deducted, but mileage reimbursement at a lesser rate may produce a differential deduction. For example, mileage reimbursed by the employer at $.10 per mile will permit $.10 per mile deduction during the first 15,000 miles. The optional method may only be used on automobiles which have not previously been fully depreciated using accelerated methods of depreciation. If the vehicle is fully depreciated, the standard mileage rate is $.11 per mile.

Reimbursements made by the corporation to the professional may be either a flat $.20 per mile (a figure which will be increased from time to time by the Service) or an actual reimbursement of the expenses incurred by the professional. However, to the extent that reimbursements exceed the flat $.20 per mile rate, the employee must substantiate to the employer the actual out-of-pocket expenses incurred.[32] Some advisors feel that a professional corporation should also consider reimbursing the professional for the ''depreciation'' incurred by him on the automobile as a means to ''bail out'' additional funds. That is, the depreciation which is reimbursed is exactly covered by the depreciation deduction taken by the professional, resulting in a tax-free distribution of income. If the professional has sufficient salary to cover the depreciation taken on the automobile, the effect will be the same because the depreciation deductions will offset salary. Unless the professional faces a reasonable compensation problem (as described in Chapter 13, *infra*), the authors would advise against reimbursing the professional for depreciation expenses.

Disposition of the business automobile may also cause problems. The investment tax credit provided under Section 46 of the Code is available to the professional who personally owns his automobile and is normally prorated based on business and personal use. The professional should be aware, however, that the credit is subject to recapture in the event that the automobile is disposed of (or converted to personal use) prior to the end of the useful life on which the credit was based.[33] Similarly, any disposition of the business automobile by the professional may trigger depreciation recapture under Section 1245 of the Code. In order to avoid depreciation recapture, the business automobile may be used as a trade-in on a new vehicle or may be converted to personal use and a new business automobile purchased.[34]

(c) *Substantiating Automobile Expenses*

As described in the previous section dealing with the general expense rules, the use of automobiles by professionals and professional corporations almost always becomes an issue during any Internal Revenue Service audit. Although the Cohan Rule for estimating expenses has been specifically found to be available in computing travel expenses,[35] examining agents are increasingly reluctant to allow estimated automobile expenses where the taxpayer does not maintain a specific log, on a daily basis, indicating the mileage traveled and the purpose of the trips. For this reason, the authors advise that professionals should maintain a daily log of their travels or, at the very least, should be in a position to reconstruct daily travel through the use of an appointment calendar.

(d) *Should a Professional Lease His Automobile?*

The determination of whether a professional or his professional corporation will lease the business automobiles normally depends upon the ease of acquiring the automobiles rather than the cost, since in most situations the cost of lease payments will exceed the cost of purchasing.[36] Most automobile leases are ''open end,'' giving the lessee the ability to acquire the automobile for the residual value stated in the lease (or at least the responsibility of paying the lessor that residual value). Such leases are very similar to financing transactions, because the leasing company must borrow funds from another source such as a bank or automobile manufacturer, and an additional rate of interest must be added. Even though leasing will normally produce a slightly larger overall cost, leasing does provide a number of amenities, such as ease in purchasing and disposing of automobiles (which will normally be done by the lessor), acquiring the automobile with no down payment (an open-end lease has, in effect, a balloon payment equal to the residual value of the automobile at the end of the lease), and the ability to obtain a maintenance agreement.[37] Some accountants feel that leasing an automobile also provides an easier method of deducting automobile costs whch is less likely to be challenged by the Service. Nevertheless, it is difficult to determine whether there is any quantifiable benefit from leasing because the approach taken on audit will vary with the particular examining agent.

Consequently, the authors do not feel that it can be stated categorically that leasing automobiles by a professional or by a professional corporation is best. On the other hand, if the professional has, for other reasons, decided to lease his business automobile, it can be said that leasing will not make the deduction of automobile business expenses more difficult by either the professional or his professional corporation.

(4) Airplanes Owned by Professional Corporations

It is not unusual that a number of professionals enjoy flying and see a professional corporation (with its lower corporate tax bracket under the surtax exemption) as the perfect entity through which to buy and maintain an airplane. It can be said without question, however, that the appearance of an airplane on the balance sheet (and the associated expenses on the income statement) of a professional corporation will invite Service scrutiny.[38] On the other hand, the authors have a number of professional corporation clients which own and maintain aircraft for use in the profession. If the professional use of the aircraft can be documented by comparing the log book to specific business travel and if it can be illustrated that the use of a private plane is more advantageous to the professional corporation by, for example, conserving the professional's time, deductions for airplane ownership and operation should be allowed. However, it must be remembered that airplane expenses should be substantiated just as any other travel expense. The authors have also found that examining agents typically ask whether the professional has a pilot's license. If the professional does not have a pilot's license (and must hire a professional pilot) or if a professional does have a pilot's license but also hires a professional pilot, the authors have found that examining agents are much less likely to decide that the airplane is maintained for the personal gratification of the professional.[39]

[12.03] CONVENTION EXPENSES

(1) General Rules

Ordinary and necessary expenses incurred in the furtherance of a trade or business are deductible under Section 162 of the Code. Expenses of professionals for conventions, other than for nondeductible nonbusiness purposes, such as social or political, which meet these requirements of Section 162 are deductible.[40] However, the convention expense area is one which the Service feels is subject to abuse and such expenses will be closely scrutinized on audit (probably because professionals always seem to locate their conventions in exotic places).

Where a taxpayer attends a convention in the United States and as an incident of the trip engages in some personal activity, such as a vacation, that part of the total expense which can be allocated to the taxpayer's trade or business is deductible notwithstanding the incidental personal activities.[41] However, Section 274(c) of the Code and Regulations §1.274-4(e) have removed the allocation requirement. Consequently, expenses incurred while traveling in the United States are deductible without regard to the allocation requirements of Section 274(c) if business is the main purpose of a part business, part pleasure trip. Thus, a deduction is allowed for the entire transportation cost plus the cost of meals and lodging while in transit and at the business location.

(2) Foreign Conventions

Beginning in 1977, the deduction available for expenses for foreign conventions was severely restricted. Foreign conventions include any convention, seminar, or similar meeting held outside the United States, its possessions, its trust territory of the Pacific, and Canada and Mexico ("North America"). Deductions are allowed only with regard to two foreign conventions per year with the following restrictions:

(1) Deductible transportation cannot exceed the cost of the lowest coach or economy fair available and such transportation costs are deductible only if at least one-half of the total days of the trip are spent on business related matters.

(2) Deductions for meals, lodging and other subsistence expenses will be allowed only for days when at least six hours of business activity are scheduled and the taxpayer attends at least two-thirds of such activities.

(3) The amount of subsistence expenses for any day cannot exceed the per diem rate that applies to U.S. civil servants in that area during the calendar month that the convention begins.

(4) The taxpayer must comply with numerous reporting requirements.

Effective January 1, 1981, Section 274(h) was amended to provide new rules for foreign conventions. Under the new rules, the two-conventions limit, the economy air fare, and the per diem requirements were eliminated, and no deductions will be allowed for a foreign convention unless it is "as reasonable" for the convention to be held within North America. The authors feel that the "as reasonable" standard may be more difficult to meet than were the old rules.

Before any expenses for foreign conventions are deducted, and for that matter, before any foreign convention is attended, careful attention to these rules would be advisable.[42]

(3) Spouse's Convention Expenses

The convention expenses of an employee's spouse will, when paid by the employer, be deductible if the ordinary and necessary rules of Section 162 of the Code are met. Regulations §1.162-2(c) states as follows:

> Where a taxpayer's wife accompanies him on a business trip, expenses attributable to her travel are not deductible items unless it can be adequately shown that the wife's presence on the trip has a bona fide business purpose. The wife's performance of some incidental service does not cause her expenses to qualify as deductible business expenses. The same rules apply to any other members of the taxpayer's family who accompany him on such a trip.

These regulations provide a two-pronged test: (1) the trip must be primarily for business purposes, and (2) the wife's presence must have a bona fide business purpose and the services she performs must be other than incidental. In recent years, the Tax Court has added a third test which requires that the spouse's services must not be merely social.[43]

Those cases in which the spouse attends the convention for strictly social purposes are easily identified.[44] On the other hand, those situations in which the spouse attends the convention for a bona fide business purpose are also easily identified.[45] Obviously, the courts scrutinize the facts of each particular case to determine whether the spouse assisted the employee and a primary question is whether the spouse attended the business functions. There is, consequently, a broad area between these two extremes, such as where the spouse attends the convention at the request of the employer to provide a number of helpful but not essential duties, such as a host or hostess. The Service has continued to disallow expenses where spouses do not actually participate in the business function of the meeting.

There have, however, been a number of recent cases in which the convention expenses of spouses have been held to be deductible even though the spouse's functions appear to be merely social and the spouse did not participate in the business activities.[46] The Service has, however, continued to consider the convention expenses of spouses as an issue to be examined on audit and the Tax Court often agrees with the Service.[47] Further, the Service and the Tax Court take the position that disallowed convention expenses of spouses produce gross income for the employee.[48]

Even where a spouse's convention expenses are disallowed, the corporation and/or taxpayer-employee are entitled to deduct the travel expenses for the employee (including all automobile travel expenses), the lodging for the employee (computed at the single room rate), and all meals for the employee. Consequently, it is imperative that records of the convention be saved so that, if an audit occurs during later years, the exact expenses of the employee may be identified and deducted.[49]

[12.04] SALARIES AND OTHER COMPENSATION
PAID TO FAMILY MEMBERS

Often, professionals seek to transfer income from themselves to other members of their families in order to take advantage of lower income tax rates or to provide other employee benefits for the family members. Such payments and benefits are often subject to close scrutiny upon audit by the Service and are generally measured against a standard of reasonableness. Usually, such payments to family members are disallowed where the family members perform few or no services and any disallowed payments will be considered constructive dividends to the respective shareholder-professional.[50] It should also be remembered that salary payments to the spouse of a professional may increase the effective tax rates because FICA and FUTA taxes will be due on that salary.

[12.05] EXPENSES FOR RETIRED PROFESSIONALS

Often, professionals who are retired continue to maintain offices and deduct expenses for malpractice insurance, travel, and entertainment. Sometimes, this is simply to give the retired professional something to do during his retirement, but it may be used as a subterfuge to deduct expenses which would otherwise be personal. In Rev. Rul. 77-32,[51] the Service took the position that such expenses are not deductible. In that ruling, an anesthesiologist suspended practice indefinitely because of increases in malpractice insurance costs and because he did not expect income from his practice; he did attend educational meetings and conventions to maintain his professional expertise. The Service ruled that, because the anesthesiologist was not currently carrying on a trade or business (he planned to resume practice at some indefinite date), the expenses were not deductible under Code Section 162.[52]

[12.06] ENTERTAINMENT EXPENSES

The entertainment expenses of professional corporations, are, as they are for business corporations, deductible. However, examining IRS agents did not always take this position and in the past asserted that entertainment expenses for professionals were unethical. Due to such action, the American Medical Association notified the Commissioner of Internal Revenue that it did not consider the incurring of legitimate business entertainment expenses as unethical or contrary to public policy.[53] In fact, entertainment expenses may be absolutely necessary for certain professionals who practice specialties and depend on referrals from other professionals for the generation of fees. Although Section 162 of the Code does not specifically mention the term "entertainment expenses," expenses for entertaining customers and others are deductible expenses under Section 162(a) of the Code. Nevertheless, because the entertainment expense area is one which is subject to substantial abuse, both business and professional corporations receive very close scrutiny from the Service on these matters.

For years, the Service sought to define entertainment expenses which are deductible, and such a definition was enacted in 1962 in the form of Section 274 of the Code. However, specific criteria to be used in establishing the entertainment expenses of doctors under Section 162 had already been set forth in a Letter Ruling issued by the National Office of the Service on June 13, 1958, to the Mississippi State Medical Association,[54] which states, in principal part, as follows:

> Criteria to be used in establishing the deductibility of entertainment expenses include, but are not limited to, the following: (a) the specific purpose of the entertainment; (b) the nature of the practice of the doctor incurring the expenditure; (c) the period of time the doctor has been in practice and the number of patients he already has; (d) the percentage of his patients received by referrals; (e) names of individuals entertained and reasons why additional income could reasonably be expected from each; (f) whether or not referrals were actually received from the doctors entertained and any indication of the effect of the entertainment on these referrals; (g) the number of times individual doctors were entertained during the year inasmuch as repeated entertainment indicates a personal motive; (h) whether or not other doctors in the same type of practice in the locality have entertainment expenses.

Normally, the entire amount of the entertainment expense is deductible, including the amount expended for the taxpayer's own expenses. However, the Service has indicated that the taxpayer's own expenses may be disallowed under the decision in *Richard A. Sutter*,[55] and Section 162, if the Service finds an abuse situation.[56]

(1)   Requirements of Section 274

In order for entertainment expenses to be deductible, they must be deductible as "ordinary and necessary" under Section 162 of the Code, the general requirements of Section 274(a) must be met, and the substantiation requirements of Section 274 must be met.[57] Section 274(a) divides entertainment expenses into two categories. The first includes activity expenses which are deductible under certain circumstances, the second includes "facility" expenses which are not deductible.

Under Section 274(a)(1)(A), no deductions will be allowed for an expense related to an activity generally considered entertainment, amusement, or recreation unless the taxpayer proves the expense was "directly related to" or "associated with" the taxpayer's trade or business. Under Regulations §1.274-2(c)(2)-(7), an expenditure will be considered "directly related to" the taxpayer's trade or business if it meets any of the following requirements:

(1) At the time of the entertainment expenditure, the taxpayer had more than a general expectation of deriving some income or other specific trade or business benefit at some time in the indefinite future; during the entertainment to which the expenditure related, the taxpayer actively engaged in a business meeting, negotiation, discussion, or other bona fide business transaction, other than the entertainment, for the purpose of obtaining such income or other specified trade or business benefit; in light of all the facts and circumstances, the principal character or aspect of the combined business and entertainment activities to which the expenditure related was the active conduct of a trade or business; and the expenditure deducted was allocable to the taxpayer and persons from whom he expected business benefit to the exclusion of nonbusiness guests, if any; or

(2) Expenditures in a clear business setting, i.e., the recipient would reasonably understand that the outlay was only for business; or

(3) Compensation for services or prizes to other employees; or

(4) Club dues or fees allocable to business meals.

"Directly related" expenditures are generally thought to be those used for the generation of new business, and, as specified above, business must actually be discussed. Care should be taken in meeting this requirement, since it is possible for the general rules to be met and still be difficult to engage in the active conduct of a trade or business, such as discussions at night clubs, theaters, and sporting events, or during essentially social gatherings, such as cocktail parties.

Entertainment expenditures may also be deductible, even though not directly related to the active conduct of the trade or business, if they are "associated" with the active conduct of the trade or business and the entertainment was directly preceded or followed by a substantial bona fide business discussion. In this situation, it is not necessary for business discussions to actually occur with the entertainment as long as they occur contemporaneously, such as on the same day.[58]

(2) Facility Expenses

Under Section 274(a)(1)(B), expenses related to any facility used in entertainment will not be deductible unless the facility is used only incidentally for entertainment. Expenditures used in connection with the facility can include depreciation and operating costs, such as rent and utility charges for the facility, club dues, and other out-of-pocket expenses.

(3) Specific Exceptions to the Application of Section 274(a)

As long as the provisions of Section 162 are met, the following types of expenditures are deductible, notwithstanding Section 274(a):[59]

(1) <u>Business Meals</u>. Expenses for food and beverages furnished by an individual under circumstances which are the type generally considered to be conducive to a business discussion.

(2) Food and Beverage for Employees. Expenses for food and beverages furnished on the business premises of the taxpayer primarily for his employees.

(3) Expenses Treated as Compensation. Expenses for goods, services and facilities, to the extent that the expenses are treated by the taxpayer with respect to the recipient of the entertainment, amusement, or recreation as compensation to an employee.

(4) Reimbursed Expenses. Expenses paid or incurred by the taxpayer in connection with performance by him of services for another person under a reimbursement or other expense allowance arrangement with such other person.

(5) Recreational Expenses of Employees. Expenses for recreation, social, or similar activities primarily for the benefit of employees (other than employees who are officers, stockholders or other owners or highly compensated employees).

(6) Employee, Stockholder, Business Meetings. Expenses incurred by the taxpayer which are directly related to business meetings of his employees, stockholders, agents, or directors.

(7) Meetings of Business Leagues. Expenses directly related and necessary to attendance at a business meeting or convention of any organization described in Section 501(c)(6) and exempt from taxation under Section 501(a).

(8) Items Available to the Public. Expenses for goods, services, and facilities made available by the taxpayer to the general public.

(9) Entertainment Sold to Customers. Expenses for goods and services which are sold by the taxpayer in a bona fide transaction for adequate and full consideration.

Obviously, the requirements of Section 274 relating to entertainment expenses are quite complex and should be considered prior to any substantial expenditures.

[12.07]   CLUB DUES

Dues or fees to any social, athletic, or sporting club were required, prior to 1979, to meet the following two tests in order to be deductible: (1) they must be ordinary and necessary business expenses; and (2) they must satisfy the requirements of Section 274 that they be used primarily for business. With respect to expenses after 1978, only dues and fees paid to country clubs, civic organizations, professional organizations, and business luncheon clubs are deductible. Section 274(a)(2) of the Code.

In order to establish that club dues are ordinary and necessary business expenses, it must be proved that the club was joined for business reasons, the use of the club corresponds to business purposes, and the business benefit resulting from the membership must be shown. In addition, Section 274(a)(2)(C) requires that the taxpayer must use the club primarily (more than 50%) for business. If the club is used primarily for business, a pro rata portion (based on business use) of the club dues may be deductible. If a taxpayer uses a club less than 50% for business, no deduction for dues is allowed. The personal use of the club by the taxpayer's family is considered in determining whether the taxpayer uses the club more than 50% for business.

Clubs operated only to provide lunches in an atmosphere conducive to business discussions are not considered social clubs and as such are not subject to the dues rules of Section 274(a)(2).[60] Likewise, dues payable to professional and civic organizations, such as medical associations, are not considered social clubs and need not meet the test of Section 274.

Since most professional society dues are deductible and dues for purely sporting clubs are not, most of the questions concerning club dues revolve around the deductibility of country club dues. If a country club is used "primarily" for the enhancement of the trade or business of the professional, a pro rata portion of the dues should be deductible by him on his personal return, as long as he maintains sufficient records to establish that over 50% of the use of the club was for business purposes. Some professional corporation advisors prefer to have professionals deduct club dues on their personal returns, while others prefer to have the professional corporation deduct such dues. It is difficult to determine whether there is any practical advantage to be gained by having the club dues paid by the professional corporation, other than keeping the professional's federal income tax return "clean." In any event, the employment agreement and/or board resolutions of the corporation should require the professional employee to belong to the country club and to use it for corporate business purposes if the dues are to be deducted (either by the professional or the professional corporation).

It has generally been held that initiation fees for club memberships are considered to be capital items and are not deductible (as long as the membership lasts for more than one year).[61]

[12.08] EMPLOYEE GIFTS

Business gifts to individuals or organizations can be deducted under Section 162 of the Code.[62] However, Section 274(b) of the Code limits deductions for any gifts made directly or indirectly to any individual to $25 for each donee for the entire year. The amount of the gift depends on the cost to the donor, not the value to the donnee. The aggregate cost of gifts in excess of $25 per donee is nondeductible.

The expense for the gift generally does not include incidental expenses, such as engraving on jewelry, packaging, mailing, or insurance.[63] The $25 per annum restriction provided under Section 274(b) of the Code, the so-called "Christmas turkey" provision, was established in order to prohibit employers from providing large untaxable benefits to employees in the form of gifts. A good argument can be made that Congress should consider raising the $25 limit. ERTA has increased from $100 to $400 the amount which may be deductible by an employer for awards to an employee based on length of service, productivity or safety achievement. See Section 274(b) of the Code.

[12.09] EDUCATIONAL EXPENSES

(1) Educational Benefit Trust

In the past, owners of closely held corporations have attempted to establish methods for providing additional tax-free benefits for shareholder-employees. One of these methods was the educational benefit trust under which the corporation would agree to pay for the educational benefits of the children of selected employees, with the result that the benefit payments would be deductible by the corporation and not taxable at all or taxable to the child-recipient. During the 1970's, there was a substantial amount of controversy concerning these trusts.[64]

The Service violently contested the use of educational benefit trusts and in 1975 issued Rev. Rul. 75-448[65] which outlines the federal income tax consequences of such trusts. Under the Ruling, the corporation receives no deduction at the time it makes payments to the trusts and the employees are taxed on the amounts paid from the trusts when they are used as a payment of educational benefits.

However, in 1977 and 1978, the Seventh Circuit, affirming two earlier Tax Court decisions, rejected the educational benefit trust concept. In *Armantrout v. Commissioner*,[66] *Educo, Inc. v. Commissioner*,[67] and *Citrus Orthopedic Medical Group, Inc.*[68] employees were deemed to have received taxable income when the educational benefit trust set up by the employer paid for children's educational expenses. Payments were compensatory in nature and employees, by remaining employed, consented to having part of their earnings paid to the trust fund. The fact that the employees had no right to receive the payments directly was immaterial.

The authors recommend caution in adopting any type of educational benefit trust or other mechanism to pay the education expenses of employees' children.

(2) Education Expenses for the Professional

Regulations §1.162-5 provides the general rules for deducting educational expenses. Under these regulations, expenditures made by an individual for educational programs which are not expenditures designed to provide minimum educational requirements or to qualify the individual for a new trade or business are deductible as ordinary and necessary business expenses (even though the education may lead to a degree) if the education: (1) maintains or improves skills required by the individual in his employment or other trade or business; or (2) meets the express requirements of the individual's employer, or the requirements of applicable laws or regulations, imposed as a condition to the retention by the individual of an established employment relationship, status, or rate of compensation.

Most of the questions in the educational expense area center around the exceptions concerning expenses for minimal education requirements and qualification for a new trade or business. The following is a list of typical expense items decided under case law.[69]

(1) *Legal Profession*

Morton S. Taubman,[70] deduction denied accountant for cost of obtaining law degree since the degree qualified him for a new trade or business.

Johnson v. United States,[71] lawyer denied deduction for cost of LLM (Master of Laws) in taxation where course was taken to meet requirements of his new specialty, the practice of tax law. A different result should obtain where a tax lawyer with an established tax practice returns to law school to obtain an LLM in taxation.

Avery v. United States,[72] bar admission fees and expenses not deductible, but should be subject to amortization. Rev. Rul. 69-292,[73] deductions denied for review courses before taking CPA exam.

(2) *Medical Profession*

Leonard T. Fielding,[74] deduction denied for expenses incurred in becoming psychiatrist; he was acquiring new profession.

Rev. Rul. 72-32,[75] anesthesiologist unable to deduct expenses for refresher courses for return to practice.

[12.10] OVERHEAD INSURANCE

Since a professional's income is based upon the time he is available to perform his profession, one of the principal desires of most professionals is to assure that the practice may be continued through temporary periods of disability without undue hardship. One of the means to minimize the cash flow burden during disability is disability insurance.

Where a professional corporation purchases disability insurance on key employees, the corporation cannot deduct the premiums paid on those policies. Rev. Rul. 66-262.[76] Further, the disability income received by the corporation, regardless of amount, is wholly tax-exempt under Section 104(a)(3) of the Code and Rev. Rul. 66-262. The same result applies where the disability insurance is purchased to fund a disability buyout.

On the other hand, an ''overhead expense disability policy'' reimburses a professional or his corporation, in the event of the disability of the professional, for the expenses actually incurred by the professional in the operation of his office, including such items as rent, electricity, heat, depreciation, employees' salaries, and other fixed expenses which are normal and customary in the conduct and operation of a profession. Overhead insurance does not cover salaries, fees, drawing accounts, or other remuneration for the disabled professional (or generally any other professional working with the professional corporation).

In Rev. Rul. 55-264,[77] the Service held that any proceeds derived under the terms of an overhead insurance policy are includable in gross income under the terms of Section 61 of the Code. However, any premiums paid on such policies constitute business expenses and are deductible under Section 162 of the Code. Although the amounts received under such a policy will be considered ordinary income, the proceeds of the policy will be used to meet expenses which will be otherwise deductible and, consequently, there should be no adverse income tax effect.

The annual premium payments for overhead insurance are generally not excessive and professionals should consider the purchase of at least a minimum amount of overhead insurance to assure that the professional corporation can meet the overhead cost related to a disabled professional.

[12.11] THE USE OF LOANS IN PROFESSIONAL CORPORATIONS

Very often, professionals are required to make loans to their professional corporations or desire to borrow funds from the professional corporation. Loans to and from professional corporations may generate disastrous tax results unless properly accomplished and care should be taken to review the tax impact of such loans before they are made.

(1) Loans from the Professional Corporation to the Professional Must Be Bona Fide

(a) General Rules

When a professional corporation makes a loan to a shareholder-employee out of its earnings and profits, questions can arise with regard to whether the professional corporation is merely attempting to avoid tax on a distribution which is, in fact, a dividend. If the loan arrangement is not bona fide, the loan will be treated as a constructive dividend to the shareholder and, in all likelihood, will be taxable as ordinary income.[78] Professionals often desire to make withdrawals from their professional corporations when they need immediate cash, and the authors have found that professionals very often will make such withdrawals without consulting their advisors. Whether or not a withdrawal of corporate funds by a shareholder-employee will constitute a dividend or a loan is a question of fact involving the following considerations:

(1) Whether the amount of the withdrawal was carried on the corporate records as a loan.

(2) Whether the withdrawal is evidenced by a legally enforceable promissory note.

(3) Whether the corporation and the shareholder regard the withdrawal as an indebtedness and whether the loan has been approved by action of the board of directors.

(4) Whether the corporation had sufficient surplus to cover the loan when it was made.

(5) Whether the shareholder intended to make repayment at the time the withdrawal was made and whether a definite repayment date, in the not too distant future, was established.

(6) Whether there is security for the loan other than the signature of the shareholder.

(7) Whether the amount of the loan is reasonable considering all the facts and circumstances.

(8) Whether the provisions of state law regarding loans to shareholder-employees are satisfied.

(9) Whether an adequate rate of interest is charged on the loan.

The intent to repay appears to be treated by the courts as the most significant factor in determining whether advances constitute loans or constructive dividends. When the following factors converge, the courts appear to have little difficulty in concluding that advances by a corporation to shareholders constitute dividends: (1) no notes evidencing the indebtedness; (2) no understanding concerning repayment; (3) no agreement to pay interest and no interest charged; and (4) no security given.[79] In *Taschler v. Commissioner*,[80] loans made by the president and sole shareholder from a small loan corporation were deemed to be dividends even though they were evidenced by a demand note. The court stated, "True, a note payable on demand was given. But the taxpayer had no fear of the prospect of [the corporation] ever insisting that the note be paid." The presence of a demand note under which the amount due remains outstanding for a number of years may result in a greater emphasis upon the distribution nature of the advance. In *C.F. Williams*,[81] taxpayers withdrew large sums in each of the years 1964 to 1969 from corporations in which they were majority shareholders. The court was unable to find any intent to repay these advances, since notes were not issued until three years after the first loan and no interest was paid until five years after the first loan was made. The court also found it significant that the majority shareholders were in effective control over the corporations' intentions and actions with respect to requiring repayment.

(b) *Interest-Free Loans*

Professionals often desire to make interest-free or low-interest loans to themselves from their professional corporations. They should, however, be aware that the use of interest-free or low-interest loans from their professional corporations is an unsettled area of the tax law at the present time. There is a very real possibility that any such loans will be scrutinized by the Service on audit and will probably be challenged. In recent years, the Service has been anxious to litigate cases in this area in hopes of obtaining a favorable court decision but, as of this date, has been singularly unsuccessful.

Although the interest-free nature of a loan should be considered in determining whether the loan is a bona fide loan or a constructive dividend, the interest-free nature of a loan should not, itself, be sufficient to categorize the loan as a constructive dividend. In *Moses W. Faitoute*,[82] the court implied that once an intent to repay the loan principal is found, the interest itself will not be subject to additional scrutiny with respect to the constructive dividend in issue. In situations involving interest-free or low-interest loans from corporations to shareholders, the Service has argued that the borrowers have received an economic benefit equal to the difference between the amount of interest actually paid and the interest the shareholders would have paid had they borrowed the funds in an arm's-length transaction. In at least one case, the Service has used the prime interest rate to compute the economic benefit.[83] The Service usually contends that the economic benefit should be included in the borrower's income as ordinary income either as a dividend or as additional compensation, but if the borrower is a shareholder as well as an employee, the Service will contend that the income is a constructive dividend.

In the past, the courts that have ruled on this issue have consistently taken the position that interest-free or low-interest loans do not generate income to the borrower, pointing to the fact that the borrower would be entitled to an off-setting interest deduction and, therefore, there is no need to require inclusion in the borrower's income.[84] This holding is, of course, conditioned on the premise that the borrower would be entitled to the interest deduction. It is possible, however, that the Service could argue that taxable income should result to the borrower where the interest deduction of the borrower is limited for tax purposes, that is, that Section 265 of the Code (limiting interest on loans to carry taxes into investments) or Section 163(d) of the Code (relating to excess investment interest) may apply to the shareholder-employee. Despite the holdings in these cases, the Service, relying on dissenting opinions and critical commentary, continues to contend that interest-free or low-interest loans do generate income to the borrower.[85]

Where a corporation has existing loans from third parties and at the same time makes interest-free or low-interest loans to the shareholders, a ruling consistent with, but somewhat different from, the earlier cases, has been reached. In *Joseph Creel*,[86] shareholders received interest-free loans from their corporation but were generally required to guarantee the corporation's debt. The Tax Court refused to repudiate its prior decisions but held that the loans in this particular situation did create income to the borrowers. Because of the existing corporate loans, the Tax Court held that: (1) the corporation merely acted as the agent of the shareholders in obtaining the loans and, therefore, the corporation was not entitled to an interest deduction; (2) when the corporation paid the loans (for the shareholders) the shareholders received a constructive dividend; and (3) the shareholders received an interest deduction equal to a constructive dividend. Although this case does side-step the *Dean*[87] decision, it does produce a neutral tax result for the shareholders.

The gift tax implications of interest-free loans are set forth in *Crown v. Commissioner*,[88] which held that interest-free loans payable on demand did not result in the making of a taxable gift by the lender. In *Crown,* the taxpayer was one of three brothers who were members of a partnership which, in 1966, made loans of approximately $18,000,000 to 24 trusts previously established for the benefit of the children and other close relatives of the brothers. All of the loans were evidenced by demand notes or open accounts, neither of which made any provision for the payment of interest, except that the notes did call for the payment of 6% interest after demand. No demand for payment was made during 1967 and no interest was paid. The Service argued unsuccessfully that the right to use the money interest-free was a valuable property right and that the transfer of this property right to the trusts was subject to a gift tax.

One of the arguments raised by the Commissioner on appeal, and relied upon by the dissenting judges in the Tax Court, was that an interest-free loan constituted an "unequal exchange" within the meaning of Section 2512(b) of the Code (where property is transferred for less than adequate and full consideration in money or money's worth, then the amount by which the value of the property exceeded the value of the consideration shall be deemed a gift). The Commissioner contended that the value of the money loaned exceeded the value of the promise to repay, since the promise was evidenced by an interest-free note, and the difference constituted a taxable gift within the meaning of Section 2512(b). The court in *Crown* rejected this argument, noting that the value of the promise to repay the loan could not be determined with certainty because a transfer of the economic benefit would not be complete until such time as the lender demanded repayment. Thus, the interest-free loans made in *Crown* did not result in a taxable gift.

Interest-free loans from professional corporations to shareholders should not be subject to gift tax, but intra-family loans from a professional corporation to a family member of a controlling shareholder may be subject to scrutiny under gift tax considerations. Such loans may result in a constructive dividend from the professional corporation to the shareholder, followed by an interest-free loan from a shareholder to the other family member. On the other hand, the gift tax situation can be avoided through the use of demand notes and the constructive dividend question concerning the bona fide nature of the loans may be satisfied through the use of an agreement between the shareholder and the corporation that the note will be repaid as soon as possible by the shareholder.

So far, the Service has focused only on the income tax treatment of the shareholder who borrows funds from the corporation. However, it is possible that the Service may soon turn its attention to the income tax treatment of the corporation. If this occurs, the Service will probably use arguments under Section 482 of the Code (allocation of income and deductions between related trades or businesses), the substance over form argument, or the assignment of income argument[89] to obtain a reallocation of income to the corporation. While there is very little authority for such a result, the authors would not be surprised to see it proposed by the Service.[90]

The authors feel that, before interest-free loans are made to a shareholder-professional, care should be taken to determine the exact effect of making a loan with a realistic interest rate.[91] For example, as long as the professional has not reached levels of compensation which would be considered unreasonable and as long as the professional is otherwise eligible to deduct the interest which would be payable to the professional corporation, interest payable to the professional corporation should result in little or no extra tax or lessened cash flow. Assuming that interest is payable to the corporation, the taxpayer will take a deduction for that interest. The interest paid will potentially be considered taxable income to the corporation, but the interest received could be used to make additional contributions to qualified retirement plans or be retained in the corporation to purchase capital equipment (while all income generated from the professional practice—some of which would normally be required to be retained in the corporation for capital improvements—will be paid to the professional).

(2) Loans from Professionals to Professional Corporations

As illustrated in section [5.10], *supra*, the capital of a professional corporation need not be overly endowed. For this reason, it is sometimes necessary for professionals to make short-term loans to their professional corporations for working capital purposes. As long as such loans are evidenced by promissory notes, are for a short duration, are authorized by the board of directors of the corporation, and are eventually repaid, such loans should be considered bona fide loans and not contributions to capital. On the other hand, where the corporation is thinly capitalized, where the loans are made for extended periods, and where loans are made without corporate authorization or the use of promissory notes, the Service may contend that such loans constitute additional contributions to capital and, consequently, the repayment of such loans constitutes a constructive dividend.[92]

[12.12] CONSTRUCTIVE DIVIDENDS

Where a shareholder receives a personal benefit from the professional corporation, either in the form of the payment by the corporation of his personal expenses, the receipt of unreasonable compensation, or the benefit of an interest-free loan, the Service generally takes the position that the receipt of such benefit takes the form of a constructive dividend.[93] The Service takes this position because a larger effective tax is produced. Dividends paid from a corporation to a shareholder are not deductible and, consequently, must be paid with after-tax dollars. Also, dividends received by a shareholder are taxable as ordinary income to the extent of the earnings and profits of the corporation under Section 301 of the Code. Consequently, a constructive dividend produces a so-called "double tax" because of the tax at the corporate level and the tax at the shareholder level.

Because of the additional tax that may be produced by a constructive dividend, it is normally preferable to provide, in employment agreements or bylaws, that amounts which may potentially be subject to constructive dividend treatment, such as the payment of personal expenses or the retention by the shareholder of excess expense reimbursements, shall be considered compensation or, if not considered compensation, repaid to the professional corporation. See the shareholder employee's employment agreement at section [10.01](1), *supra*, and the bylaws at section [6.04], *supra*.

EXHIBIT 1

EXPENSE REPORT

Employee _____

Date _____

Place _____

Purpose _____

_____

_____

*Expenses (Please Itemize):

_____ $ _____

_____   _____

_____   _____

_____   _____

_____   _____

_____   _____

_____   _____

_____   _____

_____   _____

_____   _____

Total Expense $ _____

Advance Issue $ _____

Amount Reimbursable to Corporation $ _____

           or

Amount Due Employee $ _____

*If any of your expenses were charged, please indicate where appropriate and show credit account to which they were charged.

NOTES TO CHAPTER 12

1. See generally Prentice-Hall *Federal Taxes*, ¶11,000.
2. For a listing of many of these definitions, see Prentice-Hall *Federal Taxes* at ¶11,010.
3. 290 U.S. 111 (1933).
4. For a general discussion, Prentice-Hall *Federal Taxes*, ¶11,031.
5. *Commissioner v. Lincoln Electric Co.*, 176 F.2d 815 (6th Cir. 1949), *cert. denied*, 338 U.S. 949 (1950).
6. *New Colonial Ice Co. v. Helvering*, 292 U.S. 435 (1934).
7. *Cohan v. Commissioner*, 39 F.2d 540 (2d Cir. 1930), remanding 11 B.T.A. 743. Also see Prentice-Hall *Federal Taxes* at ¶41,277.
8. Section 274(d) of the Code and Treas. Regs. §1.274-5.
9. See *Sanford v. Commissioner*, 50 T.C. 823 (1968), *aff'd*, 412 F. 2d 201 (2d Cir. 1969), *cert. denied*, 396 U.S. 841 (1969).
10. See section [12.06], *infra*, for a complete description.
11. Treas. Regs. §1.446-1(c)(i) provides that expenditures of a cash basis taxpayer must actually be made. Rev. Rul. 68-643, 1968-2 C.B. 76 (interest may not be prepaid for more than 12 months). Business insurance premiums paid in advance for a period of more than one year are, in general, not currently deductible because the benefit of such payment is deferred. The Service and, by and large, the courts, have consistently applied a rule permitting cash basis corporations to deduct only the pro rata portion of the insurance premium which applies to the current year. See *Commissioner v. Boylston Market Association*, 131 F.2d 966 (1st Cir. 1942). However, in certain instances taxpayers may be able to deduct prepayments where, for example, they have uniformly treated insurance premiums as business expenses in the year the premiums are paid, even though part of the expense related to a later year. See *Waldheim Realty & Investment Co. v. Commissioner*, 245 F.2d 823 (8th Cir. 1957), reversing and remanding 25 T.C. 1216 (1956).
12. See, generally, Section 267 of the Code.
13. Rev. Rul. 57-502, 1957-2 C.B. 118. Also, see Prentice-Hall *Federal Taxes* at ¶11,180, for a discussion of the cases, especially *Robert O. Eder*, 42 T.C.M. 585, ¶81,408 P-H Memo T.C. (1981) and the shareholder [10.01](1), employee's employment agreement at section *supra*, which requires the employee to incur such expenses.
14. See, generally, the table of professional expenses contained in Prentice-Hall *Federal Taxes* at ¶1125.
15. See Treas. Regs. §1.162-2(b)(2).
16. See IRS Publication No. 17 (1980), page 67.
17. Rev. Rul. 55-109, 1955-1 C.B. 261, and Rev. Rul. 59-371, 1959-2 C.B. 236. See *Edwin R. Curphey*, 73 T.C. 766 (1980), and Letter Ruling 8023052. See, generally, Prentice-Hall *Federal Taxes* at ¶11,425.

18. The fact that tools are transported in a car that would have been used for commuting in any event does not make the cost of commuting deductible. However, transportation costs in excess may be deductible if he can show additional costs are incurred by carrying tools (but based on the *same* mode of transportation). Rev. Rul. 75-380, 1975-2 C.B. 59. This rule, as a practical matter, will probably not permit additional deductions by professionals.

19. 1976-2 C.B. 86.

20. Prentice-Hall *Federal Taxes* at ¶11,426.

21. Section 2 of Public Law 95-427, October 7, 1978, amended by Section 2 of Public Law 96-167, December 29, 1979.

22. See also *Edwin R. Curphey, supra*, at note 17.

23. *Sanders v. Commissioner*, 439 F.2d 296, 299 (9th Cir. 1971).

24. 41 A.F.T.R. 2d 78-762, (D.C. Mont., 1977).

25. 38 T.C.M. 147, ¶79,038 P-H Memo T.C. (1979).

26. See *ON-RI-GA Medical Professional Association*, 1978-183 T.C. Memo.

27. 37 T.C.M. 1847, ¶78,465 P-H Memo T.C. (1978).

28. 38 T.C.M. 557, ¶79,122 P-H Memo T.C. (1979).

29. See *Andrew W. Shea*, 38 T.C.M. 1178, ¶79,303 P-H Memo T.C. (1979). See Letter Ruling 8014016, which disallows as commuting expenses emergency trips by a doctor from his home to the hospital. Also see Prentice-Hall *Professional Corporation Guide*, Vol. VIII, Report Bulletin No. 6, June 6, 1980, and cases reported at Prentice-Hall *Federal Taxes* at ¶14,426(95).

30. For a complete list of cases relating to professionals, see Prentice-Hall *Federal Taxes* at ¶11,425-11,434. Also, see Osborne, ''Careful Planning Can Increase Professional's Deductions for Travel and Entertainment,'' 4 *Taxation for Lawyers* 90 (1976), and Rosen, ''Travel Expenses—The Amount of Deduction Depends on Personal Element Mixed in With Business,'' 5 *Taxation for Lawyers* 264 (1977).

31. The rates under the optional method are usually increased annually. See IRS Form 2106.

32. See Rev. Rul. 74-433, 1974-2 C.B. 92, and Treas. Regs. §1.274-5.

33. See Treas. Regs §1.47-2(a)(2)(iii) (Example (1)) for an example of conversion of property to personal use.

34. Under Treas. Regs. §1.1245-1(a), a disposition does not include conversion to personal use. Rev. Rul. 69-487, 1969-2 C.B. 165. A gift to the spouse of a professional will also not be a disposition. Section 1245(b)(1) of the Code. Treas. Regs. §1.1245-4(a).

35. *Russell A. Bufalino*, ¶76,110 P-H Memo T.C.

36. The actual, total cost of lease payments should be greater than a purchase, but the monthly payment under a lease will usually be less than a purchase. This occurs because the lessor ''finances'' a larger portion of the purchase cost for the lessee by leaving a balloon payment at the end of the lease, i.e., the

residual. Sometimes lease costs only slightly exceed purchase costs due to the leasing company's ability to purchase automobiles at "dealer's cost" and possibly obtain funds at favorable interest rates.

37. Leasing also eliminates the necessity of the professional negotiating the purchase and eventual sale of the automobile. Also, in the event the automobile is a "lemon," the lessor should assist in negotiating with the dealer and the manufacturer.

38. See, for example, *Henry A. Sherry*, ¶75-337 P-H Memo T.C. (airplane deduction denied to lawyer).

39. See *Harbor Medical Corporation*, 38 T.C.M. 1144, ¶79,291 P-H Memo T.C. (1979) (medical corporation could not deduct the cost of owning and operating airplane).

40. See *Wolfe v. McCaughn*, 17 A.F.T.R. 10007 (D. Pa. 1933).

41. See Treas. Regs. §1.162-2(b).

42. See Rev. Rul. 79-425, 1972-2 C.B. 81, and Rev. Rul. 74-292, 1974-1 C.B. 43, where foreign convention expenses of professionals were disallowed.

43. See *Fenstermaker*, 37 T.C.M. 898, ¶78,210 P-H Memo T.C. (1978).

44. See Prentice-Hall *Federal Taxes* at ¶11,356(15).

45. See *Duncan v. Brookwalter*, 11 A.F.T.R. 2d 1383, 216 F. Supp. 301 (D.C. Missouri 1963) (doctor's wife, who was his partner and assistant, accompanied doctor on convention and expenses were allowed). Also see Prentice-Hall *Federal Taxes*, ¶11,356(10).

46. See *Warwick v. U.S.*, 236 F. Supp. 761 (E.D. Virginia 1964) (spouse accompanied husband to entertain European customers and wives); *U.S. v. Disney*, 413 F.2d 783 (9th Cir. 1969) (deduction allowed where spouse attended convention to cultivate close and cordial relationships); *Wilkins v. U.S.*, 348 F. Supp. 1282 (N.D. Nebraska 1972), (deduction permitted by Inspector General of the Foreign Service Department of State for wife's trips abroad); and *Bank of Stockton*, 1977-24 T.C. Memo (expenses of wives deductible since they facilitated personal contact among bankers).

47. See *Fenstermaker, supra*, at note 43, where the expenses of attendance of wives at a technical trade show were disallowed.

48. See *Fenstermaker, supra*, to note 43, and Letter Rulings 7902008, 7902012, 7902013, 7902016, 7902017, and 7902018. See, however, *U.S. v. Gotcher*, 401 F.2d 118 (5th Cir. 1978), which reached the opposite result and held that no taxable income would result if the taxpayer-employee could illustrate that there was no economic gain or that the gain did not benefit the taxpayer personally.

49. For general references, see: Shaddock, "The Tax Consequences of a Spouse's Convention Expenses," 29 *Baylor Law Review* 585 (1977).

"Expenses of Wives Can Be Business Related," 18 *Taxation for Accountants* 211 (April, 1977).

Price, "Traveling With Your Wife May Be Taxing," 28 *Federal Bar Journal* 75 (1968).

50. See, generally, Prentice-Hall *Federal Taxes* at ¶11,567.

51. 1977-1 C.B. 38.

52. Also, see *Estate of Henry Sussman,* 37 T.C.M. 1430, ¶78,344 P-H Memo T.C. (1978).

53. See letter to Commissioner dated February 21, 1955, published at ¶76,292 Prentice-Hall *Federal Taxes* (1957).

54. Set forth in ¶54,636 of Prentice-Hall *Federal Taxes* (1960).

55. 21 T.C. 170 (1954), acq. 1954-1 C.B. 6.

56. See Rev. Rul. 63-144, 1963-2 C.B. 129.

57. The substantiation requirements are discussed at section [12.01](2), *supra.*

58. See Treas. Regs. §1.274-2(d)(3)(ii).

59. See Section 274(e) of the Code.

60. See Treas. Regs. §1.274-2(e)(3)(ii).

61. See I.T. 2414, VII-1 C.B. 229, declared obsolete by Rev. Rul. 67-466, 1967-2 C.B. 427; IRS Publication 234 (1979), page 61; *Whitney v. Commissioner,* 73 F.2d 589 (3rd Cir. 1934); *Grace National Bank of New York,* 15 T.C. 563 (1950), *aff'd per curiam,* 189 F.2d 966 (7th Cir. 1951); *Kenneth D. Smith,* 1965-169 T.C. Memo; *Mercantile National Bank of Dallas,* 30 T.C. 84 (1958); *Duval Motor Company,* 28 T.C. 42 (1957).

62. Treas. Regs. §1.162-15.

63. Treas. Regs. §1.274-3(c).

64. See Henkel & Hackett, ''An Analysis of Education Benefit Trusts, How They Work, the Advantages, and the Problems,'' 42 *J. Taxation* 346 (1975).

65. 1975-2 C.B. 55.

66. 570 F.2d 210 (7th Cir. 1978), *aff'g per curiam* 67 T.C. 966 (1977).

67. 557 F.2d 617 (7th Cir. 1977).

68. 72 T.C. No. 43 (1979).

69. A complete listing of the applicable case law can be found at Prentice-Hall *Federal Taxes,* ¶1,504.

70. 60 T.C. 814 (1973).

71. 332 F. Supp. 906 (D.C. Louisiana 1971), 27 A.F.T.R. 2d 71-1239.

72. 76-2 U.S.T.C. ¶9694, 38 AFTR 2d 76-6073 (N.D. Iowa 1976).

73. 1969-1 C.B. 84.

74. 57 T.C. 761 (1972).

75. 1977-1 C.B. 38.

76. 1966-2 C.B. 105.

77. 1955-1 C.B. 11, also see Letter Ruling 7730007.

78. See Section 301 of the Code.

79. See, for example, *Chism's Estate v. Commissioner,* 322 F.2d 956 (9th Cir. 1963).

80. 440 F.2d 72 (3rd Cir. 1971).

81. ¶78,306, P-H Memo. T.C.

82. 38 B.T.A. 32 (1938), *acq.* 1938-2 C.B. 10.

83. *Albert Suttle,* T.C. Memo. 1978-393.

84. *J. Simpson Dean,* 35 T.C. 1083 (1961); *Albert Suttle,* T.C. Memo 1978-393, 46 A.F.T.R. 2d 80-5413 (4th Cir. 1980); *Herman M. Greenspun,* 72 T.C. 931 (1979); *Estate of Benjamin Liechtung,* 40 T.C.M. 1118, ¶80,352 P-H Memo T.C. (1980); *William G. Martin,* 39 T.C.M. 531 (1979); *Haworth H. Parks,* 40 T.C.M. 1228, ¶80,382 P-H Memo T.C. (1980).

85. See Letter Ruling 7731077 regarding the nontaxable treatment of interest-free loans to unrelated customers.

86. 72 T.C. 1173 (1979).

87. Note 83, *supra.*

88. 585 F.2d 234 (7th Cir. 1979), *aff'g.* 67 T.C. 1060 (1977).

89. All discussed at section [9.01], *supra.*

90. See, Roth, ''Can Lender be Charged with Receiving Taxable Income as a Result of an Interest-Free Loan?'' 52 *J. Taxation* 136 (1980).

91. For a general discussion of this topic, see: Edwards, ''What Planning Opportunities Does CA-7's No Gift Holding in *Crown* Open Up?'' 50 *J. Taxation* 163 (March, 1979); Duhl and Fine, ''Interest-Free Loans in the Tax Court: Is *Dean* Weakening Under IRS Attacks?'' 50 *J. Taxation* 322 (December 1979).

92. See generally, Section 385 of the Code and the Treas. Regs. thereunder. At the time the *Desk Book* went to press, the Treasury Department announced that it was reconsidering the Treas. Regs. under Section 385 (which had caused a great deal of concern among members of the tax bar).

93. *Anderson,* 1976-28 T.C. Memo; *Gardner* 1976 T.C.M. 76-349; *Norman S. Brandes, M.D., Inc.,* 1979-38 T.C.M. However, there is no automatic constructive dividend rule. See *Palo Alto Town & Country Village, Inc.,* 565 F.2d 1388 (9th Cir. 1977). Also see Worthy, ''Accidental Dividends,'' December, 1973, *Taxes* 724.

CHAPTER **13**

Deductibility of Compensation And Reasonableness

[13.01] WHAT IS THE PROBLEM AND WHAT IS AT STAKE?

Compensation paid for services is deductible as an ordinary and necessary business expense under Section 162 of the Code in accordance with Regulations §1.162-7. Regulations §1.162-7(a), stating that there may be included among the ordinary and necessary expenses paid or incurred in carrying on any trade or business a "reasonable allowance for salaries or other compensation for personal services actually rendered," thus provides a two-pronged test for deductibility. The second prong of the test, that services must actually be rendered, is usually not a factor; it is the first prong of the test, that of reasonableness, which causes difficulties.

Most closely held corporations, including professional corporations, are potentially subject to the reasonable compensation question because the owners of the corporation, themselves, set compensation levels. Professional corporations may be considered even more susceptible because often little, if any, earnings are retained on an annual basis. The reasonable compensation question arises because shareholder-employees would prefer to pay out all of the earnings of the corporation as compensation, which will make the earnings nontaxable to the corporation and taxable only to the shareholder-employees at the maximum 50% rate provided under Section 1348 of the Code (under ERTA the maximum tax under Section 1348 is repealed because, for taxable years beginning after December 31, 1981, the maximum tax rate on any income is 50%). It should be realized, however, that the shareholder-employees of closely held and professional corporations actually have dual capacities, as shareholders and as employees, and they must be compensated in each capacity. If the shareholder-employees of closely held and professional corporations compensate themselves only as employees, the Service may determine that a portion of the compensation actually represents a return to the shareholders on the invested capital in the corporation, and that portion of the compensation will be declared unreasonable. If this occurs, potential "double" taxation of the unreasonable portion of the compensation occurs because that portion will be considered nondeductible to the corporation and will be taxable to the professional employee (prior to 1982 at rates potentially in excess of 50%) i.e., constructive dividends are not subject to the maximum tax rate limits provided under Section 1348 of the Code).

For years prior to 1982, Section 1348 of the Code provides a 50% maximum income tax rate for all income generated through personal services; both current and deferred compensation are covered. The effect of Section 1348 is to limit to 50%, the federal income tax on personal service income. For example, if Attorney A receives a $200,000 salary from his professional corporation (and files a joint return for 1980), all taxable income over $60,000 would (without Section 1348) be subject to rates in excess of 50%. The general effect of Section 1348 is to limit to 50% the tax rates on Attorney A's salary in excess of $60,000. Section 1348 will, however, have the effect of pushing unearned income (interest, dividends, etc.) into higher brackets. If Attorney A had another $10,000 of interest (and total taxable income of between $162,400 and $215,400) the interest would be subject to a 68% tax rate. The effect of Section 1348 is to skip the rates between 50% and 68% and tax the unearned income at the highest tax rate which would have been applicable without the limitation provided in Section 1348. Taxing unearned income at such higher rates is consistent with the tax tables, however.

For taxable years beginning after December 31, 1981, the maximum tax on any type of income is 50%. This change, brought about by ERTA, substantially reduced the "double" tax problem created by unreasonable compensation.

Obviously, the reasonable compensation problem only applies to those professional employees who are also shareholders of the professional corporation. While some commentators feel that professionals should begin considering the reasonable compensation problem when salaries exceed $50,000 per year,[1] the authors feel that reasonable compensation may become an issue where a professional employee receives compensation in excess of 100% of his billings, or it can otherwise be shown that a significant amount of the compensation of the professional is attributable to work of associates or income earned from the use of equipment. While there have been very few cases involving the reasonable compensation of professionals, professional advisors should constantly be aware of the reasonable compensation problem and take steps to avoid its application.

[13.02] HOW IS REASONABLE COMPENSATION DETERMINED?

(1) Factors

The determination of the reasonableness of the compensation paid to an employee is made on the facts and circumstances of each particular case. However, through the years, a number of factors to be considered in determining reasonable compensation have been distilled from the case law regarding general business corporations. These factors are as follows:

(1) Is compensation paid to the shareholders of the corporation in roughly the same percentage as they own stock?

(2) How does compensation paid from the corporation relate to compensation paid from the professional practice prior to incorporation.?[2]

(3) What type of work is performed by the employee, what are his duties, and has he assumed additional duties in the recent past?

(4) What is the experience of the employee and does he have any particular expertise or background, technical skills, inventive or managerial ability?

(5) What amount of time and energy does the employee devote to the work of the corporation?

(6) To what extent is the production of the corporation due to the work of the employee?

(7) Was the employee inadequately compensated during the early years of the formation of the business due to insufficient cash flow?

(8) How much compensation is paid to similar employees in comparable businesses?

(9) To what extent do market and economic factors have an impact on the success of the business?

(10) Is compensation set with the proper corporate formalities and for clearly stated reasons?

None of the above factors is determinative in the question of reasonable compensation, although probably the most important factor is that of comparable salaries in comparable businesses.[3] This factor often presents a problem for the taxpayer because the Service can review the tax returns of other similar businesses to reach its conclusions (although these will not specifically be cited to the taxpayer), while the taxpayer often finds it difficult to obtain comparable salary figures, although they are sometimes obtainable through trade associations.

(2) What Is Compensation?

For purposes of determining the reasonableness of a shareholder's compensation, all direct and indirect benefits, including salary payments, employee benefits, and retirement plan contributions (whether or not vested) are generally considered within the term "compensation." Although examining Internal Revenue Service agents often overlook these forms of compensation and deal primarily with salaries and bonuses, care should be taken to include all forms of compensation in making projections regarding reasonableness. See, for example, the projections in Exhibit 1 at the end of this chapter.

Section 404(a) of the Code permits deductions for contributions to qualified retirement plans and requires that employer contributions must satisfy the conditions under either Section 162 or Section 212 of the Code in order to be deductible for income tax purposes. Thus, it is possible for the amounts contributed to a qualified retirement plan, when added to the direct compensation paid to the employee, to cause the total compensation to be considered unreasonable. In *Angelo D. Bianchi*,[4] a dentist incorporated his practice and adopted a pension plan covering himself and his dental assistant. During the corporation's first fiscal year, which was only seven days long, the corporation made an initial contribution to the pension plan of approximately $17,000, producing a net operating loss. The court held that the contribution to the plan and compensation paid to the doctor during the corporation's first taxable year were unreasonably high and nondeductible.[5]

Where excess compensation is found to be unreasonable, the amount of the retirement plan contribution allowed is based upon the allowable direct compensation paid the employee. Any disallowed retirement plan contribution may be reallocated among the other employees or returned to the employer, according to the terms of the plan.[6]

(3)   McCandless Tile—The Automatic Dividend Rule

In considering whether amounts paid to an employee are compensatory, courts normally review the dividend history of the corporation, the availability of funds in the corporation to pay dividends, and the amounts paid to the employee as a percentage of gross and net income. The ultimate test for determining the existence of dividends appeared to have been established in the case of *Charles McCandless Tile Service v. United States*.[7] In that case, the corporation conducted a ceramic tile contracting business and, although it was profitable, no dividends were paid to the shareholders of the corporation. Mr. McCandless and his son, as the officers, directors, and sole shareholders of the corporation, together received compensation amounting to approximately 54% of the net profits of the corporation. In determining to what extent the amounts paid to the shareholders were dividends, the court determined that a reasonable return on the investment of the shareholders was justified and concluded that "a return on equity capital equal to 15% of the net profits (before salaries and federal income taxes) would have been reasonable and justified in each of the years under review." The court further stated:

Even a payment deemed reasonable, however, is not deductible to the extent that it is in reality a distribution of corporate earnings and not compensation for services rendered. . . . We think it clear that any return on equity capital is so conspicuous by its absence as to indicate, given all the facts, that the purported compensation payments necessarily contained a distribution of corporate earnings.

The holding in *McCandless* produced the so-called "automatic dividend rule" which provides that, even though compensation may be reasonable, a return on invested capital must be made to the shareholders. Although professional corporations normally have a smaller amount of invested capital than do regular mercantile enterprises, the *McCandless* holding has been held applicable in personal service situations.[8]

Fortunately, the automatic dividend rule established in *McCandless* was rejected by several courts and, in 1979, the Service rejected the automatic dividend rule and agreed that the nonpayment of dividends would be only one significant factor in determining the deductibility of compensation.[9] Some commentators feel that, after the issuance of Rev. Rul. 79-8, the *McCandless* rule has been converted into a "semi-automatic dividend rule."[10]

[13.03] REASONABLE COMPENSATION IN PROFESSIONAL CORPORATIONS

(1) Early Professional Service Cases

There have been very few cases involving the reasonableness of compensation paid to professionals. The two leading cases are *Klamath Medical Service Bureau v. Commissioner*,[11] and *McClung Hospital, Inc.*[12] In *Klamath*, a corporation entered into agreements with its stockholder-physicians to provide medical and surgical services under certain prepaid medical plans sold to local businesses. The Ninth Circuit found that compensation paid by the corporation was deductible up to 100% of the base fee billings and the excess was nondeductible. It was also found that amounts paid to the physicians in excess of 100% of their billings were not reasonable compensation (the contracts did not permit payment in excess of 100%). The facts of the *Klamath* case do differ, however, from that of a typical professional corporation because a typical professional corporation will derive fees only from professional services and not from service contracts and from operating hospitals as in the *Klamath* case.

Subsequent to the *Klamath* case, the Tax Court decided *McClung Hospital*, citing *Klamath* as authority. In *McClung*, the court held that compensation paid to physicians in an amount equal to their entire billings without reduction for expenses or uncollectable accounts was reasonable compensation for the services rendered. In reaching this decision, the Tax Court cited *Klamath* for the position that payments to individual doctors up to 100% of billings was deemed to be reasonable compensation for services rendered.

Although some commentators feel that *Klamath* and *McClung* are "scarcely more than two ten-year old straws in an uncertain wind,"[13] they have been and remain the leading cases in the area. Assuming that they are controlling, they establish the rule that compensation for professional services not exceeding 100% of billings is deductible. However, is compensation payable at a rate of 100% of billings, irrespective of collections and overhead expenses, reasonable where such costs would reduce the professional's *net* profit, if he were operating alone, to 60% of his gross billings? Do *Klamath* and *McClung* apply even where the labors of associates produce cash flow sufficient to cover operating expenses, thereby permitting the professional to receive compensation up to 100% of his gross billings? On the other hand, should professionals be limited to compensation equal only to 100% of billings? Consider, for example, the senior partner in a large law firm who may bill a reduced number of hours because he is constantly in the process of obtaining new business and meeting with clients in order to maintain existing business, spending hours which would not be chargeable.

It appears that *Klamath* and *McClung* are not the final word, but they give some guidance in determining reasonable compensaiton, particularly to smaller professional groups where fees earned from the work of associates and staff members and fees from the use of equipment, such as X-ray machines, are not material factors.

Regulations §1.1348-3(a), dealing with the maximum tax on personal service income, offers some indication of what professional compensation should be considered reasonable. It provides, in part, that:

> The entire amount received by an individual for the performance of personal services, such as services performed by a doctor, dentist, lawyer, architect, or accountant, shall be treated as earned income if the individual is himself invidually and personally responsible for the services performed, even though he employs assistants to perform part or all of such services.
>
> . . . The practice of his profession by a doctor, dentist, lawyer, architect, or accountant will not, as such, be treated as a trade or business in which capital is a material income-producing factor even though the practitioner may have a substantial capital investment in the professional equipment or in the physical plant constituting the office from which he conducts his practice since his capital investment is regarded as only incidental to his professional practice.

Under the above rules, an unincorporated professional, who is not subject to reasonable compensation rules, may treat all of his professional income, whether produced through the help of associates or through the use of equipment, as personal service income and it will be subject to the 50% maximum tax rate.

(2)   Recent Cases Involving Service Corporations[14]

Medical Collection Corporation.[15] The Tax Court found that $260,000 of the $360,000 paid to the president-stockholder of the corporation over a two-year period was reasonable compensation. The court noted that the president had started the company and built it up over the years.

Isaacson, Rosenbaum, Spiegelman & Freidman, P.C. v. United States.[16] A professional legal corporation failed to have questions of reasonable compensation certified to the state supreme court. The corporation made payments out of accumulated earnings to employees who were also corporate directors, without regard to the amount of services each rendered. Characterization of payments as reasonable compensation for purposes of federal taxation is controlled, not by the state law, but by Section 162. This case is still pending.

Nor-Cal Adjustors.[17] A corporation involved in the insurance adjusting business paid its shareholder employees a base salary, extra compensation based on billings, and a bonus in the same percentage as shareholdings. The bonus was deemed to be unreasonable compensation.

Auburn & Associates, Inc. v. United States.[18] The court allowed a deduction to a closely held corporation for high salaries paid to two employees who were under-compensated for their salaries during the initial years of the corporation.

Petro-Chem Marketing Co. v. United States.[19] Involved the deductibility of compensation paid to the stockholder-employees of the corporation whose sole activity was dealing in petro-chemical products. It was conceded that the entire success of the corporation depended on the personal efforts of the stockholder-employees who bought and sold petro-chemical products in a highly sophisticated field. The Court of Claims held that compensation was excessive, citing *McCandless Tile*. The court specifically noted that part of the earnings were produced simply through market fluctuations and not the efforts of the shareholder-employees.

Eduardo Catalano, Inc.[20] The taxpayer was a professional corporation, the sole shareholder of which was a noted architect. As remuneration for his services, the shareholder received both direct compensation from the corporation and deferred compensation paid to a pension plan on his behalf. The Commissioner contended that a portion of this compensation package represented a dividend payment to the shareholder. The Tax Court held that the salary paid to the shareholder was reasonable compensation for services rendered. Payments were made to the shareholder without threatening the financial status of the corporation and compensation amounts were determined prospectively as to anticipated earnings, rather than retrospectively as to immediate past performance of the corporation.

Home Interiors and Gifts, Inc.[21] Salaries, bonuses, and commissions paid as a percentage of a corporation's sales that were paid to its key officers were reasonable compensation. The amounts were comparable to other corporations similarly situated and the key officers were responsible for phenomenal success of corporation. Commissions they received were not disproportionate to those received by other employees. The prosperity of the corporation was shared with stockholders.

Anthony La Mastro.[22] A professional corporation, electing to be treated as a Subchapter S corporation, made contributions to a pension plan during its first taxable year, which consisted of only 14 days. The deduction for the contribution produced a net operating loss for the short taxable year. The Tax Court held that the contribution was, in part, unreasonable compensation and the deduction and the net operating loss produced were reduced accordingly.

Pepsi-Cola Bottling Co. of Salina, Inc. v. Commissioner.[23] Contingent compensation formula for majority shareholder not upheld, even though adopted and enforced in good faith, It was, in fact, an arrangement between the stockholder and herself as an employee.

Bianchi v. Commissioner.[24] In determining reasonable compensation for a professional in a professional corporation, prior earnings as a self-employed practitioner are relevant.

Helen L. Foos.[25] Compensation in excess of $1,000,000 (based on percentage of profits) determined to be reasonable for coal brokerage business. Taxpayer analogized business to professional corporation.

A report of Service audits compiled by the Professional Corporation Committee of the Tax Section of the American Bar Association reported 14 audits across the United States raising the reasonable compensation issue. The audits involve 10 medical or dental corporations, two legal corporations, one accounting corporation, and one medical-legal corporation. Five of the medical audits were settled with no change and one of the legal audits was settled with no change. The overall salary range of the no-change audits was from $30,000 to $750,000, while the range for the other audits was $28,000 to $450,000. This and the other information submitted did not permit the A.B.A. to reach any conclusions regarding predictable patterns of reasonable compensation audits.

[13.04] REDUCING THE CHANCE OF UNREASONABLE COMPENSATION

(1) Documentation

All compensation paid to professionals should be paid to them pursuant to duly executed employment agreements which are executed at the beginning of the fiscal year and are authorized by the board of directors. Further, at the time the agreements are authorized, or at the time raises are granted, the reasons for granting such raises should be reviewed by the board of directors and contained in appropriate minutes. Such minutes should include, among other things, statements regarding the responsibilities, skill, and income earned by the professional. It is also advisable to avoid sudden increases in compensation and to retain a small amount of retained earnings in the professional corporation annually, i.e., $1,000 to $2,000, and steps should be taken to avoid net operating losses in a professional corporation since they appear to attract the attention of the Service.

(2) Bonuses

Care should be taken to avoid year-end bonuses, particularly if they are noncontractual, discretionary bonuses. Regulations §1.162-9 specifically mentions bonuses as an area which may generate unreasonable compensation. Any bonuses which are granted should be contractually established bonuses pursuant to the employment agreement of the shareholders and should be based upon a quantifiable figure, such as production, and should not be a percentage of the net profit of the corporation. Also, if possible, bonuses should be paid periodically during the year and not paid entirely at year end.

(3) Salaries

Salaries should either be a stated dollar amount or they should be based upon production. Some professional corporation advisors recommend using a stated salary which will be established in the professional's employment agreement at the beginning of each fiscal year. This salary will be placed sufficiently high so that all compensation which is anticipated to be paid to the professional during the year can be paid within the stated salary figure without creating a bonus. Further, the employment agreement of the professional will provide that any salary which cannot be paid at the end of the fiscal year of the corporation due to the cash flow of the corporation will be canceled. Care should be taken to avoid setting excessively high salaries so that large amounts of unpaid salary will not remain at the end of the fiscal year.

Compensation based upon formulae are also specifically recognized as acceptable under Regulations §1.167-7(b)(2). If such formulae are negotiated at arm's length, are reasonable when made, and are not merely an attempt to allocate the net profits of the corporation among the shareholders, such formulae will normally be upheld and compensation paid under them will be deemed to be reasonable. However, the Service takes the position that, in closely held corporations, such formulae are seldom negotiated at arm's length and are, usually, merely subterfuges whereby the stockholders divide the profits of the corporation. If compensation formulae are used in a professional corporation, they should be based, not upon the net profits of the corporation, but upon the production of each individual professional, such as calculating compensation as a percentage of the net collections of the professional. If formulae are based on production, and are generally not in the same proportion as are stockholdings, they should be upheld and compensation paid under them should be considered reasonable, since it reflects the activities of the professional.

(4) Subchapter S

In the past, some commentators have felt that the election by a professional corporation of status under Subchapter S will insulate the professionals from charges of unreasonable compensation. However, the reasonable compensation rules apply equally to regular and Subchapter S corporations.[26]

(5) Consumer Price Index

During recent years, the Consumer Price Index, published by the U.S. Department of Labor, has increased dramatically and some advisors feel that indexing professionals' salaries to the Index provides a safe harbor for compensation increases.

(6) Payment of Dividends

The authors feel that it is essential that professional corporations pay dividends. However, this dividend should be smaller than that normally paid by a business corporation and should be at least a "substantial, insignificant dividend."[27] The dividend paid by a professional corporation should normally be computed as a percentage of investment capital and not under the *McCandless* rule, which would require a dividend of 15% of earnings before compensation and taxes. It is difficult to determine what percentage of capital should be paid out as a dividend, but if the dividend becomes so insignificant that it becomes a token dividend, most commentators feel that it will be disregarded.[28] However, since professional corporations normally have a substantially smaller amount of capital, payment of dividends should not be that significant.[29]

It is felt by some, however, that some value should be allocated to goodwill in computing the amount of the dividend to be paid by professional corporations. While it can be argued that professional corporations generally do not have goodwill, it must be recognized that the names of some large law, accounting, and medical practices do have substantial value. At least one court has ascribed goodwill to a professional medical practice in a divorce situation.[30] In *Barton-Gillet Company*,[31] the Tax Court, in determining that a dividend was due to the shareholder of a personal service corporation, concluded that a reasonable return should be paid upon capital, including not only invested and accumulated capital, but also goodwill. The goodwill issue was not mentioned, however, in the subsequent case of *Nor-Cal Adjustors*.[32] In addition, the former Chief Counsel of the Internal Revenue Service, K Martin Worthy, indicated in an article in the July, 1970, issue of *Medical Economics*, that goodwill should be included in valuing the capital of a professional corporation for purposes of dividends and that a dividend rate of from between 15% and 30%, per annum, of invested capital, would be appropriate, with a higher percentage dividend being applied in situations where a professional maintained a "monopoly" on the profession.

In early cases regarding the sales of professional practices, which involved the characterization of the income as either ordinary income or capital gain, the Service took the position that transferable "goodwill" does not attach to the business of the professional man or firm or to any business, the success of which depends solely upon the professional skill, ability, integrity, and other personal characteristics of the owner.[33] The courts did, however, reject this position and, over the years, the position of the Service has changed slightly. In Rev. Rul. 60-301,[34] the Service held that no goodwill is transferred, even where a firm name is transferred, if the business is dependent solely upon the skill and personal characteristics of an owner. In Rev. Rul. 64-235,[35] the Service agreed that it would no longer take the position that, as a matter of law, a one-man professional corporation cannot have salable goodwill. However, in Rev. Rul. 70-45,[36] the Service held that, when a new professional is admitted to a practice, there may be a partial transfer of goodwill.

As a final step in determining the amount of dividend to be paid, the professional should compute the additional cost of the dividend prior to making his decision. For example, if $10,000 of corporate profits will be used to constitute the dividend and if the corporation is in the 17% bracket and the shareholder is in the 50% bracket, the additional cost of the use of the $10,000 for the payment of the dividend is determined as follows: $1,700 will be paid in corporate tax, leaving a dividend of $8,300 to be paid to the professional; without the dividend the corporation will pay no tax, the shareholder will pay $5,000 in tax and have $5,000 in hand; with the dividend, the corporation will pay $1,700 in tax, the individual will pay $4,150 in tax on the $8,300 dividend and will have $4,150 in after-tax cash. By receiving a dividend, rather than compensation, the individual receives $850 less cash after taxes. That is, the individual must pay 50% tax on the $1,700 paid by the corporation producing an extra tax of $850.

(7) Repayment Clauses

In the case of *Vincent E. Oswald*,[37] the Tax Court held that, where a shareholder-employee has a pre-existing obligation to repay to the corporation any amounts of compensation determined on audit to be considered unreasonable, the shareholder-employee will receive a deduction for such repayments in the year in which they are repaid. The Service has agreed to follow the *Oswald* decision and has outlined the requirements in Rev. Rul. 69-115,[38] and the *Oswald* rationale has, again, recently been upheld in *John G. Paul*.[39]

Many professional corporation advisors recommend the use of *Oswald* clauses because, where the corporation is in a lower income tax bracket than the professional, the repayment provision may result in a lower overall tax payable to the government. For this reason, they feel that examining agents will be reluctant to assert a reasonable compensation argument when they must report to their supervisors that they have reduced the overall tax payable to the government. On the other hand, such repayments may be held until later years and subsequently repaid, as compensation, to the affected professional. Further, some professionals appear reluctant to agree to such a repayment provision. Generally, *Oswald* clauses are more suited to smaller corporations.

One definite drawback to the use of *Oswald* clauses which has been mentioned by commentators for some years and recently reiterated in dicta in the case of *Castle Ford, Inc.*,[40] is that the use of an *Oswald* clause may, itself, indicate that the shareholders feel that their compensation may be approaching unreasonable levels. The authors feel that, in most situations, the adoption of an *Oswald* clause by a professional corporation is merely a preventive measure and not an indication that compensation is unreasonable.

If an *Oswald* clause is chosen, it may be placed either in the employment agreement for the employee or in the bylaws of the corporation. Some professional corporation advisors prefer to place the *Oswald* clause in the corporate bylaws in order to avoid the problem raised in *Castle Ford*. That is, the clause will be available if needed, but usually will not appear to the examining agent, since examining agents generally review corporate minute books, but seldom read bylaws in their entirety. As a final precaution, repayment under *Oswald* clauses should be conditioned upon the deductibility of the repayment to the shareholder so that the repayment is not considered a contribution of capital. See the discussion in section [6.04](4), *supra*, and the comment to paragraph 4 of the shareholder employment agreement contained in section [10.01], *supra*.

EXHIBIT 1

XYZ CLINIC, P.C.
COMPENSATION HISTORY
1978, 1979, and 1980 proforma

SHAREHOLDER TOTAL	1978	1979	1980
Salaries	$336,000	$336,000	$336,000
Bonuses	-0-	60,000	60,000
Fringe Benefits (approximate)	3,000	5,000	5,000
Retirement Plans (approximate)	90,000	90,000	90,000
Total Compensation	$429,000	$491,000	$491,000
Dividends	-0-	$ 1,000	$ 10,000
Gross Income	$547,500	$703,300	$725,000
Profit			
Net before tax	4,400	14,600	30,000
Net before compensation and tax	443,400	505,600	521,000
Net before taxes and bonuses	N/A	74,600	90,000
Invested Capital	12,000	20,600	40,000
Compensation/Gross Income	78%	70%	68%

	1978	1979	1980
Compensation/Net Profit before compensation and taxes	99%	97%	94%
Bonuses/Net Profit before taxes and bonuses	N/A	80%	67%
.25 × Invested Capital	3,000	5,150	10,000
.15 × Net Profit before compensation and tax	65,000	75,840	78,150
Dividends/Net Profit before compensation and tax	0%	.2%	2%
Dividends/Invested Capital	0%	4.8%	25%

NOTES TO CHAPTER 13

1. See Eaton, *supra,* Chapter 7, note 1.
2. See *Irby Construction Company*, 290 F.2d 842 (Ct. Cl., 961), and *Robert A. Young*, 38 T.C.M. 957, ¶79,242 P-H Memo T.C. (1979).
3. See Treas. Regs. §1.162-7(b)(3).
4. 66 T.C. 324 (1976), *aff'd* without a published opinion, 553 F.2d 93 (2d Cir. 1977).
5. Also see *Edwin's Inc. v. United States,* 77-1 U.S.T.C. ¶9265, 39 AFTR 2d 77-1161 (W.D. Wis. 1977) (on remand from the 7th Circuit), 501 F.2d 675 (7th Cir. 1974), and *Quinn v. United States*, 77-1 U.S.T.C. 9369, 40 AFTR 2d 77-5097 (D. Md. 1977).
6. Rev. Rul. 67-341, 1967-2 C.B. 156.
7. 442 F.2d 1336 (Ct. Cl. 1970).
8. See *Barton-Gillet Co., *T.C. Memo. 1970-157, *aff'd per curiam* 442 F.2d 1343 (4th cir. 1971).
9. Rev. Rul. 79-8, 1979-1 C.B. 92.
10. See Battle, ''The Use of Corporations by Persons Who Perform Services to Gain Tax Advantages,'' 57 *Taxes* 797, at 810 (1979); *Eduardo Catalano, Inc.,* T.C. Memo. 1979-183.
11. 261 F.2d 842 (9th Cir. 1958), *aff'd* 29 T.C. 399 (1957), *cert. denied,* 359 U.S. 966 (1959), *acq.* 1960-2 C.B. 5.
12. T.C. Memo. 1960-86.
13. Eaton, *supra*, Chapter 7, note 1, at §11.03[3].
14. For further references, see:

    Schwartz, ''Meeting Attacks on the Professional Corporation: Organization Problems; Section 482; Reasonable Compensation; Retirements and Liquidations,'' 32 *NYU Inst. Fed. Tax*. 859, at 876 (1974);

    Cooke, ''Deduction for Return of Disallowed Corporate Payments Depends on Prior Agreement,'' 5 *Taxation for Accountants* 326 (1976).

    Warren and Dunkle, ''Professional Corporations,'' *La Notes*, October, 1971, Vol. 8, Page 1.

    Reimer, ''Shareholder-Employee Compensation—How to Minimize

Chances of IRS Disallowance,'' 5 *Taxation for Lawyers* 356 (1976).

Tannenbaum, "How to Prevent the IRS From Claiming that an Employee's Compensation is a Disguised Dividend,'' 4 *Taxation for Lawyers* 288 (1976).

Hoffman, "Heeding Significant Factors Improves the Odds for 'Reasonable' Compensation,'' March, 1979, *J. Taxation* 150.

Horsley and Dray, "Compensating Stockholders of Professional Corporations: Analysis,'' March, 1971, *J. Taxation* 146.

Holden, "Has the Court of Claims Adopted an 'Automatic Dividend' Rule in Compensation Cases?'' 32 *J. Taxation* 331 (June, 1970).

Capouano, "Tax Advantages and Disadvantages of Professional Corporations,'' 58 *A.B.A.J.* 758, 760 (1972).

Jones, "Is There a Dividend Requirement for Professional Corporations?'' 34 *J. Taxation* 139 (1979).

15. 36 T.C.M. 1074, ¶77,266 P-H Memo T.C. (1977).

16. 44 A.F.T.R. 2d 79-5382 (Ct. Cl., 1979).

17. 30 T.C.M. 837, ¶71,200 P-H Memo T.C. (1971), *aff'd.* 503 F.2d 100 (9th Cir. 1974).

18. 366 F. Supp. 457 (W.D. Pa. 1971).

19. 602 F.2d 959 (Ct. Cl., 1979).

20. 38 T.C.M. 763, ¶79,183 P-H Memo T.C. (1979).

21. 73 T.C. 1142 (1980).

22. 72 T.C. 377 (1979).

23. 528 F.2d 176 (10th Cir. 1976).

24. 66 T.C. 324 (1976), *aff'd* in an unpublished opinion, 553 F.2d 93 (2d Cir. 1977).

25. T.C. Memo 1981-61.

26. See section [5.15], *supra.*

27. A phrase coined by Mr. Harry V. Lamon, Jr., in an address to ALI-ABA course, "Qualified Plans, Insurance, and Professional Corporations—III,'' February 21, 1974, in Phoenix, Arizona.

28. Kalish and Lewis, "Professional Corporations Revisited,'' 28 *Tax Lawyer* 487 (1975).

29. See Rev. Rul. 57-141, 1957-1 C.B. 14, and Ford and Page, "Reasonable Compensation: Continuous Controversy,'' 5 *Journal of Corporate Tax* 307 (1979). Reduced capital should permit reduced dividends, see *Helen L. Foos,* T.C.M. 863, ¶81,061 P-H Memo T.C. (1981).

30. See *Golden v. Golden,* 75 Cal. Rep. 735 (1968), in which a court included $32,000 as goodwill in valuing the husband's community property where he earned between $35,000 and $55,000 during the three years prior to his divorce.

31. T.C. Memo. 1970-157.

32. See section [13.03](1), *supra*.

33. See Rev. Rul. 57-480, 1957-2 C.B. 47.

34. 1960-2 C.B. 15.

35. 1964-2 C.B. 18.

36. 1970-1 C.B. 17.

37. 49 T.C. 645 (1968), acq. 1968-2 C.B. 2.

38. 1969-1 C.B. 50.

39. 67 T.C. 286 (1976). Also, see Rev. Rul. 79-311, 1979-2 C.B. 25, which outlines the proper tax treatment for amounts to be repaid to the corporation and proper accounting for FICA and FUTA taxes previously withheld.

40. T.C. Memo. 1967-157.

PART III

EMPLOYEE BENEFITS

CHAPTER **14**

Maximizing Fringe Benefits in The Professional Corporation

[14.01] PERQUISITES GENERALLY

The area of fringe benefits, or perquisites, has been in a constant state of flux since the establishment of the federal income tax almost 70 years ago. This confusion occurs primarily because of the very broad definition of the term ''gross income'' under Section 61(a) of the Code, which provides that gross income includes ''all income from whatever source derived, including . . . compensation for services . . .'' However, over the years, there have been added to the Code a number of statutory exemptions from gross income. The most notable exemption from gross income is, of course, that for gifts and inheritances, which appear to have no direct connection with compensation, although this is not always the case. See, for example, *Commissioner v. Duberstein*,[1] where the Supreme Court held that a Cadillac transferred in appreciation of business leads was considered gross income.

In the employment context, the fringe benefit concept takes on a special meaning for professional corporations, because fringe benefits which fall within the applicable statutory and Service exclusions permit deductible payments to be made by the professional corporation without a resulting inclusion of income by the professional. At the present time, there are a number of specific fringe benefits which are available to the professional corporation, and they are as follows:

(1) Qualified Retirement Plans

Qualified pension and profit sharing plans which meet the requirements contained in Section 401, *et seq.*, of the Code permit employers to make contributions to a plan for the benefit of employees, as long as the plan meets the various qualification requirements and is not discriminatory in favor of officers, shareholders, or highly compensated individuals (see Chapter 15, *infra*, for a detailed discussion of qualified retirement plans). Contributions to qualified retirement plans are deductible by the employer and not taxable to the employees until distributions from the plans are received. Further, earnings on contributions are not taxable to the plan (or the corporation or the employees).

(2) Accident and Health Plans

Generally, amounts received by employees under accident or health plans as reimbursement for medical expenses or for the loss of a member of the body are not includable in an employee's gross income. Accident and health insurance premium payments are also generally deductible by the professional corporation and are not considered income to the employees. See Sections 104, 105 and 106 of the Code. Further, amounts received as disability payments under wage continuation plans are not, to a limited extent, considered income to employees. See Section 105(d) of the Code. For a general discussion of these provisions, see section [14.03], *infra*.

(3) Employee Death Benefits

Employee death benefits provided by a professional corporation which are not in excess of $5,000 are excludable from the gross income of the beneficiaries and the estate of the deceased employee under Section 101(b) of the Code. See section [14.05], *infra*.

(4) Meals and Lodging

Under Section 119 of the Code, gross income does not include the value of meals or lodging which are provided for employees "for the convenience of the employer."

(5) Group Life Insurance

Section 79 of the Code excludes from an employee's gross income the cost of the first $50,000 of group term life insurance paid by the employer. Special rules apply for group permanent insurance provided by the employer. See section [14.02], *infra*.

In order to qualify as excludable from the income of the employee, fringe benefits must generally be provided under a "plan" for *all* of the employees of the employer. Although it is generally permissible to provide different benefits for different classes of employees, fringe benefit plans which discriminate in favor of officers, highly compensated employees, or shareholders, without regard to their status as employees, are subject to close scrutiny by the Service. Any fringe benefit "plan" provided by professional corporations should demonstrate that the benefits provided are based purely on the employment relationship.[2]

Due to the broad definition of "income" provided in Section 61 of the Code, it would appear that the value of any benefits flowing from the employer to the employee, which are not specifically excluded under the available statutory exemptions, should be considered gross income to the employee. However, a number of nonstatutory exemptions have been provided over the years by the administrative practices of the Service. The primary nonstatutory exception is for facilities and privileges, such as entertainment, medical services, or discounts on purchases furnished to employees. These benefits are not considered wages subject to federal income tax withholding under Regulations §31.3401(a)-1(b)(10) if they are of a relatively small value or offered to employees generally and are merely a means of the employer promoting the goodwill and efficiency of its employees. Although the Regulations do not specifically provide for an exemption from income (but only from withholding), such fringe benefits are generally not considered income by the Service.

Obviously, it is difficult both to value and to withhold income tax on benefits which are provided by an employer in kind to an employee. Also, since most employee fringe benefits are provided under plans which are not required to be filed with the Service (except for qualified retirement plans), abuse in the fringe benefit area is only discoverable by the Service on audit. Consequently, the fringe benefit area is of constant interest to the Service which has, for years, attempted to provide general rules under which the value of fringe benefits may be determined and taxed to employees.

In 1975, the Treasury made its most venturesome attempt to define fringe benefits by issuing a Discussion Draft of Proposed Regulations §1.61-16 and Proposed Amendments of Regulations.[3]

The discussion draft of Proposed Regulations §1.61-16 provides general rules in determining whether fringe benefits constitute taxable compensation for employees; they are as follows:

(1) If the value of the benefit provided is so small as to make accounting for it unreasonable or administratively impractical, the benefit is not taxable to the employee.

(2) The benefit is generally not taxable to the employee if it is incidental to the employer's business (such as air fare discounts for airline employees), is not

limited to highly paid employees, and does not create an additional cost for the employer.

(3) If the fringe benefit is not excludable under either of the two foregoing rules, then the taxable status of the benefit is determined by reviewing all of the facts and circumstances. Among the more important factors to be considered are whether the cost to the employer is not significant in relation to the value, whether the benefit is a reimbursement of a greater than usual time of expense which was incurred by the employee for a purpose normally thought to be primarily personal, whether the benefit is an insubstantial amount in comparison to the employee's salary, and whether the benefit is provided primarily to insure the employee's safety by protecting against risk encountered in the employment relationship.

The Discussion Draft was obviously introduced in order to produce comment and criticism, which it did. Under substantial pressure from the business community, the Treasury withdrew the Discussion Draft on September 28, 1976. Nevertheless, the Service, under the administration of President Carter, continued to scrutinize fringe benefit programs, particularly those of closely held and professional corporations. For this reason, it is important that the professional and his advisors assure that the fringe benefit programs which are provided by the professional corporation are sanctioned either by statutory or regulatory exemption. Otherwise, the value of the fringe benefit provided will probably be considered a constructive dividend by the Service.

However, responding to overwhelming Congressional pressure, the Reagan administration agreed to a moratorium on the fringe benefit Regulations and Section 801 of ERTA prohibits the issuance of Regulations until December 31, 1983.

[14.02] LIFE AND DISABILITY INSURANCE

(1) Group Term Insurance Under Section 79

One of the most favorable and often used benefits available to professionals through incorporation is group term life insurance under Section 79 of the Code. Section 79 of the Code was enacted in 1964 to provide a statutorily accepted fringe benefit, under which employers may provide, on a tax-free basis, group term life insurance protection for employees of up to $50,000. Section 79 covers only group term life insurance (which may have a permanent feature) and does not cover travel, accident, or health insurance. Group term life insurance under Section 79 provides the following advantages for the professional:

(1) The premiums paid by the professional corporation are deductible.
(2) The professional is not taxable on the premium payments, except to the extent that more than $50,000 of coverage is provided.

(3) To the extent that the professional is taxed on coverage in excess of $50,000, the professional is taxed at favorable Table I rates under the Regulations.

(4) The professional owns the policy and may assign it to his spouse or a trust, thus removing the insurance proceeds from his estate if the assignment is made more than three years before the date of death. Further, any insurance proceeds received under the policy are, as with other insurance, tax-free under Section 101(a) of the Code.

(5) Group term life insurance is often provided on a guaranteed issue basis without the necessity of the professional proving insurability.

Group term insurance is generally provided under a master policy with a commercial insurance company, but may be provided under individual policies (as is the case in many closely held and professional corporations).

Thus, group term life insurance provides an excellent method of providing additional insurance for the professional with tax deductible dollars. As with other types of term insurance, group term life insurance has, however, the disadvantage that premiums do escalate in later years and coverage will terminate automatically upon retirement (unless the professional corporation agrees to continue the policy). Further, where the professional corporation employs fewer than 10 employees, group term life insurance under Section 79 of the Code may not be available without proof of insurability.

(a) *General Rules*

In order to qualify as a group term insurance plan under Section 79 of the Code and under Regulations §1.79-1, a group term insurance plan must satisfy the following requirements:

(1) *Term Insurance*
Term insurance must be provided.
(2) *Permanent Insurance.*

An insurance policy that includes permanent insurance or a cash surrender value may be part of a Section 79 plan if:

(a) The policy or the employer designates in writing the part of the death benefit that is group term life insurance.

(b) The part designated as group term life insurance must correspond to a detailed formula provided in the regulations.

(c) Employees must be given an option to elect to receive or to be excluded from the permanent coverage.

(d) The death benefit designated as group term insurance must not be reduced because of an employee's election to be excluded from the permanent coverage.

(3) *Death Benefit.*

A group term insurance plan adopted by an employer must provide a general death benefit that is excludable from gross income under Section 101(a) of the Code. Under Regulations §1.79-1(f)(3), travel insurance, health insurance, and accident insurance (including amounts payable under double indemnity clauses) do not provide general death benefits and may not be included in Section 79 plans.

(4) *Coverage Must Be Provided Under a Plan*
    For a Group of Employees.

Group term insurance coverage must be provided under a *plan* arranged by the professional corporation for a *group* of its employees. The plan must cover a group of employees that includes either all of the employees of the professional corporation or a class of employees which is determined solely on the basis of age, marital status, or factors related to employment. The coverage requirements for group term insurance are not as restrictive as those applicable to qualified retirement plans under Section 401, *et seq.* [4] Regulations §1.79-0 specifically states that factors relating to employment include membership in a union, duties performed, compensation received, length of service, or participation in the employer's pension, profit sharing or accident and health plans (even where such plans require employee contributions). The Regulations state that stock ownership is not a factor related to employment and prior regulations specifically stated that insurance which was available only to stockholders would not qualify as a Section 79 plan. [5]

Only employees in the common-law sense or former common-law employees may obtain the income exclusion provided under Section 79 of the Code. Insurance provided for corporate directors is not available for coverage under Section 79. [6] Thus, it is important for a professional corporation to cover all full-time employees under the group Section 79 plan in order to make coverage for the professionals available. Since the cost of group term life insurance for staff employees is usually minimal, there is normally very little burden placed upon the professional corporation by providing coverage for them. Further, insurance coverage may be provided under Section 79 for an employee's spouse and dependents if it is incidental (i.e., does not exceed $2,000 on any one life). [7]

In plans covering 10 or more full-time employees, the insurer may require evidence of insurability, including a medical examination. [8] However, in plans covering fewer than 10 full-time employees, eligibility and amount of coverage may be based only on evidence of insurability which may be determined through the use of a medical questionnaire completed by the employee, rather than by a physical examination. [9] Further, in plans covering fewer than 10 full-time employees, additional voluntary medical information furnished by the employee may not be made the basis of a premium rate determination. [10]

Special rules apply for determining the existence of a Section 79 plan if the covered group is at all times during the calendar year fewer than 10 employees. In general, where (at all times during the calendar year) fewer than 10 employees are covered, a plan will exist only if the plan benefits all full-time employees who are insurable, or all full-time employees (without regard to insurability) who are represented by an organization such as a union, which organization carries on substantial activities in addition to obtaining insurance. The plan may require a waiting period for new employees of up to six months and may exclude part-time employees (whose customary employment is not more than 20 hours per week or five months in any calendar year) and employees over age 65.[11]

(5) *Insurance Provided Under a Policy Carried Directly or Indirectly by the Employer*

This requirement of the Regulations is met if the employer pays any part of the cost (directly or indirectly) or arranges for the payment by the employees and charges at least one employee less than a Table I cost and at least one other employee more than the Table I cost. Group term coverage may be provided by a master policy or by a group of individual policies.

(6) *Insurance Coverage*

In order to constitute a group term plan under Section 79,[12] the amount of insurance provided to covered employees must be based on a formula that precludes individual selection. The Regulations state that factors such as salary, years of service, or position, or a combination of such factors, are permissible. In addition, the Regulations permit amounts to be subject to employee contributions to the plan. Thus, most group term insurance plans under Section 79 provide coverage based either upon the status as a professional (versus nonprofessional employees) or status as an officer.

In order for plans with fewer than 10 full-time employees to qualify under Section 79, the amount of coverage must be either: (1) a uniform percentage of salary; or (2) based upon coverage (established by the insurer under which no bracket exceeds two and one-half times the next lower bracket and the lowest is at least 10% of the highest bracket). The accepted method of meeting this requirement is to provide coverage of $50,000 for professional employees who are officers of the corporation, $25,000 of coverage for professional employees who are not officers of the corporation (or $25,000 coverage for the office manager if there are no such professionals), and $10,000 of coverage for all staff employees. For a number of years, some professionals felt that they could meet these coverage requirements by providing a middle bracket (such as that for non-officer professionals) even though there would probably never be anyone to fill that bracket. However, Rev. Rul. 80-220[13] provides that these requirements will be met only if there is actual coverage in the classification necessary to meet these requirements (i.e., $25,000 of insurance must be provided for some employees).

The Regulations provide no special coverage rules (either based on percentages or amounts) on plans with more than 10 full-time employees. Consequently, it has been felt that such plans could provide widely divergent coverage for the first $50,000 (i.e., $50,000 for officers and $10,000 for all other employees). However, in 1980, the Service issued Rev. Proc. 80-22[14] which provides that the Service will no longer issue rulings as to whether a group insurance plan for 10 or more employees qualifies as group term insurance if the amount of insurance is not computed in accordance with the rules applicable for plans for fewer than 10 employees. The impact of this recent Service position is not clear since there is no justification for it in the Regulations.

It is also possible to superimpose additional coverage (over $50,000) under Section 79 plans. However, care should be taken to assure that when such coverage is provided the formula used for providing such insurance precludes individual selection. In a Technical Advice Memorandum issued as Letter Ruling 7852013,[15] an employer established a group term insurance plan for the benefit of 41 employees. The amount of basic coverage varied for five classes of employees stated in the plan with class amounts ranging from $5,000 to $50,000. In addition, the president, who was the sole shareholder, received $1,000,000 in group term insurance coverage and his son, who was a vice president, received $500,000 of group term insurance coverage. The Service stated that the coverage of the president and vice president was not group term insurance since the amount of their coverage was not based upon a formula that precluded individual selection. Although the group term plan covered more than 10 employees, the Service referred to the rules applicable to plans covering fewer than 10 employees and noted that the amount of coverage of the president and vice president was not a uniform percentage of their salary and that the amount of coverage was 42 and 22 times the coverage of the next lowest class (so that the two and one-half rule was not satisfied). This Technical Advice Memorandum suggests that, where disproportionate amounts of group term coverage are provided for key employees, the Service may treat this coverage as a separate plan under which the coverage test applicable to plans covering fewer than 10 employees would apply. The most probable tax consequence would be for the Service to treat the payment of the additional premium as a constructive dividend to the owners.

(7) Compliance with State Law

In order to constitute a group term insurance plan under Section 79 of the Code, the arrangement must satisfy any state law requirements applicable to group term insurance. Hence, the exemption under Section 79 is not available for amounts of insurance in excess of the maximum amount which may be provided by a single contract of group term life insurance under applicable state law, irrespective of the general $50,000 allowance.[16] If a plan provides for group term coverage in excess of the amount permitted under state law, the employee will be taxed on the actual premium for any coverage exceeding the state law maximum and not the Table I cost of such coverage.[17]

(b) Income Tax Consequences of Group Term Life Insurance to Employees

Prior to the Revenue Act of 1964, former Regulations §1.61-(d)(2) provided that "premiums paid by an employer on policies of group term life insurance covering the lives of his employees are not gross income to his employees, even if they designate the beneficiaries.'' This exemption from taxation was not subject to any dollar limitation. However, with the advent of Section 79(a) of the Code, this rule was changed and Section 79 provides for the inclusion in the gross income of an employee of an amount equal to the cost of group term life insurance on his life provided for all or part of such year under a policy carried by his employer, but only to the extent that such cost exceeds the sum of (1) the cost of $50,000 of insurance, and (2) the amount (if any) paid by the employee toward the purchase of such insurance. The $50,000 limitation applies to all coverage provided by all employers in the aggregate in the case of an employee covered by plans of more than one employer.

Regulations §1.79-3 prescribes the rules for determining the cost of group term life insurance on an employee's life which is to be included in his gross income pursuant to the rules of inclusion set forth in Section 79(a). Such amount is determined by computing the cost of the portion of group term life insurance on the employee's life to be taken into account for each ''period of coverage'' (defined as any one-calendar-month period, or part thereof, during the employer's taxable year during which the employee is provided group term life insurance on his life), aggregating the cost so determined, then reducing that amount by the amount paid by the employee toward the purchase of the group term life insurance. Table I of the Regulations, which is set forth in full below, determines the cost for each $1,000 of group term life insurance on an employee's life for each one month period. The cost of the portion of the group term life insurance on each employee's life for each period of coverage for one month is obtained by multiplying the number of thousands of dollars of such insurance coverage (computed to the nearest 10th) which is provided during each period by the appropriate amount set forth in Table I.

TABLE I

Uniform Premiums for $1,000
of Group Term Life Insurance Protection

Five-Year Age Bracket	Cost per $1,000 of Protection for One Month Period
Under 30	$ .08
30 to 34	$ .10
35 to 39	$ .14
40 to 44	$ .23
45 to 49	$ .40
50 to 54	$ .68
55 to 59	$1.10
60 to 64	$1.63

Employees older than age 64 are treated as if they fall within the 60 to 64 age bracket.

The net premium cost of group term life insurance as provided in Table I applies only to the cost of group term life insurance subject to the rules of inclusion set forth in Section 79(a). Thus, in determining the amount to be included in the employee's gross income, only the cost of the portion of insurance coverage in excess of $50,000 is taken into account. There is no requirement for income tax withholding on the amount included in the employee's income. However, the employer must list the cost of such insurance for each employee for each year on Form W-2, in accordance with the instructions to that Form, but only to the extent that such cost is taxable to the employee under Section 79(a). Amounts subject to income tax under Section 79(a) will be subject to the maximum 50% tax on personal service income provided under Section 1348 of the Code.[18]

Section 79 group term life insurance provides a very economical method for providing life insurance protection for those individuals within a professional corporation who desire additional insurance coverage. Although the Table I rates are generally thought to be very low because they are based on old income tax regulations, such rates were also based on old mortality tables. The increased longevity of individuals has, currently, permitted life insurance companies to provide lower-cost term insurance, sometimes approaching the Table I costs. However, even if the cost of term insurance does approach the Table I cost, the requirement that the employee only report as taxable income the amount of such premium will provide an exceptional benefit. For example assume that a 60-year-old physician incorporated his professional practice and has a marginal income tax rate (federal, state and local) of 65% and that the incorporated medical practice provides $300,000 of group term life insurance for him. The annual Table I cost of $250,000 of excess coverage is $5,000 to the physician and the cost of including that amount in his income in tax dollars will be approximately $3,250. If the physician were to provide such insurance himself, the pre-tax bonus necessary to provide sufficient funds to pay tax on the excess coverage would be in excess of $9,000. Also, assuming that the annual premium on such excess coverage would approach $6,000 if such coverage were obtained separately by the physician, the pre-tax income necessary to pay such premium would be in excess of $17,000. Section 79 group term insurance can be provided in lieu of nonqualified deferred compensation. By providing such additional insurance, the professional corporation can assure the professional that what would have been an unfunded liability of the corporation will be paid in the event of his death, and it can be paid to his wife or to a trust, thus eliminating estate taxes. On the other hand, group term coverage normally terminates upon retirement, and the professional should carefully weigh the benefits of such coverage versus any direct reduction in deferred compensation.

Problems may arise in the professional corporation setting where one or more of the professionals do not qualify for group term insurance due to medical problems. If additional fringe benefits are provided to the professional who cannot qualify for group term insurance, care should be taken not to create a *de facto* cafeteria plan, since such a *de facto* plan would probably not qualify under the cafeteria plan rules. See section [14.04], *infra*.

For purposes of computing taxable income resulting from a plan providing group term insurance in excess of $50,000, all employee contributions to the plan will be allocable to coverage in excess of $50,000. Thus, an employee's contributions are subtracted in full from the amount that would otherwise be taxable to him. An employee cannot, however, carry over from year to year any unused portion of his contributions. As can be seen from the example of the incorporated physician above, a significant tax benefit occurs where the professional does not contribute toward the plan and it is probably preferable to avoid employee contributions.

Section 79(b) of the Code provides several exceptions to the general rule that group term coverage in excess of $50,000 is taxable to the insured employee. If either of the following exceptions is applicable, no portion of the premiums paid by the employer is includable in the gross income of the employee:

(1) Code Section 79(b)(1) exempts group term coverage after an employee has terminated employment with the employer and has reached retirement age or has become disabled within the meaning of Section 72(m)(7) of the Code. The continuation of group term insurance for retired employees may become excessively expensive, but this exception does provide the basis for retired lives reserve plans discussed in detail in section 7.02[3], *infra*.

(2) Code Section 79(b)(2) exempts group term coverage under which the employer is directly or indirectly a beneficiary or under which a charity (under Section 170(c)) is the sole beneficiary.

(3) Code Section 79(b)(3) exempts group term coverage provided by a qualified pension, profit sharing or stock bonus plan. However, the "P.S. 58 cost" of insurance provided for by such plans will be currently taxable to the employees and there is no minimum tax-free amount comparable to the $50,000 Section 79 limit. See section [15.02] (14), *infra*, for a detailed discussion of the use of life insurance in qualified retirement plans.

(c) *Income Tax Consequences of Group Term Insurance to the Employer*

In general, premiums paid by an employer for group term life insurance on the lives of its employees are currently deductible.[19] Employer contributions will not, however, be deducted unless, when considered with all of the employee's other compensation, they qualify as "reasonable compensation." No deduction will be allowed for the cost of coverage on the life of an employee, however, if the employer is the beneficiary under the policy, either directly or indirectly.[20] The Service has privately held that, where company-paid group term life insurance is used to fund a buy-sell agreement between the shareholders of a corporation, the employer cannot deduct the premium since the premium payments are not related to the employer's trade or business.[21]

(d) *Gift Tax Consequences Applicable to Group Term Life Insurance*[22]

Under Rev. Rul. 76-490,[22] the Service stated its position regarding the gift tax consequences of a transfer of a group term policy. Under that ruling, an employee transferred to an irrevocable trust all of his rights, title, and interest in a group term policy. Under the terms of the trust, the employee's beneficiary was to receive the full proceeds of the policy immediately upon the death of the employee. The ruling states that the initial transfer to the trust did not constitute a taxable gift since the employee's interest in the group policy had no ascertainable value at the time of the transfer due to the fact that the employer could terminate the plan at any time. The ruling further states, however, that each time the employer paid a group term premium, the employee was deemed to have made an indirect transfer to the trust of the employer premiums paid on behalf of the employee and such indirect transfer is subject to gift tax under Code Section 2501. Further, the ruling states that the gift so created was not a gift of a future interest and therefore qualified for the $3,000 annual gift tax exclusion of Code Section 2503(b). Under ERTA, for transfers made after December 31, 1981, the annual gift tax exclusion is $10,000 per donee.

In Rev. Rul. 79-47,[23] the same basic facts existed as in Rev. Rul. 76-490, except that the trustee of the irrevocable trust was required, rather than to make immediate payments of the proceeds of insurance to the beneficiary, to hold the proceeds of insurance and to pay income to the employee's children and the corpus to his grandchildren. The Ruling stated that the employer's payment of group term premiums would constitute a taxable gift by the employee to the trust but that the gift would not qualify for the Code Section 2503(b) $3,000 annual exclusion because of the failure to require immediate payment to the grantor's beneficiary.

In several recent private letter rulings, the Service has, however, indicated that there are methods under which the gift created under Rev. Rul. 76-490 can be considered a present interest under Code Section 2503(b). In Letter Ruling 8006109, a donor proposed to transfer group term life insurance and $1,000 in cash to an irrevocable insurance trust. The trust contained withdrawal powers which would have permitted the beneficiaries to withdraw $3,000 annually under *Crummey v. Commissioner*.[24] The Service ruled that the transfer of the policy to the trust would qualify as a present interest and that when the premium payments were made by the employer such payments would also constitute a present interest. Consequently, in the event that a beneficiary of an irrevocable life insurance trust has the power to withdraw trust assets annually, either in the form of cash or in the form of the insurance policy itself, the present interest requirements of Section 2503(b) should be satisfied.

(e) *Estate Tax Considerations Applicable to Group Term Life Insurance*

In general, the broad principles of Section 2042 require inclusion of group term insurance in the employee's gross estate if he has any incidents of ownership in the policy. Where all of the incidents of ownership have been transferred to another by the employee at least three years prior to his date of death, exclusion from estate taxation of the proceeds will be achieved.[25] Further, a majority shareholder who has transferred all of the incidents of ownership of a policy will not be considered to continue to have an incident of ownership merely because the corporation can discontinue the group plan.[26] The Service has also, after several years of indecision, determined that where the employer changes insurance carriers (and consequently new assignments must be made by the employee), a new three-year period under Section 2035 of the Code will not commence.[27] It should be noted, however, that the general applicability of Section 2035 was removed by ERTA, but that Section 2035 will continue to apply to transfers of life insurance policies within three years of death.

(f) *Plan Document*

Plans of group life insurance under Section 79 should be set forth in writing and adopted by appropriate resolution of the professional corporation. Care should also be taken to assure that the rights of employees under ERISA, as described in section [14.10], *infra*, are granted. The following is a form of Section 79 plan which may be adopted.

X, Y, AND Z, P.C.

GROUP INSURANCE PLAN

WHEREAS, the X, Y, and Z, P.C. ("Employer") desires to restate its existing plan of group insurance for its employees classified below; and

WHEREAS, such plan of group insurance is designed to qualify for the tax benefits available under Section 79 of the Internal Revenue Code and Section 1.79 of the Income Tax Regulations;

NOW, THEREFORE, effective _____, the Employer hereby establishes the following plan of group insurance:

A. Name of Employer: _____
   Address of Employer: _____
                            _____
   Type of Business Entity: _____

B. Eligible Employees:

   The term "employees" shall mean all employees whose customary employment is for more than 20 hours per week or more than five months in any calendar year. All employees employed by the Employer on the effective date of this Plan shall be eligible to participate immediately. Any person becoming an employee on a later date shall be eligible to participate on the first day of the month following six months of employment.

C. Benefits:

   (1) Benefits shall be provided to eligible employees through group insurance as described in the attached schedule.

   Premiums for the insurance set forth in the attached schedule shall be paid for by the Employer.

The insurance set forth in the attached schedule shall be initially provided through the following contract:

Policy Number: _____

Issued by: _____

(2) In addition to the benefit set forth in Section C(1), employees who are members of Classes 1 and 2 shall be eligible for additional term life insurance in the amount of $200,000 and $100,000, respectively.

Policies under Section C(2) shall be issued only to those employees eligible for same who elect to participate and make appropriate application therefor, and provide such information and submit to such examination as the life insurance company shall require.

D. Miscellaneous Provisions:

(1) The fiduciary under this Plan shall be the Employer.

(2) The administrator of this Plan shall be the Employer.

(3) The Employer may amend or terminate this Plan at any time, and shall have the power and authority to adopt policies or regulations with respect to the administration of the Plan as it may deem reasonable.

(4) The _____ Life Insurance Company is not a party to this Plan, and its liability is limited to the terms of the policies it issues pursuant hereto.

(5) It is the intent of the Employer that this Plan and the policies issued hereunder qualify for certain tax benefits as a plan of group life insurance under Section 79 of the Internal Revenue Code and Section 1.79 of the Income Tax Regulations. The classes of employees herein set forth and the formula for determining amounts of insurance have been established on a basis intended to preclude individual selection. It is further intended that this Plan provide group term life insurance protection for at least 10 full-time employee at some time during a calendar year.

E. Effective Date:

This Plan is effective as of _____, 19___.

X, Y, AND Z, P.C.

By: _____
                                 President

BENEFIT SCHEDULE

Benefits shall be provided to eligible employees in accordance with the following schedule:

Class 1	Officers	$50,000
Class 2	Professional Employees Who are Not Officers	$25,000
Class 3	All Other Employees	$10,000

(2) Group Permanent Insurance

Prior to November 4, 1976, insurance companies were permitted to market a very attractive group "permanent" insurance product as a supplement to group term plans. However, on that date the Service gave notice that it was suspending the issuance of Private Letter Rulings regarding the tax consequences of group permanent insurance programs. During the next several years, various forms of Proposed Regulations were issued which finally became permanent on May 14, 1979. These Regulations[28] provide specific limitations for those situations in which group permanent insurance may be a part of a group term program. The new Regulations generally provide for a larger portion of the premium for the permanent insurance to be taxable to the employee and, consequently, group permanent insurance under Section 79 of the Code has become less attractive. Generally, excess group term life insurance, retired lives reserve insurance, or split dollar insurance will provide a better premium value. Group permanent insurance should not, however, be overlooked, and the professional and his advisors should closely scrutinize any group permanent product offered and review with their counsel the impact of such a group permanent insurance program under the Regulations, which are quite complicated.

(3) Retired Lives Reserve

Retired lives reserve insurance originated in the 1940's and became a sanctioned tax concept only in 1969.[29] Basically, retired lives reserve insurance is a group term insurance product which provides favorable tax consequences to the employer corporation due to the interplay between the taxation of regular business corporations and the rules regarding the taxation of life insurance companies.

A retired lives reserve is a fund for continuing group term life insurance on employees after retirement. Accordingly, a prerequisite to the establishment of a retired lives reserve program is the existence of a group term life insurance program.[30] The statutory basis for retired lives reserve lies in Section 79(b)(1), which provides that Section 79(a) will not apply to the cost of group term life insurance which is provided under a policy carried directly or indirectly by an employer after an individual has terminated employment and either has reached the retirement age or is disabled. The need for retired lives reserve arises because most group term insurance ceases upon an employee's termination of employment, or becomes so prohibitively expensive that the employer must discontinue coverage. Consequently, retired lives reserve is a method for the continuation of group term coverage for retired employees through the establishment of a pre-retirement reserve to accumulate funds to be used for the future payment of premiums. Such a fund assures the employer that amounts will be available to provide for the payment of premiums and provides security to the retiring employee that his coverage will not be canceled. Such objectives are particularly important to highly paid employees of professional corporations.

The overriding factor in evaluating the desirability of establishing a retired lives reserve program will be the income tax consequences to the employer and the employee and also the estate and gift tax consequences to the employee. Typically, the following tax consequences are sought:

    (1) Current deductibility of employer contributions to the reserve;

    (2) Excludability from employee's gross income of employer contributions to the reserve and income earned by the reserve, both during employment and when applied after retirement for the purchase of insurance;

    (3) Excludability of the proceeds of the insurance from the gross income of a beneficiary.

In many cases, employees will also be concerned about the possibility of planning techniques that will permit them to exclude the proceeds of the insurance from their gross estates as well as to avoid adverse gift tax consequences during life. Other than the indication in Section 79(b) that premium payments for retired employees need not be included in their gross incomes, there is no statutory authority for the tax treatment of retired lives reserve insurance and the tax consequences of retired lives reserve insurance has been established over the years through public and private rulings by the Service. At this time, however, the tax consequences of retired lives insurance are somewhat more tenuous due to the announced policy of the Service to suspend the issuance of rulings on retired lives reserve insurance.[31] The authors understand that, while the Service does not explicitly favor the abolition of the retired lives reserve concept, it does favor the lessening of the tax benefits (i.e., the total deductibility to the employer without inclusion in income of employees). The following discussion outlines the tax benefits sought through retired lives reserve insurance.

(a) *Current Deductibility of Employer Contributions and Nontaxability of Earnings of Reserve*

Rev. Rul. 69-382,[32] provides that, if the following conditions are satisfied, employer contributions will be currently deductible, assuming that such contributions are otherwise deductible under Section 162:[33]

    (1) The balance of the reserve must be used solely for the purpose of providing group term insurance coverage for current or retired employees as long as any current or retired employee remains alive.

    (2) Contributions must be made on a level basis and be no greater than is necessary to allocate the cost of post-retirement group term insurance coverage over the working lives of the employees involved. However, Rev. Rul. 73-599[34] states that, if contributions in excess of the ratable amount necessary for level funding are made, such excess contributions may be carried over and deducted in future years.

    (3) The employer must have no right of reversion of amounts in the reserve as long as any current or retired employee remains alive.

    (4) In Rev. Rul. 73-599 and Rev. Rul. 77-92,[35] the Service held that the reservation by the employer of the right to recover a retired lives reserve fund held

by an insurance company for the purpose of transferring the reserve to a Section 501(c)(9) trust, or to another insurance carrier that will continue the retired lives reserve program, will violate the requirement of Rev. Rul. 69-478, providing that the employer may not retain the right to recover any portion of the reserve so long as any active or retired employee remains alive. In each of these rulings, the employer could have, under the terms of the plan, elected to retain the reserve rather than transfer the reserve. However, the Service has ruled[36] that the reservation of the right to transfer funds from the original insurance carrier to a new carrier, unaccompanied by a right to retain the funds, would not constitute an impermissible reservation of rights.

(5) Assets of the reserve may be owned by a nonexempt trust, a voluntary employee association exemption under Section 501(c)(9), or a segregated account held by a life insurance company.

(6) Upon termination of the retired lives reserve arrangement and after the death of all employees who were at any time covered under the plan, any remaining funds in the reserve may revert to the employer.

(b) *Income Tax Consequences to Employees*

The Service has not challenged the principle that transfers by the employer to the reserve are not included in the gross income of the employee at the time the transfer is made. It appears, however, that an argument could be made for requiring inclusion in an employee's income of employer contributions under the principles of Section 83(a) of the Code at the time the employee acquires a vested right to have future insurance premiums paid from the reserve. The failure of the Service over the past 10 years, since the enactment of Section 83, to apply Section 83 to retired lives reserve provides some measure of assurance that inclusion under Section 83 will not become a problem in the future.

Further, under Code Section 79(b)(1), the payment of post-retirement group term insurance from the reserve will not result in gross income to the recipient, and the payment of proceeds upon the death of the employee will be excluded from the gross income of the beneficiary under Section 101(a).

(c) *Estate Tax Treatment*

Retired lives reserve insurance with respect to which all incidents of ownership have been transferred more than three years before the date of death should be excludable from the estate of the employee.[37]

(d) *Gift Tax Planning*

Where an employee assigns his rights in his retired lives reserve policy to a third party while he is employed, a gift tax problem may be created annually when the employer makes deposits to the reserve. Rev. Rul. 76-490,[38] held that, when an employee assigned a group term life insurance policy to an irrevocable trust, the employer's payment of the term insurance premium would constitute an indirect transfer to the trust on an annual basis. Also, in Rev. Rul. 79-47,[39] the Service indicated that the amount of the annual gift made upon the assignment of a group term policy will be the amount of the premium. These rulings would indicate that, if the employee has any rights under the retired lives reserve policy which he can assign, the amounts paid by the employer into the reserve may constitute an annual gift. However, some advisors believe that no pre-retirement gift tax problem exists because the employee has no vested interest in the contributions made by the employer or in the reserve fund itself. That is, until retirement, the employee merely has an expectancy which may not mature into a vested interest.

In many cases, an employee's right in the employer's continued payment of retired lives reserve insurance is contingent upon service until retirement. It is possible that, upon retirement (or upon the occurrence of some other condition that causes the employee's rights to vest), the taxable gift which occurs is the present value of a vested right to receive the benefit of future payments. Such a conclusion would seem to be the logical result under Rev. Rul. 76-490 and Rev. Rul. 79-47.[40] The occurrence of a large taxable gift upon retirement may, however, be avoided by the use of a forfeiture provision (i.e., in the event a retired employee enters competition with his employer).

(e) *Practical Problems with Retired Lives Reserve Insurance*

As previously indicated, the tax benefits of retired lives reserve insurance are based, to a large extent, upon the available income tax advantages (i.e., total deductibility of premium payments by employer and exclusion of premium payments from income during and after retirement by employee). In addition to the substantial gift tax problems which arise when an employee terminates his employment and becomes fully "vested" in his retired lives reserve insurance, another major practical problem exists because the employer is not entitled to receive a refund of the reserve amounts. This may cause particular problems in professional corporations where, for some reason, the professional corporation is forced to discontinue the plan or where the professional, for whom the insurance was funded, dies prior to retirement. If the professional does die prior to retirement, amounts placed in the reserve to fund his post-retirement insurance will not inure to his benefit and must be held, probably for a number of years, in the reserve.

Also, the tax benefits of retired lives reserve, since they are not established by statutory authority, are subject to change by the Service, and the authors anticipate that any such changes would apply on a prospective basis for new policies and for policies in existence on the date of the change (for amounts placed in the reserve after that date). Authority for such a result appears in the effective date provisions established for amendments to the group permanent regulations.[41]

Due to these problems, the authors recommend that very serious considerations be given before any retired lives reserve plan is adopted and that professionals consider other types of insurance, such as additional group term and split dollar insurance.

(4) Split Dollar Insurance

(a) *General Description*

Split dollar insurance is a method of providing insurance for selected employees and can produce favorable income and estate tax results. Unlike group term life insurance, the premiums paid by a corporation under a split dollar arrangement are not deductible. Also, under most split dollar arrangements, the employee must either report a portion of the premium as income or contribute toward the payment of the premium. However, because of the availability of the corporate surtax exemption, split dollar insurance is an excellent vehicle for providing additional whole life insurance coverage for only the professional employees of a professional corporation at low corporate tax rates. While there are a myriad of split dollar arrangements which may be employed, this section describes only those arrangements which are specially suited to the professional corporation and the needs of the professional.

Split dollar insurance generally permits the joining of two parties in connection with the purchase of a whole life insurance policy, where one of the parties has a need for insurance protection and the other party has the ability and desire to pay the premiums. Split dollar insurance is most commonly used between employer and employee, but it may also be used between individuals, trusts, partnerships, or corporations. Split dollar arrangements are established by written agreements which specify the respective obligations of the parties for the payment of premiums and designate the entitlement of the parties to the rights and benefits of the policy. The structuring of the split dollar arrangement is critical since subtle variations in the form of the arrangement may result in significant tax consequences. A copy of a typical "collateral assignment" split dollar arrangement is attached to this subsection. Split dollar insurance does not require approval by the Service or any other federal agency. Also, unlike group term insurance, the employer has complete freedom to select those employees who will participate in any split dollar arrangements and there is no requirement that all employees, or a particular class of employees, be covered. The authors recommend, however, that split dollar arrangements which are established be based upon employment status rather than shareholder status.

Split dollar arrangements are commonly used to provide life insurance protection for key employees, to fund stockholders' cross-purchase agreements, and to provide funds for nonqualified deferred compensation arrangements and salary continuation arrangements.

(b) *Ownership of the Split Dollar Policy*

The insurance policy used in connection with a split dollar arrangement may be owned either by the professional corporation, the professional, or some third party (the spouse of the professional, his children, or a trust). There are two common methods of ownership known as the "endorsement method" and the "collateral assignment method."

Under the endorsement method of ownership, the professional corporation applies for and owns the policy, including the incidents of ownership. Under this method, the professional corporation endorses to the professional (or his designated beneficiary) a portion of the death benefits payable (typically the excess of the face value of the policy over the aggregate amount of the premiums paid by the employer). Unless the professional assigns the death benefit to a third party, it will be included in his estate. Even where an assignment is made, the death benefit may be included in the estate of a controlling shareholder of a professional corporation. For these reasons, the collateral assignment method of ownership is most often used in the professional corporation setting.

Under the collateral assignment method of ownership, the subject insurance policy is owned by the employee (or by a third party, such as his spouse, his children, or a trust). The owner of the policy then enters into an agreement with the professional corporation under which the professional corporation agrees to pay a portion of the premium in exchange for an assignment (the collateral assignment) of the policy and a portion of the death proceeds sufficient to reimburse the corporation for the funds advanced toward permium payments. The ability to permit third parties, such as a trust, to be the owner of a split dollar policy under the collateral assignment method is a very important aspect, since it permits the professional to obtain insurance and, yet, effectively excludes the majority of the proceeds of that insurance from his estate. Where the split dollar policy is owned by someone other than the professional, care should be taken to assure that the wording of the collateral assignment does not grant to the professional corporation any incidents of ownership. If the corporation were to obtain incidents of ownership, it is possible that the estate tax exclusions sought would not be obtained. The collateral assignment form attached to this subsection specifically addresses this issue.

The income tax consequences of both the collateral assignment method and the endorsement method are identical.[42] In either case, the employee will be taxed annually on the economic benefit provided under the split dollar arrangement. This occurs, even if, under the collateral assignment method, the policy is endorsed to or owned by a third party.[43]

During the 1960's, the Service took the position that the collateral assignment method was, in effect, a loan from the corporation to the shareholder. Even though this position has been changed (under Rev. Rul. 64-368, no loan exists and only an economic benefit is conferred annually), the effect of the collateral assignment method under standard accounting practices and under most state laws is that a loan exists between the corporation and the shareholder. For this reason, the collaterial assignment method may be unavailable in those states which prohibit loans between a corporation and its officers, directors, or shareholders.

The type of split dollar method chosen will also have an impact on the ability of the employee to obtain and/or transfer the policy upon his termination of employment or retirement. The transfer for value problem (under Section 101(a) of the Code) will normally not exist under the collateral assignment method since the employee or the third party will also be the owner of the policy. However, a transfer for value problem may exist under the endorsement method. If the employee is the insured under an endorsement method (which is normally the case), a transfer for value problem will generally not exist. If the policy is transferred to the employee (which is not a transfer for value) and then given by the employee to his spouse, a gift, but not a transfer for value, to the spouse will have occurred. On the other hand, if the employee would prefer that his spouse own the policy (without creating a three-year waiting period under Section 2035—as is created on his gift of the policy) and the policy is transferred directly from the employer to the spouse, a transfer for value will have occurred. However, if the insured is the employee's spouse, a purchase of the policy from the corporation by the employee will be a transfer for value and, if the policy is held by the employee until the death of his spouse, the proceeds will be taxed as ordinary income to the extent they exceeded the purchase price of the insurance contract. Obviously, these transfer problems can be avoided by prior planning and the use of the collateral assignment method if it is intended that the employee's spouse will ultimately be the owner of the policy.

(c) *Payment of Premiums*

The obligation to pay the premiums and the right to receive benefits under the split dollar arrangement will be determined by the split dollar agreement. The most common methods of allocating the payment of premiums and the corresponding right to reimbursement are as follows:

(1) *Basic Method*

Under the basic method which was approved in Rev. Rul. 64-328, the employer pays the portion of the premium equal to the annual increase in the cash surrender value of the policy, and the employee pays the balance of the premium. Upon the termination of the agreement or the death of the employee, the employer receives an amount equal to the greater of the cash surrender value of the policy or the amounts advanced toward the payment of premium. The employee then receives the balance of the policy proceeds, if any.

This method, although receiving approval from the Service, is very seldom used because it requires the employee to make large payments during the first few years of the split dollar arrangement. In the later years, the employee's contribution becomes smaller or is reduced to zero, but the employee is still taxed on the P.S. 58 cost of the insurance protection provided and the employee may not carry over prior contributions (in excess of the P.S. 58 cost[44] for earlier years) to reduce the taxable P.S. 58 cost in later years.

(2) *Employer-Pay-All*

Under this arrangement, the employer pays the entire premium and the employee is taxed on the P.S. 58 cost of the insurance protection, but the employer cannot deduct the amount on which the employee is taxed. Upon the death of the employee or the termination of the arrangement, the employer receives an amount equal to the aggregate of the employer premium payments and the employee receives the balance of the proceeds. Although the employer-pay-all plans have not been subject to attacks by the Service, they have been the subject of concern by commentators who feel that the Service may eventually take the position that an employer-pay-all plan is not a "split dollar" plan because the employee does not contribute toward the payment of the premium (and, therefore, the employee should be taxed on the full amount of the premium payment made by the employer.)[45] The authors feel, however, that the Service would have difficulty in sustaining this position because the employer does receive a portion of the insurance proceeds.[46]

(3) *Level Contributions*

Under this arrangement, the amount paid annually by the employee toward the premium obligation is a level amount, with the corporation paying the balance of the premium. Upon the termination of the split dollar arrangement or the death of the employee, the employer receives a return of the amount advanced by it and the employee receives the balance of the proceeds. The advantage of this arrangement is that the employee's contribution does not increase in the later years, and this should facilitate personal financial planning. This method will, however, normally result in an employee contributing in excess of the P.S. 58 cost in early years and less than the P.S. cost in later years, with the excesses of early years being unavailable to offset the underpayments in later years which produce taxable income.

(4) *Employee Pays P.S. 58 Cost*[47]

Under this arrangement, the employee pays the portion of the premium equal to the P.S. 58 cost and the employer pays the balance. Upon the termination of the arrangement or the death of the employee, the employer receives a return of the aggregate premium payments advanced and the employee receives the balance. This is, in most cases, the best method of allocation since the employee will only be required to pay the amount that otherwise would be taxable as the P.S. 58 cost. Many employers enter into so-called "P.S. 58 cost bonus plans" whereby the amount of the P.S. 58 cost (or sometimes double the amount of the P.S. 58 cost in order to take taxes into account) is given to the employee to permit him to pay the portion of the premium. This normally results in a lowering of the overall effective tax rate for the corporation and the employee since, even in the employer-pay-all situation, the P.S. 58 cost which the employee must report as income is not deductible by the employer.

This arrangement will normally provide a smaller cost for the employee during earlier years, when he is younger, and a correspondingly increased cost in later years. For this reason, the split dollar agreement should permit the employee to purchase the employer's interest in the policy or to freeze the employer's interest through the use of policy loans to pay premiums. Section 264 of the Code requires that, in order to secure an interest deduction on life insurance policy loans, four annual premium payments must be made during the first seven years. Consequently, after the first four years, the split dollar arrangement may be frozen and, from that point, the security interest of the corporation remains unchanged and the subsequent premium payments may be made through cash value loans, with the only cash outlay being tax deductible interest paid by the employee.

(d) *Treatment of Policy Dividends.*

Policy dividends are often used as a source of purchasing additional insurance protection, since otherwise the employee's protection is diminished by virtue of the employer's increasing interest in the face value of the policy. Structuring of the policy dividends must, however, be accompanied by a review of the various tax consequences. There are a number of alternative methods of using policy dividends, and Rev. Rul. 66-110,[48] sets forth the tax consequences as follows:

(1) *Deposit*

If policy dividends are held on deposit for the employer, neither the employee nor the employer is taxable on them. However, if policy dividends are held on deposit for the employee, the employee must report as income the full amount of the dividend.

(2) *Reduction of Employer Contributions*

If policy dividends are used to reduce employer contributions, the dividends will be nontaxable under Section 72(e) to the extent that, in the aggregate, they do not exceed the aggregate prior employer contributions. However, although dividends used to reduce employer contributions do not result in direct taxable income to the employee, they do result in a slightly increased P.S. 58 cost because the taxable dividends reduce the required employer contribution and, thus, increase the insurance protection provided for the employee (the insurance protection provided for the employee is the face amount of the policy less amounts required to reimburse the employer).

(3) *Reduction of Employee Contributions*

To the extent dividends are used to reduce employee contributions, the dividends will result in gross income to the employee.

(4) *Fifth Dividend Option*

If the dividends are applied to the purchase of additional term insurance in an amount equal to the cash value of the policy (the "fifth dividend option"), the dividends will, in full, constitute gross income to the employee.

(5) *Paid-Up Insurance*

If the dividends are used to purchase paid-up insurance in which the employee has a non-forfeitable interest, the dividends will be fully taxable to the employee. On the other hand, if the dividends are used to purchase paid-up insurance in which the employer is entitled to the cash value, then only the P.S. 58 cost of that additional insurance is taxable to the employee.

(e) *Income Tax Consequences of Split Dollar Life Insurance.*

(1) *Income Tax Consequences to the Employer*

Premium payments made by the employer are not deductible since the employer is a beneficiary under the policy.[49] Even if the employee contributes the entire annual P.S.58 cost toward the payment of the premium, the employer will not be entitled to a deduction.[50] Further, the advances toward the payment of split dollar premiums which appear on the books of the professional corporation as an asset will be taken into consideration for purposes of determining whether the corporation has violated the accumulated earnings tax provisions. See section [9.04], *supra*, for a discussion of these provisions. However, to the extent that the split dollar arrangement can be viewed as an indemnification of the corporation for the economic loss of the key employee, the policy should be viewed as a reasonable business need, thus making accumulations reasonable.[51]

(2) *Income Tax Consequences to the Employee*

The income tax treatment of split dollar arrangements depends upon the date on which the plan was enacted. Plans in effect on November 14, 1964, continue to be governed under the tax treatment prior to that date and are "grandfathered." However, the Service has stated in a Technical Advice Memorandum, issued as Letter Ruling 7832012 that where a pre-November 14, 1964, split dollar policy is transferred to another employee after 1964 under the same split dollar plan, the tax consequences to the transferee employee will be governed by the law applicable to post-November 13, 1964, plans. Of course, any amounts which are actually paid by the employee toward the purchase of the split dollar insurance or amounts which are taxable to the employee under the split dollar arrangement are not deductible by the employee.[52]

(3) *Pre-November 14, 1964, Split Dollar Plans*

The tax consequences of pre-November 14, 1964, split dollar plans are provided under Rev. Rul. 55-713,[53] which held that where an employer enters into a split dollar arrangement with an employee in which the employer is required to pay a portion of the premium equal to the increase in the cash value of the policy annually and the employee is required to pay the remainder of the premium (where the employer is entitled to the proceeds of the policy equal to the cash surrender value of the policy and the balance of the proceeds are paid to the employee), the arrangement will be treated as an interest-free loan to the employee in an amount equal to the increases in the cash surrender value. Such an interest free loan would not result in income to the employee or in a deduction to the employer, and the proceeds payable to the employer and employee on the employee's death would be excluded from gross income under Section 101(a). The courts have held that where the employer paid premiums in excess of the annual increase in cash value, including the premium paid for one year term insurance payable to the employee, such excess would be gross income to the employee.[54]

(4) *Post-November 13, 1964, Split Dollar Plans*

In response to prompting by Congress[55] the Service reconsidered its position taken in Rev. Rul. 55-713 and revoked that position for plans established and policies purchased after November 13, 1964, with the issuance of Rev. Rul. 64-328.[56] Rev. Rul. 64-328 sets forth the "economic benefit" rule which provides that a split dollar arrangement will not be treated as an interest-free loan but results in the earnings from the investment element of the life insurance contract being used to provide current life insurance protection for the employee. Consequently, the ruling holds that the employee must include annually, in his gross income, the value of the economic benefit conferred through the life insurance protection, which is equal to the P.S. 58 cost of the life insurance protection provided, less the amount of premiums paid by the employee. If the insurer has published one-year term insurance rates which are lower than the P.S. 58 rates, such rates may be used to compute the one-year term cost of insurance protection.[57] As a practical matter, the authors have found that the term rates of a large number of insurance companies are lower than the P.S.58 cost and may be used in computing the economic benefit.

The principles announced in Rev. Rul. 64-328 have been expanded and defined in several subsequent rulings. Rev. Rul. 79-50[58] held that where a split dollar insurance arrangement benefits a shareholder who is not an employee, the P.S. 58 cost will be taxed to the shareholder as a distribution under Section 301 of the Code, i.e., taxable as a dividend to the extent of the corporation's earnings and profits. Also, Rev. Rul. 78-420[59] holds that where a split dollar arrangement is entered into for the benefit of an employee and he assigns all of his rights to the policy to a third party (e.g., his spouse, an irrevocable trust, or another beneficiary), the P.S. 58 cost would be included in the employee's gross income since the employee will continue to receive the economic benefit from the split dollar arrangement and the employee will be treated as making an annual transfer by gift to the owner of the policy in an amount equal to the value of the life insurance protection provided. The ruling further provides, however, that the employee would only be required to report as income an amount equal to the P.S. 58 cost, reduced by the premiums paid by the third party.

(f) *Gift Tax Consequences of Split Dollar Insurance.*

The transfer by an employee of his interest in a split dollar arrangement to a third party will constitute a taxable gift.[60] A taxable gift will also occur during each year that the split dollar arrangement remains in effect.[61]

The value of the initial transfer should be equal to the net cash value of the policy (unencumbered by repayment obligations to the corporation), and the value of the annual gift will be the value of the annual insurance protection provided, reduced by premium contributions made by the owner of the policy. The gift tax consequences are the same whether the employee transfers his interest in an existing split dollar policy to his beneficiary or whether the employee's beneficiary directly enters into a split dollar arrangement with the employer. In either case, the employee confers a benefit on his beneficiary.[62]

The transfer of a split dollar insurance policy to, or the origination of a split dollar insurance policy in, an irrevocable life insurance trust containing appropriate *Crummey* powers (see section [14.02](1)(d), *supra*) should be sufficient to create a present interest in the annual insurance protection provided by the employer and thus the annual gift tax exclusion under Section 2503(b) should be available.

(g) *Estate Tax Consequences of Split Dollar Insurance*

If the insured employee retains any interest in the split dollar policy, whether under an endorsement or a collateral assignment arrangement, the proceeds payable to the employee's beneficiary will be included in his estate under Section 2042.[63] The portion of the proceeds payable to the employer will not be directly included in the employee's gross estate because the employee either will not retain any incidents of ownership over such portion of the proceeds (under the endorsement method) or because the employee's estate should be entitled to a deduction under Section 2053(a)(3) in the amount of the employer's claim for the payment under the split dollar plan (under the collateral assignment method). It should be noted, however, that if the employee is a stockholder in the corporation, the value of the stock of the corporation will include the amounts due to the corporation under the split dollar arrangement which should, as a practical matter, increase the value of his stock.

An employee may remove split dollar insurance from his estate by making an irrevocable transfer to a third party of all incidents of ownership over the policy at least three years prior to his date of death.[64] After the assignment, if the annual gift resulting from the economic benefit provided is not covered by the annual gift tax exclusion under Section 2503(b), the value of the insurance protection for the three years prior to the decedent's death, but not the full proceeds payable to the beneficiary under the policy, will be included in the employee's estate.[65] However, if the annual economic benefit is fully covered by the annual gift tax exclusion, neither the annual economic benefit nor the proceeds should be included in the employee's estate.[66]

A special estate problem arises where a corporation enters into a split dollar arrangement with an employee who owns more than 50% of the voting stock of the corporation. Generally, any retention by the employer corporation of ownership attributes in the portion of the policy payable to the employee's beneficiary will cause such portion to be included in the employee's gross estate even though the employee does not directly own any incidents in the policy.[67] If a corporation's *majority* shareholder is a party to a split dollar arrangement with the corporation and the majority shareholder transfers (more than three years prior to his death) his entire interest in the split dollar arrangement to his intended beneficiary in an effort to exclude the proceeds from his gross estate, the following alternative results will occur depending upon the manner in which the split dollar policy is owned:

(1) *Endorsement Method*

If the corporation is the owner of the policy and retains all incidents of ownership, other than the right to name the beneficiary of the employee's portion of the policy, the corporation's incidents of ownership will be attributed to the majority shareholder and the proceeds payable to the corporation will be included in the shareholder's gross estate. See Rev. Rul. 76-274 (Situation 1).[68]

(2) *Collateral Assignment Method*

If the third-party owner of a split dollar insurance policy under a collateral assignment owns all the incidents of ownership, other than the right to borrow against the policy up to the amount of the premiums paid by the corporation and the right to receive an amount equal to the aggregate premiums paid by the corporation, the corporation will not be considered to have any incidents of ownership *in the portion of the policy that is payable to the third-party owner*. As a result, there will be no attribution of incidents of ownership to the majority shareholder with respect to the portion of the policy payable to the owner and, consequently, that portion of the policy will be excluded from the estate of the majority shareholder. See Regulations §§20.2042-1(c)(6) and Rev. Rul. 76-274, (Situation 3).

In many small professional corporations, it is possible that one of the professionals may be a majority shareholder. In such professional corporations, it is, therefore, advisable that the collateral assignment method of providing split dollar insurance be used if estate tax exclusion is intended. The authors have found that, as a practical matter, the collateral assignment method of providing split dollar insurance is almost always used in professional corporations, whether or not majority shareholders exist.

The following collateral assignment split dollar forms are adapted from the Massachusetts Mutual Life Insurance Company forms appearing at Prentice-Hall *Estate Planning Manual*, ¶2005:

SPLIT DOLLAR INSURANCE AGREEMENT

AGREEMENT made this _____ day of _____, 19___, by and between _____ (the "Owner"), and _____ (the "Corporation"), a Georgia corporation.

WHEREAS, the Corporation recognizes the unique and essential services of _____ (the "Employee") to the Corporation and his contributions to the Corporation; and

WHEREAS, the Corporation has determined that its best interests would be served by entering into a split dollar life insurance arrangement with the Owner, whereby the Corporation will assist the Owner in maintaining certain life insurance for the benefit and protection of the Employee's family by contributing from time to time toward payment of premiums due on the policy of the Owner on the Employee's life; and

WHEREAS, the Corporation enters into the following Agreement subject to the condition that such policy be assigned to the Corporation as security for repayment of any amounts which the Corporation may contribute toward payment of any premiums due on such policy;

NOW, THEREFORE, for and in consideration of the premises and other valuable consideration, it is hereby agreed between the parties as follows:

ARTICLE I

APPLICATION FOR INSURANCE

1.1 Owner has applied to _____ Life Insurance Company (the ''Insurer'') for an insurance policy (the ''Policy'') on the life of _____, in the face amount of $_____, which Policy has been issued to and is owned by the Owner. The Policy number is _____ and the Policy is subject to the terms of this Agreement.

ARTICLE II

OWNERSHIP OF POLICY

2.1 The Owner shall retain and may exercise all rights and privileges of ownership with respect to the Policy, except as otherwise hereinafter provided.

2.2 The Corporation shall have no rights of ownership with respect to the Policy, but the Policy is subject to the terms of this Agreement and the provisions of the collateral assignment of the Policy by the Owner securing Owner's obligation to the Corporation under this Agreement.

ARTICLE III

ELECTION OF DIVIDEND OPTION

3.1 (Alternative One—Dividends Applied Toward Reduction of Premiums.) All dividends declared by the Insurer on the Policy shall be applied to reduce the premiums payable on the Policy and shall reduce the amount the Corporation is required to advance under paragraph 4.1.

(Alternative Two—Dividends Applied to Buy Additional Paid Up Insurance.) All dividends declared by the Insurer on the Policy shall be applied to purchase additional paid up insurance on the life of the Employee.

(Alternative Three—Dividends Applied to Buy Term Insurance and Additional Paid Up Insurance.) All dividends declared by the Insurer on the Policy, or any part thereof as may be necessary, shall be applied to purchase one-year term insurance on the life of the Employee in an amount equal to the guaranteed cash value of the Policy as of the next Policy anniversary and any balance of the dividend shall be applied to buy additional paid up insurance. Whenever the dividend is not adequate to purchase the required amount of term insurance, the entire dividend shall be applied to purchase whatever amount of term insurance the dividend will purchase.

(Alternative Four—Dividends Applied to Buy Term Insurance and Any Balance is Used to Reduce Premiums.) All dividends declared by the Insurer on the Policy, or any part thereof as may be necessary, shall be applied to purchase one-year term insurance on the life of the Employee in an amount equal to the guaranteed cash value of the Policy as of the next Policy anniversary and any balance of the dividend shall be applied toward payment of any premium then due on the Policy. Whenever the dividend is not adequate to purchase the required amount of term insurance, the entire dividend shall be applied to purchase whatever amount of term insurance the dividend will purchase.

(Alternative Five—Dividends to be Accumulated.) All dividends declared by the Insurer on the Policy shall be accumulated by the Insurer until the Owner directs how the accumulated dividends shall be applied.

(Alternative Six—Dividends Paid to Policy Owner in Cash.) All dividends declared by the Insurer on the Policy shall be paid to the Owner in cash.

3.2 The Owner has elected the dividend option described in the foregoing paragraph 3.1 of this ARTICLE III and agrees to give the Corporation sixty (60) days advance written notice prior to any change or termination of the dividend option as selected by the Owner hereunder. In the event the Corporation determines that such change or termination of the dividend option adversely affects the security interest of the Corporation hereunder or under the Collateral Assignment, this Agreement may be terminated by the Corporation upon thirty (30) days advance written notice to the Owner, in which event the provisions of ARTICLE IX and ARTICLE X hereinafter set forth shall become effective and operative. In the event the Corporation determines that such change or termination does not affect its security interest hereunder or under the Collateral Assignment, a conforming amendment shall be made to this Agreement to reflect such change or termination.

ARTICLE IV

PAYMENT OF PREMIUMS ON POLICY

4.1 On or before the due date of each annual premium on the Policy, the Corporation will advance to the Owner an amount equal to that portion of the annual premium which exceeds the cost of the portion of such insurance which the beneficiary or beneficiaries named by the Owner and designated in the Policy would be entitled to receive if the Employee died during the Policy year for which such annual premium is paid. The foregoing cost shall be determined pursuant to Rev. Rul. 64-328, 1964-2, C.B. 11, and Rev. Rul. 55-747, 1955-2 C.B. 228, as amplified by Rev. Rul. 66-110, 1966-1 C.B. 12, and Rev. Rul. 67-154, 1967-1 C.B. 11.

4.2 Upon receipt of the amount which the Corporation shall contribute under paragraph 4.1 of this ARTICLE IV toward payment of the premiums due on the Policy, the Owner will pay the full amount of the premiums due on the Policy to the Insurer. The payment of the premium shall be made by the Owner on the date the premium is due and within the grace period allowed by the Policy for the payment of the premium.

ARTICLE V

OWNER'S OBLIGATION TO CORPORATION

5.1 The Owner shall be obligated and hereby agrees to repay to the Corporation the aggregate amount which the Corporation advances to the Owner pursuant to paragraph 4.1 of ARTICLE IV of this Agreement. This obligation of the Owner to the Corporation shall be payable as provided in ARTICLE VIII and ARTICLE X of this Agreement.

ARTICLE VI

ASSIGNMENT OR TERMINATION OF POLICY

6.1 The Owner will collaterally assign the Policy to the Corporation as security for the repayment of the amounts which the Corporation advances to the Owner under paragraph 4.1 of ARTICLE IV of this Agreement. The collateral assignment will be in the form attached hereto as Schedule "A" (the "Collateral Assignment") and will not be altered or changed without the consent of the Corporation.

6.2 While this Agreement is in force and effect, the Owner will neither sell, surrender nor otherwise terminate the Policy without first giving sixty (60) days advance written notice to the Corporation. In the event the Corporation determines that such sale, surrender or termination of the Policy adversely affects the security interest of the Corporation hereunder or under the Collateral Assignment, this Agreement may be terminated by the Corporation upon thirty (30) days advance written notice to the Owner, in which event the provisions of ARTICLE IX and ARTICLE X hereinafter set forth shall become effective and operative. In the event the Corporation determines that such sale, surrender or termination does not affect its security interest hereunder or under the Collateral Assignment, a conforming amendment shall be made to this Agreement to reflect such sale, surrender or termination.

ARTICLE VII

ADDITIONAL POLICY BENEFITS AND RIDERS

7.1 The Owner may apply for and secure such additions and riders to the Policy as are provided by the Insurer for the benefit of the Owner.

7.2 Upon written request by the Corporation, the Owner will apply for and secure such additions and riders to the policy as are provided by the Insurer for the benefit of the Corporation.

7.3 The cost or additional premium attributable to any such addition or rider shall be paid by the party which will benefit from or be entitled to receive the proceeds of such addition or rider.

ARTICLE VIII

DEATH CLAIMS

8.1 Upon the death of the Employee, the Corporation shall be entitled to receive a portion of the death benefits payable under the Policy. The amount which the Corporation will be entitled to receive shall be the aggregate amounts of its contributions, pursuant to paragraph 4.1 of ARTICLE IV of this Agreement, toward the payment of premiums due on such policy. The receipt of this amount by the Corporation shall constitute satisfaction of the Owner's obligation under ARTICLE V of this Agreement.

8.2 Upon the death of the Employee, the beneficiary or beneficiaries named by the Owner and designated in the Policy shall be entitled to receive the amount of the death benefits provided under the Policy in excess of the amount payable to the Corporation under paragraph 8.1 of this ARTICLE VIII. This amount shall be paid under the settlement option in the Policy elected by the Owner.

ARTICLE IX

TERMINATION OF AGREEMENT

9.1 This Agreement shall terminate on the occurrence of any of the following events:

(a) Cessation of the Corporation's business.

(b) Ninety (90) days written notice given by either party to the other.

(c) Termination of employment of the Employee.

(d) Bankruptcy, receivership or dissolution of the Corporation.

(e) Election of the aggrieved party if either the Corporation or the Owner fails for any reason to make the contribution required by ARTICLE IV of this Agreement toward payment of any premiums due on the Policy, provided that any election to terminate this Agreement under this clause must be made within ninety (90) days after the failure to make the required contribution occurs.

(f) Repayment in full by the Owner of the contributions made by the Corporation under paragraph 4.1 of ARTICLE IV of this Agreement toward payment of the premiums due on the Policy. The Corporation agrees that upon receipt of such repayment the Corporation will release the Collateral Assignment of the policy made by the Owner pursuant to ARTICLE VI of this Agreement.

ARTICLE X

DISPOSITION OF POLICY ON TERMINATION
OF AGREEMENT

10.1 In the event this Agreement is terminated pursuant to subparagraphs 9.1 (a), (b), (c), (d) or (e) of ARTICLE IX of this Agreement, the Owner shall have ninety (90) days in which to repay the Corporation the aggregate amount which it has contributed toward payment of the premiums due on the Policy under paragraph 4.1 of ARTICLE IV of this Agreement. Upon receipt of this amount, the Corporation shall release the Collateral Assignment of the Policy. In the event the Owner does not repay the amount which the Corporation has contributed within said ninety (90) day period: (1) the Corporation may enforce any rights which it has under the Collateral Assignment of the Policy and may take whatever other action it deems appropriate, at law or in equity, to collect, or to cause the Owner to repay to the Corporation, the amount due the Corporation by the Owner under ARTICLE V of this Agreement, and (2) the Owner agrees, promptly upon any such termination, to surrender the Policy to the Insurer for cancellation and to direct the Insurer to apply the proceeds of such cancellation to the repayment of the amount due by the Owner to the Corporation pursuant to this Agreement.

ARTICLE XI

DEATH OF OWNER

11.1 In the event of the death of the Owner during the continuance of this Agreement, this Agreement shall not terminate and the Corporation shall continue to perform according to the Agreement with the Owner's successor in interest in the Policy, if such successor in interest executes a new or supplemental agreement by which such successor in interest will be bound by the terms and provisions of this Agreement and, provided, further, that such successor in interest executes a collateral assignment with respect to the Policy. The Owner's personal representative and, following administration of the Owner's estate, the distributee of the Owner's estate who acquires the Owner's interest in and ownership of the Policy shall, respectively, within 30 days from the date of the Owner's death or from the date of distribution of the Policy to such distributee, as the case may be, promptly notify the Corporation of such event and within 30 days following the date of postmark of such notice execute such new or supplemental agreement and collateral assignment.

11.2 In the event the Owner's successor in interest to the Policy does not enter into such a new or supplemental agreement and collateral assignment with the Corporation as provided in paragraph 11.1 of this ARTICLE XI, then this Agreement shall terminate as of the death of the Owner and the provisions of ARTICLE X of this Agreement shall become fully effective and operative.

ARTICLE XII

INSURER NOT A PARTY

12.1 The Insurer (a) shall not be deemed to be a party to this Agreement for any purpose or in any way responsible for its validity; (b) shall not be obligated to inquire as to the distribution of any monies payable or paid by it under the Policy on the Employee's life acquired pursuant to the terms of this Agreement; and (c) shall be fully discharged from any and all liability under the terms of any policy issued by it, which is subject to the terms of this Agreement, upon payment or other performance of its obligations in accordance with the terms of such policy.

ARTICLE XIII

AMENDMENT OF AGREEMENT

13.1 This Agreement shall not be modified or amended except by a writing signed by the Corporation and the Owner. This Agreement shall inure to the benefit of and shall be binding upon the heirs, personal representatives, successors and assigns of each party to this Agreement.

ARTICLE XIV

AGREEMENT OF FURTHER PERFORMANCE

14.1 Each of the parties, for itself and its heirs, personal representatives, successors and assigns, agrees to take such further action, do such other things, and execute such other writings as shall be necessary and proper to carry out the terms and provisions of this Agreement.

ARTICLE XV

NOTICES

15.1 Any notices required or permitted hereunder shall be sufficiently given if sent by registered or certified mail, postage prepaid, or personally delivered, addressed or delivered as follows:

Owner: _____

Corporation: _____
_____
_____

or to such other addresses as shall be furnished in writing by either party to the other party; and any such notice shall be deemed to have been given, if mailed, as of the date mailed, and, if personally delivered, as of the date delivered.

ARTICLE XVI

NO WAIVER

16.1 No waiver of a breach or any provision of this Agreement shall be construed to be a waiver of any breach of any other provision of this Agreement or of any succeeding breach of the same provision. No delay in acting with regard to any breach of any provision of this Agreement shall be construed to be a waiver of such breach.

ARTICLE XVII

COUNTERPARTS

17.1 This Agreement is executed in multiple counterparts, each of which shall be deemed an original and together shall constitute one and the same agreement.

ARTICLE XVIII

STATE LAW

18.1 This Agreement shall be subject to and shall be construed under the laws of the State of Georgia.

IN TESTIMONY WHEREOF, the Corporation, pursuant to the proper corporate authority, has caused this Agreement to be signed on its behalf and its seal to be affixed and attested by its proper officers and the Owner has hereunto subscribed his name and seal, all as of the day and year first above set forth.

_____ (SEAL)
                Owner

(CORPORATE SEAL)   By: _____

ATTEST:

By: _____
        Secretary

(Alternative Provision for use where
the policy is owned by an irrevocable
life insurance trust)

ARTICLE XI

TERMINATION OF THE

IRREVOCABLE TRUST

11.1 In the event of the termination of the _____ Irrevocable Trust during the continuance of this Agreement, this Agreement shall not terminate and the Corporation shall continue to perform according to the Agreement with the Owner's successor in interest in the Policy, if such successor in interest executes a new or supplemental agreement by which such successor in interest will be bound by the terms and provisions of this Agreement and, provided, further, that such successor in interest executes a collateral assignment with respect to the Policy. The Owner's successor in interest shall, within 30 days from the date of the termination of the Owner, promptly notify the Corporation of such event and within 30 days following the date of postmark of such notice execute such new or supplemental agreement and collateral assignment.

11.2 In the event the Owner's successor in interest to the Policy does not enter into such a new or supplemental agreement and collateral assignment with the Corporation as provided in paragraph 11.1 of this ARTICLE XI, then this Agreement shall terminate as of the termination of the Owner and the provisions of ARTICLE X of this Agreement shall become fully effective and operative.

SCHEDULE "A"

ASSIGNMENT OF LIFE INSURANCE POLICY AS COLLATERAL

KNOW ALL MEN BY THESE PRESENTS THAT:

For value received, the undersigned hereby assigns, transfers and sets over to _____, its successors and assigns (herein called the "Assignee") the herein described portion of the death benefit under Policy No. _____ issued by _____ Life Insurance Company (herein called the "Insurer") and any supplementary contracts issued in connection therewith (said policy and contracts being herein called the "Policy"), upon the life of _____, subject to all of the terms and conditions of the Policy and to all superior liens, if any, which the Insurer may have against the Policy. The undersigned by this instrument agrees, and the Assignee by the acceptance of this assignment agrees, to the conditions and provisions herein set forth.

It is understood and agreed by the Assignee and the undersigned that:

(1) The Assignee shall have the sole right to collect from the Insurer only the portion of the proceeds of the Policy described in Paragraph 3 hereof when it becomes a claim by death or maturity AND THAT ALL OTHER RIGHTS UNDER THE POLICY, INCLUDING, BY WAY OF ILLUSTRATION AND NOT LIMITATION, THE RIGHT TO SURRENDER THE POLICY, THE RIGHT TO MAKE POLICY LOANS, THE RIGHT TO DESIGNATE AND CHANGE THE BENEFICIARY, AND THE RIGHT TO ELECT AND TO RECEIVE DIVIDENDS, ARE RESERVED EXCLUSIVELY TO THE OWNER OF THE POLICY AND ARE EXCLUDED FROM THIS ASSIGNMENT AND DO NOT PASS BY VIRTUE HEREOF AND MAY BE EXERCISED BY THE OWNER ON THE SOLE SIGNATURE OF THE OWNER. NOTHING HEREIN SHALL AFFECT FUNDS, IF ANY, NOW OR HEREAFTER HELD BY THE INSURER FOR THE PURPOSE OF PAYING FUTURE PREMIUMS UNDER THE POLICY.

(2) This Assignment is made as collateral security for and is limited to the liabilities of the undersigned to the Assignee, either now existing or that may hereafter arise with respect to premiums advanced for the Policy by the Assignee, (all of which liabilities secured or to become secured are herein called "Liabilities") under ARTICLE IV of that certain Split Dollar Insurance Agreement of even date herewith, a copy of which is attached hereto as Exhibit "A".

(3) Under this Assignment, the Insurer will only be obligated, and have the authority, to distribute to the Assignee that portion of the death proceeds of the Policy equal to the then existing Liabilities. In the event of the death of _____ while the Policy and this Assignment are in force, the death proceeds of the Policy shall be divided into two parts by the Insurer as follows:

a. One part shall be equal to the Liabilities of the undersigned to the Assignee as described in Paragraph 2 hereof, and

b. The other part shall be equal to the remainder of the death proceeds.

The part of the death proceeds of the Policy described in Subparagraph (a) shall be distributed to the Assignee and the part described in Subparagraph (b) shall be distributed to the beneficiaries designated under the Policy; provided, however, that no distributions shall be made until the division of death proceeds into the above-described parts has been agreed upon in writing by Assignee and said beneficiaries and said writing has been delivered to and accepted by the Insurer.

(4) Any balance of sums received hereunder by the Assignee from the Insurer in excess of the then existing Liabilities, matured or unmatured, shall be paid promptly by the Assignee to the persons entitled thereto under the terms of the Policy had this Assignment not been executed;

(5) The Assignee, not having any right to obtain policy loans from the Insurer, will not take any steps to borrow against the Policy.

(6) The Assignee will upon request forward without unreasonable delay to the Insurer the Policy for endorsement of any designation or change of beneficiary or any election of an optional mode of settlement; provided, however, that any such designation, change or election shall be made subject to this assignment and to the rights of the Assignee hereunder.

(7) Except as otherwise provided in any other document evidencing Liabilities owing to the Assignee from the undersigned, its successors and assigns, if any, the Assignee shall be under no obligation to pay any premium on the Policy. The principal of, or interest on, any loans or advances on the Policy, or any other charges on the Policy, shall be an obligation of the undersigned and not an obligation of the Assignee.

(8) In the event of any conflict between the provisions of this Assignment and provisions of any evidence of any Liability, with respect to the Policy or rights of collateral security therein, the provisions of this Assignment shall prevail.

(9) The undersigned declares that no proceedings in bankruptcy are pending against it and that its property is not subject to any assignment for the benefit of creditors.

Signed and sealed this ___ day of _____, 19___.

_____
                            Owner

_____
                           Address

THE FOREGOING ASSIGNMENT IS HEREBY ACCEPTED THIS _____ DAY OF _____, 19___.

_____

(CORPORATE SEAL)

ATTEST: By: _____
                                          President

_____
Secretary

This Summary Plan Description covers those matters which must be communicated to you as required by the Employee Retirement Income Security Act of 1974 (ERISA), which is administered by the United States Department of Labor.

SPLIT DOLLAR INSURANCE PLAN
FOR EMPLOYEES OF

_____

The Plan Sponsor and Administrator is _____, whose address is _____, _____. The telephone number is _____. The Employer Identification Number (EIN) of the Plan Sponsor is _____. The Plan Number assigned to this Plan by the Plan Sponsor is _____. The general administration of this Plan is provided by the Plan Sponsor.

It is not anticipated that it will ever be necessary to have a lawsuit about this Plan; however, if a lawsuit is to be brought, legal process may be served on the Plan Sponsor and Administrator at the above address.

This Plan provides a means whereby the Corporation contributes toward the payment of premiums due on life insurance policies carried on the lives of certain of its employees. The Board of Directors of the Corporation reserves unto itself the right to determine which of its employees are eligible to participate in the Plan. The provisions of this Plan are attached hereto as Exhibit "A".

As a participant in this Plan, you are entitled to certain rights and protections under ERISA. ERISA provides that all Plan participants shall be entitled to:

1. Examine, without charge, at the Plan Administrator's office all Plan documents, including contracts and copies of all documents filed by the Plan with the U.S. Department of Labor, such as detailed annual reports and Plan Descriptions, and

2. Obtain copies of all Plan documents and other Plan information upon written request to the Plan Administrator, who may make a reasonable charge for all such copies.

In addition to creating rights for Plan participants, ERISA imposes duties upon the people who are responsible for the operation of employee benefit plans. The people who operate this Plan, called "fiduciaries", have a duty to do so prudently and in the interest of you and other Plan participants and beneficiaries. No one, including your employer, may fire you or otherwise discriminate against you in any way to prevent you from obtaining a welfare benefit or exercising your rights under ERISA. If your claim for a welfare benefit is denied in whole or in part, you must receive a written explanation of the reason for denial. You have the right to have the Plan review and reconsider your claim.

Under ERISA, there are steps you can take to enforce the above rights. For instance, if you request materials from the Plan Administrator and do not receive them within 30 days, you may file suit in a federal court. In such a case the court may require the Plan Administrator to provide the materials and pay you up to $100 a day until you receive the materials, unless the materials were not sent because of reasons beyond the control of the Plan Administrator. If you have a claim for benefits which is denied or ignored, in whole or in part, you may file suit in a state or federal court. If it should happen that Plan fiduciaries misuse the Plan's money, or if you are discriminated against for asserting your rights, you may seek assistance from the U.S. Department of Labor, or you may file suit in federal court. The court will decide who should pay court costs and legal fees. If you are successful the court may order the person you have sued to pay these costs and fees. If you lose, the court may order you to pay these costs and fees, if, for example, it finds your claim is frivolous. If you have any questions about this Plan, you should contact the Plan Administrator. If you have any questions about this statement or about your rights under ERISA, you should contact the nearest Area Office of the U.S. Labor-Management Services Administration, Department of Labor.

ACTION BY THE
DIRECTORS OF

_____

We, _____, _____, and _____, constituting all of the Directors of _____ (the ''Corporation''), do unanimously consent to, ratify, approve, and adopt, under Section 22-710 of the Georgia Business Corporation Code, the following statements and resolutions:

WHEREAS, _____ in his official capacity as _____ of the Corporation has stimulated the business activities of the Corporation; and

WHEREAS, the loss of Mr. _____ as an officer and employee of the Corporation would seriously impair the Corporation's operations, profits and financial stability; and

WHEREAS, in order to retain the services of Mr. _____ the Corporation is willing to enter into a split dollar insurance plan with Mr. _____'s wife, _____, in order that she may carry insurance on his life;

NOW, THEREFORE, it is resolved that:

1. The officers of the Corporation are authorized to enter into a split dollar life insurance agreement with _____, with respect to a policy of insurance on the life of _____, _____ of the Corporation, provided that the death benefits of the policy are collaterally assigned to the Corporation as security for the repayment of the amounts which the Corporation will contribute toward payment of the premiums due on the policy pursuant to the terms of the split dollar insurance agreement.

2. _____ shall be the owner of the policy and shall have the right to name the beneficiary of the proceeds payable on the insured's death in excess of the amount due to the Corporation under the split dollar agreement to secure the Corporation's contributions toward the premium payments.

3. The Treasurer of the Corporation is hereby authorized, until otherwise directed, to contribute an amount toward payment of each annual premium due on

the policy. This amount shall be paid to _____ and shall be the sum required to pay the annual premium on the policy less the ''P.S. 58'' cost of such policy which shall be paid by _____.

4. The officers of the Corporation or any of them, and in the discretion of the one or more of them acting in the matter, are fully authorized, empowered and instructed, in the name and on behalf of the Corporation, to take all action, do all things and execute all writings as shall be necessary to carry out the foregoing.

Unanimously consented to, adopted, approved, and ratified this _____ day of _____, 19___.

_____

_____

_____

(5) Key Man Life Insurance

Key man life insurance is life insurance which is purchased by the professional corporation on the lives of the professionals. It can either be term insurance or whole life insurance, and although it is generally not considered to be a direct fringe benefit it may be used to finance fringe benefits or other corporate needs, such as stock retirement agreements and deferred compensation agreements.

The authors have found that in most instances professional corporations do need *some* key man life insurance. However, the amount of key man life insurance will depend on the facts and circumstances of each situation and, in general, only a relatively small amount (in the neighborhood of $100,000 per professional) is necessary. However, where the corporation has substantial deferred compensation requirements which must be met or where the professional corporation owns substantial assets, such as office buildings and equipment, more key man life insurance may be necessary. It is important that a professional corporation not over-insure its needs because excess insurance will simply produce a windfall for the surviving professionals (see section [11.02] (3), *supra*, for a complete discussion of the use of insurance in valuing professional corporations). Further, any additional insurance needs of the professionals should be handled through other types of personal insurance, such as additional group term life insurance or split dollar insurance, in order to remove the proceeds of that insurance from the estates of the professionals. Additional key man insurance, in excess of necessary amounts, will simply increase the value of the professional corporation and, consequently, the estates of the professionals. The authors have also found that, while term insurance does provide low cost life insurance protection, it is advisable to consider the use of whole life insurance as key man insurance because the policies will generally be kept for an extended period of time and will not be canceled in later years (as might be done with personal term insurance when college education expenses are met, for example).

Using key man insurance to fund stock retirement agreements, deferred compensation agreements, or other corporate benefits is normally advantageous in the professional corporation because of the availability of the corporate surtax exemption. Section 264 of the Code expressly prohibits deductions for premiums paid on life insurance covering any officer or employee of a corporation or any person financially interested in the corporation if the corporation is either directly or indirectly a beneficiary under the policy. Since key man insurance premiums must be paid with after-tax dollars, the availability of the lower corporate tax rates will permit the professional corporation to purchase key man insurance at rates below 20% (based on the first $50,000 of taxable income of the professional corporation), as opposed to the 50% rates which would probably be applicable in a partnership setting. Although the corporation must use after-tax dollars to pay the premium on key man insurance, the following other benefits are available:

(1) Death proceeds under the policy are excluded from gross income of the corporation under Section 101(a). See Letter Ruling 7730037.
(2) Policy dividends are excluded from the corporation's gross income to the extent that they do not exceed prior premium payments. Section 72(e).
(3) Borrowing against the policy does not result in gross income, and interest on policy loans will be deductible as long as the "four out of seven" rule of Section 264 is met.
(4) The annual increase in the cash value of the policy will not be considered taxable income to the corporation.[69]
(5) If the policy is surrendered for its cash value, the amount received will be included in gross income only to the extent that it exceeds the aggregate of the premiums paid less amounts previously received. Section 72(e)(1)(B).

Premiums paid on key man life insurance which is owned by and payable to the corporation are not taxable to the insured professional if he has no interest in the policy.[70] However, where the employee either owns the life insurance policy or has incidents of ownership in a life insurance policy on which the corporation pays premiums, the individual must report the premium payments as taxable income.[71] Some professional corporation advisors feel that permitting the corporation to make premium payments on policies owned by the professionals will create a tax advantage for the professionals because the professionals will only be required to report the premium payment as income and will not be required to use after-tax compensation to make the premium payments. While such payments will generally be considered compensation to the professionals, the authors feel that, in the professional corporation setting, IRS agents are more likely to attempt to restructure premium payments as constructive dividends. Such payments may also raise questions regarding whether the compensation and benefits provided to the professionals, taken together, are reasonable. Further, where there is no evidence to indicate that the premium payments were intended as compensation (such as minutes of a meeting of a board of directors—which professionals often overlook) such premium payments may be considered as dividends.

(6) Disability Insurance and Salary Continuation Plans

(a) *Disability Insurance*

The establishment of a professional corporation permits professionals a means of deducting disability insurance premiums which are otherwise nondeductible to individual proprietors or partners. The authors feel that all professionals should seriously consider obtaining personal disability insurance and should review the need for disability insurance with their professional advisors and insurance agents. In making this review, the following points should be considered:

(1) Most disability policies are now being offered with a "residual" feature, which permits a professional to return to work on a part-time basis and continue to receive partial disability payments. For example, if the professional returns to work and earns one-third of the income which he earned prior to his disability, the disability payments will be reduced by one-third. Without a "residual" feature, disability policies are usually "all or nothing" policies, requiring the professional to be totally disabled in order to receive any benefits whatsoever.

(2) Longer waiting periods prior to the commencement of disability benefits substantially reduce disability premiums. For this reason, waiting periods of 90 to 180 days should be considered and, normally, the professional's employment agreement will be structured so that his salary will be continued by the professional corporation during this disability waiting period.

(3) Care should be taken to assure that the disability policies are noncancellable by the carrier and provide lifetime coverage (or at least coverage to age 65).

Where the professional corporation pays the premiums on personal disability insurance policies for the professional (these may be either group disability policies or individual disability policies) the amounts paid by the professional corporation are deductible under Section 162.[72] Further, as long as the disability insurance is provided by the professional corporation under a "plan" of providing accident or health benefits, the disability premiums paid by the corporation need not be reported as income by the employee. The plan may be discriminatory and cover only a select number of employees, but the authors feel that the plan should be structured so as to preclude individual selection and should cover groups of employees, such as officers.[73] Any disability proceeds payable under the policies (where the corporation pays the premium) must be included by the professionals as taxable income since there is no exclusion under Section 104 of the Code.

On the other hand, where the professional pays the disability insurance premium (which will be nondeductible to him), any disability benefits will be nontaxable to him under Section 104. The dramatically different tax effect of disability proceeds based on whether the professional or the professional corporation paid the premium has led some professionals to enter into arrangements whereby the professional pays the disability premiums on January 1 of every year and, if the professional does not become disabled by the following December 31, the professional corporation reimburses him for the premium payment. Professionals who adopt this arrangement feel that they have completely covered all eventualities because, if they become disabled during the year, they will have made the premium payments themselves so that disability benefits will be nontaxable but, if they do not become disabled, the corporation will reimburse them for the premium payments. The authors feel that such an arrangement violates the spirit, if not the letter, of Sections 104, 105, and 106 and would not recommend its adoption. Further, the authors feel that, after a review of several years of premium payments, a competent IRS agent could challenge this arrangement.

Although the authors do not favor the year-end reimbursement arrangement, they do favor utilization of both employer-and employee-paid premiums. The authors feel that professionals should consider permitting the professional corporation to pay the premiums on the more expensive individual disability policies which are maintained by the professional. Due to ongoing interest and other tax deductions which will be generated by the professional's existing assets, a moderate amount of taxable income following disability will probably not produce an unacceptable amount of income tax. On the other hand, if the professional maintains group disability policies, which normally have smaller premiums, the authors feel that the professionals should consider paying these premiums personally so that disability benefits received under these policies will be tax-exempt.

(b) *Salary Continuation Arrangements*

Prior to 1977, Section 105(d) of the Code permitted an employee to exclude from taxable income $100 per week for disability payments when made by the employer. However, by virtue of amendments under the Tax Reform Act of 1976, the maximum amount excludable ($5,200 per year) is reduced on a dollar-for-dollar basis by the taxpayer's adjusted gross income (including disability income) in excess of $15,000. Thus, if the taxpayer receives $5,200 in disability income and $15,000 (or more) in other income, which together equals $20,200 (or more) he will not be entitled to any exclusion for disability payments. As a result of these restrictions, self-insured disability income plans have very little tax appeal for professionals because most disabled professionals will be planning on disability income in excess of $20,000 in any event. Consequently, following the Tax Reform Act of 1976, employment agreements for professionals have generally omitted self-insured disability salary continuation payments.

[14.03] HEALTH AND MEDICAL PLANS

(1) Self-Insured Health and Medical Reimbursement Plans

Where the professional corporation provides a plan to reimburse employees for uninsured health and medical benefits, such benefit payments are deductible by the corporation under Section 162 and excludable by the employees from income under Section 105 of the Code. In the Revenue Act of 1978, very restrictive nondiscrimination requirements were placed on such plans and effectively eliminated such plans (or caused a drastic reduction of benefits) for all but the smallest professional corporations.

(a) *Rules Prior to January 1, 1980*

Prior to the amendments by the Revenue Act of 1978, professional corporations could provide uninsured health and medical reimbursement plans for their employees on a discriminatory basis as long as a "plan" was provided for the "employees" of the professional corporation under Regulations §1.105-5. In order for a plan to exist, no particular legal pattern was required and it was not necessary that the plan be in writing or that the employees' rights to benefits under the plan be enforceable. However, the plan was required to be in effect on the date the expenses were incurred, the employees were required to have knowledge of the plan, and the plan was required to be administered in accordance with its terms. Further, the plan was required to be for "employees." The plan was permitted to cover one or more employees in their capacity as employees (not shareholders). It was generally considered that such plans could apply to all the officers of a professional corporation (as long as there were either professionals who were not officers who could not participate or as long as there were nonprofessional officers who would participate) and could provide a reimbursement benefit equal to a percentage of compensation. Although there were a number of cases involving uninsured health and medical reimbursement plans which discriminated in favor of shareholders (not employees),[74] such plans were generally recognized by the Service as long as benefits were provided on some rational basis for a class of employees which could be ascertained on criteria other than shareholder status.

(b) *Revenue Act of 1978*

With the enactment of the Revenue Act of 1978, very stringent requirements were placed on insured medical reimbursement plans, effective after December 31, 1979.[75]

Generally, such plans are prohibited from discriminating in favor of highly compensated individuals under specific rules regarding participation and benefits. Participation rules for uninsured health and medicial reimbursement plans are very similar to those required for qualified retirement plans. Generally, an uninsured health and medical reimbursement plan discriminates with regard to the eligibility to participate unless: (a) the plan benefits 70% or more of all employees or 80% or more of all employees who are eligible to benefit under the plan, if 70% or more of all employees are eligible to benefit under the plan; or (b) employees participate under a classification set up by the employer and found by the Service not to be discriminatory. For purposes of the eligibility requirements, employees may be excluded from participation if they have not completed three years of service, have not attained age 25, are part-time employees (whose weekly employment is less than 35 hours and whose employment is customarily less than nine months), are included in a collective bargaining agreement, or are nonresident aliens who receive no income from U.S. sources. The benefits which must be provided under such a plan are required to be identical for all participants, that is, the same dollar amount of benefits and not benefits based upon a percentage of compensation (as is permitted under qualified retirement plans). The terms of the plan must be set forth in a written plan document.

The term "highly compensated individual" is defined as an individual who is (1) one of the five highest-paid officers, (2) a shareholder who owns (either actually or constructively) more than 10% value of the stock of the corporation, or (3) among the highest-paid 25% of all employees (including the five highest-paid officers, but not including employees who are properly excluded from participation). Any amount which is paid under a health and medical reimbursement plan to a "highly compensated individual" which is in excess of the benefits provided for other participants is considered an "excess reimbursement" and must be reported as income by the highly compensated individual, presumably as compensation and not as a constructive dividend.

Health and medical reimbursement plans can be designed however, to provide discriminatory medical benefits for "diagnostic procedures" for employees (but not their dependents). Regulations §1.105-11(g)(1) defines the term "diagnostic procedures" to include "routine medical examinations, blood tests, and X-rays" but to exclude "expenses incurred for treatment, cure, or testing of an unknown illness or disability, or treatment or testing for a physical injury, complaint or specific symptom of a bodily malfunction." For example, a routine dental examination with X-rays is considered a medical diagnostic procedure, but X-rays or treatment for a specific complaint are not. In addition, such procedures do not include any activity undertaken for exercise, fitness, nutrition, or recreation, or the general improvement of health.

Obviously, such restrictive requirements placed upon uninsured health and medical reimbursement plans, requiring nondiscriminatory participation rules and the same dollar amount of benefits for all participants, have essentially eliminated nondiscriminatory health and medical reimbursement plans for all but the smallest professional corporations.[76] In some larger professional groups, the authors have found that nondiscriminatory plans are maintained on a reduced basis (such as a

$300 limit per employee per year). However, it is possible to provide nondiscriminatory health and medical benefits as a part of a cafeteria plan discussed in section [14.04], *infra*.

(c) *Alternatives Under the Nondiscriminatory Rules*

With the adoption of the nondiscriminatory rules, effective January 1, 1980, professional corporations have the following alternatives:

(1) *Have No Plan, Maintain the Existing Discriminatory Plan, or Adopt a Nondiscriminatory Plan*

Obviously, the elimination of the medical reimbursement plan will mean the elimination of benefits. On the other hand, the adoption of a nondiscriminatory medical reimbursement plan, depending upon the number of staff employees in the professional corporation and the level of benefits may become excessively expensive. Some professionals are considering maintaining the existing discriminatory health and medical reimbursement plans because excess benefits will only be considered as additional compensation. They reason that better tax benefits are obtained by simply including $2,000 of excess benefits in income (with an after-tax cost of $1,000) than by being required to expend $2,000 of after-tax compensation (with an effective tax cost of $2,000, assuming a 50% tax bracket) to make such payments. There is, however, no indication in the Regulations that such excess payments will not be considered to be constructive dividends and the authors anticipate that the Service will take this position. Consequently, the authors feel that professionals who maintain their existing discriminatory medical reimbursement plans are not proceeding without risk.

(2) *Diagnostic Medical Reimbursement Plans*

As an alternative to adopting no plan or adopting a nondiscriminatory plan, professionals might consider adopting a diagnostic medical reimbursement plan which at least will cover annual physicals. Obviously, such a plan has reduced usefulness for physcians, but it may provide minimum benefits for other professionals. A form of discriminatory medical reimbursement plan is attached to this subsection.

(3) *Insured Medical Reimbursement Plans*

A number of insurance carriers are offering "insured" medical reimbursement plans which, acccording to the sales literature, are exempt from the nondiscrimination rules of Section 105(h). Most of these plans operate in a similar fashion which, in effect, is simply a servicing arrangement whereby the insurance company charges a fee for establishing a plan and then assures that payment of medical expenses is made (with a concomitant 10% to 15% service charge to the professional corporation). The Regulations specifically state that a plan underwritten by a policy of insurance or prepaid health care which does not involve "the shifting of risk" and is a "cost plus" arrangement will be considered a self-insured plan.[77] The authors feel that many of the "insured" medical reimbursement plans being offered at this time do not adequately shift the risk of medical expenses from the professional corporation to the insurer and will not qualify as nondiscriminatory, insured plans. The authors feel further that any professional considering an "insured" medical reimbursement plan should not adopt such a plan unless a Private Letter Ruling has been issued by the Service with regard to that plan or the professional can obtain an opinion regarding the effect of the plan from competent legal counsel.

(4) *Insurance*

Since bona fide insurance plans are exempt from the nondiscrimination rules of Section 105(h), it is possible for professional corporations to obtain additional medical insurance with regard to certain classes of employees. For example, a professional corporation could adopt a plan of providing not only personal but dependent health and medical insurance coverage for officers and providing insurance benefits which are more favorable than those provided for non-officer employees (such as lower deductibles, higher daily rates, dental care, etc.)

DIAGNOSTIC
MEDICAL REIMBURSEMENT PLAN
OF

_____

_____., a Georgia professional corporation (hereinafter referred to as the "Corporation") hereby establishes this Health and Medical Reimbursement Plan (hereinafter called the "Plan") for the benefit of its officers (hereinafter referred to as "Officers").

1. Reimbursement for Medical Diagnostic Expenses

(a) Effective _____, and for every successive year thereafter until terminated as provided herein, the Corporation will reimburse on an annual basis, any Officer of the Corporation who is employed by the Corporation on a full-time basis for those expenses for medical diagnostic procedures (as defined in Treasury Regulations §1.105-11(g), as now or hereafter amended) of such Officer. An Officer shall be considered employed on a full-time basis for purposes of this Plan if he or she customarily works at least nine (9) months in each year and thirty (30) hours in each week. Expenses for medical diagnostic procedures as so defined in Treasury Regulations §1.105-11(g) include all amounts paid for such procedures as routine medical examinations, blood tests, and X-rays, including annual physical examinations and routine dental examinations, and ordinary and necessary travel expenses primarily for an allowable diagnostic procedure; however, such expenses do not include expenses incurred for the treatment, cure or testing of a known illness or disability, or treatment or testing for a phsycial injury, complaint or specific symptom of a bodily malfunction. Diagnostic procedures do not include any activity undertaken for exercise, fitness, nutrition, recreation, or the general improvement of health. The diagnostic procedures must be performed at a facility which provides no services (directly or indirectly) other than medical and ancillary services.

(b) The Corporation may, in its discretion, pay any or all of the above described expenses directly in lieu of making reimbursement therefor. In such event, the Corporation shall be relieved of all further responsibilities with respect to those particular medical diagnostic expenses.

(c) The annual reimbursement to, or payment on behalf of, an Officer shall be limited to two thousand dollars ($2,000).

(d) Any Officer applying for reimbursement under this Plan shall submit to the Corporation annually, by _____, all bills for verification by the Corporation prior to payment. A failure to comply herewith may, at the discretion of the President of the Corporation, terminate the right of such Officer to reimbursement for that year.

(e) Reimbursement or payment shall be made by the Corporation within forty-five (45) days after the last date on which bills may be submitted.

2. Other Insurance

Reimbursement or payment under this Plan shall be made by the Corporation only in the event and to the extent that such reimbursement or payment is not provided for under any insurance policy or policies, whether owned by the Corporation or the Officer or under any other health and accident plan or wage continuation plan. In the event that there is such a policy in effect, providing for reimbursement in whole or in part, then to the extent of the coverage under such policy or plan, the Corporation shall be relieved of any liability hereunder.

3. Purpose

It is the intent of the Corporation that the benefits payable under this Plan shall be excludable from the gross incomes of the participants under Section 105 of the Internal Revenue Code of 1954, as amended, and that this Plan shall be deemed a discriminatory, self-insured medical reimbursement plan providing diagnostic benefits only under Section 105(h) of the Internal Revenue Code of 1954, as amended, and the Treasury Regulations which may be promulgated thereunder from time to time. To the extent that the terms of this Plan shall at any time constitute, or this Plan shall be operated in such a manner as to cause discrimination in favor of highly compensated participants under Section 105(h) or the Regulations thereunder, other than to the extent permitted for diagnostic procedures, the terms and operation of the Plan shall be modified to cause the Plan not to so discriminate.

4. Coverage

Any person now or hereafter becoming employed by the Corporation on a full-time basis and who is an Officer of the Corporation shall be eligible for the benefits provided under this Plan. A copy of this Plan shall be given to all such Officers of the Corporation.

5. Termination

This plan shall be subject to termination or amendment at any time hereafter by affirmative vote of a majority of the Board of Directors of the Corporation, provided that such termination or amendment shall not affect any right to claim for reimbursement for medical diagnostic expenses under the provisions of Paragraph 1(a), arising prior to such termination or amendment.

(CORPORATE SEAL)

ATTEST:

_____

_____   By: _____
Secretary   President

                                               Date: _____

(2) Health and Medical Insurance.

In today's society, group health and medical insurance is an indispensable element of survival. As a practical matter, all professionals must have it and, to some extent, must provide it for their employees. However, for a professional practicing as a proprietor or as a partner, the expenses for the professional's own health and medical insurance are only deductible under the general medical expense rules of Section 213 of the Code (one-half of the premium up to $150 with remainder of the premium only being deductible to the extent the total medical expenses exceed 3% of adjusted gross income). Consequently, as a practical matter, the amount of premiums in excess of $150 is usually never deductible by a professional, although payments for his common-law employees are deductible.

Upon incorporation, premiums paid by the corporation for the health and medical insurance of the common-law employees and the professional will be deductible by the professional corporation, as long as the "plan" requirements of Regulations §1.105-5 are met.[78] Further, if health insurance benefits are provided under a "plan" for employees, the professional corporation may discriminate among classes of employees with regard to benefits and may provide increased coverage (by way of dependent coverage or by way of additional insurance coverage) for the officers of the corporation.[79]

[14.04] CAFETERIA PLANS

(1) General

The Revenue Act of 1978 provides new rules for all written cafeteria plans (sometimes referred to as "flexible benefit plans") for plan years beginning after December 31, 1978. A cafeteria plan is a plan which permits participants to choose the benefits which they would like to receive from among those benefits offered by the employer, some of which may be taxable and some nontaxable.

Cafeteria plans which meet the requirements of Section 125 of the Code will permit employer contributions to be excluded from the gross income of employees to the extent that nontaxable benefits are selected. Nontaxable benefits include group term life insurance up to $50,000 in coverage, disability benefits, accident and health benefits, and group legal services to the extent that such benefits are excludable from gross income. Cafeteria plans may also provide deferred compensation as a nontaxable benefit, but subject to the rules applicable to cash or deferred profit sharing plans. See Section 125(d)(2) of the Code.

Notwithstanding these general rules, amounts contributed to a cafeteria plan for highly compensated employees (an employee who is an officer, a more-than-5% shareholder, or within the highest-paid group of all employees, or an employee who is a spouse or dependent of such an individual) will be included in gross income to the extent that the highly-compensated employee *could have* selected taxable benefits, unless the plan meets certain anti-discrimination requirements regarding coverage, eligibility, and contributions or benefits.

(2) Participation

Participation in a cafeteria plan will not be discriminatory if the plan meets the nondiscriminatory classification test applicable to qualified plans under Section 410(b)(1)(B), that is, if the benefit classification of employees is found by the Secretary of the Treasury not to discriminate in favor of employees who are officers, shareholders, or highly compensated. Further, a nondiscriminatory cafeteria plan may not require more than three years of employment for participation and the employment requirement for all employees must be identical. In addition, an employee who has satisfied the employment requirement and who is otherwise entitled to participate in the plan must commence participation no later than the first day of the first plan year after the employment requirement is satisfied.

(3) Contributions and Benefits

According to the Congressional Committee Reports,[80] a plan will not be discriminatory regarding contributions and benefits if the total benefits and nontaxable benefits attributable to highly compensated employees, measured as a percentage of compensation, are not significantly greater than the total benefits and nontaxable benefits attributable to other employees (measured on the same basis) provided the plan is not otherwise discriminatory.

A cafeteria plan which provides health benefits will not be considered as discriminatory if: (i) contributions on behalf of each participant include an amount which equals either 100% of the cost of health benefit coverage under the plan of the majority of highly compensated participants who are similarly situated (e.g., the same family size) or are at least equal to 75% of the cost of the most expensive health benefit coverage elected by any similarly situated plan participant; and (ii) the other contributions or benefits provided by the plan bear a uniform relationship to the compensation of plan participants. Although no Regulations have been issued on cafeteria plans under Section 125 of the Code, many advisors feel that it is possible, under these special health benefit rules, to provide uninsured medical reimbursement plan benefits (described in section [14.03], *supra*). For example, if each employee is given the opportunity to receive $2,000 of his compensation in cash, or have it applied by the employer to pay uninsured medical expenses, or have it applied toward the payment of health and accident insurance coverage, the plan should be nondiscriminatory. A form of such a plan is attached to this subsection.

Cafeteria plans can provide an excellent method of providing benefits for employees of a professional corporation. However, it is possible to have the requirements of cafeteria plans imposed on benefits provided to professionals where there is no intent to adopt a cafeteria plan. For example, where a professional is unable to obtain disability insurance which is generally provided for the professionals by the professional corporation, it might be argued that a cafeteria plan exists where his other benefits, such as group term life insurance, are increased to assure that he receives the same dollar amount of benefits as the other professionals. Although, as a practical matter, such adjusting may occur in a professional corporation setting, the authors feel that such adjustment should not be contractually required. Although the Service has, to date, not made an attempt to create *de facto* cafeteria plans in the professional corporation area, the authors would not be surprised if such an attempt were made.

XYZ, P.C.
EMPLOYEE CAFETERIA BENEFIT PLAN

WHEREAS, the Congress of the United States has enacted legislation in the form of Sections 105 and 125 of the Internal Revenue Code of 1954 ("Code") which is designed to encourage employers to offer flexible employee benefit plans to their employees on a nondiscriminatory basis; and

WHEREAS, the Board of Directors of XYZ, P.C. ("Employer") has determined that it is in the best interest of employees of the Employer to adopt a flexible employee welfare benefit plan which will supplement existing non-flexible plans and benefits, and thereby better enable eligible employees to provide for health and medical care in a flexible and cost effective fashion in accordance with Sections 105 and 125 of the Code;

NOW, THEREFORE, in order to accomplish these purposes, the Board of directors of the Employer has by appropriate resolution adopted the XYZ, P.C. Employee Cafeteria Benefit Plan ("Plan") as hereinafter stated to be effective as of _____, 19 ___.

It is intended that this Plan meet all the requirements of Sections 105 and 125 of the Code for purposes of exclusion of health and medical benefits from gross income of the eligible employees, and the Plan shall be interpreted, wherever possible, to comply with such terms of the Code.

1. <u>Purpose.</u> The purpose of this Plan is to enable eligible employees of the Employer to choose among the benefits provided by the Employer under this Plan in such fashion as best suits their individual circumstances, and further to encourage and help provide for expanded, but cost effective, health benefits for each eligible employee and medical benefits for each eligible employee and his or her spouse and dependents. It is the intention of the Employer that this Plan qualify as a "cafeteria plan" within the meaning of Section 125 of the Code, and that any health or medical benefits paid under the Plan be eligible for exclusion from gross income under sections 105 or 106 of the code. The Employer presently provides, and may continue to provide, a variety of other employee benefits to some or all of its employees on a non-elective basis. The benefits provided under this Plan shall be in addition to and not in lieu of such other benefits, and such other benefits shall not constitute a part of this Plan.

2. <u>Effective Date.</u> The Effective Date of this Plan shall be _____, 19___. Except as otherwise provided in Section 6, the records of the Plan shall be kept on the basis of the fiscal year running August 1 through July 31 (the "Plan Year").

3. <u>Eligibility.</u> All Full-Time Employees of the Employer shall be eligible to participate in this Plan. Full-Time Employees are employees who customarily work both at least 35 hours per week and at least 9 months per year. For purposes of this Plan, the term "hour" shall have the following meaning:

(a) Each hour for which an employee is paid or entitled to payment, for the performance of duties for the Employer during the applicable computation period.

(b) Each hour for which an employee is paid, or entitled to payment, by the employer on account of a period of time during which no duties are performed (irrespective of whether the employment relationship has terminated) due to vacation, holiday, illness, incapacity (including disability), layoff, jury duty, military duty or leave of absence. For purposes of this subparagraph (b), a payment shall be deemed to be made by or due from Employer regardless of whether such payment is made by or due from the Employer directly, or indirectly through, among others, a trust, fund, or insurer, to which the Employer contributes or pays premiums and regardless of whether contributions made or due to the trust fund, insurer or other entity are for the benefit of particular employees or are on behalf of a group of employees in the aggregate.

(c) Each hour for which back pay, irrespective of mitigation of damages, is either awarded or agreed to by the Employer. The same hours of service shall not be credited both under paragraph (a) or paragraph (b), as the case may be, and under this paragraph. Crediting of hours of service for back pay awarded or agreed to with respect to periods described in paragraph (b) shall be subject to the limitations set forth in that paragraph.

(d) For purposes of determining hours of service for reasons other than the performance of duties and for crediting of hours of service to computation periods, the rules of DOL Reg. Secs. 2530.300b-2(b) and (c) are hereby specifically incorporated by reference.

4. <u>Participation</u>. Each employee who is eligible to participate in the Plan under Section 3 (an "Eligible Employee") shall become a Participant in the Plan (a "Participant") on the Effective date of the Plan if on the Effective Date he or she is a Full-Time Employee of the Employer and has completed at least one year of service with the Employer. Each other eligible Employee shall become a Participant on the first day of the first Plan Year beginning after he or she has completed one year of service with the Employer if on such day he or she is a Full-Time Employee of the Employer. For purposes of this section, the term one year of service shall mean the 12-month period commencing on the date of employment of an employee and ending on the day immediately preceding the anniversary thereof. A Participant who terminates or is discharged from employment with the Employer shall cease to be a Participant in the Plan on the effective date of such termination or discharge.

5. <u>Benefits.</u> From the effective Date of the Plan and for so long as this Plan is continued, the Employer shall provide to each Participant for each calendar month a cafeteria benefit in the total amount of $100. Each Participant may elect to receive this benefit, in accordance with the procedures set forth in Section 8, and subject to the limitations set forth in Sections 6 and 7, either (a) as a health or medical benefit; or (b) as a cash benefit; or (c) as a combination benefit.

(a) <u>Health or Medical Benefit</u>. If a Participant elects receipt of the health or medical benefit, then Employer shall pay to such Participant or to third parties on behalf of such Participant such amounts as he or she has expended or incurred while a Participant for health or medical care for himself or herself and his or her spouse and dependents. Amounts incurred for health or medical care shall include amounts incurred for medical expenses as defined in Section 213(e) of the code, including, without limitation, amounts incurred or paid for physicians', surgeons', and dentists' fees, hospital charges (including laboratory and X-ray fees), costs of prescription and other ethical medicines and drugs, costs of medical related aids such as eyeglasses, and tuition payments for schooling for dependent children who are either handicapped or hyperactive or who have learning disabilities, provided, however, that any amounts for medical diagnostic procedures directly provided by Employer to any employee on a non-elective basis shall not be considered part of this Plan. Amounts incurred for health or medical care shall also include costs of medical and hospitalization insurance, accident and health insurance, disability insurance, and dental insurance, provided, however, that any insurance coverage directly provided by Employer to any employee on a non-elective basis shall not be considered part of this Plan.

(b) <u>Cash Benefit</u>. If a Participant elects receipt of the cash benefit then Employer shall pay to such Participant such amount in a lump sum.

(c) <u>Combination Benefit</u>. If a Participant elects the combination benefit, then Employer shall pay to or on behalf of such Participant the appropriate amount in accordance with Sections 5(a) and/or 5(b) as the case may be.

6. <u>Limitation.</u> No Participant shall be entitled to receive more than $100 as a health or medical benefit, cash benefit or combination benefit for any calendar month under this Plan, or more than $1200 as a health or medical benefit, cash benefit or combination benefit for any Plan Year under this Plan, provided, however, that if a Participant incurs expenses that would qualify under Section

5(b) except for the limitation of the immediately preceeding sentence, then such expenses may be carried forward to future calendar months in which he or she is a Participant.

7. Claim Procedure. Claims for health or medical benefits, cash benefits, or combination benefits under this Plan shall be made on forms maintained by the Employer.

(a) Health or Medical Benefit. Each Participant shall be entitled to elect reimbursement of medical expenses, by filing, on a form provided by the Employer, within 15 days after the end of each calendar month, a request for reimbursement of medical expenses incurred or paid by the Participant to a third party since Participant became a Participant in this Plan, together with such evidence of indebtedness to, or of such payment to, the third party as shall be required by the Employer in accordance with rules uniformly applied. Payment of medical benefits normally shall be made on the last day of the calendar month immediately following the calendar month with respect to which the reimbursement claim is filed or deemed filed. Each Participant shall be entitled to elect payment of the costs of medical and hospitalization insurance, accident and health insurance, disability insurance, or dental insurance by filing on a form provided by the Employer, within an election period to be prescribed by the Plan Administrator, a request for periodic payment to the particular third party insurer. Employer's sole obligation in such event shall be to pay such costs to such insurer in a timely fashion, and Employer shall assume no obligation under any policy or contract of insurance.

(b) Cash Benefit. Each Participant shall be entitled to elect the cash benefit, by filing, on a form provided by the Employer, a request for payment of such benefit in a lump sum. If for any month a Participant fails to elect any other benefit, such Participant shall be deemed to have elected to receive a full cash benefit. Payment of cash benefits normally shall be made on the last day of the calendar month with respect to which the cash benefit claim is filed or deemed filed, provided, however, that any Participant may elect, by filing on a form provided by the Employer, to receive payment of net cash benefits due on the last day of December and on the last day of July in any Plan Year.

(c) Combination Benefit. Each Participant shall be entitled to elect the combination benefit, by filing, on a form provided by the Employer, a request for payment of benefits in accordance with the provisions of Sections 7(a) and/or (b).

(8) Review Procedure. If any claim for benefits under this Plan is denied in whole or in part, the claimant shall be furnished promptly by the Employer with a written notice (a) setting forth the reason for the denial, (b) making reference to pertinent Plan provisions, (c) describing any additional material or information from the claimant which is necessary and why, and (d) explaining the claim review procedure set forth herein. Failure by the Employer to respond to a claim within a reasonable time shall be deemed a denial. Within 60 days after denial of any claim for benefits under this Plan, the claimant may request in writing a review of the denial by the Plan Administratory. Any claimant seeking review hereunder is entitled to examine all pertinent documents, and to submit issues and comments in writing. The Plan Administrator shall render a decision on review of a claim not later than 60 days after receipt of a request for review hereunder. The decision of

the Plan Administrator on review shall be in writing and shall state the reason for the decision, referring to the Plan provisions upon which it is based. Such decision of the Plan Administrator on review shall be final and conclusive.

9. <u>Administration</u>. The Plan Administrator shall have authority and responsibility to control and manage the operation and administration of this Plan under rules uniformly applied. The Plan Administrator shall be one or more Employees appointed by the Board of Directors of the Employer.

10. <u>Funding</u>. This Plan shall be funded by the Employer from the general assets of the Employer and all contributions to the Plan shall be designated and deemed to be Employer contributions. No separate fund or trust shall be established, segregated or maintained and nothing contained herein shall impose on any officers or directors of the Employer any personal liability for any benefits due a Participant or beneficiary pursuant to this Plan.

11. <u>Amendment and Termination</u>. This Plan may be amended or terminated at any time by the Board of Directors of the Employer; provided, however, that termination shall not affect the right of any Participant to claim a medical benefit for amounts incurred for medical care prior to termination to the extent such amount is payable under the terms of this Plan prior to the calendar month immediately following the calendar month in which the Plan is terminated.

12. <u>Entire Plan Stated</u>. This document sets forth the entire Plan. No other employee benefit or employee benefit plan which is, or may hereafter be, maintained by the Employer on a non-elective basis shall constitute a part of this Plan.

IN WITNESS WHEREOF, the Employer has caused this Plan to be executed this the _____ day of _____, 19___, to be effective as of _____, 19___.

EMPLOYER:
XYZ, P.C.

(CORPORATE SEAL)
ATTEST:

By: _____
President

_____
Secretary

DELEGATION OF RESPONSIBILITIES PURSUANT TO ERISA

The following fiduciary has accepted the duties and responsibilities delegated to it under the Plan pursuant to ERISA until its successors are duly appointed and qualified, this _____ day of _____, 19___.

PLAN SPONSOR:
XYZ, P.C.

(CORPORATE SEAL)

By: _____

President

ATTEST:

_____

Secretary

PLAN ADMINISTRATOR:

_____

XYZ, P.C.
EMPLOYEE CAFETERIA BENEFIT PLAN
MASTER BENEFIT ELECTION FORM

To: Plan Administrator

From: _____

Participant

I understand that the XYZ, P.C. Employee Cafeteria Benefit Plan entitles me to elect medical, health or cash benefits or a combination thereof, in a total amount of $100 per month or $1,200 per Plan Year so long as I remain a Participant in the Plan. I hereby elect the following benefit(s) under the XYZ, P.C. Employee Cafeteria Benefit Plan:

1. ☐ I request that you begin paying monthly premiums to the _____ Insurance company or to the insurer identified in the attached contract, commencing on _____, 19___. I understand that I cannot revoke this election for a 12 month period, and subject to that restriction, direct that you continue to pay such premiums until I direct you in writing to the contrary, or until I cease to be a Participant in this Plan.

2. ☐ I request reimbursement of medical expenses. Prior to the 15th day of each month I will submit invoices and/or receipts evidencing such expenses incurred since I became a Participant in the Plan. If the total amount exceeds $100, I request payment on such total amount each month until fully paid or until I cease to be participant in this Plan. I understand that amounts due will be paid on the last day of the month in which I submit the invoices and/or receipts.

3. ☐ I request payment of a cash benefit equal to the difference between $100 per month and the amounts elected under paragraphs 1 and 2 above. I request that this amount be paid:

   A. ☐ *Monthly.*

   B. ☐ *On December 31 and July 31 of each Plan Year.*

_____

Participant

Approved:

_____

Plan Administrator

_____

Date

_____

Date

455

XYZ, P.C.
EMPLOYEE CAFETERIA BENEFIT PLAN
MONTHLY BENEFIT ELECTION FORM

TO: PLAN ADMINISTRATOR

FROM: _____
               PARTICIPANT

For period ended _____, 19___:

☐ Monthly insurance perium .... $ _____

☐ Medical expenses .... $ _____

☐ Cash .... $ _____

        Total (cannot exceed $100
                 for any month) .... $ _____

                  Less ....   −$100

☐ Medical expense carryover .... $ _____

                        Approved:

_____   _____
Participant   Plan Administrator

_____
Date   Date

[14.05] $5,000 DEATH BENEFIT

By incorporating, professionals may take advantage of the income tax exclusion under Section 101(b) which provides for $5,000 of death benefits. Section 101(b) provides that up to $5,000 of death benefits will be exempt from income taxation if paid by or on behalf of the employer as a death benefit to the employee's estate or beneficiary. Generally, this death benefit is available whether the $5,000 exclusion is paid voluntarily or under the professional's employment agreement. However, the $5,000 exclusion is not available with respect to amounts which the employee had a nonforfeitable right to receive while living.

Payments in excess of $5,000 will be taxed as income in the form of deferred compensation, constructive dividends (if paid to a shareholder), or non-taxable gifts. For a number of years, the position of the Treasury was that amounts paid in excess of the $5,000 death benefit were always taxable income.[81] Although the Service has retreated somewhat from this position, and conceded that gifts may, in certain circumstances, be made, it generally considers voluntary death benefits to be compensation.[82] The courts are somewhat divided on the issue of whether death benefit payments are to be considered tax-free gifts or taxable compensation and each case must be decided on its own facts.

In order to be deductible by the employer, death benefits must qualify as ordinary and necessary business expenses under Section 404(a)(5) of the Code.[83] Consequently, if the payments constitute additional reasonable compensation for the employee's services, the payments will be deductible. On the other hand, payments made in the form of gifts will not be deductible by the employer. If payments in excess of $5,000 made to the spouse of the deceased employee constitute nondeductible gifts, the first $5,000 in death benefits should, nevertheless, be deductible if paid as compensation.

If the $5,000 (or greater) death benefit provided for the employee is simply a survivor benefit and he has no right to any post-retirement income or benefits, the benefits should not be includable in the employee's estate.[84] However, in determining whether the employee had any post-retirement benefits, all benefits which accrue to the employee due to his employment (except qualified retirement plan benefits) are treated as one contract for purposes of Section 2039(a).[85] Thus, it is possible for the $5,000 death benefit, when provided in the employee's employment agreement, to be excluded from his estate in the absence of other nonqualified deferred compensation, salary continuation, or disability benefits. On the other hand, if such other benefits are provided in the employment agreement, it is possible that the $5,000 death benefit will be included in the employee's estate. The existing cases and rulings in the area specifically emphasize the nature of the other post-retirement and disability benefits paid. Since most professionals will receive some form of post-retirement or disability benefits under their employment agreements, such benefits should be compared to the existing case law and rulings, if the $5,000 death benefit will also be included in the employee's employment agreement and if estate tax exclusion is sought.

On the other hand, if the $5,000 death benefit payment is not made under the professional's employment agreement but is merely a voluntary payment on the part of the professional corporation, such payment will not be included in the employee's estate.[86] Even in view of the possibility that contractual death benefits may be included in the professional's estate, the authors believe that it is preferable to provide for the $5,000 death benefit in the professional's employment agreement and, thereby, assure that the benefit will be paid (which will be excludable from the income of the estate of the beneficiary and will be deductible by the professional corporation). During the tax reform discussions which occurred in 1979 and 1980, the $5,000 death benefit under Section 101(b) of the Code was slated for repeal since it was felt that it only provided benefits for highly compensated individuals. While the $5,000 death benefit can be granted upon a discriminatory basis and, generally, it is only granted to professional employees, it continues to have explicit statutory approval, and the authors feel that it should be employed.

[14.06]   SICK-PAY PLANS

(1)   Authority for Sick-Pay Plans

With the planned increase in the Social Security wage base for the coming years (see section [2.07], *supra*), it may be beneficial for professional corporations to adopt formal sick-pay plans. Under such plans, amounts paid to employees during period of absence from work due to personal injury or sickness do not constitute "wages" for purposes of the FICA and FUTA taxes.[87]

Section 3101 of the Federal Insurance Contributions Act ("FICA")[88] imposes an old age, survivors, and disability insurance tax and a hospital insurance tax on the "wages" received by employees, and Section 3102 requires that these taxes be withheld from the employees' "wages." Furthermore, Section 3111 of FICA imposes an old age, survivors, and disability insurance tax and a hospitalization insurance tax (based on employee "wages") on employers.

Section 3121(a) of FICA defines "wages" to include all remuneration for employment, excluding:

> The amount of any payment (including any amount paid by employer for insurance or annuities, or into a fund, to provide for any such payment) made to, or on behalf of, an employee or any of his dependents under a plan or system established by an employer which makes provision for his employees generally (or for his employees generally and their dependents) for a class or classes of his employees (or for a class or classes of his employees and their dependents), on account of—
>
> (a) retirement, or
> (b) sickness or accident, disability, or
> (c) medical or hospitalization expenses in connection with sickness or accident disability, or
> (d) death.

The Service has, following the plain meaning of Section 3121(a) of FICA, held that payments for earned sick leave made to an employee for periods of absence from work due to illness are payments made pursuant to a plan or system of the type described in Section 3121(a) of FICA and are, therefore, excluded from the term "wages" and are not subject to FICA tax (either by employee or by employer).[89] However, the Service has taken the position that this exemption from FICA tax applies only to payments made on account of the *personal* injury or sickness of employees and that amounts paid to the employee on account of illness of an immediate family member are not exempt from FICA tax.[90] Although the statutory language of Section 3121(a) of FICA and the regulations thereunder appear to provide support for a contrary position (i.e., that payments to an employee on account of a dependent's sickness do not constitute "wages,"), the legislative history supports the position that payments to an employee due to the illness of a dependent are not exempt from FICA tax.

Section 3301 of the Federal Unemployment Tax Act (FUTA)[91] imposes a tax on every employer equal to 3.4% (less the applicable credit for state unemployment insurance) of the ''wages'' paid by the employer during the calendar year. Section 3306(b) of FUTA, which defines the term ''wages'' contains a definition identical to that contained in Section 3121(a) of FICA (i.e., payments on account of personal accident and sickness are excluded).[92] However, for FUTA purposes, the term ''wages'' is limited to the first $6,000 of remuneration paid to an employee during a year (exclusive of remuneration excluded from wages).[93]

For many years, the Social Security Administration has taken the position that it is not necessary for sick-pay plans to be written. However, with the advent of ERISA, all employee benefit plans (including welfare plans, such as a sick plan) must be written.[94] Included at the end of this subsection is a form of sick-leave plan which can be adopted by a professional corporation. Also included is a request-for-benefits form which requires the employee to specifically delineate the reason for his or her absence (so that sick pay will not be paid on account of absences due to the illness of dependents).

(2)   Utility and Future Sick-Pay Plans.

Most professional corporations provide some form of sick-leave arrangement for employees, whether sick leave is permitted for a specific number of days per year. The establishment of a sick-pay plan should not affect the normal sick-leave policies of the professional corporation but should permit the employer (and the employee) to save portions of the FICA and FUTA taxes on sick-leave payments. Because of the limitations on ''wages'' for FICA and FUTA purposes, sick-leave plans will have little effect for employees earning more than $6,000 (for FUTA purposes) per year or earning more than $29,700 in 1981 (the FICA wage base for 1981).

During the tax reform discussions of 1980, the elimination of the FICA and FUTA tax breaks for sick-pay plans was under consideration.[95] Although the benefits of sick-pay plans may, at some future date, be eliminated, the authors feel that in professional corporations with more then ten staff employees sick-pay plans should be considered because they provide a benefit which justifies the additional bookkeeping costs.

SICK AND EMERGENCY LEAVE PLAN

OF

DOW & ROWE, P.C.

Doe and Rowe, P.C., a Georgia Professional Corporation (hereinafter referred to as the ''Corporation'') hereby established this Sick and Emergency Leave Plan (hereinafter referred to as the ''Plan'') for the benefit of its nonprofessional employees.

459

1. Purpose of the Plan

This Plan is established to provide benefits for nonprofessional employees of the Corporation for periods during which they are absent from work on account of personal injury or sickness or other emergency.

2. Participation

Any person now or hereafter becoming employed by the Corporation on a full-time basis in a nonprofessional capacity shall be eligible for the benefits provided under this Plan, and a copy of this Plan shall be given to all full-time nonprofessional employees of the Corporation. An employee shall be considered as employed on a full-time basis after he or she has been an employee of the Corporation for thirty (30) days and if he or she customarily works at least (30) hours per week. Also, an employee shall be considered employed in a nonprofessional capacity if he or she is not licensed to practice law or is not a graduate of an accredited law school.

3. Benefits and Claim Procedure

Subject to the restrictions hereinafter set forth, during those periods when an employee covered by this sickness is absent from work on account of personal injury or sickness or other emergency, the Corporation shall pay to employee the salary, less the applicable federal and state withholding taxes, which the employee would have received had he or she actually been present at work.

Whenever an employee of the Corporation is absent from work on account of personal injury or sickness or other emergency, the employee must, on the day on which he or she returns to work, certify to the office manager of the Corporation (hereinafter referred to as the "Office Manager"), that he or she has been absent from work due to personal injury or sickness or other emergency. Upon receipt of the employee's certification, the Office Manager shall determine the benefits due to the requesting employee according to the following schedule:

Term of Employment	Benefit Period
Less than 6 months	1 week per year
6 or more months	2 weeks per year

and shall determine, in his sole discretion, whether the employee shall be entitled to benefits under this Plan for the period during which such employee was absent from work. The determination of whether to award benefits shall be made by the Office Manager on the basis of the circumstances of each particular case, and the Office Manager is authorized to withhold benefits under this Plan when he believes, among other things, that an employee claiming benefits has previously received a reasonable amount of benefits hereunder.

The payment of benefits hereunder shall be made with the next scheduled salary payment after the Office Manager determines that the employee is entitled to such benefits.

If an employee's claim for benefits hereunder is wholly or partially denied, the Office Manager will furnish, within a reasonable time after such disallowance, a written notice stating the specific reason or reasons for the denial, pointing out the Plan provisions on which the denial is based and a description of any additional material or information needed to give the claim further consideration, together with the reason it is needed. This notice will also contain an explanation of the claim review procedures of the Plan.

If a claim has been wholly or partially denied, the employee making the claim may ask to have the claim reviewed. The employee or someone authorized to represent the employee should make a written request for review to an executive officer of the Corporation within sixty (60) days after notice of denial is received. Arrangements will then be made to have the claim reviewed, fully and fairly, by the Board of Directors of the Corporation. The employee or his representative may review documents pertinent to the claim and submit issues and comments in writing. Within sixty (60) days after receipt of a request for review, the Board of Directors will furnish a written decision. If it is determined that benefits or additional benefits are due, payment will be made promptly. The written decision will set forth specific reason or reasons for the decision and the Plan provisions on which the decision is based.

4. Funding

The benefits to be paid under this Plan will be paid from the general assets of the Corporation and the Corporation has not insured its obligation hereunder. Employees of the Corporation are not required to contribute toward the cost of the Plan.

5. Other Emergency, Including Sickness or Injury of Children, Spouses, and Other Relatives

Employees of the Corporation will be entitled to benefits hereunder not only for those days on which they are absent from work due to their own injury or sickness but, when approved by the Office Manager, also for absence from work due to other emergencies, including the sickness or injury of their children, spouses, and other relatives.

6. Tax Status of Benefits

It is the intention of the Corporation that the benefits payable under this Plan shall: 1) be eligible for the exclusion from the gross incomes of the employees, to the extent provided by Section 105 and 106 of the Internal Revenue Code of 1954; and 2) not be classified as wages for purposes of the Federal Insurance Contributions Act (Chapter 21, Subtitle C, Internal Revenue Code of 1954) and the Federal Unemployment Tax Act (Chapter 23, Subtitle C, Internal Revenue Code of 1954). However, in determining whether benefits payable hereunder are classified as wages for purposes of the Federal Insurance Contributions Act and the Federal Unemployment Tax Act, benefits paid for absence from work due to other emergency, including the sickness or injury of any person other than the employee, whether or not a dependent or relative of the employee, shall not be considered absence from work due to an employee's personal injury or sickness.

7. Amendment and Termination

This Plan may be amended and shall be subject to termination at any time hereafter by the affirmative vote of a majority of the Board of Directors of the Corporation, provided that such amendment or termiantion shall not affect the right of any employee to claim benefits for days prior to such amendment or termination on which the employee was absent from work and for which the Corporation has agreed to compensate the employee hereunder.

8. Effective Date and Plan Year

This Plan shall be effective as of _____, and the records of the Plan shall be maintained on the basis of a Plan Year ending _____.

DOE & ROWE, P.C.

By: _____

President

Date: _____

SICK AND EMERGENCY LEAVE

REQUEST FOR BENEFITS

NAME: _____

DAYS ABSENT FROM WORK: _____

REASON FOR ABSENCE: ( ) PERSONAL INJURY OR SICKNESS
DESCRIBE: _____

OTHER EMERGENCY, INCLUDING INJURY OR SICKNESS OF RELATIVE OR DEPENDENT
DESCRIBE: _____

I HEREBY REQUEST BENEFITS UNDER THE SICK AND EMERGENCY LEAVE PLAN OF DOE & ROWE, P.C., FOR THE ABOVE DAYS ON WHICH I WAS ABSENT FROM WORK.

_____
EMPLOYEE'S SIGNATURE

DATE: _____

ACTION TAKEN: ( ) APPROVED
               ( ) DENIED

_____
OFFICE MANAGER
DATE: _____

[14.07] FICA BONUS PLANS

FICA bonus plans work somewhat like sick-pay plans due to the exclusion from the definition of the term ''wages'' for FICA purposes of the amount of the employee's share of the FICA tax which is paid for the employee by the employer. As with sick-pay plans, FICA bonus plans are only effective for those employees with earnings below the Social Security wage base.

FICA taxes must be paid both by the employee and the employer, the employee's share being withheld from his income during each pay period. The amount of FICA taxes paid by an employee must be included in his income, and he receives no deduction for the payment. Under a FICA bonus plan, an employer wishing to grant a bonus to an employee will, instead of granting a flat dollar bonus to the employee, agree to pay the employee's share of his FICA taxes for him. That is, if an employee's share of his FICA taxes on his base salary is $1,000 and the employer desires to give the employee a bonus of $1,000, granting the bonus in the conventional method would only increase the amount of FICA taxes due because FICA taxes would also be paid upon the bonus. If, however, the employer used the $1,000 to pay the employee's FICA taxes, the $1,000 would not be considered "wages" for purposes of the FICA tax and would result in a FICA savings to both the employee and the employer. Of course, the amount of the FICA taxes paid for the employee by the employer is considered income to the employee.

There are a number of ways of computing the exact FICA bonus which will result in a maximum tax savings for the employer and the employee, and any professional interested in adopting a FICA bonus plan should consult his accountant. However, before adopting a FICA bonus plan, professionals should consider that there are a number of practical problems encountered with FICA bonus plans, not the least of which is a communication problem. Since a FICA bonus plan is, to say the least, an unconventional method of granting a bonus, most employees will probably not understand that they (in addition to the employer) will receive a net benefit from the FICA bonus plan. Consequently, it is usually necessary to explain the FICA bonus plan in some detail to the employees. Also, once a FICA bonus plan is adopted for one year, employees often anticipate that it will be continued in future years. Such employee anticipation can present a problem in later years when the employer may not desire to grant a bonus equal to the employee's share of the FICA tax. This is especially true with increasing the FICA wage base and FICA rates.

Effective December 31, 1980, Section 3121(a)(6) was amended[96] to eliminate FICA bonus plans by defining wages to include FICA taxes paid by the employer. Consequently, the benefit once obtained through FICA bonus plans has been removed.

[14.08] PERSONAL FINANCIAL CONSULTING SERVICES

Personal financial consulting services provided by a corporation for select employees have generally been considered a neutral fringe benefit. Under Rev. Rul. 73-13,[97] the Service has ruled that corporations may pay the cost of outside consulting and investment services for employees and deduct this payment as additional compensation, as long as the executive includes the payment as gross income.The executive may, of course, deduct the portion of the payment which relates to tax advice, under Section 212 of the Code. Some professionals are taking a more aggressive approach and maintain that a moderate amount of personal financial consulting services may be provided for them and deducted by their professional corporations, without the necessity of including the cost of those services in income. The rationale for this approach is that, without these consulting services, the executive will not understand the benefits which the professional corporation is providing for him and will be less likely to desire to continue his employment with the professional corporation. The authors feel that this argument has substantial justification in the business corporation context, particularly with large corporations in which the executives are not totally aware of management policies and the reasons for providing certain benefits. On the other hand, the authors feel that providing substantial personal financial consulting services to the controlling professionals of a professional corporation is subject to scrutiny by the Service (and possible treatment as a constructive dividend). Consequently, the authors feel that all personal financial consulting services which are provided to the professionals by the advisors to the professional corporation, other than incidental advice, should be paid directly by the professionals.

[14.09]   MISCELLANEOUS FRINGE BENEFITS

Some professional corporations also provide miscellaneous fringe benefits for professional employees. Such benefits include burglar alarm systems, the payment of home telephone charges, club dues, automobile expenses, etc. Providing such fringe benefits generally does raise Service audit questions, and the authors feel that such benefits should be provided only if their cost would be deductible if paid by the professional directly. For example, if the professional has a family telephone number and a separate professional telephone number at his home, the professional telephone costs could be entirely deductible. A portion (based on business usage) of the personal telephone costs may also be deductible.[98] Further, if the professional maintains drugs and other medical equipment in his home and it is necessary to provide a security system to protect these items, there are grounds for permitting the professional corporation to pay for the system. For a discussion of club dues and automobile expenses, see sections [12.07] and [12.02], *supra*. The authors feel that professional corporations should avoid providing "questionable" fringe benefits, but should definitely provide reimbursement (or the professional should pay for and deduct on his own return) for bona fide expenses related to the professional practice.

[14.10] ERISA CONSIDERATIONS

Many fringe benefits which are provided under "plans," such as group term insurance, group permanent insurance, retired lives reserve programs, split dollar insurance, disability insurance, medical reimbursement plans, cafeteria plans, and sick-pay plans, are considered employee welfare plans under Section 3(1) of ERISA. Employee welfare plans are, in general, subject to Parts 1, 4 and 5 of Title 1 of the Department of Labor provision of ERISA, relating, respectively, to reporting and disclosure, fiduciary responsibility, and administration and enforcement.

(1) General Reporting and Disclosure Requirements

The general reporting and disclosure requirements of ERISA are applicable to employee welfare plans, which are described under Section 3(1) of ERISA as:

> any plan, fund, or program which was heretofore or is hereafter established or maintained by an employer or by an employee organization, or by both, to the extent that such plan, fund, or program was established or is maintained for the purpose of providing for its participants or their beneficiaries, through the purchase of insurance or otherwise, ... medical, surgical, or hospital care or benefits, or benefits in the event of sickness, accident, disability, death or unemployment, or vacation benefits, apprenticeship or other training programs, or day care centers, scholarship funds, or prepaid legal services . . .

This definition, obviously, describes most of the benefits previously described in this chapter.

Under the fiduciary responsibility requirements of ERISA, every employee welfare plan must be established and maintained pursuant to a written plan document.[99] Also, every welfare plan must provide an established "funding policy" in order to carry out the objectives of the plan.[100] However, the Department of Labor has recognized that in certain unfunded plans, such as group term life insurance plans, no funding policy need be established.[101] On the other hand, in the case of a retired lives reserve program, a funding policy may be required.

Every employee welfare plan must also contain the following:

(1) A description of the "named fiduciaries," and a description of the allocation and responsibilities among them;

(2) A procedure for amending the plan or determining who has authority to amend the plan; and

(3) The method for making payments.

Moreover, ERISA requires that, generally, all assets be held in trust. This requirement is not, however, applicable where the assets consist of insurance contracts or assets held by insurance companies.[102] Insurance contracts may be held by the employer but should be held in a safe and prudent manner.

(a) *Reports to the Internal Revenue Service and the Department of Labor*

Welfare plans must file annual reports on Forms 5500 or 5500-C with the Service, which will forward copies to the Department of Labor. Except for certain exemptions described below, professional corporations will generally be required to comply with the following reporting and disclosure requirements:

(1) *Summary Plan Description*

A summary plan description of the plan must be filed with the Department of Labor, within 120 days after the plan become effective.[103] Also, an up-dated summary plan description must be filed with the Secretary of Labor every five years.[104] Changes or material modifications in the summary plan description must also be filed with the Department of Labor.

(2) *Annual Reports*

An annual report must also be filed with the Department of Labor but, for this purpose, the Form 5500 or 5500-C filed with the Service (which is sent to the Department of Labor by the Service) will suffice.

(3) *Terminal Reports*

The administrator of a plan must also file reports with the Department of Labor concerning the termination of any welfare plan.[105]

(b) *Reports to Participants and Beneficiaries*

(1) *Summary Plan Description*

The administrator of a welfare plan is required to furnish to each participant and beneficiary a summary plan description within 90 days following participation.[106] The content of summary plan descriptions is generally defined in Labor Regulations §2520.102-3, and a detailed list of the aspects which should be included in the summary plan description are set forth in section [15.02](2)(b), *infra*. The authors feel, however, that since most welfare and fringe benefit plans are short in length, the best method of preparing a summary plan description is to provide a basic statement of ERISA rights with a copy of the plan attached thereto. A copy of such summary plan description follows at the end of this subsection.

Every fifth year an updated summary plan description must be distributed to participants and, of course, amendments to the summary plan description must also be distributed to participants.

(2) *Summary Annual Report*

Each participant and beneficiary must be furnished with a summary annual report.[107]

(3) *Miscellaneous*

Participants must also be furnished with an explanation of why benefits have been denied, and the documents of the plan must generally be made available to the participants.[108]

(c) *Exemptions*

Most welfare plans provided by professional corporations will be wholly or partially exempt from the reporting and disclosure requirements under one or more of the following:

(1) *Small Welfare Plans.*

Labor Regulations §2520.104-20 contains an exemption for welfare plans that have fewer than 100 participants (at the beginning of each year), and under which benefits are paid under either, or both of the following:

(a) As needed from the general assets of the employer; or

(b) Exclusively through insurance contracts or policies, the premiums of which are paid by the employer from its general assets (certain other rules apply to insurance plans which permit contributions by participants).

Such plans are not required to file a copy of the summary plan description (or modifications), annual reports, or terminal reports with the Department of Labor. Also, such plans are not required to furnish financial statements and summary annual reports to participants and beneficiaries. However, such plans must meet the other reporting and disclosure requirements, such as furnishing plan documents to the Secretary of Labor on request, and keeping plan records. Further, participants and beneficiaries of such plans must be furnished a summary plan description.

Similar rules apply for certain group insurance arrangements of two or more unaffiliated employers which fully insure one or more welfare plans.[109]

(2) *Top Hat Plans*

A limited exemption under Labor Regulations §2520.104-24 is provided for welfare plans which are maintained primarily for providing benefits for a select group of management or highly compensated employees and for which benefits are unfunded and are provided merely from the employer's general assets or are provided exclusively through insurance contracts. Such plans are exempt from all reporting and disclosure requirements except for the requirement that documents be furnished to the Department of Labor upon request. There is, however, no definition in the Regulations concerning the term "unfunded" plans. The question of whether a plan is a "funded" plan may become crucial since funded plans are subject to the fiduciary requirements of Title 1 of ERISA. For a further discussion of funded and unfunded plans, see section [16.01], *infra*.

(3) *Larger Welfare Plans*

If an insured welfare plan covers more than 100 participants, it is subject to the full reporting and disclosure requirements of ERISA, except that certain items need not be completed in the annual report (Form 5500, Form 5500-C, or Form 5500-K). See Labor Regulations §2520.104.44.

SUMMARY PLAN DESCRIPTION

This Summary Plan Description covers those matters which must be communicated to you as required by the Employee Retirement Income Security Act of 1974 (ERISA), which is administered by the United States Department of Labor.

MEDICAL EXPENSE REIMBURSEMENT PLAN
FOR EMPLOYEES OF
_____

The Plan Sponsor and Administrator is _____ whose address is _____. The telephone number is _____. The Employer Identification Number (EIN) of the Plan Sponsor has not yet been received from the Internal Revenue Service. The Plan Number assigned to this plan by the Plan Sponsor is _____. The fiscal records of this plan are maintained on the same accounting period adopted by this Employer for federal income tax purposes.

It is not anticipated that it will ever be necessary to have a lawsuit about this plan; however, if a lawsuit is to be brought, legal process may be served on the Plan Administrator at the above address.

The plan provides for reimbursement of medical care expenses on behalf of an employee [, his (her) spouse, and/or dependents]. The requirements for being covered under this plan, the provisions concerning termination of coverage, a description of the plan benefits (including any limitations and exclusions which may result in reduction or loss of benefits) are shown on the attached Exhibit ''A''. The procedures to be followed in presenting claims for benefits are described in this attachment.

The general administration of this plan is provided by the Plan Sponsor. The cost of the plan and all expenses are paid by the Plan Sponsor from its general assets. Participants are not required to contribute toward the cost of the plan.

If a claim is wholly or partially denied, the Plan Sponsor will furnish, within a reasonable time after proofs of claim are received, a written notice stating the specific reason or reasons for the denial, pointing out the plan provisions on which the denial is based, and a description of any additional material or information needed to give the claim further consideration, together with the reason it is needed. The notice will also contain an explanation of the plan's claim review procedures.

If a claim has been denied or partially denied, the person making the claim may ask to have the claim reviewed. The claimant or someone authorized to represent the claimant should make a written request for review to an executive officer of the Plan Sponsor within sixty (60) days after notice of denial is received. Arrangements will then be made to have the claim reviewed, fully and fairly, by the Board of Directors of the Plan Sponsor. The claimant or his representative may review documents pertinent to the claim and submit issues and comments in writing. Within sixty (60) days after receipt of a request for review, the Board of Directors will furnish a written decision. If it is determined that benefits or additional benefits are due, payment will be made promptly. The written decision will set out the specific reason or reasons for the decision and the plan provisions on which the decision is based.

As a participant in this plan, you are entitled to certain rights and protections under the Employee Retirement Income Security Act of 1974 (ERISA). ERISA provides that all plan participants shall be entitled to:

Examine, without charge, at the Plan Administrator's office all plan documents, including insurance contracts and copies of all documents filed by the plan with the U.S. Department of Labor, such as detailed annual reports and plan descriptions;

Obtain copies of all plan documents and other plan information upon written request to the Plan Administrator. The Administrator may make a reasonable charge for the copies.

In addition to creating rights for plan participants, ERISA imposes duties upon the people who are responsible for the operation of the employee benefit plan. The people who operate your plan, called "fiduciaries" of the plan, have a duty to do so prudently and in the interest of you and other plan participants and beneficiaries. No one, including your employer, may fire you or otherwise discriminate against you in any way to prevent you from obtaining a welfare benefit or exercising your rights under ERISA. If your claim for a welfare benefit is denied in whole or in part you must receive a written explanation of the reason for denial. You have the right to have the Plan Administrator review and reconsider your claim. Under ERISA, there are steps you can take to enforce the above rights. For instance, if you request materials from the Plan Administrator and do not receive them within 30 days you may file suit in a federal court. In such a case the court may require the Plan Administrator to provide the materials and pay you up to $100 a day until you receive the materials, unless the materials were not sent because of reasons beyond the control of the Administrator. If you have a claim for benefits which is denied or ignored, in whole or in part, you may file suit in a state or federal court. If it should happen that plan fiduciaries misuse the plan's money, or if you are discriminated against for asserting your rights, you may seek assistance from the U.S. Department of Labor, or you may file suit in a federal court. The court will decide who should pay court costs and legal fees. If you are successful, the court may order the person you have sued to pay these costs and fees. If you lose, the court may order you to pay these costs and fees, for example, if it finds your claim is frivolous. If you have any questions about your plan, you should contact the Plan Administrator. If you have any questions about this statement or about your rights under ERISA, you should contact the nearest Area Office of the U.S. Labor-Management Service Administration, Department of Labor.

NOTES TO CHAPTER 14

1. 363 U.S. 278 (1960).

2. See generally Treas. Regs. §1.79-1 and §1.105-5; *Bogene, Inc.,* 27 T.C.M. 730 (1968) and *Edward D. Smithback,* 28 T.C.M. 709 (1969).

3. Prop. Treas. Regs. (Discussion Draft) §1.61-16, 40 *Federal Register* 41118 (1975). It should be noted that, ordinarily, regulations are issued in proposed form with a request that taxpayers comment on the proposed regulations. After the comments are reviewed, the regulations are then issued in final form.

4. The Age Discrimination in Employment Act ("ADEA") permits employees to continue to work until age 70. Care should be taken to assure that the plan of group term insurance comports with AREA. Note Treas. Regs. §1.79-2(b)(3)(iii), indicating that retirement age may be considered age 65.

5. Treas. Regs. §1.79-1(b)(1)(iii)(B) specifically superseded by the existing regulations under T.D. 7, 623 (May 14, 1979).

6. See *Maurice A. Enright,* 56 T.C. 1261 (1971).

7. Treas. Regs.§1.61-2(d)(2)

8. See Rev. Rul. 71-576, 1971-2 C.B. 88.

9. Treas. Regs. §1.79-1(c).

10. Rev. Rul. 75-528, 1975-2 C.B. 35.

11. See Treas. Regs. §1.79-1(c).

12. See Treas. Regs. §1.79-1(c)(2).

13. 1980-33 I.R.B. 6.Also see Letter Ruling 8025032.

14. 1980-26 I.R.B. 26.

15. See also Letter Ruling 8014003.

16. Treas. Regs. §1.79-1(b)(1)(i), Rev. Rul. 69-423, 1969-2 C.B. 12.

17. Treas. Regs. §1.79-1(e).

18. Treas. Regs. §1.1348-3(a)(1)(i)(c).

19. Code Section 162(a), Treas. Regs. §1.264-1, Rev. Rul. 56-400, 1956-2 C.B. 116.

20. See Section 264(a) of the Code. Also see Section 79(b)(2)(A), Rev. Rul. 66-203, 1966-2 C.B. 104; Rev. Rul. 70-148, 1970-1 C.B. 60. However, where the employer is a nominal beneficiary, i.e., is required to pay the proceeds to the beneficiary of the employee, the employer will not be considered the owner. Rev. Rul. 72-2, 1972-1 C.B. 19.

21. See Letter Ruling issued to Century Planning Corporation dated June 28, 1962, signed by Arthur Singer, Acting Director, Tax Ruling Division.

22. 1976-2 C.B. 300. Many advisors feel that the position of the Service in this ruling regarding a gift of the annual premium is incorrect. See Kroll note 7-22A, at §5.1[13].

23. 1979-1 C.B. 312.

24. 397 F. 2d 82 (9th Cir. 1968), *rev'g.* 25 T.C.M. 772 (1966). Also see Letter Ruling 8021058.

25. See Rev. Rul. 69-54, 1969-1 C.B. 221 and *Landorf v. U.S.*, 408 F. 2d 461 (Ct. Cl., 1969). However, the amount of the premium for the last three years may be includable in the estate of the shareholder. See Kroll, *Legal and Tax Planning Forms*, Vol. 2 "Compensation: Insurance and Survivor Benefits" (1980) §5.1[13]. However, if the amount of the annual premium is covered by annual gift tax exclusion under Section 2503, no portion of the premium should be includable in the employee's estate.

26. Treas.Regs. §20.2042-1(c)(6). Also see *Estate of Lumpkin v. Commissioner*, 474 F. 2d 1092 (5th Cir. 1973) and *Estate of Connelly v. U.S.*, 551 F. 2d 545 (3d Cir. 1977) regarding whether the taxpayer has retained all incidents of ownership.

27. Rev. Rul. 80-289, 1980-43 I.R.B. 16, revoking Rev. Rul. 79-231, 1979-2 C.B. 323.

28. Treas. Regs.§1.79-1.

29. See Rev. Rul. 69-382, 1969-2 C.B. 28, Rev. Rul. 69-478, 1979-2 C.B. 29.

30. Retired lives reserve insurance is subject to the "plan" requirements of Section 79 and it is possible that superimposing substantial amounts of retired lives reserve insurance upon an existing group term insurance plan may cause the plan to violate the requirements of Section 79 because the plan does not preclude individual selection.

31. See Rev. Proc. 80-22, 1980-26, I.R.B. 26.

32. 1969-2 C.B. 28.

33. Benefits provided under retired lives reserve insurance should be included in determining whether compensation is reasonable.

34. 1973-2 C.B. 40, as modified by Rev. Rul. 77-92, 1977-1 C.B. 41.

35. *Id.*

36. Letter Ruling 8042168.

37. See Rev. Rul. 71-497, 1971-2 C.B. 329 (Situation 1). However, for cases which may provide the contrary result, see *Bel v. U.S.*, 452 F. 2d 633 (5th Cir. 1972), and its progeny.

38. 1976-2 C.B. 300. Rev. Rul. 76-490 is discussed more fully at section [14.02] (1), *supra.*

39. 1979-1 C.B. 312.

40. See Roberts and Klein,"Estate Taxation of Group Term Life Insurance," *CLU Journal*, October, 1978; and Lewis, "Retired Lives Reserve Takes the Witness Stand," *The Financial Planner*, Vol. 8, No. 8, August, 1979, p. 28.

41. See section [14.02](2), *supra.*

42. Rev. Rul. 64-328, 1964-2 C.B. 11.

43. Rev. Rul. 78-420, 1978-2 C.B. 67.

44. See note 7-47, *infra.*

45. See Hamblen, ''Split Dollar Life Insurance and the Controlling Stockholder—Still Useful with Prudent Planning,''Prentice-Hall *Successful Estate Planning Ideas and Methods*, ¶2005, and Wise, *Business Insurance Agreements* (Massachusetts Mutual Life Insurance Company, 1970).

46. See Treas. Regs. §1.161-2 (d) (2) (ii) (A); also see Kroll, *supra*, note 7-22A at §4.1[2]for a similar opinion.

47.

P.S. 58 Rate
One-Year Premium Cost for $1,000
Life Insurance Protection

Age	Cost	Age	Cost
15	$1.27	46	$6.78
16	$1.38	47	$7.32
17	$1.48	48	$7.89
18	$1.52	49	$8.53
19	$1.56	50	$9.22
20	$1.61	51	$9.97
21	$1.67	52	$10.79
22	$1.73	53	$11.69
23	$1.79	54	$12.67
24	$1.86	55	$13.74
25	$1.93	56	$14.91
26	$2.02	57	$16.18
27	$2.11	58	$17.56
28	$2.20	59	$19.08
29	$2.31	60	$20.73
30	$2.43	61	$22.53
31	$2.57	62	$24.50
32	$2.70	63	$26.63
33	$2.86	64	$28.98
34	$3.02	65	$31.51
35	$3.21	66	$34.28
36	$3.41	67	$37.31
37	$3.63	68	$40.59
38	$3.87	69	$44.17
39	$4.14	70	$48.06
40	$4.42	71	$52.29
41	$4.73	72	$56.89
42	$5.07	73	$61.89
43	$5.44	74	$67.33
44	$5.85	75	$73.23
45	$6.30		

47. These rates are published in Rev. Rul. 57-747, 1955-2 C.B. 228.

48. 1966-1 C.B. 12.

49. Section 264(a) of the Code and Treas. Regs. §1.264-1.

50. Rev. Rul. 64-328 1964-2 C.B. 11.

51. See *Emeloid Co.,Inc. v. Commissioner*, 189 F. 2d 230 (3rd Cir. 1951).

52. Section 264(a) of the Code.

53. 1955-2C.B. 23.

54. See *Arnold Genshaft*, 64 T.C. 282 (1975), *acq*. 1976-1 C.B. 22.

55. See H.R. Report No. 749, 88th Congress, 1964-1 (Part II) C.B. 125 at 186 and S. Report No. 830, 88th Congress, 1964-1 (Part II) C.B. 505, at 585.

56. 1964-2 C.B. 11.

57. Rev. Rul. 66-110, 1966-1 C.B. 12.

58. 1979-1 C.B. 138.

59. 1978-2 C.B. 67.

60. Treas. Regs. §25.2511-1(h)(8), Rev. Rul. 78-420, 1978-2 C.B. 67.

61. Rev. Rul. 76-490, 1976-1 C.B. 300.

62. See Rev. Rul. 78-420, 1976-2 C.B. 278, (Situation 2).

63. *Eleanor M. Schwager*, 64 T.C. 783 (1975).

64. Sections 2042 and 2035 of the Code. *Bel v. U.S.*, 452 F. 2d 683 (5th Cir. 1971); also see section [14.02](i)(e) *supra*.

65. Section 2503(b) of the Code.

66. Section 2035(b) of the Code.

67. Treas. Regs. §20.2042-1(c)(6); also see *Estate of Levy*, 70 T.C. 80 (1978), holding these regulations to be valid.

68. 1976-2 C.B. 278.

69. *Theodore H. Cohen*, 30 T.C. 1055 (1958), *acq*. 1964-1 C.B. 4.

70. See *Casale v. Commissioner*, 247 F.2d 440 (1957); Rev. Rul. 59-184, 1959-1 C.B. 65.

71. Treas. Regs. §1.62-2(d)(2).

72. Rev. Rul. 58-59, 1958-1 C.B. 88.

73. Treas. Regs. §1.105-5.

74. See *Allen v. Larkin*, 48 T.C. 629 (1967), *aff'd,* 394 F.2d 494 (1st Cir. 1968); *Samuel Levine*, 50 T.C. 422 (1968); *Edward and Mary Smithback*, 1969-136 T.C. Memo; *Estate of John Leidy*; 75-340 T.C. Memo; *Bogene, Inc.*, 1968-147 T.C. Memo; *Sebastian Bongiovanni*, 35 T.C.M. 586, ¶76,131 P-H Memo T.C. (1976), and *John H. Kennedy, Inc.*, 36 T.C.M. 878, ¶77,210 P-H Memo T.C. (1977).

75. See Section 105(h) of the Code and Treas. Regs. *1.105-11*.

76. The authors understand that some IRS agents have attempted to disallow uninsured medical reimbursement plans where all employees are covered and all employees are professionals (there are no staff employees), but there is no basis for such a position.

77. In fact, the "cost plus"language was not included in the Proposed Regulations issued in early 1980 but is included in the final regulations (issued January 15, 1981), probably as a response to such "insured" plans.

78. Treas. Regs. §1.162-10 (a); Rev. Rul. 58-90, 1958-1 C.B. 88; Rev. Rul. 56-632; 1956-2 C.B. 101; Rev. Rul. 210, 1953-2 C.B. 114.

79. Section 106; Treas. Regs. §106-1; Treas. Regs. §1.79-3(f); Rev. Rul. 58-90, 1958-1, C.B. 88, Rev. Rul. 56-632, 1956-1 C.B. 101.

80. House Report 95-1445, page 64, and Senate Report No. 95-1263, page 75.

81. Rev. Rul. 60-326, 1960-2 C.B. 32.

82. See Rev. Rul. 60-102, 1960-2 C.B. 37.

83. Treas. Regs. §1.404.(a)-12.

84. Section 2039 (a) of the Code; *Estate of Fusz*, 46 T.C. 214 (1966), *acq.* 1962-2 C.B. 2; Rev. Rul. 76-380; 1976-2 C.B. 27.

85. Treas. Regs. §20.2039-1 (b).

86. See *Estate of Barr*, 40 T.C. 227 (1963), acq. (in result only) 1978-1 C.B. 1.

87. See Sections 3121 (a) and 3306 (b) of the Code. Also see Rev. Rul. 65-275, 1965-1 C.B. 385; Rev. Rul. 78-392, 1978-2 C.B. 251; Rev. Rul. 80-303, 1980-45 C.B. I.R.B. 10; and Private Letter Ruling 7717004.

88. Subtitle C, Chapter 21 of the Code.

89. Rev. Rul. 65-275, 1965-1 C.B. 285.

90. Rev. Rul. 68-189, 1968-1 C.B. 421.

91. Subtitle C, Chapter 23 of the Code.

92. See Treas. Regs. §31.3306(b)(2)-1, Rev. Rul. 65-275, 1965-1 C.B. 421.

93. Treas. Regs. §31.3306(b)(1)-1.

94. See ERISA Sections 3(1), 3(3) and 402(a).

95. See Prentice-Hall *Federal Taxes*, No. 32, Vol. LXI, July 16, 1980, ¶60,353.

96. Under H.R. 7765, the Omnibus Reconciliation Act of 1980.

97. 1973-1 C.B. 142.

98. See *B. Morgan Heflin, Inc.*, 1979-62 T.C.M. (10% of orthodontist's home telephone expense deductible).

99. See Section 402(a)(1) of ERISA.

100. See Section §402(b)(1) of ERISA.

101. ERISA Interpretive Bulletin 75-5, juuestion F-5.

102. See Sections 403(b)(1) and (2) of ERISA.

103. Section 102 of ERISA and Labor Regs. §2520.104(a)-2.

104. See Labor Regulations §2520.104(a)-2.

105. See Labor Regulations §2520.101-1.

106. See Section 104(b)(1) of ERISA.

107. Labor Regulations §2520.104(b)-10(a).

108. Sections 503 and 104(b) of ERISA, respectively.

109. See Labor Regulations §2520.104.21.

CHAPTER **15**

Qualified Retirement Plans

[15.01] CHOICE OF PLAN

As described in the initial chapter of the Desk Book, adoption of a qualified retirement plan, unencumbered by the H.R. 10 limitations, is one of the major benefits which may be obtained through the incorporation of a professional practice. Such a plan permits current income tax deductions by the professional corporation, a deferral of income tax until receipt (actual or constructive) by the professional, tax-exempt earnings during the existence of the trust, exemption of the trust from the claims of the creditors of both the professional and the professional corporation, and the availability of favorable treatment under the income and estate tax rules upon the payment of benefits from the plan. Although most of these tax advantages may be obtained by the unincorporated professional under an H.R. 10 plan, corporate qualified plans offer much greater flexibility in design and operation and more permissible benefit alternatives than are available for H.R. 10 plans. However, it should be noted that, if the professional corporation elects to be taxed as a Subchapter S corporation, several of the H.R. 10 restrictions will become applicable to the corporation's qualified plan. Unless specifically stated otherwise, the discussion in this chapter relates to qualified plans maintained by corporations that do not have in effect elections to be taxed under Subchapter S.

This chapter will provide a general overview of the various types of qualified plans which are available to, and generally used by, professional corporations, a description of those factors which aid in choosing a particular type of qualified retirement plan, and a description of various administrative and operational problems which are encountered by professional corporations.

Once the decision to establish a qualified retirement plan is made by the professional corporation, care should be taken to assure that the plan is designed to meet the goals of the various professionals. The decision regarding the type and design of the qualified retirement plan to be established is almost as crucial as the decision regarding the incorporation.

The incorporation of a professional practice does not, through some form of alchemy, create funds where none existed before. A portion of the income received from the professional practice must be used to pay overhead (including rent, staff salaries, etc.), another portion must be used to provide direct compensation to the professional, and the remainder may be used to provide fringe benefits and qualified retirement plan benefits. Probably the most important aspect of choosing the appropriate qualified retirement plan is determining the amount of contributions that can be made on an annual, recurring basis to the plan. If the income of the professional practice is entirely exhausted with the payment of overhead expenses and the payment of direct compensation to the professional, funds will obviously not be available to make contributions to the plan. On the other hand, if the professional feels his life style can be maintained on a reduced amount of direct compensation, funds will be available for the plan. In other words, the funds which will be contributed to a qualified retirement plan of a professional corporation are those "profits" in excess of the funds needed to meet overhead expenses and provide fringe benefits and living expenses for the professional. Thus, the professional is simply deferring a portion of his current income until later years. At the same time, he also defers income taxes on that income. For example, if a professional earning a salary of $90,000 per year establishes a qualified retirement plan into which $20,000 per year is contributed for him, he has only reduced his net take-home pay by $10,000 (assuming the 50% tax bracket), while enabling a $20,000 contribution to the plan.

The choice of qualified retirement plans is probably easiest in a one-man professional corporation and probably most difficult in professional corporations with fewer than 10 professionals, particularly where there is wide divergence in the ages of the various professionals. It has been the authors' experience, that, generally, the older professionals have seen the "writing on the wall" and desire to create as many retirement benefits as their incomes will allow, while the younger professionals prefer to defer little or nothing. Professionals should not proceed with the establishment of a qualified retirement plan (or even choosing one) without seeking the advice of their attorneys and accountants. Even if the professionals desire to adopt one of the many available master plans (see Section [15.02] (7), *infra*), the assistance of the attorney and accountant should be sought prior to the adoption of the plan. Only by reviewing the various needs and desires of the professionals, in conjunction with the legal ramifications of the plan, can the most appropriate plan for the professional corporation be chosen.

This discussion is not intended to provide exhaustive treatment of all aspects of qualified retirement plans, but merely to review those aspects which are particularly applicable to professional corporations, so that the professional and his advisors will not overlook them in designing the qualified retirement plan. For an extensive explanation of all aspects of qualified retirement plans, reference should be made to the Prentice-Hall *Pension and Profit Sharing Service*.

(1) Regular Profit Sharing Plans

A profit sharing plan is normally the first type of qualified retirement plan which a professional should consider adopting. Profit sharing plans are among the many types of ''defined contribution'' plans. The common characteristic of all defined contribution plans is that such plans provide individual accounts for each participant (although all plan assets are normally commingled for investment purposes). A participant's benefit under a defined contribution plan is based solely on the amount in the participant's account. Section 414(i) of the Code. This arrangement provides a certain measure of security from the standpoint of funding for the employer maintaining the plan, because the plan does not promise any specific level of benefits, and therefore if the plan suffers poor investment experience, the employer will not be called upon to underwrite the unanticipated shortfall in funds necessary to provide benefits. A necessary corollary to the employer's security in funding is that participants will bear the burden of poor investment experience and reap the benefit of favorable investment experience.

Under a profit sharing plan, contributions may be made only out of the profits of the professional corporation (current and/or accumulated) and contributions may be totally discretionary on the part of the professional corporation or may be made mandatory in the event there are sufficient profits (i.e., contributions equal to 5% of compensation but not to exceed current profits). For purposes of determining current or accumulated profits out of which contributions may be made, the plan may define ''profits'' consistent with generally accepted accounting principles. If a professional corporation has profits as determined under generally accepted accounting principles, contributions may be made even if there are no current or accumulated profits from a tax standpoint.[1] Amounts which are contributed to a profit sharing plan are allocated to the participants based on their compensation as a percentage of the entire compensation of all participants. However, if the profit sharing plan is integrated with Social Security (as discussed in section [15.01] (7) (d), *infra*), a participant's compensation that is not in excess of the taxable wage base may be disregarded in allocating all or a portion of the employer's contributions. Amounts which are allocated are then held by the trustee of the plan, and, on an annual basis, the earnings, losses and forfeitures of the plan are allocated to the accounts of the participants. There is no guaranteed retirement benefit under a profit sharing plan, because a retiring participant is entitled to receive only the amount in his account, which may be more or less than the total of the contributions actually made to the account, depending upon the investments made by the trustee.

In a profit sharing plan, forfeitures (the unvested portion of an account of a participant whose employment is terminated prior to becoming fully vested, see section [15.01] (7)(b), *infra*) are reallocated among the remaining participants. Forfeitures, thus, increase the accounts of those participants who continue employment with the professional corporation. The allocation of forfeitures is usually based on the current compensation of the remaining participants in the year in which the forfeiture occurred. Allocation of forfeitures may be based on other factors, such as the account balances of all remaining participants; however, if this results in officers, shareholders, or highly compensated participants receiving forfeitures that are a larger percentage of current compensation than is the case with rank-and-file employees, the plan will lose its qualified status.[2] To prevent possible disqualification, profit sharing plans should, as a rule, avoid allocating forfeitures on any basis other than current compensation. Section 404(a)(3) of the Code limits deductible contributions to a profit sharing plan to 15% of the compensation of all plan participants. However, if a contribution of less than 15% is contributed during a given year, the amount of such shortfall may be carried over to a subsequent year, although total contributions to a profit sharing plan for a given year may not exceed 25% of the compensation of all plan participants for the given year.

In addition to the annual contribution limitation which is applied to the plan in the aggregate, Section 415(c) of the Code provides a limitation with regard to "annual additions" with respect to the account of each participant. See section [15.02](11), *infra*, for a description of the annual addition limitations.

The authors feel that profit sharing plans should be the first type of plan considered by a professional corporation, primarily because profit sharing plans allow the amount of contributions to fluctuate, dependent entirely upon the determination of the board of directors of the corporation. Profit sharing plans can be very useful for new professional corporations which desire to implement some type of qualified retirement plan but are unsure of exactly how successful the corporation will be. Profit sharing plans are also very useful in a professional corporation which has wide fluctuations in income on an annual basis. Although the contributions to a profit sharing plan are discretionary, professionals should be aware that in order to establish and maintain a qualified plan, the plan must actually be a "plan" as defined in Regulations §1.401-1, which requires substantial and recurring contributions.[3] It is generally felt that in order to meet this test, contributions must be made at least every three years. In any event, however, the failure to make contributions because of insufficient profits will not disqualify the plan.[4]

The following is an example of the allocation of a profit sharing plan contribution for a professional corporation with four employees where a contribution of 15% of compensation is made:

Allocation of unintegrated Profit Sharing Plan Contribution:
15% of total compensation of $205,900:

Participant	Compensation	Contribution Allocation
Professional	$175,900.00	$26,385.00
Staff Employee	12,000.00	1,800.00
Staff Employee	10,000.00	1,500.00
Staff Employee	8,000.00	1,200.00
TOTAL	$205,900.00	$30,885.00

Although the professional receives the larger contribution, his contribution is based on the same percentage of compensation (15%) as that granted to the staff employees. It is, however, possible to integrate the contributions under a profit sharing plan with the Social Security taxes which the corporation must pay. Generally, under a profit sharing plan, integration with Social Security benefits will provide that contributions be allocated in the following manner: first to those participants whose compensation is in excess of the Social Security wage base, in an amount equal to 7% of such excess, and second to all participants as their compensation relates to total compensation. See section [15.01](7)(d), *infra*, for a detailed discussion of integration. If the profit sharing plan in the above example were integrated with Social Security benefits, the allocations would be as follows:

Allocation of the same $30,885.00 contribution under an
integrated profit sharing plan using the 1980
Social Security wage base of $25,900:

Participant	Contribution Allocation
Professional @ $175,900	$27,914.87
Staff Employee @ $12,000	1,188.05
Staff Employee @ $10,000	990.04
Staff Employee @ $8,000	792.04
TOTAL	$30,885.00

Obviously, an integrated profit sharing plan provides a larger allocation for the professional. An important factor that should be considered in making the decision of whether to integrate a profit sharing plan is that an integrated profit sharing plan may not permit distributions of accounts prior to retirement, death or other separation from service.[5] In contrast, nonintegrated profit sharing plans may provide for distributions to participants (even if they remain employed) after a period of deferral of as little as two years, or the attainment of a stated age, or the prior occurrence of some event demonstrating financial need. A form of profit sharing plan and trust is attached to this chapter as Exhibit 1.

(2)   Cash or Deferred Profit Sharing Plans

Cash or deferred profit sharing plans permit employees to decide, on an individual basis, whether to receive the yearly cash contributions allocated to their accounts or defer those amounts until retirement. Until 1978, there were many questions concerning the use of cash or deferred profit sharing plans because of the uncertainty relating to the qualification requirements for such plans and the income and estate tax constructive receipt issues. The Revenue Act of 1978 added new rules to the Code, which specifically address the qualification requirements and the constructive receipt issues.

Section 402(a)(8) of the Code now provides that, if a profit sharing plan meets the special requirements for cash or deferred plans provided in Section 401(k) of the Code, the amounts that an employee elects to defer under such a plan will not be treated as having been "distributed or made available," and will not be considered constructively received for income or estate tax purposes. Consequently, as long as the plan satisfies the requirements of Section 401(k) of the Code, employees will be required to recognize income only to the extent that they elect to take plan contributions in cash; deferred contributions will not be taxed until distributed or made available.

The new statutory rules of Section 401(k) of the Code require that cash or deferred profit sharing plans satisfy the general qualification rules for profit sharing plans, as well as comply with the following three additional requirements:

(a)   *Distribution Rule*

The distribution rule provides that amounts deferred may not be distributable to participants or other beneficiaries before retirement, death, disability, separation from service, hardship or attainment of age 59½. The deferred amounts may not be distributable merely by reason of completion of a stated period of participation or the lapse of a fixed number of years.

(b)   *Vesting Rule*

The vesting rule requires that any employer contributions elected to be deferred by an employee must be nonforfeitable. This rule does not require that amounts that are automatically deferred be fully vested, only that the amounts deferred pursuant to the employee's election be nonforfeitable.

(c) *Participation and Discrimination Rule*

Under this rule, a cash or deferred plan satisfies the general nondiscrimination requirements regarding contributions and coverage if, for the plan year, the employees who are eligible to participate satisfy the normal coverage requirements applicable to qualified retirement plans (Section 410(b)(1) of the Code) and if the contributions of the employer on behalf of eligible employees satisfy the special percentage deferral rule explained below.

Either of two tests must be met in order to satisfy the rule. First, the actual deferral percentage for the highly compensated employees cannot be more than the actual deferral percentage for all other employees multiplied by 1.5 (the "1.5 Test"). The second test has two parts: (a) the actual deferral percentage for the highly compensated employees cannot exceed the actual deferral percentage for all other eligible employees by more than three percentage points; and (b) the actual deferral percentage for the highly compensated employees cannot exceed the actual deferral percentage of all other eligible employees by more than a multiple of 2.5 (the 3% Test"). Under this rule, the term "highly compensated employee" is defined as any employee who is more highly compensated than two-thirds of all eligible employees taking into account only compensation that is covered by the plan. Also, the "actual deferral percentage" for a group of employees (the highly compensated group or the group consisting of the other eligible employees) is the average for the group of the ratios (computed separately for each employee in the group) where each ratio is equal to the dollar amount of employer contributions that the employee elects to defer divided by the total amount of compensation received by the employee that is covered by the plan.

The most restrictive rule contained in Section 401(k) is the participation and discrimination rule. This rule can be best understood through the use of an example. Consider an employer with 24 employees and a cash or deferred payment profit sharing plan that allocates to each employee 10% of his compensation. The actual deferral percentages among the lowest two-thirds of the employees are as follows: eight employees defer one-fifth of their allocation under the plan and receive the balance in cash (2.0% deferral) and eight employees defer one-fourth of their allocation under the plan and receive the balance in cash (2.5% deferral). As a consequence, the actual deferral percentage of the lowest-paid two-thirds is 2.25% (i.e., average of 2.0% and 2.5%). Applying the 1.5 Test, the higher-paid one-third of the employees cannot elect, as a group, to defer more than 3.375% of the allocations available to them and must receive the balance in cash so that the actual deferral percentage of the higher-paid one-third will not exceed 3.375% (1.5 times 2.25%—the actual deferral percentage for the lower-paid two-thirds). Applying the 3% Test, the actual deferral percentage available to the highly compensated employees as a group could be not more than 5.25%, i.e., the 2.25% actual deferral percentage of the lower-paid employees increased by three percentage points. An actual deferral percentage of 5.25% additionally does not violate the "2.5 times" requirement of the 3% Test since 2.25% times 2.5 is 5.625%, which is greater than 5.25%. This example illustrates that the objective of providing each employee with an independent choice of whether to defer or receive the contributions currently is subject to the participation and discrimination rule. A higher-paid employee's income could be significantly increased in a year in which he is unable to defer the full amount he wishes because the lower-paid employees chose to defer very little. That is, if the lower-paid employees do not elect to defer any contributions, the highly paid employees will not be entitled to defer any contributions.

The adverse results of complying with the actual deferral percentage rules may be partially ameliorated by providing in the plan that a minimum percentage of the allocation must be automatically deferred each year, so that the election allowed by the plan only applies to a portion of the allocations. A properly drafted provision would guarantee that at least one of the actual deferral percentage rules will be satisfied and, therefore, the higher-paid employees could predict the minimum amount that they will be entitled to defer each year. For example, if a plan allocated to each employee 10% of his compensation and provided that 6⅔% *must* be deferred and the remaining 3⅓% was subject to election, the higher-paid employees could elect full deferral of the 3⅓% even if lower-paid employees elected to defer no portion of the 3⅓%. The 1.5 Test would be satisfied since 1.5 times 6⅔% is 10%. If the plan allocated to each employee 5% of his compensation, providing that 2% *must* be deferred and the remaining 3% was subject to election, the higher-paid employees could elect full deferral of the 3% even if the lower-paid employees elected to defer no portion of the 3%. In this case, the 3% Test would be satisfied (2.5 times 2% is 5%, and 2% plus 3% is 5%). Obviously, this type of provision requiring a high percentage of automatic deferral will decrease the amount available for take-home cash. For an employee making $150,000 per year, a mandatory deferral of 6⅔% would provide deferral discretion over only $5,000. As is apparent, the rules governing cash or deferred plans create a substantial administrative burden while producing only a minimum amount of flexibility.

An alternative to a cash or deferred profit sharing plan is to provide a profit sharing plan which permits a participant to withdraw his vested benefits after a period of two years. Regulations §1.401-1(b)(ii) provides that a profit sharing plan must provide a definite predetermined formula for allocating the contributions made to the plan among the participants and for distributing the funds accumulated under the plan *after a fixed number of years*, the attainment of a stated age, or upon the prior occurrence of some event, such as layoff, illness, disability, retirement, death or severance of employment. Rev. Rul. 71-295,[6] provides that the term "fixed number of years" is considered to mean at least two years. Therefore, a profit sharing plan may provide that an employee may elect to have his vested benefits distributed to him two years after such amounts have been credited to his account. Additionally, if an employee has participated for at least five years, the employee may elect to have his entire vested account distributed to him, including employer contributions made during the preceding two years, since the Service acknowledges five years as constituting a significant period of deferral.[7] Such provisions must be carefully drafted to insure that the employee has not "constructively received" such amounts when he does not elect to withdraw the benefits. If an amount is determined to be constructively received, it must be included in income even though the employee does not elect to receive the amount and does not actually receive the amount. Such early distribution options could serve to provide to the highly paid employees the ability to withdraw funds as needed; however, a detrimental consequence of permitting such early receipt elections, from the standpoint of the highly paid employees, is that the plan may not be integrated with Social Security.

Both a cash or deferred plan and a profit sharing plan with early distribution options will permit employees to withdraw retirement funds on a current basis. They do, however, defeat the overall purpose of all *retirement* plans, which is obviously the accumulation of retirement benefits. Also, such plans provide less incentive for employees to remain with the corporation until retirement. For these reasons, the authors feel that cash or deferred plans and profit sharing plans with early distribution options, while they are perfectly acceptable and, in some cases, may meet the divergent needs of the various professionals, should only be adopted where there has been careful consideration of the impact of these plans upon the retirement planning of the professionals.

(3) Profit Sharing Thrift Plans

Employee contributions may be a feature (either mandatory or voluntary) of any profit sharing plan. As a general rule, voluntary employee contributions in the aggregate may not exceed 10% of the compensation paid to an employee during his participation in the plan.[8] As a general rule, mandatory contributions (the minimum contribution required as a prerequisite for participation) may not for any year exceed 6% of compensation paid to the employee for the year in question.[9] Where employee contributions to a profit sharing plan, are permitted such a plan is often called a "contributory" plan. Where employer contributions are based on the amount or rate of employee contributions, such a plan is normally called a "thrift" (or savings) plan. Thrift plans have increased in popularity with both large and small corporations and normally have several attractive features, such as the following:

> (1) Employee contributions are normally made through payroll deductions; an employee receives no company contributions unless he has authorized payroll deductions.

(2) The company contribution is not tied to current profits but the company usually contributes a fixed dollar amount (such as $1.00) for each dollar contributed by the employee.

(3) Such a plan usually provides "class year" vesting, and permits the participants to withdraw the employer's contributions after they have become vested.

(4) Prior to 1982, an employee was not entitled to a deduction for his contributions, but this is possible after ERTA. See section [15.02](10), *infra*.

Thrift plans have generally received an enthusiastic employee response, which is somewhat unusual, since a regular profit sharing plan would normally provide the same type of benefits without the requirement of employee contributions. It is probably not the employee contributions which have generated the employee enthusiasm, however, but merely the class year vesting concept, which, in effect, turns the profit sharing thrift plan into a short-term savings account-type plan.

As a general rule, thrift plans offer the same benefits to a professional corporation as do profit sharing plans. Consequently, thrift plans are usually not thought of as a major type of profit sharing plan for use by professional corporations. However, thrift plans can serve a definite need in the professional corporation setting where professionals have divergent retirement desires. That is, the amount which is deferred for the professionals will be directly related to their own voluntary contributions and can, thus, be adjusted annually. On the other hand, if a thrift plan is adopted and the direct compensation of those professionals who do not contribute to the thrift plan (and consequently do not receive employer contributions) is adjusted upward, it is entirely possible that a *de facto* cash or deferred plan may exist (which would probably be discriminatory because the low-paid employees were not afforded the cash or deferred option).

(4)   Pension Plans

Pension plans, as opposed to profit sharing plans, must provide for definitely determinable benefits. Further, under pension plans, contributions are mandatory, irrespective of corporate profits, in an amount necessary to fund the benefits provided by the plan. Further, forfeitures created in pension plans do not increase the benefits of the individual participants but merely reduce the annual contributions required by the employer.[10]

(a)   *Defined Benefit Pension Plans*

Defined benefit pension plans provide specified benefits for employees which must be funded irrespective of corporate profits or losses. As a general rule, defined benefit pension plans provide greater benefits (to the extent that employer contributions are allocated to fund pensions) for older employees than for younger employees.[11] Further, defined benefit pension plans are often very useful in professional corporations where older professionals desire to defer a substantial amount of current income until retirement. The increased potential for deferral by use of a defined benefit pension plan results from the fact that, whereas the largest employer contribution that may be made to the account of an employee in a defined contribution plan (which includes profit sharing and money purchase pension plans) is (as of 1981) $41,500 (or if smaller, a contribution equal to 25% of compensation), a defined benefit plan may be funded by deductible employer contributions in an amount sufficient to provide an annual pension (as of 1981) of up to $124,500 (or if smaller, a pension equal to 100% of average compensation for a participant's 3 highest consecutive years of employment). These maximum dollar figures are increased each year to adjust for inflation.

In addition, if an employee has not been employed by the employer maintaining the plan for at least 10 years as of his date of retirement, the maximum limit for pensions must be reduced by 10% for each year of employment less than 10. A technique that is often available to increase the size of the maximum deductible pension plan contribution, particularly for senior employees, is to use a benefit formula that gives credit for service with the employer prior to the effective date of the plan. One limitation on the rate at which past service costs may be funded is, if the unfunded cost of past and current service benefits attributable to any 3 individuals is more than 50% of the unfunded cost of past and current service benefits of all participants covered by the pension plan, the cost attributable to such 3 individuals cannot be funded over fewer than 5 years.[12]

Although the ability to defer large amounts of compensation through deductible contributions to defined benefit pension plans may work well in some professional corporations, it may create problems in others. For example, once the older professional has retired, the younger professionals will be required to continue funding under the existing plan (or terminate it). This problem can be particularly acute if an older professional in a small professional corporation was credited with a significant amount of past service at the time the plan was established, and this past service credit is not fully funded by the date on which the older professional retires. In this case, the remaining younger professional finds his professional corporation making contributions to fund the pension of a person who no longer performs services for the professional corporation, and the temptation to terminate the plan can be overwhelming. Since the majority of the contributions of the employer goes toward the funding of the retirement benefits of those employees closest to retirement, defined benefit pension plans work well in larger corporations where there is a sufficient number of employees at various age levels to assure a level method of funding benefits over a number of years. On the other hand, in a small professional corporation with one younger professional and one older professional, the majority of the employer contribution will be used to fund the benefit of the older professional, thus leaving the younger professional (after the retirement of the older professional) with a virtually unfunded benefit. As long as the aspects of defined benefit pension plans are understood, they can prove useful in a professional corporation setting.

The annual contributions required under a defined benefit pension plan must be determined actuarially, based upon the ages of the participants, the earnings of the trust fund, inflation, etc. Consequently, the administration of a defined benefit pension plan is normally more costly than that of a profit sharing plan or a money purchase pension plan. Further, defined benefit plans (except those maintained by an employer whose principal business is providing services and which at no time covers more than 25 active participants) are generally subject to the pension benefit guaranty provisions of Title IV of ERISA. The exception from Title IV coverage for professional service employers whose plans at no time cover more than 25 active participants specifically includes, pursuant to ERISA Section 4021(c)(2)(B), employers whose principal business is the performance of professional services and which are owned or controlled by physicians, dentists, chiropractors, osteopaths, optometrists, other licensed practitioners of the healing art, attorneys, public accountants, public engineers, architects, draftsmen, actuaries, psychologists, social or physical scientists and performing artists.

The Pension Benefit Guaranty Corporation (PBGC) in a series of recent opinion letters[13] has taken the position that the professional service provider exception does not apply to opticians, food brokers, artists, designers, real estate brokers, individuals in advertising and public relations, foresters, and river boat pilots. The rationale of the PBGC in these opinion letters is that these occupational groups are outside of the exception because the occupations involved do not require a prolonged course of specialized intellectual instruction and are not predominently intellectual in character. Pension plans that are subject to Title IV must pay annual premiums to the PBGC of $2.60 per participant per year—and for this purpose ''participant'' includes all actual participants plus former participants or their beneficiaries that are currently receiving or that have a future right to receive plan benefits. If a plan subject to Title IV of ERISA is terminated and has insufficient assets to pay benefits guaranteed by the PBGC, the employer becomes liable to the PBGC in an amount equal to the lesser of 30% of the employer's net worth or the value of the unfunded ''guaranteed benefits'' under the plan.

There are also other important restrictions, the so-called ''5717 limitations,'' contained in Regulations § 1.401-4(c), on amounts payable with respect to the 25 highest paid employees at the time the plan is established (or at the time benefits are substantially increased). These limitations may have a substantial impact on professional corporations because they will generally come into play if a lump-sum distribution is payable with respect to a participant within 10 years after the plan is established (or amended to substantially increase benefits) or if the plan is terminated within its first 10 years (or within 10 years of an amendment that substantially increases benefits). Further, if the plan is underfunded within such first 10 years, these limitations may apply beyond 10 years.

The different types of defined benefit plans are described below.

(1) *Fixed Benefit Plans*

Fixed benefit plans generally define benefits in terms of a specified percentage of a participant's average monthly compensation for the three or five highest-paid consecutive years of service out of his last 10 years of service. However, these benefits are generally phased in over a period, such as 15 years of service. For example, each participant might be entitled at normal retirement age to an annuity for his or her life equal to 25% of his or her average monthly compensation for the highest five consecutive years of service out of his or her last 10 years of service. If the participant has completed less than 15 years of service at his or her normal retirement age, the annuity determined under the immediately preceding sentence will be reduced one-fifteenth for each year of service less than 15 which the participant has then completed.

A fixed benefit plan may be especially advantageous in a professional corporation where there are a limited number of professionals in their mid to late forties or early fifties (and intend to work at least 10 more years). For example, assume that a company has the following employees:

Employee	Age	Years of Service	Salary
Older Professional	55	20	$100,000
Younger Professional	30	5	$ 30,000
Staff Employee	30	5	$ 10,000

Assume further that the normal retirement benefit formula is 25% of a participant's average monthly compensation for the highest five consecutive years of service out of the last 10 years of service. Finally, ignoring interest considerations and salary increases and assuming that a total of $500,000 will be needed to fund the older professional's benefit at age 65, $150,000 will be needed to fund the younger professional's benefit at age 65, and $50,000 will untimately be needed to fund the staff employee's benefit at age 65. Based on these assumptions, $500,000 must be funded over 10 years for the older professional; hence, the contribution on his behalf must be $50,000 or 50% of his annual compensation. In contrast, $50,000 must be funded over 35 years for the staff employee, producing an annual contribution of under $1,500 or less than 15% of the staff employee's annual compensation. If an interest assumption had been added to this example the disparity in the percentage of compensation required to fund the older versus the younger professional's benefit would be even more pronounced since the contributions made on behalf of the younger professional will have a much longer period of time to compound interest and hence even smaller contributions would be needed to fund the younger professional's benefit (a dollar invested at 8% return for 10 years is worth $2.16, for 35 years it will be worth $14.79). Admittedly, this example does not conform to accepted actuarial practice, but the authors feel that it does illustrate that disproportionate percentage of the employer contributions will be allocated to the older professional.

(2) Unit Benefit Plans

Unit benefit plans usually define the pension to be received by the participant based on some type of increasing formula that takes into account both years of service and compensation, such as the following:

(I) CAREER AVERAGE UNIT BENEFIT PLANS

Under this type of plan, each participant is credited with a benefit for each year of service, and the benefit is based on the participant's compensation for that particular year of service. For example, assume that a participant who is age 55 when first employed is entitled to a benefit equal to 1% of his or her compensation for each year of service. If such participant earns the compensation shown in the first column below, his or her annual benefit accrual and annual pension benefit will be as follows:

	Compensation	Benefit
Year One	$ 50,000	$ 500
Year Two	$ 55,000	$ 550
Year Three	$ 60,000	$ 600
Year Four	$ 65,000	$ 650
Year Five	$ 70,000	$ 700
Year Six	$ 80,000	$ 800
Year Seven	$ 85,000	$ 850
Year Eight	$ 90,000	$ 900
Year Nine	$ 95,000	$ 950
Year Ten	$100,000	$1,000
Annual Pension Equals:		$7,500

(II) FINAL AVERAGE UNIT BENEFIT PLANS

Under this type of plan, each participant is credited with a benefit for each year of service, and the benefit is based on a participant's average compensation for a particular period of time, generally the highest five consecutive years out of the last 10 years. For example, assume a benefit formula of 1% for each year of service multiplied by a participant's highest five consecutive years of service out of the last 10 years. Assume further that the participant was age 55 when initially employed and worked ten years and that his or her compensation is as shown in the career average unit benefit plan example above. The average compensation for the highest five consecutive years of service out of the last 10 years of service is $90,000. Since he or she has completed 10 years of service, he or she will be entitled to an annual pension of 10% of $90,000, or $9,000.

A unit benefit plan will principally be advantageous when the professional employees either have, or are expected to have, many years of service. A career average unit benefit plan, as opposed to a final average unit benefit plan, will serve to avoid a large unfunded liability and accelerated funding during later years in the event of substantial salary increases. The benefits under a career average unit benefit plan, however, are not likely to keep pace with inflation.

(3) *Flat Benefit Plans*

Benefits under a flat benefit plan are not dependent upon a participant's compensation. Under the pure type of flat benefit plan, the participant will be entitled to a flat monthly pension at normal retirement, such as $200, irrespective of his or her length of service or compensation. Alternatively, the monthly pension at normal retirement could be defined in terms of a specified dollar amount, such as $20, multiplied by the participant's years of service. Flat benefit plans are usually adopted only in collectively bargained plans between labor and management.

In the professional corporation setting, a fixed benefit final average earnings plan will usually provide the most appropriate type of defined benefit plan. Normally, after careful consideration of personal savings, investments, and anticipated Social Security benefits, a professional will be able to determine the amount of income continuation from the qualified plan that he or she feels is necessary to provide adequate retirement security. This amount will be based on the receipt of a certain percentage of the compensation the professional was accustomed to earning prior to retirement. Since continuation during retirement of a certain style of living is the objective, a final average pay formula will usually be selected. The plan's actuary will make assumptions regarding the anticipated impact of inflation on salaries, so the plan will be funded from the outset to provide a benefit that allows for inflation. Once this income continuation percentage is formulated, it will become the cornerstone of the pension plan benefit formula. Of course, if several professionals are involved, a collective decision must be made regarding the income continuation percentage.

Once the income continuation percentage (assume 60%) is determined, the benefit formula must also be determined. The flat benefit plan approach is completely out of the question since it fails to take compensation into account. A unit benefit plan is a plausible alternative; however, it is likely that in many cases the professionals will be uncertain as to how long they will remain in service with the professional corporation and, in many cases, age differences among the professionals would result in a wide divergence of benefits (based on a percentage of salary) if a unit benefit approach is used. The professionals might, therefore, agree upon a fixed benefit formula under which any participant who serves 15 or more years will be entitled to a full 60% pension, with persons serving fewer than 15 years receiving 1/15th of the full benefit for each year of service.

As previously discussed, defined benefit plans (and particularly fixed benefit plans that require only a 10-or 15-year minimum period of service for full benefits) create a greater funding obligation for the older participants. Acknowledging this fact, the compensation package of older professionals versus younger professionals may be equitably adjusted after adoption of the qualified pension plan so that current compensation of younger professionals will be reduced to a lesser extent than that of the older professionals. This kind of adjustment often equates to the financial realities and desires of the professionals (the younger professionals generally want almost all their compensation paid currently, while older professionals are more cognizant of their retirement needs and therefore are more willing to relinquish current compensation to provide for retirement security). In addition, the younger professionals often are faced with the personal expenses of starting a home and family that the older professionals have already experienced. If the younger professionals should desire to shelter more current compensation than required to fund their defined benefits, the professional corporation could consider adopting a defined contribution plan in addition to the defined benefit plan. Furthermore, if desired, the defined contribution plan could be drafted in such a manner that the older professionals would be excluded from participation.[14]

(b) *Target Benefit Plans*

Under a target benefit plan, benefits are defined in terms of formulae which are the same as those for defined benefit plans. However, employer contributions, earnings, and losses are actuarially allocated to individual accounts for the plan participants, and actual pensions are based upon the amounts in the respective individual accounts. Thus, a target benefit plan is simply a pension plan which sets as its goal a pension to be funded by the amount on hand. The employer only has an obligation to make the contribution called for under the plan formula, and no contribution with regard to the actual benefit provided. A target benefit plan is, consequently, a hybrid-type arrangement combining some of the characteristics of a defined benefit plan with those of a defined contribution plan. The targeted benefit provided under the plan is not an actual promise for the participant and the actual benefit which will be paid will be based upon what is actually in the participant's account (based on the required contribution under the plan formula). Consequently, the target benefit plan closely resembles a money-purchase pension plan.[15]

The following considerations should be reviewed in connection with a target benefit plan:

(1) The PBGC provisions of Title IV or ERISA do not apply to target benefit plans.

(2) The 5717 limitations do not apply to target benefit plans.

(3) It is sometimes difficult to determine whether a target benefit plan discriminates in favor of the highly paid employees and, consequently, actuar-

ial allocations are required. These allocations may prove quite costly.

(4) The annual additional limitations which apply to target benefit plans are those of defined contribution plans.

(c) *Money-Purchase Pension Plans*

Money-purchase pension plans are also hybrid plans. Money-purchase pension plans must contain a formula that determines the amount of employer contributions in a manner that is not subject to the employer's discretion and is not based on profits. Amounts contributed to the plan are allocated to accounts set up for the participants and there are no guaranteed benefits under the plan. Consequently, upon retirement, the participant will be entitled only to the benefit that can be obtained from his account (i.e., money-purchase). Money-purchase pension plans typically provide for a contribution based upon a stated percentage of a participant's annual compensation and such plans may be integrated with Social Security benefits. Under the integration formula generally adopted in money-purchase pension plans, there may be a 7% differential between wages below and above the Social Security wage base (i.e., the employer may contribute 0% for compensation below the wage base and 7% for compensation above the wage base, or 3% of compensation below the wage base and 10% of compensation above the wage base). The maximum employer contribution which may be made to a money-purchase pension plan is the lesser of 25% of a participant's annual compensation or $41,500 (in 1981, subject to adjustment for inflation in later years). The following table illustrates a fully integrated money-purchase pension plan, with a contribution formula of 3% of compensation up to the Social Security wage base (of $25,900 for 1980) plus 10% of all compensation in excess of that wage base. This table should be compared with the table illustrating the integrated profit sharing plan in Section [15.01](1), *supra*:

Participant	Contribution Allocation
Professional @ $175,900	$15,777.00
Staff Employee @ $12,000	$ 360.00
Staff Employee @ $10,000	$ 300.00
Staff Employee @ $8,000	$ 240.00
	$16,677.00

In considering the adoption of a money-purchase pension plan, the professional should take note of the following facts:

(1) Contributions are mandatory and are in proportion to compensation. This is similar to the allocation under a profit sharing plan and in contrast to the possibility of disproportionately higher contributions on behalf of higher-paid employees under fixed rate plans, unit benefit plans, and target benefit plans.

(2) The PBGC provisions of Title IV of ERISA do not apply nor do the 5717 limitations.[16]

(3) A money-purchase pension plan is a defined contribution plan for purposes of the annual addition limitation under Section 415 of the Code.

Since money-purchase pension plans are defined contribution plans, they are very similar in many respect to profit sharing plans. The two most obvious differences are that contributions are mandatory and that forfeitures (as with pension plans) must reduce employer contributions. A form of money-purchase pension plan is included in this Chapter as Exhibit 2.

(5) Combinations of Plans

(a) *Defined Contribution Plans*

Target benefit plans, money-purchase pension plans, and profit sharing plans are all classified as "defined contribution plans" because benefits are determined by the participant's individual account balance. Under Section 415 of the Code, the "annual additions" which may be made to such plans on account of a participant must be aggregated, with the maximum annual allocation equaling the lesser of (a) 25% of the participant's compensation for the year or (b) $41,500 (for 1981, which figure is adjusted annually for cost of living increases).

A combination of defined contribution plans provides an excellent method for professional corporations, which do not wish to assume the burden of adopting a defined benefit plan, to increase benefits. For example, if a professional corporation adopts both a profit sharing plan and a money-purchase pension plan (which is integrated with Social Security), the annual employer contribution which is provided for the professional employee can reach 25% of his compensation. Further, a required contribution is only necessary under the money-purchase pension plan and the contribution under the profit sharing plan can be funded only if net profits are available. The table below illustrates the combination of a profit sharing plan and a money-purchase pension plan, which operates in tandem to provide the maximum annual addition limitation for the professional employee:

EXAMPLE OF PROFIT SHARING PLAN AND INTEGRATED
MONEY-PURCHASE PENSION PLAN

Allocation of contributions where corporation maintains a nonintegrated profit sharing plan and an integrated money-purchase pension plan (integration is based on 3% of compensation up to the Social Security wage base of $25,900 for 1980 plus 10% of compensation over that amount). The profit sharing plan contribution is adjusted to assure that the professional does not exceed the maximum annual additional limitation for 1980 of $36,875. The contribution to the profit sharing plan is computed by first determining the money-purchase pension plan contribution required to be made for the professional:

$$($175,900) - ($25,900) = $150,000$$
$$\times \quad .10$$
$$\$\ 15,000$$
$$($\ 25,900) \times (.03) \quad = \quad 777$$
$$\$\ 15,777$$

Since 25% of the professional's $175,900 compensation exceeds $36,875, the maximum limitation on employer contributions to the professional's accounts for both the profit sharing and money purchase plans will be $36,875. Since a contribution of $15,777 was required to be made to the professional's account in the money-purchase plan, the maximum contribution to the professional's profit sharing account will be $36,875 less $15,777 or $21,098. This results in a profit sharing contribution that is $21,098/$175,900, or 11.99% of the professional's compensation. Accordingly, the professional corporation will make a contribution to the profit sharing plan that is equal to 11.99% of the compensation earned by all participants included in the profit sharing plan.

Participant	Profit Sharing Plan	Money-Purchase Pension Plan	Total Allocation
Professional @ $175,900	$21,098.00	$15,777.00	$36,875.00
Staff Employee @ $12,000	$ 1,439.32	$ 360.00	$ 1,799.32
Staff Employee @ $10,000	$ 1,199.43	$ 300.00	$ 1,499.43
Staff Employee @ $8,000	$ 959.54	$ 240.00	$ 1,199.54
Total	$24,696.29	$16,677.00	$41,373.29

The reason why the professional in the above table *needed* to have a money purchase plan in addition to a profit sharing plan, is that if only a profit sharing plan were maintained the maximum deductible contribution would be limited to 15% of compensation paid during the year. Therefore the 25% of compensation ceiling under Code Section 415 could not be fully utilized. On the other hand, the professional could have adopted only a money-purchase plan having a contribution formula that would by itself require the maximum contribution allowed; however, if such a money-purchase plan were used, the full 25% of compensation contribution would have been required (since money purchase contributions are mandatory). If in a given year the professional corporation experienced cash flow problems and could not make the required contribution, a nondeductible excise tax equal to 5% of the deficiency could be imposed under Section 4971 of the Code, and if a timely correction of the deficiency were not made, an additional nondeductible excise tax equal to 100% of the deficiency could be imposed. In order to ameliorate the inflexible funding requirement created by exclusive use of a money-purchase plan, and in order to avoid the inability to make a full 25% of compensation employer contribution created by exclusive use of a money-purchase plan requiring a part of the total benefit that the employer feels reasonably certain could be paid even in cash lean years, plus a profit sharing plan under which the annual contribution is determined solely at the discretion of the employer. The money-purchase plan is the plan that should be integrated so that the professional will always receive the full benefit of integration even in those years when substantial contributions are not made to the profit sharing plan.

(b) *Defined Benefit and Defined Contribution Plans*

If a professional desires to defer more than the 25% or $41,500 limit applicable to defined contribution plans, the only alternative is to adopt either a defined benefit plan or a combination of plans that includes both a defined benefit and a defined contribution (money purchase or target benefit) plan.

Any combination of both defined benefit and defined contribution plans must satisfy the so-called "1.4 rule." In general, this means that the *sum* of (a) the *percentage of* the maximum permissible benefit that is actually provided by the defined benefit plan (the defined benefit plan fraction) and (b) the *percentage of* the maximum annual additions (that could have been made for all years of employment with an employer) that were actually made on behalf of a participant (the defined contribution plan fraction) cannot exceed 140%. For 1980, the maximum permissible defined benefit for a participant is the lesser of $110,625 or 100% of a participant's average compensation for his highest three consecutive years of employment with the employer maintaining the plan. For 1980, the maximum permissible annual additions for a participant is the lesser of $36,875 or 25% of a participant's compensation from the employer received during the year. The 1.4 rule is perhaps best understood by use of an example.

Example of 1.4 Rule

> *Hypothesis*: Professional A was first employed by Professional Corporation (P.C.) in 1970. In 1982, P.C. establishes both a defined benefit plan and a money-purchase pension plan and these were the first qualified retirement plans ever maintained by P.C. for Professional A. If P.C. had contributed the maximum permissible annual additions on behalf of Professional A for all of the years of employment of Professional A by P.C. since his date of hire in 1970, the aggregate amount contributed through the end of 1982 would be $200,000. Professional A's compensation in 1980, 1981 and 1982 (his 3 high consecutive years) is $100,000 per year.
>
> *Result:* The maximum amount that P.C. can contribute to Professional A's money purchase account in 1982 is $25,000 (25% of $100,000). This will result in a defined contribution plan fraction of $25,000/$200,000 or .125. Since the defined contribution plan fraction is less than .4 or 40%, the defined benefit plan could provide Professional A with a

pension equal to $100,000 and the 1.4 Rule would not be violated since his fractions would equal 12.5% plus 100% or 112.5%.

Changing the facts slightly, if P.C. had established the money purchase plan prior to 1982 and the annual additions actually made to the plan up to and including 1982 equaled $100,000, then Professional A's defined contribution plan fraction would be $100,000/$200,000 or 50%. Under these changed facts, Professional A's projected pension benefit could be no greater than $90,000 resulting in a defined benefit plan fraction of $90,000/$100,000 or 90%, which, when added to Professional A's defined contribution plans fraction of 50%, creates a total of 140% which satisfies the 1.4 Rule. Combinations of defined benefit and defined contribution plans maintained by the same employer should be drafted with appropriate "fail-safe" provisions that will make a violation of the 1.4 Rule impossible.

If a combination involves a defined benefit plan and a profit sharing plan, one further limitation may pose problems. The deductible contributions under the combined plans may not exceed the greater of 25% of the compensation paid to the plan participants during the year or the employer contributions required to satisfy the minimum funding standards (which are only applicable to defined benefit plans, target plans, and money purchase pension plans). Hence, if a defined benefit plan and a profit sharing plan maintained by the same employer cover the same employees, and if the contributions under the defined benefit plan equal 20% of the compensation paid to such participants during the year, the deductible contribution to the profit sharing plan will be limited to only 5% of the compensation paid to the participants during the year. Therefore, where the objective is to defer as much compensation as possible, consistent with the 1.4 Rule limitation, the defined contribution plan selected must be a plan that is subject to the minimum funding standards (a target benefit or money purchase plan). An important consideration that must be kept in mind by professionals who are contemplating this maximum deferral route is that the plans needed to obtain this objective *must* be funded at the minimum funding level of Section 412 of the Code, and failure to so fund the plans each year will result in imposition of nondeductible excise taxes under Section 4971 of the Code. Hence the advantage of maximum deductibility carries with it a price tag of somewhat limited funding flexibility.

(6) Simplified Pension Plans

The Revenue Act of 1978 established the Simplified Employee Pension (SEP) for years beginning after 1978. Effectively, a SEP is not a qualified plan but is, instead, a plan for contributing to a group of individual retirement accounts (SEP-IRAs).[17]

The principal drawback of a SEP is that contributions on behalf of a given individual are limited to the lesser of 15% of compensation or $7,500 (under ERTA

$15,000 for taxable years beginning after December 31, 1981—the H.R. 10 maximum applicable to defined contribution plans maintained by partnerships or sole proprietorships). A SEP generally must cover every employee who is at least age 25 and has performed any service for the employer maintaining the plan during at least three of the immediately preceding five calendar years. Contributions must be fully vested when made. Only the first $100,000 ($200,000 under ERTA for taxable years beginning after December 31, 1981) of a given employee's compensation may be taken into account under the plan, and employer contributions to the SEP-IRAs must bear a uniform relationship to the total compensation of each participant. However, if compensation over $100,000 is taken into account, the contributions for employees cannot be less than 7.5% of compensation. If the SEP is integrated with Social Security, an employer's contribution to each participant's SEP-IRA is reduced by the employer's share of Social Security tax paid on behalf of the employee. If the employer maintains other qualified retirement plans, contributions to a SEP will be treated as annual additions to a defined contribution plan for purposes of applying Code Section 415.

There are a limited number of advantages to SEP's. First, the reporting and disclosure requirements are less burdensome than those for qualified plans, but are still significant. In addition, if the employer contribution is not equal to the lesser of 15% of the employee's compensation or $1,500 ($7,500 under ERTA for taxable years beginning after December 31, 1981), the employee may contribute the amount of the difference between the employer's contributions and the lesser of 15% of compensation or $1,500 ($7,500 under ERTA for taxable years beginning after December 31, 1981), and will be entitled to a deduction for such contribution. Notwithstanding these benefits, the authors do not feel that SEP's offer a real alternative to professional corporations. The adoption of a profit sharing plan which is integrated with Social Security will provide a much greater benefit for the professionals than is available under the SEP, and the administration of a profit sharing plan is relatively simple, particularly if a prototype plan of a bank or brokerage house is adopted. Further, SEP's are very inflexible with regard to the specific terms of the plan. Since the account of each SEP participant is an IRA, a number of important incidents associated with qualified plans are lacking, for example:

(1) Excise taxes are imposed for distributions prior to age 59½ or disability;

(2) Mandatory distributions must begin at age 70½;

(3) Loans to participants are prohibited;

(4) Life insurance benefits are prohibited; and

(5) Ten-year averaging of lump-sum distributions is unavailable.

Finally, the Service has still not clarified its position with regard to when SEP's must be amended to comply with rulings and regulation changes and whether notice will be provided *by the Service* regarding such changes.

(7) Specific Qualification Aspects Relevant to Professional Corporations

(a) *Eligibility and Minimum Participation Standards*

Section 410 of the Code sets forth the minimum participation standards imposed upon all qualified retirement plans. In order to obtain qualified status, a plan may not, as a condition of participation, require that an employee complete a period of service extending beyond the later of his reaching age 25 or the completion of one year of service. Part-time employees working less than 1,000 hours during any given year may be indefinitely excluded, even if they are older than 25. In order to meet these requirements, a plan must provide that an employee who has satisfied age and service requirements participate no later than the earlier of (1) the first day of the first plan year beginning after the date on which the employee satisfied the requirements, or (2) the date six months after the date on which he satisfied such requirements.[18] Also, participation may be withheld until the completion of three years of service, but only if the plan provides for full vesting after three years of service.

In order to meet these requirements, the authors recommend that qualified retirement plans adopted by a professional corporation provide participation rules stating that participation will begin after the completion of one year of service and attainment of age 25. The authors also recommend that such participation be retroactive to the first day of the first plan year in which the later of these two requirements is met. Although it is possible to postpone participation for as much as 18 months following employment (through the use of dual entry dates which permit employees to come into the plan at six-month intervals), the authors believe that, in the interest of simplicity, a one-year participation standard should be adopted. See Article 2 of the profit sharing plan and money-purchase pension plans included in this chapter as Exhibits 1 and 2.

A plan may generally not exclude from participation employees who are beyond a specific age. However, a defined benefit plan or a target benefit plan may exclude employees who are within five years of normal retirement age when they begin employment.[19] The impact of the Age Discrimination in Employment Act (ADEA) on participation in qualified retirement plans is currently under review by the Equal Opportunity in Employment Commission. ADEA is applicable to all employers who have 20 or more employees. ADEA broadly prohibits discrimination based on age in terms, conditions, and benefits of employment and protects privately employed individuals in the age group of 40 to 70. Section 4(f)(2) of ADEA generally permits employers to observe the terms of bona fide employee benefit plans such as retirement or pension plans except that employees who are under age 70 may not be involuntarily retired pursuant to the terms of a pension plan. The Regulations currently interpreting ADEA were issued by the Department of Labor. The Regulations permit the exclusion from participation in a defined benefit plan of employees who were first employed within five years of normal retirement date.[20] The Labor Regulations also permit suspension of benefit accrual once normal retirement age is reached. The Labor Regulations permit employers to discontinue making contributions to a defined contribution plan account of a participant who has attained normal retirement age *if* the employer does not also maintain a defined benefit plan in which the participant participates. If the employer maintains more than one defined contribution plan in which an employee participates (and no defined benefit plans), the Labor Regulations permit employer contributions to cease in any *one* defined contribution plan designated by the employer at normal retirement age. For example, if an employer maintains a money purchase plan and a profit sharing plan, at the employee's normal retirement age the employer could cease making contributions to one or the other of the plans, but not both. Jurisdiction over ADEA has passed from the Department of Labor to the EEOC, and EEOC has indicated that it may revise certain of the Labor Regulations.

Section 410(b) specifies minimum eligibility standards which provide that in order to be qualified the plan must benefit 70% or more of all employees or 80% or more of the employees who are eligible to benefit under the plan if 70% or more of all employees are eligible to benefit. The plan may also qualify under classifications established by the employer and found by the Secretary of the Treasury to be nondiscriminatory. Normally the classification test requires the plan to cover a reasonable cross-section of employees in all compensation ranges.[21] The minimum eligibility requirements usually do not present a problem for professional corporations unless groups of professional corporations or partnerships are involved. If there are several professional corporations or partnerships involved, Sections 414(b), (c), and (m) provide that all employees and all corporations and partnerships which are members of a controlled group are treated as if employed by a single employer. The major problem in the controlled group context is the definition of a brother-sister controlled group. Under Regulations §1.414(c), this generally means two or more organizations conducting trades or business: (a) if the same five or fewer persons own singly or in combination a "controlling interest" of each organization ("controlling interest" means ownership of 80% of the total combined voting power of all classes of stock entitled to vote or at least 80% of the total value of shares of all classes of stock); and (b) if, taking into account the ownership of each such person only to the extent such ownership is identical with respect to each such organization, such persons are in "effective control" of each corporation ("effective control" means ownership of stock possessing more than 50% of the total combined voting power of all classes of stock entitled to vote or 50% of the total value of shares of all classes of stock of such corporation).

The crux of the problem is that the Service has taken the position that a brother-sister grouping exists where stock of each entity exists singly or in combination. For example, where Dr. A owns 100% of his Professional Corporation and 55% of Corporation X and Mr. B owns 45% of Corporation X, ownership is as follows under the two tests listed above:

| | Test (a) | | Test (b) | |
| | Percent of Stock Ownership | | Percent of Indentical Ownership | |
	P.C.	Corp. X	P.C.	Corp. X
Dr. A	100	55	55	55
Mr. B.	--	45	--	--
Total	100	100	55	55

In this situation, Dr. A and Mr. B together own 100% of both corporations. The Service, in relying on Regulations §1.1563-1(a)(3), takes the position that Mr. B's stock ownership in Corporation X should be counted, and, consequently, that the computation of the 80% rule under Test (a) should show that Corporation X qualifies as a controlled corporation, as does P.C. On the other hand, the Tax Court has in *Fairfax Auto Parts of Northern Virginia, Inc. v. Commissioner*,[22] held that Mr. B's ownership in the corporation cannot be taken into account for purposes of the 80% test because Mr. B does not own stock in both P.C. and Corporation X. Thus, it was held that the 80% test was not satisfied.[23]

Thus, the rules of Section 401 (qualification standards), Section 410 (participation), Section 411 (vesting), and Section 415 (limitations on benefits and contributions) are applied to all members of the controlled group as if all of the employees worked for the employer adopting the plan. The rules under Section 404 (deductions) and Section 412 (funding) are generally applied only with respect to members of the controlled group which adopt the same plan.

There are also special rules under Section 414(m) of the Code relating to controlled groups of service corporations, and these are discussed in Chapter 19, *infra*.

(b) *Vesting and Benefit Accrual*

Section 411 of ERISA provides the minimum vesting standards and permits the adoption of three types of vesting schedules, two of which are commonly used. The first is so-called "cliff-vesting." A cliff vesting schedule requires full vesting for a participant with at least 10 years of service, but no vesting for a participant with fewer than 10 years of service. The second common statutory vesting schedule calls for the so-called "graded vesting" schedule. A graded vesting schedule calls for at least 25% vesting after five years of service and annual vesting increases every year thereafter so that the participant will be 100% vested after 15 years of service.

Notwithstanding these statutorily provided vesting schedules, the Service has recently required that professional corporations use the so-called "4-40 vesting schedule" unless it can be shown that the turnover rate of highly paid employees is not appreciably lower than the turnover rate among the rank-and-file employees.[24] The 4-40 vesting schedule calls for vesting as described below:

Years of Service	Nonforfeitable Percentage
1	0
2	0
3	0
4	40
5	45
6	50
7	60
8	70
9	80
10	90
11	100

The longest permissible vesting schedule has, of course, advantages. The vesting schedule is obviously an inducement to employees to continue employment until they are fully vested. Nonetheless, if a participant's employment is terminated before he or she is fully vested, benefits which are forfeited will be distributed to the advantage of the other participants under the plan or will serve to reduce employer contributions. Forfeitures may be substantial if the employee turnover rate is high.

During 1980, the Service made a concerted attempt to enforce vesting schedules which are significantly more restrictive than the 4-40 schedule, specifically the three-year vesting schedule for closely held and professional corporations where the owners typically do not terminate their employment. There is, however, specific authority in the legislative history of ERISA that vesting at a rate more rapid than the 4-40 rate is not required, notwithstanding a substantial turnover rate among staff employees, unless there is actual misuse in operation of vesting to deny participants' accrued benefits.[25] The authors feel that the 4-40 vesting schedule is appropriate and should be adopted for most professional corporations, unless a shorter vesting schedule is desired. The 4-40 schedule should provide a sufficient deferral period during the first three years of employment to eliminate short-term employees from the vesting rules and the schedule should provide, during later years of employment, vesting which will induce employees to remain with the corporation.

(c) *Past Service*

Past service with former employers may be used for determining eligibility to participate in a qualified retirement plan and accural and vesting of benefits. At one time the Service maintained that past service as a self-employed individual (partner or sole proprietor) could not be counted for purposes of a plan adopted by a corporate successor of the partnership. The Service was unsuccessful with this position in litigation,[26] and it now acknowledges that a corporate qualified plan may include service with a prior partnership or as a sole proprietor for purposes of participation, vesting and benefit accrual.[27]

Until recently, the Service maintained that if past service credit is given for purposes of benefit accrual in a defined benefit plan, the plan provisions giving past service credit must prohibit "duplication of benefits," that is, the crediting of benefits under two plans simultaneously.[28] In Rev. Rul. 80-349[29], the Service reversed its position and stated that prevention of "duplication of benefits" was not mandatory; however, the ruling implied that where duplication of benefits does exist it may result in discrimination, thereby disqualifying the plan.

The Service also takes the position that using prior service for purposes of eligibility, vesting, and benefit accrual is subject to nondiscrimination rules and may disqualify a plan where no staff employees received past service credit for their service with a former employer (or possibly where none of the existing staff employees were employed with the former employer).[30] Consequently, the authors generally do not recommend that past service credit be granted for service with predecessor employers unless there are also staff employees who were employed by the predecessor organization.

(d) *Integration with Social Security Benefits*

In computing contributions to a qualified retirement plan, the Service permits an employer to take into consideration its contributions to the Social Security system. For example, in 1981 an employer pays a Social Security tax equal to 6.65% of the first $29,700 of compensation paid for each employee. Since this tax will not be paid with respect to compensation above $29,700, a somewhat larger contribution or benefit is permitted with respect to compensation in excess of the Social Security wage base. This concept of taking into account Social Security taxes and computing contributions of benefits under a qualified plan is known as "integration." Although the Service has, in the last several years, discussed the possibility of attempting to eliminate integration, the authors feel that professionals should definitely review the possibility of adopting integrated plans and should not hesitate to adopt those plans if they so desire.[31] The present state of the law governing Social Security integration is based on Regulations §1.401-3(c) and Rev. Rul. 74-446.[32] Profit sharing plans and money-purchase pension plans are generally integrated with the Social Security wage base with a 7% integration factor. Thus, in both a money-purchase pension plan and in a profit sharing plan, the account of each participant may be credited with a contribution equal to 7% of the compensation earned by the participant during the plan year that was in excess of the Social Security wage base. Any employer contribution in excess of the amount allocated under the preceding sentence is then allocated to the accounts of all participants in an amount equal to a uniform percentage of all compensation earned. See the examples of integrated profit sharing plans and money-purchase pension plans combined in sections [8.01](1) and (4)(c), *supra*.

A defined benefit pension plan is integrated with Social Security if the benefit provided by the plan, when added to the benefit provided by the employer-financed portion of Social Security, results in a combined benefit that is a uniform percentage of the compensation paid by the employer to each participant in the plan. Basically, there are three types of integrated defined benefit plans: excess plans, step-rate plans and offset plans.

(1) *Excess Plans*

An excess plan pays a benefit based solely upon an employee's compensation in excess of a certain amount which is referred to as the plan's "integration level." The plan provides proportionately greater benefits to higher-paid participants since higher-paid participants will have a greater proportion of their compensation exceeding the integration level. For example, if Participant A's compensation is $10,000 and Participant B's compensation is $20,000, a nonintegrated defined benefit plan could provide a benefit to B that is no greater than twice the benefit provided to A. However, if the plan is integrated at an integration level of $8,000, then only $2,000 of A's compensation and $12,000 of B's compensation is taken into account in computing the benefits, and therefore the plan can provide B a benefit that is 6 times greater than the benefit provided to A. Note that in this example if A's compensation had been less than the $8,000 integration level, A would not accrue any benefit.

The maximum *integration level* for an individual is determined by averaging the Social Security wage bases in effect during the individual's working career ending with his participation in the plan. Since the Social Security wage base has increased over the years, and will no doubt continue to increase in the future, a plan's integration level may be drafted to automatically increase (with respect to active participants) with the Social Security wage base. Once a permissible integration *level* has been determined, the second critical variable to be determined is the integration *rate*. The integration rate is the retirement benefit provided by the plan expressed as a percentage of compensation in excess of the integration level. The range of permissible integration rates will depend upon whether the plan is a fixed benefit plan or a unit benefit plan.

In an integrated fixed benefit plan, the benefit is normally expressed as a fixed percentage of the excess of the final average compensation over the integration level. For example, assume that a plan provided a defined benefit equal to the excess of average compensation for the last five years of participation over $8,000 times 25%. This integrated benefit represents an integration *level* of $8,000 and an integration rate of 25%. The greatest integration *rate* permitted for a fixed benefit plan that provides no benefit other than a life annuity at age 65 is 37½%. If a participant has fewer than 15 years of service with the employer maintaining the plan, this 37½% rate may be phased in no more rapidly than 2½% per year. Thus, for example, if a participant retires with only 8 years of service with the employer, the greatest integration rate that may be used for the participant will be 8 times 2½% or 20%.

A participant's compensation with respect to which a fixed benefit plan's integrated benefit is determined normally must be averaged over a period of at least five consecutive years. This is to prevent the creation of a large integrated benefit based on only one or two year's compensation. An average over three or four years is permitted, however, but in this case the maximum permissible integration rate is reduced.[33]

A unit benefit plan provides a unit of benefit for each year of service. An integrated unit benefit excess plan provides a unit of benefit equal to the excess of compensation over the plan's integration level multiplied by the plan's integration rate. Thus, for example, if the benefit were (average compensation in the last five years of service in excess of $8,000) times (1½%) times (years of service), the integration level would be $8,000 and the integration rate would be 1½%. The maximum permissible integration rate is 1.0% for final average unit benefit plans providing solely a straight life annuity at age 65. Such a plan may use an integration level determined in the same manner as for fixed benefit plans. The maximum permissible integration rate for a career average unit benefit plan is 1.4% and the integration level for such a plan may equal only the Social Security wage base in each year for which benefits are accrued. That is, for *each* year of service a participant earns a benefit equal to 1.4% of the excess of compensation earned in that year over the Social Security wage base in effect for that year.

If a plan provides benefits other than a straight life annuity beginning at age 65 the integration rate for either fixed benefit or unit benefit plans must be reduced; e.g., there is a pre-retirement death benefit, if early retirement before age 65 is permitted, if the retirement benefit is other than a single life annuity. These adjustments are rather tedious and complex; however, the important fact for the individual contemplating adoption of an integrated plan to bear in mind is that, in order to add benefits other than an annuity for life beginning at age 65, the maximum permitted amount of integrated retirement benefits will normally decrease.

(2) *Step-rate Plans*

A fixed benefit or unit benefit plan that provides an *integrated* benefit based on compensation in excess of the plan's integration level may *in addition* provide a nonintegrated benefit for compensation whether above or below the integration level. Such plans are referred to as step-rate plans, and can be thought of as a combination of integrated excess plan and a nonintegrated plan. For example, a fixed benefit plan could provide, as a sole benefit, a straight life annuity beginning at age 65 of 30% of participant's final 5 years average pay up to $8,000 plus 37½% of his final 5 years average pay in excess of $8,000. This formula is acceptable since it provides the same benefit as an integrated excess plan paying 37½% of compensation in excess of $8,000 plus a nonintegrated plan paying 30% of compensation.

(3) *Offset Plans*

An offset plan determines a defined benefit under which no participant and no part of compensation is excluded because of a minimum compensation level. But the benefit so determined is then reduced or ''offset'' by a percentage of the participant's Social Security benefit. For example, a fixed benefit offset plan could provide a benefit equal to 25% of participant's final five years average pay minus one-half of the participant's Social Security old age pension. The maximum permitted percentage offset for a plan that provides only a straight life annuity at age 65 is an offset of 83⅓% of the participant's Social Security benefit. Analogous to the case with excess plans, when offset plan benefits provided are other than a straight life annuity beginning at age 65, the maximum permissible percentage offset must be reduced.

(e) *Payment of Benefits*

Benefits normally become payable under qualified retirement plans upon the termination of employment (prior to retirement), disability, death, or retirement of the participant. The vesting schedule established under the plan will apply to benefits payable upon termination of employment (prior to the normal retirement date). Upon death, disability, and reaching normal retirement age, participants will generally be fully vested. In drafting qualified retirement plans for a professional corporation, questions often arise with regard to when benefits should be paid to employees who terminate employment prior to reaching normal retirement age. Some retirement plans provide, and some advisors recommend, that qualified retirement plans actually be *retirement* plans and that benefits should be postponed until actual retirement. Under this arrangement, an employee who terminates participation at age 30 must wait until either the normal or early retirement date established under the plan before benefits can be received. Those who support this approach also state that it will prohibit professionals who leave the professional corporation from receiving their benefits and using those benefits to fund a competing professional practice. Although providing "retirement" benefits for participants and prohibiting competition by departing professionals is important, the authors feel that it is probably best to provide in qualified retirement plans of professional corporations that benefit payments be made to terminating participants as soon after termination as possible. If the benefits of terminated employees are withheld until retirement, such employees will remain participants under the plan and must, on an annual basis, be furnished with annual reports and various other documents required under the reporting and disclosure regulations. Providing current benefits to terminated participants should eliminate the proliferation of partially vested participants which will occur over the years as staff employees constantly leave the professional corporation.

With the advent of ERISA, various rules were enacted with regard to providing annuities to participants under qualified retirement plans. In general, if a *"life annuity"* is available to the participant, he must also have available to him a "joint and survivor" annuity. A "life annuity" means an annuity which requires the survival of the participant or his spouse as one of the conditions for payment. For example, (1) an annuity for the participant's life, and (2) an annuity of 10 payments or until the participant's death, whichever first occurs, would both constitute life annuities and would invoke the joint and survivor requirements, but an annuity for a period of 30 years certain is not a life annuity and would not cause the joint and survivor provisions to apply to the plan.[34] While the joint and survivor annuity rules do provide protection, they also provide rules regarding notice which must be given to employees which are unduly burdensome to plan administrators. Since, in practice, the authors have found that most professional corporations have overlooked the notice and other requirements of the joint and survivor annuity Regulations, the authors generally recommend that the defined contribution qualified retirement plans of professional corporations do not provide an annuity option. The profit sharing plan and money purchase plans included in this chapter as Exhibits 1 and 2, respectively, provide that benefits may be distributed in a lump sum, periodically over 10 years or in any combination. While the requirements of the joint and survivor annuity regulations have been avoided, the authors feel that employees will not have been prejudiced by the removal of the joint and survivor annuity benefit because they should be in a position to obtain an annuity, if one is desired, through rolling over a lump-sum distribution of their account into an individual retirement account or an individual retirement annuity as permitted under Section 402(a)(5) of the Code. If a rollover is made, the participant will not be taxed on the initial distribution of funds from the plan (prior to the rollover) but upon subsequent distributions from the individual retirement account or annuity.

[15.02] ADMINISTRATIVE CONSIDERATIONS— PREVENTING POTENTIAL PROBLEMS

(1) General Administration of the Plan

Professionals are often too busy to handle their own personal financial affairs and, as a result, the administrative aspects of the qualified retirement plans adopted by professional corporations are often overlooked. It is important that qualified retirement plans be administered properly because, it they are not, it is possible that such plans may become ''discriminatory in operation'' and be disqualified by the Service.

Once a qualified retirement plan is established, one professional should be assigned the responsibility of dealing with the attorney, the accountant, the trustee, and the investment manager (if all of these exist). Also, in establishing the plan, some consideration should be given to who will perform the technical administrative functions of the plan, such as filing annual reports and making annual allocations. Under defined benefit pension plans, these functions are almost always performed by the actuary, since an actuarial analysis is necessary to compute the benefit annually. The normal fee for actuaries for most professional corporation defined benefit plans ranges from $500 to $2,000 per annum, depending upon the number of employees and the complexity of the plan. Most problems arise, however, under defined contribution plans where it is not necessary to have an actuary. In many such plans, the trustee of the plans is a local bank and, normally, the bank will offer administrative services. However, not all banks seek out professional corporation plans because they are usually smaller plans (at least in the scope of the bank's overall employee benefit area) and not all professionals desire to have banks act as trustee and invest plan funds (generally due to the conservative nature of most banks). Many brokerage houses and retirement plan consulting firms offer administrative services for defined contribution plans. Further, some accounting firms will assist a professional corporation in its annual administrative function (but most accounting firms will do so only if there are fewer than 10 employees—due to the complexity of the allocations when more than 10 employees are involved). The administrative services for defined contribution plans should normally run between $500 and $1,500 per year per plan (depending on the number of participants and the activity in the plan).

The fees for administering qualified retirement plans on an annual basis may be paid either by the trust or by the professional corporation. The authors generally recommend that such fees be paid by the professional corporation as they are deductible by the corporation. Further, payment of such fees by the plans would reduce the funds which will eventually be available to fund retirement benefits.

The authors also generally recommend that the professional corporation, and not one of the professionals, be designated as the plan administrator. To designate an individual as the plan administrator requires obtaining a separate employer identification number for the individual, and changing plan administrators if the individual leaves the professional corporation. In addition, the individual would be subject to suits by disgruntled participants.

(2)   Reporting and Disclosure Requirements of ERISA

The following are the reporting and disclosure requirements for qualified retirement plans.[35]

(a) Plan Description

Under Sections 102 and 104 of ERISA, the administrator of each qualified retirement plan must file a plan description with the Secretary of Labor within 120 days after the plan is adopted and every five years thereafter. A description of material modifications to the plan must also be filed within 210 days after the close of any year in which changes occur. This requirement is satisfied by filing the summary plan description with the Department of Labor and by filing summaries of any amendments to the plan that materially modify its terms.

(b) Summary Plan Description

A summary plan description, prepared in a manner calculated to be understood by the average plan participant, must be provided to participants and beneficiaries within 120 days after the plan is adopted. A copy must also be filed with the Department of Labor within that 120-day period. Further, a summary description of material modifications must be furnished to participants and beneficiaries within 210 days after the end of the plan year in which such modifications occur and the summary plan description must be provided to new employees within 90 days after they become participants.

The required contents of the summary plan description are described in Labor Regulations §2520.102-3 and include a general statement of the benefits provided under the plan and the manner in which the plan operates. An example of a summary description is included in this chapter as Exhibit 3.

Plans with fewer than 100 participants are required to file a form 5500-R in two out of every three years. This form is a brief registration statement and gives the Service, the Department of Labor and the Pension Benefit Guaranty Corporation an overview of the plan. Every third year the plan must file the appropriate Form 5500 or 5500-C.

(c) *Participant's Benefit Statements upon Request*

Upon the written request of a participant or beneficiary, the plan administrator must supply, without charge to the participant or beneficiary, a statement based on the latest available information of his or her total accrued benefit, the percentage of accrued benefits that are nonforfeitable, or the date upon which benefits will become nonforfeitable.[36] The plan administrator is not required to provide more than one such benefit statement during any 12-month period.[37] The Department of Labor has issued Proposed Regulations §2520.102-2(a)(6) under which plans need not furnish benefit statements on request if at least once during every 12-month period a benefit statement is furnished to all participants and beneficiaries; however, participants and beneficiaries would be entitled to one duplicate copy of their statement upon written request.

(d) *Furnishing Other Documents Relating to the Plan*

The plan administrator must make available for inspection by participants and beneficiaries copies of the plan document and trust agreement, copies of any collective bargaining agreement or contract under which the plan was established or is maintained, a copy of the latest annual report filed with the Service, and a copy of the latest summary plan description.[38] No charge may be made for exercising the right to inspect these documents. If the participant or beneficiary requests copies of these documents, copies must be provided, but a reasonable charge not in excess of the actual cost of reproducing the documents may be required, but no charge may be made for the postage or handling involved in providing requested documents.[39] Not later than nine months after the close of a plan year, the plan administrator must furnish each participant and each beneficiary receiving benefits, a "summary annual report" that summarizes the annual report that was sent to the Service. The format for this report is prescribed in Labor Regulations §2520.104b-10.

(3)   Adoption of Plans and Adoption of Amendments

A qualified retirement plan may be adopted at any time prior to the close of the employer's taxable year and become effective retroactive to the first day of the employer's taxable year. For example, a calendary year employer could adopt a qualified defined benefit plan on December 31, 1981, with an effective date of January 1, 1981, and the employer could contribute and deduct for 1981 at any time prior to the date for filing the 1981 tax returns, including extensions, the amount necessary to pay the normal cost for the entire 1981 plan year plus an amount necessary to amortize the cost of past service credit (if any) provided for in the plan.

An employer that adopts (or amends) a qualified plan is permitted to file with the Service during a period referred to as the "remedial amendment period" a request that the Service make a determination that the provisions of the plan as adopted (or as amended) satisfy the requirements of the Code for qualification. The significance of filing the determination request during the remedial amendment period, is that, if a request is filed during that period and the Service determines that changes are necessary to cause the plan to be qualified, the needed changes may be made *retroactive* to the effective date of the plan (or the effective date of a plan amendment) so that the plan will be qualified from its initial effective date (or remain qualified since the effective date of an amendment).[40] If a request for a determination is filed after the close of the remedial amendment period, and the Service discovers deficiencies in the plan, retroactive cure of the deficiencies may not be possible. Where the plan year corresponds to the employer's taxable year, the remedial amendment period for initial qualification (or for a plan amendment) will extend until the date for filing the employer's tax return (including extensions) for the first taxable year of the employer in which the plan (or the amendment) is effective. The remedial amendment period may be extended at the discretion of the Service, but the Service does not extend the period where failure to file timely a determination letter request was due merely to oversight.

It should be remembered that the period for *adopting* a qualified retirement plan by an employer ends with the last day of the first taxable year of the employer for which the plan is effective. Although contributions may be made after the end of the employer's taxable year and may be deducted for the year to which they apply, the plan itself may not be adopted retroactive to a taxable year that ended prior to the date of adoption. See *Engineered Timber Sales*,[41] in which the Tax Court held that, where the employer had adopted a trust agreement and the employer's board of directors had passed a resolution to adopt a plan prior to the expiration of the employer's first taxable year for which the plan was to be effective, but no enforceable plan was drafted until the following taxable year of the employer, no deductions would be permitted for the first taxable year for which the plan was made effective.

A plan that satisfies all the requirements of the Code for qualification and that receives a favorable determination letter is not guaranteed to be qualified *forever*. Two distinct classes of events could occur that would disqualify the plan: (1) the plan might *in operation* become disqualified—for example the plan administrator might improperly exclude some rank-and-file employees and thereby cause the plan to discriminate;[42] or (2) the legal requirements applicable to qualified plans might change—for example by issuance of new or modified Treasury Regulations or with a new revenue ruling.[43] Generally, when there is a change in applicable law, a plan will remain qualified if the plan is amended not later than the close of the plan year following the plan year in which the change in law occurred, and the amendment is made effective as of the first day of the plan year following the plan year in which the change in law occurred. It is critical that plan administrators, or their counsel, keep abreast of changes in the laws applicable to qualified plans so that timely plan amendments may be adopted.

(4) Loans to Participants

A loan from a qualified retirement plan to a participant of that plan is a prohibited transaction under Section 406(a)(1)(B) of ERISA and Section 4975(c)(1)(B) of the Code. However, Section 408(b)(1) of ERISA and Section 4975(d)(1) of the Code provide an exemption from the prohibited transaction rules where the following requirements are met:

(1) Loans are made to all participants and beneficiaries on a reasonably equivalent basis;

(2) Loans are not made available to highly compensated employees, officers, or shareholders in an amount greater than the amount made available to other employees (this requirement will not be violated, however, merely because the plan permits all plan participants to borrow the same percentage of their vested accrued benefits even though officers, shareholders and highly compensated employees may, as a group, have larger vested accrued benefits than rank-and-file employees);

(3) Loans are made in accordance with specific provisions regarding such loans set forth in the plan;

(4) Loans bear a reasonable rate of interest; and

(5) Loans are adequately secured.

As the amounts in an existing qualified retirement plan accumulate, the professionals often desire to borrow those funds so that they can, in effect, "pay interest to themselves." The availability of loans from qualified retirement plans does, in times of inflation, provide a real source of funds, and the authors believe that, as long as the loans are made within the exemption provided in Section 408(b)(1) of ERISA, they can provide an attractive source of financing to plan participants. Loans cannot, however, be made either directly or indirectly to the professional corporation without obtaining a specific exemption from the Department of Labor. The authors feel that loans can be made to participants if the following criteria are met:

(1) Either the plan or the administrative committee of the plan sets forth the specific reasons for loans, such as medical emergencies, second mortgages, college costs, etc., and they are followed for high-paid and low-paid employees alike.

(2) The interest rates which are charged by the plan are equivalent to rates which would be charged by local banks on similar loans and the loans, themselves, carry the terms which can be obtained locally from banks. Some District Directors are taking the position that qualified plans cannot permit loans to extend beyond a ten-year period. While there is no authority for this position, the authors recommend that loans not extend beyond the normal retirement date of the particular participant.

(3) The loan must be represented by a bona fide promissory note.

(4) Loans should be made only to the extent of the vested account balance of the participant, with the vested account balance acting as security. If loans in excess of the vested account balance of the participant are made, the plan should have the vested account balance as security plus other security, such as listed stocks and bonds, or a second mortgage. Any security taken by the plan should be segregated from the assets of the professionals and held by the trustee.

(5) Loans should be made in a consistent, business-like manner and loan applications should be executed by the participant desiring to borrow.

(6) Loans made by a participant should be earmarked investments of that participant's account so that, if that participant does default on the loan, only that participant and not the other participants will suffer.

(7) Although the commercially available interest rate should be charged on the loans, care should be taken that state usury laws are not violated.

(8) Loans from defined benefit plans should be made only to the extent of the accrued vested benefit.

A rather subtle problem may arise in the case of loans from a pension plan (defined benefit or money purchase plan). One of the characteristics of qualified pension plans is that such plans may not make distributions to participants prior to separation from service or attainment of normal retirement age. A *loan* from a pension plan does not violate this distribution limitation since bona fide loans are not plan distributions. A problem may arise, however, if the security for a loan from a pension plan is the vested accrued benefit of the participant. If the participant defaults on a plan loan and the only asset out of which collection may be made is the participant's vested accrued benefit, the satisfaction of the loan by reduction of the participant's accrued benefit could constitute a premature distribution that would disqualify the plan. A similar problem could arise in the case of loans from integrated profit sharing plans, since distributions from integrated profit sharing plans are prescribed prior to separation from service or attainment of normal retirement age. In order to avoid the premature distribution problem, the authors suggest that pension and integrated profit sharing plans that provide for loans to participants require adequate security for such loans *other than* the participant's accrued benefit.

(5) Bonding Requirements of ERISA

Section 412 of ERISA requires that every fiduciary and every person who handles funds or other property of a qualified retirement plan must be bonded, and that the bond shall be not less than 10% of the amount of the funds handled. While such bonds, ("ERISA bonds") are inexpensive and can be obtained as a rider to the general fidelity insurance of the professional corporation, they are often overlooked. Further, questions arise with regard to who "handles" funds and what are the "funds" handled? For these reasons, the authors feel that it is prudent to require that all professionals (if they are trustees or members of a plan administrative committee) be bonded and that the bond be in the amount of 10% of the funds in the plan.

(6) Investments

ERISA does not require any specific type of investment to be maintained by any type of qualified retirement plan. However, Section 404 of ERISA requires that fiduciaries exercise the care, skill, prudence, and diligence that a "prudent man acting in a like capacity and familiar with such matters" would use and also requires diversifying investments unless it is clearly prudent not to do so. These standards can normally be met by investments which are generally available, such as listed stocks and bonds. However, since a qualified trust is tax-exempt, the authors feel that an effort should be made to maximize the annual income under the trust in order to take advantage of the compounding effect which the tax-exempt status provides. Obviously, tax shelters and other investments with tax-favored status provide very little benefit to a tax-exempt trust and as such the authors feel that they should generally be avoided.

Often, professionals desire to leverage the ability of their qualified retirement plans to purchase various assets, such as real estate. Where the assets are purchased within a qualified retirement plan and funds are borrowed to acquire those assets or the assets are purchased through the use of purchase money indebtedness, the income generated from the sale of those assets will be partially taxable to the trust (which is normally tax-exempt) as if it were a regular taxable entity. This rule also applies to margin accounts.[44] There are, however, certain exceptions with regard to the purchase of real estate where the property is purchased from the owner and the owner takes back a second mortgage.

Many qualified retirement plans of professional corporations will have assets of less than $500,000 and, therefore, such plans may be unable to obtain the services of a registered investment advisor to handle investments. Consequently, the management of fund assets will fall to the trustee, be it a bank or the professionals themselves. If the professionals themselves are the trustees of the plan, they should take steps to assure that all assets held by the plan are segregated from their personal assets and from the assets of the professional corporation. Also, as trustees, the professionals will be responsible for the investments of the plan.

Most professionals either do not have the time or are not adept at investing large sums of money and, consequently, often the investment of assets of a qualified retirement plan of a professional corporation falls to a stockbroker or to an investment company. If a local stockbroker is employed, it should be recognized that he will generally not be considered a fiduciary unless he exercises discretionary control or authority over the fund or renders investment advice for a fee (most stockbrokers have disclaimers which eliminate them from the fiduciary responsibility rules of ERISA).

Further, many qualified retirement plans of professional corporations are invested in ''guaranteed investment contracts'' with insurance companies. While these contracts appear to offer a good annual return, professionals should be fully aware of the implications of investing in such contracts, since they usually involve some type of termination discount or some type of extended payout upon termination.

Very often, the investment ideas of the professionals will differ, and it is possible to provide in a qualified retirement plan that the participants will have the ability to earmark (direct the investment of) their accounts. Under an earmarking arrangement, the participant will have the authority to direct the trustee with regard to the vested balance of his account. Earmarking exists only in defined contribution plans and is not available with respect to defined benefit plan assets derived from employer contributions, although defined benefit plans that permit voluntary employee contributions may permit employees to earmark their voluntary employee contribution accounts. Further, if a participant does earmark the investment of his account, the fiduciary will be relieved of liability for a loss by reason of the participant's control.[45]

Section 314 of ERTA has imposed a substantial restriction on the investment of earmarked accounts by adding Section 408(n) of the Code which treats the investment in collectibles in an individually directed account as a distribution to the participant. Collectibles are works of art, rugs, antiques, metals, gems, stamps, coins, alcoholic beverages and other tangible personal property designated by the Secretary of the Treasury. Section 408(n) only applies to collectibles acquired after December 31, 1981. Collectibles continue to be permissible investments for the general retirement plan account, however. It should also be recognized, however, that participants may not direct the investment of their accounts into items such as oriental rugs, expensive foreign cars, and oil paintings which are collected by the professional and used personally, since such use would constitute a prohibited transaction and would result in the imposition of excise taxes under Section 4975 of the Code. Such exotic assets may be an appropriate investment for the general account of the plan if they are fully insured and held by a third party so that the professional does not receive any personal benefit from them. Further, some investment managers feel that the type of investment should vary with the type of plan, that is, that a defined benefit pension plan with a definite fixed benefit which must be reached should be invested in interest-bearing bonds, preferred stocks, and blue chip stocks. On the other hand, they feel that since there is no definite retirement benefit provided under profit sharing plans and money purchase plans, they may be invested in higher-risk assets. The authors believe that while the character of investments may vary from defined benefit to defined contribution plans, security of principal is an essential element to any investment strategy under any qualified retirement plan.

Following ERISA, it was felt that corporate trustees should be employed in order to minimize the risk of suit against the professional. However, in the six years following ERISA, although there have been a number of suits under ERISA, there have been few suits against professionals who have acted as trustees under their qualified retirement plans. For this reason, the authors feel that professionals should feel free to act as trustees of the qualified retirement plans established by their professional corporations. If professionals do choose to serve as trustees, plan administrators, or to perform other services for the plan, they normally must do so without pay (other than reimbursement of expenses properly and actually incurred); since Section 408(c)(2) of ERISA prohibits persons who already receive full-time pay from an employer from receiving compensation from the plan other than expense reimbursement. Care should be taken, however, to assure that the investment of the plan's assets, particularly the amounts credited to the accounts of the staff employees, be done in a conservative manner.

Whether the professionals act as trustee or whether a bank is employed to do so, the rights and duties of the trustee must be prescribed either in the plan itself or in a separate trust documeent. Although many plans and trust documents are one unified document, the authors recommend establishing a plan and a separate trust agreement. In this manner, the plan need only be executed by the corporation whereas the trust agreement must be executed by the corporation and the trustee. Consequently, if the corporation decides to amend the plan, it need only pass a board resolution and sign the amendment; the signature of the trustee is not necessary.

(7) Master Plans Versus Individually Designed Plans

A number of banks, brokerage houses, and insurance companies offer master or prototype plans which can be adopted by professional corporations. These plans have received a master determination letter and can be adopted by the professional corporation without the necessity of seeking further Service approval. Such plans can be adopted by the completion of an adoption agreement under which a number of alternatives can be selected, such as participation rules and vesting schedules.

Master plans appear to offer an attractive alternative to professionals because they can be executed with very little assistance from the attorney and accountant of the professionals and, consequently, with a minimum fee. Professionals should be aware, however, that most master plans are offered by entities which are selling a service (banks, brokerage houses, and insurance companies all sell investment services, with administrative services). Master plans also have the following drawbacks:

(1) Master plans usually offer less flexibility than do individually designed plans since the professional only has a choice of the terms contained in the adoption agreement.

(2) Master plans may contain hidden problems because the terms of the master plan may be acceptable generally by the Service but may, in the particular situation of the professional corporation, create problems. Although the representatives of the company offering the master plan will be knowledgeable about the plan, the authors have found that they typically do not scrupulously review the plan in light of the particular situation of the professional corporation. This is particularly true in situations where provisions in the master plan may eventually produce discrimination in operation.

(3) Once a master plan is adopted, it may be difficult to terminate that plan and transfer assets to a successor trustee. Most master plans contain a provision which states that the assets may only be transferred to a plan which has received a determination letter from the Service. Consequently, if the professional corporation desires to terminate the master plan arrangement and transfer the funds to an individually designed plan, the delay in obtaining the determination letter (at least six to eight months) will delay the transfer of the funds.

(4) Master plans may have hidden administrative costs which must be borne by the plan or the employer. This is particularly true with so-called ''deposit administration'' plans maintained by insurance companies.

(5) Further, the fees of the attorney and accountant for the professional corporation will probably not be insubstantial if they are requested to review and comment on the master plan proposed. Problems often are identified upon a review of a master plan because master plans are not tailor-made to deal with the individual needs of any specific business. Where the attorney of the professional corporation is called upon to review and interpret provisions of master plans, the time required and, therefore, the fees charged are often significantly greater than if the attorney had drafted an individually designed plan for the corporation since it is much easier for the attorney to work with plans with which he is familiar than to undertake a complete examination of new plans.

Professionals should be alert to some organizations offering plans which appear to be master or prototype plans but which are, in fact, individually designed plans. The authors are aware of a number of insurance companies that engage in this practice and, in fact, draft individually designed retirement plans for professionals. Professionals encountering this arrangement should carefully assess the potential problems which may arise in adopting an individually designed plan which has been drafted by someone other than the attorney for the professional corporation as there is a greater possibility that problems may arise under such a plan than may arise under a master or prototype plan. Further, drafting such plans and the accompanying trust agreements is generally considered by the American Bar Association to be the unauthorized practice of law.[46]

Because qualified retirement plans are such an important part of the benefits which may be obtained through incorporation, the authors feel that, in most instances, professionals should consider adopting individually designed plans which have been coordinated by their attorney and accountant. By adopting individually designed plans, the professional corporation can assure that the plan initially meets its needs, creates no latent problems and that, as the Service rules relating to qualified plans change in the future, the attorney and accountant will be on hand to make appropriate amendments.

(8) Prohibited Transactions

Section 406 of ERISA and parallel provisions of Section 4975 of the Code prohibit employee benefit plans from engaging in certain types of transactions. The provisions of Section 4975 of the Code only apply to qualified *retirement* plans, while the provisions of Section 406 of ERISA apply to both *retirement* plans (whether or not "qualified" under the Code) and *welfare* plans (medical, accident, layoff, etc. benefit plans). Violations of the prohibited transaction provisions of the Code can result in the imposition of a nondeductible excise tax equal to 5% of the "amount involved" in the transaction for each year that the transaction continues. An additional excise tax of 100% of the amount involved is imposed if correction is not made upon notice by the Service. A fiduciary who permits a prohibited transaction (to which Section 406 of ERISA applies) to occur may be held personally liable under Section 4409 of ERISA for any loss to the plan resulting from the transaction.

Transactions that constitute prohibited transactions are absolutely forbidden, regardless of the financial or economic soundness of the transaction and regardless of whether the transaction offers the plan a more attractive financial opportunity than is available elsewhere. Generally the defense of good faith, innocence and reasonable lack of knowledge that a transaction is prohibited will not prevent imposition of the excise tax under Code Section 4975, but a violation of Section 406 of ERISA can be avoided with this defense.

The specific transactions prohibited are certain transactions between plans and "parties in interest." ERISA Section 3(14) enumerates a rather broad class of persons who constitute parties in interest with respect to a plan. Parties in interest include all plan fiduciaries, including the plan administrator, trustee or custodian of plan assets, any person who provides services to a plan, the employer whose employees are covered by the plan, a relative (spouse, ancestor, lineal descendent or spouse of a lineal descendent) of any of the foregoing individuals, and any employee, officer, director or 10% (direct or indirect) shareholder of the employer who maintains the plan. A prohibited transaction will occur if there is a direct or indirect:

(1) sale, exchange, or leasing of any property between a plan and a party in interest;

(2) lending of money or other extension of credit between a plan and a party in interest;

(3) furnishing of any goods, services, or facilities between a plan and a party in interest;

(4) transfer of any plan assets to, or use of any plan assets by or for, the benefit of a party in interest; or

(5) acquisition of securities of the employer under certain circumstances or in excess of certain maximum amounts.

In addition, certain dealings by fiduciaries will constitute prohibited transactions. Specifically, a fiduciary is prohibited from dealing with assets of the plan for his own personal gain, representing any person in a transaction involving the plan in which the party represented has interests adverse to the plan, and receiving a kickback from any person in connection with a transaction involving assets of the plan.

Section 4975 of the Code and Section 408(b) of ERISA contain a number of "statutory exemptions" from the prohibited transaction provisions. For example, the statutory exemption dealing with loans to participants has been discussed in section [15.02](4), *supra*. Other statutory exemptions include exemptions:

(1) to provide reasonable services necessary to establish or operate the plan,

(2) to permit bank trustees to invest plan assets in savings accounts and pooled investment accounts of the bank and to provide ancillary banking services to the plan,

(3) to permit fiduciaries to receive reasonable compensation for services (unless they are full-time employees of the employer), and

(4) to permit fiduciaries who are plan participants to receive plan benefits as they become payable.

In addition to the statutory exemptions, Section 408(a) of ERISA and Section 4975(c)(2) of the Code permit administrative exemptions from the prohibited transaction rules to be granted. Administrative exemptions may be granted in favor of a particular transaction (an "individual" exemption) or a class of transactions ("class" exemptions). Individual exemptions apply only to the specific transaction for which the exemption was granted, and will not authorize an identical transaction engaged in by different parties. Class exemptions generally exempt any present, past or future transaction that satisfies the requirements of the exemption.

Requests for prohibited transaction exemptions are filed with the Department of Labor. It normally takes from 4 to 6 months for an exemption request to be finally resolved and nearly 90% of the requests for exemptions are *denied*. In order to obtain an administrative exemption, a plan must complete a rather tedious application in which it must be demonstrated that the exemption if granted would be, (1) administratively feasible, (2) in the interest of the plan, its participants and beneficiaries, and (3) protective of the rights of participants and beneficiaries of the plan. Chances for approval are increased if the applicant can show that, due to independent safeguards, the transaction provides a "no lose" opportunity for larger financial benefit to the plan than other available investment alternatives. Until recently, the Department of Labor was reluctant to authorize transactions involving continuing transactions between the plan and parties in interest (e.g., loans and leases). However, it has recently granted a number of such continuing transaction exemptions, including several that have permitted improved real property to be contributed to a plan and leased back to the employer.[47]

(9) Contributions

The determination of the deductibility of contributions to a qualified retirement plan is generally made pursuant to Section 404 of the Code. The amounts which may be deductible as contributions to a qualified pension plan (defined benefit or money purchase) are determined under Section 404(a)(1).

An employer may contribute to a pension plan (defined benefit or money purchase) and deduct the amount necessary to pay the normal cost of plan benefits plus the amount necessary to amortize past service liabilities. The normal cost of a defined benefit plan must be calculated by the plan's actuary. The normal cost of a money purchase plan is determined by the plan's benefit formula, for example, 10% of participants' compensation. Generally, past service liabilities are created by plan amendments that increase the rate at which benefits accrue for prior service and by plan provisions that grant past service benefits upon establishment of the plan. Past service liabilities attributable to all participants may be amortized over as many as 30 years or as few as 10 years. Alternatively, past service liabilities may be amortized over the remaining future service of each employee, but if over 50% of plan costs are attributable to three or fewer individuals, past service liabilities attributable to those three or fewer individuals may not be amortized over fewer than five years.

The deductibility for contributions for profit sharing plans is determined under Section 404(a)(3), which sets a basic deduction limit for profit sharing contributions of 15% of the compensation otherwise paid or accrued during the taxable year to all beneficiaries of the plan. If an employer contributes an amount in excess of the deduction limits for a particular year, the excess payment is deductible in succeeding years. On the other hand, if a contribution made to a profit sharing plan is less than 15% of the annual total compensation, the difference between the amount actually contributed and the 15% of annual compensation may be carried forward as a deductible amount in a succeeding taxable year, but the total deduction in any later year may not exceed 25% of compensation.[48]

If amounts are deductible under both pension plans and profit sharing plans, the employer may first deduct the entire amount deductible with respect to the pension plans. If the amount deductible on account of the pension plans is less than 25% of the participants' compensation for the plan year, the employer can make up the difference by making additional contributions to profit sharing plans. If the employer's contribution to the pension plans exceed 25% of the participants' compensation for the plan year, then no amount may be deducted for the profit sharing plans.[49] Contributions must also satisfy the applicable contribution and benefit limitations of Section 415 of the Code.

The contribution to qualified retirement plans by professional corporations are considered general business expenses. Consequently, in order for an employer to obtain a deduction for such expenses under Section 404, the expenses must be ordinary and necessary under Section 162 of the Code. In determining whether deductions to qualified retirement plans are ordinary and necessary, the questions of reasonable compensation (discussed in Chapter 13, *supra*) must be considered. When determining reasonable compensation for an employee, all benefits are taken into account, including contributions under qualified retirement plans. Consequently, if the reasonableness of the compensation to the professional is challenged, a challenge may also be made to the qualified retirement plan or benefits and a portion of the deduction for contributions may be disallowed or the Service may attempt to disqualify the plan. If discrimination results from contributions attributable to unreasonable compensation, a defined contribution plan may avoid disqualification by permitting the reallocation to other employees of any contribution determined to be unreasonable.[50]

The reasonable compensation requirement may be a particular problem where the first year of the professional corporation is a short first year and large contributions are made, particularly where large amounts of income are held over and paid during the first few months of incorporation in order to permit larger contributions to the qualified plans.[51]

Under Section 404 of the Code, deductions are generally allowed in the year in which they are made. However, under ERISA, an amendment was made to Section 404(a)(6) of the Code to permit a deduction for a particular year to be taken where the contribution for that year is made on or before the filing of the federal income tax return (plus extensions thereof). In order to obtain a deduction under Section 404(a)(6) of the Code, the contribution for a year must be paid to the plan on or before the due date for filing the federal income tax return (plus extensions, if any), must be allocated on the books of the plan in the same manner as they would have been allocated if they had been actually contributed on the last day of the plan year, and must be deducted on the federal income tax return.[52] The initial contributions to a qualified retirement plan may also be made during the grace period. That is, although it is absolutely necessary to adopt the plan prior to the end of the fiscal year of the employer, no contribution to that plan need be made (even though the trust may be a "dry trust" under local law) until the time for filing the corporation's federal income tax return.[53] However, the authors recommend that upon the establishment of a qualified plan the trust of that plan be funded with a $100 contribution even though the remainder of the contribution will be made at a later date.

(10) Voluntary Employee Contributions

(a) *Nondeductible Contributions*

Qualified retirement plans may permit voluntary employee contributions of up to 10% of an employee's compensation.[54] This 10% limit is a maximum limitation for all plans, so that if 10% is contributed under a profit sharing plan nothing may be contributed under a money purchase pension plan.[55] However, the 10% voluntary contribution is cumulative so that the contribution may be made equal to 10% of the employee's aggregate compensation for all years that he has been a participant.[56] Furthermore, the 10% limitation is not reduced or affected by amounts rolled over or directly transferred from another qualified plan.

Voluntary employee contributions are also subject to the annual addition limitations under Section 415 of the Code. Under the Section 415 limitations, a voluntary contribution to the plan of 6% of a participant's compensation will not constitute an annual addition since annual additions arising from voluntary contributions are defined to be the *lesser* of (i) voluntary contributions in excess of 6%, or (ii) 50% of the voluntary contributions made for the plan year.

For years prior to 1982, plans which permit voluntary employee contributions should also be drafted so that the employee will not be considered to have "constructively received" the earnings on the voluntary contributions. While plans should always permit an employee to withdraw his voluntary contributions, restrictions should be placed upon the ability of an employee to withdraw the earnings on his voluntary contributions. Without such restrictions, the employee will be taxed on an annual basis on the earnings on his voluntary contributions. The Service currently takes the position that a restriction on the withdrawal of earnings on voluntary contributions which prohibits an employee from participating in a plan for six months will be sufficient to eliminate the constructive receipt problem. However, the authors feel that a much less restrictive requirement will eliminate the constructive receipt problem, and Section 314(c) of ERTA has eliminated this problem for taxable years beginning after December 31, 1981 by providing that a participant will be taxable only on distributions when they are received. See Section 402(a) of the Code.

The ability of an employee to make voluntary employee contributions to a qualified retirement plan is an excellent benefit, which creates for the employee the ability to defer income taxes on the earnings in the voluntary account. That is, any voluntary employee contributions must be made with after-tax dollars, but the earnings on the amounts contributed voluntarily by the employee remain tax-exempt until withdrawn by him. Consequently, the employee may take advantage of the compounding effect of tax-exempt earnings through the use of voluntary employee contributions. Voluntary employee contributions are particularly useful for deferring income until later years when it will be needed, such as for the expenses of college educations for children.

(b) *Deductible Contributions*

ERTA represents a significant departure from prior law by permitting a participant in a qualified retirement plan to receive a deduction for a voluntary contribution to that plan or an IRA in an amount equal to the lesser of $2,000 ($2,500 for married individuals) or the compensation of the individual. See Section 219 of the Code. However, such deductible contributions are subject to the general IRA limitations (they cannot be withdrawn prior to attaining age 59½ or becoming disabled without a 10% penalty) and such amounts are not subject to the special taxation provided for lump sum distributions. On the other hand, mandatory distribution at age 70½ (which is required for IRA's) is not required. In the case of SEPs, deductible voluntary employee contributions will be allowed (in addition to the regular deductible contribution described in the preceding paragraph) in an amount equal to the lesser of: (i) 15% of compensation or (ii) the amount contributed by the employer and included in gross income (but not in excess of $7,500).

No deductions are allowed for individuals who are age 70½. In order for a deductible employee contribution to be made to a qualified retirement plan, the plan must specifically permit such contributions.

(11) Annual Addition Limitation

Section 415 of the Code provides limitations on the annual benefits which may be provided under qualified retirement plans. Under Section 415(b)(1), the employer may not fund a defined benefit plan benefit which is greater than the lesser of $124,500 (for 1981) or 100% of the participant's average compensation for his highest three consecutive calendar years.

Under defined contribution plans, the contributions and other additions with respect to a participant may not exceed the lesser of $41,500 (for 1981) or 25% of the participant's compensation. For purposes of determining the annual addition, the following allocations are considered: (1) the employer contributions; (2) the lesser of the employee contributions in excess of 6% of his compensation or one-half of the employee contributions; and (3) the forfeitures allocated to his account.

(12)   Qualifying Plans with the Internal Revenue Service

Although obtaining a determination letter with regard to a retirement plan is not a prerequisite for having a "qualified" plan, obtaining a determination letter does permit the professional corporation to receive advance determination of the qualified status of the plan. For this reason, the authors feel that all plans which are intended to be qualified plans should be filed with the District Director of the local Service office for qualification. If plans are filed for determination during the remedial amendment period (discussed at section [15.02](3), *supra*), and qualified status is not received, the plans may be amended retroactively to permit qualified status, or the contributions may be returned to the employer. Further, the authors believe that all amendments to a plan or trust document, other than ministerial amendments, such as the change of the trustee or the change of the name of the plan, should be filed with the Service for continued qualification.

The receipt of a determination letter from the District Director is not, however, a carte blanche to qualified status. The determination letter merely states that, on the facts and law which exist as of the date of qualification, the plan in *form* meets the qualification rules. Further changes in the facts relating to the employer and the employees and changes in the rules and regulations of the Service may later disqualify the plan. In *Wisconsin Nipple & Fabricating Corporation v. Commissioner*,[57] the court upheld the Commissioner's retroactive revocation of determination letters (issued in 1960 and 1962) where a later Revenue Ruling (issued in 1971) indicated that the plan discriminated in favor of a prohibited group. The Seventh Circuit clearly places responsibility on the taxpayer for "keeping abreast of current developments in the law to be assured that the plan is still in compliance." For this reason, the authors feel that professionals should continue to monitor the status of their retirement plans with their professional advisors to assure that they remain qualified.

Rev. Proc. 72-6,[58] at Section 1.04 states "a favorable determination letter on a profit sharing plan, stock bonus plan, or bond purchase plan, or on the exempt status of a related trust, if any, is not required as a condition for obtaining the benefits pertaining to the plan or trust."

(13)   Discrimination in Operation

Obviously, qualified retirement plans may be disqualified if they fail to meet the specific statutory requirements provided under Section 401, *et seq.*, of the Code such as minimum participation rules, vesting rules, etc. However, it is possible for qualified retirement plans to be disqualified due to the manner in which they have been operated, even though determination letters have been issued on those plans. Due to the propensity of professionals to ignore their affairs, disqualification due to discrimination in operation presents a substantial risk to plans operated by professional corporations.

In addition to the specific statutory requirements for qualified plans, Section 401 also contains several rather vague prohibitions. For example, under Section 401(a)(2), the plan must be used for the "exclusive benefit" of participants and their beneficiaries. Further, under Section 401(a)(3) a plan may not discriminate in favor of the "prohibited group," composed of officers, shareholders, and highly compensated individuals. Regulations §1.401-1(b)(3) provides a general overview of what may constitute impermissible discrimination:

> The plan must benefit the employees in general, although it need not provide benefits for all of the employees. Among the employees to be benefited may be persons who are officers and shareholders. However, a plan is not for the exclusive benefit of employees in general if, by any device whatever, it discriminates either in eligibility requirements, contributions, or benefits in favor of employees who are officers, shareholders, . . . or highly compensated employees.

It is often difficult to determine the "prohibited group" in many corporations. The Service has taken the position that the term "highly compensated" is a relative rather than an absolute term. It is often thought that employees making in excess of $25,000 per year may be considered highly compensated.[59] However, in a professional corporation, it is very easy for the Service to determine the highly compensated employees, i.e., the professionals.

Those situations in which a qualified retirement plan is diverted to the use of the professionals or the professional corporation are often obvious (i.e., a loan of all qualified plan funds to the professional, etc.). However, even if the terms of a plan in *form* comply with the statutory requirements, it is possible that in *operation* benefits and contributions may discriminate in favor of the prohibited group, even though there is no intention that they do so. It is difficult to anticipate when discrimination in operation may occur, but the following are a few examples:

(a) *Erroneous Administration of Plan Provisions*

In several cases, the participation provisions of qualified retirement plans (which are otherwise qualified) were inadvertently not followed, leading to disqualification of the plans due to discrimination in operation. In *Myron v. U.S.*,[60] five eligible employees were excluded from coverage for two consecutive years and the company's contributions were allocated only to the account of the corporation's sole shareholder. The lower court found that the exclusion was inadvertent but nevertheless concluded this innocent error justified disqualification. In affirming, the Seventh Circuit Court of Appeals agreed that even inadvertent failure in coverage could be a proper basis for denying qualification.[61]

Several such cases specifically involve professional and service corporations. In *Allen Ludden*,[62] Allen Ludden and Betty White (the well-known actor and actress) formed a corporation (Albets) which adopted a money-purchase pension plan and a profit sharing plan for the benefit of the corporation's employees. The plans, as written, met the requirements for qualification and determination letters were issued by the Service. Through a bookkeeping error, the only staff employee of Albets, a production secretary, was inadvertently excluded from participation in the plan even though she met the plan's participation requirements. The Service argued, and the court held, that the exclusion of the production secretary constituted discrimination in favor of highly compensated officers in violation of Sections 401(a)(3)(B) and 401(a)(4) of the Code and failed to meet the minimum coverage provisions of Section 401(a)(3)(A) (pre-ERISA).

In *Forsyth Emergency Services, P.A.*,[63] a professional corporation was engaged in emergency medical services and operated the emergency room facilities at Forsyth Memorial Hospital in Winston-Salem, North Carolina. The corporation was owned by three physicians who adopted a money-purchase pension plan which received a determination letter from the Service. During 1972 and 1973, certain nonprofessional employees of the corporation were inadvertently omitted from coverage under the retirement plan. However, in August of 1975, after this fact was brought to the corporation's attention by the Service, additional contributions were made so that allocations could be made for these nonprofessional employees for the years in which they were excluded. The exclusion of the nonprofessional employees resulted from a misreading of the plan by the professional advisor to the corporation.

The court held that the plan did not meet the eligibility requirements for coverage and that the plan discriminated in operation. The court further held that discrimination in operation could not be cured by retroactively funding contributions accrued, but unallocated, to the nonprofessional employees (even if such retroactive allocation was made voluntarily by the corporation). The court noted that, because the plan covered primarily professional employees, the plan did not cover a cross section of all employees. In examining the question of whether a retroactive cure for discrimination was available, the court stated that it found no support in the Code, the Regulations, or the case law which would permit retroactive correction.

Cases like *Ludden* and *Forsyth* are dramatic examples of the problems which can occur due to the inadvertent errors of the professionals, even where they seek the advice of their professional advisors. The Service has, however, somewhat relented from the position in *Ludden* and *Forsyth*. In Private Letter Ruling 7949001 a corporation was permitted to reallocate contributions to its money-purchase pension plan and profit sharing plan so that the plans would qualify under Section 401 of the Code. Under this ruling, the corporation adopted a prototype plan in 1973 and made contributions in 1973, 1974, and 1975. On audit, the Service held that the eligibility requirements of the plan were not followed and that one part-time employee was included and that three full-time employees were excluded from coverage. The Service ruled that the entity sponsoring the prototype plan was in error (and not the corporation) and since the mistake was one of fact and not one of law, and since no distributions had been made from the plan, the corporation would be allowed to restructure the plan to meet the coverage requirements.

In 1980, the Service promulgated Document 6651, "IRS Employee Plans Restoration Guidelines." Under these guidelines retroactive relief is available for a variety of plan deficiencies. In the case of plans that are discriminatory, restoration is accomplished by increasing benefits to defined benefit plans or making make-up contributions to defined contribution plans. Under the Guidelines such correction will reinstate the qualified status of the plan, but will not restore qualified plan status treatment of employer contributions made during a period for which the plan was discriminatory. As a result, contributions to defined benefit plans during open years for which there was discrimination will normally be disallowed, and contributions to defined contribution plans for open years for which the plan was discriminatory will be deductible only when employees become vested in their individual accounts.[64]

(b) Exclusion of Service Personnel

If the professional corporation makes an express attempt to categorize people who would normally be considered to be employees as independent contractors or employees of third-party organizations, the plan may discriminate in favor of the prohibited group by denying participation to staff employees. For a complete discussion of this topic, see Chapter 19, *infra*, discussing partnerships and professional corporations.

(c) Withdrawals from Qualified Plans

A profit sharing plan may permit participants to withdraw all or part of their vested benefits provided that such contributions have been allocated to their accounts for at least two years.[65] However, if such withdrawals are subject to the approval of a plan administrative committee and no withdrawals are permitted, except by member of the prohibited group, such operation will be discriminatory in favor of the prohibited group and will cause the plan to be disqualified.[66]

(d) Opting Out

Due to the often divergent needs of professionals, some professionals consider placing a provision in qualified retirement plans permitting employees to "opt out" of the plan. There appears to be little for the employer to lose by placing such a provision in a plan. However, if the number of persons opting out is substantial, the plan may create coverage problems. Also, if the plan permits an employee to opt out, this type of provision should be disclosed in the summary plan description. If the plan is administered so that only high-paid individuals are permitted to opt out and their compensation is correspondingly increased, the plan may be considered a *de facto* cash or deferred profit sharing plan. There is, however, no general prohibition against permitting high-paid employees to opt out of the plan as long as their compensation is not otherwise increased; most District Directors do not view the opting out of high-paid employees as a disqualifying event.

On the other hand, if low-paid employees opt out of the plan, the plan may be considered discriminatory against them.[67]

(e) *Definition of the Term "Compensation"*

Although most qualified retirement plans provide benefits based upon the compensation listed in the employee's Form W-2 (the "basic compensation"), such compensation would normally include both contractual and voluntary bonuses paid to the employees. Such a definition should normally not cause problems. However, in a professional corporation setting, if the professional employees normally receive substantial bonuses and the staff employees receive small or no bonuses, the plan may be considered discriminatory, if bonuses are used to figure contributions.[68]

(f) *Employee Turnover*

If a qualified retirement plan is adopted by a corporation and, during the pendency of the plan, the staff employees of the corporation regularly terminate their service or are fired prior to becoming vested, the plan may be considered to have a discriminatory vesting schedule, particularly if the schedule is less favorable than the 4-40 schedule.[69]

Further, the use of so-called "last day rules" in qualified retirement plans may prove discriminatory if, due to the turnover statistics of the employer, they generally have been applied only against staff personnel. Last day rules provide that an employee will not be entitled to receive an allocation of employer contributions for a particular plan year of a defined contribution plan unless he is employed at the end of that plan year. Since such rules exclude from participation in employer contributions employees who terminate service during the year, they generally apply only to staff personnel in a professional corporation setting, as the professionals generally remained employed. For this reason, the authors recommend that last day rules be eliminated from plans established by professional corporations in order to avoid potential discrimination in operation.[70]

(g) *Tax Consequences of Disqualification*

If a plan is disqualified because it discriminates in operation, the following tax consequences will occur:

(1) The trust will lose its tax-exempt status under Section 501(a), making the trust income taxable to the trust.

(2) Section 402(b) will govern the taxability of employer contributions to the beneficiaries of the trust. Generally, contributions will be included in the employees' income under Section 83 to the extent they have a vested right to such benefits. Employer contributions that are taxable to the employee are considered part of current compensation, requiring the withholding of taxes by the employer.

(3) The contributions of the employer will be deductible only to the extent that the employees are vested and only if separate accounts are maintained to record the interest of each participant.[71] As a result, deduction of employer contributions to nonqualified defined contribution plans will be delayed for the period of years necessary for employer contributions to vest, and employer contributions to non-qualified defined benefit plans will simply not be deductible. Because of this possible loss of deduction, the authors recommend that plans incorporate provisions which require employer contributions to revert to the employer within one year of the disallowance of a deduction under Code Section 404 with respect to the contribution.[72]

(14) Insurance

Qualified retirement plans may maintain insurance on the lives of the participants. There are a number of advantages and disadvantages to maintaining insurance in a qualified plan; they are as follows:

Advantages:

    (1) The possibility of an immediate and substantial benefit is secured without the necessity of relying on plan investments.

    (2) Life insurance proceeds, like other investments, may be exempt from estate tax when paid to a beneficiary in other than a lump sum.

    (3) Life insurance purchased by a qualified retirement plan is purchased with "tax deductible" dollars.

    (4) The proceeds of the life insurance policy are received income-tax-free by the trust and the "at risk" portion of the proceeds are received tax-free by the beneficiary. The "at risk" portion is the excess of the face value of the policy over its cash surrender value immediately prior to death.

Disadvantages:

    (1) The cost of life insurance protection (the P.S. 58[73] cost) is currently taxed to the employee.

    (2) Adequate death benefits may be provided outside a qualified retirement plan through the uses of other types of insurance, such as split dollar arrangements and group term insurance.

    (3) The payment of life insurance premiums by the trust will reduce the amount of cash available to fund retirement benefits.

    (4) Life insurance (even whole life insurance) historically provides a low-yield investment.

Since the purpose of a qualified retirement plan is to provide *retirement benefits*, life insurance protection may be provided only if it is "incidental."[74] As a result, the following limitations are placed on life insurance maintained in qualified plans:

(a) *Profit Sharing Plans*

A profit sharing plan is a plan established to provide, primarily, benefits, the distribution of which are deferred.[75] However, as previously mentioned, profit sharing plan funds may be distributed after the funds have been accumulated for a "fixed number of years," which is at least two years.[76] A current distribution of funds before accumulation for a fixed number of years may cause a profit sharing plan to lose its qualified status. Consequently, premiums for life insurance may be paid out of funds which have been accumulated for two or more years without causing disqualification of the plan.[77] On the other hand, insurance premiums paid out of funds which have not been accumulated for at least two years are considered to be distributions to the employee. The purchase of life insurance with funds which have not been accumulated for two years will be considered incidental (and hence will not be considered distributions) if the following occur:

(1) In the purchase of ordinary life insurance, the aggregate life insurance premiums for each participant are less than one-half the aggregate contributions allocated to that participant at any particular time, without regard to trust earnings and capital gains and losses, and the plan requires the trustee to convert the entire value of the life insurance policy at or before the employee's retirement into cash or to provide periodic income so that no portion of such value may be used to continue life insurance protection beyond retirement.[78]

(2) In the purchase of term insurance, the aggregate life insurance premiums for each participant do not exceed 25% of the total amount of funds allocated to the participant's account.[79] The limitations on the purchase of life insurance protection do not apply to voluntary employee contributions.[80]

Notwithstanding that it is permissible for qualified profit sharing plans to maintain life insurance on the lives of the employees, the authors generally recommend that profit sharing plans not be used as life insurance vehicles. It is possible that, in certain years, a profit sharing plan may not be funded and this may place the profit sharing plan in a position in which there are not sufficient funds to pay the premiums without causing disqualification.

(b) *Defined Benefit Pension Plans*

A defined benefit pension plan funded with life insurance will be deemed to provide an incidental (and hence permissible) pre-retirement death benefit if either:

(1) less than 50% of the employer contributions credited to each participant's account is used to purchase ordinary life insurance policies on the participant's life, even if the death benefit consists of both the face amount of the

policies and the amount of other contributions credited to the participant's retirement benefit; or

(2) the death benefit is funded by ordinary life insurance providing 100 times a participant's anticipated monthly normal retirement benefit and the pre-retirement death benefit does not exceed the greater of, (a) the proceeds of the 100 times life insurance policy, or (b) the reserve under the 100 times life insurance policy plus the participant's account in the auxiliary fund.[81]

A defined benefit pension plan will not constitute a qualified plan if all of the employer's contributions are used for the purchase of ordinary life insurance policies on the lives of the participants.[82]

A post-retirement death benefit is considered incidental if it does not exceed 50% of the base salary in the year before retirement and costs less than 10% of the total cost of funding pension plan benefits other than the post-retirement death benefit.[83]

(c) Money-Purchase Pension Plans

A money-purchase pension plan may provide incidental pre-retirement death benefits which meet the tests applicable either for profit sharing plans or defined benefit pension plans.[84]

(d) Tax Treatment

Employer contributions made to a qualified retirement plan which are used to pay insurance premiums are deductible by the employer, as are other contributions. However, the cost of the insurance provided under a qualified plan is treated as a current distribution to the participant and must be included in the participant's income for the year in which the premium is paid. The result is the same without regard to the type of policy purchased. The employee is taxed on the cost of the insurance protection if either the proceeds are payable to his estate or to a beneficiary or if the proceeds are payable to the trustee of the plan but the trustee is required by the terms of the plan to pay all proceeds over to the beneficiary of the participant. A participant is not taxed on the purchase of "key man" insurance by a qualified retirement plan where the proceeds of the insurance are payable into the general assets of the plan. The amount of current taxable income to the participant is measured by the pure insurance protection under Regulations §1.72-16. The rates to be used are the one-year term rates established under Rev. Rul. 55-747 or the so-called "P.S. 58 rates."[85] However, if the insurance company's rates for individual one-year term policies available to all standard risk customers are lower than the P.S. 58 rates, the lower rates may be used.[86]

Where individual group term life insurance is provided under a qualified retirement plan, the cost of the entire amount of protection is taxable to the employee and no part is exempt.[87] It is important to note that the P.S. 58 costs which have been taxed to the employee for life insurance protection may be recovered tax-free from the benefits received under the policy.[88] Tax-free recovery of the P.S. 58 cost will be available only if the benefits are ultimately received from the insurance contract with respect to which the P.S. 58 costs were included in gross income. If, however, the life insurance policy is surrendered and the proceeds are used to purchase an annuity, or the proceeds are distributed in cash, tax-free recovery of the P.S. 58 basis will be forfeited.[89]

[15.03] DISPOSITION OF H.R. 10 PLANS UPON INCORPORATION

Upon incorporation of a professional practice, questions often arise with regard to the proper disposition of the H.R. 10 plan of the predecessor partnership or proprietorship. Upon incorporation, these three alternatives are available:

(1) Freezing the H.R. 10 Plan

Many tax advisors recommend that the existing H.R. 10 plan be "frozen." That is, no further contributions will be made to the plan, and benefits of participants other than owner-employees who are under age 59½ are either distributed in a lump sum or held for distribution under the normal distribution provisions of the plan (as elected by participants in a one-time irrevocable election offered for an election period that expires prior to the date on which distributions may be made under the election). Earnings on amounts that are not distributed will continue to compound tax-free and the frozen plan will simply constitute another deferred compensation benefit which will be payable at a later date. Generally, savings and loan institutions, as opposed to banks, offer lower minimum fees and, consequently, professionals should consider transferring frozen H.R. 10 plans to savings and loan institutions.

(2) Termination of Plan and Distribution to Participants

If the owner-employee of the H.R. 10 plan is over 59½, he may receive a distribution of funds, along with the common law employees, upon its termination. However, if the owner-employee is under age 59½ and a distribution is made, a 10% penalty tax on the premature distribution will be assessed under Section 72(m)(5) of the Code unless the distribution (reduced by any amounts contributed by the owner-employee as an employee) is rolled over within 60 days into an individual retirement account or individual retirement annuity. The rollover will constitute a premature distribution and, therefore, will prohibit the owner-employee from participating as an owner-employee in any other H.R. 10 plan for a period of five years;[90] however, there will not be an excise tax imposed as a result of the premature distribution since Section 72(m)(5) of the Code only imposes an excise tax on amounts that are included in gross income, and given a rollover of the entire H.R. 10 distribution (less employee contributions), no amount is included in gross income.[91] Furthermore, the five-year suspension only applies to participation in another H.R. 10 plan; the owner-employee who receives a premature distribution from an H.R. 10 plan may immediately participate in a qualified retirement plan maintained by his corporate employer.[92] It should be noted, however, that a distribution from an H.R. 10 plan on behalf of any self-employed participant may not be rolled over into another H.R. 10 plan or corporate qualified plan either directly[93] or through a conduit IRA.[94]

(3) Termination of Plan and Transfer of H.R. 10 Funds to Qualified Retirement Plans of the New Professional Corporation

The assets of an existing H.R. 10 plan may be transferred from the trustee of the H.R. 10 plan directly to the trustee of the successor professional corporation qualified retirement plan (without passing through the hands of participants) without creating a premature distribution, as long as the special requirements of H.R. 10 plans for the owner-employees are observed. In Rev. Rul. 71-541,[95] the Service approved the transfer of H.R. 10 plan assets to a profit sharing plan provided that (1) the trustee would always be a bank, (2) separate accounts would be maintained for funds transferred on behalf of each owner-employee, (3) no payment of benefits would be made from the separate accounts on or before the owner-employee reached age 59½ or became disabled, and (4) distribution from the owner-employee's account had to begin prior to the end of the taxable year in which he attains age 70½. Care should be taken to assure that the special restrictions applicable to transferred accrued benefits of owner-employees are observed. For example, in Private Letter Ruling 8014076, the Service held that where an owner-employee's H.R. 10 account was transferred to a successor corporate plan and the former owner-employee obtained a loan from the corporate plan that reflected his transferred H.R. 10 accrued benefit, the former owner-employee had received a "benefit" attributable to the H.R. 10 plan which would be treated as a premature distribution subject to the 10% excise tax of Section 72(m)(5) of the Code.

Some professionals desire to transfer frozen H.R. 10 accounts to the trustee of the successor qualified plans in an attempt to aggregate funds for investment purposes. The special provisions applicable to the transferred H.R. 10 plan funds need only apply to them, and not to the remainder of the funds in the successor corporate plans, and the aggregation of both the H.R. 10 plans and the corporate plan funds for investment purposes is permissible. Paragraph 10.21 of the form profit sharing plan included in this Chapter as Exhibit 1 provides a mechanism for transferring frozen H.R. 10 plan assets to a successor profit sharing plan. In a number of private letter rulings, the Service has continued to affirm that H.R. 10 plan assets may be transferred to a successor corporate plan without creating a premature distribution.[96]

The special H.R. 10 plan requirements (bank trustees, etc.) apply only if the H.R. 10 plan covered owner-employees. If the H.R. 10 plan did not cover owner-employees, only the age 70½ restriction must be used. As a practical matter, professional H.R. 10 plans will cover owner-employees and the staff employees' compensation will be paid out prior to the transfer of the H.R. 10 plan to the successor corporate plan.

[15.04] TAXATION OF BENEFITS

(1) Income and Estate Tax Consequences of Distributions on Termination

Qualified retirement plans are normally established because of the obvious tax advantages that they offer at the time they are adopted: the corporation is able to deduct contributions currently and participants defer inclusion of contributions in income until amounts are distributed or made available. The professional should not overlook the important, and unique, tax opportunities that are available upon the ultimate distribution of benefits. This section will deal with the unique tax aspects of benefits received upon termination of participation in a qualified retirement plan. The tax treatment of certain pre-retirement benefits such as life insurance, pre-retirement profit sharing plan distributions, and loan provisions has been dealt with previously and will not be repeated here.

The alternative forms in which benefits may be paid will be controlled by the provisions of the qualified plan. In an individually designed plan the professionals involved may assure that the benefit provisions are drafted in such a manner as to be consistent with the tax planning and business needs of the professionals. As explained below, certain vauluable tax advantages are available only if a participant's entire accrued benefit is paid to him in a lump-sum distribution. Notwithstanding the specialized tax treatment available only to lump-sum distributions, the professionals may decide to limit the circumstances under which lump sums are paid for business reasons—e.g., to prevent a departing professional from using a lump-sum payment as a financial springboard for setting up a competing practice. The initial step in determining the best method of minimizing tax consequences of a distribution of plan benefits is to determine the permissible benefit options that are available. If the participant's vested accrued benefit (i.e., the vested amount in the participant's profit sharing or money purchase account, or the value of the participant's vested defined benefit) is less than $1,750, the plan may, and often does, give the plan administrator the option to involuntarily "cash out" the participant at termination by paying the participant the lump-sum value of the vested accrued benefit.[97]

In most situations, the professional will, upon retirement, have a choice that includes: (1) receiving a lump-sum distribution of his benefit: (2) receiving payments for a fixed number of years certain; or (3) receiving payments in the form of an annuity measured by the participant's expected lifetime (a "life annuity") or the combined lifetime of the participant and some third person such as the spouse or designated beneficiary of the participant (a "joint and survivor annuity). It is quite common for defined contribution plans (profit sharing and money purchase) to eliminate the life annuity option so that the plan will be able to avoid compliance with the burdensome joint and survivor annuity rules; however, defined benefit plans almost always offer some form of life annuity.

Once the professional determines the options that are available, he or she should consider the following issues as they apply to each alternative:

(1) What are the immediate income tax consequences of this form of distribution?
(2) What are the long-term income tax consequences of this form of distribution?
(3) What are the estate tax consequences of this form of distribution?
(4) Is this form of distribution coordinated with the professional's personal retirement planning?

For taxable years beginning after December 31, 1981, a participant will be taxable on benefits only when actually received. Prior to 1982, a participant was taxable on benefits when actually or constructively received. See Section 402(a) of the Code.

(a) Consequences of Lump-Sum Distributions

A lump-sum distribution, in general terms, is a distribution of the balance of a participant's account (and in certain cases more than one plan maintained by an employer must be aggregated) within one taxable year of the recipient, which distribution is made as a result of the participant's death or separation from service or after the employee attains age 59½. Complexities and potential pitfalls for the unwary abound in the area of lump-sum distributions, and professional advice should normally be sought in advance if this alternative is selected. If a lump sum is received, the professional is faced with the critical decision of determining whether to "roll the distribution over" into an individual retirement plan or to retain the distribution and elect to have it taxed under the special 10-year averaging rule of Section 402(e) of the Code. Accumulated deductible employee contributions are not considered for purposes of lump sum distributions.

(b) Tax Consequence of 10-Year Averaging

A recipient of a lump-sum distribution will be taxed under 10-year averaging only if this method of taxation is elected.[98] An election to use 10-year averaging is made by filing Form 4972 with the recipient's income tax return. This election can be made or revoked at any time during the period in which the income tax return for one year of receipt of the distribution can be amended (i.e., within three years of the filing deadline). Ten-year averaging may be elected only once after the recipient attains age 59½ and may only be elected if the participant whose accrued benefit is distributed was an active participant in the plan (including certain predecessor plans) for at least 5 years.[99]

In general, the amount of tax imposed on a lump-sum distribution will be 10 times the amount of tax that would be imposed under Selection 1(c) of the Code if an unmarried individual received one-tenth of the lump sum, assuming that this one-tenth amount constituted the only income received for the taxable year and further assuming that the zero bracket amount (standard deduction) did not apply to the individual.[100] If the distribution is less than $70,000, the tax is further reduced by a minimum distribution allowance under Section 402(e)(1)(D) of the Code. Furthermore, if the participant was an active participant prior to 1974, a portion of the lump sum equal to the fraction of the participant's total active participation that occurred prior to 1974, will be subject to tax as long-term capital gains (Section 402(a)(2) of the Code), unless the recipient elects to have the entire distribution taxed under the 10-year averaging rule (Section 402(e) (4) (L)). The table below indicates the amount of tax that would be imposed on a lump-sum distribution of various amounts (assuming that no portion is taxed as capital gains), as well as the percentage of the distribution that would be paid to satisfy the tax imposed:

Amount of Lump Sum	Tax Imposed	Percentage of Distribution Required to Pay Income Taxes
$ 20,000	$ 1,400	7.00%
100,000	19,150	19.15%
250,000	68,490	27.40%
500,000	193,320	38.66%
1,000,000	516,170	51.62%

The above table indicates that, if the amount of the distribution is small, the 10-year averaging election will create a very attractive tax rate. On the other hand, the recipient of a $1,000,000 distribution would never elect lump-sum treatment, since such recipient would pay a lower tax by treating the distribution as ordinary income subject to the 50% maximum tax on personal service income under Selection 1348 of the Code. Although pensions are included in personal service income under Section 1348(b) (1) (A) of the Code, amounts taxed under the 10-year averaging rule are specifically excluded from personal service income under Selection 1348 (b) (1) (B) (i) of the Code. Persons contemplating the use of 10-year averaging should consider not only the immediate tax impact but also the long-term tax consequences: once the distribution is received, earnings generated by the distribution are exposed to immediate taxation and, depending upon the investment medium selected, might be exposed to the 70% tax rates applicable to unearned investment income. However, for taxable years beginning after December 31, 1981, ERTA eliminates this problem by establishing a maximum income tax rate of 50%. Once distributed, a lump sum is also subject in full to estate taxation. Finally, lump-sum recipients might be tempted to increase current expenditures for un-needed or luxury items, so that a large portion of the lump sum might not be available to provide for future retirement security.

(c) *Rollover of Lump Sums*

The alternative to electing 10-year averaging of a lump-sum distribution is rolling over (i.e., transferrring) all or any part of the lump sum into an individual retirement account ("IRA") or individual retirement annuity. An amount must be rolled over *no later than* 60 days after receipt of a lump-sum distribution.[101] Therefore, one should plan in advance and identify the specific vehicle to be used for the rollover prior to receipt of the distribution. If a recipient changes his mind after completing a rollover, the rollover may be revoked with a minimum financial penalty if action to revoke is taken prior to the time for filling an income tax return (including extensions) for the taxable year in which the lump sum was received.[102] Such timely action will avoid a 10% penalty tax on early receipt of the amount rolled over; however, if the recipient is younger than 59½ in the year of receipt of a revoked IRA rollover, the 10% penalty will still apply to income on the rollover that is returned.[103] In addition the financial institution that maintains the IRA may impose interest or adminstrative cost penalties for early revocation. Once the IRA is revoked, the recipient may elect 10 year averaging of his distribution.

Rollover of a lump sum is available even if the participant whose accrued benefit is distributed was not an active participant in the plan for five years or any other minimum period. Furthermore, a rollover may be accomplished even if the recipient has previously elected 10-year averaging after age 59½[104] The entire amount received in a lump-sum distribution need not be rolled over,[105] and any amount not rolled over will be subject to tax at ordinary income rates; prior to 1982 tax rates will be limited by the 50% maximum tax under Code Section 1348.[106] A recipient cannot elect 10-year averaging of a portion of a lump sum that is not rolled over, but he may be able to use regular income tax averaging under Section 1301 *et seq* of the Code as a result of rolling over only part of a lump sum. The amount of a lump sum that represents employee contributions may not be rolled over but will be retained by the recipient tax-free.[107] Income attributable to employee contributions may, however, be rolled over.[108] A recipient must either rollover the identical property distributed or may sell the property distributed (during the period of up to 60 days between receipt of a lump sum and its rollover) and roll over the proceeds of sale.[109] No gain or loss will be recognized on such sales to the extent the proceeds are rolled over. A rollover is available not only to a participant who receives a lump sum, but also to the spouse of a participant who receives a lump sum on account of the participant's death.[110]

The immediate tax consequence of a rollover is that taxation of benefits is deferred for the amount rolled over until it is actually distributed from the IRA. Distributions from the IRA may begin at any time after the year in which the owner of the IRA reaches age 59½ (an earlier distribution would result in a 10% excise tax under Section 408(f) of the Code). Once age 59½ is attained and prior to reaching age 70½, distributions from the IRA are up to the discretion of the owner. Furthermore, there is no "constructive receipt" from an IRA, so that the owner can have the ability to demand, at any time, all or any part of the IRA, and such discretion will not result in any part of the IRA being taxed before it is actually received.[111] Amounts actually distributed from an IRA are taxed as ordinary income, and, prior to 1982, such distributions are subject to the 50% maximum tax limitation of Section 1348 of the Code. One cannot receive a lump sum from an IRA and elect 10-year averaging on the amount received; therefore, in most cases the decision to use an IRA will foreclose use of 10-year averaging.

Once age 70½ is attained (or beginning with the year of the rollover if in that year the owner is older than 70½),[112] the owner of an IRA must have an amount distributed from the IRA that is a certain fraction of the balance in the IRA at the beginning of the year. Failure to receive the minimum required distribution results in an excise tax under Section 4974 of the Code equal to 50% of the amount by which the required distribution exceeds the actual distribution. The fraction of the IRA that must be distributed has a numerator equal to the number of calendar years beginning after the owner attains age 70½ and a denominator equal to the life expectancy of the owner (or combined expectancies of the owner and his spouse as of the owner's 70th birthday.[113] The single life expectancy of a male age 70 is 12.1 years and of a female age 70 is 15 years. The joint life expectancy at age 70, if husband and wife are the same age, is 18.3 years.[114] Rather than receiving payments for a period certain, an annuity for the life of the participant or joint lives of a participant and his spouse may be purchased at age 70½ —this option might be attractive to an individual who is relying upon a rollover IRA as the principal source of retirement income.

Summarizing the key characteristics of the alternative of using a rollover IRA, this alternative will create no initial income taxation since neither the rollover nor the return of employee contributions is subject to tax. In the long term, the IRA alternative may be used to defer taxation of benefits distributed from a qualified plan; however, since voluntary employee contributions cannot be rolled over, use of the IRA rollover forecloses further deferral of income earned on voluntary employee contributions. Any amount remaining in an IRA on the death of the participant will be excluded from the participant's estate provided that the beneficiary of the IRA is not the participant's estate and distributions to the beneficiary from the IRA are made in uniform amounts over at least three years.[115] The use of a rollover IRA will undoubtedly increase the likelihood that the participant will retain his plan benefits to provide retirement income, rather than using the distribution for current expenditures as might be the case if 10-year averaging is utilized with a lump-sum distribution.

(d) *Receipt of Periodic Retirement Benefits from the Professional Corporation's Plan*

Rather than receiving a lump-sum distribution, a participant could elect to receive a distribution from the qualified corporate plan over a fixed number of years. One advantage of this alternative is that payments may commence prior to age 59½ and there is no inflexible requirement that distributions begin no later than age 70½; however, the manner of distribution elected by a participant must result in distributions to the participant over his life expectancy having a present value on the date benefits commence that is at least 50% of the present value of the participant's total vested accrued benefit.[116]

Receipt of benefits in the form of installments directly from the corporate plan involves a certain amount of inflexibility in scheduling the rate of payment, since, in order to avoid constructive receipt, a participant must irrevocably elect the manner of distribution within 60 days after benefits could first be elected to commence being paid.[117] It is possible, however, for the plan to permit acceleration of the schedule of payment elected if the participant encountered financial hardship. Furthermore, the plan could permit even a retired participant to receive a loan from the corporate plan (in contrast, loans from or secured by IRA's are prohibited.)[118] If an employee has a large amount of voluntary contributions, he might prefer electing installments from the plan rather than receiving and rolling over a lump sum, since employee contributions may not be rolled over, and, therefore, earnings attributable to employee contributions would lose their tax shelter under the rollover alternative, but would remain tax sheltered if benefits were distributed in installments from the plan.

An amount distributed from a qualified corporate plan after the death of the participant (other than an amount attributable to employee contributions) will be excluded from the participant's gross estate provided that such amount is payable to a beneficiary other than the participant's estate and provided that 10-year averaging of the distribution is not elected.[119] As an alternative, the beneficiary could elect 10-year averaging of a lump-sum benefit remaining in the plan, but the amount would then be included in the participant's estate. As a third alternative the spouse of the participant may be given a lump-sum distribution which could be rolled over into an IRA by the spouse.[120] A rollover by the surviving spouse may be accomplished without loss of the participant's estate tax exclusion.[121] In any event, appropriate tax advice should be sought with regard to the various elections (and possible tax consequences) which occur upon the death of a professional.

In summary, a participant may prefer receiving deferred benefits directly from a corporate plan, particularly if the participant has a large amount of voluntary employee contributions and is able to formulate an irrevocable choice of distribution option at the time of retirement. This alternative permits continued deferral of income taxation of accrued benefits and of earnings on accrued benefits (including earnings on employee contributions). This alternative also preserves the employee's estate tax exclusion on employer-derived accrued benefits, although earnings attributable to employee contributions are includable in the participant's estate under this alternative (but not under the IRA alternative to the extent such earnings are rolled over). This alternative might be best suited for the professional corporation that employs only one professional since, after the professional participant retired, the plan could be frozen, minimizing the opportunity for later events to disqualify the plan, alter the investment strategy, or modify the administration in a manner that would be to the detriment of the retired professional.

EXHIBIT 1

[AMENDMENT AND RESTATEMENT
OF THE]
PROFIT SHARING PLAN FOR THE EMPLOYEES
OF

_____

This Profit Sharing Plan contains appropriate provisions to draft an amendment and restatement of an existing plan or to draft a new plan. Various options and plan provision elections are set forth in brackets.

Prepared by:
Lamon, Elrod & Harkleroad, P.C.
2500 Peachtree Center-Cain Tower
229 Peachtree Street, N.E.
Atlanta, Georgia 30043

INDEX TO THE
[AMENDMENT AND RESTATEMENT
OF THE]
PROFIT SHARING PLAN FOR THE EMPLOYEES
OF

_____

(Introduction for Amended and Restated Plan)

AMENDMENT AND RESTATEMENT

OF THE

PROFIT SHARING PLAN FOR THE EMPLOYEES

OF

_____

WHEREAS, _____
("Employer") established the _____ PROFIT SHARING PLAN effective
_____; and

WHEREAS, effective _____, said Plan was amended and restated to meet
the requirements of the Internal Revenue Code of 1954 ("Code"), as amended by
the Employee Retirement Income Security Act of 1974 ("ERISA"); and

WHEREAS, the Board of Directors has determined that it is in the best
interest of Plan Participants and Beneficiaries to make further modifications to said
Plan in light of recent regulations and rulings promulgated under the Code and
ERISA;

NOW, THEREFORE, in order to accomplish these purposes, the Board of
Directors of the Employer has by appropriate resolutions adopted the amended and
restated _____ PROFIT SHARING PLAN ("Plan") as hereinafter stated to be
effective as of _____.

It is intended that this restated Plan, together with the Trust Agreement,
meets all the requirements of the Code and ERISA, and the Plan shall be interpreted, wherever possible, to comply with the terms of the Code and ERISA and all
formal regulations and rulings issued under the Code and ERISA.

[Alternate Introduction for New Plan]

PROFIT SHARING PLAN FOR THE EMPLOYEES

OF

_____

WHEREAS, _____ ("Employer") desires to establish the
_____ profit sharing plan to encourage employment longevity and assist

employees in planning for their retirement by permitting them to share in the Net Profits of the Employer; and

WHEREAS, said Plan is intended to meet the requirements of the Internal Revenue Code of 1954 (''Code''), as amended by the Employee Retirement Income Security Act of 1974 (''ERISA''); and

NOW, THEREFORE, the Board of Directors of the Employer does by appropriate resolution adopt the _____ PROFIT SHARING PLAN (''Plan'') as hereinafter stated to be effective as of _____.

ARTICLE I

DEFINITIONS

As used in this Plan and the accompanying Trust Agreement the following terms shall have the following meanings unless a different meaning is plainly required by the context:

1.01 The term *''Annual Addition''* in respect of any Participant shall mean the sum (for any Plan Year) of—

    (a) The Employer Contributions to the Trust in respect of said Plan Year;

    (b) The lesser of—

        (i) The amount of the Employee Contributions, if any, in said Plan Year in excess of six percent (6%) of his Basic Compensation received in said Plan Year, or

        (ii) One-half (1/2) of the Employee Contributions to the Trust in said Plan Year; and

    (c) Forfeitures credited to said Participant's account in respect of said Plan Year; provided that the Employee Contributions mentioned in (b) above shall be determined without regard to Rollover Contributions from any individual retirement account, if any.

1.02 The term *''Attained Age''* shall mean the age, in years, of an Employee as of the last anniversary of his date of birth.

1.03 The term *''Basic Compensation''* shall mean a Participant's [total compensation paid by the Employer during the Plan Year and reported on the Participant's Federal Income Tax Withholding Statement (Form W-2), including regular compensation, overtime pay, and commissions, but excluding non-contracted bonuses, expense account allowances, and Employer Contributions to this and any other retirement or welfare plan established by the Employer, to the extent that such excluded items are reported on the Form W-2.] [total compensation paid by the Employer during the Plan Year, including salary, overtime pay, commissions, and bonuses, as reported on the Participant's Federal Income Tax Withholding Statement (Form W-2).]

1.04 The term *''Beneficiary''* shall mean any person or persons (or a trust) designated by a Participant in such form as the Plan Administrator may prescribe to receive any death benefit that may be payable hereunder if such person or persons survive the Participant. This designation may be revoked at any time in similar manner and form. In the event of the death of the designated Beneficiary prior to the death of the Participant, the Contingent Beneficiary shall be entitled to receive any death benefit. See Section 5.18 if neither the Beneficiary nor Contingent Beneficiary survivies the Participant or if no Beneficiary or Contingent Beneficiary has been effectively named.

1.05 The term *"Board of Directors"* shall mean the Board of Directors of the Employer.

1.06 The term *"Contingent Beneficiary"* shall mean the person or persons (or a trust) duly designated by the Participant to receive any death benefit from the Plan in the event the designated Beneficiary does not survive the Participant.

1.07 The term *"Defined Benefit Plan"* shall mean any plan which is not a Defined Contribution Plan.

1.08 The term *"Defined Benefit Plan Fraction"* for any Plan Year, with respect to a particular participant, shall mean a fraction;

(a) The numerator of which is his projected annual benefit under the plan, including any other plan required to be aggregated under Section 415(h) of the Code, (determined as of the close of the Plan Year), and

(b) The denominator of which is his projected annual benefit under the plan, including any other plan required to be aggregated under Section 415(h) of the Code, (determined as of the close of such Plan Year) if the plan provided the maximum benefit allowable under (i) Code Section 415(b)(1)(A), or if lesser (ii) one hundred percent (100%) of such participant's average compensation for his highest three (3) consecutive Plan Years of participation.

1.09 The term *"Defined Contribution Plan"* shall mean a plan which provides for an individual account for each participant and for benefits based solely on the amount contributed to the participant's account, and any income, expenses, gains, and losses, and any forfeitures of accounts of other participants which may be allocated to such participant's account.

1.10 The Term *"Defined Contribution Plan Fraction"* with respect to a particular participant for any Plan Year shall mean a fraction;

(a) The numerator of which is the sum of the Annual Additions to his account, inclucing Annual Additions to his account in any other plan required to be aggregated under Section 415(h) of the Code, as of the close of such Plan Year, and

(b) The denominator of which is the sum of the maximum amount (consistent with Code Section 415(c)(1)) of Annual Additions to his account which could have been made for such Plan Year and for each prior Plan Year of Service with the Employer, including any other employer required to be aggregated under Section 415(h) of the Code, and including service prior to the Effective Date.

1.11 The term *"Directed Investment Employee Contributions Account"* shall mean an account established for the purpose of segregating from the general assets of the Trust Fund and separately accounting for a Participant's voluntary Employee Contributions. A Directed Investment Employee Contributions Account shall be established only upon the written directions of a Participant and shall be:

(a) Credited with:

(1) The amount of Employee Contributions the Participant so directs the Trustee to allocate to such account; and

(2) Earnings generated by the assets in such account; and

(b) Reduced by:

(1) Withdrawals from such account; and

(2) Losses, if the computation of investment earnings generated by the assets in such Account results in a negative figure; and

(3) Administrative expenses, as determined by the Trustee, attributable to such account.

A Participant's Directed Investment Employee Contributions Account shall be invested in accordance with the written instructions of the Participant to the Trustee, provided however, that no investment shall be made that would constitute a prohibited transaction under the Code or ERISA. The Plan Administrator may prescribe procedures under which directions required to be given to the Trustee under this Section may be given to the Plan Administrator and communicated by the Plan Administrator to the Trustee.

1.12 The term *"Early Retirement Date"* shall mean the later of (a) the last day of the Plan Year during which an Employee attains age [fifty-five (55)] or (b) the last day of the Plan Year in which such Employee completes ten (10) Years of Service.

1.13 The term *"Effective Date"* shall mean the original effective date of the Plan, _____ .

1.14 The term *"Employee"* shall mean each individual employed by the Employer.

1.15 The term *"Employee Accounts"* shall mean a Participant's Employee Contributions Account (if such an account exists for the Participant) and the Participant's Directed Investment Employee Contributions Account (if such an account exists for the Participant).

1.16 The term *"Employee Contributions Account"* shall mean a bookkeeping account established for the purpose of separately accounting for a Participant's voluntary Employee Contributions that are commingled with all voluntary Employee Contributions held in the Trust Fund. Employee Contributions will be accounted for in an "Employee Contributions Account" unless the Participant directs the Trustee, in writing, to account for his voluntary Employee Contributions in a Directed Investment Employee Contributions Account, as described in Section 1.11 hereof. A Participant may at any time file a written request with the Trustee to have all or any part of the balance in his Employee Contributions Account transferred to a Directed Investment Employee Contributions Account, or may at any time file a written request with the Trustee to have all or any part of his Directed Investment Employee Contributions Account transferred to an Employee Contributions Account, provided, however, that the Trustee may require that any transfers from a Directed Investment Employee Contributions Account to the Trust

541

Fund be made in cash, to the extent that the assets in the Directed Investment Employee Contributions Account are unacceptable to the Trustee, and provided further, that the Participant's Employee Accounts shall be charged with the administrative expense attributable to any such transfer as determined by the Trustee. A Participant's Employee Contributions Account shall be:

    (a) Credited with:

        (1) The amount of Employee Contributions contributed to the Trust other than contributions for which the Participant makes a written election to have allocated to his Directed Investment Employee Contributions Account; and

        (2) The Participant's proportionate share of the net gains of the Trust Fund determined under Section 4.02; and

    (b) Reduced by:

        (1) Withdrawals and benefits paid from such account; and

        (2) The Participant's proportionate share of the net losses of the Trust Fund as determined under Section 4.02.

1.17 The term *"Employer"* shall mean _____, a _____ corporation with principal offices located at _____, _____; its successors and assigns, and, subject to the provisions of Section 10.08, any company into which the Employer may be merged or consolidated or to which all or substantially all of its assets may be transferred.

1.18 The term *"Fiduciary"* shall mean and include the Trustee, Plan Administrator, Plan Sponsor, Investment Manager, and any other person who—

    (a) Exercises any discretionary authority or discretionary control respecting management of the Plan or exercises any authority or control respecting management or disposition of its assets;

    (b) Renders investment advice for a fee or other compensation, direct or indirect, with respect to any moneys or other property of the Plan, or has any authority or responsibility to do so;

    (c) Has any discretionary authority or discretionary responsibility in the administration of the Plan; or

    (d) Is described as a "fiduciary" in Section 3(14) or (21) of ERISA or is designated to carry out fiduciary responsibilities pursuant to this Plan and the Trust Agreement to the extent permitted by Section 405(c)(1)(B) of ERISA.

1.19 The term *"Hour of Service"* shall mean:

    (a) Each hour for which an Employee is paid, or entitled to payment, for the performance of duties for the Employer during a Plan Year.

    (b) Except as otherwise provided in this Subsection (b), each hour for which an Employee is paid, or entitled to payment from the Employer on account of a period of time during which no duties are performed (irrespective of whether the employment relationship has terminated) due to vacation, holiday, illness, incapacity (including disability), layoff, jury duty, military duty or leave of absence. An Employee shall be entitled to 40 Hours of Service for each work week that consists of a period described in the preceding sentence.

(1) No more than 501 Hours of Service will be credited under this Subsection (b) to an Employee on account of any single continuous period during which the Employee performs no duties (whether or not such period occurs in a single Plan Year).

(2) Hours of Service shall not be credited on account of a period during which an Employee is paid or entitled to payment and with respect to which no duties are performed, if such payment is made or due under a plan maintained solely for the purpose of complying with applicable workmen's compensation, or unemployment compensation or disability service laws, or if the payment merely reimburses the Employee for a medical or medically related expense incurred by the Employee.

(3) For purposes of this Subsection (b) a payment shall be deemed to be made by or due from the Employer regardless of whether such payment is made by or due from the Employer directly, or indirectly through, among others, a trust fund or insurer, to which the Employer pays premiums and regardless of whether contributions made or due to the trust fund, insurer or other entity are for the benefit of a particular Employee or are on behalf of a group of Employees in the aggregate.

(c) Each hour for which back pay, irrespective of mitigation of damages, is either awarded or agreed to by the Employer. The same Hours of Service shall not be credited under Subsection (a) or Subsection (b) and under this Subsection (c). The crediting of Hours of Service for back pay awarded or agreed to with respect to periods described in Subsection (b) shall be subject to the limitations described in Paragraphs (1), (2) and (3) of Subsection (b).

The crediting of Hours of Service shall be subject to all the rules contained in Paragraphs (b) and (c) of the United States Department of Labor Regulations §2530.200b-2. For purposes of this Section 1.19, service for any employer required to be aggregated with the Employer under Code Section 414(b) or (c) shall be treated as service for the Employer. [For purposes of vesting in this Plan, no period of service prior to the Effective Date shall be counted.]

[The Hours of Service for an Employee who is compensated for the Plan Year solely on the basis of commissions, as opposed to salary or hourly pay, shall be deemed to equal the quotient of such Employee's Basic Compensation divided by the lowest minimum wage under the Fair Labor Standards Act of 1938, as amended, in effect at any time during the Plan Year.] (Optional language where commissioned sales persons will participate in the plan.)

1.20 The term "*Investment Manager*" shall mean any Fiduciary (other than a trustee or named fiduciary) who—

(a) Has the power to manage, acquire, or dispose of any asset of the Plan;

(b) Is a bank, insurance company, or an investment advisor registered under the Investment Advisers Act of 1940; and

(c) Has acknowledged in writing that he is a fiduciary with respect to the Plan.

1.21 The term *"Net Profits"* shall mean the net operating profits of the Employer for any Plan Year or Plan Years computed according to its normal accounting practices, excluding any extraordinary gains or losses from non-operational activities.

(a) The term *"Current Net Profits"* refers to the Net Profits for a particular Plan Year, which Net Profits shall be determined prior to taking into account either the income taxes for such Plan Year or the contributions for such Plan Year to this or any other plan qualified under the Code. Unless the context clearly requires to the contrary, all references to "Net Profits" in this Plan shall be references only to "Current Net Profits."

(b) The term *"Accumulated Net Profits"* refers to the Net Profits for all Plan Years prior to the particular Plan Year and does take into account both income taxes and qualified plan contributions for all such prior Plan Years.

1.22 The term *"Normal Retirement Date"* shall mean the later of (a) the last day of the month coincident with or immediately preceding the Employee's [sixty-fifth (65th)] anniversary of his date of birth or (b) the 10th anniversary of the Employee's date of initial participation in the Plan.

(Option 1—Use for a New Plan)

[1.23 The term *"One Year Break in Service"* shall mean a Plan Year during which the Participant has not completed more than five hundred (500) Hours of Service.]

(Option 2—Use for an Amended and Restated Plan Where There Has Been a Switch in Computation Periods From Employment Year to Plan Year for Purposes of Vesting Credit).

[1.23 The term *"One Year Break in Service"* shall mean, for any anniversary of the date of employment occurring before _____, 19__, a 12-month period commencing on a given anniversary of the date of employment during which the Participant has not completed more than 500 Hours of Service. If the Participant does not complete more than 500 Hours of Service during the 12-month period commencing on the anniversary of the date of employment immediately preceding _____, 19__, the computation period for determining whether the Participant incurs successive One Year Breaks in Service shall continue to be based on anniversaries of the date of employment until more than 500 Hours of Service are completed during one such computation period. Except as provided in the two immediately preceding sentences, the term "One Year Break in Service" shall mean a Plan Year during which the Participant has not completed more than 500 Hours of Service.]

1.24 The term *"Participant"* shall mean an Employee who has met the requirements of Article II for participation hereunder.

(a) A Participant shall become an *"Active Participant"* in accordance with Article II and shall remain an "Active Participant" until such time as he incurs a One Year Break in Service; is cashed-out or is in the process of being cashed-out under Section 5.11; retires pursuant to Section 5.01, 5.02, or 5.03; or becomes Totally and Permanently Disabled. An "Active Participant" shall be entitled to his allocable share of Employer Contributions, forfeitures, and earnings or losses of the Trust Fund; provided, however, notwithstanding any other provisions of this Plan to the contrary, no allocation of earnings or losses of the Trust Fund shall be made to a new Participant during his first Plan Year of participation if the allocation formula described in Section 4.02(a)(2)(C) is in effect for such first Plan Year of participation and if such Participant has no prior years account balance on which to base such allocation as is necessary to the formula provided under Section 4.02(a)(2)(C) hereof. Notwithstanding any provision of this Section or Plan to the contrary, a Retired, Disabled, Former, or Terminated Participant who is re-employed and continues in the employ of the Employer through the last day of the Plan Year which includes the date or re-employment shall be an "Active Participant" for the Plan Year of re-employment, even though he completes five hundred (500) or fewer Hours of Service during such Plan Year, and shall be entitled to all of the rights of an "Active Participant" except as provided in the last sentence of Section 5.11. Otherwise, no Participant who completes five hundred (500) or fewer Hours of Service during the Plan Year and thus incurs a One Year Break in Service with respect to such Plan Year shall be regarded as an "Active Participant" for such Plan Year.

(b) A *"Terminated Participant"* is one who has not retired or become disabled under Section 5.01, 5.02, 5.03, or 5.05 and who has received the full distribution to which he is entitled pursuant to Section 5.06 and 5.07 following a One Year Break in Service, has been cashed-out or is in the process of being cashed-out as of the applicable Valuation Date pursuant to Section 5.11, or has incurred a One Year Break in Service but has no vested interest and is therefore entitled to no distribution or cash-out. No allocations of Employer Contributions, forfeitures, or earnings or losses shall be made to "Terminated Participants".

(c) A *"Retired Participant"* or *"Disabled Participant"* is one who is entitled to a distribution pursuant to Section 5.01, 5.02, or 5.03 following retirement, or pursuant to Section 5.05 following Total and Permanent Disability. "Retired Participants" and "Disabled Participants" who have not elected pursuant to Section 5.01, 5.02, 5.03, or 5.05 to take their Profit Sharing Accounts as of the Valuation Date immediately preceding their dates or retirement or the dates on which they were determined to be Totally and Permanently Disabled and for whom separate accounts have not been established under Section 5.09 prior to the Valuation Date in question shall be entitled to allocable shares of earnings or losses for the particular Plan Year and to allocable shares of Employer Contributions and forfeitures if more than five hundred (500) Hours of Service were completed during the Plan Year.

(d) A *"Former Participant"* is one who has incurred a One Year Break in Service, but has not retired pursuant to Section 5.01, 5.02, or 5.03 or become Totally and Permanently Disabled, and who has not yet received a full distribution of his vested interest under Section 5.07 or 5.11. Prior to full distribution, or segregation of his Profit Sharing Account and Employee Accounts pursuant to Section 5.09, a "Former Participant" shall be entitled to share in earnings or losses of the Trust Fund, but shall not be entitled to share in Employer Contributions or forfeitures.

[____ The term *"Participation Date"* shall mean each _____ and _____ beginning with _____.] (For use with two entry dates. If used, all succeeding Sections must be renumbered.)

1.25 The term *"Plan Administrator"* shall mean the [Employer.] [individual so named as provided in Article VII.]

1.26 The term *"Plan Anniversary Date"* shall mean the last day of the Plan Year. The Plan Anniversary Date initially shall be _____.

1.27 The term *"Plan Sponsor"* shall mean the Employer.

1.28 The term *"Plan Year"* shall mean the accounting period adopted by the Employer for federal income tax purposes, which period begins _____ and ends the following _____. [For all purposes of this Plan, the Plan Year shall also constitute the "limitation year" for purposes of Section 415 of the Code.]

1.29 The term *"Profit Sharing Account"* shall mean the account established on behalf of a Participant to which shall be credited (a) the amount of Employer Contributions allocated to the Participant pursuant to Section 3.01; (b) the Participant's proportionate share of any forfeitures; and (c) the Participant's proportionate share, attributable to his Profit Sharing Account, of the net gains of the Trust Fund determined in accordance with Section 4.02 hereof. From said account there shall be deducted the Participant's proportionate share, attributable to his Profit Sharing Account, of the net losses (if any) of the Trust Fund as determined in accordance with Section 4.02.

1.30 The term *"Service in the Armed Forces"* shall mean service in the armed forces of the United States which is required under the Military Selective Service Act or which is voluntary, if such voluntary enlistment is for a period not in excess of four (4) years, provided that the Employee reapplies for employment with the Employer within the time period required by federal law for the preservation of benefits.

1.31 The term *"Total and Permanent Disability"* or *"Totally and Permanently Disabled"* shall mean a physical or mental condition arising after an Employee has become a Participant which totally and permanently prevents the Participant from [performing the normal duties for which he is employed.] [engaging in any occupation or employment for remuneration or profit, except for the purpose of rehabilitation not incompatible with a finding of total and permanent disability.] The determination as to whether a Participant is totally and permanently disabled shall be made (i) on medical evidence by a licensed physician designated by the Plan Administrator, (ii) on evidence that the Participant is eligible for disability benefits under any long-term disability plan sponsored by the Employer but administered by an independent third party, or (iii) on evidence that the Participant is eligible for total and permanent disability benefits under the Social Security Act in effect at the date of disability. Total and Permanent Disability shall exclude disabilities arising from:

(a) Chronic or excessive use of intoxicants, drugs, or narcotics; or

(b) Intentionally self-inflicted injury or intentionally self-induced sickness; or

(c) A felonious act or enterprise on the part of the Participant; or

(d) Service in the Armed Forces where the Participant is eligible to receive a government-sponsored military disability pension.

1.32 The term *"Trust Agreement"* shall mean the agreement entered into between the Employer and the Trustee [contemporaneously with the execution of this Plan,] [on _____,] as it may subsequently be amended from time to time.

1.33 The term *"Trustee"* shall mean the Trustee or Trustees named in the Trust Agreement.

1.34 The term *"Trust Fund"* or *"Trust"* shall mean all cash, securities, life insurance, and real estate, and any other property held by the Trustee pursuant to the terms of the Trust Agreement, together with income therefrom.

1.35 The term *"Valuation Date"* shall mean the same day as the Plan Anniversary Date.

1.36 The term *"Year of Service"* shall mean, for the purpose of determining eligibility to participate herein: (1) the 12-month period commencing on the date of employment of an Employee and ending on the day immediately preceding the anniversary thereof, during which 12-month period the Employee completes at least 1,000 Hours of Service, and (2) any Plan Year commencing after the Employee's date of employment or re-employment during which he completes at least 1,000 Hours of Service. [For purposes of determining initial eligibility to participate in this Plan, all service with the sole proprietorship of _____ shall be counted.] For all other purposes, the term "Year of Service" shall mean [(a) a 12-month period commencing on the date of employment of an Employee or the anniversary of such date (provided such date or anniversary comes before _____), in which 12-month period such Employee completes at least 1,000 Hours of Service, or (b)] a Plan Year commencing on or after _____, in which an Employee completes at least 1,000 Hours of Service. (Final option contains language for switch over from employment year to plan year for purposes of vesting credit.)

1.37 Any words herein used in the masculine shall be read and be construed in the feminine where they would so apply. Words in the singular shall be read and construed as though used in the plural in all cases where they would so apply.

(Alternate Participation for New Plans)

ARTICLE II

PARTICIPATION

2.01 <u>Participation</u>. Any Employee shall become [a Participant as of the first day of the Plan Year in which he completes his first Year of Service, provided that the Employee is an employee of the Employer on the last day of such first Year of

Service.] [eligible to participate when he meets both of the following requirements:

(a) He must have completed his first Year of Service with the Employer for purposes of determining eligibility, and

(b) He must have attained age [twenty-five (25).]

The Employee shall be entitled to participate for the entire Plan Year during which he meets the later of the above requirements, provided that he is an employee of the Employer when such later requirement is met.] A Retired, Disabled, Former, or Terminated Participant who later returns to the employ of the Employer shall again become a Participant on his date of re-employment. Notwithstanding any provision of this Plan to the contrary, a Retired, Disabled, Former, or Terminated Participant who is re-employed and continues in the employ of the Employer shall be an Active Participant for the Plan Year of re-employment, even though he completes not more than "five hundred (500) hours of Service during such Plan Year, and shall be entitled to all of the rights of an Active Participant except as provided in the last sentence of Section 5.11.

2.02 Rights of Participants. All Participants shall be bound by the terms of the Plan, including all amendments hereto made in the manner authorized herein. Participants shall also be entitled to all of the rights and privileges afforded thereby, including those granted specifically by the Code and ERISA, which are hereby adopted by references as a part of this Plan.

(Alternate Participation for An Amended and Restated Plan)

ARTICLE II

PARTICIPATION

2.01 Participation. Any Employee who has qualified as a Participant under the Plan in effect immediately prior to the effective date of this amendment shall remain a Participant. Commencing with the effective date of this amendment, any Employee who is not a Participant shall become [a Participant as of the first day of the Plan Year in which he completes his first Year of Service, provided that the Employee is an employee of Employer on the last day of such first Year of Service.] [eligible to participate when he meets both of the following requirements:

(a) He must have completed his first Year of Service with the Employer for purposes of determining eligibility, and

He must have attained age [twenty-five (25).]

The Employee shall be entitled to participate for the entire Plan Year during which he meets the later of the above requirements, provided that he is an employee of Employer when such later requirement is met.] A Retired, Disabled, Former, or Terminated Participant who later returns to the employ of the Employer shall again become a Participant on his date of re-employment. Nowithstanding any provision of this Plan to the contrary, a Retired, Disabled, Former, or Terminated Participant who is re-employed and continues in the employ of the Employer shall be an Active Participant for the Plan Year of re-employment, even though he completes not more than five hundred (500) Hours of Service during such Plan Year, and shall be entitled to all of the rights of an Active Participant except as provided in the last sentence of Section 5.11

2.02 Rights of Participants. All Participants shall be bound by the terms of the Plan, including all amendments hereto made in the manner authorized herein. Participants shall also be entitled to all of the rights and privileges afforded thereby, including those granted specifically by the Code and ERISA, which are hereby adopted by references as a part of this Plan.

(Alternate Participation for two entry dates. If this is used you must add the definition of *"Participation Date."*)

2.01 Participation. An Employee who has qualified as a Participant under the Plan in effect immediately prior to the effective date of this amendment shall remain a Participant. Commencing with the effective date of this amendment, any Employee who is not a Participant shall become eligible to participate when he [completes one (1) Year of Service.] [meets both of the following requirements:]

(a) He must have completed one (1) Year of Service with the Employer; and

(b) He must have Attained Age twenty-five (25).]

An eligible Employee shall be admitted to the Plan on the Participation Date coincident with or next following his completion of the requirement[s]. A Retired, Disabled, Former, or Terminated Participant who later returns to the employ of the Employer shall again become a Participant on his date of re-employment. Notwithstanding any provision of this Plan to the contrary, a Retired, Disabled, Former, or Terminated Participant who is re-employed and continues in the employ of the Employer shall be an Active Participant for the Plan Year of re-employment, even though he completes not more than five hundred (500) Hours of Service during such Plan Year, and shall be entitled to all of the rights of an Active Participant except as provided in the last sentence of Section 5.11.

2.02 Rights of Participants. All Participants shall be bound by the terms of the Plan, including all amendments hereto made in the manner authorized herein. Participants shall also be entitled to all of the rights and privileges afforded thereby, including those granted specifically by the Code and ERISA, which are hereby adopted by reference as a part of this Plan.

ARTICLE III

PROFIT SHARING CONTRIBUTIONS

3.01 Employer Contributions.

(a) Mandatory Contributions. For each Plan Year, the Employer shall contribute to the Trust, to be held and administered by the Trustee according to the terms of the Trust Agreement, an amount out of its Current Net Profits equal to ____ percent (___%) of such Current Net Profits.

(b) Optional Contributions. For each Plan Year, the Employer may make an additional contribution from its Current or Accumulated Net Profits, in such amount as shall be determined solely by the Board of Directors on or before the time prescribed by law for filing the Employer's Federal income tax return (including extensions thereof) for the taxable year of the Employer in which falls the last day of the Plan Year. The amount of such contribution shall be paid to the Trustee on or before the time prescribed by law for filing the Employer's Federal income tax return (including extensions thereof) for the taxable year of the Employer in which falls the last day of the Plan Year.

(Alternate Section 3.01—For fully discretionary Contributions.)

3.01 Employer Contributions. For each Plan Year, the Employer shall make a contribution from its Current or Accumulated Net Profits, in such amount as shall be determined solely by the Board of Directors. The amount of such contribution shall be paid to the Trustee on or before the time prescribed by law for filing the Employer's Federal income tax return (including extensions thereof) for the taxable year of the Employer in which falls the last day of the Plan Year.

3.02 Reversion of Employer Contributions. Employer Contributions computed in accordance with the provisions of Section 3.01 shall revert to the Employer under the following circumstances:

(a) In the case of an Employer Contribution which is made by the Employer by reason of a mistake of fact, such contribution shall be returned to the Employer within one (1) year after the payment of the contribution.

(b) If the Plan, as [adopted] [amended] effective _____, or [as amended] thereafter, does not qualify under Section 401(a) of the Code, Employer Contributions subsequent to the effective date of such amendment or adoption, as appropriate, shall be returned to the Employer within one (1) year after the date of denial of qualification of the Plan.

(c) If any Employer Contribution is determined by the Internal Revenue Service to be non-deductible under Section 404 of the Code, then such Employer Contribution, to the extent that it is determined to be non-deductible, shall be returned to the Employer within one (1) year after the disallowance to the deductions.

(Option 1—Contribution Allocated Pro Rata.)

[3.03 Allocation of Employer Contributions. As soon as possible after the Employer has determined and paid the amount of the Employer Contributions for a Plan Year, such Employer Contributions shall be allocated by the Plan Administrator as of the Valuation Date coincident with the close of the Plan Year for which such contributions are made. Only Active Participants, and Retired and Disabled Participants who have not elected pursuant to Section 5.01, 5.02, 5.03, or 5.05 to take their Profit Sharing Accounts and Employee Accounts as of the Valuation Date immediately preceding their dates of retirement or the dates on which they were determined to be Totally and Permanently Disabled, who complete more than five hundred (500) Hours of Service during the Plan Year ending with the

Valuation Date in question, and for whom separate accounts have not been established under Section 5.09 prior to the Valuation Date in question, shall be eligible to share in the allocation. Each such Participant's share in the Employer Contributions shall be that amount which bears the same ratio to the total Employer Contributions for that Plan Year as such Participant's Basic Compensation from the Employer for that Plan Year bears to the Basic Compensation for that Plan Year of all Participants entitled to share in the allocation.]

(Option 2—Allocation of Contributions
Integrated with Social Security Wage Base)

[3.03 Allocation of Employer Contributions. As soon as possible after the Employer has determined and paid the amount of the Employer Contributions for a Plan Year, such Employer Contribution shall be allocated by the Plan Administrator as of the Valuation Date coincident with the close of the Plan Year for which such contributions are made. Only Active Participants, and Retired and Disabled Participants who have not elected pursuant to Section 5.01, 5.02, 5.03, or 5.05 to take their Profit Sharing Accounts and Employee Accounts as of the Valuation Date immediately preceding their dates of retirement or the dates on which they were determined to be Totally and Permanently Disabled, who complete more than five hundred (500) Hours of Service during the Plan Year ending with the Valuation Date in question, and for whom separate accounts have not been established under Section 5.09 prior to the Valuation Date in question, shall be eligible to share in the allocation.]

(a) The Employer Contributions and forfeitures as described in Section 5.06, not in excess of seven (7%) percent of the amount by which each eligible Participant's Basic Compensation exceeds the Social Security Wage Base in effect for said Plan Year (herein refered to as "excess compensation"), shall be allocated to each such eligible Participant's Profit Sharing Account in proportion to the ratio which his excess compensation for such Plan Year bears to the total excess compensation of all eligible Participants.

(b) The balance of the Employer Contributions, and forfeitures as described in Section 5.06, over the amount allocated under subparagraph (a) hereof, shall be allocated to each eligible Participant's Profit Sharing Account in proportion to the ratio which his Basic Compensation for such Plan Year bears to the Basic Compensation of all eligible Participants for such Plan Year.]

3.04 Voluntary Employee Contributions.

(a) Limitation on Amount of Employee Contributions. For each Plan Year a Participant may, but need not, contribute to the Trust an amount not to exceed 10% of his Basic Compensation paid or accrued for all Plan Years in which he has been a Participant in the Plan; provided, however, that the aggregate sum of voluntary contributions of any Participant held at any time in such Participant's Employee Accounts shall not exceed 10% of the Participant's Basic Compensation paid or accrued for the current and such prior Plan Years. Such voluntary contributions by Participants shall not reduce the Employer Contributions, and such contributions as may be made by a Participant, together with all earnings allocated

551

thereto, shall at all times be fully vested in such Participant. Voluntary contributions may be made directly to the Trustee, or a Participant may (with the consent of the Employer) direct the Employer, in writing, to withhold from his salary a sum which the Employer shall promptly remit to the Trustee. The payroll deduction method is entirely voluntary and optional and there is no duty on any Participant to make a voluntary contribution.

(b) Election to Withdraw Employee Contributions. A Participant may, upon ninety (90) days prior notice to the Plan Administrator, elect to receive all or any portion of the lesser of:

(1) the sum of all Employee Contributions previously made under Subsection (a) to the Plan less the sum of all prior distributions under this Subsection (b) of Employee Contributions to the Participant, or

(2) the balance of his Employee Accounts.

No penalty shall be imposed for the exercise of the election described in this Subsection (b), however, a Participant may not make more than one election under this Subsection (b) in any Plan Year.

(Option 1—Graded Suspension from
Employer Contributions)

[(c) Election to Withdraw Earnings on Employee Contributions. A Participant who withdraws all of his Employee Contributions under Subsection (b) may, upon ninety (90) days notice, elect to receive 25%, 50% 75% or 100% of the remaining balance of his Employee Accounts. A Participant who makes an election under this Subsection (c) shall be subject to a Suspension Period in accordance with the following table:

Percentage of Withdrawal of the Balance in the Employee Accounts	Suspension Period
25%	6 months
50%	8 months
75%	10 months
100%	12 months

The Suspension Period shall commence on the date on which the Participant receives the distribution as provided under this Subsection (c). Basic Compensation shall not include renumeration paid by the Employer to the Participant as compensation with respect to Hours of Service allocable to a Suspension Period and, therefore, the Participant shall receive no Employer Contributions with respect to service during a Suspension Period. A Participant may make an election under this Subsection (c) at the same time that he makes an election under Subsection (b), but may not make more than one election under Subsection (c) in any Plan Year; and, a Participant who has previously made an election under Subsection (b) during a Plan Year may not subsequently make an election under this Subsection (c) during such Plan Year.]

(Option 2—Six-Month Suspension from
Employer Contributions)

[(c) <u>Election to Withdraw Earnings on Employee Contributions.</u> A Participant who withdraws all of his Employee Contributions under Subsection (b) may, upon ninety (90) days notice, elect to receive 100% of the remaining balance of his Employee Accounts. A Participant who makes an election under this Subsection (c) shall be subject to a Suspension Period of six (6) months. The Suspension Period shall commence on the date on which the Participant receives the distribution as provided under this Subsection (c). Basic Compensation shall not include renumeration paid by the Employer to the Participant as compensation with respect to Hours of Service allocable to a Suspension Period and, therefore, the Participant shall receive no Employer Contributions with respect to service during a Suspension Period. A Participant may make an election under this Subsection (c) at the same time that he makes an election under Subsection (b), but may not make more than one election under this Subsection (c) in any Plan Year; and, a Participant who has previously made an election under Subsection (b) during a Plan Year may not subsequently make an election under this Subsection (c) during such Plan Year.]

(Option 3—No Suspension from
Employer Contribututions, but a Two-Year
Suspension from Employee Contributions
With No Make Up Period)

[(c) <u>Election to Withdraw Earnings on Employee Contributions.</u> A Participant who withdraws all of his Employee Contributions under Subsection (b) may, upon ninety (90) days notice, elect to receive 100% of the remaining balance of his Employee Accounts. A Participant who makes an election under this Subsection (c) shall be subject to a Suspension Period of twenty-four months. The Suspension Period shall commence on the date on which the Participant receives the distribution as provided under this Subsection (c). For purposes of computing the limitation on Employee Contributions under Subsection (a), Basic Compensation shall not include remuneration paid by the Employer to the Participant as compensation with respect to Hours of Service allocable to a Suspension Period, and, therefore, the Participant shall not be permitted to make Employee Contributions with respect to service during a Suspension Period. However, the allocation of Employer Contributions and forfeitures shall not be affected by such Suspension Period. A Participant may make an election under this Subsection (c) at the same time that he makes an election under Subsection (b), but a Participant who has previously made an election under Subsection (b) during a Plan Year may not subsequently make an election under this Subsection (c) during such Plan Year.]

(d) <u>Limitation of Election.</u> No election may be made under Subsection (b) or (c) by an individual who is not an Active Participant, or by an Active Participant during a Suspension Period under Subsection (c), provided, however, that an Employee who separates from service with the Employer may elect, within sixty (60) days after incurring a One Year Break in Service, subject to approval by the Plan Administrator, to receive the entire balance in his Employee Accounts.

(e) Optional Rule Regarding Frequency of Elections. Notwithstanding any provision of this Section 3.04 to the contrary, the Plan Administrator may adopt a written policy under which Participants who are not under a Suspension Period may make an election to receive amounts under Subsection (b) or (c) more frequently than is otherwise permitted under this Plan. Such policy, if adopted, shall be applied uniformly to all Participants.

3.05 Section 415 Limitations. Notwithstanding any provisions contained herein to the contrary, the Annual Addition for any Plan Year with respect to a Participant, under this Plan and under any other Defined Contribution Plan maintained by the Employer, shall not exceed the lesser of (i) twenty-five percent (25%) of the Participant's Basic Compensation for the Plan Year or (ii) $36,875 (or such amount as may be increased by regulations promulgated by the Secretary of the Treasury from time to time). Also, if an Employee is a Participant in this Plan and one or more Defined Benefit Plans maintained by the Employer, the sum of his Defined Benefit Plan Fraction and his Defined Contribution Plan Fraction shall not exceed 1.4 for any Plan Year. For purposes of this Section 3.05 and Section 3.06, the term Employer shall include any other employer required to be aggregated under Code Section 415(h) and the term Basic Compensation shall include Basic Compensation from any such other employer.

(ERISA Transitional Language)

[If an Employee was a Participant on or before September 2, 1974, in this Plan and a Defined Benefit Plan maintained by the Employer, the sum of his Defined Benefit Plan Fraction and Defined Contribution Plan Fraction for the year which includes September 2, 1974, may be in excess of 1.4 if (i) the Defined Benefit Plan Fraction is not increased by an amendment to the Defined Benefit Plan or otherwise after September 2, 1974; and (ii) contributions are not made to this Plan after September 2, 1974.]

3.06 Correction of Contributions in Excess of Section 415 Limits. In the event that, as of any Valuation Date, corrective adjustments in any Participant's Profit Sharing Account or Employee Accounts are required to comply with Section 3.05, the Annual Addition to his Profit Sharing Account and Employee Accounts shall be reduced by corrective adjustments made in the following order of precedence:

(a) Return to the Participant that portion, or all, of his Employee Contributions under Section 3.04 required to insure compliance with Section 3.05;

(b) Forfeiture of that portion, or all, of the Employer Contributions under Section 3.01 and forfeitures allocated under Section 4.02(c) required to insure compliance with Section 3.05.

Any amounts forfeited under Section 3.06(b) shall be held in a suspense account and shall be applied, subject to Section 3.05, toward funding the Employer Contributions for the next succeeding Plan Year; and, such application shall be made prior to any Employer Contributions and prior to any Employer Contributions that would constitute Annual Additions. No income or investment gains and losses shall be allocated to the suspense account provided for under this Section 3.06. If any amount remains in a suspense account provided for under this Section 3.06 upon termination of this Plan, such amount will revert to the Employer notwithstanding any other provision of this Plan.

3.07 Correction of Prior Incorrect Allocations and Previous Funding Deficiencies. Notwithstanding any provisions contained herein to the contrary, in the event that, as of any Valuation Date, adjustments in any Participant's Profit Sharing Account or Employee Accounts are required to correct any incorrect allocation of contributions, investment earnings or losses, or forfeitures, or any funding deficiency which may have occurred in a previous year, the Plan Administrator is authorized to apply, as necessary and proper, the Employer Contributions, Employee Contributions, and amounts forfeited under Section 5.06 for the Plan Year ending on such Valuation Date to correct such incorrect allocation or funding deficiency and to increase such Participant's Profit Sharing Account and/or Employee Accounts to the value which would have existed on said Valuations Date had there been no prior incorrect allocation or funding deficiency. The Plan Administrator is also authorized to take such other actions as he deems necessary to correct prior incorrect allocations or funding deficiencies.

ARTICLE IV

ALLOCATIONS AND ACCOUNTS OF PARTICIPANTS

4.01 Valuations. As of each Valuation Date, the Trustee shall determine the fair market value of the Trust Fund, and the Plan Administrator shall determine the fair market value of the Profit Sharing Account and Employee Accounts of each Participant. The value of the Profit Sharing Account and Employee Contributions Accounts of Participants as of any Valuation Date shall be equal to the value of such Accounts as of the last Valuation Date, plus or minus the applicable adjustments contained in Section 4.02. The value of the Directed Investment Employee Contributions Account of any Participant as of any Valuation Date shall be equal to the fair market value of the assets in such Account on such Valuation Date less any amount owed by such Account for administrative expenses allocable thereto.

4.02 Allocations. As of each Valuation Date, the Profit Sharing Account and Employee Contributions Account of each Participant shall be adjusted in the manner provided in this Section.

(a)(1) Earnings or Losses. The investment earnings (or losses, if the computation specified in this sentence results in a negative figure) of the Trust Fund shall be equal to (A) the fair market value of the Trust Fund (excluding amounts held in separate accounts pursuant to Section 5.09, or held in Directed Investment Employee Contributions Accounts, excluding any earmarked investments of any Profit Sharing Accounts, and excluding the value of any insurance contracts) as of the current Valuation Date; less (B) the fair market value of the Trust Fund (excluding amounts held in separate accounts pursuant to Section 5.09 or held in Directed Investment Employee Contributions Accounts, excluding any earmarked investments of any Profit Sharing Accounts, and excluding the value of any insurance contracts) as of the immediately preceding Valuation Date; plus (C) benefit payments to Participants (excluding payments from separate accounts established under Section 5.09 or from Directed Investment Employee Contributions Accounts), amounts placed in separate accounts pursuant to Section 5.09, or transferred from an Employee Contributions Account to a Directed Investment Employee Contributions Account, any amounts in a Profit Sharing Account that were transferred during the Valuation Plan Year as a segregated earmarked investment and any other disbursements from a Profit Sharing Account or Employee Contributions Account on behalf of a particular Participant since the last preceding Valuation Date; less (D) any Employer Contributions made to the Trust Fund, any Employee Contributions made to an Employee Contributions Account, any transfers from a Directed Investment Employee Contributions Account to an Employee Contributions Account since the last preceding Valuation Date, and any amounts in a Profit Sharing Account that were transferred during the Valuation Plan Year from a segregated earmarked account to the assets of the Trust Fund that are subject to investment by the Trustee. Investment earnings shall be allocated to the Profit Sharing Account and to the Employee Contributions Account of each Active Participant, and each Former Participant for whom a separate account has not been established under Section 5.09 prior to the first day of the Plan Year ending with the Valuation Date in question, and each Retired or Disabled Participant who has not elected pursuant to Section 5.01, 5.02, 5.03, or 5.05 to take his Profit Sharing Account and Employee Accounts as of the Valuation Date immediately preceding his date of retirement or the date on which he is determined to be Totally and Permanently Disabled and for whom a separate account has not been established under Section 5.09 prior to the first day of the Plan Year ending with the Valuation Date in question.

(a)(2) <u>Allocation of Earnings or Losses.</u>

(A) The amount of earnings or losses determined under Subsection (a)(1) above shall be allocated to the Profit Sharing Accounts and Employee Contributions Accounts in the manner provided in this Subsection (a)(2). For purposes of this Subsection, the term Participant shall mean only those individuals identified in Subsection (a)(1) of this Section 4.02 as entitled to share in earnings or losses.

(B) The allocation method described in Subsection (C) below shall apply for the first Valuation Date, and for all succeeding Valuation Dates unless the Plan Administrator provides written notice to all Participants having Profit Sharing Accounts or Employee Contributution Accounts that the allocation method provided for in Subsection (D) shall apply. Such written notice must be provided on or before the date on which the Summary Plan Description is initially furnished to Participants, or if later, at any time prior to the first Plan Year to which the allocation method described in Subsection (D) is to apply. With respect to Plan Years following the Plan Year commencing with the Effective Date, the Plan Administrator may change the allocation method from the method described in Subsection (C) to the method described in Subsection (D) or from the method described in Subsection (D) to the method described in Subsection (C), but only if the Plan Administrator provides written notice of such change to all Participants prior to the commencement of the first Plan Year for which the change shall apply.

(C) Under this Subsection (C), investment earnings and losses shall be allocated to each Participant, other than Participants for whom separate accounts have been established under Section 5.09 prior to the Valuation Date in question, in the ratio that the value of each Profit Sharing Account and each Employee Contributions Account of each such Participant as of the last preceding Valuation Date, minus any amount paid, segretated, or disbursed to or on behalf of the Participant under Subsection (a)(1)(C) above, since the last preceding Valuation Date, bears to the total value of the Profit Sharing Accounts of all such Participants as of the last preceding Valuation Date, minus the amounts paid, segregated, or disbursed to or on behalf of all such Participants under Subsection (a)(1)(C) above, since the last preceding Valuation Date[; provided, however, that for the first Valuation Date following the Effective Date the allocation of earnings or losses under this Subsection (C) shall be made in the same proportion that Employer Contributions or Employee Contributions allocated to each such Profit Sharing Account or Employee Contributions Account as of such first Valuation Date bears to the value of all Employer Contributions and Employee Contributions in all such accounts as of such first Valuation Date.] (Use option for new plans only.) Any Participant may request the Plan Administrator to make a Special Valuation under Section 4.04 in order to avoid prejudice to his Accounts that might otherwise occur as a result of the application of this Subsection (a)(2)(C) to such Participant's Accounts. The cost of making such Special Valuation shall be charged to the Accounts of the Participant requesting such Special Valuation. Approval of a request for s Special Valuation is subject to the discretion of the Plan Administrator and the Plan Administrator shall exercise his discretion on a non-discriminatory basis. For purposes of this Subsection (C), the value of any insurance contract shall be excluded in determining the value of any Account.

(D) Under this Subsection (D), the allocation of investment earnings or losses as of each Valuation Date shall be made on a month to month, time-weighted basis for each Participant's Profit Sharing Account and Employee Contributions Account. The Trustee shall uniformly and consistently apply procedures under which any amount transferred to or withdrawn from an Account on or prior to the fifteenth (15th) day of a calendar month shall be treated as transferred or withdrawn on the first day of the month. The Trustee shall uniformly and consistently apply procedures under which any amount transferred to or withdrawn from an Account after the fifteenth (15th) day of a calendar month shall be treated as transferred or withdrawn on the first day of the next succeeding calendar month. Amounts transferred to an Account under this Subparagraph (d) shall include Employee Contributions, Rollover Contributions, Employer Contributions, Forfeitures and amounts transferred to the Trust Fund that were earmarked or were held in Directed Investment Employee Contributions Accounts. Amounts withdrawn from an Account under this Subparagraph (D) shall include benefit payments, withdrawals, transfers to a separate account under Section 5.09, transfers to a Directed Investment Employee Contributions Account and transfers to a segregated earmarked investment. Uniform and consistent rules shall be applied in determining when a transfer or withdrawal to or from an Account occurs.

557

(b) Employer Contributions. The Profit Sharing Account of each Active Participant, and of each Retired or Disabled Participant who has not elected pursuant to Section 5.01, 5.02, 5.03, or 5.05 to take his Profit Sharing Account as of the Valuation Date immediately preceding his date of retirement or the date on which he is determined to be Totally and Permanently Disabled, who completes more than five hundred (500) Hours of Service during the Plan Year ending with the Valuation Date in question, and for whom a separate account has not been established under Section 5.09 as of the Valuation Date in question, shall be increased by any allocation of the Employer Contributions set forth in Section 3.03 hereof.

(c) Forfeitures. The aggregate value of Profit Sharing Accounts or portions thereof forfeited under Section 5.06 since the previous Valuation Date shall be allocated among the Profit Sharing Accounts of Active Participants, and of Retired and Disabled Participants who have not elected pursuant to Section 5.01, 5.02, 5.03, or 5.05 to take their Profit Sharing Accounts and Employee Accounts as of the Valuation Date immediately preceding their dates of retirement or the dates on which they are determined to be Totally and Permanently Disabled, who complete more than five hundred (500) Hours of Service during the Plan Year ending with the Valuation Date in question, and for whom separate accounts have not been established under Section 5.09 as of the Valuation Date in question, in the same proportion as the Employer Contributions, as set forth in Section 3.03 hereof.

(d) Employee Contributions. The Employee Contributions Account and/or Directed Investment Employee Contributions Account, as specified by the Participant, shall be increased by the amount of his Employee Contributions, if any, made pursuant to Section 3.04 since the immediately preceding Valuation Date. If the allocation method described in Section 4.02(a)(2)(D) is in effect for the Plan Year, Employee Contributions made pursuant to Section 3.04 since the immediately preceding Valuation Date shall be entitled to an allocable share of earnings and losses for the Plan Year, as determined under Section 4.02(a)(2)(D). If the allocation method described in Section 4.02(a)(2)(C) is in effect for the Plan Year, no allocation of earnings or losses for the Plan Year shall be made with respect to any Employee Contributions made pursuant to Section 3.04 since the immediately preceding Valuation Date, but Employee Contributions made on or before the immediately preceding Valuation Date and not withdrawn prior to the Valuation Date in question shall be entitled to an allocable share of earnings or losses for the Plan Year, as determined under Section 4.02(a)(2)(C).

4.03 Determinations of Value. In determining the value of the Trust Fund, the Profit Sharing Accounts, and the Employee Accounts, the Trustee and the Plan Administrator shall exercise their best judgment, and all such determinations of value shall be binding upon all Participants and their Beneficiaries. All allocations shall be deemed to have been made as of the Valuation Date, regardless of when actual allocations were made.

4.04 Special Valuations. Notwithstanding anything to the contrary expressed or implied herein, the Plan Administrator (with the consent of the Trustee) may direct on a non-discriminatory basis a special valuation date in order to avoid prejudice either to continuing Participants or to terminating Participants. Such special valuation date shall be deemed equivalent to a regular valuation date, except that the allocations under Section 4.02(b) and (c) shall not be made.

4.05 _Separate Allocations for Each Affiliate._ In the event that affiliated or subsidiary corporations become signatory hereto, completely independent records, allocations, and contributions shall be maintained for each corporation. The Trustee may invest all funds in Profit Sharing Accounts and Employee Contribution Accounts without segregating assets between or among signatory Employers. Separate Profit Sharing Accounts and Employee Accounts shall be established by each Employer for each Participant employed by any such Employer. Forfeitures arising with respect to one Employer's Former or Terminated Participants shall be allocated only among the Profit Sharing Accounts of that Employer's Participants and shall not be allocated throughout the affiliated group of Employers.

ARTICLE V

PAYMENTS OF BENEFITS TO PARTICIPANTS

5.01 _Normal Retirement._ When a Participant reaches his Normal Retirement Date and retires, he shall become entitled to the full value of his Profit Sharing Account and Employee Accounts (a) as of the Valuation Date immediately preceding his Normal Retirement Date, appropriately adjusted to take into account his Employee Contributions and any payments or distributions to or for him since such Valuation Date, or (b) as of the Valuation Date coincident with or immediately following his Normal Retirement Date, whichever he elects on or before his Normal Retirement Date. Any election by a Participant to take his Profit Sharing Account and Employee Accounts as of the Valuation Date immediately preceding his Normal Retirement Date shall make such Participant ineligible to receive further allocations of Employer Contributions, forfeitures, and earnings or losses unless he is subsquently re-employed by the Employer. Any election by a Participant to take his Profit Sharing Account and Employee Accounts as of the Valuation Date coincident with or immediately following his Normal Retirement Date shall entitle such Participant, for the Plan Year during which he retires, to: (1) an allocable share of earnings or losses and (2) an allocable share of Employer Contributions and forfeitures if he completes more than five hundred (500) Hours of Service during such Plan Year; but the distribution to such Participant shall not commence during the Plan Year in which he retires. A failure on the part of the Participant to make any election on or before his Normal Retirement Date shall be deemed to constitute an election to take the full value of his Profit Sharing Account and Employee Accounts as of the Valuation Date coincident with or immediately following his Normal Retirement Date.

5.02 _Late Retirement._ In the event that a Participant continues as an Employee of the Employer following his Normal Retirement Date in accordance with the Employer's employment practices or in accordance with the applicable law, such Participant shall continue to be an Active Participant under the Plan until his retirement and, upon his retirement, he shall become entitled to the full value of his Profit Sharing Account and Employee Accounts (a) as of the Valuation Date immediately preceding his date of retirement, appropriately adjusted to take into account his Employee Contributions and any payments or distributions to or for him since such Valuation Date, or (b) as of the Valuation Date coincident with or immediately following his date of retirement, whichever he elects on or before his date of retirement. Any election by a Participant to take his Profit Sharing Account and Employee Accounts as of the Valuation Date immediately preceding his date of retirement shall make such Participant ineligible to receive further allocations of Employer Contributions, forfeitures, and earnings or losses unless he is subsequently re-employed by the Employer. Any election by a Participant to take his Profit Sharing Account and Employee Accounts as of the Valuation Date coincident with or immediately following his date of retirement shall entitle such Participant, for the Plan Year during which he retires, to: (1) an allocable share of earnings or losses and (2) an allocable share of Employer Contributions and forfeitures if he completes more than five hundred (500) Hours of Service during such Plan Year; but the distribution to such Participant shall not commence during the Plan Year in which he retires. A failure on the part of the Participant to make any election on or before his date of retirement shall be deemed to constitute an election to take the full value of his Profit Sharing Account and Employee Accounts as of the Valuation Date coincident with or immediately following his date of retirement.

5.03 Early Retirement. When a Participant retires on or after his Early Retirement Date but before his Normal Retirement Date, he shall become entitled to the full value of his Profit Sharing Account and Employee Accounts (a) as of the Valuation Date immediately preceding his retirement, appropriately adjusted to take into account his Employee Contributions and any payments or distributions to or for him since such Valuation Date, or (b) as of the Valuation Date coincident with or immediately following his retirement, whichever he elects on or before the date of his retirement. Any election by a Participant to take his Profit Sharing Account and Employee Accounts as of the Valuation Date immediately preceding his date of retirement shall make such Participant ineligible to receive further allocations of Employer Contributions, forfeitures, and earnings or losses unless he is subsequently re-employed by the Employer. Any election by a Participant to take his Profit Sharing Account and Employee Accounts as of the Valuation Date coincident with or immediately following his date of retirement shall entitle such Participant, for the Plan Year during which he retires, to: (1) an allocable share of earnings or losses and (2) to an allocable share of Employer Contributions and forfeitures if he completes more than five hundred (500) Hours of Service during such Plan Year; but the distribution to such Participant shall not commence during the Plan Year in which he retires. A failure on the part of the Participant to make any election on or before his date of retirement shall be deemed to constitute an election to take the full value of his Profit Sharing Account and Employee Accounts as of the Valuation Date coincident with or immediately following his date of retirement.

5.04 Death Benefit. If a Participant dies while an Active Participant under the Plan, his Beneficiary or Beneficiaries shall be entitled to the full value of his Profit Sharing Account and Employee Accounts (a) as of the Valuation Date immediately preceding his date of death, appropriately adjusted to take into account his Employee Contributions and any payments or distributions to or for him since such Valuation Date, or (b) as of the Valuation Date coincident with or immediately following his date of death, whichever his Beneficiary or Beneficiaries unanimously elect within sixty (60) days following the date of death. If the Beneficiary or Beneficiaries fail to unanimously elect option (a) within the sixty (60) day election period such Beneficiary or Beneficiaries shall be deemed to have elected option (b). If the Beneficiary or Beneficiaries unanimously elect option (a) such Profit Sharing Account and Employee Accounts shall be ineligible to receive, further allocations of Employer Contributions, forfeitures, or earnings or losses. If such Beneficiary or Beneficiaries elect or are deemed to elect option (b), the deceased Participant shall for all purposes be regarded as an Active Participant as of the Valuation Date coincident with or immediately following his date of death and shall be entitled to: (1) an allocable share of earnings or losses as of such Valuation Date and (2) an allocable share of Employer Contributions and forfeitures as of such Valuation Date if the deceased Participant completed more than five hundred (500) Hours of Service during the Plan Year in which the death occurs; but the distribution with respect to such deceased Participant shall not commence during the Plan Year in which he dies.

5.05 Disability. When it is determined that a Participant is Totally and Permanently Disabled, the Plan Administrator shall certify such fact to the Trustee, and such Disabled Participant shall be entitled to receive the full value of his Profit Sharing Account and Employee Accounts (a) as of the Valuation Date immediately preceding the date the Plan Administrator determines he became Totally and Permanently Disabled, appropriately adjusted to take into account Employee Contributions and any payments or distributions to or for him since such Valuation Date, or (b) as of the Valuation Date coincident with or immediately following the date the Plan Administrator determines he became Totally and Permanently Disabled, whichever the Participant or his legal representative elects not later than the thirtieth (30th) day following the Plan Administrator's determination of Total and Permanent Disability. Any election by a Participant or his legal represenatative to take his Profit Sharing Account and Employee Accounts as of the Valuation Date immediately preceding the effective date of the Plan Administrator's determination shall make such Participant ineligible to receive further allocations of Employer Contributions, forfeitures, and earnings or losses unless he is subsequently re-employed by the Employer. Any election by a Participant or his legal representative to take his Profit Sharing Account and Employee Accounts as of the Valuation Date coincident with or immediately following the date of the Plan Administrator's determination shall entitle such Participant, for the Plan Year during which the determination is made, to: (1) an allocable share of earnings or losses and (2) an allocable share of Employer Contributions and forfeitures if he completes more than five hundred (500) Hours of Service during such Plan Year; but the distribution to such Participant or legal representative shall not commence during the Plan Year in which the determination is made. A failure on the part of the Participant or his legal representative to make any election on or before the thirtieth (30th) day following the Plan

Administrator's determination of Total and Permanent Disability shall be deemed to constitute an election to take the full value of his Profit Sharing Account and Employee Accounts as of the Valuation Date coincident with or immediately following the effective date of the Plan Administrator's determination.

5.06 _Termination._ Whenever the employment of a Participant is terminated for reasons other than normal, early or late actual retirement under Sections 5.01, 5.02, or 5.03 hereof, death under Section 5.04, or Total and Permanent Disability under Section 5.05, and as a result of such termination said Participant incurs a One Year Break in Service, he shall become entitled to the following:

(a) _Filing of Claim._ Upon incurring a One Year Break in Service, the Participant may file a written claim for benefits with the Plan Administrator requesting distribution of the nonforfeitable percentage of his Profit Sharing Account and of his Employee Accounts determined as of the Valuation Date coincident with the completion of his One Year Break in Service. Alternatively, such Participant may elect to defer receipt of the nonforfeitable percentage of his Profit Sharing Account and his Employee Accounts determined as of the Valuation Date coincident with the completion of his One Year Break in Service. If the Participant makes such an election to defer receipt (or fails to file a claim for benefits within a reasonable period of time after incurring a One Year Break in Service), or if the Plan Administrator does not approve an election to receive benefits upon termination, the nonforfeitable percentage of his Profit Sharing Account and his Employee Accounts, determined as of the Valuation Date coincident with the completion of his One Year Break In Service, shall be segregated and held in a separate account in accordance with Section 5.09. For purposes of this Section, the Participant's nonforfeitable percentage of his Profit Sharing Account shall be based upon the Former or Terminated Participant's total number of completed Years of Service, computed without regard to any Years of Service completed after the One Year Break in Service. Such nonforfeitable percentage shall be determined from the following schedule:

Completed Years of Service	Nonforfeitable Percentage	Forfeitable Percentage

That portion of the Profit Sharing Account to which the Former or Terminated Participant is not entitled shall be segregated and reallocated in accordance with Section 4.02(c).

(b) _Review of Claim._ The Plan Administrator shall review any claim for benefits filed in accordance with Subsection (a) and shall, in its discretion (which shall be exercised in a uniform and non-discriminatory manner), either authorize an immediate commencement of distribution in accordance with Section 5.07 or shall direct that the nonforfeitable percentage of the Participant's Profit Sharing Account and his Employee Accounts shall be segregated and held as a separate account in accordance with Section 5.09.

(c) Treatment of Separate Accounts. If, under Subsection (a), the Participant elects or is deemed to elect deferred receipt of the nonforfeitable percentage of his Profit Sharing Account and Employee Accounts determined as of the Valuation Date coincident with the completion of his One Year Break in Service, or if under Subsection (b) the Plan Administrator directs that such amount be held in a separate account in accordance with Section 5.09, the Participant, upon filing a written claim, shall be entitled to the then balance of such separate account (which shall be distributed in the manner elected under Section 5.07) as of his Normal Retirement Date or as of his Early Retirement Date if he had completed at least ten (10) Years of Service before incurring a One Year Break in Service.

(d) Mandatory Distribution. Irrespective of whether the Participant files a written claim, or elects to defer receipt under Subsection (a), the Plan Administrator, in its discretion, may direct payments in a lump sum to such Participant if such Participant incurs a One Year Break in Service and if the vested portion of his Profit Sharing Account does not then exceed $1,750.00.

5.07 Method of Payment. Subject to the provisions of Sections 5.08 and 5.11, a Participant separating from service in accordance with Section 5.01, 5.02, 5.03, 5.05, or 5.06, or his Beneficiary in the event of the Participant's death, shall request a manner and time for commencement of distribution of any benefits under the Plan as provided hereinafter. The request by the Participant or the Beneficiary shall be in writing and shall be filed with the Plan Administrator at least thirty (30) days before distribution is to be made and shall be subject to approval by the Plan Administrator. Upon the approval of the Plan Administrator, one of the following alternative forms of distribution of the Participant's Profit Sharing Account and Employee Accounts shall be selected by the Participant or Beneficiary:

(a) A lump-sum distribution in cash or in kind, provided that no "in kind" distribution may be made of a life annuity;

(b) Periodic installments (either monthly or annually) for a period not to exceed ten (10) years; or

(c) Any combination of the above.

Notwithstanding the foregoing, if the Participant is the person making the election, he shall not elect installments extending beyond either the life expectancy of the Participant or the joint life expectancies of the Participant and his spouse, if any.

In the absence of an election by the Beneficiary within nine (9) months following a Participant's death the Beneficiary, or all of the Beneficiaries collectively, shall be deemed to have elected monthly installments for a period of four (4) years.

5.08 Commencement of Benefits. Any payment of benefits to the Participant shall begin not later than sixty (60) days after the last day of the Plan Year in which the *latest* of (a), (b), or (c) occurs:

(a) The Participant's Normal Retirement Date;

(b) The tenth (10th) anniversary of the date the Employee became a Participant;

(c) The Participant's separation from service.

Under no circumstances, however, shall any benefits be paid until a written claim therefor is filed with the Plan Administrator.

5.09 <u>Separate Accounts</u>. As soon as practical after the amount that is distributable to a Former, Retired, or Disabled Participant or to the Beneficiary of a deceased Participant is finally determined, if his distribution will either be paid in installments or be delayed more than six (6) months if payable in a lump sum, his Profit Sharing Account and Employee Accounts shall be segregated from other Trust Fund assets and invested in a separate account. The investment of such separate account shall be in such federally insured savings accounts as are determined by the Trustee, [including savings accounts maintained by the Trustee,] with all interest earned on such investments credited to such accounts and all disbursements charged thereto. Such accounts may be held in cash, but only for a limited period between investments, or as a reserve to meet installment distributions. In the event of the death of a Participant to whom periodic installments are being paid, or are due to be so paid, prior to receipt of the full interest in such account, the remaining balance of such separate account shall be paid in installments to the Beneficiary or Contingent Beneficiary in accordance with the schedule elected by the Participant under Section 5.07

(Section 5.10 is drafted pursuant to Georgia Law; it may vary from state to state.)

5.10 <u>Beneficiaries</u>. If, at the time of a Participant's death while benefits are still outstanding, his named Beneficiary does not survive him, the benefits shall be paid to his named Contingent Beneficiary in accordance with the terms of Section 5.07. If a deceased Participant is not survived by either a named Beneficiary or Contingent Beneficiary (or if no Beneficiary or Contingent Beneficiary was effectively named), the benefits shall be paid, in the discretion of the Plan Administrator, in a lump sum to the person or persons or in periodic installments, as provided in Section 5.07, to the person or persons in the first of the following classes of beneficiaries with one or more members of such class then surviving: the Participant's (a) widow or widower, (b) children, (c) parents, (d) brothers and sisters, or (e) executors and administrators. If the Beneficiary or Contingent Beneficiary is living at the death of the Participant, but such person dies prior to receiving the entire death benefit, the remaining portion of such death benefit shall be paid in a single sum to the estate of such deceased Beneficiary or Contingent Beneficiary.

5.11 <u>Cash-Out Procedure upon Discharge or Resignation</u>. If the Participant, on or before the date of his termination of employment by reason of discharge or resignation or within a reasonable period of time thereafter (but not later than the Valuation Date for the Plan Year during which such termination occurs), requests in writing that the Plan Administrator distribute to him the vested portion of his Profit Sharing Account and his Employee Accounts, the Plan Administrator may, in its sole discretion, direct the Trustee to pay such amount to the Participant within sixty (60) days following his request, notwithstanding that the Participant shall not then have incurred a One Year Break in Service. The Participant's Profit Sharing Account and Employee Accounts shall be determined as of the Valuation Date immediately preceding the date of his termination, and such Participant's vested interest shall be determined as of his date of termination. Once the Plan Administrator issues the directive for the Trustee to pay the Participant, the cash-out shall be deemed to be in process or pending. The nonvested portion of a Participant's Profit Sharing Account that is not distributed to him at the time of the cash-out shall be forfeited if the Participant does not effect a buy-back in accordance with Section 5.12, and such forfeited amount will be reallocated in accordance with Section 4.02(c). Such reallocation shall be made on the Valuation Date coincident with the Participant's incurring a One Year Break in Service, or, if the Participant does not incur a One Year Break in Service, but fails to repay the cash-out as provided in Section 5.12 hereof within two years of his reemployment date, such reallocation shall be made on the Valuation Date coincident with or immediately following the second anniversary of such reemployment. No earnings or losses shall be allocated to the amount that is returned to the Participant's Profit Sharing Account under Section 5.12 or reallocated as a forfeiture under the immediately preceding sentence. Absent a buy-back by the Participant under Section 5.12, the actual payment of benefits under this Section 5.11 shall satisfy all obligations of the Trust to such Participant, and such Participant shall be entitled to no allocations of Employer Contributions, forfeitures, or earnings or losses as of the Valuation Date coincident with or immediately following his termination of employment, absent a buy-back prior to such Valuation Date, even though the cashed-out Participant resumes his employment with the Employer on or before such Valuation Date.

5.12 Buy-Back Procedure. A Terminated Participant who has received a cash-out of benefits pursuant to Section 5.11, and who returns to the employ of the Employer before a One Year Break in Service has occurred, shall be permitted to repay the cash-out amount to the Trust Fund within two (2) years following the date of his return, and thereby restore his benefits under the Plan determined as of the Valuation Date immediately preceding the actual payment of the cash-out.

5.13 Reemployment After One Year Break in Service.

(a) A Former or Terminated Participant who is reemployed after incurring a One Year Break in Service shall not be entitled to receive credit for vesting purposes for Years of Service earned prior to the One Year Break in Service except as follows:

(1) If he had a non-forfeitable right to all or a portion of his account balance derived from Employer Contributions at the time of his termination of employment, he shall receive credit for Years of Service earned prior to his One Year Break in Service upon his completion of a Year of Service following the date of his reemployment; or

(2) If he did not have a non-forfeitable right to all or any portion of his account derived from Employer Contributions at the time of his termination of employment, he shall receive credit for Years of Service earned prior to his One Year Break in Service if (i) he completes a Year of Service after his re-employment, and (ii) at the time he completes such Year of Service his number of consecutive One Year Breaks in Service is less than

his aggregate Years of Service earned before his initial One Year Break in Service.

(b) All Years of Service earned after a One Year Break in Service shall be disregarded in determining a Participant's non-forfeitable percentage in his Profit Sharing Account balance attributable to Employer Contributions prior to the One Year Break in Service.

5.14 Special Rule for Directed Investment Employee Contributions Accounts. Notwithstanding any other provision of this Plan to the contrary, the amount in a Directed Investment Employee Contributions Account that is available for distribution shall be the value of such account on the date on which the distribution is made, less any amount owned by such Account for administrative expenses allocable thereto.

[5.15 Loans to Participants. The Plan Administrator may, in its sole discretion, direct the Trustee to make a loan or loans from the Trust Fund to any Participant to relieve unusual financial hardship, such as, but not limited to, the illness of a Participant or a member of a Participant's immediate family, or for the purpose of establishing or preserving the home in which a Participant resides, or for the purpose of education of children, in a total amount not in excess of the value [of the vested portion] of such Participant's Profit Sharing Account. The Plan Administrator shall adopt and follow uniform and non-discriminatory rules for repayment of such loans in a period certain at the prevailing rate of interest being charged by [the Trustee]. [commercial banks in _____.] The Plan Administrator shall direct the Trustee to obtain from the Participant such note and security as it may require. Notwithstanding the provisions of Section 10.09, in the event of failure to repay the principal or interest according to its terms, or should the Participant's employment terminate prior to full repayment thereof, in addition to any other remedy provided in the loan instruments or by law, the Plan Administrator may direct the Trustee to charge against the vested portion of his Profit Sharing Account which secures the loan the amount required to fully repay the loan. No distribution shall be made to any Participant, unless and until all unpaid loans to such Participant have either been paid in full or deducted from the Profit Sharing Account of the Participant. This Section authorizes only the making of bona fide loans and not distributions, and before resort is made against the vested portion of a Participant's Profit Sharing Account for his failure to repay any loan, such other reasonable efforts to collect the same shall be made by the Plan Administrator as it deems reasonable and practical under the circumstances. [All loans made under this Section shall be considered investments of the Trust Fund unless the Trust Agreement specifically permits, and a Participant so directs, that the loans be earmarked investments of his Account.] Under no circumstances, however, shall an unpaid loan be charged against a Participant's vested interest so long as he remains employed by the Employer.]

ARTICLE VI

CLAIMS PROCEDURE

6.01 Filing of Claim. A Plan Participant or Beneficiary shall make a claim for Plan benefits by filing a written request with the Plan Administrator upon a form to be furnished to him for such purpose.

6.02 _Denial of Claim._ If a claim is wholly or partially denied, the Plan Administrator shall furnish the Participant or Beneficiary with written notice of the denial within sixty (60) days of the date the original claim was filed. This notice of denial shall provide (1) the reason for denial, (2) specific reference to pertinent Plan provisions on which the denial is based, (3) a description of any additional information needed to perfect the claim and an explanation of why such information is necessary, and (4) an explanation of the Plan's claim procedure.

6.03 _Review of Denial._ The Participant or Beneficiary shall have sixty (60) days from receipt of denial notice in which to make written application for review by the Plan Administrator. The Participant or Beneficiary may request that the review be in the nature of a hearing. The Participant or Beneficiary shall have the rights (1) to representation, (2) to review pertinent documents, and (3) to submit comments in writing.

6.04 _Decision upon Review._ The Plan Administrator shall issue a decision on such review within sixty (60) days after receipt of an application for review as provided in Section 6.03.

(Options Drafted for Employer or Individual to Serve as
Plan Administrator—Must Redraft for a Committee)

ARTICLE VII

THE PLAN ADMINISTRATOR

7.01 _Designation._ [The Plan Administrator shall be the Employer. The Plan Administrator shall keep a permanent record of its actions with respect to the Plan which shall be available for inspection by appropriate parties as provided in the Code and ERISA.]

[The Board of Directors of the Employer shall name one of its members or an officer of the Employer, to be known as the Plan Administrator, to administer the Plan, keep records of individual Participant benefits, and notify the Participants of the amount of their benefits annually.

The original Plan Administrator shall be _____. The Plan Administrator shall serve until his resignation or dismissal by the Board of Directors of the Employer and a vacancy shall be filled in the same manner as the original appointment. No compensation shall be paid the Plan Administrator from the Trust Fund for his services. The Plan Administrator shall keep a permanent record of his actions with respect to the Plan which shall be available for inspection by appropriate parties as provided in the Code and ERISA.]

7.02 _Responsibilities in General._ Subject to the limitations of the Plan, the Plan Administrator shall from time to time establish rules for the administration of the Plan and transaction of its business. The records of the Employer, as certified to the Plan Administrator, shall be conclusive with respect to any and all factual matters dealing with the employment of a Participant. The Plan Administrator shall interpret the Plan and shall determine all questions arising in the administration, interpretation, and application of the Plan, and all such determinations by the Plan Administrator shall be conclusive and binding on all persons, subject, however, to the provisions of the Code and ERISA.

7.03 Payment Orders. The Plan Administrator shall direct the Trustee in writing to make payments from the Trust Fund to Participants who qualify for such payments hereunder. Such written order to the Trustee shall specify the name of the Participant, his Social Security number, his address, and the amount and frequency of such payments.

7.04 No Discrimination. The Plan Administrator shall not take action or direct the Trustee to take any action with respect to any of the benefits provided hereunder or otherwise in pursuance of the powers conferred herein upon the Plan Administrator which would be discriminatory in favor of Participants who are officers, shareholders, or highly compensated employees, or which would result in benefiting one Participant, or group of Participants, at the expense of another or in discrimination between Participants similarly situated or in the application of different rules to substantially similar sets of facts.

7.05 Requests by Trustee for Instructions. The Trustee may request instructions in writing from the Plan Administrator on any matters affecting the Trust and may rely and act thereon.

7.06 Allocations. The Plan Administrator shall be responsible for the determination of Profit Sharing Accounts, and Employee Accounts. The Trustee shall segregate Directed Investment Employee Contributions Accounts but need not segregate Profit Sharing Accounts or Employee Contributions Accounts either among Participants or among employers for investment purposes, except as indicated in Section 5.09.

ARTICLE VIII

THE TRUST FUND AND TRUSTEE

8.01 Existence of Trust. The Employer has entered into a Trust Agreement with the Trustee to hold the funds necessary to provide the benefits set forth in this Plan.

8.02 Exclusive Benefit Rule. The Trust Fund shall be received, held in trust, and disbursed by the Trustee in accordance with the provisions of the Trust Agreement and this Plan. No part of the Trust Fund shall be used for or diverted to purposes other than for the exclusive benefit of Participants, Retired Participants, Disabled Participants, their Beneficiaries, or Contingent Beneficiaries under this Plan , or the payment of reasonable administrative expenses. No person shall have any interest in, or right to, the Trust Fund or any part thereof, except as specifically provided for in this Plan or the Trust Agreement or both.

8.03 Removal of Trustee. The Board of Directors may remove the Trustee at any time upon the notice required by the terms of the Trust Agreement, and upon such removal or upon the resignation of a Trustee, the Board of Directors shall appoint a successor Trustee.

8.04 _Powers of Trustee._ The Trustee shall have such powers to hold, invest, reinvest, or to control and disburse the funds as at that time shall be set forth in the Trust Agreement or this Plan.

8.05 _Integration of Trust._ The Trust Agreement shall be deemed to be a part of this Plan, and all rights of Participants or others under this Plan shall be subject to the provisions of the Trust Agreement.

ARTICLE IX

AMENDMENT AND TERMINATION

9.01 _Right to Amend._ The Employer reserves the right at any time, by action of its Board of Directors, to modify or amend, in whole or in part, any or all of the provisions of the Plan, including specifically the right to make such amendments effective retroactively, if necessary, to bring the Plan into conformity with regulations promulgated under the Code or ERISA which must be complied with so that the Plan and Trust Fund may continue to remain qualified and to preserve the tax-exempt status of the Trust. No modification or amendment shall make it possible for Trust assets to be used for, or diverted to, purposes other than the exclusive benefit of Participants and their Beneficiaries.

9.02 _Right to Terminate._ The Employer may, by action of its Board of Directors, terminate the Plan and the Trust.

9.03 _Vesting upon Termination._ If the Plan is terminated by the Employer or its contributions to the Trust are completely discontinued, the Profit Sharing Accounts of Participants as of the date of termination or complete discontinuance of contributions shall immediately become non-forfeitable.

9.04 _Distributions upon Termination._ If the Plan is terminated, the interest of each Participant shall be distributed in a lump sum or in periodic installments, in cash or in kind (provided that no "in kind" distribution may be made of a life annuity), or shall continue to be held in Trust at the discretion of the Plan Administrator as provided in Article V hereof.

9.05 _Vesting upon Partial Termination._ In the event a partial termination occurs, the accounts of those Participants affected shall become non-forfeitable and shall be held or distributed in accordance with the provisions of Section 5.07.

ARTICLE X

MISCELLANEOUS PROVISIONS

10.01 _Prohibition Against Diversion._ There shall be no diversion of any portion of the assets of the Trust Fund other than for the exclusive benefit of Participants and their Beneficiaries.

10.02 _Prudent Man Rule._ For purpose of Part 4 of Title I of ERISA, the Employer, the Trustee, and the Plan Administrator shall each be Fiduciaries and shall each discharge their respective duties hereunder with the care, skill, prudence, and diligence under the circumstances then prevailing that a prudent man acting in a like capacity and familiar with such matters would use in the conduct of an enterprise of a like character and with like aims. Without limiting the generality of the above, it is specifically provided that the appointment and retention of any parties pursuant to ARTICLE VII of the Plan are "duties" of the Employer for purposes of this Section.

10.03 Responsibilities of Parties. The Employer shall be responsible for the administration and management of the Plan except for those duties specifically allocated to the Trustee or Plan Administrator. The Trustee shall have exclusive responsibility for the management and control of the assets of the Plan except for the investment of assets held in Directed Investment Employee Contributions Accounts. The Plan Administrator shall have exclusive responsibility for all matters specifically delegated to it by the Employer in the Plan. The Employer shall be deemed the Plan Sponsor for all purposes of ERISA.

10.04 Report Furnished Participants. The Plan Administrator shall furnish to each Plan Participant, and to each Beneficiary receiving benefits under the Plan, within the time limits specified in the Code and ERISA, each of the following:

(a) A Summary Plan Description and periodic revisions;

(b) Notification of amendments to the Plan;

(c) A Summary Annual Report which summarizes the Annual Report filed with the Department of Labor.

10.05 Reports Available to Participants. The Plan Administrator shall make copies of the following documents available at the principal office of the Employer for examination by any Plan Participant or Beneficiary:

(a) The Profit Sharing Plan and Trust Agreement; and

(b) The latest annual report.

10.06 Reports upon Request. The Plan Administrator shall furnish to any Plan Participant or Beneficiary who so requests in writing, once during any twelve-month period, a statement indicating, on the basis of the latest available information—

(a) The total benefits accrued; and

(b) The non-forfeitable benefits, if any, which have accrued, or the earliest date on which benefits will become non-forfeitable.

The Plan Administrator shall also furnish to any Plan Participant or Beneficiary who so requests in writing, at a reasonable charge to be prescribed by regulation of the Secretary of Labor, any document referred to in Section 10.05.

10.07 Rollover Contributions and Direct Transfers from Other Qualified Retirement Plans. Notwithstanding any provisions contained herein to the contrary, a Participant shall be entitled:

(a) To transfer (or cause to be transferred directly) to the Trust to be held as part of his Employee Contributions Account or his Directed Investment Employee Contributions Account (i) the redemption proceeds of a retirement bond, (ii) cash and other property received by him in one or more distributions together constituting a qualifying rollover distribution from or under another qualified trust or qualified plan or an employee annuity or custodial account, (iii) an amount paid or distributed out of an individual retirement account or individual retirement annuity or retirement bond consisting of a prior rollover contribution from a qualified trust or annuity plan, (iv) cash or other property representing his account or benefits in another qualified plan or qualified trust, which shall be transferred directly from said plan or trust to the Trust, or (v) any combination of the above;

(b) Upon at least sixty (60) days written notice to the Plan Administrator, and only with the consent of the Plan Administrator, to cause his entire account, to the extent that it has vested, to be transferred on his behalf, in the form of cash or other property (in one or more distributions together constituting a lump sum distribution), directly to a qualified trust or an annuity plan.

Any amount so transferred to or from this Trust is herein called a "Rollover Contribution." Any Rollover Contribution to the Trust, together with the earnings thereon, shall be fully vested.

10.08 Merger or Consolidation of Employer. If the Employer is merged or consolidated with another organization, or another organization acquires all or substantially all of the Employer's assets, such organization may become the Employer hereunder by action of its Board of Directors and by action of the Board of Directors of the prior Employer, if still existent. Such change in Employers shall not be deemed a termination of the Plan by either the predecessor or successor Employer.

10.09 Non-Alienation or Assignment. None of the benefits under the Plan are subject to the claims of creditors of Participants or their Beneficiaries, and will not be subject to attachment, garnishment, or any other legal process whatsoever. Neither a Participant nor his Beneficiaries may assign, sell, borrow on, or otherwise encumber any of his beneficial interest in the Plan and Trust Fund, nor shall any such benefits be in any manner liable for or subject to the deeds, contracts, liabilities, engagements, or torts of any Participant or Beneficiary. If any Participant or Beneficiary shall become bankrupt or attempt to anticipate, sell, alienate, transfer, pledge, assign, encumber or change any benefit specifically provided for herein, or if a court of competent jurisdiction enters an order purporting to subject such interest to the claim of any creditor, then such benefit shall be terminated and the Trustee shall hold or apply such benefit to or for the benefit of such Participant or Beneficiary in such manner as the Plan Administrator, in its sole discretion, may deem proper under the circumstances.

10.10 Plan Continuance Voluntary. Although it is the intention of the Employer that this Plan shall be continued and its contributions made regularly, this Plan is entirely voluntary on the part of the Employer, and the continuance of the Plan and the payments thereunder are not assumed as a contractual obligation of the Employer.

10.11 Suspension of Contributions. The Employer specifically reserves the right, in its sole and uncontrolled discretion, to modify, suspend contributions to the Plan (in whole or in part) at any time or from time to time and for any period or periods, or to discontinue at any time the contributions under this Plan.

10.12 Agreement Not An Employment Contract. This Plan shall not be deemed to constitute a contract between the Employer and any Participant or to be a consideration or an inducement for the employment of any Participant or Employee. Nothing contained in this Plan shall be deemed to give any Participant or Employee the right to be retained in the service of the Employer or to interfere with the right of the Employer to discharge any Participant or Employee at any time regardless of the effect which such discharge shall have upon such individual as a Participant in the Plan.

10.13 Payments to Minors and Others. In making any distribution to or for the benefit of any minor or incompetent Participant or Beneficiary, or any other Participant or Beneficiary who, in the opinion of the Plan Administrator, is incapable of properly using, expending, investing, or otherwise disposing such distribution, then the Plan Administrator, in his sole, absolute, and uncontrolled discretion may, but need not, order the Trustee to make such distribution to a legal or natural guardian or other relative of such minor or court appointed committee of any incompetent, or to any adult with whom such person temporarily or permanently resides; and any such guardian, committee, relative, or other person shall have full authority and discretion to expend such distribution for the use and benefit of such person; and the receipt of such guardian, committee, relative, or other person shall be a complete discharge to the Trustee, without any responsibility on its part or on the part of the Plan Administrator to see to the application thereof.

10.14 Unclaimed Benefits. If any benefits payable to, or on behalf of, a Participant are not claimed within a reasonable period of time from the date of entitlement, as determined by the Plan Administrator, and following a diligent effort to locate such person, the Plan Administrator shall file a Form SSA or any successor form with the annual report for the appropriate Plan Year with respect to such Participant and shall set up a separate account pursuant to Section 5.09 for such Participant. If the Participant or his Beneficiary or Contingent Beneficiary does not file a claim for benefits prior to the Valuation Date of the Plan Year during which such Participant's seventieth (70th) birthday occurs, such Participant shall be presumed dead and the post-death benefits, if any, under this Plan shall be paid to his Beneficiary if he is then living and can be located following a diligent search, or to the person or persons specified under Section 5.10 if the Beneficiary is not then living or cannot be located.

10.15 Governing Law. This Plan shall be administered in the United States of America, and its validity, construction, and all rights hereunder shall be governed by the laws of the United States under ERISA. To the extent that ERISA shall not be held to have preempted local law, the Plan shall be administered under the laws of the State of _____. If any provision of the Plan shall be held invalid or unenforceable, the remaining provisions hereof shall continue to be fully effective.

10.16 Headings No Part of Agreement. Headings of sections and subsections of the Plan are inserted for convenience of reference. They constitute no part of the Plan and are not to be considered in the construction thereof.

10.17 Merger or Consolidation of Plan. This Plan and Trust shall not be merged or consolidated with, nor shall any assets or liabilities be transferred to, any other plan, unless the benefits payable to each Participant if the Plan was terminated immediately after such action would be equal to or greater than the benefits to which such Participant would have been entitled if this Plan had been terminated immediately before such action.

10.18 Amendment of Former Vesting Schedule.

(a) Election of Former Vesting Schedule. In the event the vesting schedule of this Plan is amended [or the vesting schedule of any preceding plan is amended by adoption of this amendment and restatement], any Participant who has completed at least five (5) Years of Service and whose vested interest is at any time adversely affected by such amendment may elect to have his vested interest in Employer Contributions determined without regard to such amendment by notifying the Plan Administrator in writing during the election period as hereinafter defined. The election period shall begin on the date such amendment is adopted and shall end no earlier than the latest of the following dates:

    (i)   The date which is 60 days after the date the amendment is adopted;

    (ii)   The date which is 60 days after the day the Plan amendment becomes effective; or

    (iii)   The date which is 60 days after the day the Participant is issued written notice of the amendment by the Employer or Plan Administrator.

Such election shall be available only to an individual who is a Participant at the time such election is made, and such election shall be irrevocable.

(b) No Divestiture by Reason of Amendment. If the vesting schedule of this Plan is amended [or the vesting schedule of any preceding Plan is amended by adoption of this amendment and restatement] the nonforfeitable percentage of a Participant's Profit Sharing Account not attributable to Employee Contributions (determined as of the later of the date such amendment is adopted or becomes effective) shall be at least the nonforfeitable percentage computed under the Plan as of the later of such dates without regard to the amendment.

10.19 Indemnification. The Employer hereby agrees to indemnify any current or former Employee or member of the Board of Directors of the Employer to the full extent of any expenses, penalties, damages, or other pecuniary loss which such current or former Employee or member of the Board of Directors may suffer as a result of his responsibilities, obligations, or duties in connection with the Plan or fiduciary activities actually performed in connection with the Plan. Such indemnification shall be paid by the Employer to the current or former Employee or member of the Board of Directors to the extent that fiduciary liability insurance is not available to cover the payment of such items, but in no event shall such items be paid out of Plan assets.

Notwithstanding the foregoing, this indemnification agreement shall not relieve any current or former Employee or member of the Board of Directors serving in a fiduciary capacity of his fiduciary responsibilities and liabilities to the Plan for breaches of fiduciary obligations, nor shall this agreement violate any provision of Part 4 of Title I of ERISA as it may be interpreted from time to time by the United States Department of Labor and any courts of competent jurisdiction.

[10.20 Special Provisions Required by Subchapter S Status of Employer. For all Plan Years in which the Employer is an electing small business corporation (a "Subchapter S Corporation"), as defined in sections 1371 through 1379 of the Code, and to the extent necessary to maintain the qualified status of the Plan under section 401(a) of the Code for all Plan Years in which the Employer has ceased to be a Subchapter S Corporation, the following special provisions shall apply, notwithstanding any other provisions of this Plan to the contrary:

(a) Basic Compensation. For purposes of this Plan, the Basic Compensation of each Participant employed by a Subchapter S Corporation shall not exceed $100,000 per year.

(b) Taxability of Contributions. Any Participant who is classified as a "shareholder-employee" ("Shareholder-Employee") within the meaning of section 1379(d) of the Code for any portion of a Plan Year shall include in his gross income, for his taxable year in which or with which the taxable year of the Employer ends, the excess of the amount of contributions paid to the Plan on his behalf which is deductible under section 404(a)(1), (2), or (3) of the Code by the Employer for its taxable year over the lesser of:

(i) 15% of the compensation received or accrued by such Participant from the Employer during its taxable year, or

(ii) $7,500.

As used herein, the term "compensation" means all compensation for personal services actually rendered, except that for which a deduction is allowable under a plan that qualifies under section 401(a) of the Code, including a plan that qualifies under section 404(a)(2) of the Code.

(c) Forfeitures. The Profit Sharing Accounts or portions thereof forfeited under Section 5.06 which are attributable to contributions deducted or deductible under section 404(a)(3) of the Code for any taxable year in which the Employer was a Subchapter S Corporation shall be allocated pursuant to Section 4.02(c) in the following manner:

(i) such forfeitures shall be allocated solely to Participants other than Shareholder-Employees, or

(ii) if there are no such other Participants, such forfeitures shall be repaid to the Employer not later than the 15th day of the third month following the close of the taxable year of the Employer in which such forfeitures arose.

Such forfeitures shall be computed, at the option of the Plan Administrator, under the "Apportionment Method" or the "Direct Tracing Method" described in Proposed Treasury Regulations §1.1379-1(c).]

[10.21 Receipt of Funds From Prior HR-10 Plan. Anything in this Plan to the contrary notwithstanding (except for the provisions of Section 10.17), the Trustee may receive and hold, as a part of the Trust Fund, assets (hereinafter referred to as the "transferred assets," which shall be deemed to include all increments allocable to such transferred assets) transferred directly from the trustee or custodian of any other retirement plan (hereinafter referred to as the "transferor plan") which is qualified under Section 401(a) of the Code, and which benefits one or more owner-employees as that term is defined in Section 401(c)(3) of the Code (hereinafter "owner-employee"). In applying the provisions of this Section 10.21, the following special provisions shall apply:

(a) The transferred assets and all rights to or derived therefrom shall be at the time of the transfer and at all times thereafter fully nonforfeitable and vested in the respective Participants (and in the proportions) to which such transferred assets had been allocated under the transferor plan.

(b) The Trustee shall not be liable or responsible for any acts or omissions in the administration of any transferor plan and the trusts thereunder of any other person or entity who was trustee, custodian or other fiduciary under any prior plan, the Trustee shall be held harmless from such liability or responsibility.

(c) Except as otherwise provided in this Section 10.21, all transferred assets shall be administered and distributed in the same manner as provided under the Plan.

(d) The Trustee shall keep a separate and identifiable fund with respect to the transferred assets (which may be commingled for investment pruposes with other assets of the Trust), designated as "transferred fund", and the separate account within the transferred fund of each Participant shall be adjusted annually in the manner specified in Article IV hereof, treating for this purpose the transferred fund as if it were the entire Trust Fund.

(e) If the transferor plan shall be a plan benefiting one or more owner-employees, the following special provisions shall apply:

(i) No payment shall be made from the transferred fund to any Participant who was an owner-employee under the transferor plan unless he is either disabled or has attained the age of 59½ years. For purposes only of the foregoing sentence "Disability" shall mean inability to engage in any substantial gainful activity by reason of any medically determinable physical or mental impairment which can be expected to result in death or to be of long continued and indefinite duration.

(ii) The entire interest of each Participant must actually be distributed to such Participant:

(1) In the case of a Participant, other than a Participant who is or has been an owner employee under the transferor plan, no later than the last day of the taxable year of such employee in which he attains age 70½; or not later than the last day of the taxable year in which he retires, whichever is later, and

(2) In the case of a Participant who is, or has been an owner-employee under the transferor plan, not later than the last day of the taxable year in which he attains age 70½.

(f) If a Participant who was an owner-employee under the transferor plan dies after receiving a portion of his benefits under the Plan but before the full value of his interest in the transferred fund has been distributed to him, such Participant's entire remaining interest in the transferred fund must either be distributed to his beneficiary within five years or be used within that period to purchase an immediate annuity for such beneficiary; however, this requirement is not mandatory if the distribution of such interest has commenced and such distribution is for a term certain over a period not extending beyond the joint life and survivor expectancy of the Participant and his spouse.

(g) The Trustee having control over the transferred assets shall always be a "Bank" as required in Section 401(d)(1) of the Code and the Regulations thereunder.]

IN WITNESS WHEREOF, the Employer has caused this [Amendment] [Agreement] to be executed this the ___ day of _____, 19___, to be effective as of _____.

EMPLOYER:

_____

(CORPORATE SEAL)

ATTEST:

By: _____
President

_____
Secretary

DELEGATION OF RESPONSIBILITIES PURSUANT TO ERISA

The following fiduciary has accepted the duties and responsibilities delegated to it under the Plan pursuant to ERISA until its successors are duly appointed and qualified, this ____, day of _____, 19___.

PLAN SPONSOR [AND
PLAN ADMINISTRATOR]:

_____

(CORPORATE SEAL)

ATTEST:

_____   By: _____
Secretary   President

[PLAN ADMINISTRATOR:

_____]

[AMENDMENT AND RESTATEMENT
OF THE]
[PROFIT SHARING] TRUST AGREEMENT
OF

_____

This Profit Sharing Trust Agreement form may be used in conjunction with Exhibit 2 as a Money-Purchase Pension Trust Agreement by removing references to directed investment employee contributions accounts and references to the Profit Sharing Plan contained herein.

Prepared by:
Lamon, Elrod & Harkleroad, P.C.,
2500 Peachtree Center-Cain Tower
229 Peachtree Street, N.E.
Atlanta, Georgia 30043

INDEX TO THE
[AMENDMENT AND RESTATEMENT
OF THE]
[PROFIT SHARING] TRUST AGREEMENT
OF

_____

[AMENDMENT AND RESTATEMENT
OF THE]
[PROFIT SHARING] TRUST AGREEMENT
OF

INTRODUCTION

AGREEMENT made as of the ___day of _____, 19___, by and between _____, a corporation organized and existing under the laws of the State of _____("Employer"), and _____ ("Trustee"),

WITNESSETH

[WHEREAS, effective _____, Employer established a qualified [Profit Sharing] Trust Agreement and amendments thereto were adopted on _____ and _____; and

WHEREAS, by the terms of Section _____ authority rests in the Board of Directors of the Employer to amend said Trust Agreement; and

WHEREAS, certain modifications are necessary for the Trust Agreement to meet the requirements of the Employee Retirement Income Security Act of 1974; and]

WHEREAS, [in order to accomplish these purposes,] the Board of Directors of the Employer at a meeting thereof held on the _____ day of _____, 19___, specifically approved and adopted by resolution the [amended and restated] [Profit Sharing] Plan of _____, to be effective as of _____, 19___;

NOW, THEREFORE, in consideration of the premises and of the mutual covenants herein contained, it is agreed by and between the Employer and the Trustee as follows:

ARTICLE I

ESTABLISHMENT OF TRUST

1.01 _Manner of Establishment._ Employer has adopted a qualified [Profit Sharing] Plan for the exclusive benefit of certain of its Employees and their Beneficiaries, and intends to make regular and continuing contributions as provided in the Plan. The funds and other assets that will, from time to time, be contributed to the Trustee by Employer are to be administered as a Trust and that Trust is hereby created. All assets held in Trust by the Trustee shall be held in Trust and controlled and managed exclusively by the Trustee, except as herein expressly provided or as provided in ERISA Section 403(a). Employer intends that the Trust shall constitute a part of the Plan, the provisions of which are herein incorporated by reference, which will meet the requirements of the Employee Retirement

Income Security Act of 1974 ("ERISA") and qualify under Section 401(a) of the Internal Revenue Code of 1954 as amended ("Code"), and thereby obtain a tax-exempt status under Section 501(a) of the Code.

ARTICLE II

GENERAL DUTIES OF THE PARTIES

2.01 <u>Duties of Employer</u>. Employer shall make contributions to the Trust Fund in cash or property acceptable to the Trustee. Such contributions shall be valued at fair market value at the time of contribution. The Trustee shall notify Employer in writing of the unacceptability of a contribution within three (3) days after receipt by the Trustee. Employer shall keep accurate books and records with respect to its Employees, their service with the Employer and their Basic Compensation.

2.02 <u>Duties of Trustee.</u> The Trustee shall hold all acceptable property received by it. Such property, together with the income therefrom, shall constitute the Trust Fund. The Trustee shall manage and administer the Trust pursuant to the terms of this Trust Agreement without distinction between principal and income and without liability for the payment of interest thereon. The Trustee shall have no duty or authority to compute any amount to be paid to it by the Employer. The Trustee shall not be responsible for the collection of any contributions to the Trust Fund.

2.03 <u>Named Fiduciaries"</u>. The Employer identifies the Trustee and the Plan Administrator as "Named Fiduciaries". The Plan Administrator shall have sole and exclusive responsibilities (other than that herein specifically conferred upon the Trustee) for establishing and carrying out the funding policy and the methods of funding as set forth in the Plan, this Trust Agreement, and the rules and regulations, if any, adopted by the Plan Administrator, all of which shall be consistent with ERISA and all regulations promulgated thereunder. The Plan Administrator shall have sole discretion to allocate and to delegate, by written communications directed to the Employer, the Trustee, and each Participant and Beneficiary of the Plan, any or all of his fiduciary responsibilities, to persons designated by him. An Investment Manager may be named by the Plan Administrator as provided in ERISA Section 402(c)(3) without necessity of an amendment to the Trust Agreement and after prior written notice to the Employer, to the Participants and Beneficiaries of the Plan, and to all Named Fiduciaries of the Plan. By executing this Trust Agreement, each Named Fiduciary specifically consents to be a Named Fiduciary within the meaning of ERISA. Any person designated as Fiduciary herein may serve in more than one fiduciary capacity with respect to the Plan and may employ persons to render advice with regard to any responsibility such Named Fiduciary has under the Plan.

2.04 <u>Foreign Assets</u>. Except as otherwise authorized by regulations promulgated by the Secretary of Labor, the Trustee may not maintain any indicia of ownership of any asset outside the jurisdiction of the District Courts of the United States.

ARTICLE III

POWERS AND SPECIFIC DUTIES OF THE TRUSTEE

3.01 Powers. The Trustee shall have the power to invest and reinvest the Trust Fund [subject to the direction of the Plan Administrator in writing pursuant to Section 3.03 and] subject to the right of Participants to direct the investment of their Voluntary Employee Contributions through Direct Investment Employee Contributions Accounts. Such investments and reinvestments may include, but are not limited to the following: any type of security, including, but not necessarily limited to, common stocks or preferred stocks; open-end or closed-end mutual funds; corporate bonds, debentures, or convertible debentures; commercial paper; bankers' acceptances or certificates of deposit, [including certificates of deposit of the Trustee bank;] U.S. Treasury bills, notes or bonds; improved or unimproved real estate located in the United States; participations in any common trust fund or commingled fund for the investment of Qualified Pension and Profit Sharing Plan Assets which may be established and maintained from time to time by the _____; and to lend the funds of the Trust to others, except as prohibited by ERISA or the provisions of the Plan, upon receipt of adequate security, including chattel mortgages or first or second loan deeds, at a reasonable rate of interest.

The Trustee shall have full power to do all such acts, take all such proceedings and exercise all such rights and privileges, whether herein specifically referred to or not, as could be done, taken or exercised by the absolute owner thereof, including, but without in any way limiting or impairing the generality of the foregoing, the following powers and authority:

(a) To retain the same for such period of time as the Trustee in its sole discretion shall deem prudent;

(b) To sell the same, at either public or private sale, at such time or times and on such terms and conditions as the Trustee shall deem prudent;

(c) To consent to or participate in any plan for the reorganization, consolidation or merger of any corporation, the security of which is held in the Trust, and to pay any and all calls and assessments imposed upon the owners of such securities as a condition of their participating therein. In connection therewith, to consent to any contract, lease, mortgage, purchase or sale of property, by or between such corporation and any other corporation or person;

(d) To exercise or dispose of any right the Trustee may have as the holder of any security to convert the same into another or other securities, or to acquire any additional security or securities, to make any payments, to exchange any security or to do any other act with reference thereto which the Trustee may deem prudent;

(e) To deposit any security with any protective or reorganization committee, and to delegate to such committee such power and authority with relation thereto as the Trustee may deem prudent, and to agree to pay and to pay out of the Trust such portion of the expenses and compensation of such committee as the Trustee may deem proper;

(f) To renew or extend the time of payment of any obligation due or becoming due;

(g) To grant options to purchase any property;

(h) To compromise, arbitrate or otherwise adjust or settle claims in favor of or against the Trust, and to deliver or accept in either total or partial satisfaction of any indebtedness or other obligation any property, and to continue to hold same for such period of time as the Trustee may deem appropriate;

(i) To exchange any property for other property upon such terms and conditions as the Trustee may deem proper, and to give and receive money to effect equality in price;

(j) To execute and deliver any proxies or powers of attorney to such person or persons as the Trustee may deem proper, granting to such person such power and authority with relation to any property or securities at any time held for the Trust as the Trustee may deem proper;

(k) To foreclose any obligation by judicial proceeding or otherwise;

(l) To sue or defend in connection with any and all securities or property at any time received or held for the Trust, all costs and attorney's fees in connection therewith to be charged against the Trust;

(m) To manage any real property in the same manner as if the Trustee were the absolute owner thereof;

(n) To borrow money, with or without giving security;

(o) To cause any securities held for the Trust to be registered and to carry any such securities in the name of a nominee or nominees;

(p) To hold such portion of the Trust as the Trustee may deem necessary for the ordinary administration of the Trust and disbursement of funds as directed in Section 3.02 in cash, without liability for interest, by depositing the same in any bank [including the Trustee bank,] subject to the rules and regulations governing such deposits, and without regard to the amount of any such deposits; and

(q) To invest in life insurance contracts on the lives of key employees of the Employer, payable on death to the Trustee as beneficiary. (Such insurance contracts shall be vested exclusively in the Trustee for the benefit of the Trust as a whole and shall not be distributed in kind to a Participant in satisfaction of any interest he may have in the Trust Fund.)

3.02 Dealings with Plan Administrator. The Trustee shall from time to time, on the written directions of the Plan Administrator, make distribution from the Trust to such persons, in such manner, in such amounts and for such purposes as may be specified in such directions. The Trustee shall be under no liability for any distribution made by it pursuant to the directions of the Plan Administrator and shall be under no duty to make inquiry as to whether any distribution directed by the Plan Administrator is made pursuant to the provisions of the related Plan and this Section, except to the extent required of a prudent Co-Fiduciary under ERISA. The Trustee shall not be liable for the proper application of any part of the Trust if distributions are made in accordance with the written directions of the Plan Administrator as herein provided, nor shall the Trustee be responsible for the adequacy of the Trust to meet and discharge any and all payments and liabilities under the related Plan.

[3.03 Earmarked Investments. At any time, each Participant under the Plan may request, in writing and on the form provided by the Plan Administrator, that the nonforfeitable portion of his [Profit Sharing] Account, or any uniform lesser amount as determined by the Plan Administrator, be invested in any form of investment selected by the Participant; provided, however, that such transaction shall not constitute a prohibited transaction within the meaning of Section 4975 of the Code.

When a Participant has so earmarked the nonforfeitable portion of his [Profit Sharing] Account or any portion thereof, the Plan Administrator shall so direct the Trustee hereunder. The Trustee shall segregate on his books the amounts so earmarked, and the amount so segregated shall not share in and shall not affect the net income, net loss, net appreciation, and net depreciation of the unsegregated Trust Fund. Such segregated account shall hereafter be referred to as a ''separate account''.

All expenses attributable to any earmarked investment shall be charged against the [Profit Sharing] Account or separate account of the Participant earmarking the nonforfeitable portion of his [Profit Sharing] Account. Under no circumstances, however, shall the credit to the Participant's separate account immediately following the earmarked investment exceed the nonforfeitable portion standing to such Participant's credit in his [Profit Sharing] Account and separate account immediately following the investment, taking into account the reduction in his [Profit Sharing] Account or separate account resulting from the expense of making the earmarked investment.

As used herein, the term ''nonforfeitable portion'' of a Participant's [Profit Sharing] Account shall mean that amount to which the Participant is entitled at that point in time when the schedule as set forth in Section 5.06 of the Plan is applied to his Profit Sharing Account.

3.04 Liability for Earmarked Investments and for Directed Investment Employee Contributions Accounts. In the event that a Participant in the Plan elects to earmark the investment of the nonforfeitable portion of his [Profit Sharing] Account, pursuant to Section 3.03 hereof, and/or in the event that a Participant elects to establish a Directed Investment Employee Contributions Account under the Plan, he shall not be deemed to be a Fiduciary with respect to the Plan by reason of such earmarking, or by reason of establishing such Directed Investment Employee Contributions Account, and neither the Trustee, the Plan Administrator nor any other Fiduciary with respect to the Plan shall be liable for any loss or breach resulting from the exercise of such Participant's right to earmark his [Profit Sharing] Account or to establish a Directed Investment Employee Contributions Account, except to the extent provided by Section 4975 of the Code.

The Trustee shall have the right to resign in accordance with Section 7.01 rather than to make a particular earmarked investment or permit a particular investment in a Directed Investment Employee Contributions Account. If the

Trustee does so resign, it shall not incur any liability to the Participant or any other party by reason of not making the earmarked investment or by reason of not permitting a particular investment in a Directed Investment Employee Contributions Account.]

3.05 Prohibited Transactions. The Trustee shall not accept or act upon direction from the Plan Administrator or any other person to engage in a transaction known by the Trustee to be a "prohibited transaction" under ERISA. In the event of any uncertainty or dispute respecting any such proposed transaction, the Trustee shall not be required to act or be liable to any person for failing so to act on such direction unless and until a final administrative or judicial determination shall be obtained by any person interested in such transaction and duly served upon the Trustee and the Trustee shall thereafter have had a reasonable opportunity to comply with such direction if it is determined to be lawful under the terms of the Plan and ERISA in the opinion of legal counsel.

3.06 Manner of Payment. The Trustee may make any payment required to be made by it hereunder, by mailing to the person or entity a check or delivering the property directed to be distributed by the Plan Administrator, at the last known address as may have last been furnished the Trustee.

3.07 Restriction on Exercise of Powers; Prudent Man Rule. The Trustee, the Plan Administrator, and all other Fiduciaries with respect to the Plan are required to discharge their duties solely in the interests of Participants and Beneficiaries and for the exclusive purpose of providing benefits to Participants and Beneficiaries and defraying reasonable expenses of administration; with the care, skill, prudence and diligence, under the circumstances then prevailing, that a prudent man acting in a like capacity and familiar with such matters would use in the conduct of an enterprise of like character and with like aims; by diversifying the investments so as to minimize the risk of large losses unless under the circumstances it is clearly prudent not to do so; and in accordance with the Plan, this Trust Agreement, the rules and directions of the Plan Administrator and the provisions of Title I or ERISA.

3.08 Life Insurance. As directed in writing by the Plan Administrator, the Trustee shall have the following powers and duties with respect to any ordinary or term life insurance policy held in the Trust for the benefit of a Participant:

(a) To apply in writing for ordinary or term insurance to be issued on the life of any insurable Participant in the Plan in an amount to be determined by the Plan Administrator. However, the aggregate premiums for ordinary insurance in the case of each Participant shall be less than one-half of the aggregate of the Employer Contributions allocated to him at any particular time, and the aggregate premiums for term insurance in the case of each Participant shall be less than one-quarter of the aggregate of the Employer Contributions allocated to him at any particular time. Any such policy shall be issued by any legal reserve life insurance company authorized to sell such policy in the state of issue and selected by the Plan Administrator. Each such policy shall be a contract between the insurer and the Trustee, and shall be held by the Trustee as an asset of the Trust for the benefit of the insured Participant. Any other provision to the contrary notwithstanding, the

Trustee shall convert into cash the entire value, if any, of a life insurance contract held for the benefit of a Participant at or before such Participant's retirement, shall convert the value, if any, of the life insurance policy into a non-transferable annuity or other non-transferable form providing periodic income so that no portion of such value may be used to continue life insurance protection beyond retirement, or shall distribute such life insurance contract to the Participant.

(b) To exercise all rights, options and benefits provided by any policy or permitted by any insurer with respect to any policy issued by it, including the right to change any provision which shall become inoperative upon the retirement of any Participant.

(c) To pay premiums on any policy held in the Trust; accumulate dividends; and apply dividends in reduction of premiums. Any dividends payable with respect to any policy as to which there shall be no further premiums due shall be paid in cash to the Trustee and added to the insured Participant's Profit Sharing Account in the Trust Fund.

(d) To name the beneficiary of any such policy and change such beneficiary from time to time and to select the method of settlement to be effective upon the maturity of any such policy and change any such method of settlement. No Participant shall have the right to direct the Trustee with respect to any of such matters without the consent of the Plan Administrator.

No insurance company which shall issue any policy, as hereinabove provided, shall be a party to this Trust Agreement. The liability of any such insurance company shall be only as provided in any policy which it may issue and such company shall not be considered a Named Fiduciary hereunder, provided, however, that if such insurance company shall undertake to invest Plan assets in an unallocated investment medium, such insurance company shall also be considered a Named Fiduciary hereunder.

3.09 Third Parties. All persons dealing with the Trustee are released from inquiring into the decision or authority of the Trustee and from seeing to the application of any monies, securities or other property paid or delivered to the Trustee.

3.10 Co-Fiduciaries. Anything in the Trust Agreement or the Plan to the contrary notwithstanding, each Fiduciary with respect to the Plan acknowledges, by participating in the execution of this Trust Agreement or by consenting directly or indirectly, orally or in writing, to act as a Fiduciary with respect to the Plan, that he is responsible for carrying out his own duties in accordance with the standards set forth under ERISA and all regulations promulgated thereunder. Each Fiduciary shall be responsible for the actions or failure to act of all other Fiduciaries with respect to the Plan if he knowingly participates, approves, acquiesces in or conceals a breach committed by another such Fiduciary; or if his failure to exercise reasonable care in the administration of his own duties enables the breach to be committed. Each Fiduciary is required to act prudently in the delegation or allocation of responsibilities to other persons. In the event that there are Co-Trustees acting hereunder, each Trustee will be responsible for participating in the administration of the Plan and for exercising reasonable care to prevent the other from committing a breach. If the Plan or the Trust Agreement or any written rule or direction of the Plan Administrator shall by agreement allocate responsibilities among Co-Trustees, only the Trustee to whom the responsibilities are delegated will be responsible for the breach unless the other Trustee or Trustees knowingly participate therein. In the event that an Investment Manager other than the Trustee is appointed pursuant to this Trust, no Trustee shall be liable for the acts or omissions of such Investment Manager, or be under any obligation to invest or manage the assets of the Plan which are subject to management by an Investment Manager as such term is defined in ERISA Section 3(38). Nothing in the Plan or the Trust Agreement shall be deemed to enlarge the responsibilities or liabilities of any Trustee or Co-Trustee or any other Fiduciary with respect to the Plan beyond those imposed by ERISA and all regulations promulgated thereunder.

3.11 Liabilities of the Trustee. The Trustee shall not be liable for any losses incurred by the Trust by reason of any lawful direction to invest communicated to the Trustee by the Plan Administrator in accordance with Section 3.08 [or by any Participant in exercise of his power to earmark investments for his own Account,] or to establish and maintain a Directed Investment Employee Contributions Account except with respect to any transaction entered into by the Trustee which is prohibited by ERISA and as to which the Trustee is a Fiduciary, party-in-interest or disqualified person as defined by ERISA. Nothing herein shall exculpate or relieve the Trustee from liability for any losses to the Trust incurred by his negligence, bad faith or knowing participation in a breach of trust. The Trustee warrants and represents that he is not prohibited from serving as Trustee hereof because of certain disabilities provided in ERISA Section 411.

ARTICLE IV

SETTLEMENT OF ACCOUNTS

4.01 General Records. The Trustee shall maintain accurate records and detailed accounts of all investments, receipts, disbursements, and other transactions hereunder. Such records shall be available at all reasonable times for inspection by the Plan Administrator, the Employer, or any Fiduciary, Participant or Beneficiary or authorized representative of such persons; provided, however, that Participants and Beneficiaries shall be entitled to inspect only those records relating to their own Accounts. The Trustee shall submit or cause to be submitted in a timely manner to the Plan Administrator such information as the Plan Administrator may reasonably require in connection with the preparation of the various reports required to be made by ERISA to various regulatory agencies and to Plan Participants and Beneficiaries. In the absence of fraud or bad faith, the valuation of the Trust by the Trustee shall be conclusive on all parties affected by this Trust.

4.02 Annual Accounting. Within sixty (60) days following the close of each Plan Year the Trustee shall file with the Plan Administrator a written accounting setting forth a description of all property purchased and sold and all receipts, disbursements, and other transactions effected by it during such period. Further, the Trustee shall list property held by it at the end of such period and such list shall include a valuation of each asset at its fair market value as determined at the close of the Plan Year. The Plan Administrator may approve such accounting by written notice of approval delivered to the Trustee or by failure to object in writing to the Trustee within sixty(60) days from the date upon which the account was delivered to the Plan Administrator. Upon receipt of written approval of the account, or upon the passage of said period of time without written objections having been delivered to the Trustee, such acccounting shall be deemed to be approved, and the Trustee shall be released and discharged as to all items, matters and things set forth in such accounting as if such accounting had been settled and allowed by a decree of a court of competent jurisdiction.

4.03 <u>Agents</u>. The Employer or the Plan Administrator, or both, at any time may employ any person or entity as an agent to perform any act, keep any records or accounts, or make computations which are required of them under the Code or ERISA. Such employment shall not be deemed to be contrary to or inconsistent with the provisions of this Trust Agreement. Nothing done by such person or corporation as agent for the Employer or the Plan Administrator shall change or increase in any manner the responsibility or liability of the Trustee hereunder, unless such agent shall be deemed to be a Fiduciary with respect to the Plan, and the Trustee shall have failed to meet the standards imposed by Sections 3.07 and 3.10 hereof.

ARTICLE V

DURATION AND TERMINATION OF TRUST

5.01 <u>Duration and Termination</u>. It is the intention of Employer that this Trust and the Profit Sharing Plan to which it relates shall be a permanent plan of benefits administered for the exclusive benefit of Employer's participating Employees and their Beneficiaries. However, the Employer retains complete discretion to terminate the Plan and Trust, and upon such termination the Trust shall be distributed by the Trustee as and when directed by the Plan Administrator, in accordance with the provisions of the Plan, this Trust Agreement, the Code and Section 403(d)(1) of ERISA. From and after the date of termination of the Trust, and until the final distribution of the Trust, the Trustee shall continue to have all the powers provided under this Trust Agreement necessary and expedient for the orderly liquidation and distribution of the Trust.

5.02 <u>Continuation of Plan.</u> If the related Plan is terminated or discontinued, the Employer may elect not to terminate the Trust. In that event, the Trust shall be administered as though the related Plan was in full force and effect throughout the entire period of its existence. If the Trust is subsequently terminated pursuant to Section 5.01, the Trust Fund shall be distributed as directed by the Plan Administrator in accordance with the provisions of the Plan, this Trust Agreement, the Code and Section 403(d)(1) of ERISA.

ARTICLE VI

AMENDMENTS

6.01 Amendments. This Trust Agreement may be amended at any time by a written agreement executed by the Employer. However, such amendment shall not operate to cause any part of the Trust Fund, other than such part as is required to pay taxes and administration expenses, to be used for, or diverted to, purposes other than for the exclusive benefit of Employer's participating Employees and their Beneficiaries.

ARTICLE VII

RESIGNATION OR REMOVAL OF TRUSTEE

7.01 Method. The Trustee may resign or may be removed by the Employer. The resignation or removal shall be effective thirty (30) days after receipt of written notice of such resignation or removal. Upon such resignation or removal, Employer shall appoint a Successor Trustee to whom the resigning or removed Trustee shall transfer all of the assets of the Trust Fund then held by it as expeditiously as possible. Such Successor Trustee shall thereupon succeed to all of the powers and duties given to the Trustee by this Trust Agreement. Within sixty (60) days of such transfer of the Trust assets, the resigning or removed Trustee shall render to the Employer an accounting in the form and manner prescribed in Section 4.02. Unless Employer shall within sixty (60) days after the receipt of such accounting file with the resigning or removed Trustee written objections thereto, the accounting shall be deemed to have been approved, and the resigning or removed Trustee shall be released and discharged as to all items, matters and things set forth in such accounting, as if such accounting had been settled and allowed by a decree of a court of competent jurisdiction.

ARTICLE VIII

TAXES, EXPENSES AND COMPENSATION OF TRUSTEE

8.01 Manner of Payment. The Trustee shall deduct from and charge against the Trust Fund any taxes paid by it which may be imposed upon the Trust Fund or income thereon which the Trustee is required to pay with respect to the interest of any person therein; provided, however, that any taxes [attributable to an earmarked investment or] attributable to a Directed Investment Employee Contributions Account shall be paid out of and deducted from the separate account established for [such earmarked investment or] such Directed Investment Employee Contributions Account, [as the case may be]. The Trustee is not authorized to pay any excise or other tax levied upon any disqualified person imposed by reason of such person's engagement in any prohibited transaction. The Trustee is also not authorized to purchase any errors and ommissions insurance for Fiduciaries not permitted by Section 410(b)(3) of ERISA.

8.02 Trustee Compensation. Employer shall pay to the Trustee reasonable compensation for its services as Trustee hereunder at the rate to be agreed upon from time to time and reimburse the Trustee for its reasonable expenses. The Trustee shall have a lien on the Trust Fund for such compensation and for any reasonable expenses, including attorney's fees, and the same may be withdrawn from the Trust Fund if not paid within a reasonable time by the Employer. No compensation (other than reasonable expenses) shall be paid to a Trustee who is a full-time Employee of the Employer.

ARTICLE IX

IMPOSSIBILITY OF DIVERSION

9.01 Diversion. No part of the corpus or income of the Trust Fund shall be used for, or diverted to, purposes other than for the exclusive benefit of Participants or their Beneficiaries.

ARTICLE X

GOVERNING LAW

10.01 Governing Law. This Trust shall be administered in the United States of America, and its validity, construction and all rights hereunder shall be governed by the laws of the United States under ERISA. To the extent that ERISA shall not be held to have preempted local law, the Trust shall be administered under the laws of the State of _____. If any provision of this Agreement shall be held invalid or unenforceable, the remaining provisions hereof shall continue to be fully effective.

ARTICLE XI

SPENDTHRIFT PROVISION

11.01 Spendthrift Provision. No Participant or Beneficiary entitled to any benefits under this Trust Agreement shall have any right to assign, pledge, transfer, hypothecate, encumber, commute or anticipate his interest in any benefits under this Trust. Such benefits shall not in any way be subject to any legal process of levy of execution or attachment or garnishment proceedings in connection with the payment of any claim against any such person.

ARTICLE XII

QUALIFICATION

Notwithstanding any other contrary provisions of this Trust, it is intended that this [amended] Trust and the related [amended] Plan shall qualify for tax exemption and qualification under the Internal Revenue Code of 1954, as amended by ERISA. However, if the Trust or said Plan fails to qualify, the Employer shall have the right to amend this Trust pursuant to ARTICLE VI, or the Plan pursuant to ARTICLE IX thereof.

IN WITNESS WHEREOF, Employer and Trustee have caused this [Amendment] [Agreement] to be executed by their duly authorized officers and their seals to be hereunto affixed, this _____ day of _____, 19___.

EMPLOYER:

(CORPORATE SEAL)

ATTEST:

By: _____
President

_____
Secretary

PLAN ADMINISTRATOR:

_____

TRUSTEE:

(CORPORATE SEAL)

By: _____
Duly Authorized Officer

ATTEST:

_____
Duly Authorized Officer

EXHIBIT 2

[AMENDMENT AND RESTATEMENT
OF THE]

_____

MONEY-PURCHASE PENSION PLAN

This Money-Purchase Pension Plan form contains appropriate provisions to draft an amendment and restatement of an existing plan or to draft a new plan. Various options and plan provision elections are set forth in brackets. This plan is integrated with Social Security wage base.

Prepared by:
Lamon, Elrod & Harkleroad, P.C.
2500 Peachtree Center-Cain Tower
229 Peachtree Street, N.E.
Atlanta, Georgia 30043

INDEX TO THE

[AMENDMENT AND RESTATEMENT

OF THE]

MONEY-PURCHASE PENSION PLAN

(Introduction for Amended and Restated Plan)

AMENDMENT AND RESTATEMENT

OF THE

_____

MONEY-PURCHASE PENSION PLAN

WHEREAS, _____("Employer") established the _____; and MONEY-PURCHASE PENSION PLAN effective _____; and

WHEREAS, effective _____, said Plan was amended and restated to meet the requirements of the Internal Revenue Code of 1954 ("Code"), as amended by the Employee Retirement Income Security Act of 1974 ("ERISA); and

WHEREAS, the Board of Directors has determined that it is in the best interest of Plan Participants and Beneficiaries to make further modifications to said Plan in light of recent regulations and rulings promulgated under Code and ERISA;

NOW, THEREFORE, in order to accomplish these purposes, the Board of Directors of the Employer has by appropriate resolutions adopted the amended and restated _____ MONEY-PURCHASE PENSION PLAN (''Plan'') as hereinafter stated to be effective as of _____.

It is intended that this restated Plan, together with the Trust Agreement, meet all the requirements of the Code and ERISA, and the Plan shall be interpreted, wherever possible, to comply with the terms of the Code and ERISA and all formal regulations and rulings issued under the Code and ERISA.

(Alternate Introduction for New Plan)

MONEY-PURCHASE PENSION PLAN

WHEREAS, _____ (''Employer'') desires to establish the _____ MONEY-PURCHASE PENSION PLAN to encourage employment longevity and assist employees in planning for their retirement; and

WHEREAS, said Plan is intended to meet the requirements of the Internal Revenue Code of 1954 (''Code''), as amended by the Employee Retirement Income Security Act of 1974 (''ERISA''); and

NOW, THEREFORE, the Board of Directors of the Employer does by appropriate resolution adopt the _____ MONEY-PURCHASE PENSION PLAN (''Plan'') as hereinafter stated to be effective as of _____.

ARTICLE I

DEFINITIONS

As used in this Plan and the accompanying Trust Agreement the following terms shall have the following meanings unless a different meaning is plainly required by the context:

1.01 The term ''*Account*'' shall mean the account established on behalf of a Participant to which shall be credited (a) the amount of Employer Contributions allocated to the Participant pursuant to Section 3.01; (b) the Participant's proportionate share, attributable to this Account, of the net gains of the Trust Fund determined in accordance with Section 4.02 hereof. From said Account there shall be deducted the Participant's proportionate share, attributable to this Account, of the net losses (if any) of the Trust Fund as determined in accordance with Section 4.02 hereof.

1.02 The term ''*Annual Addition*'' in respect of any Participant shall mean the sum (for any Plan Year) of—

(a) The Employer Contributions to the Trust in respect of said Plan Year;

(b) The lesser of—

    (i) The amount of the Employee contributions, if any, in said Plan Year in excess of six percent (6%) of his Basic Compensation received in said Plan Year, or

    (ii) One-half (1/2) of the Employee contributions to the Trust in said Plan Year; and

(c) Forfeitures credited to said Participant's Account in respect of said Plan Year; provided that the Employee contributions mentioned in (b) above shall be determined without regard to rollover contributions from any individual retirement account, if any.

1.03 The term *"Attained Age"* shall mean the age, in years, of an Employee as of the last anniversary of his date of birth.

1.04 The term *"Basic Compensation"* shall mean a Participant's [total compensation paid by the Employer during the Plan·Year and reported on the Participant's Federal Income Tax Withholding Statement (Form W-2), including regular compensation, overtime pay, and commissions, but excluding non-contracted bonuses, expense account allowances, and Employer Contributions to this and any other retirement or welfare plan established by the Employer to the extent that such excluded items are reported on the Form W-2.] Total compensation paid by the Employer during the Plan Year, including salary, overtime pay, commissions, and bonuses, as reported on the Participant's Federal Income Tax Withholding Statement (Form W-2).]

1.05 The term *"Beneficiary"* shall mean any person or persons (or a trust) designated by a Participant in such form as the Plan Administrator may prescribe to receive any death benefit that may be payable hereunder if such person or persons survive the Participant. This designation may be revoked at any time in similar manner and form. In the event of the death of the designated Beneficiary prior to the death of the Participant, the Contingent Beneficiary shall be entitled to receive any death benefit. See Section 5.10 if neither the Beneficiary nor Contingent Beneficiary survives the Participant or if no Beneficiary or Contingent Beneficiary has been effectively named.

1.06 The term *"Board of Directors"* shall mean the Board of Directors of the Employer.

1.07 The term *"Contingent Beneficiary"* shall mean the person or persons (or a trust) duly designated by the Participant to receive any death benefit from the Plan in the event the designated Beneficiary does not survive the Participant.

1.08 The term *"Contributions"* shall mean the Employer Contributions made pursuant to Section 3.01

1.09 The term *"Defined Benefit Plan"* shall mean any plan which is not a Defined Contribution Plan.

1.10 The term *"Defined Benefit Plan Fraction"* for any Plan Year, with respect to a particular participant, shall mean a fraction;

(a) The numerator of which is his projected annual benefit under the plan, including any other plan required to be aggregated under Section 415(h) of the Code (determined as of the close of the Plan Year), and

(b) The denominator of which is his projected annual benefit under the plan, including any other plan required to be aggregated under Section 415(h) of the Code (determined as of the close of such Plan Year) if the plan provides the maximum benefit allowable under (i) Code Section 415(b)(1)(A), or if lesser (ii) one hundred percent (100%) of such participant's average compensation for his highest three (3) consecutive Plan Years of participation.

1.11 The term *"Defined Contribution Plan"* shall mean a plan which provides for an individual account for each participant and for benefits based solely on the amount contributed to the participant's account, and any income, expenses, gains, and losses, and any forfeitures of accounts of other participants which may be allocated to such participant's account.

1.12 The term *"Defined Contribution Plan Fraction"* with respect to a particular participant for any Plan Year shall mean a fraction:

(a) The numerator of which is the sum of the Annual Additions to his account, including Annual Additions to his account in any other plan required to be aggregated under Section 415(h) of the Code, as of the close of such Plan Year, and

(b) The denominator of which is the sum of the maximum amount (consistent with Code Section 415(c)(1)), of Annual Additions to his account which could have been made for such Plan Year and for each prior Plan Year of Service with the Employer, including any other employer required to be aggregated under Section 415(h) of the Code, and including service prior to the Effective Date.

1.13 The term *"Early Retirement Date"* shall mean the later of (a) the last day of the Plan Year during which an Employee attains age [fifty-five (55)] or (b) the last day of the Plan Year in which such Employee completes ten (10) Years of Service.

1.14 The term *"Effective Date"* shall mean the original effective date of the Plan, _____.

1.15 The term *"Employer"* shall mean each individual employed by the Employer.

1.16 The term *"Employer"* shall mean _____, a _____ corporation with principal offices located at _____, _____; its successors and assigns, and, subject to the provisions of Section 10.08, any company into which the Employer may be merged or consolidated or to which all or substantially all of its assets may be transferred.

1.17 The term *"Fiduciary"* shall mean and include the Trustee, Plan Administrator, Plan Sponsor, Investment Manager, and any other person who—

(a) Exercises any discretionary authority or discretionary control respecting management of the Plan or exercises any authority or control respecting management or disposition of its assets;

(b) Renders investment advice for a fee or other compensation, direct or indirect, with respect to any moneys or other property of the Plan, or has any authority or responsibility to do so;

(c) Has any discretionary authority or discretionary responsibility in the administration of the Plan; or

(d) Is described as a "fiduciary" in Section 3(14) or (21) of ERISA or is designated to carry out fiduciary responsibilities pursuant to this Plan and the Trust Agreement to the extent permitted by Section 405(c)(1)(B) of ERISA.

1.18 The term *"Hour of Service"* shall mean:

(a) Each hour for which an Employee is paid, or entitled to payment, for the performance of duties for the Employer during a Plan Year.

(b) Except as otherwise provided in this Subsection (b), each hour for which an Employee is paid, or entitled to payment from the Employee is paid, or entitled to payment from the Employer on account of a period of time during which no duties are performed (irrespective of whether the employment relationship has terminated) due to vacation, holiday, illness, incapacity (including disability), layoff, jury duty, military duty or leave of absence. An Employee shall be entitled to 40 Hours of Service for each work week that consists of a period described in the preceding sentence.

(1) No more than 501 Hours of Service will be credited under this Subsection (b) to an Employee on account of any single continuous period during which the Employee performs no duties (whether or not such period occurs in a single Plan Year).

(2) Hours of Service shall not be credited on account of a period during which an Employee is paid or entitled to payment and with respect to which no duties are performed, if such payment is made or due under a plan maintained solely for the purpose of complying with applicable workmen's compensation, or unemployment compensation or disability service laws, or if the payment merely reimburses the Employee for a medical or medically related expense incurred by the Employee.

(3) For purposes of this Subsection (b) a payment shall be deemed to be made by or due from the Employer regardless of whether such payment is made by or due from the Employer directly, or indirectly through, among others, a trust fund or insurer, to which the Employer pays premiums and regardless of whether contributions made or due to the trust fund, insurer or other entity are for the benefit of a particular Employee or are on behalf of a group of Employees in the aggregate.

(c) Each hour for which back pay, irrespective of mitigation of damages, is either awarded or agreed to by the Employer. The same Hours of Service shall not be credited under Subsection (a) or Subsection (b) and under this Subsection (c). The crediting of Hours of Service for back pay awarded or agreed to with respect to periods described in Subsection (b) shall be subject to the limitations described in Paragraphs (1), (2) and (3) of Subsection (b).

The crediting of Hours of Service shall be subject to all the rules contained in Paragraphs (b) and (c) of the United States Department of Labor Regulations §2530.200b-2. For purposes of this Section 1.18, service for any employer required to be aggregated with the Employer under Code Section 414(b) or (c) shall be treated as service for the Employer. [For purposes of vesting in this Plan, no period of service prior to the Effective Date shall be counted.]

[The Hours of Service for an Employee who is compensated for the Plan Year solely on the basis of commissions, as opposed to salary or hourly pay, shall be deemed to equal the quotient of such Employee's Basic Compensation divided by the lowest minimum wage under the Fair Labor Standards Act of 1938, as amended, in effect at any time during the Plan Year.] (Optional language where commissioned sales persons will participate in the plan.)

1.19 The term *"Investment Manager"* shall mean any Fiduciary (other than a trustee or named fiduciary) who—

(a) Has the power to manage, acquire, or dispose of any asset of the Plan;

(b) Is a bank, insurance company, or an investment advisor registered under the Investment Advisers Act of 1940; and

(c) Has acknowledged in writing that he is a fiduciary with respect to the Plan.

1.20 The term *"Normal Retirement Date"* shall mean the later of (a) the last day of the month coincident with or immediately preceding the Employee's [sixty-fifty (65th)] anniversary of his date of birth or (b) the 10th anniversary of the Employee's date of initial participation in the Plan.

(Option 1—Use for a New Plan)

[1.21] The term *"One Year Break in Service"* shall mean a Plan Year during which the Participant has not completed more than five hundred (500) Hours of Service.]

(Option 2—Use for Amended and Restated Plan Where There Has Been a Switch in Computation Periods from Employment Year to Plan Year for Purposes of Vesting Credit.)

[1.21 The term *"One Year Break in Service"* shall mean, for any anniversary of the date of employment occuring before _____, 19___, a 12-month period commencing of a given anniversary of the date of employment during which the Participant has not completed more than 500 Hours of Service. If the Participant does not complete more than 500 Hours of Service during the 12-month period commencing on the anniversary of the date of employment immediately preceding _____, 19___, the computation period for determining whether the Participant incurs successive One Year Breaks in Service shall continue to be based on anniversaries of the date of employment until more than 500 Hours of Service are completed during one such computation period. Except as provided in the two immediately preceding sentences, the term ''One Year Break in Service'' shall mean a Plan Year during which the Participant has not completed more than 500 Hours of Service.]

1.22 The term *''Participant''* shall mean an Employee who has met the requirements of Article II for participation hereunder.

(a) A Participant shall become an *''Active Participant''* in accordance with Article II and shall remain an ''Active Participant'' until such time as he incurs a One Year Break in Service; is cashed-out or is in the process of being cashed-out under Section 5.11; retires pursuant to Section 5.01, 5.02, or 5.03; or becomes Totally and Permanently Disabled. An ''Acrive Participant'' shall be entitled to his allocable share of Employer Contributions and earnings or losses of the Trust Fund; provided, however, notwithstanding any other provisions of this Plan to the contrary, no allocation of earnings or losses of the Trust Fund shall be made to a new Participant during his first plan year of participation if such Participant has no prior years account balance on which to base such allocation as is necessary to the formula provided under Section 4.02(a) hereof. Notwithstanding any provision of this Section or Plan to the contrary, a Retired, Disabled, Former, or Terminated Participant who is re-employed and continues in the employ of the Employer through the last day of the Plan Year which includes the date or re-employment shall be an ''Active Participant'' for the Plan Year of re-employment, even though he completes five hundred (500) or fewer Hours of Service during such Plan Year, and shall be entitled to all of the rights of an ''Active Participant'' except as provided in the last sentence of Section 5.11. Otherwise, no Participant who completes five hundred (500) or fewer Hours of Service during the Plan Year and thus incurs a One Year Break in Service with respect to such Plan Year shall be regarded as an ''Active Participant'' for such Plan Year.

(b) A *''Terminated Participant''* is one who has not retired or become disabled under Section 5.01, 5.02, 5.03, or 5.05 and who has received the full distribution to which he is entitled pursuant to Sections 5.06 and 5.07 following a One Year Break in Service, has been cashed-out or is in the process of being cashed-out as of the applicable Valuation Date pursuant to Section 5.11, or has incurred a One Year Break in Service but has no vested interest and is therefore entitled to no distribution or cash-out. No allocations of Employer Contributions or earnings or losses shall be made to ''Terminated Participants''.

(c) A *''Retired Participant''* or *''Disabled Participant''* is one who is entitled to a distribution pursuant to Section 5.01, 5.02, or 5.03 following retirement, or pursuant to Section 5.05 following Total and Permanent Disability. ''Retired Participants'' and ''Disabled Participants'' who have not elected pursuant to Section 5.01, 5.02, 5.03, or 5.05 to take their Accounts as of the Valuation Date immediately preceding their dates of retirement or the dates on which they were determined to be Totally and Permanently Disabled and for whom separate accounts have not been established under Section 5.09 prior to the Valuation Date in question shall be entitled to allocable shares of earnings or losses for the particular Plan Year and to allocate shares of Employer Contributions if more than five hundred (500) Hours of Service were completed during the Plan Year.

(d) A *"Former Participant"* is one who has incurred a One Year Break in Service, but has not retired pursuant to Section 5.01, 5.02, or 5.03 or become Totally and Permanently Disabled, and who has not yet received a full distribution of his vested interest under Section 5.07 or 5.11. Prior to full distribution, or segregation of his Account pursuant to Section 5.09, a "Former Participant" shall be entitled to share in earnings or losses of the Trust Fund, but shall not be entitled to share in Employer Contributions.

[_____ The term *"Participation Date"* shall mean each _____ and _____ beginning with _____.]

(For use with two entry dates. If used all succeeding Sections must be renumbered.)

1.23 The term *"Plan Administrator"* shall mean the [Employer.] [the individual so names as provided in ARTICLE VII.]

1.24 The term *"Plan Anniversary Date"* shall mean the last day of the Plan Year. The Plan Anniversary Date initially shall be _____.

1.25 The term *"Plan Sponsor"* shall mean the Employer.

1.26 The term *"Plan Year"* shall mean the accounting period adopted by the Employer for federal income tax purposes, which period begins _____ and ends the following _____. [For all purposes of this Plan, the Plan Year shall also constitute the "limitation year" for purposes of Section 415 of the Code.]

1.27 The term *"Service in the Armed Forces"* shall mean service in the armed forces of the United States which is required under the Military Selective Service Act or which is voluntary, if such voluntary enlistment is for a period not in excess of four (4) years, provided that the Employee reapplies for employment with the Employer within the time period required by federal law for the preservation of benfits.

1.28 The term *"Social Security Wage Base"* shall mean the contribution and benefit base as determined under Section 230 of the Social Security Act, as now or hereafter amended, in effect on the particular Anniversary Date.

1.29 The term *"Total and Permanent Disability"* or *"Totally and Permanently Disabled"* shall mean a physical or mental condition arising after an Employee has become a Participant which totally and permanently prevents the Participant from [performing the normal duties for which he is employed.] [engaging in any occupation or employment for remuneration or profit, except for the purpose of rehabilitation not incompatible with a finding of total and permanent disability.] The determination as to whether a Participant is totally and permanently disabled shall be made (i) on medical evidence by a licensed physician designated by the Plan Administrator, (ii) on evidence that the Participant is eligible for disability benefits under any long-term disability plan sponsored by the Employer but administered by an independent third party, or (iii) on evidence that the Participant is eligible for total and permanent disability benefits under the Social Security Act in effect at the date of disability. Total and Permanent Disability shall exclude disabilities arising from:

(a) Chronic or excessive use of intoxicants, drugs, or narcotics; or

(b) Intentionally self-inflicted injury or intentionally self-induced sickness; or

(c) A felonious act or enterprise on the part of the Participant; or

(d) Service in the Armed Forces where the Participant is eligible to receive a government-sponsored military disability pension.

1.30 The term *"Trust Agreement"* shall mean the agreement entered into between the Employer and the Trustee [contemporaneously with the execution of this Plan,] [on _____,] as it may subsequently be amended from time to time.

1.31 The term *"Trustee"* shall mean the Trustee or Trustees named in the Trust Agreement.

1.32 The term *"Trust Fund"* or *"Trust"* shall mean all cash, securities, life insurance, and real estate, and any other property held by the Trustee pursuant to the terms of the Trust Agreement, together with income therefrom.

1.33 The term *"Valuation Date"* shall mean the same day as the Plan Anniversary Date.

1.34 The term *"Year of Service"* shall mean, for the purpose of determining eligibility to participate herein: (1) the 12-month period commencing on the date of employment of an Employee and ending on the day immediately preceding the anniversary thereof, during which 12-month period the Employee completes at least 1,000 Hours of Service, and (2) any Plan Year commencing after the Employee's date of employment or re-employment during which he completes at least 1,000 Hours of Service. [For purposes of initial eligibility, service with the sole proprietorship of _____ shall be counted.] For all other purposes, the term "Year of Service" shall mean [(a) a 12-month period commencing on the date of employment of an Employee or the anniversary of such date (provided such date or anniversary comes before _____), in which 12-month period such Employee completes at least 1.000 Hours of Service, or (b)] a Plan Year commencing on or after _____, in which an Employee completes at least 1,000 Hours of Service. (Final option contains language for switch over from employment year to Plan Year for purposes of vesting credit.)

1.35 Any words herein used in the masculine shall be read and be construed in the feminine where they would so apply. Words in the singular shall be read and construed as though used in the plural in all cases where they would so apply.

(Participation for a New Plan)

ARTICLE II

PARTICIPATION

2.01 <u>Participation</u>. Any Employee shall become [a Participant as of the first day of the Plan Year in which he completes his first Year of Service, provided that the Employee is an employee of Employer on the last day of such first Year of Service.] [eligible to participate when he meets both of the following requirements:

(a) He must have completed his first Year of Service with the Employer for purposes of determining eligibility, and

(b) He must have attained age [twenty-five (25).]

The Employee shall be entitled to participate for the entire Plan Year during which he meets the later of the above requirements, provided that he is an employee of Employer when such later requirement is met.] A Retired, Disabled, Former, or Terminated Participant who later returns to the employ of the Employer shall again become a Participant on his date of re-employment. Notwithstanding any provision of this Plan to the contrary, a Retired, Disabled, Former, or Terminated Participant who is re-employed and continues in the employ of the Employer shall be an Active Participant for the Plan Year of re-employment, even though he completes not more than five hundred (500) Hours of Service during such Plan Year, and shall be entitled to all of the rights of an Active Participant except as provided in the last sentence in Section 5.11.

2.02 Rights of Participants. All Participants shall be bound by the terms of the Plan, including all amendments hereto made in the manner authorized herein. Participants shall also be entitled to all of the rights and privileges afforded thereby, including those granted specifically by the Code and ERISA, which are hereby adopted by reference as a part of this Plan.

(Alternate Participation for Amended and Restated Plan)

ARTICLE II

PARTICIPATION

2.01 Participation. An Employee who has qualified as a Participant under the Plan in effect immediately prior to the effective date of this amendment shall remain a Participant. Commencing with the effective date of this amendment, any Employee who is not a Participant shall become [a Participant as of the first day of the Plan Year in which he completes his first Year of Service, provided that the Employee is an employee of Employer on the last day of such first Year of Service.] [eligible to participate when he meets both of the following requirements:

(a) He must have completed his first Year of Service with the Employer for purposes of determining eligibility, and

(b) He must have attained age [twenty-five (25).]

The Employee shall be entitled to participate for the entire Plan Year during which he meets the later of the above requirements, provided that he is an employee of Employer when such later requirements is met.] A Retired, Disabled, Former, or Terminated Participant who later returns to the employ of the Employer shall again become a Participant on his date or re-employment. Notwithstanding any provision of this Plan to the contrary, a Retired, Disabled, Former, or Terminated

599

Participant who is re-employed and continues in the employ of the Employer shall be an Active Participant for the Plan Year of re-employment, even though he completes not more than five hundred (500) Hours of Service during such Plan Year, and shall be entitled to all of the rights of an Active Participant except as provided in the last sentence of Section 5.11

2.02 Rights of Participants. All Participants shall be bound by the terms of the Plan, including all amendments hereto made in the manner authorized herein. Participants shall also be entitled to all of the rights and privileges afforded thereby, including those granted specifically by the Code and ERISA, which are hereby adopted by reference as a part of this Plan.

(Alternate Participation for two entry dates. If this is used you must add the definition of "Participation Date.")

2.01 Participation. An Employee who has qualified as a Participant under the Plan in effect immediately prior to the effective date of this amendment shall remain a Participant. After the effective date of this amendment, any Employee who is not a Participant whall become eligible to participate when he [completes one (1) Year of Service.] [meets both of the following requirements:

(a) He must have completed one (1) Year of Service with the Employer; and

(b) He must have Attained Age [twenty-five (25).]

An eligible Employee shall be admitted to the Plan on the Participation Date coincident with or next following his completion of the requirements.] A Retired, Disabled, Former, or Terminated Participant who later returns to the employ of the Employer shall again become a Participant on his date of re-employment. Notwithstanding any provision of this Plan to the contrary, a Retired, Disabled, Former, or Terminated Participant who is re-employed and continues in the employ of the Employer shall be an Active Participant for the Plan Year of re-employment, even though he completes nor more than five hundred (500) Hours of Service during such Plan Year, and shall be entitled to all of the rights of an Active Participant except as provided in the last sentence of Section 5.11.

2.02 Rights of Participants. All Participants shall be bound by the terms of the Plan, including all amendments hereto made in the manner authorized herein. Participants shall also be entitled to all of the rights and privileges afforded thereby, including those granted specifically by the Code and ERISA, which are hereby adopted by reference as a part of this Plan.

ARTICLE III

EMPLOYER CONTRIBUTIONS

3.01 Amount of Employer Contributions. For each Plan Year, the Employer shall contribute to the Trust, to be held and administered by the Trustee according to the terms of the Trust Agreement, the following amounts for Active Participants as of the Anniversary Date and Retired or Disabled Participants who, as of the

Anniversary Date, have not elected pursuant ot Section 5.01, 5.02, 5.03, or 5.05 to take their Accounts as of the Valuation Date immediately preceding their dates of retirement or the dates on which they were determined to be Totally and Permanently Disabled and for whom separate accounts have not been established under Section 5.09 prior to the Anniversary Date:

(a) Three percent (3%) of each such Participant's Basic Compensation up to but not exceeding the Social Security Wage Base in effect on the Anniversary Date [or twenty thousand dollars ($20,000), whichever is lesser]; and

(b) Ten percent (10%) of each such Participant's Basic Compensation in excess of the social Security Wage Base in effect on the Anniversary Date [or twenty thousand dollars ($20,000), whichever is lesser]. (Note: Use dollar figure to lock in integration level at some figure other than the Social Security wage base.)

3.02 Reversion of Employer Contributions. Employer Contributions computed in accordance with the provisions of Section 3.01 shall revert to the Employer under the following circumstances:

(a) In the case of an Employer Contribution which is made by the Employer by reason of a mistabke of fact, such Contribution shall be returned to the Employer within one (1) year after the payment of the Contribution.

(b) If the Plan, as [adopted] [amended] effective _____, or [as amended] thereafter, does not qualify under Section 401(a) of the Code, Employer Contributions subsequent to the effective date of such amendment [or adoption, as appropriate,] shall be returned to the Employer within one (1) year after the date of denial of qualification of the Plan.

(c) If any Employer Contribution is determined by the Internal Revenue Service to be non-deductible under Section 404 of the Code, then such Employer Contribution, to the extent that it is determined to be non-deductible, shall be returned to the Employer within one (1) year after the disallowance of the deduction.

3.03 Allocation of Employer Contributions. The Plan Administrator shall establish and maintain an Account in the name of each Participant and, as soon as possible after the Employer has determined and paid the amount of the Employer Contributions for a Plan Year, such Employer Contributions shall be allocated to the Participant's Accounts by the Plan Administrator in the following manner:

(a) Employer Contributions made pursuant to Section 3.01 (a) shall be allocated to each Participant's Account in proportion to the ratio that said Participant's Basic Compensation not exceeding the Social Security Wage Base in effect on the Anniversary Date [or twenty thousand dollars ($20,000), whichever is the lesser,] bears to the total Basic Compensation of all Participants not exceeding said Social Security Wage Base [for twenty thousand dollars ($20,000), whichever is the lesser].

(b) Employer Contributions made pursuant to Section 3.01 (b) shall be allocated, to each Participant's Account in proportion to the ratio that said Participant's Basic Compensation in excess of the Social Security Wage Base in effect on the Anniversary Date [or twenty thousand dollars ($20,000), whichever is the lesser,] bears to the total Basic Compensation of all Participants receiving an allocation of Employer Contributions in excess of the Social Security Wage Base in effect on the Anniversary Date [or twenty thousand dollars ($20,000), whichever is the lesser,] bears to the total Basic Compensation of all Participants receiving an allocation of Employer Contributions in excess of the Social Security Wage Base in effect on the Anniversary Date [or twenty thousand dollars ($2,000), whichever is the lesser].

Only Active Participants, and Retired and Disabled Participants who have not elected pursuant to Section 5.01, 5.02, 5.03, or 5.05 to take their Accounts as of the Anniversary Date immediately preceding their dates of retirement or the dates on which they were determined to be Totally and Permanently Disabled who complete more than five hundred (500) Hours of Service during the Plan Year ending with the Anniversary Date in question, and for whom separate accounts have not been established under Section 5.09 prior to the Anniversary Date in question, shall be eligible to share in the allocation of Employer Contributions as provided above.

3.04 <u>Section 415 Limitations.</u> Notwithstanding any provisions contained herein to the contrary, the Annual Addition for any Plan Year with respect to a Participant, under this Plan and under any other Defined Contribution Plan maintained by the Employer shall not exceed the lesser of (i) twenty-five percent (25%) of the Participant's Basic Compensation for the Plan Year or (ii) $36,875 (or such amount as may be increased by regulations promulgated by the Secretary of the Treasury from time to time). Also, if an Employee is a Participant in this Plan and one or more Defined Benefit Plans maintained by the Employer, the sum of his Defined Benefit Plan Fraction and his Defined Contribution Plan Fraction shall not exceed 1.4 for any Plan Year. For purposes of this Section 3.04 and Section 3.05, the term Employer shall include any other employer required to be aggregated under Code Section 415(h) and the term Basic Compensation shall include Basic Compensation from any such other employer.

(ERISA Transitional Language)

[If an Employee was a Participant on or before September 2, 1974, in this Plan and a Defined Benefit Plan maintained by the Employer, the sum of his Defined Benefit Plan Fraction and Defined Contribution Plan Fraction for the year which includes September 2, 1974, may be in excess of 1.4 if (i) the Defined Benefit Plan Fraction is not increased by an amendment to the Defined Benefit Plan or otherwise after September 2, 1974; and (ii) Contributions are not made to this Plan after September 2, 1974.]

3.05 <u>Correction of Contributions in Excess of Section 415 Limits.</u> In the event that, as of any Valuation Date, corrective adjustments in any Participant's Account are required to comply with Section 3.04, the Annual Addition to his Account shall be reduced by forfeiting that portion, or all, of the Employer Contributions under Section 3.01 required to assure compliance with Section 3.04.

Any amounts forfeited under this Section 3.05 shall be held in a suspense account and shall be applied, subject to Section 3.04, toward funding the Employer Contributions for the next succeeding Plan Year, and such application shall be made prior to any Employer Contributions and prior to any Employee Contributions that would constitute Annual Additions. No income or investment gains and losses shall be allocated to the suspense account provided for under this Section. If any amount remains in a suspense account provided for under this Section upon termination of this Plan, such amount will revert to the Employer notwithstanding any other provision of this Plan.

3.06 Combination of Plans. Notwithstanding any provisions contained herein to the contrary, in the event that the Employer maintains any other Defined Contribution Plan and the sum of the Annual Additions in respect of a Participant exceeds the limitations contained in Section 3.04, corrective adjustments shall not be made in said Participant's Account under this Money-Purchase Pension Plan if such other Defined Contribution Plan provides for corrective adjustments that will prevent a violation of the limitations contained in Section 3.04.

3.07 Correction of Prior Incorrect Allocations and Previous Funding Deficiencies. Notwithstanding any provisions contained herein to the contrary, in the event that, as of any Valuation Date, adjustments are required in any Participant's Account to correct any incorrect allocation of Employer Contributions, investment earnings or losses, or any funding deficiency which may have occurred in a previous year, the Plan Administrator is authorized to apply the Employer Contributions to correct such incorrect allocation or funding deficiency and to increase such Participant's Account to the value which would have existed on said Valuation Date had there been no prior incorrect allocation or funding deficiency. The Plan Administrator is also authorized to take such other actions as he deems necessary to correct prior incorrect allocations or funding deficiencies.

ARTICLE IV

ALLOCATIONS AND ACCOUNTS OF PARTICIPANTS

4.01 Valuations. As of each Valuation Date, the Trustee shall determine the fair market value of the Trust Fund, and the Plan Administrator shall determine the fair market value of the Account of each Participant. The value of the Account of each Participant as of any Valuation Date shall be equal to the value of such Account as of the last Valuation Date, plus or minus the applicable adjustments contained in Section 4.02.

4.02 Allocations. As of each Valuation Date, the Account of each Participant shall be adjusted in the following manner:

(a) Earnings or Losses. The investment earnings (or losses, if the computation specified in this sentence results in a negative figure) of the Trust Fund shall be equal to (i) the fair market value of the Trust Fund (excluding amounts held in separate accounts pursuant to Section 5.09, excluding any earmarked investments of any Accounts, and excluding the value of any insurance contracts) as of the current Valuation Date; less (ii) the fair market value of the Trust Fund (excluding amounts held in separate accounts pursuant to Section 5.09, excluding any earmarked investments of any Accounts, and excluding the value of any insurance contracts) as of the immediately preceding Valuation Date; plus (iii) benefit payments to Participants (excluding payments from separate accounts), any amounts placed in separate accounts pursuant to Section 5.09, any amounts that were transferred since the immediately preceding Valuation Date to a segregated earmarked investment, and any other disbursements from the Trust Fund on behalf of a particular Participant since the last preceding Valuation Date; less (iv) any Employer Contributions made to the Trust Fund since the last preceding Valuation Date and any amounts that were transferred since the immediately preceding Valuation Date from a segregated earmarked investment to the assets of the Trust Fund that are subject to investment by the Trustee. Investment earnings or losses shall be allocated to the Account of each Active Participant, and each Former Participant for whom a separate account has not been established under Section 5.09 as of the Valuation Date in question, and each Retired or Disabled Participant who has not elected pursuant to Section 5.01, 5.02, 5.03, or 5.05 to take his Account as of the Valuation Date immediately preceding his date of retirement or the date on which he is determined to be Totally and Permanently Disabled and for whom a separate account has not been established under Section 5.09 as of the Valuation Date in question. Such investment earnings shall be allocated in the ratio that the value of such Account (valuing insurance contracts at zero) as of the last preceding Valuation Date, minus any amount paid, segregated, or disbursed to or on behalf of the Active, Former, Retired or Disabled Participant under (iii), above, since the last preceding Valuation Date, bears to the total value of the Accounts (valuing insurance contracts at zero) of all such Participants as of the last preceding Valuation Date, minus the amounts paid, segregated, or disbursed to or on behalf of all such Participants under (iii), above, since the last preceding Valuation Date; [provided, however, that for the first Valuation Date following the Effective Date the allocation of earnings or losses shall be made in the same proportion that Employer Contributions allocated to each Account as of such first Valuation Date bears to the value of all Employer Contributions in all such Accounts as of such first Valuation Date.] (Use option for new plans only.) Any Participant may request the Plan Administrator to make a Special Valuation under Section 4.04 in order to avoid prejudice to his Account that might otherwise occur as a result of the application of the immediately preceding sentence to such Participant's Account. The cost of such Special Valuation shall be charged to the Account of the Participant requesting such Special Valuation. Approval of a request for a Special Valuation is subject to the discretion of the Plan Administrator and the Plan Administrator shall exercise his discretion in a non-discriminatory manner. No allocation of investment earnings shall be made to any Terminated Participant, to any Former Participant for whom a separate account has been established under Section 5.09 as of the Valuation Date in question, or to any Retired or Disabled Participant who has elected pursuant to Section 5.01, 5.02, 5.03, or 5.05 to take his Account as of the Valuation Date immediately preceding his date of retirement or the date on which he is determined to be Totally and

Permanently Disabled or for whom a separate account has been established under Section 5.09 as of the Valuation Date in question.

(b) Employer Contributions. The Account of each Active Participant, and of each Retired or Disabled Participant who has not elected pursuant to Section 5.01, 5.02, 5.03, or 5.05 to take his Account as of the Valuation Date immediately preceding his date of retirement or the date on which he is determined to be Totally and Permanently Disabled who completes more than five hundred (500) Hours of Service during the Plan Year ending with the Valuation Date in question, and for whom a separate account has not been established under Section 5.09 as of the Valuation Date in question, shall be increased by any allocation of the Employer Contributions (plus any amounts forfeited and applied against Employer Contributions as provided in Section 5.06) set forth in Section 3.03 hereof.

4.03 Determination of Value. In determining the value of the Trust Fund and the Accounts, the Trustee and the Plan Administrator shall exercise their best judgment, and all such determinations of value shall be binding upon all Participants and their Beneficiaries. All allocations shall be deemed to have been made as of the Valuation Date, regardless of when actual allocations were made.

4.04 Special Valuations. Notwithstanding anything to the contrary expressed or implied herein, the Plan Administrator (with the consent of the Trustee) may direct on a non-discriminatory basis a special valuation date in order to avoid prejudice either to continuing Participants or to terminating Participants. Such special valuation date shall be deemed equivalent to a regular valuation date, except that the allocation under Section 4.02(b) shall not be made.

4.05 Separate Allocations for Each Affiliate. In the event that affiliated or subsidiary corporations become signatory hereto, completely independent records, allocations, and contributions shall be maintained for each corporation. The Trustee may invest all funds without segregating assets between or among signatory Employers. Separate Accounts shall be established by each Employer for each Participant employed by any such Employer. Forfeitures arising with respect to one Employer's Former or Terminated Participants shall be allocated only to reduce future Contributions of that Employer and shall not be allocated throughout the affiliated group of Employers.

ARTICLE V

PAYMENTS OF BENEFITS TO PARTICIPANTS

5.01 Normal Retirement. When a Participant reaches his Normal Retirement Date and retires, he shall become entitled to the full value of his Account (a) as of the Valuation Date immediately preceding his Normal Retirement Date, appropriately adjusted to take into account any payments or distributions to or for him since such Valuation Date, or (b) as of the Valuation Date coincident with or immediately following his Normal Retirement Date, whichever he elects on or before his Normal Retirement Date. Any election by a Participant to take his Account as of the Valuation Date immediately preceding his Normal Retirement

Date shall make such Participant ineligible to receive further allocations of Employer Contributions and earnings or losses unless he is subsequently re-employed by the Employer. Any election by a Participant to take his Account as of the Valuation Date coincident with or immediately following his Normal Retirement Date shall entitle such Participant, for the Plan Year during which he retires, to: (1) an allocable share of earnings or losses and (2) an allocable share of Employer Contributions if he completes more than five hundred (500) Hours of Service during such Plan Year; but the distribution to such Participant shall not commence during the Plan Year in which he retires. A failure on the part of the Participant to make any election on or before his Normal Retirement Date shall be deemed to constitute an election to take the full value of his Account as of the Valuation Date coincident with or immediately following his Normal Retirement Date.

5.02 <u>Late Retirement</u>. In the event that a Participant continues as an Employee of the Employer following his Normal Retirement Date in accordance with the Employer's employment practices or in accordance with applicable law, such Participant shall continue to be an Active Participant under the Plan until his retirement and, upon his retirement, he shall become entitled to the full value of his Account (a) as of the Valuation Date immediately preceding his date of retirement, appropriately adjusted to take into account any payments or distributions to or for him since such Valuation Date, or (b) as of the Valuation Date coincident with or immediately following his date of retirement, whichever he elects on or before his date of retirement. Any election by a Participant to take his Account as of the Valuation Date immediately preceding his date of retirement shall make such Participant ineligible to receive further allocations of Employer Contributions and earnings or losses unless he is subsequently re-employed by the Employer. Any election by a Participant to take his Account as of the Valuation Date coincident with or immediately following his date of retirement shall entitle such Participant, for the Plan Year during which he retires, to: (1) an allocable share of earnings or losses and (2) an allocable share of Employer Contributions if he completes more than five hundred (500) Hours of Service during such Plan Year; but the distribution to such Participant shall not commence during the Plan Year in which he retires. A failure on the part of the Participant to make any election on or before his date of retirement shall be deemed to constitute an election to take the full value of his Account as of the Valuation Date coincident with or immediately following his date of retirement.

5.03 <u>Early Retirement</u>. When a Participant retires on or after his Early Retirement Date but before his Normal Retirement Date, he shall become entitled to the full value of his Account (a) as of the Valuation Date immediately preceding his retirement, appropriately adjusted to take into account any payments or distributions to or for him since such Valuation Date, or (b) as of the Valuation Date coincident with or immediately following his retirement, whichever he elects on or before the date of his retirement. Any election by a Participant to take his Account as of the Valuation Date immediately preceding his date of retirement shall make such Participant ineligible to receive further allocations of Employer Contributions and earnings or losses unless he is subsequently re-employed by the

Employer. Any election by a Participant to take his Account as of the Valuation Date coincident with or immeidately following his date of retirement shall entitle such Participant, for the Plan Year during which he retires, to: (1) an allocable share of earnings or losses and (2) to an allocable share of Employer Contributions if he completes more than five hundred (500) Hours of Service during such Plan Year; but the distribution to such Participant shall not commence during the Plan Year in which he retires. A failure on the part of the Participant to make any election on or before his date of retirement shall be deemed to constitute an election to take the full value of his Account as of the Valuation Date coincident with or immediately following his date of retirement.

5.04 Death Benefit. If a Participant dies while an Active Participant under the Plan, his Beneficiary or Beneficiaries shall be entitled to the full value of his Account (a) as of the Valuation Date immediately preceding his date of death, appropriately adjusted to take into account any payments or distributions to or for him since such Valuation Date, or (b) as of the Valuation Date coincident with or immediately following his date of death, whichever his Beneficiary or Beneficiaries unanimously elect within sixty (60) days following the date of death. If the Beneficiary or Beneficiaries fail to unanimously elect option (a) within the sixty (60) day election period such Beneficiary or Beneficiaries shall be deemed to have elected option (b). If the Beneficiary or Beneficiaries unanimously elect option (a) the Participant's Account shall be ineligible to receive further allocations of Employer Contributions or earnings or losses. If such Beneficiary or Beneficiaries elect or are deemed to elect option (b), the deceased Participant shall for all purposes be regarded as an Active Participant as of the Valuation Date coincident with or immediately following his date of death and shall be entitled to: (1) an allocable share of earnings or losses as of such Valuation Date and (2) an allocable share of Employer Contributions as of such Valuation Date if the deceased Participant completed more than five hundred (500) Hours of Service during the Plan Year in which the death occurs; but the distribution with respect to such deceased Participant shall not commence during the Plan Year in which he dies.

5.05 Disability. When it is determined that a Participant is Totally and Permanently Disabled, the Plan Administrator shall certify such fact to the Trustee, and such Disabled Participant shall be entitled to receive the full value of his Account (a) as of the Valuation Date immediately preceding the date the Plan Administrator determines he became Totally and Permanently Disabled, appropriately adjusted to take into account any payments or distributions to or for him since such Valuation Date, or (b) as of the Valuation Date coincident with or immediately following the date the Plan Administrator determines he became Totally and Permanently Disabled, whichever the Participant or his legal representative elects not later than the thirtieth (30th) day following the Plan Administrator's determination of Total and Permanent Disability. Any election by a Participant or his legal representative to take his Account as of the Valuation Date immediately preceding the effective date of the Plan Administrator's determination shall make such Participant ineligible to receive further allocations of Employer Contributions and earnings or losses unless he is subsequently re-employed by the Employer. Any election by a Participant or his legal representative to take his Account as of the Valuation Date coincident with or immediately following the date of the Plan Administrator's determination shall entitle such Participant, for the Plan Year during which the determination is made, to: (1) an allocable share of earnings or losses and (2) an allocable share of Employer Contributions if he completed more than five hundred (500) Hours of Service during such Plan Year; but the distribution to such Participant or his legal representative shall not commence during the Plan Year in which the determination is made. A failure on the part of the Participant or his legal representative to make any election on or before the thirtieth (30th) day following the Plan Administrator's determination of Total and Permanent Disability shall be deemed to constitute an election to take the full value of his Account as of the Valuation Date coincident with or immediately following the effective date of the Plan Administrator's determination.

5.06 Termination. Whenever the employment of a Participant is terminated for reasons other than normal, early or late actual retirement under Sections 5.01, 5.02, or 5.03 hereof, death under Section 5.04, or Total and Permanent Disability under Section 5.05, and as a result of such termination said Participant incurs a One Year Break in Service, he shall become entitled to the following:

(a) Filing a Claim. Upon incurring a One Year Break in Service, the Participant may file a written claim for benefits with the Plan Administrator requesting distribution of the nonforfeitable percentage of his Account determined as of the Valuation Date coincident with the completion of his One Year Break in Service. Alternatively, such Participant may elect to defer receipt of the nonforfeitable percentage of his Account determined as of the Valuation Date coincident with the completion of his One Year Break in Service. If the Participant makes such an election to defer receipt (or fails to file a claim for benefits within a reasonable period of time after incurring a One Year Break in Service), the nonforfeitable percentage of his Account, determined as of the Valuation Date coincident with the completion of his One Year Break in Service, shall be segregated and held in a separate account in accordance with Section 5.09. For purposes of this Section, the Participant's nonforfeitable percentage shall be based upon the Former or Terminated Participant's total number of completed Years of Service, computed without regard to any Years of Service completed after the One Year Break in Service. Such nonforfeitable percentage shall be determined from the following schedule:

Completed Years of Service	Nonforfeitable Percentage	Forfeitable Percentage

That portion of the Account to which the Former or Terminated Participant is not entitled, based on the forfeitable percentage under the above vesting schedule, shall be applied against and proportionately reduce the next ensuing Employer Contribution.

(b) Review of Claim. The Plan Administrator shall review any claim for benefits filed in accordance with Subsection (a) and shall, in its discretion (which shall be exercised in a uniform and non-discriminatory manner), either authorize an immediate commencement of distribution in accordance with Section 5.07 or shall direct that the nonforfeitable percentage of the Participant's Account shall be segregated and held as a separate account in accordance with Section 5.09.

(c) Treatment of Separate Accounts. If, under Subsection (a), the Participant elects or is deemed to elect deferred receipt of the nonforfeitable percentage of his Account determined as of the Valuation Date coincident with the completion of his One Year Break in Service, or if under Subsection (b) the Plan Administrator directs that such amount be held in a separate account in accordance with Section 5.09, the Participant, upon filing a written claim, shall be entitled to the then balance of such separate account (which shall be distributed in the manner elected under Section 5.07) as of his Normal Retirement Date or as of his Early Retirement Date if he had completed at least ten (10) Years of Service before incurring a One Year Break in Service.

(d) Mandatory Distribution. Irrespective of whether the Participant files a written claim, or elects to defer receipt under Subsection (a), the Plan Administrator, in its discretion, may direct payments in a lump sum to such Participant if such Participant incurs a One Year Break in Service and if the vested portion of his Account does not then exceed $1,750.00.

5.07 Method of Payment. Subject to the provisions of Sections 5.08 and 5.11, a Participant separating from service in accordance with Section 5.01, 5.02, 5.03, 5.05, or 5.06, or his Beneficiary in the event of the Participant's death, shall request a manner and time for commencement of distribution of any benefits under the Plan as provided hereinafter. The request by the Participant or the Beneficiary shall be in writing and shall be filed with the Plan Administrator at least thirty (30) days before distribution is to be made and shall be subject to approval by the Plan Administrator. Upon the approval of the Plan Administrator, one of the following alternative forms of distribution shall be selected by the Participant or Beneficiary:

(a) A lump sum distribution in cash or in kind, provided that no "in kind" distribution may be made of a life annuity;

(b) Periodic installments (either monthly or annually) for a period not to exceed ten (10) years; or

(c) Any combination of the above.

Notwithstanding the foregoing, if the Participant is the person making the election, he shall not elect installments extending beyond either the life expectancy of the Participant or the joint life expectancies of the Participant and his spouse, if any.

In the absence of an election by the Beneficiary within nine (9) months following a Participant's death, the Beneficiary, or all of the Beneficiaries collectively, shall be deemed to have elected monthly installments for a period of four (4) years.

5.08 Commencement of Benefits. Any payment of benefits to the Participant shall begin not later than sixty (60) days after the last day of the Plan Year in which the *latest* of (a), (b), or (c) occurs:

(a) The Participant's Normal Retirement Date;

(b) The tenth (10th) anniversary of the date the Employee became a Participant;

(c) The Participant's separation from service.

Under no circumstances, however, shall any benefit be paid until a written claim therefor is filed with the Plan Administrator.

5.09 Separate Accounts. As soon as practical after the amount that is distributable to a Former, Retired, or Disabled Participant or to the Beneficiary of a deceased Participant is finally determined, if his distribution will either be paid in installments or be delayed more than six (6) months if payable in a lump sum, his Account shall be segregated from other Trust Fund assets and invested in a separate account. The investment of such separate account shall be in such federally insured savings accounts as are determined by the Trustee, [including savings accounts maintained by the Trustee,] with all interest earned on such investments credited to such accounts and all disbursements charged thereto. Such accounts may be held in cash, but only for a limited period between investments, or as a reserve to meet installment distributions. In the event of the death of a Participant to whom periodic installments are being paid, or are due to be so paid, prior to receipt of the full interest in such account, the remaining balance of such separate account shall be paid in installments to the Beneficiary or Contingent Beneficiary in accordance with the schedule elected by the Participant under Section 5.07.

(Section 5.10 drafted pursuant to Georgia law; may vary from state to state.)

5.10 Beneficiaries. Each Participant shall designate a Beneficiary or Beneficiaries and Contingent Beneficiaries to receive benefits upon his death, and such designation may be changed from time to time by the Participant by filing a new designation with the Plan Administrator. If, at the time of a Participant's death while benefits are still outstanding, his named Beneficiary does not survive him, the benefits shall be paid to his named Contingent Beneficiary in accordance with the terms of Section 5.07. If a deceased Participant is not survived by either a named Beneficiary or Contingent Beneficiary (or in no Beneficiary or Contingent Beneficiary was effectively named), the benefits shall be paid, in the discretion of the Plan Administrator, in a lump sum to the person or persons or in periodic installments, as provided in Section 5.07, to the person or persons in the first of the following classes of beneficiaries with one or more members of such class then surviving: the Participant's (a) widow or widower, (b) children, (c) parents, (d) brothers and sisters, or (e) executors and administrators. If the Beneficiary or Contingent Beneficiary is living at the death of the Participant, but such person dies prior to receiving the entire death benefit, the remaining portion to such death benefit shall be paid in a single sum to the estate of such deceased Beneficiary or Contingent Beneficiary.

5.11 <u>Cash-Out Procedure upon Discharge or Resignation</u>. If the Participant, on or before the date of his termination of employment by reason of discharge or resignation, or within a reasonable period of time thereafter (but not later than the Valuation Date for the Plan Year during which such termination occurs), requests in writing that the Plan Administrator distribute to him the vested portion of his Account, The Plan Administrator may, in its sole discretion, direct the Trustee to pay such amount to the Participant within sixty (60) days following his termination of employment, notwithstanding that the Participant shall not then have incurred a One Year Break in Service. The Participant's Account shall be determined as of the Valuation Date immediately preceding the date of his termination, and such Participant's vested interest shall be determined as of his date of termination. Once the Plan Administrator issues the directive for the Trustee to pay the Participant, the cash-out shall be deemed to be in process or pending. The nonvested portion of a Participant's Account that is not distributed to him at the time of the cash-out, shall be forfeited if the Participant does not effect a buy-back in accordance with Section 5.12, and such forfeited amount shall be applied against and proportionately reduce future Employer Contributions. Such forfeiture shall occur on the Valuation Date coincident with the Participant's incurring a One Year Break in Service, or, if the Participant does not incur a One Year Break in Service, but fails to repay cash-out within two (2) years of his reemployment date, such forfeiture shall occur on the expiration date of the two (2) year buy-back period described in Section 5.12. No earnings or losses shall be allocated to the amount that is returned to the Participant's Account under Section 5.12, or to the amount treated as a forfeiture under the immediately preceding sentence. Absent a buy-back by the Participant under Section 5.12, the actual payment of benefits under this Section 5.11 shall satisfy all obligations of the Trust to such Participant, and such Participant shall not be entitled to share in allocations of Employer Contributions and earnings or losses as of the Valuation Date coincident with or immediately following his termination of employment, absent a buy-back prior to such Valuation Date, even though the cashed-out Participant resumes his employment with the Employer on or before such Valuation Date.

5.12 <u>Buy-Back Procedure</u>. A Terminated Participant who has received a cash-out of benefits pursuant to Section 5.11, and who returns to the employ of the Employer before a One Year Break in Service has occurred, shall be permitted to repay the cash-out amount to the Trust Fund within two (2) years following the date of his return, and thereby restore his benefits under the Plan determined as of the Valuation Date immediately preceding the actual payment of the cash-out.

5.13 <u>Reemployment After One Year Break in Service</u>.

(a) A Former or Terminated Participant who is reemployed after incurring a One Year Break in Service shall not be entitled to receive credit for vesting purposes for Years of Service earned prior to the One Year Break in Service except as follows:

(1) If he had a nonforfeitable right to all or a portion of his Account derived from Employer Contributions at the time of his termi-

nation of employment, he shall receive credit for Years of Service earned prior to his One Year Break in Service upon his completion of a Year of Service following the date of his reemployment; or

(2) If he did not have a nonforfeitable right to all or any portion of his Account derived from Employer Contributions at the time of his termination of employment, he shall receive credit for Years of Service earned prior to his One Year Break in Service if (i) he completes a Year of Service after his reemployment, and (ii) at the time he completes such Year of Service his number of consecutive One Year Breaks in Service is less than his aggregate Years of Service earned before his initial One Year Break in Service.

(b) All Years of Service earned after a One Year Break in Service shall be disregarded in determining a Participant's nonforfeitable percentage in his Account attributable to Employer Contributions prior to the One Year Break in Service.

[5.14 Loans to Participants. The Plan Administrator may, in its sole discretion, direct the Trustee to make a loan or loans from the Trust Fund to any Participant to relieve unusual financial hardship, such as, but not limited to, the illness of a Participant or a member of a Participant's immediate family, or for the purpose of establishing or preserving the home in which a Participant resides, or for the purpose of education of children, in a total amount not in excess of the value [of the vested portion] of such Participant's Account that is attributable to Employer Contributions under Section 3.01. The Plan Administrator shall adopt and follow uniform and non-discriminatory rules for repayment of such loans in a period certain at the prevailing rate of interest being charged by [the Trustee.] [commercial banks in _____.] The Plan Administrator shall direct the Trustee to obtain from the Participant such note and security as it may require. Notwithstanding the provisions of Section 10.09, in the event of failure to repay the principal or interest according to its terms, or should the Participant's employment terminate prior to full repayment thereof, in addition to any other remedy provided in the loan instruments or by law, the Plan Administrator may direct the Trustee to charge against the vested portion of his Account which secures the loan the amount required to fully repay the loan. No distribution shall be made to any Participant, unless and until all unpaid loans to such Participant have either been paid in full or deducted from the Account of the Participant. This Section authorizes only the making of bona fide loans and not distributions, and before resort is made against the vested portion of a Participant's Account for his failure to repay any loan, such other reasonable efforts to collect the same shall be made by the Plan Administrator as it deems reasonable and practical under the circumstances. [All loans made under this Section shall be considered investments of the Trust Fund unless the Trust Agreement specifically permits, and a Participant so directs that the loans be earmarked investments of his Account.] Under no circumstances, however, shall an unpaid loan be charged against a Participant's vested interest so long as he remains employed by the Employer.]

ARTICLE VI

CLAIMS PROCEDURE

6.01 Filing of Claim. A Plan Participant or Beneficiary shall make a claim for Plan benefits by filing a written request with the Plan Administrator upon a form to be furnished to him for such purpose.

6.02 Denial of Claim. If a claim is wholly or partially denied, the Plan Administrator shall furnish the Participant or Beneficiary with written notice of the denial within sixty (60) days of the date the original claim was filed. This notice of denial shall provide (1) the reason for denial, (2) specific reference to pertinent Plan provisions on which the denial is based, (3) a description of any additional information needed to perfect the claim and an explanation of why such information is necessary, and (4) an explanation of the Plan's claim procedure.

6.03 Review of Denial. The Participant or Beneficiary shall have sixty (60) days from receipt of denial notice in which to make written application for review by the Plan Administrator. The Participant or Beneficiary may request that the review be in the nature of a hearing. The Participant or Beneficiary shall have the rights (1) to representation, (2) to review pertinent documents, and (3) to submit comments in writing.

6.04 Decision upon Review. The Plan Administrator shall issue a decision on such review within sixty (60) days after receipt of an application for review as provided in Section 6.03.

(Options drafted for employer or individual to serve as Plan Administrator—must redraft for Committee.)

ARTICLE VII

THE PLAN ADMINISTRATOR

7.01 Designation. [The Plan Administrator shall be the Employer. The Plan Administrator shall keep a permanent record of its actions with respect to the Plan which shall be available for inspection by appropriate parties as provided in the Code and ERISA.]

[The Board of Directors of the Employer shall name one of its members or an officer of the Employer, to be known as the Plan Administrator, to administer the Plan, keep records of individual Participant benefits, and notify the Participants of the amount of their benefits annually.

The original Plan Administrator shall be _____. The Plan Administrator shall serve until his resignation or dismissal by the Board of Directors of the Employer and a vacancy shall be filled in the same manner as the original appointment. No compensation shall be paid the Plan Administrator from the Trust Fund for his services. The Plan Administrator shall keep a permanent record of his actions with respect to the Plan which shall be available for inspection by appropriate parties as provided in the Code and ERISA.]

7.02 <u>Responsibilities in General.</u> Subject to the limitations of the Plan, the Plan Administrator shall from time to time establish rules for the administration of the Plan and transaction of its business. The records of the Employer, as certified to the Plan Administrator, shall be conclusive with respect to any and all factual matters dealing with the employment of a Participant. The Plan Administrator shall interpret the Plan and shall determine all questions arising in the administration, interpretation, and application of the Plan, and all such determinations by the Plan Administrator shall be conclusive and binding on all persons, subject, however, to the provisions of the Code and ERISA.

7.03 <u>Payment Orders.</u> The Plan Administrator shall direct the Trustee in writing to make payments from the Trust Fund to Participants who qualify for such payments hereunder. Such written order to the Trustee shall specify the name of the Participant, his Social Security number, his address, and the amount and frequency of such payments.

7.04 <u>No Discrimination.</u> The Plan Administrator shall not take action or direct the Trustee to take any action with respect to any of the benefits provided hereunder or otherwise in pursuance of the powers conferred herein upon the Plan Administrator which would be discriminatory in favor of Participants who are officers, shareholders, or highly compensated employees, or which would result in benefiting one Participant, or group of Participants, at the expense of another or in discrimination between Participants similarly situated or in the application of different rules to substantially similar sets of facts.

7.05 <u>Requests by Trustee for Instructions.</u> The Trustee may request instructions in writing from the Plan Administrator on any matters affecting the Trust and may rely and act thereon.

7.06 <u>Allocations.</u> The Plan Administrator shall be responsible for the determination of Accounts, and the Trustee need not segregate accounts either among Participants or among employers for investment purposes, except as indicated in Section 5.09.

ARTICLE VIII

THE TRUST FUND AND TRUSTEE

8.01 <u>Existence of Trust.</u> The Employer has entered into a Trust Agreement with the Trustee to hold the funds necessary to provide the benefits set forth in this Plan.

8.02 <u>Exclusive Benefit Rule.</u> The Trust Fund shall be received, held in trust, and disbursed by the Trustee in accordance with the provisions of the Trust Agreement and this Plan. No part of the Trust Fund shall be used for or diverted to purposes other than for the exclusive benefit of Participants, Retired Participants, Disabled Participants, their Beneficiaries, or Contingent Beneficiaries under this Plan. No person shall have any interest in, or right to, the Trust Fund or any part thereof, except as specifically provided for in this Plan or the Trust Agreement or both.

8.03 <u>Removal of Trustee.</u> The Board of Directors may remove the Trustee at any time upon the notice required by the terms of the Trust Agreement, and upon

614

such removal or upon the resignation of a Trustee, the Board of Directors shall appoint a successor Trustee.

8.04 <u>Powers of Trustee.</u> The Trustee shall have such powers to hold, invest, reinvest, or to control and disburse the funds as at that time shall be set forth in the Trust Agreement or this Plan.

8.05 <u>Integration of Trust.</u> The Trust Agreement shall be deemed to be a part of this Plan, and all rights of Participants or others under this Plan shall be subject to the provisions of the Trust Agreement.

ARTICLE IX
AMENDMENT AND TERMINATION

9.01 <u>Right to Amend.</u> The Employer reserves the right at any time, by action of its Board of Directors, to modify or amend, in whole or in part, any or all of the provisions of the Plan, including specifically the right to make such amendments effective retroactively, if necessary, to bring the Plan into conformity with regulations promulgated under the Code or ERISA which must be complied with so that the Plan and Trust Fund may continue to remain qualified and to preserve the tax exempt status of the Trust. No modification or amendment shall make it possible for Trust assets to be used for, or diverted to, purposes other than the exclusive benefit of Participants and their Beneficiaries.

9.02 <u>Right to Terminate.</u> The Employer may, by action of its Board of Directors, terminate the Plan and the Trust.

9.03 <u>Vesting upon Termination.</u> If the Plan is terminated by the Employer or its contributions to the Trust are completely discontinued, the Accounts of Participants as of the date of termination or complete discontinuance of contributions shall immediately become nonforfeitable. In the event that the Employer should resume making contributions to the Trust following discontinuance, such future Employer Contributions shall be allocated in accordance with the provisions of Article III and shall be vested in accordance with Section 5.06.

9.04 <u>Distributions upon Termination.</u> If the Plan is terminated, the interest of each Participant shall be distributed in a lump sum or in periodic installments, in cash or in kind, or shall continue to be held in Trust at the discretion of the Plan Administrator as provided in Article V hereof.

9.05 <u>Vesting upon Partial Termination.</u> In the event a partial termination occurs, the Accounts of those Participants affected shall become nonforfeitable and shall be held or distributed in accordance with the provisions of Section 5.07.

ARTICLE X
MISCELLANEOUS PROVISIONS

10.01 <u>Prohibition Against Diversion.</u> There shall be no diversion of any portion of the assets of the Trust Fund other than for the exclusive benefit of Participants and their Beneficiaries.

10.02 <u>Prudent Man Rule.</u> For purposes of Part 4 of Title I of ERISA, the Employer, the Trustee, and the Plan Administrator shall each be Fiduciaries and shall each discharge their respective duties hereunder with the care, skill, prudence, and diligence under the circumstances then prevailing that a prudent man acting in a like capacity and familiar with such matters would use in the conduct of an enterprise of a like character and with like aims. Without limiting the generality of the above, it is specifically provided that the appointment and retention of any parties pursuant to ARTICLE VII of the Plan are "duties" of the Employer for purposes of this Section.

10.03 Responsibilities of Parties. The Employer shall be responsible for the administration and management of the Plan except for those duties specifically allocated to the Trustee or Plan Administrator. The Trustee shall have exclusive responsibility for the management and control of the assets of the Plan. The Plan Administrator shall have exclusive responsibility for all matters specifically delegated to it by the Employer in the Plan. The Employer shall be deemed the Plan Sponsor for all purposes of ERISA.

10.04 Reports Furnished Participants. The Plan Administrator shall furnish to each Plan Participant, and to each Beneficiary receiving benefits under the Plan, within the time limits specified in, and as required by, the Code and ERISA, each of the following:

(a) A Summary Plan Description and periodic revisions;

(b) Notification of amendments to the Plan; and

(c) A Summary Annual Report which summarizes the Annual Report filed with the Department of Labor.

10.05 Reports Available to Participants. The Plan Administrator shall make copies of the following documents available at the principal office of the Employer for examination by any Plan Participant or Beneficiary:

(a) The Money Purchase Pension Plan and Trust Agreement; and

(b) The latest annual report.

10.06 Reports Upon Request. The Plan Administrator shall furnish to any Plan Participant or Beneficiary who so requests in writing, once during any twelve-month period, a statement indicating, on the basis of the latest available information—

(a) The total benefits accrued; and

(b) The non-forfeitable benefits, if any, which have accrued, or the earliest date on which benefits will become non-forfeitable.

The Plan Administrator shall also furnish to any Plan Participant or Beneficiary who so requests in writing, at a reasonable charge to be prescribed by regulation of the Secretary of Labor, any document referred to in Section 10.05.

10.07 Rollover Contributions and Direct Transfers from Other Qualified Retirement Plans. Notwithstanding any provisions contained herein to the contrary, a Participant shall be entitled:

(a) To transfer (or cause to be transferred directly) to the Trust to be held as part of his Account and other property received by him in one or more distributions together constituting a lump-sum distribution from or under another qualified trust or qualified plan or an employee annuity or custodial account, (iii) an amount paid or distributed out of an individual retirement account or individual retirement annuity or retirement bond consisting of a prior rollover contribution from a qualified trust or annuity plan, (iv) cash or other property representing his account or benefits in another qualified plan or qualified trust, which shall be transferred directly from said plan or trust to the Trust, or (v) any combination of the above;

(b) Upon at least sixty (60) days written notice to the Plan Administrator, and only with the consent of the Plan Administrator, to cause his entire account, to the extent that it has vested, to be transferred on his behalf, in the form of cash or other property (in one or more distributions together constituting a lump-sum distribution), directly to a qualified trust or an annuity plan.

Any amount so transferred to or from this Trust is herein called a "Rollover Contributution." Any Rollover Contribution to the Trust, together with the earnings thereon, shall be fully vested but need not be segregated from the remainder of the Participant's Account unless the Trustee otherwise elects or the Participant or Plan Administrator otherwise directs.

10.08 Merger or Consolidation of Employer. If the Employer is merged or consolidated with another organization, or another organization acquires all or substantially all of the Employer's assets, such organization may become the Employer hereunder by action of its Board of Directors and by action of the Board of Directors of the prior Employer, if still existent. Such change in Employers shall not be deemed a termination of the Plan by either the predecessor or successor Employer.

10.09 Non-Alienation or Assignment. None of the benefits under the Plan are subject to the claims or creditors of Participants or their Beneficiaries, and will not be subject to attachment, garnishment, or any other legal process whatsoever. Neither a Participant nor his Beneficiaries may assign, sell, borrow on, or otherwise encumber any of his beneficial interest in the Plan and Trust Fund, nor shall any such benefits be in any manner liable for or subject to the deeds, contracts, liabilities, engagements, or torts of any Participant or Beneficiary. If any Participant or Beneficiary shall become bankrupt or attempt to anticipate, sell, alienate, transfer, pledge, assign, encumber or change any benefit specifically provided for herein, or if a court of competent jurisdiction enters an order purporting to subject such interest to the claim of any creditor, then such benefit shall be terminated and the Trustee shall hold or apply such benefit to or for the benefit of such Participant or Beneficiary in such manner as the Plan Administrator, in its sole discretion, may deem proper under the circumstances.

10.10 Plan Continuance Voluntary. Although it is the intention of the Employer that this Plan shall be continued and its contributions made regularly, this Plan is entirely voluntary on the part of the Employer, and the continuance of the Plan and the payments thereunder are not assumed as a contractual obligation of the Employer.

10.11 Suspension of Contributions. The Employer specifically reserves the right, in its sole and uncontrolled discretion, to modify, suspend contributions to the Plan (in whole or in part) at any time or from time to time for any period or periods, or to discontinue at any time the contributions under this Plan. Contributions shall be suspended only if a waiver of the minimum funding standard under Section 412 of the Code is first obtained. In the event that Contributions are thus suspended for any period, upon termination of such suspension and the resumption of Contributions the Employer shall, within a reasonable period of time, make up both the Contributions suspended and earnings thereon for those Participants who are eligible for benefits at the time of such resumption.

10.12 Agreement Not An Employment Contract. This Plan shall not be deemed to constitute a contract between the Employer and any Participant or to be a consideration or an inducement for the employment of any Participant or Employee. Nothing contained in this Plan shall be deemed to give any Participant or Employee the right to be retained in the service of the Employer or to interfere with the right of the Employer to discharge any Participant or Employee at any time regardless of the effect which such discharge shall have upon such individual as a Participant in the Plan.

10.13 Payments to Minors and Others. In making any distribution to or for the benefit of any minor or incompetent Participant or Beneficiary, or any other Participant or Beneficiary who, in the opinion of the Plan Administrator, is incapable of properly using, expending, investing, or otherwise disposing such distribution, then the Plan Administrator, in his sole, absolute, and uncontrolled discretion may, but need not, order the Trustee to make such distribution to a legal or natural guardian or other relative of such minor or court appointed committee of any incompetent, or to any adult with whom such person temporarily or permanently resides; and any such guardian, committee, relative, or other person shall have full authority and discretion to expend such distribution for use and benefit of such person; and the receipt of such guardian, committee, relative, or other person shall be a complete discharge to the Trustee, without any responsibility on its part or on the part of the Plan Administrator to see to the application thereof.

10.14 Unclaimed Benefits. If any benefits payable to, or on behalf of, a Participant are not claimed within a reasonable period of time from the date of entitlement, as determined by the Plan Administrator, and following a diligent effort to locate such person, the Plan Administrator shall file a Form SSA or any successor form with the annual report for the appropriate Plan Year with respect to such Participant and shall set up a separate account pursuant to Section 5.09 for such Participant. If the Participant or his Beneficiary or Contingent Beneficiary does not file a claim for benefits prior to the Valuation Date of the Plan Year duing which such Participant's seventieth (70th) birthday occurs, such Participant shall be presumed dead and the post-death benefits, if any, under this Plan shall be paid to his Beneficiary if he is then living and can be located following a diligent search, or to the person or persons specified under Section 5.10 if the Beneficiary is not then living or cannot be located.

10.15 Governing Law. This Plan shall be administered in the United States of America, and its validity, construction, and all rights hereunder shall be governed by the laws of the United States under ERISA. To the extent that ERISA shall not be held to have preempted local law, the Plan shall be administered under the laws of the State of _____. If any provision of the Plan shall be held invalid or unenforceable, the remaining provisions hereof shall continue to be fully effective.

10.16 Headings no Part of Agreement. Headings of sections and subsections of the Plan are inserted for convenience of reference. They constitute no part of the Plan and are not to be considered in the construction thereof.

10.17 Merger or Consolidation of Plan. This Plan and Trust shall not be merged or consolidated with, nor shall any assets or liabilities be transferred to, any other plan, unless the benefits payable to each Participant if the Plan was terminated immediately after such action would be equal or greater than the benefits to which such Participant would have been entitled if this Plan had been terminated immediately before such action.

10.18 Amendment of Former Vesting Schedule.

(a) Election of Former Vesting Schedule. In the event the vesting schedule of this Plan is amended [or the vesting schedule or any preceding plan is amended by adoption of this amendment and restatement,] any Participant who has completed at least five (5) Years of Service and whose vested interest is at any time adversely affected by such amendment may elect to have his vested interest in Employer Contributions determined without regard to such amendment by notifying the Plan Administrator in writing during the election period shall begin on the date such amendment is adopted and shall end no earlier than the latest of the following dates:

(i) The date which is 60 days after the date the amendment is adopted;

(ii) The date which is 60 days after the day the Plan amendment becomes effective; or

(iii) The date which is 60 days after the day the Participant is issued written notice of the amendment by the Employer or Plan Administrator.

Such election shall be available only to an individual who is a Participant at the time such election is made, and such election shall be irrevocable.

(b) No Divestiture by Reason of Amendment. If the vesting schedule of this Plan is amended [or the vesting schedule of any preceding Plan is amended by adoption of this amendment and restatement,] the nonforfeitable percentage of a Participant's Account (determined as of the later of the date such amendment is adopted or becomes effective) shall be at least the nonforfeitable percentage computed under the Plan as of the later of such dates without regard to the amendment.

10.19 Indemnification. The Employer hereby agrees to indemnify any current or former Employee or member of the Board of Directors of the Employer to the full extent of any expenses, penalties, damages, or other pecuniary loss which such current or former Employee or member of the Board of Directors may suffer as a result of his responsibilities, obligations, or duties in connection with the Plan or fiduciary activities actually performed in connection with the Plan. Such indemnification shall be paid by the Employer to the current or former Employee or member of the Board of Directors to the extent that fiduciary liability insurance is not available to cover the payment of such items, but in no event shall such items be paid out of Plan assets.

Notwithstanding the foregoing, this indemnification agreement shall not relieve any current or former Employee or member of the Board of Directors serving in a fiduciary capacity of his fiduciary responsibilities and liabilities to the Plan for breaches of fiduciary obligations, nor shall this agreement violate any provision of Part 4 of Title I of ERISA as it may be interpreted from time to time by the United States Department of Labor and any courts of competent jurisdiction.

[10.20 Special Provisions Required by Subchapter S Status of Employer. For all Plan Years in which the Employer is an electing small business corporation (a "Subchapter S Corporation"), as defined in sections 1371 through 1379 of the Code, and to the extent necessary to maintain the qualified status of the Plan under section 401(a) of the Code for all Plan Years in which the Employer has ceased to be a Subchapter S Corporation, the following special provisions shall apply, notwithstanding any other provisions of this Plan to the contrary:

(a) Basic Compensation. For purpose of this Plan, the Basic Compensation of each Participant employed by a Subchapter S Corporation shall not exceed $100,000 per year.

(b) Taxability of Contributions. Any Participant who is classified as a "shareholder-employee" ("Shareholder-Employee") within the meaning of section 1379(d) of the Code for any portion of a Plan Year shall include in his gross income, for his taxable year in which or with which the taxable year of the Employee ends, the excess of the amount of contributions paid to the Plan on his behalf which is deductible under section 404(a)(1), (2), or (3) of the Code by the Employer for its taxable year over the lesser of:

    (i) 15% of the compensation received or accrued by such Participant from the Employer during its taxable year, or

    (ii) $7.500.

As used herein, the term "compensation" means all compensation for personal services actually rendered, except that for which a deduction is allowable under a plan that qualifies under section 401(a) of the Code, including a plan that qualifies under section 404(a)(2) of the Code.]

[10.21 Receipt of Funds From Prior HR-10 Plan. Anything in this Plan to the contrary notwithstanding (except for the provisions of Section 10.17), the Trustee may receive and hold, as a part of the Trust Fund, assets (hereinafter referred to as the "transferred assets," which shall be deemed to include all increments allocable to such transferred assets) transferred directly from the trustee or custodian of any other retirement plan (hereinafter referred to as the "transferor plan") which is qualified under Section 401(a) of the Code, and which benefits one or more owner-employees as that term is defined in Section 401(c)(3) of the Code (hereinafter "owner-employee"). In applying the provisions of this Section 10.21, the following special provisions shall apply:

(a) The transferred assets and all rights to or derived therefrom shall be at the time of the transfer and at all times thereafter fully nonforfeitable and vested in the respective Participants (and in the proportions) to which such transferred assets had been allocated under the transferor plan.

(b) The Trustee shall not be liable or responsible for any acts or omissions in the administration of any transferor plan and the trusts thereunder of any other person or entity who was trustee, custodian or other fiduciary under any prior plan, the Trustee shall be held harmless from such liability or responsibility.

(c) Except as otherwise provided in this Section 10.21, all transferred assets shall be administered and distributed in the same manner as provided under the Plan.

(d) The Trustee shall keep a separate and identifiable fund with respect to the transferred assets (which may be commingled for investment purposes with other assets of the Trust), designated as "transferred fund", and the separate account within the transferred fund of each Participant shall be adjusted annually in the manner specified in Article IV hereof, treating for this purpose the transferred fund as if it were the entire Trust Fund.

(e) If the transferor plan shall be a plan benefiting one or more owner-employees, the following special provisions shall apply:

    (i) No payment shall be made from the transferred fund to any Participant who was an owner-employee under the transferor plan unless he is either disabled or has attained the age of 59½ years. For purposes only of the foregoing sentence "Disability" shall mean inability to engage in any substantial gainful activity by reason of any medically determinable phsyical or mental impairment which can be expected to result in death or to be of long continued and indefinite duration.

    (ii) The entire interest of each Participant must actually be distributed to such Participant:

        (1) In the case of a Participant, other than a Participant who is or has been an owner employee under the transferor plan, no later than the last day of the taxable year of such employee in which he attains age 70½; or not later than the last day of the taxable year in which he retires, whichever is later, and

        (2) In the case of a Participant who is, or has been an owner-employee under the transferor plan, not later than the last day of the taxable year in which he attains age 70½.

(f) If a Participant who was an owner-employee under the transferor plan dies after receiving a portion of his benefits under the Plan but before the full value of his interest in the transferred fund has been distributed to him, such Participant's entire remaining interst in the transferred fund must either be distributed to his beneficary within five years or be used within that period to purchase an immediate annuity for such beneficiary; however, this requirement is not mandatory if the distribution of such interest has commenced and such distribution is for a term certain over a period not extending beyond the joint life and survivor expenctancy of the Participant and his spouse.

(g) The Trustee having control over the transferred assets shall always be a "Bank" as required in Section 401(d)(1) of the Code and the Regulations thereunder.]

IN WITNESS WHEREOF, the Employer has caused this [Amendment] [Agreement] to be executed this the ____ day of _____, 19___, to be effective as of _____.

EMPLOYER:

_____

(CORPORATE SEAL)
ATTEST:

By: _____
President

_____
Secretary

DELEGATION OF RESPONSIBILITIES PURSUANT TO ERISA

The following fiduciary has accepted the duties and responsibilities delegated to it under the Plan pursuant to ERISA until its successors are duly appointed and qualified, this ____ day of _____, 19___.

PLAN SPONSOR [AND PLAN ADMINISTRATOR]:

_____

(CORPORATE SEAL)
ATTEST:
_____
Secretary

By: _____
President

[PLAN ADMINISTRATOR:

_____]

EXHIBIT 3

SUMMARY PLAN DESCRIPTION
FOR

_____

PROFIT SHARING PLAN

Effective _____

QUALIFIED RETIREMENT PLANS

_____

_____

_____

_____

Plan I.D. No. _____
Employer I.D. No. _____

This booklet provides only a summary of the Plan document itself. It is not intended to cover all matters addressed in the Plan, but instead is designed to give Plan participants and beneficiaries a general idea of their rights under the Plan. If questions arise, or if a provision of this summary is inconsistent with the formal text of the Plan, all decisions will be based on the formal text of the Plan, which will control in all instances. A copy of the Plan document is available for your inspection during regular business hours.

TABLE OF CONTENTS

Page No.

INTRODUCTION

Effective _____ your Employer adopted a Profit Sharing Plan to enable eligible employees to share in the profits of the company. You play an important part in determining profits, and the better and more efficiently you work, the greater the company profits will be and the greater your share will be.

This booklet contains a convenient summary of the Profit Sharing Plan in simple language. You should read this summary carefully to obtain an understanding of the benefits to which you may be entitled, as well as the circumstances that affect the availability of those benefits. Where a specific interpretation of the Plan is involved, or a provision of the Plan is related to a specific situation, you should consult the Plan Administrator.

DEFINITIONS

There are certain terms used in this summary with which you may not be familiar or which have specific meanings when used in explaining the Plan. These terms and their definitions are listed below. When one of these terms is used in the

623

text it is followed by an asterisk (*) to let you know that you can refer back to this section for an explanation.

1. Break in Service occurs in any Plan Year* during which you do not work more than 500 hours of service.

2. Compensation refers to the total sum paid to you by the Employer during a Plan Year* [including regular salary, overtime and commissions, but excluding non-contracted bonuses, expense account allowances and Employer contributions to this or any other benefit plan.] [including salary, overtime, commissions and bonuses.]

3. Directed Investment Employee Contributions Account refers to a separate account which may be established in accordance with your written instructions to the Trustee for the purpose of allowing you to direct the investment of any Voluntary Employee Contributions you may make. Any amount you authorize to be placed in a Directed Investment Employee Contributions Account will not share in the earnings or losses of the Trust Fund but will be credited with the earnings or debited for the losses of the investment medium you select. Neither the Plan Administrator, Trustee nor Employer assumes any liability in connection with your Directed Investment Employee Contributions Account. If you do not elect to establish a Directed Investment Employee Contributions Account, any Voluntary Employee Contributions you may make will be commingled with the general Trust Fund for purposes of investments.

4. Disability or Disabled refers to a mental or physical condition which arises after you become a participant and which totally and permanently prevents you from [performing the normal duties for which you were employed.] [engaging in any occupation for pay.] Certain types of disorders are excluded from Disability, such as those arising from excessive use of intoxicants or drugs, self-inflicted injury or self-induced sickness, or taking part in a felonious act.

5. Early Retirement Date is a date prior to your Normal Retirement Date* on which you may retire as long as you have reached age 55 and completed 10 Years of Service*.

6. Employee Accounts refers to both your Directed Investment Employee Contributions Account*, if you have established such an account, and your Employee Contributions Account*, if you elect to make Voluntary Employee Contributions and choose to leave them commingled with the general Trust Fund. You may switch funds between the two accounts, but your accounts will be charged with any administrative expenses arising from such transfers.

7. Employee Contributions Account refers to the account established for the purpose of accounting for any Voluntary Employee Contributions you may make which you do not place in a Directed Investment Employee Contributions Account*.

8. Forfeitures refers to the portion of your Profit Sharing Account* to which you are *not* entitled at the time of severance because at that time you have not completed a specified number of Years of Service*. Any amount you forfeit is reallocated to other eligible Participants.

9. Normal Retirement Date is the last day of the month immediately preceding your 65th birthday or the 10th anniversary of your participation in the Plan, whichever is later.

10. Plan Anniversary Date is the last day of the Plan Year, _____.

11. Plan Year is the fiscal period beginning on _____ and ending on the following _____. All records concerning the Plan are maintained on the basis of the Plan Year.

12. Profit Sharing Account refers to the account established in your name for purposes of crediting your share of Employer Contributuions, Forfeitures* and earnings or losses of the Trust Fund attributable to Employer Contributions.

13. Vested Benefit or Vested Amount refers to that portion of your accounts to which you are always entitled. This includes all Voluntary Employee Contributions which you may make, plus a percentage of the Employer Contributions as determined by your Years of Service*.

14. Year of Service. You must work 1,000 hours in a year to be given credit for a Year of Service. For purposes of determing your eligibility to participate in the Plan, the year is measured initially from your date of employment. For all other purposes, Years of Service are measured on a Plan Year* basis.

ADMINISTRATION

1. Q. Who is the Plan Administrator of the Plan?

   [A. The Plan Administrator of your Profit Sharing Plan is _____. His business address is _____ and he may be reached by telephone at _____. He has been appointed Plan Administrator by the Board of Directors of the Employer and serves without pay. He performs a wide range of functions including interpreting the Plan provisions, maintaining records and determining Participants' eligibility for benefits. Each year the Plan Administrator, through the Trustee, will furnish you a statement of your account in the Trust Fund.]

   [A. The people responsible for the administration of your Profit Sharing Plan are called the Administrative Committee. The people on the Administrative Committee are _____, _____, and _____. You can write to the Administrative Committee at the address of the Employer shown on the front cover, or a Committee member may be reached by telephone at _____. The members have been appointed to the Committee by the Board of Directors of the Employer and serve without pay. The Committee performs a wide range of functions, including interpreting the Plan provisions, maintaining records and determining Participants eligibility for benefits. Each year the Administrative Committee, through the Trustee, will furnish you a statement of your account in the Trust Fund.]

[A.   The Employer serves as the Plan Administrator. In this capacity the Employer performs a wide range of functions, including interpreting the Plan provisions, maintaining records and determining Participants' eligibility for benefits. Each year the Plan Administrator, through the Trustee, will furnish you a statement of your account in the Trust Fund.]

2.   Q.   Who is the Trustee of the Plan's Trust Fund?

      A.   _____, _____, is the Trustee of your Profit Sharing Trust Fund. The Trustee invests the money in the Trust Fund and annually advises the Participants of their interests in the fund, on behalf of the Plan Administrator.

3.   Q.   If it ever becomes necessary to serve the Plan with any legal papers or process to whom should such process be delivered?

      A.   Legal papers or legal process with respect to the Plan should be delivered in person by an appropriate officer of the Court from which such process issues, to the law firm of Lamon, Elrod & Harkleroad, P.C., 2500 Peachtree Center, Cain Tower, 229 Peachtree Street, N.E., Atlanta, Georgia 30043. Service of legal process may also be made on the Plan Administrator or the Trustee.

ELIGIBILITY AND PARTICIPATION

1.   Q.   When do I become eligible to participate in the Profit Sharing Plan?

    [A.   You become eligible to participate the first time you complete a Year of Service*. You will actually participate from the beginning of the Plan Year during which you completed your Year of Service*.

        Example: J.D. completes a Year of Service* between his employment date, _____, and the first anniversary of his employment date _____. His actual participation is retroactive to the first day of the Plan Year* in which he completes the Year of Service*, _____.]

    [A.   You become eligible to participate when you have completed two requirements.

        1)   You must have reached an age of at least ___ years.

        2)   You must complete a Year of Service*.

You will actually participate from the beginning of the Plan Year during which you meet the later of the above requirements.

        Example: L.B. begins work on _____. He completes a Year of Service* between then and _____, however, he is only

_____ years old and so does not yet qualify for participation. He has his _____ birthday on _____. He now has met both requirements and his participation is retroactive to the beginning of the Plan Year* in which he met the last condition, _____.]

[A. You become eligible to participate the first time you complete a Year of Service*. You will actually become a Participant on the next following _____ or _____, whichever comes first after you have completed your Year of Service.*

Examples: N.R. begins employment with the Employer on _____. He completes a Year of Service* between then and _____. He will become a Participant on _____.]

2. Q. Once I've become a Participant, how long will I continue participating in the Plan?

A. Once you have become a Participant, as long as you continue to be employed by the Employer you will continue to participate in the Plan to some degree. The number of hours you work in a Plan Year* will determine your rights to participation. It works like this:

If You Work this Many Hours In a Plan Year* You Will be Given Credit For	Your Share of Employer Contributions	Your Share of Trust Fund Earnings (or Losses)	Your Share of Forfeitures* in the Trust Fund	One Year of Service* for Vesting Purposes
1,000 or more	YES	YES	YES	YES
More than 500 but less than 1,000	YES	YES	YES	NO
Not more than 500	NO	YES	NO	NO

3. Q. What are my obligations as a Participant in the Plan?

A. From time to time when appropriate you will be required to do the following:

1) File with the Plan Administrator certain Beneficiary Designation Forms;

2) File with the Plan Administrator a claim for benefits, upon your severance of employment for any reason;

3) Notify the Plan Administrator if you wish to ["earmark" the Vested* portion of your Profit Sharing Account* or] establish a Directed Investment Employee Contributions Account*.

4) File with the Plan Administrator a written notice if you wish to make a Voluntary Employee Contributions;

5) File with the Plan Administrator a written request if you wish to withdraw any Voluntary Employee Contributions;

6) Furnish satisfactory evidence of Disability* with the Plan Administrator if you are requesting a Disability*;

7) File a written notice with the Employer if you wish to continue employment beyond your Normal Retirement Date*; and

8) Provide the Plan Administrator your new address anytime you move.

CONTRIBUTIONS

(Integrated plans use alternate clause at end of this Exhibit 3.)

1. Q. Where does the money come from that is credited to my Account?

A. There are four sources from which money may be credited to your Account.

1) <u>Employer Contributions</u>. At the end of each Plan Year* your Employer, by resolution of the Board of Directors, will decide how much of its net profits to contribute to the Trust Fund. That amount will be paid over to the Trustee.

1) <u>Employer Contributions</u>. At the end of each Plan Year* your Employer expects to make a contribution from its net profits in an amount equal to [____% of the net profits.] [____% of the total Compensation* paid to all Plan Participants during that year.] The Employer may decide to contribute more, up to certain limits set by the Internal Revenue Service. The amount will be paid over to the Trustee.

Example: [The Employers' net profit for the Plan Year*] [The total Compensation* paid by the Employer to all Participants during the year] was $50,000. The Employer will contribute ____% of that amount, or _____.

The Trustee will divide this money among the Profit Sharing Accounts* of the eligible Participants in the same proportion that each eligible Participant's Compensation * for that Plan Year is to the total Compensation* paid to all eligible Participants.

Example: The Employer contribution for a given Plan Year* is $5,000. The total Compensation* paid to all eligible Participants in that Plan Year* was $100,000. T.L.'s own Compensation* for that year was $8,000 or 8% of the total Compensation* of all eligible Participants. Therefore T.L. would be credited with 8% of the $5,000 Employer contribution, or $400.

2) <u>Voluntary Employee Contributions</u>. The Plan does not require Employees to make contributions to the Plan. You may, however, voluntarily contribute up to 10% of the Compensation* paid to you by the Employer.

> Example: K.A. earned $12,000 during the Plan Year. He may voluntarily contribute up to $1.200 to his Employee Accounts.

Voluntary Employee Contributions may be made directly to the Trustee, or your Employer will withhold them from your paycheck, whichever you direct.

You may, upon 90 days written notice to the Plan Administrator, elect to withdraw from the Trust Fund any Voluntary Employee Contributions you may have made. There is no penalty for withdrawing your Voluntary Employee Contributions, however, you may elect to do so only once in any given Plan Year*.

[Any Participant who withdraws all of his Employee Contributions may also elect to withdraw 25%, 50%, 75% or 100% of the earnings that have been allocated to his Employee Accounts*. However, if you do elect to withdraw all or any portion of your earnings, you will be subject to a suspension period from receiving Employer Contributions in accordance with the following schedule:

Percentage of Earnings Withdrawn	Suspension Period
25%	6 months
50%	8 months
75%	10 months
100%	12 months

In other words, any salary you earn during the suspension period, which will begin on the date you receive the distribution, will not be included as Compensation* for purposes of allocating Employer Contributions. You must make an election to withdraw earnings at the same time you elect to withdraw your Voluntary Employee Contributions.]

[Any Participant who withdraws all of his Employee Contributions may also elect to withdraw 100% of the earnings that have been allocated to his Employee Accounts*. However, if you elect to withdraw your earnings, you will be subject to a 24-month suspension period from making further Voluntary Employee Contributions. In other words, any salary you earn during the 24-month suspension period, which will begin on the date you receive the distribution, will not be included as Compensation* for purposes of determining the amount you are allowed to voluntarily contribute.

629

You must make an election to withdraw earnings at the same time you elect to withdraw your Voluntary Employee Contributions.]

Voluntary Employee Contributions are always 100% vested and nonforfeitable.

3) Earnings of the Trust Fund. The Trustee will invest the contributions turned over to it in various stocks, bonds and other securities. At the end of each Plan Year* the earnings on these investments, such as interest or dividends, will be divided up and added to the Profit Sharing Accounts*and Employee Contributions* of the eligible Participants. This is assuming that the Trust Fund increases in value. Sometimes investments don't work out so well. If the fund should suffer a loss, the Participants' Profit Sharing Accountants* and Employee Contributions Accounts* would be charged with their proportionate share of that loss. Allocation of earnings (or losses) on the fund to Participants' Accounts is explained by the following.

Example: The total balance of the Trust Fund at the end of the 1980 Plan Year* is $40,000. $5,000 of that total is in your account. In other words, your share of the total Trust Fund is 12-1/2%. During the 1981 Plan Year* the total $40,000 is invested so that it earns $2,000. Since 12-1/2% of the fund was yours, you will be credited with 12-1/2% of the earnings or $250.

Earnings will be allocated to your Profit Sharing Account* as described in the immediately preceding example for each Plan Year* unless the Plan Administrator advises Plan Participants, in writing, that he has elected to prorate the earnings on a daily basis, whereby your Profit Sharing Account* and Employee Contributions Account* will be valued on each day of the Plan Year* and earnings allocated accordingly.

[This Plan contains a special provision which allows you to "earmark" the Vested Benefit* of your Profit Sharing Account*. This means that you may instruct the Plan Administrator to direct the Trustee to invest the Vested Amount* in your Profit Sharing Account* in any way you choose. For example, you could direct that your Vested Benefit*be invested in Certificates of Deposit. If you do earmark your Vested Benefit*, that portion of your Profit Sharing Account* will not share in the earnings or losses of the trust fund, but rather will be credited with the earnings or losses of the investment medium which you select. As with Directed Investment Employee Contributions Accounts*, neither the Plan Administrator, Trustee or Employer assumes any liability in connection with any earmarked investments.]

4) Forfeitures*. If a Participant leaves the Employer before retirement, death, or Disability*, he may forfeit part or all of his share in

the Trust Fund (except his Voluntary Employee Contributions). Any amounts so forfeited are divided up among the Profit Sharing Accounts* of the remaining eligible Participants, in the same manner that the Employer Contributions are divided.

BENEFITS

1. Q. What will my benefits be at retirement?

   A. If you retire [at any Early Retirement Date*, or] at your Normal Retirement Date*, or at some date after your Normal Retirement Date*, you are entitled to your entire Profit Sharing Account* and Employee Accounts*; that is, all of the Employee Contributions, all of the Voluntary Employee Contributions you have made, and any earnings and Forfeitures* which have been allocated to your Accounts, minus previous withdrawals and investment losses if there have been any. You will be asked to elect whether you want the account computed as of the Plan Anniversary Date* immediately preceding or immediately following your retirement date. If you elect the date preceding, you will not receive any allocations of Employer Contributions, Forfeitures* or earnings or losses for the Plan Year* in which you retire. If you elect the date following, you will receive allocations of earnings or losses for the Plan Year* in which you retire and you will further receive allocations of Employer Contributions and Forfeitures* for the Plan Year* in which you retire if you work more than 500 hours during that Plan Year*, but you cannot begin receiving your benefits until the next Plan Year*. If you don't make any election by the date of your actual retirement, your Accounts will be treated as if you had elected the Plan Anniversary Date* immediately following your retirement date.

2. Q. What happens if I become disabled while I'm a Participant?

   A. You will be required to furnish the Plan Administrator satisfactory evidence of your Disability*. When the Plan Administrator confirms your Disability* you become entitled to your entire Profit Sharing Account* and Employee Accounts*; that is, all of the Employer Contributions, all of the Voluntary Employee Contributions you have made, and any earnings and Forfeitures* allocated to your Accounts, minus previous withdrawals and investment losses if there have been any. You (or your legal representative if you are so incapacitated that someone else is handling your affairs) will have 30 days to elect whether you want your Accounts computed as of the Plan Anniversary Date* immediately preceding or immediately following the date the Plan Administrator determines your Disability*. If you elect the date preceding, you will not receive any allocations of Employer Contributions, Forfeitures* or earnings or losses for the Plan Year* in which your Disability* is confirmed. If you elect the date following, you will receive allocations of earnings or losses for the Plan Year* in which your Disability* is determined and you will further receive allocations of Employer Contributions and Forfeitures* for the Plan Year* in which your Disability*, is confirmed if you worked more than 500 hours in the Plan Year*, but you cannot begin receiving your benefits until the next Plan Year*. If you don't make any election within the 30 day period, your account will be treated as if you had elected the Plan Anniversary Date* immediately following the date the Plan Administrator determined your Disability*.

3. Q. What happens if I die while I'm a Participant?

A. Upon your death your designated beneficiary will become entitled to your entire Profit Sharing Accounts* and Employee Accounts*; that is all of the Employer Contributions, all of the Voluntary Employee Contributions you have made, and any earnings or Forfeitures* allocated to your Accounts, minus previous withdrawals and investment losses if there have been any. Your beneficiary will have 60 days after your death to elect to have your Accounts computed as of the Plan Anniversary Date* immediately preceding or immediately following your date of death. If he elects the date preceding, there will be no allocation of Employer Contributions, Forfeitures* or earnings or losses for the Plan Year* in which your death occurs. If he elects the date following, allocations of earnings or losses will be made for the Plan Year* in which your death occurs and allocations of Employer Contributions and Forfeitures* will be made for the Plan Year* in which your death occurs if you worked more than 500 hours in that Plan Year*, but your beneficiary cannot begin receiving benefits until the next Plan Year*. If your beneficiary does not make any election within the 60 day period, your Accounts will be treated as if he had elected the Plan Anniversary Date* immediately following your date of death.

4. Q. What happens if my employment is terminated, by me or the Employer, prior to retirement, death or Disability*?

A. The main purpose of an employee benefit plan is to provide income at retirement, Disability* or death. So, if you leave the Employer for any reason before any of these occurrences your benefits will probably not be as great as if you continued employment. Of course, you are always entitled to *all* of the Voluntary Employee Contributions you have made. We are talking now about the part of your Profit Sharing Account* that came from the Employer Contributions. It all works on a formula, that means you are entitled to a certain percentage of your Profit Sharing Account* depending on the number of Years of Service* you have prior to your Break in Service*. The percentage of your Profit Sharing Account* to which you are entitled is your Vested Benefit*. You forfeit, or lose, the balance of your Profit Sharing Account*. The formula for determining your Vested Benefit* follows:

If You Have Been Credited With This Many Years Of Service*	You will be Vested in this Percent of Employer Contributions in Your Account	And You Will Forfeit This Percent

This schedule will be applied to your Profit Sharing Account* as of the last day of the Plan Year* in which your Break in Service* occurs unless an immediate cash-out is requested by you and approved by the Plan Administrator, as explained in Question 6 below.

5. Q. Once I am entitled to benefits, how will they be paid to me?

    A. You, or your beneficiary if you have died, should make a written request of the Plan Administrator for payment in any of the following ways:

    1) A lump sum;

    2) Monthly or annual installment payments for a period not to exceed 10 years; or

    3) Any combination of the above.

    If payments are to be made in installments or if a lump-sum distribution will not be made for more than 6 months, the amount to which you are entitled will be segregated from the trust fund and invested in a federally insured savings account which will accumulate the standard rate of interest.

6. Q. When do my benefit payments begin?

    A. If you retire, become Disabled* or die, you or your beneficiary may elect, with the approval of the Plan Administrator, when your benefits shall begin.

    If your employment is severed for reasons other than retirement, Disability* or death, your benefits will normally be held until the end of the Plan Year* in which your Break in Service* occurs. At that time you should file a written claim with the Plan Administrator indicating whether you want your Vested Benefit* paid to you immediately, or if you prefer to have it held in a separate account (as explained in Question 5 above) until what would have been your [Early Retirement Date* or] Normal Retirement Date* if you had not terminated. The Plan Administrator may approve or disapprove whichever election you have made, but he may not be discriminatory in reaching his decision. If you do not file your written claim within a reasonable period after the end of your Break in Service,* your Vested Benefit* will be treated as though you had requested that it be held in a separate account.

Whether or not you have filed a written claim, if your Vested Benefit* is $1750 or less the Plan Administrator may direct that you be paid out immediately after the end of your Break in Service* in a lump sum.

If you terminate before death, retirement or Disability* there is one other option available to you. At your time of resignation or discharge you may request an immedate cash-out. If the Plan Administrator approves your request, your Vested Benefit* will be computed as of the Plan Anniversary Date* immediately preceding your termination date, (without waiting until the Break in Service* occurs) and will be paid to you within 60 days after your termination. In this case you will not receive any allocation of the Employer Contributions or Forfeitures* or earnings of the Trust Fund for the Plan Year* during which you terminate. You'll be credited with a Year of Service* (in applying the vesting schedule in Question 4 above) only if you completed more than 1.000 hours during the Plan Year* in which your termination occurs.

7. Q. What happens if I terminate employment and then I'm rehired by the Employer?

A. Generally, you will be re-admitted to the Plan on your date of re-employment. Your rights and benefits under the Plan in such a situation will depend upon a number of factors including the following:

1) Your Years of Service* before your severance;

2) The length of your Break in Service*;

3) The number of hours you work in the Plan Year* of your re-employment;

4) Whether or not you have a vested interest in Employer Contributions before your severance; and

5) Whether or not your benefits were paid out to you following your severance.

Because each specific situation will represent a different combination of these factors, you should discuss it with the Plan Administrator if you are re-employed.

8. Q. Is any of the money in the Trust Fund available to me while I'm actively employed and participating in the Plan?

A. In an instance of extreme financial hardship the Plan Administrator may permit you to borrow money from the Trust Fund in an amount not to exceed your Profit Sharing Account* Vested Benefit*. The transaction will be handled in almost the same way as when you borrow money from a bank. You will be required to sign a note, pay the prevailing rate of interest being charged by banks in your area, and make repayment of definite amounts at specified times. Your account in the Profit Sharing Trust Fund will serve as collateral for the loan. Should you terminate employment before fully repaying the loan, any unpaid balance will be deducted before you receive distribution of your Vested Benefit*.

9. Q.   If I make a written request for benefits that I feel entitled to, and my request is denied, what can I do?

   A.   If your claim for benefits is denied, the Plan Administrator will give you a written explanation of the reasons for denial. If you are not satisfied with the explanation you have 60 days to request a review, which may be in the nature of a hearing, and your lawyer may represent you. Then within 60 days the Plan Administrator will issue his decision on the review. If you do not accept this decision, you have further recourse as explained below in the Statement of Rights.

STATEMENT OF RIGHTS

A.   As a Participant in the Profit Sharing Plan you are entitled to certain rights and protections under the Employee Retirement Income Security Act of 1974. ERISA provides that all Plan Participants shall be entitled to:

   1. Examine, without charge, at the Plan Administor's office all Plan documents and copies of all documents filed by the Plan with the U.S. Department of Labor, such as annual reports and Plan descriptions.

   2. Obtain copies of all Plan documents and other Plan information upon written request to the Plan Administrator. The Administrator may make a reasonable charge for copies.

   3. Receive a summary of the Plan's annual financial report. The Plan Administrator is required by law to furnish each Participant with a copy of this summary financial report.

   4. Obtain, once a year, a statement of the nonforfeitable (vested) benefits (if any) or the earliest date on which benefits will become nonforfeitable (vested). The Plan may require a written request for this statement,but it must provide the statement free of charge.

   5. File suit in a federal court, if any materials requested are not received within 30 days of the Participant's request, unless the materials were not sent because of matters beyond the control of the Administrator.The court may require the Plan Administrator to pay up to $100 for each day's delay until the materials are received.

B.   In addition to creating rights for Plan Participants, ERISA imposes obligations upon the persons who are responsible for the operations of the Plan.

   These persons are referred to as "fiduciaries" in the law. Fiduciaries must act solely in the interest of the Plan Participants and they must exercise prudence in the performance of their Plan duties. Fiduciaries who violate ERISA may be removed and required to make good any losses they have caused the Plan.

C.   Your Employer may not fire you or discriminate against you to prevent you from obtaining a benefit or exercising your rights under ERISA.

D.   If you are improperly denied a benefit in full or in part, you have a right to file suit in a federal or a state court. If Plan fiduciaries are misusing the Plan's money, you have a right to file suit in a federal court or request assistance from the U.S. Department of Labor. If you are successful in your lawsuit, the court may, if it so decides, require the other party to pay your legal costs, including attorney's fees. Likewise, if you are unsuccessful, the court in its sole discretion may order you to pay the legal costs, including attorney's fees, of the defendant(s).

E. If you have any questions about this statement or your rights under ERISA, you should contact the Plan Administrator or the Area Office of the U.S. Labor-Management Service Administration, Department of Labor.

GENERAL INFORMATION

1. Q. I understand the Federal Government issues some employee benefit plans. Are the benefits of this Plan insured?

   A. No, the government exempts profit sharing plans from the Pension Benefit Guaranty Corporation regulations and insurance. Contributions are always allocated to the individual Participants'accounts. Once the employer makes a contribution to the Plan that money may never be used for anything but the exclusive benefit of the Participants and their beneficiaries. Also if the Plan terminates or the Employer goes out of business all the money in the Participants' accounts automatically becomes 100% vested and is not forfeitable for any reason.

2. Q. I understand that this is just a summary of the Plan. May I see the actual documents?

   A. Yes, as explained in the Statement of Rights, all Plan documents are available to you. However, the Plan and Trust Agreement are legal documents and may be difficult for the layman to understand. That is why the Employer has furnished you this summary. Should any discrepancies arise between this summary and the Plan and Trust, the language in the Plan and Trust Agreement shall govern.

(Alternate clause for integrated plans)

CONTRIBUTIONS

1. Q. Where does the money come from that is credited to my account?

   A. A. There are four sources from which money may be credited to your account.

   1. Employer Contributions. At the end of each Plan Year* your Employer, by resolution of the Board of Directors, will decide how much of its net profits to contribute to the Trust Fund. That amount will be paid over to the Trustee.

      The Trustee will divide this money among the Profit Sharing Accounts* of the eligible Participants according to the formula in the Plan.

In order to understand how the formula works, you should first understand the definitions of Basic Compensation*, excess Compensation*, Excess Compensation* and Social Security wage Base* at the beginning of this Summary Plan Description.

Now, let's suppose that A, B, C, D, E and F are Plan Participants at the end of the 1981 Plan Year*, each with the following compensation:

	Basic Compensation	Social Security Wage Base	Excess Compensation
A	$ 60,000	$ 29,700	$ 30,300
B	50,000	29,700	20,300
C	32,000	29,700	2,300
D	22,000	29,700	0
E	10,000	29,700	0
F	8,000	29,700	0
Totals	$182,000		$52,900

Assuming that the Employer has made a $25,000 contribution for this Plan Year, the Trustee applies the formula mentioned above in two steps.

Step I. Seven percent (7%) of the Excess Compensation* of all Participants is allocated to the Profit Sharing Accounts* of those who had Excess Compensation*, in the same ratio as each individual's Excess Compensation* bears to the total Excess Compensation* of all Participants.

$$\begin{aligned} \$52,900 &= \text{Total Excess Compensation*} \\ \times \quad .07 &= \text{Seven Percent} \\ \$ 3,703 &= \text{Amount to be allocated under Step I} \end{aligned}$$

A will have allocated to his account 30,300/52,900 × $3,703 = $2,121
B will have allocated to his account 20,300/52,900 × $3,703 = 1,421
C will have allocated to his account 2,300/52,900 = $3,703 = 161

Total amount allocated under Step I $3,703

Under Step I, Participants D,E and F will not have any allocations made to their Profit Sharing Accounts* since their compensation did not exceed the Social Security Wage Base.

Step II. After allocating $3,703 in Step I of the total $25,000 Employer Contribution, there is still $21,297 to be allocated. The Trustee divides this amount among all Profit Sharing accounts* in the same ratio as each Participant's Basic Compensation* bears to the total Basic Compensation* of all Participants.

A will have allocated to his account 60/182 × $21,296 = $7,020.98
B will have allocated to his account 50/182 × $21,297 = $5,850.82

C will have allocated to his account 32/182 × $21,297 = $3,744.52
D will have allocated to his account 22/182 × $21,297 = $2,574.37
E will have allocated to his account 10/182 × $21,297 = $1,170.17
F will have allocated to his account 8/182 × $21,297 = $ 936.14

Total amount allocated under Step II $21,297.00

(Note: The above examples have been computed on the assumption that there were no Forfeitures* during the Plan Year*. As willbe explained in subparagraph 4 below, total Forfeitures* are added to the Employer Contribution before any of the above allocations are made.)

SUBCHAPTER S PROVISIONS

For all Plan Years* in which your Employer elects to be a Subchapter S Corporation, the following special provisions will apply:

1. No more than $100,000 of Basic Compensation* shall be considered for urposes of the Plan.

2. A Shareholder-Employee will be taxed on Employer Contributions allocated to his account in excess of the lesser of:

   (a) 15% of his Basic Compensation*; or
   (b) $7,500.

Also, no Shareholder-Employee shall be eligible to share in Forfeitures* of Employer Contributions made during years in which Subchapter S election was in effect (even if these Forfeitures* occur after the Subchapter S election is terminated). A Participant is considered a Shareholder-Employee if he owns, directly or indirectly, more than 5% of the outstanding stock of the Employer.

If you should have any questions concerning these special provisions, please contact your Plan Administrator.

NOTES TO CHAPTER 15

1. Rev. Rul. 80-252, 1980-38 I.R.B. 14, Rev. Rul. 66-174, 1966-1 C.B. 81.
2. Rev. Rul. 81-10, 1981-2 I.R.B. 8.
3. Treas. Regs. §1.401-1(b)(2).
4. See Sherwood Swan & Co., 42 T.C. 299 (1964), Rev. Rul. 80-146, 1980-23 I.R.B. 10.
5. Rev. Rul. 71-446, §15.03, 1971-2 C.B. 187.
6. 1971-2 C.B. 184.
7. Rev. Rul. 68-24, 1968-1 C.B. 150.
8. Rev. Rul. 80-350, 1980-51 I.R.B. 7.
9. Rev. Rul. 80-307, 1980-46 I.R.B. 6.

10. See Treas. Regs. §1.401-1(a)(2)(i) and §1.401(b)(l)(i).

11. In Rev. Rul. 74-142, 1974-1 C.B. 95, a professional corporation established a pension plan providing a retirement benefit of 60% of average compensation for each participant. There were only two participants under the plan, a 60-year-old professional and a 52-year-old staff employee. Because of the differences in ages and compensation, 90% of the contributions were applied to fund the benefits for the older professional. Yet, the Service ruled that the plan qualified and did not discriminate in favor of the older professional. See also *Ryan School Retirement Trust*, 24 T.C. 127 (1955).

12. Section 404(a)(1)(A)(ii) of the Code.

13. PBGC Opinion Letters 80-9 to 80-15.

14. See *James E. Thompson, Jr.*, 74 T.C. No. 65 (1980).

15. See Rev. Rul. 76-464, 1976-2 C.B. 115.

16. Section 4021(b)(11) of ERISA; Rev. Rul. 67-415, 1967-2 C.B. 383.

17. See Section 408(k) of the Code.

18. Section 410(a)(4) of the Code.

19. See Sections 401(a)(3) and 410(a)(2) of the Code and Treas. Regs. §1.410(a)-4(a)(1).

20. 29 C.F.R. §860.120(f)(l)(iv)(A).

21. See *Federal Land Bank Association of Asheville, North Carolina*, 74 T.C. No. 82 (1980), in which a thrift plan in which only 2 of 23 employees participated was held to cover a nondiscriminatory classification.

22. 65 T.C. 798 (1976), *rev'd,* 548 F.2d 501 (4th Cir. 1977), *cert. denied,* 90 S.Ct. 300 (1977).

23. A comparable result was reached in *Charles Baloian Company, Inc.,* 68 T.C. 620 (1977), but see *T.L. Hunt, Inc., of Texas v. Commissioner,* 562 F.2d 532 (8th Cir. 1977), rev'g 35 T.C.M. 966, ¶76,221 P-H Memo T.C. (1976), which held that there is no requirement that each of the five or fewer stockholders own stock in controlled corporations as a prerequisite to counting their stock in making up the 80% stock requirement.

24. See Rev. Proc. 75-49, 1975-2 C.B. 584, as modified by Rev. Proc. 76-11, 1976-1 C.B. 550.

25. See Prentice-Hall *Handbook on the Pension Reform Law,* ¶892 (1974).

26. *Farley Funeral Home*, 62 T.C. 150 (1974).

27. Tech. Advice Memo. 7742003.

28. See Rev. Rul. 62-139, 1962-2 C.B. 123, Rev. Rul. 72-531, 1972-2 C.B. 221.

29. 1980-51 I.R.B. 6.

30. See Rev. Rul. 69-409, 1969-2 C.B. 98, *Kenneth Namio Kimura*, Tax Court Petition Docket No. 10307-79 "R", filed July 13, 1979.

31. For a complete discussion of integration, see ¶8891 of Prentice-Hall *Federal Taxes*.

32. 1971-2 C.B. 187.

33. Rev. Rul. 72-276, 1972-1 C.B. 111.

34. Section 401(a)(11) of the Code and Treas. Regs. §1.401(a)-11.

35. Prentice-Hall *Pension Reporter* ¶16021, et seq.

36. Section 105(a) of ERISA.

37. Section 105(b) of ERISA.

38. Section 104(b)(2) of ERISA.

39. Labor Regulations §2520.104(b)-30.

40. Treas. Regs. §1.401(b)-1.

41. 74 T.C. No. 60 (1980).

42. *Myron v. U.S.,* 550 F.2d 1145 (9th Cir. 1977).

43. *Wisconsin Nipple & Fabricating Co. v. Commissioner*, 67 T.C. 490 (1976), *aff'd*, 581 F.2d 1235 (7th Cir. 1978).

44. *Elliot Knitwear Profit Sharing Plan*, 614 F.2d 347 (3rd Cir. 1980) *aff'g*,71 T.C. 765 (1979); Sections 511-514 of the Code; investment in partnerships (even as a limited partner) may also generate unrelated business taxable income, see Rev. Rul. 79-222, 1979-2 C.B. 236, Treas. Regs. §1.514(c)-1(a)(2) example (4).

45. Section 404(c) of ERISA.

46. "Final Opinion on Employee Benefit Planning" issued by the committee on Unauthorized Practice of Law dated October 17, 1977.

47. Prohibited Transaction Exemptions 80-78, 80-86, 80-97, and 81-1. Also see section 10.04, *infra*.

48. In one case, however, where the employer made "advance contributions" to a profit sharing plan to enable the plan to make an investment, the Tax Court found the advance to constitute a loan, and the plan was held to have debt-financed, unrelated business income as a result of the investment. *Marprowear Profit Sharing Trust v. Commissioner*, 74 T.C. No. 80 (1980).

49. Section 404(a)(7) of the Code.

50. Rev. Rul. 67-341, 1967-2 C.B. 156.

51. *Angelo J. Bianchi,* 66 T.C. 3234 (1976), *aff'd*, 553 F.2d 93 (2d Cir. 1977). *Anthony LaMaestro*, 72 T.C. 377 (1979), *Robert A. Young,* 1979-242 T.C.M. (1979).

52. Rev. Rul. 76-28, 1976-1 C.B. 106.

53. Rev. Rul. 57-419, 1957-2 C.B. 264.

54. Rev. Rul. 80-350, 1980-51 I.R.B. 7; Rev. Rul. 59-185, 1959-1 C.B. 86.

55. Rev. Rul. 69-627, 1969-2 C.B. 92.

56. Rev. Rul. 69-217, 1969-1 C.B. 115, as clarified by Rev. Rul. 74-385, 1974-2 C.B. 130.

57. See note 8-43, *supra*, *Pulver Roofing Co., Inc.,* 70 T.C. 1001 (1978), and section 8.02[3] *supra*.

58. 1972-1 C.B. 710.

59. Rev. Rul. 66-13, 1966-1 C.B. 73. Rev. Rul. 66-15, 1961 C.B. 83. *Commissioner v. Pepsi-Cola Niagara Bottling Corporation,* 399 F.2d 390 (2d Cir. 1968).

60. See note 8-42, *supra*.

61. Also see *Ma-Tran Corp.,* 70 T.C. 158 (1978).

62. 68 T.C. 826 (1977), *aff'g,* 620 F.2d 700 (9th Cir. 1980).

63. 68 T.C. 881 (1977).

64. Section 404(a)(5) of the Code.

65. Rev. Rul. 71-295, 1971-2 C.B. 184.

66. Rev. Rul. 57-587, 1957-2 C.B. 270.

67. Rev. Rul. 80-351, 1980-51 I.R.B. 7, Rev. Rul. 73-340, 1973-2 C.B. 134. Also, in *Richard F. Olma*, 38 T.C.M. 112, ¶79,286 P-H Memo T.C. (1979), pension and profit sharing plans established by a professional corporation wholly owned by two dentists failed to qualify. The plan discriminated in favor of the prohibited group because, for the years in issue, the only participants in the plan were the two dentists. Of the two other employees who met the plan's minimum service requirements, one did not meet the minimum age requirement and the other had voluntarily waived her right to participate pursuant to provisions in the plan.

68. *Perry Epstein*, 70 T.C. 439 (1978).

69. Rev. Proc. 76-11, 1976-1 C.B. 550.

70. Rev. Rul. 76-250, 1976-2 C.B. 124.

71. Section 404(a)(5) of the Code.

72. ERISA §403(c)(2)(C) permitting this type of reversion.

73. See note 47, Chapter 14, *supra*.

74. Treas. Regs §1.401-1(b).

75. *Id.*

76. Rev. Rul. 54-231, 1954-1 C.B. 150.

77. *Id.*, note 74, *supra*.

78. Rev. Rul. 73-501, 1973-2 C.B. 127; Rev. Rul. 69-421, 69-2 C.B. 59; Rev. Rul. 54-51, 1954-1 C.B. 147, as amplified by Rev. Rul. 57-213, 1957-1 C.B. 157, and Rev. Rul. 60-84, 1960-1 C.B. 159.

79. Rev. Rul. 61-164, 1961-2 C.B. 99; Rev. Rul. 66-143, 1966-1 C.B. 79; Rev. Rul. 70-611, 1970-2 C.B. 89; and Rev. Rul. 73-510, 1973-2 C.B. 386.

80. Rev. Rul. 69-408, 1969-2 C.B. 58.

81. Rev. Rul. 74-307, 1974-2 C.B. 126, clarifying Rev. Rul. 68-453, 1968-2 C.B. 163 and Rev. Rul. 73-501, 1973-2 C.B. 127.

82. Rev. Rul. 61-164, 1961-2 C.B. 99, and Rev. Rul. 54-67, 1954-1 C.B. 149.

83. Rev. Rul. 60-59, 1960-1 C.B. 154.

84. Rev. Rul. 74-307, 1970-1 C.B. 194, and Rev. Rul. 69-421, 1969-2 C.B. 59.

85. 1955-2 C.B. 228. See section [14.02](1), *supra*, for a listing of the P.S. 58 rates.

86. Rev. Rul. 66-110, 1966-1 C.B. 212.

87. Section 72 and Section 79(b)(3) of the Code.

88. Treas. Regs. §1.72-1(b).

89. Private Letter Rulings 7830082 and 7902083, and Rev. Rul. 67-336, 1967-2 C.B. 66.

90. Section 401(d)(5)(c) of the Code.

91. Rev. Rul. 78-404, 1978-2 C.B. 156.

92. Private Letter Rulings 8035101, and 8051116.

93. Section 402(a)(5)(E)(ii) of the Code.

94. Section 408(d)(3)(A)(ii) of the Code.

95. 1971-2 C.B. 209.

96. Letter Rulings 7807058, 8005022, and 8020065.

97. Section 411(a)(7)(B)(i) of the Code.

98. Section 402(e)(4)(B) of the Code.

99. Section 402(e)(4)(H) of the Code and Private Letter Rulings 8002078 and 8027025, with respect to using service in a predecessor plan to satisfy the five-year requirement.

100. Section 402(e)(1)(C) of the Code.

101. Section 402(a)(5)(C) of the Code.

102. Section 408(d)(4) of the Code and Private Letter Rulings 8044031 and 8045026.

103. Treas. Regs. §1.408-4(c)(3)(i).

104. Section 402(a)(5)(D)(i)(II) of the Code.

105. Section 402(a)(5)(A)(ii) of the Code.

106. Section 402(a)(6)(C) of the Code.

107. Section 402(a)(5)(B) of the Code.

108. Private Letter Ruling 8037034.

109. Sections 402(a)(5)(A)(ii) and 402(a)(6)(D) of the Code.

110. Section 402(a)(7) of the Code.

111. Private Letter Rulings 8008170, 8015093, and 8038101.

112. Private Letter Ruling 8044059.

113. Treas. Regs. §1.408-2(b)(6).

114. A deferred payment over 18.3 years may be very attractive because, under the formula of Treas. Regs. §1.408-2(b)(6), the required annual distribution during the first ten years will normally not even be equal to the interest earned on the IRA. This permits continued deferral of all the principal and some of the interest until future years.

115. Section 2039(e) of the Code.
116. Rev. Rul. 72-241, 1972-1 C.B. 108.
117. Rev. Rul. 59-94, 1959-1 C.B. 25.
118. Section 408(e)(2)-(4) of the Code.
119. Sections 2039(c) and 2039(f) of the Code.
120. Section 402(a)(7) of the Code.
121. Treas. Regs. §20.2039-4(c)(3).

CHAPTER 16

Nonqualified
Deferred Compensation

[16.01] GENERAL EXPLANATION

Professional corporations may adopt nonqualified deferred compensation programs identical to those adopted by regular business corporations, and the same rules of taxation cover nonqualified deferred compensation programs of both professional and regular business corporations. Unlike qualified retirement plans, nonqualified deferred compensation may be granted on a discriminatory basis, and, more often than not, is granted only to the professionals. Although nonqualified deferred compensation arrangements are often used in the professional corporation setting, they are most commonly implemented for one of the following purposes:

(1) Income Deferral

Nonqualified deferred compensation arrangements have historically been implemented in order to permit employees to defer current income until later years when, hopefully, the employee's tax bracket will be lower. The benefit of such deferral is somewhat lessened by the 50% maximum tax rate on personal service income provided under Section 1348 of the Code (and by the 50% rate established for 1982 and thereafter by ERTA) and also by the imposition of the alternative minimum tax under Section 55 which may actually cause income tax brackets in later years to be higher where the employee has deferred taxes through the use of tax shelter vehicles.

Deferral arrangements are normally used in larger professional corporations and with third-party payors. In small professional corporations, deferral arrangements will certainly provide benefits (through the ability to accumulate earnings at the lower corporate tax rates), but will probably produce net operating losses for the professional corporation (which the authors feel should be avoided) when deferred compensation payments begin. That is, if a small professional corporation accumulates earnings in earlier years to fund a nonqualified deferred compensation arrangement in later years for Professional A during his retirement, and if the other professionals (after the retirement of Professional A) withdraw a substantial amount of the annual earnings of the professional corporation, the deferred compensation payments to Professional A (which will be deductible) will normally produce net operating losses in the professional corporation for income tax purposes.

Further, deferred compensation arrangements in one-man professional corporations may actually increase the taxes due. For example, assume that under a contractual arrangement a professional corporation has accumulated $100,000 to be used to provide deferred compensation to the sole professional employee. If the professional employee dies prior to the commencement of the payment of benefits, the value of the professional corporation will be reduced by the value of the deferred compensation owed, but the value of the deferred compensation must be included in the professional's estate. Further, the beneficiaries of the professional must report the deferred compensation as income when received (although they will receive a deduction under Section 691(c) for estate taxes paid). On the other hand, if the professional were to die with $100,000 in accumulated earnings in the professional corporation, the value of the professional corporation would be increased by $100,000 for estate tax purposes, but there would be no income tax paid on the liquidation of the professional corporation due to the step-up in basis under Section 1014 in the stock of the professional corporation. Consequently, in one-man professional corporations, it is often best to use accumulated funds to provide benefits, such as split dollar insurance, which will pass outside the professional's estate.

Amounts payable under deferred compensation arrangements are considered personal service income and are, consequently, subject to the 50% maximum tax rate under Section 1348 of the Code for years prior to 1982. Further, amounts paid under nonqualified deferred compensation arrangements are deductible by the employer when paid or made available to the employee under Section 404(a)(5).

(2) Payments to Older Professionals

Very often, one of the older professionals will have begun the professional corporation, and the establishment of a deferred compensation arrangement for the older professional provides a tax deductible means whereby the younger professionals compensate him for establishing the client base of the firm. This is particularly useful in legal and accounting practices where the value of the practice is produced by established relationships with clients (rather than a medical practice where the value is essentially the amounts receivables existing on the books). The use of deferred compensation arrangements for the older professional employees often provides a method for younger professional employees to "buy in." For example, if Dr. A's professional corporation has $250,000 in accounts receivable on the books and Dr. B intends to buy a 40% interest in the corporation, it can be argued that Dr. B must, necessarily, buy a 40% interest in the existing accounts receivable. Since this would require Dr. B to pay $100,000 on the date of purchase (which may be difficult), a deferred compensation arrangement could be established so that, upon retirement or death, Dr. A will receive deferred compensation in the amount of $100,000 (possibly increased by a cost of living factor). The same type of an arrangement can be established between Dr. A and Dr. B through the use of preferred stock so that the value of the corporation upon Dr. B's entry will be frozen in preferred stock issued to Dr. A, which must be purchased from him upon his retirement. The use of the preferred stock mechanism does not, however, provide a deductible payment to the corporation and may produce adverse tax consequences to Dr. A under Section 306 of the Code (depending on the manner of the disposition of the preferred stock). See section [1.07] which describes these issues in more detail.

(3) Fringe Benefits

Most insurance companies have recently, through the use of sophisticated insurance policies with annuity features, created a mechanism for providing key man insurance which will have sufficient cash values to fund substantial retirement or disability income benefits. Such policies can provide substantial benefits for professionals in medium to large professional corporations. On the other hand, such key man insurance policies should probably not be obtained by one-man professional corporations because the proceeds of the policy and/or the value of the deferred compensation benefits must be included in the professional's estate. It would probably be wiser in a one-man professional corporation to provide some type of arrangement, such as split dollar insurance, which may be excluded from the estate of the professional.

Any arrangement of deferred compensation adopted by a professional corporation should be represented by a formal, written agreement which is adopted by the board of directors and executed by both the corporation and the professional who will receive the deferred compensation. Care should be taken to assure that the corporate resolutions authorizing the deferred compensation clearly illustrate the corporate benefit of paying the deferred compensation. See *M.S.D. Inc. v. U.S.*,[1] where payments made by a corporation to the widow of one of the founding officers of the corporation were not deductible as deferred compensation. Although there was an arrangement between the corporation and the officer to make payments in the event of his death, the arrangement was not motivated by the intention to confer a business benefit for the closely held family corporation. Thus, the payments were not "necessary" and were not deductible as a business epxense. A form of deferred compensation contract is included in this chapter as Exhibit 1.

Because most deferred compensation agreements established by professional corporations are unfunded, it is often important to provide that the deferred compensation payable by the corporation be personally guaranteed by the remaining professionals. Such personal guaranties provide assurances to the professional who will receive the deferred compensation that the other professionals will not strip the professional corporation of its assets, thereby leaving him (or his beneficiaries) with an unenforceable obligation.

Although nonqualified deferred compensation arrangements are not subject to the nondiscrimination requirements of Section 401, *et seq.*, of the Code which are imposed on qualified retirement plans, they may be subject to the requirements of Title I of ERISA. Section 3(2) of Title I of ERISA defines the terms "employee pension benefit plan" and "pension plan" to mean any plan, fund, or program which is established or maintained by an employer that provides retirement income to an employee or results in the deferral of income by employees for periods extending to the termination of employment or beyond. Thus, the first question which must be asked of any nonqualified deferred compensation arrangement is whether it constitutes a "plan" of providing deferred compensation. To the extent that deferred compensation is provided to one or two employees on a random basis, a plan probably does not exist. However, any deferred compensation provided other than on an *ad hoc* basis will probably be considered a "plan."

Even if a "plan" exists, under Title I of ERISA, "unfunded" arrangements maintained primarily for the purpose of providing deferred compensation for a select group of management or highly compensated employees are exempt. Sections 201(2), 301(a), and 401(a) of ERISA exempt such "top hat" plans from the participation, vesting, benefit accrual, funding, and fiduciary responsibility provisions. The reporting and disclosure requirements of ERISA may be satisfied by an employer who maintains such a plan by filing with the Department of Labor a single statement that includes the employer's name, address, identification number, and a declaration that the employer maintains a plan primarily for the purpose of providing deferred compensation for a select group of management or highly compensated employees, the number of such plans maintained by the employer, and the number of employees in each plan.[2] However, in order to qualify for the general exemption from Title I of ERISA, the plan must be "unfunded." At the present time, the Labor Regulations do not define the term "unfunded." The authors feel that tests similar to those provided under Section 83 of the Code, regarding the taxation of unfunded deferred compensation arrangements, should apply for Title I of ERISA. However, the Labor Department may take the position that any mechanism for funding, such as the use of insurance policies, creates a "funded" plan.[3]

[16.02] INCOME TAX TREATMENT OF DEFERRED COMPENSATION ARRANGEMENTS

The tax treatment of deferred compensation arrangements depends primarily on whether the arrangements are funded or unfunded.

(1) Funded Arrangements

Since the enactment in 1969 of Section 83 of the Code, the tax treatment of funded arrangements has been fairly well settled. Under Section 83, an employee is taxed on his interest in a funded deferred compensation arrangement where it is either (1) no longer subject to a substantial risk of forfeiture (usually the performance of future services) or (2) is transferable. The fair market value of the interest is included in the employee's income and the employer receives a corresponding deduction in the year of inclusion.

The determination of whether an arrangement is "funded" is usually based upon whether the employer has segregated assets for the benefit of the employee beyond the reach of its creditors (for example, in trust). The mere contractual obligation of an employer does not constitute a funded plan. Further, assurances provided by the employer that the deferred compensation will be paid, such as the purchase of a life insurance policy or an annuity contract, under which the employer remains the owner and a beneficiary, do not create a funded plan.[4] Nor should the personal guarantee of the other shareholders of the corporation create a funded arrangement.

(2) Unfunded Arrangements

Because of the potential tax consequences of funded arrangements, most deferred compensation arrangements are unfunded. Under an unfunded arrangement, an employee will be required to report as income the deferred amount in the year in which it is actually or constructively received. Regulations §1.451-2 provides that income is constructively received in the year in which it is "credited to his account, set apart for him, or otherwise made available so that he may draw upon it at any time, or so that he could have drawn upon it during the taxable year . . . ."

In 1960, the Service eliminated much of the confusion which existed with regard to constructive receipt through the issuance of Rev. Rul. 60-31.[5] Rev. Rul. 60-31 sanctioned the typical unfunded deferred compensation arrangement by stating that the Service will normally not look behind the contract entered into by the parties. In the late 1960's, the Service began to define its position with regard to elective deferred compensation arrangements in a number of revenue rulings. In Rev. Rul. 67-449[6] and Rev. Rul. 69-650,[7] amounts were not considered constructively received by employees where the election to defer receipt of compensation and bonuses was made prior to the time when such compensation was due.

In Rev. Proc. 71-19,[8] the Service announced guidelines to be followed in obtaining advance rulings on unfunded deferred compensation arrangements. The Service stated that a ruling would be issued where the election to defer payment was made before the beginning of the period of service for which the compensation was payable, regardless of the existence of a plan or forfeiture provisions. With respect to elections made subsequent to the beginning of the service period, substantial forfeiture provisions must impose "a significant limitation or duty which will require a meaningful effort on the part of the employee to fulfill and there is a definite possibility that the event which will cause the forfeiture could occur." A number of private letter rulings on nonqualified deferred compensation arrangements have been issued to professional corporations. See, for example, Letter Ruling 7742090, in which a professional corporation agreed to pay deferred compensation to one of its shareholders equal to 5% of the net profits of the corporation during the four fiscal years following the year in which shareholder's death, retirement, or termination of employment occurs. This Letter Ruling also provided for the personal guaranty of the payments by the remaining shareholders.

On September 7, 1977, the Service issued Information Release No. 1881 in which it stated that it was suspending the issuance of private letter rulings on nonqualified deferred compensation plans under which employees can elect to defer part of their salaries, where the deferred salaries are invested by the employer. This freeze on rulings was prompted by the Service's concern that "in substance, the employee receives the compensation and deposits it with the employer to be held for the employee's benefit." Private letter rulings are, however, being issued at the present time on nonqualified deferred compensation arrangements.[9]

(3) Proposed Treasury Department Regulations

On February 3, 1978, the Service published proposed regulations which would eliminate the tax advantages of most new, nonqualified deferred compensation arrangements.[10] Under these proposed regulations, if a taxpayer's basic compensation "is, at the taxpayer's individual option, deferred to a taxable year later than that in which such amount would have been payable but for his exercise of such option, the amount shall be treated as received by the taxpayer in such year." This language would have effectively eliminated nonqualified deferred compensation arrangements, especially in closely held and professional corporations.

Fortunately, in the Revenue Act of 1978, Congress mandated that the "taxable year of inclusion in gross income of any amount, by a private deferred compensation plan, shall be determined in accordance with the principles set forth in the regulations, rulings, and judicial decisions relating to deferred compensation which were in effect on February 1, 1980."[11] Consequently, the Service has now relented on the position taken in the proposed regulations, but the position which will be taken by the various district offices (on audit) with regard to unfunded deferred compensation arrangements is still unclear.[12]

(4) FICA and FUTA Taxes

Section 3121(a)(13) of the Federal Insurance Contributions Act (FICA) and Section 3306(b)(10) of the Federal Unemployment Tax Act (FUTA) exempt from the term "wages":

> Any payment or series of payments by an employer to an employee or any of his dependents which is paid . . . upon or after termination of an employee's employment relationship because of (i) death, (ii) retirement or disability, or (iii) retirement after attaining an age specified in the plan . . . under a plan established by the employer which makes provision for his employees generally or a class or classes of his employees (or for such employees or classes of employees and their dependents), other than any such payment or series of payments which would have been paid if the employee's employment relationship had not been so terminated.

Also, the term "wages" does not include "any payment . . . made to an employee after the month in which . . . he attains age 65 . . . if the employee did not work for the employer in the period for which such payment is made."[13]

Under these provisions, some commentators feel that nonqualified deferred compensation arrangements should generally be exempt from FICA and FUTA taxes.[14] However the Service will continue to construe these provisions very restrictively and, although it is issuing private letter rulings which exclude deferred compensation from FICA and FUTA taxes under these provisions,[15] it may be difficult for professional corporations to meet the "plan" requirements. However, amounts payable after attaining age 65 should be exempt from FICA or FUTA taxes.[16]

[16.03] METHODS FOR DEFERRING INCOME WITH THIRD-PARTY CARRIERS

(1) Insurance Companies and Health Maintenance Organizations

Whether amounts of current income can be deferred depends upon the structure of the relationship between the professional and the third-party organization.

Where the professional renders services to the individual client/patient and such services generate a right of reimbursement from the third-party payor (such as an insurance carrier, i.e., Blue Cross/Blue Shield) the Service has ruled that deferral of income may not occur. In Rev. Rul. 69-50,[17] a participating physician voluntarily entered into an agreement with a nonprofit corporation that insured the medical expenses of its subscribers. Under the agreement, the physician irrevocably elected to defer a percentage of payments that were otherwise due to him from the corporation for services rendered to patients insured by the corporation. The amounts deferred were to be paid to the physician in equal monthly installments upon the earlier of retirement or disability or, in the case of death, to the physician's beneficiary. Rev. Rul. 69-50 holds that the physician must include the deferred amounts in gross income for the year in which they were withheld by the corporation, because the physician's right to the compensation payments emanates from the medical services that are rendered to the patients insured by the corporation. The patients compensate the physician for the services by vesting the physician with a right to compensation payments from the corporation. In effect, the patients have funded their obligation to the physician with the corporation, thereby conferring an economic or financial benefit upon the physician. Because the agreement between the corporation and the physician is independent of the dealings between the patient and the physician, the inclusion of a substantial forfeiture provision in the agreement does not alter the relationship by which the patient-subscriber has conferred an economic benefit upon the physician. See Rev. Rul. 77-420.[18] Also see *U.S. v. Basye, et al.,*[19] which held that amounts set aside in trust for physicians providing services to the Kaiser-Permanente Health Maintenance Organization were considered constructively received.

On the other hand, when a professional renders services directly to the third-party organization and the fee income is generated through such services and not through services rendered to a particular patient/client, income may be deferred. In Rev. Rul. 69-474,[20] a nonprofit corporation engaged in operating a medical and hospital service program entered into an agreement with a partnership composed of physicians whereby the physicians agreed to furnish the medical services required to satisfy the medical service obligations provided in the corporation's membership contract. There was no contractual relationship between the physicians and the patients and the fees due to the physicians were paid by the corporation and were based on the average membership in the group multiplied by the per-member price in effect for that month. Thus, remuneration was not related to any particular service provided to any particular patient. Under this arrangement, amounts contributed to a nonqualified retirement plan, which was not funded by a trust or any other arrangement, were not considered constructively received by the physicians.

(2) Hospitals and Other Large Employers

In *Goldsmith v. United States*,[21] the Court of Claims found that a life insurance plan providing life, accidental death, disability, retirement, and severance benefits resulted in current income to a physician based on the "economic benefit" he received, to the extent of the value of the life, accidental death, and disability benefits, but not with respect to retirement and severance benefits.

The plan was an arrangement under which the employer promised to provide the specified benefits "out of its general assets" and in return the physician agreed to have his compensation reduced by $450 per month. On the day that the agreement was entered into, the employer entered into a contract with an insurance company, the terms of which would pay to the employer precisely the same benefits that the employer had agreed to pay the physician. The policy was owned by the employer, and the physician had no legal interest in the benefits payable from the policy other than as a general creditor of the employer. The employer could have chosen to cancel the policy and provide the benefits from its general assets without the use of insurance; however, the physician had the option to cancel the arrangement on 30 days' notice.

The court considered, but rejected, inclusion of the $450 in the physician's gross income under the theory of constructive receipt. The court stated that, since the agreement to reduce cash salary in exchange for the benefits provided by the arrangement occurred prior to the time the salary was earned, there would not be constructive receipt, even though the physician had initiated the establishment of the plan.[22] The court found instead that the physician was taxed on the "economic benefit" provided. In addition, the court found that no economic benefit was conferred by the promise to pay retirement and severance benefits since neither would commence prior to the physician's 65th birthday (some 27 years subsequent to the date of the establishment of the arrangement) and no trust or escrow agreement was established and the employer's promise to pay future benefits was not represented by a note or other writing that could be sold or assigned. On the other hand, the court found that the life, accidental death, and disability benefits conferred a taxable benefit to the physician in view of the fact that:

(1) Such benefits were payable immediately upon the physician's death or disability and, therefore, payment would not be subject to the continued financial stability of the employer until the physician's 65th birthday;

(2) The life insurance benefits effectively provided the same kind of life insurance protection that is currently taxable when provided under qualified retirement plans; and

(3) The value of the economic benefit provided by current life, accidental death, and disability benefits is readily determinable by comparison with the cost of comparable commercial insurance.

The trial judge's opinion in the *Goldsmith* case was adopted by the Court of Claims;[23] however, its impact on nonqualified deferred compensation arrangements is uncertain. This is especially true since the concept announced in *Goldsmith*, that the employee should be taxed on the economic benefit of policies purchased by the employer to provide benefits under an unfunded arrangement, is contrary to existing case law.[24] Most commentators feel that the *Goldsmith* case is simply an ill-reasoned decision by the Court of Claims and will not have a substantial impact on nonqualified deferred compensation arrangements.

EXHIBIT 1

DEFERRED COMPENSATION AGREEMENT

This Agreement, made and entered into this _____ day of _____, 19____, by and between A & B, M.D., P.C. (the "Corporation"), A, M.D. (the "Employee") and B, M.D. (the "Guarantor").

W I T N E S S E T H:

WHEREAS, the Corporation is a professional corporation organized and in good standing under the laws of the State of Georgia; and

WHEREAS, the Employee has been continuously employed by the Corporation since _____; and

WHEREAS, the Employee has performed his duties in a capable and efficient manner, resulting in substantial growth and progress to the Corporation; and

WHEREAS, the Corporation and the Guarantor highly value the services of the Employee and are desirous of retaining his services until retirement and in assisting him to provide for the contingencies of death, retirement as an employee of Corporation, and disability; and

WHEREAS, the Employee is willing to continue in the employ of the Corporation until retirement in order to secure the benefits herein conferred;

NOW THEREFORE, the parties for and in consideration of the mutual agreements, covenants and representations contained herein, do hereby agree as follows:

1. Employment. The Corporation hereby agrees to continue the employment of the Employee and the Employee hereby agrees to continue to perform his services for the Corporation pursuant to the terms and conditions contained in the Employment Agreement by and between the Corporation and the Employee, dated _____.

2. Amount of Benefits. The Corporation agrees to pay to the Employee, or to any person or persons designated by Employee to Corporation in writing, upon the death, retirement or disability of the Employee, whichever shall first occur, the following benefits:

If Death, Retirement or Disability Occurs:	Benefit
Before April 1, 1982	$47,500
On or after April 1, 1982 but before April 1, 1987	$60,000
On or after April 1, 1987	$75,000

653

3. Method of Payment of Benefits. The benefits described in Paragraph 2 shall be payable in twenty-four (24) equal monthly installments, the first installment payment to be made twelve (12) months from the date of the Employee's death, retirement as an employee of Corporation or disability, whichever shall first occur, and each subsequent installment shall be paid on the first day of each month thereafter until such benefits shall be paid in full. In the event that Employee has not designated a person or persons to receive such benefits as described in Paragraph 2, such installments shall be paid to the Employee, or, in the event of the Employee's death, to his surviving spouse, but, if no spouse shall survive the Employee, to his descendants, *per stirpes*, but, if no spouse or descendant shall survive the Employee, to the Employee's estate.

4. Disability. For purposes of this Agreement, the term "disability" shall mean Employee's inability to perform any of the duties pertaining to his profession.

5. Guaranty. Guarantor does hereby absolutely and unconditionally guarantee to the Employee, and to Employee's spouse, or other designated beneficiaries, the prompt payment and performance of all obligations of the Corporation arising from and under this Agreement. Guarantor further agrees that this guaranty shall continue in full force and effect until all of the payments due under this Agreement have been paid in full, and except as provided herein Guarantor shall not be released from his obligations hereunder so long as any claim arising out of this Agreement is not settled or discharged in full, unless, prior to Employee's death, disability, or retirement, Guarantor's employment with the Corporation shall be terminated by the Corporation without cause, in which event Guarantor's obligations hereunder shall cease. Termination of Guarantor's employment by the Corporation "without cause" shall mean termination for any reason other than:

(1) Loss by Guarantor of his license to practice medicine in the State of Georgia;

(2) Suspension of Guarantor's license to practice medicine in the State of Georgia for a period of one (1) year or more;

(3) Guarantor's addiction to narcotics, alcohol or other drugs;

(4) Declaration of personal bankruptcy by Guarantor; or

(5) The breach by Guarantor of the provisions of Paragraph 2 of his employment agreement with Corporation of even date herewith (or comparable provisions of any future or successor employment agreement between Guarantor and Corporation) which relate to the practice by Guarantor of his medical specialty solely, and the devotion of his entire professional time and his best efforts, as an employee of Corporation and the treatment and referral of patients.

If Guarantor's employment shall be terminated by the Corporation for any of the reasons listed above, or if Guarantor shall voluntarily terminate his employment with the Corporation, Guarantor expressly agrees that his obligations under this guaranty shall remain in full force and effect. Guarantor further agrees that at the time payments to Employee commence under this Agreement, or upon

Guarantor's death or his total and permanent disability, or upon termination of Guarantor's employment with Corporation as described above, any amounts that may be or become due or payable to him from the Corporation or Employee, either in payment for any shares of stock in the Corporation owned by him, or pursuant to the terms of said employment agreement between Guarantor and the Corporation, or otherwise, shall be held and retained by the Corporation or Employee and used to fund the amounts due Employee under this Agreement or to offset any claim or claims that the Employee or his designated beneficiaries may then have or may have in the future under this guaranty; provided, however, that in no event shall such amounts withheld by Corporation or Employee exceed $75,000; further provided, however, that if Guarantor dies prior to April 1, 1987, the amount of this guaranty and the amounts that may be so withheld by Corporation or Employee shall be limited as follows: if Guarantor dies before April 1, 1982, limited to $47,500 or if Guarantor dies on or after April 1, 9182 but prior to April 1, 1987, to $60,000. In the event that any amounts due to Guarantor are withheld as provided in this Paragraph 5 prior to April 1, 1987, and in the event that Employee dies or becomes disabled prior to April 1, 1987, the difference between the amount so withheld and the amount determined to be due to Employee under Paragraph 2 hereof shall be promptly refunded to Guarantor or his estate upon Employees's death or disability prior to April 1, 1987. In the event that amounts due to Guarantor are withheld as provided in this Paragraph 5, Guarantor's obligations under this guaranty shall be considered satisfied to the extent of such withheld amounts and, if such withheld amounts equal the amounts determined to be due to Employee under Paragraph 2 hereof, the Guarantor's entire obligation under this guaranty shall be considered satisfied.

6. <u>Stock Valuation.</u> The parties to this Agreement agree that no obligation or liability of the Corporation arising under this Agreement shall be taken into account for purposes of computing the value of any stock ownership interest that the Employee may have in the Corporation.

7. <u>Other Compensation Arrangements.</u> All parties agree that no deferred compensation payable under this Agreement shall be considered to be a salary, death benefit, or other compensation or benefit to the Employee, his designated beneficiaries or his estate for purposes of computing benefits to which the Employee, his designated beneficiaries, or his estate may be entitled under any pension or profit sharing plan, employment agreement, or any other compensation arrangement maintained by the Corporation for the benefit of its employees.

8. <u>Assignability.</u> The right of the Employee or his designated beneficiaries to the payment of the deferred compensation provided under this Agreement shall not be commuted, sold, assigned, transferred, pledged, encumbered or otherwise conveyed, nor shall any interest of the Employee under this Agreement be subject to any claim of any creditor of the Employee or subject to any judicial process involving the Employee.

9. <u>Binding Effect.</u> This Agreement shall be binding upon and inure to the benefit of the Corporation, its sucessors and assigns and the Employee, his designated beneficiaries, heirs, executors, administrators and legal representatives.

10. Governing Law. This Agreement shall be construed in accordance with and governed by the laws of the State of Georgia.

11. Authority. All provisions, terms and conditions of this Agreement have been duly consented to, ratified, approved, and adopted by the Board of Directors of the Corporation, and appropriate authority has been delegated to the undersigned officers of the Corporation to execute this Agreement.

12. Paragraph Headings. The paragraph headings contained in this Agreement are for convenience only and shall in no manner be construed as a part of this Agreement.

13. Entire Agreement. This Agreement constitutes the sole and entire agreement with respect to the matters contained herein, and any representation, inducement, promise, or agreement, whether oral or written, which is not embodied herein shall be of no force or effect.

14. Counterparts. For the convenience of the parties hereto, any number of counterparts may be executed, and each such executed counterpart shall be deemed to be an original instrument.

15. Severability. If any term, covenant or condition of this Agreement or the application thereof to any person or circumstance shall, to any extent, be invalid or unenforceable, the remainder of this Agreement or the application of such terms, covenants and conditions to persons or circumstances other than those as to which it is held invalid or enforceable, shall not be affected thereby and each term, covenant or condition of this Agreement shall be valid and be enforced to the fullest extent permitted by law.

IN WITNESS WHEREOF, Corporation has caused this Agreement to be executed by its duly authorized officers and its seal to be hereunto affixed, and Employee and Guarantor have hereunto set their hands and seals, all being done in triplicate originals with one original being delivered to each party on the day and year first above written.

A & B, M.D., P.C.

(CORPORATE SEAL)

ATTEST: By: _____
                Vice President

_____
Secretary

           _____ (SEAL)
         A, M.D.

           _____ (SEAL)
         B, M.D.

NOTES TO CHAPTER 16

1. 77-1 U.S.T.C. ¶9366, 39 AFTR 2d 77-1393 (M.D. Ohio 1977). Also see *Muscogie Radiology*, 78-490 T.C.M. (payments made by a professional corporation to a radiologist were found to be compensation for past and future services. The Tax Court rejected the Service's argument that the payments represented the cost of acquiring the radiologist's stock).

2. Labor Regulations §2520.104-23.

3. See, for example, *Dependahl v. Falstaff Corporation*, 491 F. Supp. 1188 (E.D. Mo. 1980), *aff'd* in part and *rev'd* in part by the Eighth Circuit (6/30/81), holding that death benefits funded through the use of key man life insurance policies create a funded plan.

4. Rev. Rul. 68-99, 1968-1 C.B. 193, and Rev. Rul. 72-25, 1972-1 C.B. 128.

5. 1960-1 C.B. 174.

6. 1967-2 C.B. 173.

7. 1969-2 C.B. 106.

8. 1971-1 C.B. 609.

9. See Letter Rulings 8021085 and 8023092 permitting the deferral of future salary payments.

10. See Prop. Regs. §1.61-16.

11. See Section 132(a) of the Act.

12. See for example, the discussion which follows regarding *Goldsmith v. U.S.*, 586 F.2d 310 (Ct. Cl. 1978), at section [16.03](2), *infra*.

13. See Sections 3121(a)(9) of FICA and Section 3306(b) of FUTA.

14. See Miller "Executive Estate Planning." 17 *NYU Institute on Fed. Tax.* 1171, 1189 (1959).

15. See Letter Ruling 8021085 and Letter Ruling 8126067 (deferred payments are excluded from "wages" except in the case of employees who terminate employment for reasons other than death, disability or retirement at an age specified in the plan of the employer).

16. Rev. Rul. 77-25, 1977-1 C.B. 301.

17. 1969-1 C.B. 140.

18. 1977-2 C.B. 172.

19. 93 S. Ct. 1080 (1973).

20. 1969-2 C.B. 105.

21. 586 F.2d 810 (Ct. Cl. 1978).

22. Rev. Rul. 60-31, 1960-1 C.B. 174.

23. 586 F.2d 810 (Ct. Cl. 978).

24. See *Casale v. Commissioner*, 247 F.2d 440 (2d Cir. 1957), where an employee who owned 98% of the stock of a corporation entered into a deferred compensation agreement with the corporation. The corporation purchased a key man life insurance policy on the employee, and the court held that the employee was not taxable on the premiums paid by the corporation.

PART IV

AFFILIATED SERVICE

ORGANIZATIONS

AND TERMINATIONS

CHAPTER 17

Professional Equipment and Office Buildings

The manner in which professional equipment and office buildings are held in a professional corporation setting will not only create tax advantages and disadvantages but also, and perhaps more importantly, practical problems which may cause disagreement among the professionals.

[17.01] OFFICE BUILDINGS

It has been the general experience of the authors that it is best to maintain professional office buildings, which are used by the professional corporation and owned by the professionals, in a separate partnership and not have them owned by the professional corporation. the authors have reached this conclusion due to the following:

(1) Advantages are normally not obtained by transferring an existing office building to a new professional corporation. If the existing office building is transferred in a tax-free Section 351 exchange which occurs upon incorporation, no gain or loss will be recognized to the transferring professionals, but the professional corporation will have a "carryover" basis in the building under Section 362 of the Code. Consequently, the professional corporation will assume the depreciated basis of the building in the hands of the professionals and will continue to depreciate

661

it from that existing basis. Also, limitations will be imposed on the use of accelerated methods of depreciation. See section [2.08], *supra*. Further, if the professionals desire to increase the basis of the building in the hands of the professional corporation, a taxable sale may be made to the corporation. A taxable sale may, however, create depreciation recapture under Section 1250 or under Section 1239 (in the event the sale is to an 80% controlled corporation). Further, the sale price will be subject to close scrutiny by the Service. It is possible, however, that such a sale may result in tax benefits through increased depreciation deductions and principal payments made with after-tax dollars (at lower corporate rates).

(2) Maintaining the building in a partnership helps to minimize the value of the professional corporation. Minimizing the value of the professional corporation not only facilitates the purchase of stock in the professional corporation by new shareholders, but it also reduces the need to pay large dividends. If the office building is maintained in the professional corporation, the retained earnings of the corporation will increase each year as the loan on the office building is amortized. As the retained earnings of the professional corporation increase, it can be argued that a corresponding increase in the dividend paid to the shareholders should occur.

(3) Maintaining the office building in a separate partnership permits shareholders to obtain some tax shelter by way of depreciation and investment tax credit against their individual incomes as opposed to providing shelter in the professional corporation at tax rates of probably less than 20%.

One of the critical questions that will arise when maintaining the office building outside of the professional corporation is the amount of rent which will be paid by the professional corporation to the partnership owning the building. In order for the professional corporation to obtain a deduction for rent under Section 162, the amount of rent must be ''ordinary and necessary.'' Lease payments between related entities are one of the items which are closely scrutinized by the Service. If lease payments are too high, the excess payments could be considered a constructive dividend.[1] On the other hand, if lease payments are too low, the Service has the ability to increase the rent under Section 482 of the Code. Consequently, care should be taken in establishing the rent, and the authors recommend that the rent charged by the partnership bear some reasonable relationship to comparable, commercially available rents. However, in determining the amount of rent, it is probably best to err on the low side, since any additional rent (over and above the deductions available in the partnership) will produce taxable income in the partnership which will not be subject to the 50% maximum tax rates under Section 1348 of the Code. This issue is eliminated for 1982 and thereafter by the maximum income tax rate of 50% established by ERTA.

Also, since ''negotiations'' with regard to the terms of the lease are not necessary, the authors recommend that a form lease (of the type which is generally available on a local basis) should be used. A form lease may lessen the inclination of an IRS agent to scrutinize the terms of the lease (including the rent). Further, the authors believe that such leases should not contain any option to purchase by the professional corporation and should run for periods of approximately five years (with cost-of-living escalators) so that an IRS agent will not be inclined to view the annual renegotiations as a means of avoiding taxes.

If the office building is maintained in a separate partnership, it is essential that the partnership agreement among the partners contain a buy-out mechanism so that the interest of a deceased, terminated, or disabled partner may be purchased. Since there is always a question of whether the lease provides for a "fair" rent, it is best that the members of the partnership owning the building be active members of the professional corporation. If wives or estates of deceased partners continue as partners, they may become unhappy with an ownership interest in a building which provides little or no cash flow. For the same reasons, it is essential that all shareholders of the professional corporation also be partners (and not just minimal partners) in the partnership owning the building. Requiring younger partners to purchase a substantial interest in the partnership owning the building always involves hardship. However, if the younger partners do not purchase a substantial interest in the building (which purchase may be made on an installment basis), they may become unhappy with the seemingly large amount of rent which is paid by the professional corporation to the partnership. Also, if only the older professionals own interests in the partnership, problems may arise as they retire and desire to sell their interests. The ownership of the partnership by all of the professionals will not only prohibit the older professionals from holding the younger professionals "hostage" by increasing the rent substantially, but it will also assure the older professionals that there will be a market for their partnership interest. A form of partnership agreement for holding professional buildings is attached to this chapter as Exhibit 1.

[17.02] PERSONAL PROPERTY

If a separate building partnership is not maintained by the professionals or if the professional corporation leases office space from a third party, the authors feel that, in the interest of simplicity, it is probably best to let the professional corporation own the professional equipment (assuming there is not a substantial amount of such equipment). On the other hand, if a separate building partnership is maintained or if there is a substantial amount of professional equipment (such as radiology equipment), the authors feel that the equipment should be maintained in the separate building partnership (or a separate partnership established simply for the equipment). In addition to the problems with structuring the rent for the equipment (which are identical to those encountered in structuring the rent for the office building discussed above), the terms of the lease of the professional equipment must be designed to assure that the investment tax credit will be available to the professionals individually. In order to qualify for the 10% investment tax credit on tangible personal property, Section 46 of the Code imposes the following additional restrictions upon noncorporate lessors (including individuals, partnerships, and Subchapter S corporations):

(1) The term of the lease must be less than 50% of the useful life of each item of property leased (included in the term for purposes of this test are all options by either the lessee or the lessor to renew the lease);[2] and

(2) For the first 12 months after the date on which the property is transferred to the lessee, the sum of all the deductions on such property allowable to the lessor under Section 162, for example, insurance and maintainence costs, but not including interest, taxes, or depreciation, must exceed 15% of the rental income produced by such property. The 15% test is applied to each item of property separately.

"New" tangible personal property, the original use of which began with the lessor, is eligible for the investment tax credit without limitation under Section 48(b) of the Code. "Used" tangible personal property subject to the investment tax credit is limited to $100,000 in each year under Section 48(c) of the Code. Also, used property does not qualify for the investment tax credit if, after acquisition by a taxpayer, the property is used by a person who used the property before the acquisition. Consequently, professionals should avoid the situation where a professional corporation uses equipment on a trial basis and then the professional (individually) purchases the equipment and leases it to the corporation. In this situation, neither the professional nor the professional corporation will be entitled to the investment tax credit on the equipment.[3]

Personal property leased by the professionals to the professional corporation should be subject to a written lease which has been approved by the board of directors of the professional corporation.

[17.03] BUILDING AND EQUIPMENT HELD BY OTHER FAMILY MEMBERS

Very often, in an attempt to more or less "gild the lily," professionals permit other family members, principally minor children, to own the office building and equipment which is leased by the professional corporation. Such arrangements can provide substantial income tax savings due to the shifting of tax brackets (minor children are normally in substantially lower tax brackets than the professional) and such arrangements usually occur only in small professional corporations (in order to avoid potential conflicts among professionals). Typically, such property is owned by minor children through trusts, Subchapter S corporations, or guardians and leased directly to the professional corporation. Such arrangements are, however, subject to very close scrutiny by the Service and it has been the authors' experience that they are usually challenged by the Service when discovered.

In challenging family lease-back arrangements, the Service often attempts to invoke the assignment of income doctrine or to reallocate income and deductions under Section 482. The Service has also taken the position that the children may be the "bare legal title" holders but are not the "beneficial" owners of the property. The leading case disallowing intrafamily lease-backs is *Mathews v. Commissioner*.[4] In *Mathews*, a funeral director and his wife transferred property used in the husband's business to a 10-year trust for the benefit of their four minor children. The husband and wife retained a reversionary interest in the property and, through a prearranged agreement with the trustee, the husband leased the property back for a reasonable rental on the date the trusts were executed. The Tax Court held for the taxpayer, but the Fifth Circuit reversed and set forth the following tests for permitting rental deductions under Section 162 in an intrafamily lease-back arrangement:

(1) The grantor must not retain substantially the same control over the property that he had before he made the gift;
(2) The lease-back should be in writing and must require payment of a reasonable rental;
(3) The lease-back must have a bona fide business purpose; and
(4) The corporation must not possess a qualifying equity in the property.[5]

Probably the most difficult of the four tests set forth in *Mathews* is the third tests requiring that a bona fide business purpose exist for such lease-back. Because of *Mathews*, many tax attorneys feel that it is impossible to structure intrafamily gift and lease-back situations which will withstand Service scrutiny. While the authors have not adopted such a pessimistic outlook, they do feel that intrafamily lease-backs should be structured with care and along the lines of those favorable cases which do exist.[6] For example, in *Richard R. Quinliven,*[7] two attorneys transferred an office building to trusts set up by them for their children and subsequently leased back office space in the building. The Tax Court examined the tests set forth in *Mathews* and held that the lease payments were deductible.

The court held that the first requirement was met because the property was transferred to an independent trustee (a bank) and the trust instruments were valid and irrevocable (for a period of ten years and six months) under state law. Moreover, the lease-back was not prearranged, and the trustee had the power under the trust agreement to sell, lease, or otherwise dispose of the property. The second requirement was met because the lease was in writing. The third requirement was met because the attorneys continued to use the property in the practice of law. With regard to the fourth test, the attorneys' reversionary interest was not held to be derived from the lease and would only become possessory after the termination of the trust.

Also see *Edwin D. Davis*[8] (the Tax Court refused to reallocate income from X-ray and physical therapy corporations to an orthopedic surgeon who established the corporations and gave the stock in those corporations to his children); *Donald O. Kirkpatrick*[9] (stock ownership of children in Subchapter S corporation was recognized; parents never attempted to control the children's stock and the ownership by the children had economic reality); *Richard A. Serbousek*[10] (rent paid by two physicians to clifford trusts established for their children held deductible); *Milton Engel v. U.S.*[11] (rental deduction permitted for rent paid by a physician to a clifford trust for the benefit of his children); and *Hobart A. Lerner, M.D., P.A.,*[12] (rental deduction permitted for rent paid by professional association to a 10-year trust established by an ophthalmologist, where children were the beneficiaries).

[17.04]   PROPERTY HELD IN CORPORATE RETIREMENT PLANS

Prior to ERISA, numerous professional corporations avoided some of the problems inherent in owning the professional offices, and obtained a good investment for their qualified retirement plans, by having their qualified retirement plans own the professional offices and lease them to the professional corporation. However, under ERISA Congress specifically enacted rules to prevent this type of transaction, and, under Sections 406 and 407 of ERISA, a lease between a professional corporation and the qualified retirement plan established by that professional corporation is a prohibited transaction and subject to the excise tax penalties established under Section 4975 of the Code.

However, in certain, unique situations it is possible to obtain from the Department of Labor a specific exemption from the prohibited transaction rules. On February 24, 1978, an exemption from the prohibited transaction rules was issued[13] to the Bethel Clinic Employees' Profit Sharing Plan and Trust. This exemption covered a transaction in which a separate building corporation agreed to sell the professional building to the professional corporation's profit sharing plan for an amount less than the fair market value (Query: does the difference between the fair market value and the sales price constitute a gift or a voluntary contribution to the plan by professionals?). The building was then leased to the professional corporation at a rate which would more than cover the interest and principal payments required to be made by the retirement plan. In the event the professional corporation defaulted on the lease payments, the plan had the option, in its sole discretion to: (i) sell the property and pay off the purchase obligation; (ii) relet the property and continue amortizing the purchase obligation; or (iii) void the lease and return the property to the seller and walk away from the unpaid balance of the purchase obligation with no further liability. The transaction is structured to provide a net annual return to the plan of approximately 11% to 12% of the appraised value of the property.

In addition to establishing a "no loss" arrangement similar to that provided in the Bethel Clinic exemption, the House and Senate Conference Committee Reports on ERISA[14] stated that, in order to obtain such an exemption, it must be established that not granting the exemption will have an adverse impact on the community. In the Bethel Clinic exemption, it was shown that, without the exemption, it was possible that the professionals might leave the community, thereby causing a shortage of physicians. A number of similar exemptions have been granted.[15]

Holding property leased to a professional corporation in a qualified retirement plan creates other problems and is a recommended solution only in an unusual situation, but professionals should be aware that it can be done.

[17.05] BUILDING CORPORATIONS

In the authors' experience, it has not been unusual to discover the situation where, not only is the professional practice incorporated, but the professional building and equipment are owned in a separate corporation (so-called "building corporations"). Normally, building corporations are begun with little thought as to the tax consequences of corporate ownership and, usually, not until some years have passed and substantial depreciation has been taken, are the tax ramifications examined.

In most small professional corporations, there is very little reason to own the professional building and equipment in corporate form. Of course, corporate form will limit the potential liabilities of the shareholders, but, where there are five or fewer shareholders, the professional corporation and the building corporation will be considered a controlled group of corporations under Section 1563 of the Code and, consequently, only one corporate surtax exemption will be permitted. Further, in the first five to six years of ownership, the "shelter" obtained through depreciation and other deductions will be trapped in the corporation and will not pass through to the shareholders. On the other hand, in large professional groups, corporate ownership of the professional building and equipment may be advantageous, if for no other reason than obtaining multiple surtax exemptions.

Building corporations should only be established where the professionals understand that, once the building and equipment are transferred to the corporation, it cannot be removed without substantial adverse tax consequences. Any liquidation of the building corporation will create depreciation recapture under Section 1250 and investment tax credit recapture under Section 47 of the Code. Further, if the corporation is liquidated under the normal liquidation rules, under Section 331, the shareholders will realize, in addition to the recapture, capital gain to the extent that the fair market value of the assets received in liquidation (less liabilities assumed) exceeds the adjusted basis of their stock.[16] Further, if the corporation is liquidated under Section 333 (a special one-month liquidation which permits liquidation of real estate corporations under more favorable terms than those provided under Section 331) the shareholders will recognize the following: (1) an amount of the gain equal to the earnings and profits of the corporation will be treated as a dividend; and (2) long-term capital gain to the extent of the cash, stock, or securities distributed in liquidation.

Because it is very difficult to "undo" a building corporation, the authors feel that professional buildings and equipment should only be placed in corporate form after a thorough determination of the short-term and long-term consequences. Further, unless definite tax advantages can be obtained through multiple surtax exemptions and unless it is intended that the building and equipment remain in corporate form indefinitely, the authors generally advise against the creation of a building corporation.

EXHIBIT 1

PARTNERSHIP AGREEMENT

THIS AGREEMENT, made and entered into the _____ day of _____, 19___, by and among _____, _____, and _____.

W I T N E S S E T H:

In consideration of the mutual covenants set forth herein, the parties hereto hereby agree as follows:

ARTICLE I

FORMATION OF PARTNERSHIP

Section 1.01. Formation of Partnership.

(a) The parties hereby enter into and form a partnership (the "Partnership") for the limited purposes and scope set forth herein. The parties hereto sometimes are referred to hereinafter collectively as the "Partners" and individually as "Partner".

(b) Except as expressly provided for herein to the contrary, the rights and obligations of the Partners and the administration and termination of the Partnership shall be governed by the partnership laws of the State of _____.

Section 1.02. Purposes and Scope of the Partnership.

(a) Prior to or contemporaneously with the execution of this Agreement and for the benefit of the Partnership, each of the Partners has agreed to acquire an undivided _____ (___) interest in the tract of land described on Exhibit "A" hereto, which tract of land is referred to hereinafter as the "Property".

(b) The Partnership shall be limited strictly to the acquisition and development of the Property, and the operation and management of improvements constructed thereon for the production of income and profit, and shall not be extended by implication or otherwise except by the written agreement of all of the Partners. The term "Development of the Property" shall mean and include acquisition of the Property; payment of all ad valorem taxes, assessments, and other impositions relating to the Property; construction of an office building and other improvements on the Property; preparation of detailed plans for the Development of the Property; leasing to third parties of space in the office building placed on the Property; and all other activities ordinarily included within the scope of the acquisition and development of land for the production of income and profit. The term "Improvements" shall mean the improvements that resulted from the Development of the Property.

(c) Nothing in this Agreement shall be deemed to restrict in any way the freedom of any party hereto to conduct any business or activity whatsoever (including the acquisition, development, and exploitation of real property) without any accountability to the Partnership or any party hereto, even if such business or activity competes with the business of the Partnership.

Section 1.03. Name of Partnership.

The business and affairs of the Partnership shall be conducted solely under the name of "_____, a general partnership," and such name shall be used at all times in connection with the Partnership business and affairs.

Section 1.04. Assumed Name Certificate.

The Partners shall execute all assumed or fictitious name certificate or certificates required by law to be filed in connection with the formation of the Partnership and shall cause such certificate or certificates to be filed in the applicable records of the County and State in which the Property is situated.

Section 1.05. Scope of Partner's Authority.

Except as otherwise expressly and specifically provided in this Agreement, none of the Partners shall have any authority to act for, or to assume any obligations or responsibility on behalf of, any other Partner or the Partnership.

Section 1.06. Principal Place of Business.

The principal place of business of the Partnership shall be _____.

ARTICLE II

MANAGEMENT

Section 2.01. Management of the Partnership.

(a) The overall management and control of the business and affairs of the Partnership shall be vested in the Partners, collectively. Except where herein expressly provided to the contrary, all decisions with respect to the management and control of the Partnership approved by the Partners shall be binding on the Partnership and all the Partners. When the phrase "Approved by the Partners" is used in this Agreement, such phrase shall mean approved in writing by a majority of the Partners. In addition, any agreement, note, deed, mortgage or other document executed by all of the Partners shall be deemed to have been Approved by the Partners without further evidence of such approval. The Partnership shall have a manager (hereafter called the "Manager") who shall be responsible for the implementation of the decisions of the Partners and for conducting the ordinary and usual business and affairs of the Partnership as more fully set forth in Section 2.03 hereof, and as limited by this Agreement.

(b) No action shall be taken, sum expended, decision made or obligation incurred by the Partnership, Manager, or any Partner with respect to a matter within the scope of any of the major decisions (hereinafter called "Major Decisions") as enumerated below, unless such of the Major Decisions has been Approved by the Partners. The Major Decisions shall include:

(1) Acquisition of any land or interest therein, other than the Property described in Exhibit "A" hereto;

(2) Financing of the Partnership, including but not limited to interim and permanent financing of the Improvements on the Property, financing operations of the Partnership, or borrowing money for any reason;

(3) Sale, or other transfer, or mortgaging or the placing or suffering of any other encumbrance on any of the Property or the Improvements thereon or any part or parts thereof;

(4) Lease or sale of space in any Improvements on the Property unless such sale or lease shall be in accordance with guidelines to be Approved by the Partners;

(5) Construction of major Improvements on the Property;

(6) Selecting or varying depreciation and accounting methods and making other decisions with respect to treatment of various transactions for federal income tax purposes, consistent with the other provisions of this Agreement;

(7) Approval of all construction and architectural contracts and all architectural plans, specifications and drawings prior to the construction of any improvements contemplated thereby;

(8) Varying or changing any portion of the insurance program required by Article III hereof;

(9) Determining whether or not distributions should be made to the Partners, except as set forth in Section 4.04 hereof;

(10) Approving each Budget pursuant to Section 2.04 hereof;

(11) Making any construction expenditure or incurring any construction obligation by or on behalf of the Partnership involving a sum in excess of $5,000.00 for any transaction or group of similar transactions except for expenditures made and obligations incurred pursuant to and specifically set forth in a Budget theretofore Approved by the Partners.

Section 2.02. Appointment and Replacement of Manager.

_____ shall serve as the Manager of the Partnership and shall discharge or cause the discharge of the duties thereof as set forth herein. The Manager may be replaced by a majority vote of the Partners.

Section 2.03. Duties of Manager.

(a) The Manager, at the expense of and on behalf of the Partnership, shall implement or cause to be implemented all Major Decisions Approved by the Partners and shall conduct or cause to be conducted the ordinary and usual business and affairs of the Partnership in accordance with and as limited by this Agreement, including the following:

(1) Protect and preserve the titles and interests of the Partnership with respect to the Property and Improvements and other assets owned by the Partnership;

(2) Pay all taxes, assessments, rents and other impositions applicable to the Property and improvements and other assets owned by the Partnership;

(3) Negotiate and enter into and supervise the performance of contracts covering the construction of any Improvements or any repairs or alterations;

(4) Lease or sell to third parties space in the Improvements in accordance with guidelines that have been Approved by the Partners;

(5) Keep all books of account and other records of the Partnership in accordance with the terms of this Agreement;

(6) Prepare and deliver to each of the Partners periodic reports not less than annually of the state of the business and affairs of the Partnership;

(7) Have an annual audit of the Partnership's books made by a certified public accountant Approved by the Partners and furnish each Partner with a copy of such annual audit including a balance sheet, a statement of the capital accounts of the Partners and a statement of income, together with the certificate of said accountant covering the results of such audit, as soon as reasonably practicable after the close of the Partnership's fiscal year, but in no event later than the date, if any, required by the Partnership's lenders or mortgagees. In addition, within seventy-five (75) days after the end of each fiscal year the Manager shall have such accountant prepare and deliver to each Partner a report setting forth in sufficient detail and such information and data with respect to business transactions affected by or involving the Partnership during such fiscal year as shall enable the Partnership and the Partners to prepare their state, federal and local income tax returns in accordance with the laws, rules and regulations then prevailing. The Manager shall have such accountant also prepare federal, state and local tax returns required of the Partnership and shall file the same after Approval by the Partners.

(8) To the extent that funds of the Partnership are available therefor, pay all debts and other obligations of the Partnership, including amounts due under interim and/or permanent financing of the Improvements and other loans to the Partnership previously Approved by the Partners and costs of construction, operation and maintenance of the Property and Improvements;

(9) Maintain all funds of the Partnership held by Manager in an account used exclusively for the Partnership in a federally insured bank or savings and loan association;

(10) Make distributions periodically to the Partners in accordance with the provisions of this Agreement;

(11) Operate, maintain, repair and otherwise manage the Property and Improvements, including the performance of such functions as the collection of rent, providing of utilities, cleaning, repair and maintenance or other services to be furnished to the Partnership or by the Partnership;

(12) Perform other normal business functions and otherwise operate and manage the business and affairs of the Partnership in accordance with this Agree-

ment) and

(13) Perform other obligations provided elsewhere in this Agreement to be performed by the Manager.

(b) The expenses of Manager that are incurred directly in connection with, and are directly related to, the business and operations of the Partnership, shall be deemed to be an expense of and shall be paid by the Partnership.

Section 2.04. Budgets.

No less often than one time each fiscal year, Manager shall prepare and submit to the Partners for their consideration a budget ("Budget") setting forth the estimated receipts and expenditures (capital, operating, and other) of the Partnership for the period covered by the Budget. When Approved by the Partners, the Manager shall implement the Budget and shall be authorized, without the need for further approval by the Partners, to make the expenditures and incur the obligations provided for in the Budget, anything to the contrary notwithstanding.

ARTICLE III

INSURANCE

Section 3.01. Minimum Insurance Requirements.

(a) The Partnership shall carry and maintain in force the following insurance, the premium for which shall be a cost and expense in connection with the operation of the Partnership:

(i) Comprehensive general liability insurance (including protective liability coverage on operations of independent contractors engaged in construction and also blanket contractual liability insurance) for the benefit of the Partners as named insureds against claims for "personal injury" liability, including without limitation, bodily injury, death or property damage liability.

(ii) Such insurance on the Property and Improvements against loss or damage and against such other hazards as any lender of funds to the Partnership shall from time to time require or, if there is no such lender or no such requirement, as may be approved by the Partners from time to time.

(b) All such aforesaid policies of insurance shall name all Partners as named insured, as their respective interests may appear. All such insurance shall be effected under policies issued by insurers and be in forms and for amounts approved by the Partners.

(c) The Partnership may carry and maintain in force certain insurance policies on the lives of the Partners in such form and in such amounts as shall be deemed necessary and as are approved by the Partners. The proceeds of such policies may be used for any purpose approved by the Partners, including the purchase of a Withdrawing Partner's interest as provided hereunder.

ARTICLE IV

CAPITAL CONTRIBUTIONS, ACCOUNTING AND DISTRIBUTION

Section 4.01. Capital Contributions.

(a) As an initial capital contribution, each of the Partners does hereby transfer to the Partnership his entire beneficial interest in the Property, free and clear of all liens and encumbrances. The Property shall be acquired and held in the names of _____, _____ and _____, as tenants in common, with each said Partner having an undivided _____ (_____) interest therein, solely for the benefit of the Partnership pursuant to the terms, conditions and provisions of this Partnership Agreement. Any other property of any kind to be owned, held, operated, or developed by the Partnership may be acquired and held in the names of _____, _____, and _____ as tenants in common, with each said Partner having an undivided _____ (_____) interest therein, and when so acquired and held, such property shall be deemed to be acquired and held solely for the benefit of the Partnership pursuant to the terms, conditions and provisions of this Partnership Agreement. Each Partner covenants and agrees with the other Partners that he shall not suffer or permit any lien or encumbrance to be placed upon the Property or any Improvements thereon with respect to such Partner's undivided _____ (_____) interest unless such lien or encumbrance is Approved by the Partners or arises from the business of the Partnership. It is the intent of the Partners that legal title to the Property and the Improvements thereon shall be vested in the Partners individually, but that beneficial title to the Property and the Improvements thereon shall be vested in the Partnership. The agreed value of each Partner's initial contribution of an undivided _____ (_____) interest in the Property to the capital of the Partnership is $_____.

(b) Upon the written request of either the Manager or a majority of the Partners at any time made, each Partner hereby agrees to contribute to the capital account of the Partnership, in accordance with that Partner's "Distribution Percentage Interest" as hereinafter defined as of the time of such request, an additional sum of money sufficient, in the aggregate for all Partners, to discharge the Partnership's obligations as they become due with respect only to the following, to-wit: (i) reductions of principal and interest on any Partnership indebtedness; (ii) real estate ad valorem taxes and assessments with respect to the Property and the Improvements thereon; (iii) insurance premiums; and (iv) any other expenses or indebtedness incurred by the Partnership which was approved by the Partners or provided for in the budget approved by the Partners pursuant to Section 2.04 of this Agreement.

(c) The Partnership shall establish for each Partner a capital account, which shall be credited with the amount of his contributions to capital, shall be credited or charged, as the case may be, with his distributive share of income, gain, loss, deduction or credit of the Partnership (as determined in accordance with Section 4.02 hereof) and shall be charged with the amounts of any distributions to him pursuant to Section 4.04 hereof.

Section 4.02. <u>Interest, Income, Profits and Distributions</u>

(a) The income, profits, and other distributions of the Partnership shall be received by the Partners in the percentages (hereinafter and hereinbefore referred to as the "Distribution Percentage Interest") set forth opposite each of their names below, to-wit:

_____	_____
_____	_____
_____	_____
_____	_____

(b) Net cash flow, as hereinafter defined, depreciation, and amortization, as such terms as used for the purposes of the Internal Revenue Code, shall be allocated to the Partners according to their respective Distribution Percentage Interests.

Section 4.03. Tax Status, Allocations and Reports.

(a) Manager shall prepare or cause to be prepared all tax returns and statements, if any, which must be filed on behalf of the Partnership, and shall submit such returns and statements to all the Partners for their approval prior to filing, and when Approved by the Partners, make timely filing thereof.

(b) Subject to the succeeding provisions of this Section for accounting and federal and state income tax purposes, except as herein otherwise specifically provided, all income, deductions, credits, gains and losses shall be allocated to the Partners in proportion to their respective Distribution Percentage Interests. Any item which is stipulated to be an expense of the Partnership under the terms of this Agreement or which would be so treated in accordance with generally accepted accounting principles shall be treated as an expense of the Partnership for all purposes hereunder, whether or not such item is deductible for purposes of computing net income for federal income tax purposes. The interest payable or distributable to any Partner shall be considered an expense when paid in determining allocable income or loss of the transaction and shall be income allocable to the Partner receiving it except when it is a return of capital.

Section 4.04. Distributions to Partners.

Within thirty (30) days after the close of each calendar quarter, the Manager shall distribute the ''Net Cash Flow'' of the Partnership for the preceding calendar quarter in accordance with the Distribution Percentage Interests of the Partners as set forth in Section 4.02 hereof. For the purposes of this Article, ''Net Cash Flow'' shall mean (1) plus (2) minus the aggregate of (3) and (4) as follows:

(1) The gross income from the Partnership assets, computed in accordance with sound cash receipts and disbursements accounting principles, including all income received from all sources whatsoever as a direct or indirect result of the ownership or operation of the Partnership assets such as, but without limitation, (i) the gross amount of all cash payments received whether as rent, additional rent, fees charged or otherwise; (ii) miscellaneous income; (iii) concession income; (iv) interest on deposits, (v) the net amount of any refund of impositions of taxes applicable to any period of this Agreement; (vi) the proceeds from the sale of any property including securities, notes or other obligations received in lieu of or in addition to such cash payments; (vii) the proceeds of any sale of personal property or fixtures now or hereafter located on the Property and Improvements, and (viii) the amount of any other consideration, tangible or intangible, received in relation to or in connection with the Property and Improvements or any appurtenance thereto (but not including (a) proceeds of insurance received and used, or to be used for the restoration of the Property and Improvements in the event of damage or destruction thereof or (b) proceeds of any sale, assignment, transfer, or mortgage as permitted herein, of the whole or any part of the interest of a party hereto) received by the Partnership, any of the Partners, the Manager or any other person on behalf of the Partnership.

(2) The amount of (i) any unused portion of any capital contributions of the Partners; (ii) any proceeds received from the mortgaging of the Property and Improvements, the refinancing (to the extent that the proceeds exceed the amount of the mortgage or deed of trust being refinanced) of any mortgage or deed of trust on the Property and Improvements or the sale of the Property and Improvements or any part thereof; and (iii) any payments received as a result of any other transactions involving the ownership, operation or maintenance of the Property and Improvements which do not come within (1) above.

(3) In accordance with sound cash basis accounting principles consistently applied, insurance charges, real estate taxes, assessments, reasonable legal expenses, water, fuel, electricity, repairs and maintenance, supplies, decorating, normal fees paid to certified public accountants, management fees and expenses, and any other items which are normally considered "operating expenses" (excluding, however, any income or franchise tax imposed by federal, state or local governments on any of the Partners in their individual capacity), plus the aggregate amount of principal and interest paid under mortgages or security deeds on the Property and Improvements and under loans incurred in connection with the Property and Improvements as well as the cost of capital acquisitions, alterations or improvements, to the extent of payments made or provided for during the fiscal year (except that in the event and to the extent that, capital acquisitions, alterations or improvements are paid for out of borrowed funds, the amount paid or provided during the fiscal year for interest and amortization on mortgages or deeds of trust or loans made for such purpose shall be deducted from Net Cash Flow in lieu of deducting the cost of such capital alterations and improvements).

(4) A reasonable reserve for budgeted tenants or purchasers' work and for interest and amortization on mortgages or security deeds and loans, real estate taxes, assessments, water charges, sewer rents, insurance, commissions and other expenses generally treated on an accrual basis, and a reasonable reserve for anticipated construction and operating expenses for future years.

In computing Net Cash Flow, no deduction shall be made for depreciation or amortization as such terms are used for the purposes of the Internal Revenue Code, it being agreed that depreciation and amortization shall be allocated to each Partner in proportion to his Distribution Percentage Interest.

Section 4.05. Accounting.

(a) The fiscal year of the Partnership shall be the calendar year.

(b) The books of account of the Partnership shall be kept and maintained at all times at the place or places approved by the Partners. The books of account shall be maintained on a cash receipts and expenditures basis in accordance with generally accepted accounting principles, consistently applied, and shall show all items of income and expense.

(c) The Manager shall prepare and furnish to each of the Partners promptly after the close of each calendar quarter an unaudited statement showing the receipts and disbursements for the Partnership for the preceding quarter, the balance in each Partner's capital account, the unpaid balance under all obligations of the Partnership, and all other information reasonably requested by any Partner. The Manager shall cause to be prepared and furnished to each of the Partners promptly after the close of each fiscal year a balance sheet of the Partnership date as of the end of the fiscal year, a related statement of income or loss for the Partnership for such fiscal year, and the same information for the fiscal year as is required to be included in the aforesaid quarterly reports, all of which shall be certified in the customary manner by an independent certified public accountant.

(d) Each Partner shall have the right at all reasonable times during usual business hours to audit, examine, and make copies of or extracts from the books of account of the Partnership. Such right may be exercised through any agent or employee of such Partner designated by him or by an independent certified public accountant designated by such Partner. Each Partner shall bear all expenses incurred in any examination made for such Partner's account.

Section 4.06. Bank Accounts.

Funds of the Partnership shall be deposited in an account or accounts used exclusively for the Partnership, in form and name approved by the Partners. Withdrawals from bank accounts shall be made by parties approved by the Partners.

Section 4.07. Failure of Partner to Contribute.

In the event a Partner fails to pay into the Partnership funds sufficient to cover his proportionate share of the indebtedness, expense or other expenditures provides for in Section 4.01(b) hereof, the remaining Partners may pay such amounts and their capital accounts and Distribution Percentage Interests shall be increased accordingly.

ARTICLE V

TERM AND TERMINATION

Section 5.01. Term.

The Partnership shall commence on the date hereof and shall continue until terminated and liquidated in accordance with the provisions hereof.

Section 5.02. Dissolution.

(a) The Partnership shall be dissolved and terminated on December 31, 2020, or prior thereto upon the happening of any of the following events:

(i) The death, bankruptcy or adjudication of insanity or incompetency of any Partner, unless the remaining Partners elect to continue the Partnership pursuant to Section 5.02(c) hereof;

(ii) The mutual consent of a majority of Partners; or

(iii) The sale of all or substantially all of the Partnership assets.

(b) In the event of the withdrawal of a Partner, for any reason, or upon the death, bankruptcy or adjudication of insanity or incompetency of any Partner (which retiring Partner, trustee of a bankrupt Partner, personal representative or executor of a deceased Partner, or committee or other representative of an insane or incompetent Partner is hereinafter referred to as the "Withdrawing Partner"), the surviving or remaining Partners shall have the right to elect to continue the business of the Partnership for the balance of the term specified in Section 5.02

hereof and any renewals hereof. Such election may be exercised by notice to the Withdrawing Partner in writing stating, in substance, that the remaining Partners have elected to continue the business of the Partnership.

(c) In the event the election to continue the business of the Partnership provided for in Section 5.02(b) is exercised, the remaining Partners shall have the option to purchase the entire interest of the Withdrawing Partner for the fair market value of his partnership interest increased by his share of Partnership profits or decreased by his share of Partnership losses for the period from the beginning of the fiscal year in which his withdrawal, death, adjudication of bankruptcy, insanity or incompetency occurred until the date of his withdrawal, death, adjudication of bankruptcy, insanity or incompetency, adjusted for contributions and distributions during such period. The establishment of the fair market value of the Partnership assets shall be approved by the Partners. The purchase price to be paid for such Withdrawing Partner's interest shall be paid in five (5) equal annual installments beginning one year after the date of the withdrawal, death, adjudication of bankruptcy, insanity or incompetency of the Withdrawing Partner. Any balance of the purchase price shall bear interest at the rate of nine per cent (9%) per annum from the date of the Withdrawing Partner's withdrawal, death, adjudication of bankruptcy, insanity or incompetency until final payment thereof is made and any part or all of the balance may be prepaid at any time. When the Withdrawing Partner shall have received the payments herein provided, he shall have no further claim upon or interest in the assets or the business of the Partnership.

(d) In the event of a termination and dissolution as hereinabove provided and if the Partnership is not continued, the Partnership shall forthwith be dissolved and terminated, and any certificates or notices thereof required by law shall be filed. The remaining Partners, the dissolving Partners or such other person(s) required or permitted by law to wind up the affairs of the Partnership, as the case may be, shall wind up and liquidate the Partnership by selling the Property and Improvements thereon, and, after paying the Partnership debts, by distributing the funds remaining in the manner provided in Section 4.04 hereof. If such remaining Partners, dissolving Partners or other person(s) decide in good faith that such sale of the Property and Improvements cannot be made on commercially reasonable terms, after the payment of or provision for the debts and obligations of the Partnership, all cash on hand and all remaining assets of the Partnership shall be distributed to the Partners in kind. A reasonable time shall be allowed for the orderly liquidation of the assets of the Partnership, the discharge of liabilities to creditors, and the distribution of any remaining funds to the Partners. Each of the Partners shall be furnished a statement prepared by the Partnership's accountants which shall set forth the assets and liabilities of the Partnership as of the date of complete liquidation.

(e) It is the intention of the Partners that all amounts payable by the Partnership under this Article V and the following Article VI to a Partner in exchange for his interest shall constitute payment for such Partner's interest in Partnership property. The payments shall be considered a distribution of Partnership property under 736(b) of the Internal Revenue Code and not a payment of income under Section 736(a) of the Internal Revenue Code.

ARTICLE VI

SALE, ASSIGNMENT, TRANSFER OR OTHER DISPOSITION

Section 6.01. Prohibited Transfer.

Except as provided in this Article VI, no Partner may sell, transfer, assign or otherwise dispose of or mortgage, hypothecate, or otherwise encumber or permit or suffer any encumbrance of all or any part of its or his interest in the Partnership unless approved by the Partners and any attempt to so transfer or encumber any such interest shall be void. Neither the Partnership nor the Partners shall be bound by any such assignment until a counterpart of the instrument of assignment, executed and acknowledged by the parties thereto, is delivered to the Partnership.

Section 6.02. Termination of Employment.

Should any Partner's employment with _____, be terminated, for any reason other than death, bankruptcy or adjudication of insanity or incompetency, such Partner's interest shall be purchased by the Partnership. The purchase price to be paid by the Partnership for such Partner's interest shall be the fair market value of his Partnership interest approved by the Partners, increased by his share of Partnership profits or decreased by his share of Partnership losses for the period from the beginning of the fiscal year in which such Partner terminates his employment with _____, until the date of such termination of employment, adjusted for contributions and distributions during such period. The establishment of the fair market value of the Partnership assets shall be Approved by the Partners. The purchase price to be paid for such Partner's interest shall be paid in five (5) equal annual installments beginning one year after the date such Partner terminates his employment with _____. Any balance of the purchase price shall bear interest at the rate of nine per cent (9%) per annum from the date of such Partner's termination of employment until final payment thereof is made, and any part or all of the balance may be prepaid at any time. When such Partner shall have received the payments herein provided, he shall have no further claim upon or interest in the assets or the business of the Partnership.

Section 6.03. Permitted Transfers.

(a) No Partner shall transfer, sell, assign, give or otherwise dispose of his Partnership interest or a part thereof, whether voluntarily or by operation of law, or at judicial sale or otherwise, to any person, unless such Partner first gives written notice to the other Partners of his intention to do so.

(b) Within sixty (60) days after the receipt of the written notice referred to in subsection (a), the Partnership may, at its option, exercisable in writing, purchase and retire the interest of the Partner desiring to sell his interest. The valuation of the interest and the terms of payment shall be the same as in Section 6.02 above except that the date of sale of the Partnership interest shall be substituted for the date of termination of employment as used in Section 6.02.

(c) If the Partnership does not exercise its option under subsection (b), the Partner giving the notice shall be free to sell, transfer, or otherwise dispose of his Partnership interest to the person or persons specified in the notice. The assignee of all or part of the Partner's interest shall not be entitled, during the continuance of the Partnership, to interfere in the management or administration of the Partnership business or affairs, require any information or account of Partnership transactions, or inspect the Partnership books. The assignee shall merely be entitled to receive, in accordance with the terms of the assignment, the profits to which the assignor otherwise would be entitled.

Section 6.04. Premature Disposition of Interest.

(a) In the event a Partner sells, assigns, or transfers his interest in the Partnership to the Partnership as provided in Section 6.02 and 6.03, above, and such Partnership interest is sold, assigned, or transferred to the Partnership before the end of three (3) years from the date on which he became Partner, the purchase price of such Partner's interest shall be deemed to equal zero (0).

(b) If such Partner sells, assigns, or transfers his interest in the Partnership as provided in Section 6.02 and 6.03 above, and such Partnership interest is sold, assigned, or transferred to the Partnership before the end of (10) years, but after the end of three (3) years, from the date on which he became a Partner, the purchase price of such Partner's interest shall be deemed to equal two-thirds (⅔) of the amount determined in Section 6.02 or 6.03 above.

(c) In the event that a Partner sells, assigns or transfers his interest in the Partnership to the Partnership as provided in Section 6.02, above, because his employment with _____, has terminated because he is physically unable to continue the practice of medicine, the purchase price of, and the payment for, his Partnership interest shall be the fair market value thereof as described in Section 6.02, above, notwithstanding the provisions of subsections (a) and (b) of this Section 6.04.

ARTICLE VII

GENERAL

Section 7.01. Notices.

(a) All notices, demands or requests provided for or permitted to be given pursuant to this agreement must be in writing. All notices, demands and requests to be sent to _____, or any assignee of the interest of said Partner hereunder pursuant hereto, shall be deemed to have been properly given or served by depositing the same in the United States mail, addressed to said Partner, postpaid and registered or certified with return receipt requested at the following address: _____.

(b) All notices, demands or requests to be sent to _____, or any assignee of the interest of said Partner hereunder pursuant hereto, shall be deemed to have been properly given or served by depositing the same in the United States mail, addressed to said Partner, postpaid and registered or certified with receipt requested at the following address: _____.

(c) All notices, demands or requests to be sent to _____, or any assignee of the interest of said Partner hereunder pursuant hereto shall be deemed to have been properly given or served by depositing the same in the United States mail, addressed to said Partner, postpaid and registered or certified with receipt requested at the following address: _____.

(d) All notices, demands and requests shall be effective upon being deposited in the United States mail. However, the time period in which a response to any such notice, demand or request must be given shall commence to run from the date of receipt on the return receipt of the notice, demand or request by the addressee thereof. Rejection or other refusal to accept or the inability to deliver because of changed address shall be deemed to be receipt of the notice, demand or request sent.

(e) By giving to the other parties at least thirty (30) days' written notice thereof, the parties hereto and their respective successors and assigns shall have the right from time to time and at any time during the term of this Agreement to change their respective addresses and each shall have the right to specify as its address any other address within the United States of America.

(f) No transferee of any interest by a Partner shall be entitled to receive a notice independent of the notice sent to the Partner making such transfer. A notice sent or made to a Partner shall be deemed to have been sent and made to all transferees, if any, of such Partner.

Section 7.02. Governing Laws.

This Agreement and the obligations of the Partners hereunder shall be interpreted, construed and enforced in accordance with the laws of the State of

_____.

Section 7.03. Entire Agreement.

This Agreement contains the entire agreement between the parties hereto relative to the formation of the Partnership to develop the Property and Improvements. No variations, modifications, or changes herein or hereof shall be binding upon any party hereto unless set forth in a document duly executed by or on behalf of such party.

Section 7.04. Waiver.

No consent or waiver, express or implied, by any Partner to or of any breach or default by the other in the performance by the other of its obligations hereunder shall be deemed or construed to be a consent or waiver to or of any other breach or default in the performance by such other party of the same or any other obligations of such Partner hereunder. Failure on the part of any Partner to complain of any act or failure to act of any of the other Partners or to declare any of the other Partners in default, irrespective of how long such failure continues, shall not constitute a waiver of such Partner of his right hereunder.

Section 7.05. Severability.

In the event any provision of this Agreement or the application thereof to any person or circumstance shall be invalid or unenforceable to any extent, the remainder of this Agreement and the application of such provisions to other persons or circumstances shall not be affected thereby and shall be enforced to the greatest extent permitted by law.

Section 7.06. Binding Agreement.

Subject to the restrictions on transfers and encumbrances set forth herein, this Agreement shall inure to the benefit of and be binding upon the undersigned

Partners and their respective legal representatives, successors and assigns. Whenever, in this Agreement, a reference to any party or Partner is made, such reference shall be deemed to include a reference of the legal representatives, successors and assigns of such party or Partner.

Section 7.07. <u>Equitable Remedies</u>.

The rights and remedies of any of the Partners hereunder shall not be mutually exclusive, i.e., the exercise of one or more of the provisions hereof shall not preclude the exercise of any other provisions hereof. Each of the Partners confirms that damages at law may be an inadequate remedy for a breach or threatened breach of this Agreement and agrees that, in the event of a breach or threatened breach of any provision hereof, the respective rights and obligations hereunder shall be enforceable by specific performance, injunction or other equitable remedy, but nothing herein contained is intended to, nor shall it, limit or affect any right or rights at law or by statute or otherwise of any party aggrieved as against the other for a breach or threatened breach of any provision hereof, it being the intention by this paragraph to make clear the agreement of the Partners that the respective rights and obligations of the Partners hereunder shall be enforceable in equity as well as at law or otherwise.

IN WITNESS WHEREOF, this Agreement is executed effective as of the date first set forth above.

_____ (SEAL)

Signed, sealed and
delivered in the presence of:

_____
Unofficial Witness

_____
Notary Public

_____ (SEAL)

Signed, sealed and
delivered in the presence of:

_____
Unofficial Witness

_____
Notary Public

_____ (SEAL)

681

Signed, sealed and
delivered in the presence of:

_____

Unofficial Witness

_____

Notary Public

VALUATION

The undersigned hereby agree that as of this _____ day of _____, 19___, the value of a _____ interest in _____, a general partnership, is $_____.

_____
_____
_____

NOTES TO CHAPTER 17

1. See *Philips Co., Inc.*, 1977-150 T.C. Memo.
2. *Bloomberg v. Commissioner*, 74 T.C. No. 102 (9/23/80). The taxpayer purchased medical equipment and furnishings in 1974 which he immediately leased to a corporation of which he was an employee under a written lease dated August 1, 1974, with a term of five years. The property had estimated useful lives of five to seven years. The lease was purportedly canceled on June 10, 1977, prior to the expiration of 50% of the useful lives of the property. *Held*: The cancellation of the lease does not permit the taxpayer to meet the conditions of Section 46(e)(3) that the lease term be less than 50% of the useful lives of the property in order for a lessor to take an investment credit on the property.
3. See Letter Ruling 8002126.
4. 61 T.C. 12 (1973), *rev'd*, 520 F.2d 323 (5th Cir. 1975), *cert. denied*, 424 U.S. 967 (1976).
5. Also see *Perry v. U.S.*, 520 F.2d 232 (4th Cir. 1974), *cert. denied*, 423 U.S. 1052 (1974) (rental payments not deductible between two physicians and a clifford trust established for their children); *Frank L. Butler*, 65 T.C. 327 (1975) (rental deductions not permitted for local office building leased from trust for minor children).
6. See generally:

   Aitken, ''Coping with the Tough New Court Tests for Deductions in Lease-Back Situations,'' 44 *J. Taxation* 47 (1976).

Patterson, "Federal Income Taxation—Transfer to and Leasebacks from a Short-Term Trust," 54 *N. Car. L. Rev.* 237 (1976).

Willis and Panzur, "Shaping the Successful Trust Lease-Back Arrangement in View of Recent Decisions," *J. Taxation* 228 (1977).

7. 37 T.C.M. 346, ¶78,070 P-H Memo T.C. (1978), *aff'd*, 595 F.2d 269 (8th Cir. 1979), *cert. denied,* 444 U.S. 996.

8. 64 T.C. 1034 (1975).

9. 36 T.C.M. 1122, ¶77,281 P-H Memo T.C. (1977).

10. 36 T.C.M. 479, ¶77,105 P-H Memo T.C. (1977).

11. 77-1 U.S.T.C. ¶9323, 37 AFTR 2d 76-751 (W.D. Pa. 1977).

12. 71 T.C. 290 (1978).

13. Prohibited Transaction Exemption 78-2, 43 Fed. Reg. 7746.

14. Prentice-Hall *Handbook on Pension Reform Law* at ¶858.

15. See Prohibited Transaction Exemptions Nos. 80-69, 80-78, 80-86, and 80-97 issued by the Department of Labor. But see a denial of such an exemption in Department of Labor Advisory Opinion No. 77-16.

16. Treas. Regs. §1.331-1(b).

CHAPTER **18**

Solving Divergent Shareholder Needs—Division of a Professional Corporation

[18.01] REASONS PROFESSIONAL CORPORATIONS DIVIDE

All too often, professionals find that, although a professional corporation does provide many tax benefits and a form that offers corporate stability, operating a professional corporation creates problems, especially when professionals have different financial planning needs and desires. For instance, some professionals prefer to contribute less, while some professionals prefer to contribute more, to qualified retirement plans, some professionals would prefer to have more conservative investments in retirement plans, some professionals would prefer that the corporation assume a greater portion of their personal business expenses, such as providing for the use of automobiles, and some professionals would prefer to provide more, while some would prefer to provide less, fringe benefits. Problems will also occur where, as in many professional corporations, shareholders receive equal salaries, irrespective of individual billings and collections. Further, in any professional setting, there is always the problem of conflicting egos.

When problems do occur, there are several courses of action that may be taken:

(1) Professionals can forget the differences (which is often easier said than done) or a compromise may be reached,

(2) Where salary disputes are encountered, it may be possible to resolve the problem by compensating professionals based on a production formula, and

(3) If the disputes are too great, the professional corporation may eventually be split into multiple corporations.

When the problems become go great that a split-up is imminent, the first question to be decided is "who leaves and who stays?" In many professional corporations (particularly those which are created from existing partnerships), it is difficult to tell who "started" the corporation and who should be permitted to maintain the existing corporate structure. Also, notwithstanding the existing corporate structure, most professionals think that they own their pro rata percentage of all assets of the corporation. In dealing with professional corporation split-ups, specific attention should be given to the following assets:

(1) Retirement Plans

The qualified retirement plans of the professional corporation are one of the most important benefits provided, and care should be taken to assure that the qualified status of the plans is not lost. Further, most professionals see qualified retirement plans as simply a mechanism for deferring what would otherwise be current income. Consequently, the professionals feel that the amounts standing to their credit in the qualified retirement plans of the professional corporation "belong" to them, irrespective of the extent to which they are vested under the plans.

(2) Accounts Receivable

Accounts receivable normally constitute the largest asset of a professional corporation and are, consequently, a major point of concern. Accounts receivable also represent the yet untaxed right of the professional corporation to receive income and any distribution of the accounts receivable to the shareholders may accelerate the corporation's recognition of income.

(3) Furniture and Equipment

Depending upon the type of professional practice, furniture and equipment may represent a substantial asset (such as X-ray equipment). Notwithstanding the amount of furniture and equipment maintained by the professional corporation, most furniture and equipment will be depreciated to a very low basis, which will produce the possibility of depreciation recapture if it is distributed to the shareholders. Further, the replacement value of the equipment will probably be in excess of the original purchase price.

(4) Client/Patient Records

In dividing a professional practice, it is important to assure that the existing clients/patients of the professional corporation continue to receive proper professional care. Although the client/patient files may be divided among the professionals based on the determination of the professionals, the files actually belong to the clients/patients and should be distributed to the professionals in accordance with the wishes of the clients/patients. Further, all clients/patients should be notified of the corporate split-up, of the location in which their records will be maintained, and of their right of access to the records. In some particularly difficult cases, the authors have found that the local professional society is often willing to assist in the resolution of ethical questions regarding client/patient records.

In effecting any professional corporation split-up, the details of the split-up and the rights and privileges of the parties should be set forth in a written separation agreement. The separation agreement should, among other things, cover at least the following:

(1) Reasons for the separation;

(2) The manner in which the separation will be effected, including the organization of new corporations and the transfer of assets to the various new corporations;

(3) The anticipated tax effect of the separation (so that there will be no misunderstanding by the parties);

(4) A list of the assets which will be transferred to each of the professionals or the successor professional entities, and the value attributable to those assets;

(5) The manner in which the corporate retirement plans will be handled;

(6) An indemnification agreement whereby the parties indemnify each other against attempts to restructure the transaction after it has been completed and under which the parties divide the various liabilities among themselves and agree to be liable for possible contingent liabilities which may arise in the future (such as liabilities due to federal income tax audits);

(7) Who will be entitled to the corporation's offices, name, telephone number, and any other licenses or intangible assets of the professional corporation. The agreement should also contain a listing of the new professional names of all successor organizations;

(8) A division of the client/patient records, with a listing of all records by name and the manner in which clients/patients will be notified;

(9) The effective date of the split-up and the date, time, and place of the closing;

(10) In the event that the professional corporation will remain in existence, those professionals who will be leaving the professional corporation

should resign as officers and employees, transfer to the professional corporation their stock certificates, duly endorsed, and sign a release for all claims against the professional corporation, including claims for additional income and claims for the accounts receivable of the corporation;

(11) Any agreement for additional compensation to be paid due to accrued but unused vacation pay. Is compensation due for unreimbursed professional expenses incurred before termination? Are professional dues and other payments, such as malpractice insurance, to be distributed pro rata through the date of termination, even if they are prepaid?

(12) The existing professional corporation must obtain a warranty from the departing professionals that they will continue to maintain malpractice insurance; and

(13) The agreement should deal with the existing personal liabilities of the departing professional, such as any personal guaranty of leases and loans.

The agreement should, obviously, be signed by all of the professionals and an executed copy of the agreement, with a complete list of exhibits, should be given to each professional. Professional corporation split-ups are, as a practical matter, one of the most difficult problems faced by professional corporation advisors, primarily due to the potential tax problems, the need to provide continued professional services, and the conflicting desires of the various professionals.

There are basically three possible approaches to dividing (on an amicable basis) a professional corporation among its shareholders:

(1) The redemption of one or more shareholder's stock coupled with a salary continuation;

(2) A tax-free restructuring under Sections 368(a)(1)(D) and 355; and

(3) A complete liquidation of the professional corporation.

Since many professionals feel that, notwithstanding the corporate structure, they are simply practicing together, they often feel that they should be allowed to remove their pro rata shares of the assets of the corporation without incurring any tax burden. Consequently, one of the main objectives of any professional corporation split-up is to defer (or at least not accelerate) income taxation to the existing professional corporation and the professionals. On the other hand, in creating such a deferral, it is important that the existing employee benefits of the professional corporation not be so changed that they are unsuitable following the split-up.[1]

It should be realized that, if the professionals are not able to reach an amicable agreement regarding the split-up of the corporation, those shareholders owning a majority of the voting stock of the corporation will generally control what occurs. Consequently, the professionals should remember that, absent a shareholders' agreement of the type discussed in section [6.05], *supra*, majority voting control is very important in an unstable professional corporation.

[18.02] REDEMPTION AND CONTRACTUAL SALARY CONTINUATION

In most professional corporation split-ups, the professional corporation will stay in existence and one or more of the professionals will leave the corporation. When this occurs, the employment of the departing professional will be terminated and he will be entitled to receive all benefits granted to him under his employment agreement and other deferred and current compensation agreements of the professional corporation. He will also, generally, be entitled to receive the value of his stock under the stock retirement agreement of the professional corporation. Under most stock retirement agreements, the departing professional will be entitled to receive only a dollar value payment and will not be entitled to any of the specific assets of the corporation, such as office equipment or accounts receivable. Generally, the value established under the stock retirement agreement will compensate the departing professional for the ''net book'' value of the stock in the professional corporation, which will exclude accounts receivable. The departing professional will, on the other hand, be compensated for his ''share'' of the accounts receivable on the books of the professional corporation by the continuation of three to five months' salary payments. See generally, section [11.02], *supra.*

In general, the departing shareholder should be entitled to capital gain and installment sales treatment with regard to the redemption proceeds paid to him under the stock retirement agreement.[2] Further, the salary continuation granted to the departing professional should be considered personal service income under Section 1348 of the Code (as either deferred or current compensation) and should be subject to the 50% maximum tax for years prior to 1982. The professional corporation will receive a deduction for the salary continuation, which will at least partially offset the income resulting from the latest collection of the accounts receivable, which were generated through the efforts of the departing professional. The professional corporation will not be entitled to a deduction for the payments made to the departing shareholder on the redemption of his stock (other than interest payments made on installment sales) and no recognition of gain (except for depreciation recapture) will occur upon the distribution by the professional corporation of appreciated property in redemption of the stock of the departing professional (but there is no comparable nonrecognition provision for appreciated property distributed in satisfaction of the professional corporation's salary continuation obligation).[3]

The Service could take the position that the entire amount paid to the departing professional (including salary continuation) is paid for the redemption of his stock, in which case the professional corporation would not be entitled to a deduction for any of the payments. This question is really one of intent: whether the professional corporation intended that the salary continuation payments to the departing professional be compensation.[4] The Service could also take the position that the entire transaction constitutes a "D" reorganization, irrespective of the labels placed on the transaction by the parties. The Service could also take the position that the collapsible corporation provisions of Section 341 of the Code apply. However, the chances of the Service prevailing on either such argument are minimal and would only be enhanced if the departing professional receives substantial in kind distributions and subsequently reincorporates.

The redemption and salary continuation method of dividing a professional corporation minimizes the disruption of the professional practice, although client/patient files must still be divided. The fact that pre-existing agreements (such as the stock retirement agreement and the employment agreement) govern the rights of the parties, should reduce friction if the terms of those agreements are reasonable (although some professionals will always feel that they are receiving less than their "fair" share of the assets of the professional practice). The redemption and salary continuation technique is generally preferable where only a few of the professionals desire to depart and it may have definite disadvantages where, for example, the accounts receivable retained by the professional corporation are insufficient to satisfy the contractual salary continuation obligation.

[18.03] LIQUIDATION

In order to treat all shareholders equally, the professionals may consider a possible complete liquidation of the professional corporation under Section 331 and a pro rata distribution of assets to the shareholders. Such a liquidation will, however, generate a substantial amount of additional income tax.

(1) Treatment of Corporation

Section 336 provides, in general, that no gain or loss will be recognized by a corporation on the distribution of property in a complete liquidation. However, there will be recapture of depreciation under Section 1245(a) (for personal property) and under Section 1250(a) (for real property) and recapture of investment tax credit under Section 47(a). Further, if property is distributed which has previously been expensed or charged off (such as supplies) the corporation will realize ordinary income to the extent of the lower of the value of such property or its unconsumed cost.[5] Further, if the professional corporation has used a bad debt reserve (most professional corporations use a specific charge-off method for bad debts), the corporation must recognize income to the extent of the tax benefit attributable to the reserve, which is found by experience to be unneeded or recoverable. Further, all of the accounts receivable must be taken into income by the professional corporation, either on the grounds that the liquidating distribution constitutes an assignment of income or on the grounds that such realization is necessary to reflect income clearly.[6] Therefore, the corporate nonrecognition provisions under Section 336 offer little assistance, as a general rule, in the context of the liquidating professional corporation, with the probable outcome of such a liquidation being the bunching of income without corresponding deductions.

It has been suggested by some commentators[7] that the one-month liquidation available under Section 333 may avoid the problem generated by accounts receivable (i.e., that they must be taken into income at the corporate level). Although Section 333 requires careful planning and has several drawbacks, the Regulations under Section 333 require that the corporation's earnings and profits must be computed on the accrual basis up to the date of liquidation.[8] Consequently, it is likely that the accounts receivable must be treated as income at least for purposes of computing the earnings and profits which will be taxed to the shareholders as an ordinary dividend upon the Section 333 liquidation. Therefore, a liquidation under Section 333 appears to provide no solution to the accounts receivable problem.[9]

(2) Shareholders

Under Section 331, each shareholder will also realize capital gain equal to the difference between the fair market value of the property which he receives in the liquidation and the adjusted basis of his stock in the professional corporation. The shareholders will, however, receive an increase (to fair market value) in the adjusted basis of the property received in the liquidation under Section 334.

If the accounts receivable of the professional corporation are distributed to the shareholders, it is possible that they will not only be taxed at the corporate level but taxed again when the shareholders recognize gain on the distribution (and the shareholders will receive no cash with which to pay the taxes due). Consequently, it is probably best to distribute assets in the plan of liquidation but to retain in the corporation the accounts receivable and to distribute the cash generated from the collection of those receivables.

Upon the liquidation of a professional corporation, it may be possible that the professionals receive the goodwill of the professional corporation, upon which tax must be paid under Section 331 of the Code. If a substantial amount of goodwill does exist and can be shown, a liquidation under Section 333, although it will not avoid the accounts receivable problem, may avoid immediate gain on the goodwill. Gain will be, however, only deferred because a portion of the basis of the shareholders' stock must be allocated to the goodwill, and this will, naturally, decrease the adjusted basis of the other assets, including those on which depreciation may eventually be claimed.[10]

(3) Liquidation and Reincorporation

If all of the physicians reincorporate immediately following the liquidation, the Service may persuasively argue that there has been no real liquidation. Instead, the Service will argue that the transaction is tantamount to a "D" or "F" reorganization under Section 368. As a result, all property not contributed to the new corporations will be considered to constitute "boot" and will be taxable to the professionals as a dividend to the extent of the professional corporation's earnings and profits.[11] Because of the potential problems involved, a professional corporation generally should not be liquidated unless all of the professionals desire to discontinue practice and a number of the professionals will practice in unincorporated form. If a number of the professionals intend to remain with the corporation, a contractual salary continuation and redemption plan should be adopted. On the other hand, if all professionals intend to practice through professional corporations, consideration should be given to a tax-free split-up of the professional corporation under Sections 368(a)(1)(D) and 355 of the Code.

[18.04] TAX-FREE REORGANIZATION UNDER SECTIONS 368(a)(1)(D) AND 355

The Internal Revenue Code contains provisions which permit the division of one corporation into multiple corporations if certain specified requirements are satisfied. In most professional corporation settings, a reorganization known as a "split-up" will probably be selected. Under a split-up, the professional corporation will create as many wholly owned subsidiaries as there are shareholders. Then, each shareholder's employment agreement and a proportionate percentage of the assets will be distributed to each subsidiary corporation. The professional corporation will then be dissolved in accordance with state law, and the stock of the various subsidiary corporations will be distributed to the respective professionals so that each professional will receive only the stock of the corporation which holds his employment agreement and his share of the corporate assets.

In many jurisdictions, the stock of professional corporations may only be held by professionals. Thus, in those jurisdictions, it is impossible for professional corporation to create a subsidiary which is also a professional corporation. Therefore, in order to consummate a split-up, the subsidiaries which are initially created by the professional corporation will be business corporations and after the split-up these corporations will either be merged into newly created professional corporations which will be formed by the various professionals or the various professionals will amend the articles of incorporation of these corporations in order to convert them into professional corporations.[12]

Under a split-up, none of the professionals will remain with the existing professional corporation, which will pass out of existence. On the other hand, if certain of the professionals desire to remain with the existing professional corporation a "split-off" can be created with exactly the same tax consequences as a split-up.[13] A split-up (or split-off) imposes potential income tax liabilities on both the professional corporation, through the creation of subsidiaries and its eventual liquidation, and the shareholders of the professional corporation, through the receipt of the stock of the subsidiary corporations. Consequently, extreme care should be taken in executing a split-off or split-up and, where possible, an advance ruling from the Service should be obtained.[14]

(1) Tax Impact on Professional Corporation

In general, Section 351 of the Code, which provides for nonrecognition of gain on the transfer of assets to corporations controlled by the transferor, will permit the creation of subsidiary corporations by the professional corporation without adverse tax consequences. It is also generally accepted that even the transfer of accounts receivable by a cash method taxpayer (i.e., from the professional corporation to the subsidiaries) will qualify for nonrecognition under Section 351. See the discussion at section [5.01](3), *supra*. However, an exception to the nonrecognition rules of Section 351 will apply where the aggregate liabilities transferred exceed the aggregate adjusted basis of the property transferred. Section 357(c) provides for the recognition of gain in the event that the subsidiaries created by the professional corporation assume liabilities or take assets subject to liabilities and the sum of such liabilities exceeds the adjusted basis of the assets transferred. Accounts payable and other expenses which would be deductible when paid by the subsidiary corporations are not considered liabilities for purposes of this rule. See the discussion at section [5.01](1), *supra*.

(2) Tax Impact on Shareholders

In general, a shareholder receiving stock in the split-up of a professional corporation will not recognize gain if the following statutory conditions under Section 355 are satisfied:

(1) The distribution to the shareholder consists solely of stock or securities in the wholly owned subsidiary of the professional corporation. Section 355(a)(1)(A). Section 355(a)(3) treats as "boot" (i.e., distributed property other than stock or securities of the subsidiaries) any stock of the controlled corporation if acquired by the professional corporation in a transaction which occurs within five years of the distribution and in which gain or losses are recognized in whole or in part. Thus, recognition of gain by the professional corporation under Section 357(c) at the time of the transfer of the assets to the subsidiary corporations could result in the full recognition of gain to the professional receiving the stock of such subsidiary.

(2) The reorganization must not be principally a device for distributing the earnings and profits of a professional corporation or the subsidiaries. Section 355(a)(1)(B). In a typical split-up of a professional corporation, the reorganization should not be considered a device for distributing earnings and profits because the

transaction would produce capital gain or loss in the absence of Section 355.[15] Although a prearranged sale of the distributed stock often requires the recognition of gain, simultaneous or subsequent nontaxable exchanges (such as the merger of the newly created subsidiaries into newly formed professional corporations as may be required under state law) are permissible.[16]

(3) Immediately prior to the distribution, the professional corporation had no assets other than the stock of the controlled subsidiaries and each of the controlled subsidiaries is engaged immediately after the distribution in the active conduct of a trade or business. Section 355(b)(1)(B). The trade or business must have been actively conducted during the five-year period ending on the date of the distribution. Section 355(b)(2). A potential problem may arise where one of the professionals has practiced for less than five years. Unless the five-year rule applies to the ''practice'' as a whole (which the author's feel is preferable) or unless professionals are able to ''tack'' the professional corporation's period of practice to their period of practice, there will be a violation of the five-year rule and the potential for recognition of gain by the shareholders of the professional corporation on the distribution of the stock in the subsidiary corporations. That is, if the requirements of Section 355 are not met, the transaction will be treated as a complete liquidation of the professional corporation, subject to Section 331, so that the shareholders of the professional corporation will recognize capital gain or loss, depending upon whether the value of the liquidating distribution (i.e., the stock of the newly created subsidiary corporations) exceeds or is less than the adjusted basis of their stock in the professional corporation. The Service has conceded that the division of a single business is permissible.[17] Consequently, the professional corporation should be considered a single business, notwithstanding the fact that some of the professionals may not have a five year trade or business (have been in practice for five years) and the active business requirement of Section 355 should be met. There are, however, no cases or published revenue rulings directly on this point, and the authors feel that, for this reason, a private letter ruling is warranted, if time permits.

(4) The transaction must serve a valid corporate business purpose.[18] In general, the authors feel that there are usually ample facts to support a valid corporate business purpose in the division of most professional corporations; however, the Service may take the position that there exist simply the irreconcilable personal (and not management) differences among the shareholders, which amount only to a personal business purpose and not a corporate business purpose.[19]

[18.05] TREATMENT OF QUALIFIED RETIREMENT PLAN BENEFITS

Upon the division of a professional corporation, two major problems arise with regard to qualified retirement plan benefits. The first problem arises with regard to the portion of such benefits to which the terminating professionals are entitled and the second problem relates to how (and when) the terminating professionals will be taxed on these benefits.

(1) Vesting of Forfeitable Interests

Most professionals see qualified retirement plans simply as a mechanism to defer current income until a future date. Consequently, they view themselves as fully vested in all amounts contributed on their behalf to qualified retirement plans, and they feel that, upon termination of employment, they should be entitled to all amounts contributed for them, notwithstanding the vesting schedule adopted under the plans. In order to create full vesting for the departing professionals, the following alternatives are available:

(a) *Amendment of Vesting Schedule*

The vesting schedule for the professional corporation's qualified retirement plans could be amended to provide a vesting schedule short enough to permit full vesting for those professionals who are terminating employment. Such a shortened vesting schedule will, however, be applicable to all common-law employees of the professional corporation and must, generally, be applied in the future on a continuing basis by the professional corporation.

(b) *Termination of the Plan*

Since, under Section 411(d)(3) of the Code, the termination of a qualified retirement plan requires full vesting of all participants, it would be possible for the professional corporation to terminate its plans and provide full vesting.

(c) *Partial Termination*

Under Section 411(d)(3), partial terminations of qualified retirement plans also require full vesting of the account balances of affected participants. Partial terminations generally occur where a substantial number of participants leave the plan due to business curtailment or otherwise. It is generally thought that a 20% reduction in participation during one year or a 25% reduction in participation over two years will be considered a partial termination.[20] Where a partial termination occurs, the board of directors of the professional corporation should adopt a resolution confirming that a partial termination has occurred.

(d) *Additional Payments*

The plan administrator of the professional corporation's qualified retirement plans may treat the separation from service of the professional as a simple termination of employment not requiring full vesting. In such situations, many professional corporations give ''bonuses'' to the departing professionals (but not the common-law employees who accompany them) which approximate their forfeitable plan interests. The authors feel that such payments are unwise because they create the distinct possibility of discrimination in operation in favor of the prohibited group under Section 401(a)(4) of the Code and may lead to the disqualification of the plans.

(e) *Split-Off Plans*

In the event that a split-off or split-up of a professional corporation occurs, the various new professional corporations may adopt plans comparable to the existing plan and full vesting will not be required. The new plans will simply continue the existing terms and assets, giving past service credit for the term of employment with the initial professional corporation.[21]

(2) Portability Options

With the enactment of ERISA in 1974, numerous portability options were created. The effect of these options, which is important in the split-up of professional corporations, is to permit a participant in a qualified retirement plan to maintain the status of his plan account, by moving that account into a new qualified retirement plan, without creating a current tax liability. There are numerous portability options available to professionals in a split-up, not the least of which are the following:

(a) *Direct Transfers to Qualified Trusts*

In the event that a professional corporation is dissolved or liquidated (or following a split-off or split-up), account balances in the existing qualified retirement plans may be transferred, from trustee to trustee, to new qualified retirement plans maintained by the new professional corporations. Such transfers do not create constructive receipt on the part of participants if participants are not given the election to receive distributions in lieu of transfers.[22]

(b) *Spin-Off Plans*

Under Proposed Regulations §1.414(1)-1(b)(4), a spin-off plan amounts to a plan division and is accomplished by having one or more of the split-off or split-up professional corporations adopt the existing plan (making name changes and minor amendments, as appropriate) and by transferring assets representing the account balances of the employees of the adopting professional corporation to the trust maintained by such professional corporation. Participants are not considered to have constructively received their benefits and full vesting is not required; the split-off plans may maintain the vesting schedule of the predecessor plan.

(3) Rollovers

Sections 402(a)(5) and (6) of the Code permit the "rollover" (transfer) of lump-sum distributions and distributions made upon the termination of qualified retirement plans to new qualified retirement plans and individual retirement accounts without the recognition of current income. The requirements for lump-sum distributions are generally discussed in section [15.04], *supra*. The statutory requirements relating to tax-free rollovers are very technical and should be reviewed each time a rollover is anticipated.

NOTES TO CHAPTER 18

1. For a general discussion of the topic of dividing professional corporations, see:

   Lee, "Termination or Division of Professional Service Organizations," 1977 Southern Federal Tax Institute.

   Lee, "Termination of Interest in the Professional Corporation," 36 *NYU Institute on Fed. Tax* 123.

   Gorlick, "Who Gets the Office? . . . And Other Problems of Corporate Divorce," November 15, 1976, *Medical Economics*, page 213.

   Lee, "How to Salvage Tax Benefits When a Professional Corporation Disbands," 45 *J. Taxation* 14 (1976).

   Eaton, note 1, Chapter 7, *supra*, Section 6.10 and Section 9.05.

   Dykes, "Two Recent Letter Rulings Define IRS' Position on Tax-Free Break Up of P.C.'s: What Can Be Done," February, 1979, *J. Taxation* 92.

   Strobel, "Reorganizations of Professional Corporations: An Analysis of Some Recent Private Letter Rulings," May, 1980, *Taxes* 347.

2. Sections 302(a) and (b) and Section 453 of the Code.
3. Section 311(d) of the Code.
4. *Ted N. Steffen*, note 2, Chapter 11, *supra*.
5. Rev. Rul. 77-67, 1977-1 C.B. 33, and Rev. Rul. 74-396, 1974-2 C.B. 106.
6. Bitker and Eustice, note 2, Chapter 5, *supra*, ¶11.62, *Jud Plumbing and Heating*, 153 F.2d 681 (1976).
7. Eaton, note 1, Chapter 7, *supra,* Section 13.03.
8. Treas. Regs. §1.333-4.
9. Lee, *supra*, note 1, *supra*, 36 *NYU Inst. on Fed. Tax,* at 130.
10. Rev. Rul. 66-81, 66-1 C.B. 64.
11. *Jack D. Ringwalt v. U.S.,* 549 F.2d 89 (8th Cir. 1977), *cert. denied,* 97 S.Ct. 2950 (1977). Bitker and Eustice, note 2, Chapter 5, *supra*, ¶11.54.
12. See Letter Ruling 7743001 and 7810013.
13. In a split-off, one or more shareholders continue to own stock in the existing professional corporation and subsidiaries are created and stock distributed to those professionals who leave (split-off from) the professional corporation.
14. For examples of recent letter rulings see:

    Letter Ruling 8023030—A professional corporation is owned by two doctors and operates three offices. It wishes to split-off one of the offices to one of the shareholders, with whom the others have a disagreement. The Service ruled that this transaction will be tax-free, conditioned on the signing of a closing agreement providing for reorganization of income by the successor corporation when income items are paid or disposed of.

Letter Ruling 8018084—Six orthodontists, each working at a different location, formed a corporation. After incorporation, each shareholder doctor continued to operate his own individual office as a separate cash basis unit with his own employees. However, the accounting and billing was centralized. Now, common shareholder differences have arisen and each doctor wants to practice alone "in order to provide better services to his patients." Accordingly, the corporation will transfer to each of the six new corporations the assets related to the business conducted at each of these six locations, etc. Initially, the existing corporation will hold all stock for the new corporation. It will then transfer the stock of one of the six subsidiaries to the doctor who has operated the business at a particular location in exchange for his shares in the original corporation, and so on for the remaining dentists. The Service ruled that the transaction should be a Type D reorganization with no recognition of gains or loss to the shareholders or the new corporation.

Letter Ruling 8016036—Professional corporation has three physicians who provide medical services. Due to the disputes between two of the physicians and the remaining physician, the association will transfer all of its assets to the three newly organized corporations in exchange for stock. The association will then distribute all the stock with the first new corporation to the first physician. The other two physicians will each receive the stock of one of the remaining corporations. The association will then end its existence. The Service ruled that this corporation split-up and preliminary reorganization will be tax-free.

Letter Ruling 8009039—Proposed transfer by corporation D of half its assets and liabilities to corporation C for its stock followed by D's distribution of C stock to one of its two shareholders for a shareholder's D stock will then be valid Type D reorganization. No gain or loss will be recognized to (and no amount will be included in income of) shareholder on receipt of C stock for his D stock. Rulings are conditioned on C entering a closing agreement (released with ruling). D is incorporated legal partnership of A and B who own its stock equally. Disagreements between them as to the direction of growth of D led to the split-off plan.

Letter Ruling 7810013—A professional corporation, engaged in the practic of law, employs 81 people, including 37 attorneys, and has 16 shareholders, including A and B. The corporation's office in city X represents liability insurance carriers, and its business has developed to the point where 100% of its practice consists of defending alleged tortfeasors for and on behalf of respective carriers. Numerous conflicts have arisen because several attorneys in the rest of the firm represent plaintiffs in tort litigation. To eliminate conflicts, the corporation will transfer all of its assets from its office in city X to a new corporation, Q, in exchange for all of the stock of Q and its assumption of related liabilities. Assets include furniture, equipment and accounts receivable. The professional corporation will then distribute all of its

Q stock to A and B in exchange for their entire stock interest in the professional corporation (the stock is of equal value). Even though more Q stock will later be sold to A and B and others, A and B will continue to hold more than 80%. The professional corporation's transfer of assets and liabilities to Q, in exchange for capital Q stock, to be distributed to A and B for their P stock, will be a Type D reorganization, with no recognitional gain or loss to P or Q. And A and B will not recognize gains or loss since transaction qualifies as Section 355 split-off. Rulings are conditioned upon corporation Q entering a closing agreement, a copy of which is included with the ruling.

15. See Rev. Rul. 64-102, 1964-1 C.B. 136, Rev. Rul. 71-383, 1971-2 C.B. 180, Rev. Rul. 71-384, 1971-1 C.B. 181, and Prop. Treas. Regs. §1-355-2(c).

16. See *Commissioner v. Morris Trust*, 367 F.2d 794 (4th Cir. 1966); Rev. Rul. 68-603, 1968-2 C.B. 148; and Prop. Treas. Regs. §1.355-2(c)(2).

17. See Prop. Treas. Regs. §1.355-1; *Edmond P. Coady*, 33 T.C. 771 (1960), *acq.*, 1965-1 C.B. 4, *aff'd*, 289 F.2d 490 (6th Cir. 1961).

18. Treas. Regs. §1.355-2(c) and Prop. Treas. Regs. §1.355-2(b).

19. See, however, *Estate of Moses L. Parshelsky v. Commissioner*, 303 F.2d 14 (2d Cir. 1962), holding that a shareholder's business purpose constitutes a corporate business purpose in a closely held corporation.

20. See Sections 4043(b)(3) and 4062(e) of ERISA. Also see Treas. Regs. §1.411(d) providing a facts and circumstances test.

21. See Letter Ruling 7841059 and L.R. 8103078 based on Rev. Rul. 67-181, 1967-1 C.B. 23; Rev. Rul. 67-213, 1967-2 C.B. 27.

22. See Rev. Rul. 55-317, 1955-1 C.B. 329; Rev. Rul. 67-213, 1962-2 C.B. 149; Rev. Rul. 55-368, 1955-1 C.B. 40.

CHAPTER **19**

Partnerships of Professional Corporations

Amicable split-offs or split-ups of professional corporations are sometimes effected in order to permit the continuation of the joint professional practice and eliminate the potential conflicts which exist with regard to retirement plans and fringe benefits. Also, some professionals in a professional partnership may desire to incorporate while others do not. When these situations occur, professionals often desire to continue the practice of their profession through a partnership which consists of partners, some of whom may be professional corporations. Professional partnerships which include professional corporations as partners operate in much the same way as professional partnerships without corporate partners. However, partnerships of professional corporations create special problems with regard to state law, ethical considerations, and federal income taxation.

[19.01] STATE LAW AND ETHICAL CONSIDERATIONS

Most professional corporation acts do not contain provisions which prohibit a professional corporation from engaging in the practice of a profession through a partnership. Most state acts specifically make the general business corporation provisions applicable to professional corporations. Since under most state corporate laws corporations may engage in business as general partners in partnerships, professional corporations are also permitted to engage in the practice of a profession as a general partner in a professional partnership.

Obviously, the offering of professional services is also subject to ethical constraints designed to protect the public. The authors are unaware of any professional ethical rules which would prohibit the use of partnerships of professional corporations. In fact, the American Bar Association and many states have recently acted to permit legal partnerships of professional corporations, as long as the public has notice of the legal relationship existing between the partnership and the professional corporations.[1]

[19.02]   FEDERAL INCOME TAX QUESTIONS

Although the operation of a group of professional corporations as a partnership does not technically contravene any of the federal income tax laws, regulations or rulings, there are a number of considerations involved in determining whether a partnership of professional corporations will provide the benefits sought. The most important, and potentially hazardous, consideration is determining whether the Service will recognize the form of the transaction, and there are several major avenues of attack open to the Service, such as disregarding the corporate entity and reallocating income from the professional corporation partners to the professionals themselves. For a complete discussion of the tax principles described below, see Chapter 9, *supra*.

(1)   Recognition of Professional Corporation Partners for Tax Purposes

The intended tax consequences flowing from the recognition of a professional corporation as a partner in a professional partnership may be lost if the professional corporation is disregarded for tax purposes, and the professional corporation may be disregarded if it is merely a corporation in form but not in substance. The classic "substance over form" case in the context of professional practices is *Jerome J. Roubik*.[2] In *Roubik*, four radiologists who previously had been engaged in separate practices, went through the formalities of joining together in a single professional corporation. However, after incorporation, the radiologists continued to conduct their practices essentially as they had prior to incorporation. Thus, although receipts and expenses were accounted for through the corporate books, all of the receipts and expenses were separately allocated to the appropriate radiologist. The only shared expense was that for bookkeeping. Further, each radiologist continued to work out of his own pre-incorporation location, continued to own (and depreciate) his own equipment, and in some cases continued to render statements in his own name. Finally, three of the radiologists continued to practice, pursuant to service contracts they had individually executed prior to incorporation, with various hospitals and clinics. The Service took the position that the corporation was little more than a bookkeeping operation and that, since the radiologists had not changed the substance of their pre-incorporation practices, all income was properly attributable to them individually. The Tax Court agreed with the Service and held that the corporation should be ignored since the radiologists themselves were the true "earners" of the income.

Although *Roubik* did not involve the specific attempt of professionals to practice their profession through a partnership of professional corporations, it is a clear example of the concern of the Service with the substance of any given transaction or arrangement, and it stands as a particular warning to professionals that extreme care must be taken in conducting a professional practice through a corporation.

The Service has, however, in Rev. Rul. 72-4,[3] specifically recognized that a personal service corporation and its sole shareholder can be separately recognized for tax purposes. The shareholder can be recognized as an employee, even though the corporation was incorporated to deal exclusively in the services of its only employee who is also the principal or sole shareholder.[4]

The Service has recently attacked a partnership of professional corporations where many of the corporate and partnership formalities were overlooked. In a Technical Advice Memorandum issued as Letter Ruling 8031028 (August 8, 1980), the National Office held that income was taxable to a physician personally (and not his professional corporation) even though the corporation was not a sham where:

(1) there was no written partnership agreement for the partnership of professional corporations,

(2) the physician did not formally assign his partnership interest to the professional corporation,

(3) the physician had no written employment agreement or covenant not to compete with his professional corporation,

(4) the insurance policies of the partnership were not changed to extend coverage to the professional corporation,

(5) the physician was the sole employee of the professional corporation,

(6) the professional corporation had no debt other than the cost of establishing and maintaining a qualified retirement plan, and

(7) the professional corporation made a substantial loan to the physician and retained corporate earnings in cash.

This latest Technical Advice Memorandum is another indication that the Service is continuing to scrutinize partnerships of professional corporations.

(2) Reallocation of Income

In its attempts to re-characterize transactions and arrangements for tax purposes, the Service may use statutory provisions in addition to the basic "substance over form" theory employed in *Roubik*. A particularly effective provision is Section 482 which permits the Service to allocate income and deductions among taxpayers in order to clearly reflect income.

In order for a partnership of professional corporations to achieve the desired results, it is necessary that the professional corporations be taxed on their distributive shares of partnership income and that the shareholder-employees of the professional corporations be taxable only on the compensation paid to them by their respective professional corporations. Section 482 may be asserted in an effort to reallocate income away from the professional corporation and to its shareholder-employee on the theory that the distributive share of partnership income was earned by the shareholder.

The service may take the position that it is the professional shareholder-employees and not the professional corporations who are, in fact, the members of the partnership because it is their personal efforts which actually create the partnership income. If such a position were to prevail, all professional income would be attributable to the individual shareholder-employees as opposed to the professional corporations. The Service has, over the years, had considerable success in reallocating income under Section 482 between a sole shareholder and his corporation.

For instance, in *Borge v. Commissioner*,[5] the taxpayer was deemed, for purposes of Section 482, to own or to control two businesses (an entertainment business and a poultry business) and a portion of the entertainment compensation paid to his corporation was reallocated to him personally. The reallocation was predicated on the finding that the taxpayer merely assigned a portion of his entertainment income to his corporation and the corporation did nothing to earn or assist in earning that income. In the case of *Richard Rubin*,[6] the controlling shareholder had corporation A enter into a management contract with corporation B, whereby the controlling shareholder, as an employee of corporation A, would provide management services for corporation B. The controlling shareholder carried on a separate trade or business of rendering managerial services and thus fell within the ambit of Section 482 and income was reallocated from corporation A to the shareholder. Also see *Edwin C. Davis*,[7] which illustrates the application of Section 482 in the professional corporation context. There, the Service was unsuccessful in attempting to allocate income from X-ray and physical therapy corporations to an orthopedic surgeon who set them up and then gave the stock to his children.

Although there has been no case or ruling directly relating to the reallocation under Section 482 of income between a professional corporation (as a member of a professional partnership) and its shareholders, there is a possibility that the Service could attempt to do so.

(3) Taxable Years and Termination of the Partnership

There are various rules relating to the taxation of partnerships which should be examined when forming a partnership of professional corporations, such as:

(1) Section 706(b)(1): a partnership may not change to or adopt a taxable year other than that of its principal partners (a principal partner is a partner having an interest of 5% or more in partnership profits or capital), without permission from the Secretary of the Treasury.

(2) Section 706(b)(2): a principal partner may not change to a taxable year other than that of the partnership, without permission from the Secretary of the Treasury.

(3) Section 706(c): the partnership's taxable year is required to close upon certain events.

(4) Section 708(b): a partnership shall be considered as terminated if, within a 12-month period, there is a sale or exchange of 50% or more of the total interest in partnership capital and profits.

(4) Conclusion

The possibility that the professional corporations may not be recognized for tax purposes under the *Roubik* rationale or that income may be allocated either away from the professional corporation partners or among them in a different fashion under Section 482 represents a formidable, but not insurmountable, obstacle to the operation of a partnership of professional corporations. The determination of whether to apply the *Roubik* rationale or Section 482 is essentially a factual one and proper adherence to both the form and substance of rendering professional services as a corporate partner in a professional partnership should minimize the risk in this area. At the very least, the parties should take steps to insure that the professional corporations are the actual earners of the income.

The professional corporations should enter into employment agreements with the professional employees and should, in fact, retain and exercise control over the professionals' employment. The professional employees should be prohibited from entering into contracts in their individual names and all contracts should be in the names of the professional corporations or the partnership. Also, the professional corporations must hold themselves out to the public as rendering professional services by insuring that all statements, letterheads, office signs, business cards, telephone listings, building directories and similar business practices reflect the status of the professional corporations. A written partnership agreement should be made and consideration should be given to placing all leases, insurance policies, and other contractual agreements in the name of the professional partnership. Also, the professional partnership should hold itself out to the public as such and should also hold itself out to the Service as a partnership by obtaining an employer identification number as a partnership, by making employer tax deposits for its common-law employees, and by filing partnership income tax returns.

If, in fact, the Service prevails in disregarding the corporate entities, the professional corporations' qualified retirement plans will probably be disqualified and the employees of the corporations will lose the other employee benefits, such as group term life insurance, health and medical reimbursement plans, etc. However, if income is reallocated under Section 482, it is possible that the corporations' qualified retirement plans would not be disqualified, but plan contributions could be disallowed as deductions since the corporations would not be considered as having income and would pay no compensation.

[19.03] QUALIFIED RETIREMENT PLANS

The operation of qualified retirement plans in a partnership of professional corporations may create potential problems. On December 28, 1980, President Carter signed into law Section 414(m) of the Code, which requires that, in a partnership of professional corporations, all employees of the corporations and the partnership will be treated as employed by one employer. Under this new legislation, partnerships of professional corporations will no longer be entitled to discriminate in favor of professionals in providing qualified retirement plans. An examination of the state of the law prior to the new legislation, an analysis of the new legislation, and a recommendation with regard to the new legislation and what actions should be taken while Regulations are pending, follow below.

(1) Revenue Ruling 68-370—The IRS States Its Position

Until December 28, 1980, the rules for employee participation in the qualified retirement plans of partnerships of professional corporations were clearly stated by the Service. Through Rev. Rul. 68-370,[8] the Service ruled that a corporation which participated in a joint venture with another corporation would be required to take employees of the joint venture into account in determining whether the corporation's profit sharing plan met the requirements of Section 401(a). The Service viewed the joint venture of the two corporations as a partnership, a partnership that was not itself a taxable entity, but merely the aggregate of the constituent partners. Therefore, the establishment of the requisite employment relationship between the partnership and the common-law employees of the partnership also established such relationship between each corporate partner and such employees for purposes of Section 401.

The important effect of this conclusion was to attribute to each corporate partner the common-law employment relationship that existed between the partnership and the individual employees. Thus, since the employees of the joint venture were considered employees of the corporate partners, the Service held that such employees, and a pro rata share of the compensation paid to them, must be taken into account by each corporate partner in determining whether the qualified plan of each corporate partner met the coverage and nondiscrimination requirements set forth in Section 401(a).

(2) Packard/Burnetta Cases and Sections 414(b) and (c)

In *Ronald C. Packard*,[9] three dentists, practicing in a partnership, formed a service corporation to which all nonprofessional employees were transferred. The service corporation owned the office building in which the partnership was located and provided bookkeeping and general staff services and facilities to the partnership and to other dentists not in the partnership.

The Tax Court held that the profit sharing plan adopted by the partnership (which covered only the dentists-partners) was qualified. The court reached this decision after determining that: (1) the service corporation was formed for a bona fide business purpose and was not a subterfuge; and (2) the service personnel were directed and controlled by, and therefore, under the familar common-law test, were employees of, the service corporation as opposed to the partnership. The court emphasized the following factors:

(1) The service corporation marketed a complete package of services incidental to the practice of dentistry and sold this complete service not only to the partnership, but also to three independent dentists;

(2) The fees paid to the service corporation was not limited to a percentage of wages and expenses, but rather was a percentage of gross billings with respect to subscribers;

(3) The relationship between the service corporation and the subscribers was formalized in a written lease and management contract; and

(4) The partnership and the other subscribers were entitled to specify only the results to be accomplished by the service personnel while the service corporation maintained the right to control, hire and fire service personnel.

Sections 414(b) and (c), which were added by ERISA, were the first attempt of Congress to prevent avoidance of the anti-discrimination rules through the use of multiple corporations. Sections 414(b) and (c) basically incorporate the rules provided in Section 1563 for determining a "controlled group" of corporations (for corporate surtax exemption purposes). Under Sections 414(b) and (c) all controlled organizations must be aggregated for purposes of testing the minimum participation and other rules. However, because the tests of Section 1563 are very restrictive, Sections 414(b) and (c) were not entirely successful in eliminating abuse.

It should be noted that *Packard* involved tax years prior to the enactment of Section 414(b) and (c) of the Code. If the *Packard* situation arose today, the likely, and proper, result would be that under Section 414(c), the service employees would be treated as employed by the dental partnership, since the three dentists were in a single partnership and had the requisite degree of control in both the partnership and the service corporation.

The Tax Court again used the common-law employee attribution test in *Edward L. Burnetta, O.D., P.A.*[10] In that case, an opthalmologist and an optometrist formed separate professional corporations and adopted qualified retirement plans. Subsequently, they contracted with a service corporation, owned by the accountant for the professional corporations, to provide service personnel. As originally conceived, the service corporation was to be responsibile for the selection, hiring, training and supervision of all service personnel for a number of unrelated professional corporations. In practice, however, the selection, hiring, training and supervision of the service personnel were maintained by the respective professional corporations. Thus, the Tax Court held that the service personnel were employees of the professional corporations for whom they worked, and, consequently, the qualified retirement plans did not meet the coverage requirements of Section 401(a)(3)(A) (pre-ERISA).

The Tax Court distinguished the *Packard* decision on the basis that in *Packard* the taxpayers were able to establish under the common-law employee test that control over the service personnel in fact rested in the service corporation, not in the partnership. If Sections 414(b) and (c) had been in existence, their strict application to this case, without consideration of the common-law employee test espoused under Rev. Rul. 68-370, would have resulted in the opposite conclusion.

(3) The Kiddie Case—Pre-ERISA

In the pre-ERISA case of *Thomas Kiddie, M.D., Inc.,*[11] the Tax Court, discussing partnership law instead of the common-law employee/employer rules, thoroughly confused the area of employee participation in qualified plans of professional partnerships. Dr. Kiddie's professional corporation provided pathological services to a hospital. In 1972, the corporation created a partnership with another professional service corporation to provide pathological services, with each corporation owning 50% of the partnership. The staff employees of Dr. Kiddie's corporation then became employees of the partnership and Dr. Kiddie's corporation adopted a qualified pension plan.

The court held that the staff employees were employees of the partnership and were properly excluded from Dr. Kiddie's pension plan. The court, holding that the Section 707(b) "greater than 50% test" should apply for purposes of Section 401(a)(3), refused to attribute the partnership's employees to Dr. Kiddie's corporation because it owned only 50% of the partnership and, therefore, did not control the partnership. Whether Dr. Kiddie's corporation controlled the partnership's employees and, thus, was their employer, was not examined by the Tax Court.

(4) The IRS Position After Kiddie

The Service refused to follow *Kiddie* and continued to follow Rev. Rul. 68-370. For instance, in Letter Ruling 7834059, three professional corporations each held a one-third interest in the capital and profits of a law partnership with six full-time employees. One of the professional corporations proposed the adoption of a profit sharing plan. The Service ruled that this corporation could adopt a profit sharing plan, complying with the coverage and nondiscrimination requirements of Section 401(a), even if the other two corporations and the partnership did not adopt such a plan. Further, the employees of the partnership would be considered the full-time employees of the professional corporation and would participate in the profit sharing plan to the extent of one-third of their compensation received from the partnership. If the professional corporations included the six employees of the partnership as participants in their qualified retirement plans, if any, to the extent of one-third of their compensation received from the partnership, then the participation and nondiscrimination requirements of Section 401(a) of the Code would be satisfied. The Service then stated:

> It is our conclusion that the conclusion stated in Rev. Rul. 68-370 has not been affected by the enactment of the Employee Retirement Income Security Act of 1974 and that it still may be relied upon for authority that the employees of a partnership or joint venture are considered employees of each member or partner for purposes of testing for coverage and nondiscrimination in contributions or benefits. We believe that Sections 414(b) and (c) do not establish exclusive rules for aggregation of employees for these purposes. It is our belief that Congress in enacting ERISA did not seek to erode the established rules of the Internal Revenue Service pertaining to such matters, but rather sought to extend the coverage and nondiscrimination requirements of the Code with respect to affiliated business entities regardless of whether any employee of a member of the control group performs services for another member of the control group.[12]

(5) The Garland Case—Post-ERISA

An approach similar to that taken by the Service in Letter Ruling 7834059 was rejected by the Tax Court in its unfortunate opinion in *Lloyd M. Garland, M.D., F.A.C.S., P.A.*[13] Petitioner, a professional medical corporation, formed a partnership with a physician, and each partner owned a 50% interest in the partnership. The professional corporation adopted a pension plan which did not cover the common-law employees of the partnership. Dr. Garland felt that his professional corporation was not required by either Section 414(b) or Section 414(c) to cover the partnership's employees under the plan. Nevertheless, the Service determined that the plan did not qualify under Section 401(a) because it did not comply with the antidiscrimination provisions of Sections 401(a)(4) and 410(b)(1).

The Tax Court held, directly contrary to the position stated in Letter Ruling 7834059, that Sections 414(b) and 414(c) *are the exclusive* means for determining whether the employees of affiliated entities should be aggregated for purposes of applying the antidiscrimination provisions. Further, the Tax Court held that, since the professional corporation did not control the partnership's employees, they were properly excluded from participation in the plan. The reasoning in *Kiddie* was followed, totally ignoring the logic and desirability of using the common-law employee test as used in Rev. Rul. 68-370 as an alternative means of compliance with the antidiscrimination provisions.

(6) Did the "Loophole" Become a Noose?

Section 414(m) is effective for plan years ending after November 30, 1980, for new plans, and plan years beginning after that date for existing plans. Section 414(m) provides rules for the aggregation of employees of certain separate organizations for purposes of applying tests to various benefit plans. It is an emphatic response to the absurd results which have received judicial approval in *Kiddie* and *Garland*, but applies *only* to service organizations.[14]

For purposes of defining qualified pension plans under Section 414(m), all employees of members of an "affiliated service group" will be treated as employed by a single employer. An "affiliated service group" consists of a service organization and one or more other organizations, service or not, which are related. The broad definition of organization includes a corporation, partnership or "other organization." Section 414(m)(2) defines an affiliated service group as follows:

A first organization (FSO) and one or more of the following:

1. any service organization (A-ORG) which—
   (a) is a shareholder or partner in the FSO, and
   (b) regularly performs services for the FSO or is regularly associated with the FSO in performing services for third persons, and

2. any other organization (B-ORG) if—
   (a) a significant portion of the business of such organization is the performance of services for the FSO or A-ORG of a type historically performed in the service field by the FSO or A-ORG employees, and
   (b) 10% or more of the interest of the B-ORG is held by persons who are officers, highly compensated employees, or owners of the FSO or A-ORG.

The only Service pronouncement to date concerning the interpretation of Section 414(m) appears in Rev. Rul. 81-105.[15] Rev. Rul. 81-105 (a complete copy of which is attached to this subsection as Exhibit 1) illustrates that most abusive situations have been eliminated by the "A-ORG" and "B-ORG" tests established under Section 414(m).

The "A-ORG" test eliminates the use of a typical partnership of professional corporations to discriminate against staff employee participation in qualified retirement plans. That is, the partnership is the FSO because it provides services and the corporate partners are A-ORGs since they are regularly associated with the FSO in performing services (or regularly perform services for the FSO). Example 1 of the Rev. Rul. 81-105 illustrates this result.

The "B-ORG" test also eliminates the ability of professionals to "loan out" staff employees to related service organizations. Example 2 of Rev. Rul. 81-105 illustrates the B-ORG rule as follows:

> Corporation S provides secretarial services. Corporations A and B, both of which are professional corporations formed by doctors, each own a portion of S. A owns 11 percent of the stock of S and B owns eight percent of the stock. Approximately one-third of S's services are performed for A and one-third for B, while the other one-third are performed for other firms. A and B each maintain a retirement plan (Plan A and Plan B) and each plan covers the corporation's only employee. None of the statutory exclusions of Section 410(b) of the Code applies.
>
> Under Section 414(m)(2), Corporations A and B may each be designated as separate FSO's. Corporation S is a B-ORG for A because a signficant portion of S's business is the performance of services for A, the services are of a type historically performed in the FSO's service field by its employees, and 11 percent of the interest in S is held by owners of the FSO. S is not a B-ORG for B because the owners of B do not hold 10 percent or more of the interest in S.

It is interesting to note that Rev. Rul. 81-105 does not discuss the possible application of the A-ORG rule to Example 2, presumably on the grounds that S is not a "service organization" or that neither A nor B is "regularly associated" with S in performing services. Obviously, there are a number of terms such as "regularly performs," "service organization," and "other organization" which must be defined in future Regulations.

Neither Section 414(m) nor Rev. Rul. 81-105 defines the type of qualified plan which must be provided for the employees of an affiliated service group. Section 414(m)(l) simply states that "all employees of the members of an affiliated service group shall be treated as employed by a single employer." That is, the same discrimination standards apply to the entire group, which means that rank and file employees must have benefits that are comparable to those of the officers, shareholders, and highly paid employees. This has sometimes been called the "best plan" approach (the rank and file employees must have benefits provided under the best of the various retirement plans of the affiliated group members).

(7) Alternatives for Dealing with Section 414(m)

(a) *Regulations Under Section 414(m)*

A number of practitioners feel that the Regulations under Section 414(m) should be drafted to reestablish the pro rata test established under Rev. Rul. 68-370. Section 414(m) was enacted to eliminate the abuses of *Kiddie* and *Garland* with regard to basic participation criteria. Requiring a "best plan" approach goes much farther than simply requiring participation; it drastically changes the level of benefits for staff employees and mandates an unduly complicated "comparability" of benefits.[16] Further, some practitioners argue that there is little rationale in requiring that, where only one professional corporation (in a partnership of 10 professional corporations) adopts a qualified retirement plan, the staff employees of the partnership must be provided an identical plan for 100% of their incomes, irrespective of the fact that the activities of the professional corporation only account for one-tenth of the income of the staff employees.

In any event, there is sufficient authority for the Treasury to promulgate Regulations adopting the "best plan" and not the pro rata approach. Section 414(m)(l) requires that "all employees of the members of an affiliated service group shall be treated as employed by a single employer." There is little question concerning the discrimination rules which apply to a single employer—plans for highly compensated employees will not be qualified unless plans for staff employees are comparable. Consequently, practitioners should expect that the Regulations to be issued will adopt the best plan approach since the Service has so indicated in Rev. Rul. 81-105.

Obviously, the enactment of Section 414(m) places a premium on sophisticated planning, which will probably entail the use of defined benefit plans for affiliated service organizations (with the objective of reducing the required contributions for rank and file employees). Pending the issuance of Regulations under Section 414(m), steps should be taken to either: (1) avoid the application of the best plan approach (under the technical ownership rules of Section 414(m)) or (2) meet the requirements of the best plan approach. In either event, a ruling under Rev. Proc. 81-112[17] should be obtained from the National Office and/or appropriate District Office of the Service to assure qualification.

(b) Avoiding Application of Section 414(m)

If an "affiliated service group" exists under Section 414(m), it must be assumed that the "best plan" rules will apply. Consequently, there exists an incentive for avoiding the technical ownership rules of Section 414(m). Groups of professionals and professional corporations should be able to avoid Section 414(m) by the use of the following forms of group practice:

1. *Space Sharing Arrangements.* Where professional corporations simply share space and where each corporation employs its own employees, Section 414(m) will not be applicable. There is no common ownership and no partnership and, consequently, the A-ORG and B-ORG tests are avoided.

2. *Of Counsel Arrangements.* Where only one professional desires to establish qualified retirement plans, he can separate himself from the professional partnership and then incorporate his practice. The crucial factor under Section 414(m) is control. If neither the newly-separated professional corporation nor the

professional is a partner in the partnership but is only an independent contractor no "affiliated service group" should exist. However, in order to establish such an independent (contractor) relationship, the separating professional must give up all voting control and ownership in the professional partnership and this might not be palatable to most "senior partners" (i.e., the likely candidates for establishing such "of counsel" professional corporations).

3. *Service Bureau and Third-Party Arrangements.* As long as there is no (or less than 10%) ownership by a professional corporation or a professional in an organization providing staff personnel, there should be no need to cover the staff personnel under the qualified retirement plans of the professional corporation. The *Garland* case held that Section 414 is the *exclusive* test for determining affiliated service groups, apparently to the exclusion of the common-law employee/employer test. The enactment of Section 414(m) following *Garland* has apparently codified this holding and the Service has also agreed. See Example 2 of Rev. Rul. 81-105 indicating that employees of a service bureau need not be considered employees of a professional corporation under Section 414(m) where the owners of the professional corporation own less than 10% of the service bureau.

The common-law employee/employer test should still retain some vitality and service bureau arrangements should be reviewed very closely, especially where under local law the staff employees must be supervised by professionals (e.g., nurses). In addition, Section 414(m)(6) gives the Secretary of the Treasury broad discretion to "prescribe such regulations as may be necessary to prevent avoidance with respect to service organizations, through use of separate organizations," of the coverage and discrimination requirements applicable to qualified plans. It is quite possible that an organization that is structured for the purpose of avoiding the technical requirements for aggregation under the specific tests of Section 414(m)(2)(A) and (B) will be required to be treated as a single organization under Regulations prescribed to prevent avoidance.

Although Section 414(m) applies the stock attribution rules of Section 267, it would also be technically possible to permit the staff employees to be employed by related parties whose stock would not be attributable to the professional corporations or the owners of the professional corporations (e.g., mothers-in-law or the associates of the professional practice).

(8) Structuring Plans to Satisfy the Section 414(m) Requirements

In many situations it will not be feasible to structure ownership of related entities in such a manner that creation of an affiliated service group within the meaning of Section 414(m) will be avoided. In such situations the coverage and nondiscrimination requirements of Section 401(a)(4) and 410(b)(1) must be satisfied for the entire affiliated service group. For purposes of discussion it will be assumed that the affiliated service group consists of: (1) a partnership which employs all or a majority of the rank and file employees and may also employ one or more professionals, and (2) one or more corporate partners that employ an incorporated former partner. In this setting, each of the professional corporations will adopt a qualified retirement plan.

There are two basic approaches under which the affiliated service group could satisfy the coverage and discrimination tests. These approaches are summarized immediately below and are developed in greater detail in the discussion that follows:

The "Fair Cross Section" Approach. Each professional corporation could employ a sufficient cross section of the employees of the affiliated service group so that a plan covering solely the employees of the adopting professional corporation would be deemed to cover a nondiscriminatory classification of employees, and therefore will satisfy the coverage and nondiscrimination requirements.

The "Comparable Plan/Best Plan" Approach. If a professional corporation that adopts a plan does not employ a nondiscriminatory cross section of the employees of the affiliated service group, then the partnership that employs the bulk of the rank and file employees must establish a qualified plan, often referred to as the "core plan," which provides contributions or benefits at least as favorable as the "best plan" maintained by any professional corporation that is part of the affiliated service group.

(a) *The "Fair Cross Section" Approach*

(1)   A HYPOTHETICAL CASE

Suppose a professional service partnership contains 10 partners, 20 associates, and 30 staff personnel. Assume the senior partner transferred his partnership interest to his wholly owned professional corporation, and the professional corporation adopted a defined benefit plan that will provide a benefit equal to 100% of final five year average pay subject to the dollar ceiling of Section 415(b)(1)(A). If the senior partner were the sole employee of his professional corporation, the plan clearly would not satisfy the minimum coverage requirements of Section 410(b)(1), and the partnership would be required to adopt a "comparable" plan. Funding the partnership's comparable plan might constitute a prohibitive financial burden for the partnership to undertake, and the senior partner may be required to settle for a plan providing a benefit of substantially less than 100% of compensation, or he may be discouraged from adopting any qualified retirement plan at all.

As an alternative, suppose that, in lieu of the partnership's adoption of a comparable plan, an attempt is made to have the senior partner's professional corporation employ a nondiscriminatory classification of the affiliated service group's employees, so that coverage of the professional corporation's employees would constitute a nondiscriminatory classification within the meaning of Section 410(b)(1)(B).

The basic issue presented by the alternative approach is: how many rank and file employees must the professional corporation employ to accomplish the objective of covering a nondiscriminatory classification? Although definitive authority does not exist on this issue, it is possible that, if as few as one or two rank and file employees are transferred to the professional corporation (for example the senior partner's secretary and an assistant), the professional corporation's plan may pass the classification and nondiscrimination tests.

This approach should not be taken absent a favorable IRS determination based on a full disclosure of all the facts. In addition, it might be best to provide full and immediate vesting under this approach to prevent discrimination in operation under Section 411(d)(1). Obtaining a determination letter for this approach might require administrative appeals and even declaratory judgment proceedings in the Tax Court; but in many circumstances the potential cost savings might justify the effort involved. Consideration of the merit of this approach must focus on the administrative and judicial interpretation of the nondiscriminatory classification test described in Section 410(b)(1)(B).

(2) LEGAL BASIS FOR THE "FAIR CROSS SECTION" APPROACH

Section 410(b)(1) provides two alternative tests—a *percentage test* and a *classification test*—which define the minimum participation requirements for qualified retirement plans. In the case of an affiliated service group, these tests will be applied as if all employees of the affiliated service group were employed by a single employer. A plan (or several plans that are designated as a single plan) maintained by one or more members of an affiliated service group will satisfy the *percentage test* if it benefits at least 70% of all employees of the affiliated service group or if it benefits at least 80% of the employees who are eligible to participate and at least 70% of all employees of the affiliated service group are eligible. A plan satisfies the *classification test* if it benefits a classification of employees of the affiliated service group established by the employer which the Internal Revenue Service determines is not discriminatory in favor of the "prohibited group"—officers, shareholders and highly-compensated employees.

A qualified plan need only satisfy *one* of the two minimum participation tests. Satisfaction of the minimum participation requirements is an ongoing requirement. The requirement must be satisfied at least one day of each quarter of each plan year. See Section 401(a)(6). Once it is shown that the plan's *coverage* satisfies the minimum participation rules, the nondiscrimination requirement will only apply to the individuals who are actually participating and the exclusion of persons not covered by the plan will not cause the plan to violate the nondiscrimination requirement. See Rev. Rul. 79-348.[18]

A plan covering only one professional corporation in an affiliated service group will rarely satisfy the percentage test and, therefore, will not be qualified unless the classification test is satisfied. Regulations §1.410(b)-1(d)(2) interprets the classification test of Section 410(b)(1)(B) as follows:

> The determination as to whether a plan discriminates in favor of employees who are officers, shareholders, or highly-compensated is made on the basis of the facts and circumstances of each case, *allowing a reasonable difference* between the ratio of such employees benefited by the plan to all such employees of the employer and the ratio of the employees (other than officers, shareholders, or highly compensated) of the employer benefited by the plan to all employees (other than officers, shareholders, or highly compensated). A showing that a specified percentage of employees covered by a plan are not officers, shareholders, or highly compensated, is not in itself sufficient to establish that the plan does not discriminate in favor of employees who are officers, shareholders, or highly compensated. (Emphasis added.)

The Regulation states that there can be a "reasonable difference" between the ratio of:

prohibited group participants
all prohibited group employees of the employer
and the ratio of:
nonprohibited group participants
all nonprohibited group employees of the employer

Furthermore, a showing that a specified percentage of employees covered by the plan are not in the prohibited group, "*is not in itself* sufficient to establish that the plan does not discriminate..." Applying this Regulation to the preceding hypothetical case, and assuming that the 10 partners and 10 of the 20 associates are in the prohibited group, the ratios applicable to the senior partner's professional corporation are as follows:

Alternative One: Plan covers senior partner and two rank and file employees:

$$\frac{\text{prohibited participants}}{\text{all prohibited group employees of the employer}} = \frac{1}{20} = 5\%$$

$$\frac{\text{nonprohibited group participants}}{\text{all nonprohibited group employees of the employer}} = \frac{2}{40} = 5\%$$

$$\text{percentage of nonprohibited group participants} = \frac{2}{3} = 67\%$$

Alternative Two: Plan covers senior partner and one rank and file employee:

$$\frac{\text{prohibited group participants}}{\text{all prohibited group employees of the employer}} = \frac{1}{20} = 5\%$$

$$\frac{\text{nonprohibited group participants}}{\text{all nonprohibited group employees of the employer}} = \frac{1}{40} = 2.5\%$$

$$\text{percentage of nonprohibited group participants} = \frac{1}{2} = 50\%$$

Based upon the Regulation's stipulation that there may be a "reasonable difference between the percentage of covered prohibited group employees and the percentage of covered nonprohibited group employees," it appears that the plan might satisfy the Regulations under Alternative One and may also satisfy the Regulations under Alternative Two, in which the percentages vary on a 2 to 1 ratio and 50% of the participants are nonprohibited group employees. See, *Federal Land Bank Associates of Asheville, North Carolina.*[19]

Section 401(a)(5) of the Code states that a classification will not be discriminatory merely because it is limited to salaried or clerical employees. Regulations §1.401-3(d) states that the enumeration of permissible classifications in Section 401(a)(5) is not intended to be exclusive and that a plan's coverage could possibly be limited to the employees of "designated departments" or "other classifications" so long as the effect of the classification does not discriminate in favor of the prohibited group. In determining whether a classification results in discriminatory coverage, Regulations §1.410(b)-1(d)(2), quoted above, states that a showing that a specified percentage of the participants are nonprohibited group employees is not in itself sufficient to establish that coverage is not discriminatory. In practice, however, the administrative rulings and judicial decisions which have disqualified plans for failure to satisfy the classification test of Section 410(b)(1)(B) have uniformly involved situations in which the plan covered a *greater number* of prohibited group participants than nonprohibited group participants and, therefore, could be said to be maintained *primarily* for employees in whose favor discrimination is prohibited. The following cases and rulings are illustrative:

(1) Rev. Rul. 66-14.[20] An employer's salaried employees' profit sharing plan covered 6 of a total of 60 employees and 5 of the 6 covered (83%) were in the prohibited group. The employer did not maintain a qualified retirement plan covering nonsalaried employees. The ruling held the classification to be discriminatory. Similarly, Rev. Rul. 69-398.[21]

(2) Rev. Rul. 70-200.[22] A salaried employees' profit sharing plan covered 40 of the employer's 150 employees. Of the 40 covered employees, 22 were officers, shareholders, highly compensated or supervisory employees. However, all but the 4 highest-paid participants were compensated in the same general compensation range as the 110 excluded hourly employees. Notwithstanding the fact that 22 of 40 participants were in the prohibited group, the Service stated that the plan covered a nondiscriminatory classification of employees since the plan covered employees in all compensation ranges, and those in lower and middle compensation brackets were covered in more than nominal numbers. Similarly Rev. Rul. 66-12.[23]

(3) Rev. Rul. 74-255.[24] A salaried employees' profit sharing plan covered 7 of employer's 80 employees. Four of the covered employees were the highest-paid employees and were shareholders. The other three covered employees were the lowest-paid employees of the employer. The Service held that the plan did not cover a nondiscriminatory classification since "the classification results in covering *primarily* employees in whose favor discrimination is prohibited." Similarly, Rev. Rul. 74-256.[25]

(4) Rev. Rul. 79-337.[26] An employer's salaried employees' plan covered 2 of a total of 20 employees. Both of the participants were officers and shareholders, and each was compensated at a substantially higher rate than the hourly employees. The employer did not maintain a qualified retirement plan for the nonsalaried employees. The ruling held the classification to be discriminatory. In arriving at this conclusion the ruling used the following test:

> If the use of a salaried or clerical classification, *or any other classification*, results in covering *primarily* employees in whose favor discrimination is prohibited, the requirements of Section 410(b)(1)(B) of the Code are not met. (Emphasis added).

This test *suggests* that, if a classification results in coverage of a *number* of rank and file employees that *equals or exceeds* the number of prohibited group participants so that the plan does not "primarily" cover prohibited group employees, the classification will not be discriminatory. As previously mentioned, however, Regulations §1.410(b)-1(d)(2) provides that a classification is not assured of being nondiscriminatory merely because a specified percentage of the participants are not in the prohibited group.

(5) *Duguid & Sons, Inc. v. United States.*[27] The court sustained the disqualification of a salaried employees' plan which covered three of nine employees. In this case, 100% of the covered employees were members of the prohibited group.

(6) *Ed & Jim Fleitz, Inc.*[28] The Tax Court sustained the Commissioner's disqualification of a plan where 100% of the covered employees were members of the prohibited group. The Tax Court's opinion established a critical legal principle regarding the burden of proof applicable in a case of alleged discriminatory coverage. Noting that Section 410(b)(1)(B) refers to "a classification set up by the employer and *found by the Secretary* not to be discriminatory....," the court held that, "the question of whether or not discrimination exists is a question of fact which must first be determined by the Commissioner, and his determination should not be set aside unless it is found to be arbitrary or an abuse of discretion." Accordingly, where the Service alleged a classification to be discriminatory, the employer will have the burden of proving that the Service's determination is arbitrary or an abuse of discretion. Compare, *King v. United States*[29], holding that taxpayer will

have only the normal burden of proof in overcoming the presumptive correctness of the Commissioner's determination that a classification is discriminatory. *King* sustained the Commissioner's finding of discriminatory coverage of a salaried employees' plan that covered 25 of 145 employees where 14 participants were in the prohibited group.

(7) *Commissioner v. Pepsi-Cola Niagara Bottling Corp.*[30] The Second Circuit, reversing the Tax Court, upheld the Commissioner's disqualification of a salaried employees' profit sharing plan that covered six of the employer's 14 full-time employees. In two of the three years in issue, all of the covered employees received greater compensation than the highest-paid noncovered employee, and in one of the years in issue this was so in the case of five of the six covered employees. Finding the term "highly compensated" could reasonably be interpreted by the Commissioner to be applied on a relative basis to the employees of the employer in question, the Second Circuit concluded that the Commissioner's determination under Section 410(b)(1)(B) of discriminatory classification must be given "a shade more than its usual substantial weight."

(8) *George Loevsky.*[31] A salaried employees' plan covered 13 of 151 employees. No plan was maintained for the nonsalaried employees and 61.5% of the participants were members of the prohibited group. The Tax Court sustained the Commissioner's determination that the classification was discriminatory finding that such determination "cannot be said to have been arbitrary, unreasonable or an abuse of discretion."

(9) *Liberty Machine Works, Inc.*[32] A salaried employees' plan covered four of the employer's 80 employees. Two of the four employees were members of the prohibited group and constituted the *entire* class of prohibited group employees. When the Service denied the employer's request for an advance determination letter on the basis of discriminatory coverage, the employer amended the plan to permit participation by two additional rank and file employees. The court sustained the Commissioner's finding that the plan did not cover a nondiscriminatory classification. In this case, the classification was held discriminatory even though the plan covered four rank and file employees and only half that number of prohibited group employees. However, this result seems justifiable in light of the fact that the plan covered 100% of the prohibited group members and only 5% of the rank and file employees.

(10) *Babst Services, Inc.*[33] The plan in question covered only 4 of the employer's 55 employees, and 3 of the 4 covered employees (75%) were in the prohibited group. The Tax Court sustained the Commissioner's determination that the plan's coverage was discriminatory.

(11) *Wisconsin Nipple & Fabricating Corp.*[34] The court sustained the disqualification of a plan that covered 6 of 22 permanent employees, where 5 of the 6 covered employees (83%) were in the prohibited group.

(12) *Forsyth Emergency Services*.[35] The plan covered 3 prohibited group members and excluded three full-time rank and file employees in one of the years in issue. In the second year in issue the plan covered 3 prohibited group members and 1 rank and file employee and excluded six full-time rank and file employees. The Tax Court sustained the Commissioner's determination that this coverage was discriminatory.

(13) *Myron v. United States*.[36] Where contributions were made on behalf of the employer's sole shareholder, to the exclusion of five eligible rank and file employees, the court sustained the Commissioner's determination that the plan's coverage was discriminatory. In this case, 100% of the individuals benefitting under the plan were in the prohibited group.

(14) *Allen Ludden*.[37] Where contributions were made on behalf of the employer's two 50% shareholders and no contributions were made on behalf of the sole, full-time rank and file employee, the court sustained the Commissioner's determination that the plan's coverage was discriminatory. In this case, 100% of the individuals benefiting under the plan were in the prohibited group.

(15) *Pulver Roofing Co.*[38] For the taxable years in issue, approximately 75% of the participants in the plan were members of the prohibited group, and the percentage of nonprohibited group employees covered was approximately 5% of such employees. Under these circumstances the Commissioner's finding of discriminatory coverage was sustained.

(16) *Federal Land Bank Association of Asheville, North Carolina*.[39] An employer established a thrift plan under which all full-time employees who satisfied a nominal service requirement could elect to have the employer withhold 6% of their compensation as an employee contribution to the plan. The employer contributed a matching contribution of 3% of compensation for each participant. For the first plan year of the plan only two of the employer's 23 eligible employees elected to participate in the plan. One of these two participating employees was a prohibited group member and the other employee was a nonprohibited group member. The employer and the Service stipulated that of the 23 eligible employees 9 were in the prohibited group. Accordingly, for the year in issue, 50% of the participants were prohibited group employees and 50% were nonprohibited group employees. Furthermore, the percentage of participating prohibited group employees was 11% and the percentage of participating nonprohibited group employees was 7%.

The plan's coverage clearly failed to meet the percentage test of Section 410(b)(1)(A) and the Commissioner determined that the plan failed to cover a nondiscriminatory classification of employees under Section 410(b)(1)(B) because the plan covered a mere 8.6% of all employees and therefore failed to benefit "employees in general" or represent a "fair cross section" of the employees eligible to participate. The Commissioner argued that to satisfy the classification test the plan must benefit employees from substantially all compensation levels.

The Tax Court noted that the Commissioner's determination of discriminatory coverage "should not be overturned unless the taxpayer demonstrates it was arbitrary, unreasonable or an abuse of discretion." The Tax Court also acknowledged that the fair cross section test is a valid test for determining discriminatory classifications, particularly where the employer limits participation to a certain class of employees, and participation is "dominated by" employees who are in the prohibited group. The court held, however, that neither the Code nor the Regulations require a plan to satisfy a fair cross section test as a requirement to nondiscriminatory coverage.

The court held that to sustain a finding of discriminatory coverage, discrimination in favor of the prohibited group must exist independent of whether a fair cross section of employees is covered. The court stated that the participation of one member of the prohibited group did not tip the coverage scales in favor of the prohibited group. The court therefore reversed the Commissioner's disqualification of the plan and held the plan to be qualified for the year in issue. This statement implies the Tax Court's position that a plan's coverage will not be discriminatory where at least 50% of the participants are nonprohibited group employees; however, the court was impressed by the fact that the participation was open to all employees and, therefore, it is unclear if the result would have been the same if the eligibility provisions of the plan had limited the eligible participants to a classification containing only the two employees who participated.

(b) *The "Comparable Plan/Best Plan" Approach*

If the plan of a single member of an affiliated service group does not cover a nondiscriminatory classification of the employees of the affiliated service group, an alternative approach to satisfying the minimum coverage requirement is to take into account more than one plan maintained by the affiliated service group to satisfy the coverage requirement. Section 410(b)(1) and Regulations §1.401-3(f) provide that two or more plans designated by the employer as constituting parts of a single plan will be treated as a single plan for purposes of determining whether the coverage test is satisfied. An affiliated service group consisting of a partnership of professional corporations may therefore designate the plan(s) of corporate partner(s) and a plan maintained by the partnership as a single plan for purposes of satisfying the minimum coverage requirements. Any plans so aggregated will be qualified only if they do not discriminate in favor of the prohibited group. Hence such plans must be "comparable plans" with respect to the contributions or benefits provided under the plans.

Rev. Rul. 70-183[40], states the basic framework for evaluating comparability of qualified retirement plans. In order to satisfy the nondiscrimination requirement of Section 401(a)(4), plans may provide *either* nondiscriminatory contributions *or* nondiscriminatory benefits. See Rev. Rul. 69-253.[41] Accordingly, Rev.

Rul. 70-183 holds that two (or more) deferred compensation plans will, when considered as a single plan, not be discriminatory if:

(i) The plans are both defined benefit plans and provide comparable benefits.

(ii) The plans are both defined contribution plans (profit sharing, stock bonus or money purchase pension plans) and provide comparable contributions.

(iii) One plan is a defined benefit plan and the other plan is a defined contribution plan and the plans provide either comparable contributions or comparable benefits.

(1)   COMPARABLE DEFINED BENEFIT PLANS

Two defined benefit plans provide *comparable benefits* if the benefits provided at normal retirement age under both plans are the same percentage of compensation of participants who have similar service under the plans. In addition to the requirement that projected normal retirement benefits must be the same, the cases of *E.F. Higgens Co., Inc.*[42] *Liberty Machine Works, Inc.,*[43] *Loper Sheet Metal, Inc.,*[44] and *Claude M. Davis,*[45] establish that benefits will be comparable only if the following conditions are satisfied (or appropriate adjustment is made to compensate for variations in these conditions):

(i) Both plans use the same normal retirement age;

(ii) Both plans use the same vesting schedule (or benefits as adjusted under Rev. Rul. 74-166[46] are comparable);

(iii) Both plans provide similar death, disability, early retirement and late retirement benefits to similarly situated participants;

(iv) Both plans contain similar provisions for crediting service (if any) to participants who continue to work beyond normal retirement age; and

(v) Provisions for loans from the plan to participants, if such provisions exist, are similar in both plans.

Unfortunately, very little guidance is available for evaluating and qualifying variations in plans. Numerous comparability issues may arise from plan variations. For example, it is unclear how comparability would be established if: (1) one defined benefit plan provided a benefit of 50% of *career average* pay and another provided a benefit of 30% of *final average* pay, (2) one plan provided loans to participants while the other did not allow loans but had more rapid vesting or provided slightly greater normal retirement benefits, (3) both plans provide similar normal retirement benefits but provide different methods for determining "actuarially equivalent" alternative benefits—e.g., one plan uses a lump sum interest conversion factor equal to the Pension Benefit Guaranty Corporation rate in effect for valuing immediate annuities while the other plan uses the past 10 years average prime rate at a named financial institution.

Rev. Rul. 72-181[47] holds that, where an employer maintains separate defined benefit plans for its rank and file employees and for the prohibited group, and where such separate plans provide benefits that are similar in all respects, the mere fact that an unanticipated future termination of the prohibited group plan could cause benefits to vest for the prohibited group prior to vesting for the rank and file plan will not cause the prohibited group plan to be treated as providing discriminatory benefits.

Rev. Rul. 74-166[48] provides a mathematical formula for establishing comparability of benefits where prohibited group employees are covered under a plan that provides for more rapid vesting than the vesting schedule applicable to a plan covering rank and file employees. The formula increases the benefits deemed provided to the prohibited group employees for purposes of comparing their benefits to benefits of rank and file employees. The ruling states that if vesting applicable to rank and file employees is more rapid than vesting applicable to the prohibited group, the benefits of the rank and file employees are not subject to adjustment.

(2) COMPARABLE DEFINED CONTRIBUTION PLANS.

Two defined contribution plans provide *comparable contributions* if the amount of employer contribution to each plan is the same percentage of compensation. This determination may be made by taking into account employer contributions to Social Security. Comparability of defined contribution plans will be determined without regard to the vesting provisions under the plans since vesting relates to benefits rather than to contributions. It is likely that provisions for loans, disability, death and early retirement benefits will also be disregarded when comparing defined contribution plans since these provisions also relate to benefits rather than contributions.

(3) COMPARABILITY OF DEFINED BENEFIT AND DEFINED CONTRIBUTION PLANS.

(i) Comparing Contributions in Defined Benefit and Defined Contribution Plans.

A defined contribution plan and a defined benefit plan will satisfy the nondiscrimination requirement by reason of providing *comparable contributions* if the employer contribution to each plan is the same percentage of the aggregate compensation of the employees covered under each plan. In effect, the defined benefit plan is treated as a defined contribution plan and then compared with the defined contribution plan.

(A) *Effect of Variations In Vesting Schedules When Comparing Contributions.*

In Rev. Rul. 71-503[49] an employer contributed 5% of compensation to a fixed benefit pension plan for hourly employees and contributed 5% of compensation to a profit sharing plan for salaried employees. All of the salaried employees were members of the prohibited group. The hourly plan did not provide for any vesting for participants who terminated prior to age 65. The salaried plan provided for immediate vesting of all contributions. At issue was whether the two plans, when treated as a single plan, provided *contributions* on a nondiscriminatory basis. It was stipulated that turnover among hourly employees was high. The Service ruled that the salaried employees' plan was discriminatory with respect to *both* contributions *and* benefits and, therefore, failed to qualify under Section 401(a). The Service reasoned that both contributions and benefits that are vested are more valuable to participants than contributions and benefits that are forfeitable.

In Rev. Rul. 74-165[50], the Service revoked Rev. Rul. 71-503. Rev. Rul. 74-165 stated that, since in Rev. Rul. 71-503 the employer contributed the *same percentage* of each participant's compensation to the hourly fixed benefit plan and the salaried profit sharing plan, the plans did not discriminate with respect to *contributions*.

Rev. Rul. 74-165 held that vesting applied to benefits, not contributions, and it was therefore inappropriate to consider vesting when comparing contributions. Under the logic of Rev. Rul. 74-165, comparability of *contributions* should not be affected by variations in the plans concerning loan provisions, ability to direct investments, or death, disability, or early retirement benefits, since such variations affect benefits provided to participants rather than contributions made by the employer.

*(B)   Comparability of Contributions Must Be Satisfied
On a Year by Year Basis.*

Rev. Rul. 74-156 considered the following additional fact situation not covered by Rev. Rul 71-503. An employer established a profit sharing plan for hourly employees under which the employer contributed 7% of annual compensation *less forfeitures*. The employer also established a salaried employees' money purchase pension plan which required annual contributions of 5%. Each of the salaried employees was a member of the prohibited group. The salaried plans provided full and immediate vesting whereas the hourly plan had less rapid vesting.

In the second and third plan years, employer contributions to the hourly profit sharing plan were reduced to 5.2% and 4.8% respectively as a result of forfeitures. The ruling held that the plans were nondiscriminatory in the first and second plan years, but (absent a showing of Social Security integration) discriminated in the third plan year as a result of application of forfeitures to reduce employer contributions. Thus, when comparing contributions, the test for comparability must be satisfied *each plan year* independent of contributions made in other plan years.

*(C)   Impact of Integration Upon Comparability
of Contributions.*

In Rev. Rul. 70-580,[51] an employer maintained a money purchase pension plan for hourly employees and contributed 8% of the hourly employees' compensation to the money purchase plan. The employer also maintained a profit sharing plan for salaried employees and contributed 10% of salaried employees' compensation to the profit sharing plan. Each of the salaried employees was a member of the prohibited group.

Although the plans did not purport to be integrated, for the years in issue the sum of the employer's contributions on behalf of each participant in the money purchase and profit sharing plans plus the employer's contributions under the Social Security Act on behalf of each such participant provided a combined contribution that was a greater percentage of compensation for the hourly employees than for the salaried employees. The ruling held that the plans, when considered together, provided a nondiscriminatory integrated contribution for each participant for the years in issue.

The ruling further stated that since it would be impossible to predict the levels of compensation of participants in future years, an advance determination letter would not be issued in these circumstances. In order to obtain an advance determination regarding comparability of contributions or benefits, plans should be drafted to specifically take into account integration.

Rev. Rul. 70-580 has been superceded by Rev. Rul. 81-202 (8/24/81) which provides complicated "guidelines" for determining comparability.

(ii) Comparable Benefits in Combinations of Defined Benefit and Defined Contribution Plans.

(A)   General Principles and Problem Areas.

A defined contribution plan and a defined benefit plan will satisfy the nondiscrimination requirement by reason of providing *comparable benefits* if the employer contributions to the defined contribution plan will fund a normal retirement benefit for the defined contribution plan participant that is the same percentage of compensation as the benefit provided by the defined benefit plan, provided that other provisions of the plans which affect benefits are comparable (e.g., loan provisions, vesting provisions and provisions regarding disability, early and late retirement or death). Although the basic concept of comparable benefits is rather simple, in practice a number of difficult questions arise, such as:

(1) Assuming that the prohibited group is primarily covered by defined benefit plan(s), must the defined contribution plan provide a benefit for *each* defined contribution plan participant that is the same percentage of compensation as is provided by the defined benefit plan, or is it sufficient that the defined contribution plan provide such a comparable benefit for a class of employees that, when considered with the defined benefit plan, will cover a nondiscriminatory classification of employees?

(2) In determining comparability in connection with a request for an advance determination letter, is it sufficient to project benefits based on continuation of both plans indefinitely with their existing benefit formulas, or must comparability be tested on a year-by-year basis?

(3) How may comparability be established when the plans contain (a) different vesting schedules, (b) different eligibility requirements, different disability, early and late retirement or death benefit provisions, (c) different loan provisions, and (d) different earmarking provisions, etc.?

The applicable administrative and case law sheds some light on these issues but falls far short of resolving them. Most precedents involve defined benefit plans which covered rank and file unionized employees and defined contribution plans which covered the prohibited group (salaried employees). This occurred because prior to ERISA unionized employee could not be excluded for purposes of testing coverage and discrimination and, therefore, comparability of collectively bargained flat benefit pension plans and salaried only defined contribution plans became the issue for resolution.

In contrast, in the typical affiliated service group situation involving a combination of defined benefit and defined contribution plans, the prohibited group will be covered by the defined benefit plans and the rank and file employees will be covered by the defined contribution plans. Although the earlier precedents may be applied by analogy, the fit is often less than perfect.

(B)   Specific Examples of Testing Defined Benefit/Defined Contribution Combinations for Comparable Benefits

1. Rev. Rul. 70-183[52] compared a defined benefit plan/defined contribution plan combination maintained by an employer consisting of:

a. A pension plan for hourly employees providing a maximum annual benefit of $100 per year of service, payable at normal retirement age of 65; and

b. A profit sharing plan for salaried (prohibited group) employees providing for contributions in an amount determined annually by the employer's board of directors.

The ruling concluded that the plans were discriminatory for the three plan years in issue because they discriminated with respect to both contributions and benefits.

In testing for discriminatory benefits the ruling compared the $100 per year benefit that was accrued by the *highest paid* hourly employee, with the compensation received by the highest paid hourly employee ($10,000), to arrive at a projected pension benefit per year of service under the hourly employee's plan, of 1% of compensation. The ruling computed the pension benefit under the salaried profit sharing plan by computing the pension at age 65 that could be funded at the close of each of the 3 years in issue with the funds on hand at the end of each such year. This resulted in a pension for salaried employees of 3.0% of compensation at the end of the first year, 5.9% of compensation at the end of the second year, and 8.7% of compensation at the end of the third year. Since the profit sharing plan provided the prohibited group with benefits equal to a larger percentage of compensation than the pension plan provided to the rank and file employees, the Service found the profit sharing plan to discriminate.

Rev. Rul. 70-183 indicates that, where the defined contribution plan is of the profit sharing variety, in which no set rate of employer contributions is assured, and projection of forfeitures cannot be predicted in advance, the test for discriminatory *benefits* must be made on a year-by-year basis rather than by actuarially projecting the benefit to be derived from future employer funding.

A disturbing aspect of Rev. Rul. 70-183 is that in computing the benefit provided to the rank and file employees, the ruling compared the $100 annual benefit per year of service to the *highest* (as opposed to the *average*) compensation of any hourly employee. For example, if the *average* compensation of the hourly workers was $5,000, a $100 annual benefit per year of service would constitute a 2% of compensation benefit rather than the 1% rate computed by the ruling. Since Sections 401(a)(4) and 410(b)(1)(B) only require a nondiscriminatory benefit to be provided to a nondiscriminatory classification of employees, the benefit comparison should be made with respect to a level of compensation reflecting a fair cross section of the rank and file employees rather than the highest-paid member of the rank and file group.

2. In *Loper Sheet Metal, Inc.*[53] an employer established a profit sharing plan covering only salaried employees. The sole participants in the profit sharing plan were the employer's two 50% shareholders. The employer contributed 15% of each participant's compensation to the profit sharing plan for the years in issue. The employer also contributed to a defined benefit pension plan which covered the employee's collectively bargained hourly employees. For the years in issue, the employer contributions to the pension plan ranged from 2.46% to 2.94% of the compensation of the hourly employees. The court held the profit sharing plan to discriminate with respect to contributions since the 15% of compensation contributed to the profit sharing plan exceeded the less than 3% of compensation contributed to the pension plan.

The court then considered whether the two plans discriminated with respect to benefits. In making this comparison, the court observed:

> When we turn to making the requisite comparison of benefits payable under the pension and profit-sharing plans, we run into some difficulty for we are essentially comparing apples and oranges. Pension plans provide for definitely determinable benefits. Profit sharing plans, on the other hand, provide for contributions and do not purport to spell out a definitely determinable benefit to be paid upon retirement. Since the contributions to the profit sharing trust may vary from one year to the next dependent upon many extraneous factors, it is obviously impossible to predict with any degree of precision the benefits to be paid on some future occasion.
>
> To circumvent this dilemma we compared the benefits that are payable under the pension and profit sharing plans, we run into some difficulty during the years in question. [The court then added the following footnote.] It follows from this approach that the effect of our holding is limited to the years before us. 53 T.C. at 391.

The court implemented this comparison by first computing the annual pension expressed as a percentage of compensation earned under the pension plan for each year of service, based upon the *average* compensation of the hourly employees. The court then computed the annual pension at age 65 expressed as a percentage of compensation that could be funded for each of the profit sharing participants. The court computed this projected pension as of the close of each of the years in issue based upon: (i) the average compensation of each profit sharing participant at the close of each of the years in issue, (ii) the account balance of each participant at the close of each year, and (iii) an assumed rate of return of 4% per year on the account until the participant's 65th birthday. This method of analysis indicated that the benefit that could be funded under the profit sharing plan as of the close of each of the years in issue was a greater percentage of average compensation than the benefit earned by the participants in the pension plan. Therefore the court found the profit sharing plan to discriminate with respect to benefits.

The court stated that its finding of discrimination was also supported by the following "further evidences of prohibited discrimination":

a. The profit sharing plan had a more rapid vesting schedule. The court, quoting from *Hall v. United States*[54] stated, "vesting is an important benefit in any pension plan and is one which must be considered in reaching a decision as to whether a plan is discriminatory as to benefits."

b. The profit sharing plan permitted participants to borrow from the plan whereas the pension plan did not. The court viewed the availability of loans as an added *benefit* provided by the profit sharing plan.

c. The profit sharing plan provided that employer contributions would be continued for employees who served beyond normal retirement age, whereas the pension plan ceased benefit accrual at age 65. Although the oldest participant in the profit sharing plan was age 50, the court characterized the potential for extended participation as an added benefit.

d. The profit sharing plan had more favorable provisions for payment of benefits on death or disability than the pension plan.

The *Loper* decision indicates that comparability of benefits may be made by comparing the annual percent of compensation benefit provided for the prohibited group with the annual percent of compensation benefit provided to the rank and file employee whose compensation reflects the *average* compensation of the nonprohibited group. This is an important distinction from the approach taken in Rev. Rul. 70-183, in which the Service used the compensation of the highest paid rank and file employee as the basis for comparing benefits.

In *Loper*, as in Rev. Rul. 70-183, the comparison of benefits was made at the end of *each* year based upon the cumulative benefit funded or accrued as of the end of each year. The *Loper* decision specifically observed that the effect of its holding was limited to the years in issue. Since defined contribution plans by definition provide only the benefit that can be funded by actual account balances, it appears that the comparison of the *benefit* provided by employer contributions to a defined contribution plan to the *benefit* provided by employer contributions to a defined benefit plan must be tested *each year* to assure that benefits remain comparable.

The use of a money-purchase pension plan rather than a profit sharing plan as the defined contribution plan will increase the predictability of account balances by eliminating forfeitures and eliminating the limitation of contributions being limited to profits; however, even under a money-purchase pension plan, unanticipated variations in income or losses may cause actual benefits to vary substantially from initial projections in anticipated benefits and thereby create discrimination in operation when comparison to a defined benefit plan is made.

3. In *Peter F. Mitchell, Corp.*[55] the Tax Court considered comparability of benefits in a profit sharing plan maintained for salaried employees and two pension plans maintained for unionized hourly employees. The employer had only 3 salaried employees, and 2 of these were in the prohibited group. The employer attempted to demonstrate that the profit sharing plan would, if funded to normal retirement age, provide, on an integrated basis, a benefit that was no greater percentage of compensation than the pension plan benefit. The Tax Court rejected the employer's rationale, stating:

> The petitioner did not establish that the *comparative method* used by its witness for attempting to make a "projection" of benefits to be realized under the respective pension plans... has ever received the stamp of approval of either the respondent's regulations or rulings, or any other authoratative source.... In the absence of convincing evidence and proof that the method of comparisons and projections of benefits used by petitioner's witness is a valid method supported by a recognizable authority, we are obliged to conclude in this case that the attempted projection of benefits cannot be found to be a valid basis for holding that petitioner's profit sharing plan for its three salaried employees was not discriminatory in their favor with respect to benefits to be derived by the employees covered by that plan, for the purpose of satisfying the requirements of section 401(a)(4). 28 T.C.M. at 428.

The method of analysis used by the employer to compare benefits in *Mitchell* attempted to project benefits at normal retirement age based on future earnings of participants rather than the year-by-year analysis employed in *Loper* and Rev. Rul. 70-183. The *Mitchell* decision indicates that to prevail against the Commissioner's challenge of discriminatory benefits, a taxpayer must adhere to the comparative technique approved by the Service in Rev. Rul. 70-183.

4. *Liberty Machine Works, Inc.*[56] also considered comparability of *benefits* in a salaried employees' profit sharing plan and a collectively bargained

hourly employees' pension plan. The *Liberty Machine Works* opinion did not attempt to project the dollar amount of benefits that could be funded by the profit sharing plan as compared to the pension plan. Rather, the decision concluded that the profit sharing benefits were not comparable because the profit sharing plan provided for: (1) more rapid vesting, (2) more favorable death and disability benefits, and (3) continued eligibility for employer contributions for service performed after normal retirement age, whereas benefits accrued under the pension plan ceased at normal retirement age.

Liberty Machine Works indicates that, if conditions affecting entitlement to benefits are more favorable in the plan covering the prohibited group, benefits will not be comparable. See *E.F. Higgins & Co., Inc.*[57] which reached a similar conclusion.

(C) Special Considerations Involving H.R. 10 Plans

If a partnership is a member of an affiliated service group, any plan maintained by the partnership *and participated in by a 10% unincorporated partner* (an owner-employee) must satisfy the H.R. 10 requirements of Section 401(d), and, if the plan is a defined benefit plan, the special requirements of Section 401(j). Of particular importance are the following considerations:

1. Section 401(d)(3) specifies that a plan covering an owner-employee must cover every other employee except nonconsenting owner-employees. Thus, if one 10% partner elects to participate, all partners (other than 10% partners) *must* also participate. This restriction would also eliminate the possiblity of excluding associate professionals which may be available in medium to large size professional practices under the 70% participation test of Section 410(b)(1)(A).

2. Section 401(b)(2) requires full and immediate vesting under a plan that includes an owner-employee.

3. Section 401(d)(6) prohibits defined contribution plans which cover owner-employees, from integrating contributions with Social Security unless not more than one-third of the deductible contributions to the plan benefit owner-employees. Section 401(j)(4) prohibits a defined benefit plan which covers an owner-employee from integrating benefits with Social Security *without regard to* the percentage of contributions made on behalf of owner-employees. It is uncertain whether, for purposes of *comparing benefits* in an H.R. 10 *defined contribution* plan covering an owner-employee with benefits provided by another plan maintained by the affiliated group, benefits that could be provided under the H.R. 10 plan can take into account integration with Social Security, since an H.R. 10 defined benefit plan that benefits an owner-employee may not be integrated.

These added restrictions should be carefully evaluated in connection with the decision to permit unincorporated 10% partners to participate in the "core" plan.

(9) Suggestions to Practitioners

Although the administrative and judicial authority regarding comparability raises more issues than it answers, the following suggestions should be kept in mind in structuring comparable plans:

(1) Make the comparable plans as similar as possible. Do not use defined benefit/defined contribution combinations unless there is a good reason for doing so. If the professional corporations' plans will be defined benefit plans, consider using an integrated defined benefit core plan that provides a benefit that is the same percentge of pay as the "best" defined benefit plan adopted by a member of the affiliated service group. By using a "fractional" accrued benefit formula (Section 411(b)(1)(C)) the cost of funding benefits for the rank and file participants of the core plan can be kept to a minimum.

(2) Consider structuring the core plan to make the prohibited group (e.g. doctors, attorney's CPA's, etc.) ineligible to participate in the core plan. Prohibited group members who desire deferred compensation may separately incorporate and establish their own plans. Do not allow the prohibited group to opt in and out of the core plan since this could raise an issue of whether the plan is in practice a "cash or deferred" arrangement which must comply with Section 401(k) to be qualified.

(3) If one plan is a defined contribution plan while the other is a defined benefit plan and if comparability of *benefits* is the test relied upon:

(i) Use a money purchase pension plan rather than a profit sharing plan since funding will be more predictable due to the absence of reallocation of forfeitures and the ability to contribute irrespective of profits.

(ii) Projection of future benefits that may be funded by the defined contributions should be developed for purposes of initially establishing benefit levels and securing a determination letter from the Service. However, in each succeeding year after establishment of the plans, comparability of benefits based on actual account balances should be tested to assure that discrimination in benefits does not arise in practice.

(iii) The defined benefit plan should be fully integrated so that comparison may be made to the integrated benefit that could be funded by the defined contribution plan.

(iv) Comparability of benefits should be established if a nondiscriminatory classification of defined contribution participants may be provided a benefit that is the same percentage of compensation as the benefit provided to the prohibited group. The cases discussed earlier relating to nondiscriminatory classifications of coverage should provide guidance in this area.

(4) A final suggestion of critical importance is to seek advance administrative approval of comparability from the Key District Director of Internal Revenue Service by following the procedure set out in Rev. Proc. 81-12 wherever an

affiliated service group exists or may exist. The courts have repeatedly held that the Commissioner's determination of whether a plan's coverage is nondiscriminatory is entitled to "a shade more than its usual substantial weight," *Commissioner v. Pepsi-Cola Niagara Bottling Corp.*[58], and will be overturned only if it is "found to be arbitrary or an abuse of discretion." See *Ed & Jim Fleitz, Inc.*[59] Therefore, absent an advance ruling regarding comparability, an employer will be faced with a heavy burden of proof should the Service challenge coverage as discriminatory.

Section 5.03 of Rev. Proc. 81-12 provides that failure to indicate in a determination letter request that there is or may be an affiliated service group and to provide the information specified in Rev. Proc. 81-12 will constitute an omission of a material fact and will result in the applicant being unable to rely on the determination letter concerning the effect of Section 414(m).

Section 5.04 of Rev. Proc. 81-12 provides that determination letters issued for determinations that have considered questions arising under Section 414(m) will specifically state that the implications of Section 414(m) were considered and that the plan satisfies the qualification requirements of such section. Section 5.04 of Rev. Proc. 81-12 further provides, "Absent such a statement pertaining to Section 414(m), a determination letter does not apply to any qualification issue arising by reason of Section 414(m)." Accordingly, in addition to requesting that a determination letter address any existing or potential Section 414(m) issues, practitioners should take care to review the favorable determination letter to asure that the letter specifically addresses Section 414(m).

The availability under Rev. Proc. 81-12 of an advance administrative determination regarding satisfaction of the requirements of Section 414(m) offers the only available solution to the numerous as yet unanswered questions concerning the comparability of plans. Pending issuance of Regulations under Section 414(m) and other administrative guidelines regarding comparability, the best advice for the practitioner is to structure plans of affiliated service groups so as to provide actuarially comparable benefits and leave resolution of the unanswered issues to the determination letter procedure provided in Rev. Proc. 81-12.

EXHIBIT 1

Rev. Rul. 81-105, I.R.B. 1981-12, 27. Employees' trusts—Definitions and special rules—Affiliated service groups—Nondiscrimination requirements.— Information is provided with respect to when various businesses will be considered an affiliated service group and how this aggregation affects the retirement plans maintained by members of the group; Rev. Ruls. 68-370 and 75-35 made obsolete.

SECTION 1. PURPOSE

This Revenue Ruling provides guidance with respect to the application of section 414(m) of the Internal Revenue Code, as added by the Miscellaneous Revenue Act of 1980, Pub. L. 96-605, (1981-6 I.R.B. 21), 24. The guidance emphasizes the interaction of section 414(m) of the Code with the nondiscrimination requirements of sections 410(b) and 401(a)(4) in response to questions that have arisen as to how those sections interact. This revenue ruling also obsoletes Rev. Rul. 68-370, 1968-2 C.B. 174 and Rev. Rul. 75-35, 1975-1 C.B. 131.

SEC. 2. APPLICABLE LAW

.01 Section 414(m)(1) of the Code provides that, for purposes of certain employee benefit requirements designated in section 414(m)(4), except to the extent otherwise provided in regulations, all employees of the members of an affiliated service group shall be created as employed by a single employer.

.02 Section 414(m)(2) defines an affiliated service group as a first service organization (FSO) and one or more of:

(1) any service organization (A-ORG) which is a shareholder or partner in the FSO and which regularly performs services for the FSO or is regularly associated with the FSO in performing services for third persons, and

(2) any other organization (B-ORG) if

(A) a significant portion of the business of that organization is the performance of services for the FSO or A-ORG of a type historically performed in the service field of the FSO or A-ORG by employees, and

(B) 10 percent or more of the interest of the B-ORG is held by persons who are officers, highly compensated employees, or owners of the FSO or A-ORG.

.03 The list of employee benefit requirements in section 414(m)(4) of the Code includes the following:

(1) Section 410(b) which requires that, to satisfy the requirements of section 401(a), a retirement plan must cover either a certain percentage of employees or a classification of employees that does not discriminate in favor of employees who are officers, shareholders, or highly compensated (the prohibited group).

(2) Section 401(a)(4), which requires that to satisfy the requirements of section 401(a), either the contributions or the benefits under a retirement plan must not discriminate in favor of the prohibited group.

SEC. 3. EXAMPLES

.01 Example 1—

(1) Facts—P, a law partnership consists of corporate partners A, B, C and 10 individual partners. Each of the partners owns less than 10% of the partnership. The partnership employs as common law employees some lawyers, paralegals, and clerical employees. The partnership has a qualified plan, Plan P, covering some but not all of the common law employees. Corporations A and B each have only one employee, the sole shareholder. Corporation A maintains a retirement plan, Plan A. Corporation B maintains no plan. Corporation C employs the sole shareholder, a lawyer employee, and three clerical employees. Corporation C maintains a retirement plan, Plan C, for all its employees. Corporations A, B, and C regularly perform services for P. No individual is a participant in more than one plan and none of the statutory exclusions of section 410(b) applies.

(2) Determination of who are employees of a single employer under section 414(m) of the Code—In order to determine whether the employees covered by Plans A and C satisfy the coverage requirements of section 410(b), it first must be determined what employees are considered as employed by a single employer. Under section 414(m)(2), the partnership, P, may be designated as a FSO. Corporations A, B, and C are partners in the FSO, and regularly perform services for the FSO. Accordingly Corporations A, B, and C are A-ORGS. Because Corporations A, B and C are A-ORGS for the same FSO, Corporations A, B, and C and the FSO constitute an affiliated service group. Consequently all the employees of Corporations A, B, C, the common law employees of P, and the partners of P are considered as employed by a single employer, and must be taken into account when testing whether the coverage requirements of section 410(b) are satisfied. This group is hereafter called the total aggregated employees.

(3) Determination of whether Plan A satisfies the coverage and nondiscrimination requirements—Plan A covers only one employee, the sole shareholder of Corporation A. Because none of the statutory exclusions of section 410(b) of the code applies, One participant does not satisfy the percentage tests in section 410(b)(1)(A) when compared to the total aggregated employees. Because Plan A covers only prohibited group employees and the total aggregated employees contain several rank and file employees, the non-discriminatory classification test of section 410(b)(1)(B) is not satisfied, either. When a plan does not, considered alone, satisfy the requirements of section 410(b), the employer may designate other plans of the employer to be considered as a unit with the first plan. Such plans, considered as a unit must, among other things, satisfy the coverage and non-discrimination requirements.

Assuming Plan P were so designated, the first question to consider is whether a plan covering only Employee A and the participants of Plan P satisfies the requirements of either section 410(b)(1)(A) or (B) of the Code when compared to the total aggregated employees. (Alternatively, the employer may designate Plans A, C, and P as a unit or simply Plans A and C as a unit.) If neither coverage test is satisfied, Plan A is not a qualified plan. If either coverage test is satisfied, in order for Plan A to be qualified, Plans A and P, considered as a unit must also satisfy the non-discrimination requirements of section 401(a)(4). In making this determination the rules for testing discrimination, including rules which permit imputing social security benefits, apply. In testing for discrimination, all the compensation paid by the affiliated service group to the participants of Plan P is considered, without regard to the percentage ownership of Corporation A in the partnership.

(4) Determination of whether Plan C satisfies the coverage and nondiscrimination requirements—Plan C covers one shareholder, one lawyer employee, and three clerical employees. Coverage of five participants is not adequate to satisfy the percentage tests of section 410(b)(1)(A) of the Code when compared to the total aggregated employees. Whether the non-discriminatory classification test of section 410(b)(1)(B) would be satisfied by Plan C if its participants are compared to the total aggregated employees depends on additional facts and circumstances not herein provided. See section 1.410(b)-1(d)(2) of the Income Tax Regulations. If section 410(b)(1)(B) were satisfied, the nondiscrimination requirements of section

401(a)(4) would be applied considering the participants of Plan C only (without considering the participants of Plans A or P). However, if the requirements of section 410(b)(1)(B) were not satisfied by Plan C alone, then the plan could be considered in combination with other plans, as described in (3).

.02 Example 2.—

(1) Facts—Corporation S provides secretarial services. Corporations A and B, both of which are professional corporations formed by doctors, each own a portion of S. A owns 11 percent of the stock of S and B owns eight percent of the stock. Approximately one-third of S's services are performed for A and one-third for B, while the other one-third are performed for other firms. A and B each maintain a retirement plan (Plan A and Plan B) and each plan covers the corporation's only employee. None of the statutory exclusions of section 410(b) of the Code applies.

(2) Determination of who are employees of a single employer under section 414(m) of the Code—In order to determine whether the employees covered by Plans A and B satisfy the coverage requirements of section 410(b), it first must be determined which employees are considered as employed by a single employer. Under section 414(m)(2), Corporations A and B may each be designated as separate FSO's. Corporation S is a B-ORG for A because a significant portion of S's business is the performance of services for A, the services are of a type historically performed in the FSO's service field by employees, and 11 percent of the interest in S is held by owners of the FSO. S is not a B-ORG for B because the owners of B do not hold 10 percent or more of the interest in S.

Because Corporation S is a B-ORG for Corporation A/FSO, the two constitute an affiliated service group. Consequently, all the employees of A and S are considered as employed by a single employer and must be taken into account when testing whether the coverage requirements of section 410(b) are satisfied. Corporation B is not part of an affiliated service group with either Corporation A or S. Thus, the employee of B is not aggregated with any other employees for purposes of testing coverage.

(3) Determination of whether Plan A satisfies the coverage and nondiscrimination requirements—Plan A covers only one employee, the sole shareholder of Corporation A. Because none of the statutory exclusions of section 410(b) of the Code applies, one participant does not satisfy the percentage tests of section 410(b)(1)(A) when compared to the total employees of the A and S affiliated service group. Because Plan A covers only prohibited group employees and the total aggregated employees of the affiliated service group include rank and file employees, the nondiscriminatory classification test of section 410(b)(1)(B) is not satisfied, either. Accordingly, unless a sufficient number of the employees of S were covered by Plan A or by another plan so that at least one of the tests of section 410(b) were satisfied, Plan A is not a qualified plan. If, however, section 410(b) were satisfied, the single plan or combination of plans which satisfied that section must also satisfy the nondiscrimination requirements of section 401(a)(4). As in Example 1, the normal rules apply in testing for discrimination under section 401(a)(4) and all the compensation paid to the employees of Corporation S is

considered, without regard to the percentage ownership of Corporation A in Corporation S.

(4) Determination of whether Plan B satisfies the coverage and nondiscrimination requirements—Because Plan B covers the only employee of Corporation B, and the corporation is not a part of any affiliated service group, Plan B satisfies both sections 410(b) and 401(a)(4) of the Code.

.03 Example 3.—

(1) Corporations A and B are professional corporations formed by doctors (A and B). Corporation A and Corporation B each own one-half of P, a lock repair shop. Corporations A and B utilize the services of P, however, these corporations are an insignificant portion of P's customers.

(2) Under the rules of section 414(m)(2) of the Code there is no affiliated service group based on these facts. Considering A or B corporations as a FSO, P is not a B-ORG for either FSO because the services performed by P are not of a type historically performed by employees in the service field of the FSO. Furthermore, the service performed for A and B Corporations is not a significant portion of P's business.

(3) Considering P as a FSO, A and B Corporations are not A-ORGS for P because they are not regularly associated with P in performing service for third persons.

SEC. 4. AREAS OF LAW AFFECTED BY SECTION 414(m) OF THE CODE

This section provides a list of some, but not all, other requirements for retirement plans which are affected by section 414(m)(2) of the Code.

Code Section	Effect
410(a)	(a) All service in the affiliated service group must be counted.
	(b) Year that employment begins is based on the entire affiliated service group.
411	(a) All service in the affiliated service group must be counted.
415	(a) All benefits and annual additions from the affiliated service group are aggregated.
	(b) All compensation from the affiliated service group is aggregated.
401(a)(5) (Rev. Rul. 71-446,	(a) Multiple intergration rules of section 17 apply to the entire affiliated service group.
1971-2 C.B. 187)	(b) All service in the affiliated service group must be counted.
408(k)	(a) All service in the affiliated service group must be counted.
	(b) Discrimination is tested considering all contributions by and compensation from the affiliated service group.

SEC. 5. EFFECTIVE DATE

This revenue ruling shall apply to plan years ending after November 30, 1980. However, in the case of a plan in existence on November 30, 1980, the amendments made by this section shall apply to plan years beginning after that date.

SEC. 6. EFFECT ON OTHER DOCUMENTS

Rev. Ruls. 68-370 and 75-35 are obsoleted.

NOTES TO CHAPTER 19

1. American Bar Association Disciplinary Rule DR2-102(C), Florida Bar Opinion 79-1, Oklahoma Bar Association Legal Ethics Opinion No. 283, Arizona Bar Association Opinion No. 77-9, Alabama Bar Association Opinion RO-332, New York State Bar Ethics Opinion No. 509, Greater Cleveland bar Association Opinion No. 103.
2. Note 16, Chapter 9, *supra*.
3. 1972-1 C.B. 105. Also see Letter Ruling 8130049.
4. Also see Rev. Rul. 75-67, 1975-1 C.B. 169, and Rev. Rul. 75-250, 1975-1 C.B. 1972, which removed the spectre of the personal holding company tax from one-man professional corporations.
5. Note 31, Chapter 9, *supra*.
6. Note 19. Chapter 9, *supra*.
7. Note 5, Chapter 10, *supra*.
8. 1968-2 C.B. 174.
9. 63 T.C. 621 (1975).
10. 68 T.C. 387 (1977), government appeal dismissed *nolle pros*. (10th Cir. 1978).
11. 69 T.C. 1055 (1978).
12. The Service took the same position in Letter Ruling 7902086 and Letter Ruling 7905020, the latter of which, for the most part, is restated in 13 other Letter Rulings (7905025, -026, 030, 036, -037, -038, -042, -044, -050, -053, 060, -061, -063).
13. 73 T.C. 5 (1979).

14. A complete text of Section 414(m) is as follows:

(m) EMPLOYEES OF AN AFFILIATED SERVICE GROUP.—

(1) IN GENERAL. —For purposes of the employee benefit requirements listed in paragraph (4), except to the extent otherwise provided in regulations, all employees of the members of an affiliated service group shall be treated as employed by a single employer.

(2) AFFILIATED SERVICE GROUP. —For purposes of this subsection, the term 'affiliated service group' means a group consisting of a service organization (hereinafter in this paragraph referred to as the 'first organization') and one or more of the following:

(A) any service organization which—
(i) is a shareholder or partner in the first organization, and
(ii) regularly performs services for the first organization or is regularly associated with the first organization in performing services for third persons, and

(B) any other organization if—
(i) a significant portion of the business of such organization is the performance of services (for the first organization, for organizations described in subparagraph (A), or for both) of a type historically performed in such service field by employees, and
(ii) 10% or more of the interests in such organization is held by persons who are officers, highly compensated employees, or owners of the first organization or an organization described in subparagraph (a)(i).

(3) SERVICE ORGANIZATIONS. —For purposes of this subsection, the term 'service organization' means an organization the principal business of which is the performance of services.

(4) EMPLOYEE BENEFIT REQUIREMENTS. —For purposes of this subsection, the employee benefit requirements listed in this paragraph are—

(A) paragraph (3), (4), (7), and (16) of section 401(a),
(B) sections 408(k), 410, 411, and 415,
(C) section 105(h), and
(D) section 125.

(5) OTHER DEFINITIONS. —For purposes of this subsection—

(A) ORGANIZATION DEFINED. —The term ''organization'' means a corporation, partnership, or other organization.
(B) OWNERSHIP. —In determining ownership, the principles of section 267(c) shall apply.

(6) PREVENTION OF AVOIDANCE. —The Secretary shall prescribe such regulations as may be necessary to prevent the avoidance with respect to service organizations, through the use of separate organizations, of any employee benefit requirement listed in paragraph (4).

15. 1981-12 I.R.B. 27. This ruling declares Rev. Rul. 68-370 obsolete. For a general discussion of the best plan rule see Neal and Conaway, ''New Section

414(m) Limits Qualified Plan Abuse by Affiliated Service Organizations,'' May 1981 *J. Taxation* 258.

16. For additional viewpoints, see Sacher, ''Using Qualified 'Multiple-Employer Plans' for Partnerships of P.C.s: A Current Appraisal,'' 53 *J. Taxation* 216 (October, 1980). Mr. Sacher recommends the establishment of a plan (or plans) at the partnership level which will cover all of the partnership's employees (the professionals being covered under the professional corporations' plans) and provide benefits comparable to those provided under the plans of the professional corporations. While such a plan, termed a ''multiple-employer plan,'' may possibly eliminate the administrative burden of the authors' approach, it may involve the complexities of drafting a single plan encompassing all of the benefits of the various corporate plans. The effect of such an approach taken to its logical conclusion might be a decision by the Service to require the best provisions of *each plan*, even though a ''best plan'' approach is not required. However, rules of comparability do exist. See Rev. Rul. 69-253, 1969-1 C.B. 129; 70-183, 1970-1 C.B. 103 amplifying Rev. Rul. 66-15, 1966-1 C.B. 96 revoking Rev. Rul. 71-503, 1971-2 C.B. 20-6; and 74-166, 1974-1 C.B. 97.

For other view points, see Byam, ''Professional Organization Retirement Plans: Excluding Service Employees,'' 66 *A.B.A.J.* 790 (June 1980); Grant and Ward, ''Will *Garland* case now permit partnerships of P.C.'s to avoid qualified plan rules?'', 52 *J. Taxation* 2 (January, 1980).

17. 1981-14 I.R.B. 42, which prescribes the procedures for obtaining rulings on whether particular entities are members of an affiliated service group and for obtaining determination letters on the qualified employee benefit plans established by members of affiliated service groups.

18. 1979-2 C.B. 161.

19. 74 T.C. No. 82 (1980).

20. 1966-1 C.B. 75.

21. 1969-2 C.B. 58.

22. 1970-1 C.B. 101.

23. 1966-1 C.B. 72.

24. 1974-1 C.B. 93.

25. 1974-1 C.B. 94.

26. 1979-2 C.B. 189.

27. 67-2 U.S.T.C. ¶9717, 20 AFTR 2d 5725 (N.D.N.Y. 1967).

28. 50 T.C. 384 (1968).

29. 74-1 U.S.T.C. ¶9341, 33 AFTR 2d 74-954 (D. Neb. 1974).

30. 399 F.2d 390 (2d Cir. 1968).

31. 55 T.C. 1144 (1971).

32. 62 T.C. 621 (1974).

33. 67 T.C. 131 (1976).

34. 67 T.C. 490 (1976), *aff'd*, 581 F.2d 1235 (7th Cir. 1978).

35. 68 T.C. 881 (1977).
36. 550 F.2d 1145 (9th Cir. 1977).
37. 68 T.C. 826 (1977), *aff'd*, 80-1 U.S.T.C. ¶9188 (9th Cir. 1980).
38. 70 T.C. 1001 (1978).
39. 74 T.C. No. 82 (1980).
40. 1970-1C.B. 104.
41. 1969-1 C.B. 129.
42. 75 T.C. No. 76 (1980).
43. 62 T.C. 621 (1974).
44. 53 T.C. 385 (1969).
45. 28 T.C.M. 425 (1969).
46. 1974-1 C.B. 97.
47. 1972-1 C.B. 113.
48. 1974-1 C.B. 97.
49. 1971-2 C.B. 206.
50. 1974-1 C.B. 96.
51. 1970-2 C.B. 90.
52. 1970-1 C.B. 104.
53. 53 T.C. 385 (1969).
54. 398 F.2d 383 (8th Cir. 1968).
55. 28 T.C.M. 425 (1969).
56. 62 T.C. 621 (1974).
57. 74 T.C. No. 76 (1980).
58. Note 30, *supra*.
59. Note 28, *supra*.

INDEX

INDEX

INDEX